Catalog of
American Car
ID Numbers
1950-59

Compiled by the Staff of Cars & Parts Magazine

Published by
Amos Press Inc.
911 Vandemark Road
Sidney, Ohio 45365

Publishers of
Cars & Parts
The Voice of the Collector Car Hobby Since 1957

Cars & Parts Collectible Series
High Performance Cars
Collectible Trucks
Collector Car Annual
Cars of the '50s
Cars of the '60s

Catalog of American Car ID Numbers 1960-69
Catalog of American Car ID Numbers 1970-79
Catalog of Chevy Truck ID Numbers 1946-72
Catalog of Ford Truck ID Numbers 1946-72

Salvage Yard Treasures
A Guide to America's Salvage Yards

Distribution by Motorbooks International Publishers and Wholesalers
P.O. Box 2, Osceola WI 54020 USA

Printed and bound in the United States of America

Library of Congress Cataloging-In-Publication Date
ISBN 1-880524-04-X

ACKNOWLEDGMENTS

The staff of *Cars & Parts* Magazine devoted more than a year to the research and development of the Catalog of American Car ID Numbers 1950-59. It has been a labor-intensive project which required assistance from hundreds of collectors, clubs, researchers, and a tremendous amount of research at car shows, swap meets and auctions.

This book wouldn't have been possible without very special help from the following:

American Automobile Manufacturers Association

Dan Kirchner - Researcher

Jim Wirth - Researcher

Jim Benjaminson

Automotive History Collection of the Detroit Public Library

Thank you for making this book possible.

Catalog of
American Car
ID Numbers
1950-59

Compiled by the Staff of Cars & Parts Magazine

INTRODUCTION

Authentication has become such a critical issue within the old car hobby that the need for a comprehensive, accurate and dependable identification guide has become quite apparent to anyone involved in buying, selling, restoring, judging, owning, researching or appraising a collector vehicle. With this indepth and detailed ID guide, the staff of Cars & Parts magazine has compiled as much data as possible on the years covered to help take the fear out of buying a collector car.

Deciphering trim codes, verifying vehicle identification numbers (VIN), interpreting body codes and authenticating engine numbers will become a much easier process with this guide at your side. Putting this previously obscure information at your fingertips has not been a simple task, but one worth the tremendous investment, time and money spent on its production.

Each car manufacturer used a different system of identification and changed them frequently in the 50's. The *Cars & Parts* staff has developed the most consistent information possible from year to year for each manufacturer. Some data are not pre-sented due to lack of availability, space, time considerations, and the researchers' inability to verify sources.

Each corporation, division, year, model, VIN, body plate and engine number required decisions about what to print. The staff of *Cars & Parts* is justifiably proud of this book and invites your comments. Additional information is especially welcome.

The information contained in the Catalog of American Car ID Numbers 1950-59 was compiled from a variety of sources including original manufacturers' catalogs (when available) and official shop manuals. The *Cars & Parts* staff and researchers made every attempt to verify the information continued herein. However, many manufacturers made changes from year-to-year and model-to-model, as well as during mid-year production. And, in some instances, conflicting information and reports surfaced during the course of our indepth research. As a result, *Cars & Parts* can not guarantee the absolute accuracy of all data presented in this ID catalog.

HOW TO USE THIS CATALOG

SAMPLE: VIN (VEHICLE IDENTIFICATION NUMBER)

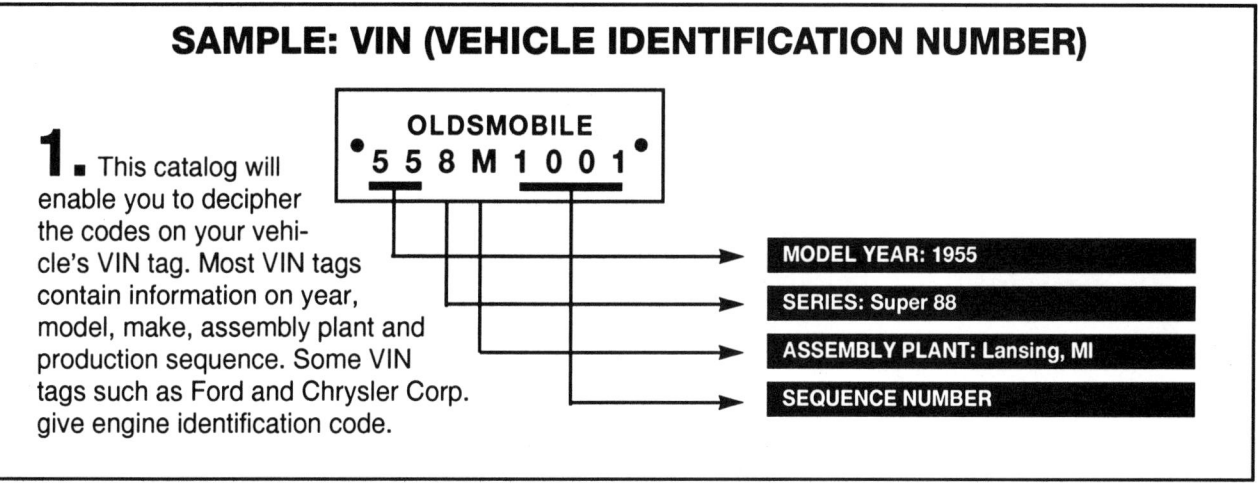

1. This catalog will enable you to decipher the codes on your vehicle's VIN tag. Most VIN tags contain information on year, model, make, assembly plant and production sequence. Some VIN tags such as Ford and Chrysler Corp. give engine identification code.

OLDSMOBILE
5 5 8 M 1 0 0 1

MODEL YEAR: 1955

SERIES: Super 88

ASSEMBLY PLANT: Lansing, MI

SEQUENCE NUMBER

SAMPLE: BODY NUMBER PLATE

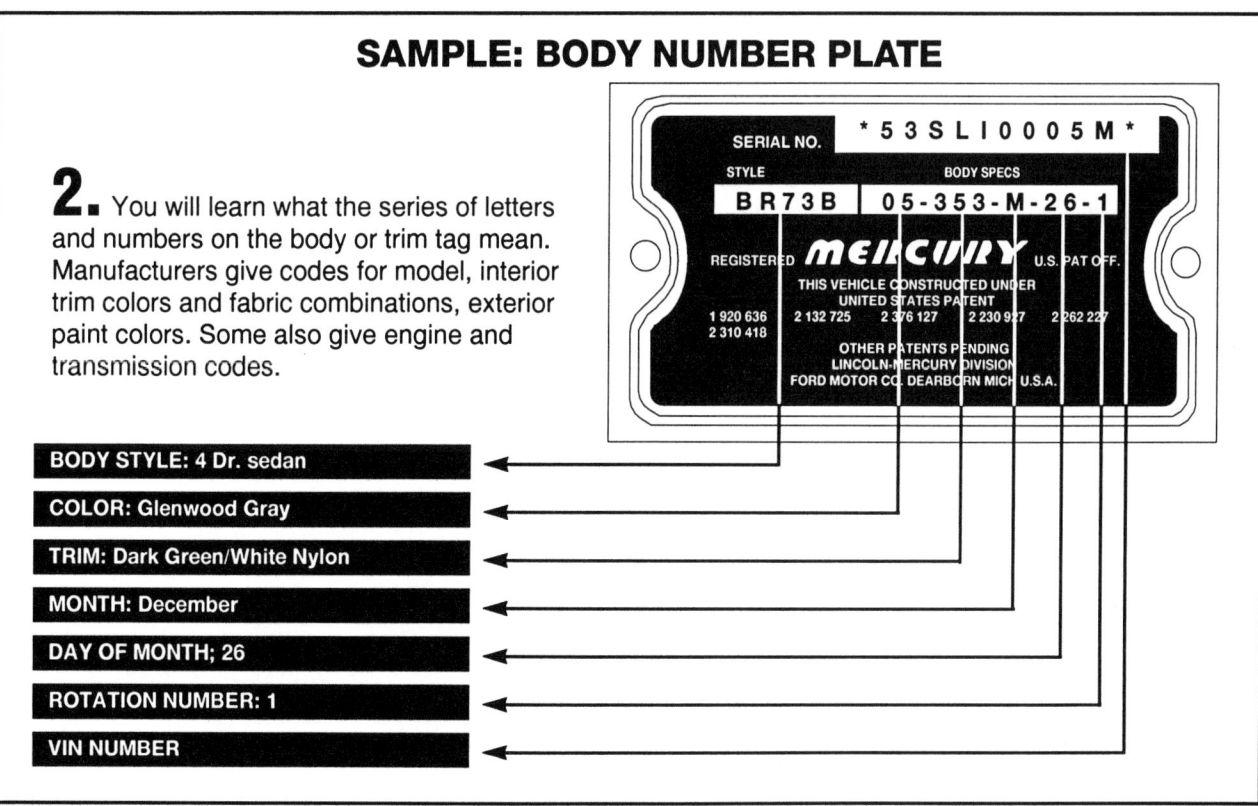

2. You will learn what the series of letters and numbers on the body or trim tag mean. Manufacturers give codes for model, interior trim colors and fabric combinations, exterior paint colors. Some also give engine and transmission codes.

SERIAL NO. * 5 3 S L I 0 0 0 5 M *

STYLE — B R 7 3 B

BODY SPECS — 0 5 - 3 5 3 - M - 2 6 - 1

REGISTERED **MERCURY** U.S. PAT OFF.

THIS VEHICLE CONSTRUCTED UNDER UNITED STATES PATENT

1 920 636   2 132 725   2 376 127   2 230 927   2 262 227
2 310 418

OTHER PATENTS PENDING
LINCOLN-MERCURY DIVISION
FORD MOTOR CO. DEARBORN MICH U.S.A.

BODY STYLE: 4 Dr. sedan

COLOR: Glenwood Gray

TRIM: Dark Green/White Nylon

MONTH: December

DAY OF MONTH; 26

ROTATION NUMBER: 1

VIN NUMBER

SAMPLE: ENGINE NUMBER

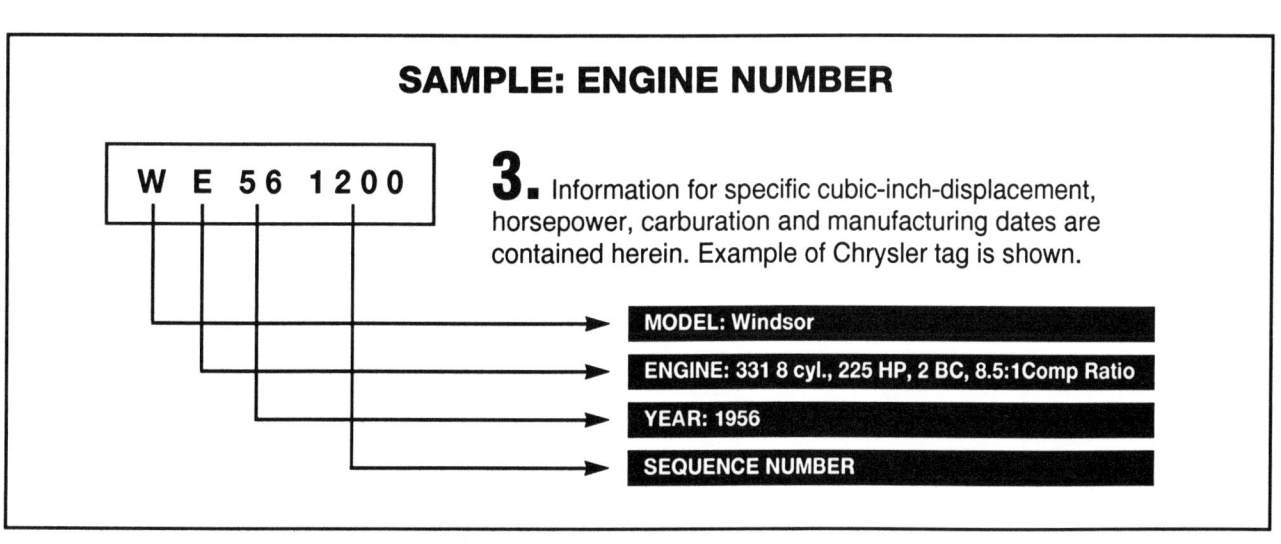

W E 56 1200

3. Information for specific cubic-inch-displacement, horsepower, carburation and manufacturing dates are contained herein. Example of Chrysler tag is shown.

MODEL: Windsor

ENGINE: 331 8 cyl., 225 HP, 2 BC, 8.5:1 Comp Ratio

YEAR: 1956

SEQUENCE NUMBER

1950 CHRYSLER WINDSOR

1950 CHRYSLER TOWN & COUNTRY

1950 CHRYSLER TOWN & COUNTRY

1950 CHRYSLER TOWN & COUNTRY

VEHICLE IDENTIFICATION NUMBER

```
• SERIAL NUMBER •
  70,058,001
```

The serial number is located on the left front door hinge post. It indicates the series/model based on numerical sequence.

MODEL NAME	MODEL CODE	ASSEMBLY PLANT	STARTING NUMBERS
Royal, 6-cyl.	C48S	Detroit	70,058,001
		Los Angeles	65,004,001
Windsor, 6-cyl.	C48W	Detroit	70,794,001
		Los Angeles	67,011,001
Saratoga, 8-cyl.	C49K	—	6,774,501
New Yorker, 8-cyl.	C49N	—	7,119,001
Town & Country, 8-cyl.	C49N	—	7,411,501
Crown Imperial, 8-cyl.	C50	—	7,813,501
Imperial	C49N	—	7,146,001

THE BODY NUMBER PLATE is located on the cowl under the hood. Chrysler did not have body style codes, paint codes or trim codes appearing anywhere on the car. When ordering parts, it was necessary to furnish the factory with both the serial number and body plate number. We have attempted to list codes for paint and trim combinations when available.

```
BODY  NUMBER
XXX  XXXX
BRIGGS BODY, DETROIT MICHIGAN
```

BODY TYPES

ROYAL - C48S - MODEL 481

BODY TYPE	CODE
2-Dr. Club coupe	2
4-Dr. sedan	5
4-Dr. sedan L.W.	5
4-Dr. Town & Country station wagon, 6-pass. L.W.	9
4-Dr. station wagon, 6-pass L.W.	9

WINDSOR - C48W - MODEL 482

BODY TYPE	CODE
2-Dr. Club coupe, 6-pass.	2
4-Dr. sedan	5
Convertible	3
2-Dr. Newport	22
4-Dr. Traveler	6
4-Dr. sedan L.W.	5
4-Dr. limo, 8-pass. L.W.	7

SARATOGA - C49K - MODEL 491

BODY TYPE	CODE
2-Dr. Club coupe	2
4-Dr. sedan	5

NEW YORKER - C49N - MODEL 492

BODY TYPE	CODE
2-Dr. Club coupe	2
4-Dr. sedan	5
Convertible	3
2-Dr. Newport	22
4-Dr. wood station wagon	9

TOWN & COUNTRY - C49N

BODY TYPE	CODE
2-Dr. Newport	22

IMPERIAL - C49N

BODY TYPE	CODE
4-Dr. sedan	5
4-Dr. deluxe sedan	5

CROWN IMPERIAL - C50

BODY TYPE	CODE
4-Dr. sedan	7
4-Dr. limo, 8-pass.	8

THE COLOR CODE indicates the paint color used on the vehicle.

COLOR	CODE
Haze Blue	5
Racine Blue	6
Newport Blue	7
Fog Green	20
Gulf Green	21
Scotch Green	22
Juniper Green Metallic	23
Shell Gray	35
Stone Gray	36
Gunmetal Metallic	37
Canyon Gray Metallic	42
Pearl Tan	45
Tobacco Brown	46
Indian Brown Metallic	48
Seal Brown	57
Crown Maroon	60
Victoria Red	61
Pagoda Cream	65

TWO-TONE COLORS

COLOR	CODE
Tampa Beige/Black	70
Tampa Beige/Juniper Green Poly	71
Tampa Beige/Indian Brown Poly	72
Black/Quaker Gray	73
Black/Shell Gray	74
Gunmetal Gray Poly/Stone Gray	75
Tobacco Brown/Pearl Tan	76
Scotch Cream/Fog Green	77
Racine Blue/Haze Blue	78

NOTE: The first code identifies the upper color and the second identifies the lower color.

THE TRIM CODE indicates the color and material scheme used on the vehicle.

ROYAL/SARATOGA TRIM

COLOR	CLOTH	VINYL	LEATHER	CODE
Gray	•			27
Tan	•			28
Green	•			29
Blue			•	41
Red			•	42
Tan			•	43
Green			•	44

WINDSOR TRIM

COLOR	CLOTH	VINYL	LEATHER	CODE
Maroon/Tan	•			13
Green/Green	•			14
Blue/Gray	•			15
Red/Red			•	17
Gray	•			30
Gray/Blue			•	41
Gray/Red			•	42
Gray/Tan			•	43
Gray/Green			•	44
Beige/Blue*	•		•	45
Beige/Red*	•		•	46
Beige/Tan*	•		•	47
Beige/Green*	•		•	48
Green/Green*	•		•	49
Blue*			•	59
Red*			•	60
Tan*			•	61
Green*			•	62
Beige/Blue#	•		•	78
Beige/Red#	•		•	79
Beige/Tan#	•		•	80
Beige/Green#	•		•	81
Green/Green#	•		•	82

* Convertible only

Newport only

NEW YORKER TRIM

COLOR	CLOTH	VINYL	LEATHER	CODE
Red/Red	•		•	17
Green	•			32
Blue	•			33
Gray	•			34
Tan	•			35
Gray/Blue		•		41
Gray/Red		•		42
Gray/Tan		•		43
Gray/Green		•		44
Green/Green*	•	•		49
Beige/Blue*	•	•		50
Beige/Red*	•	•		51
Beige/Tan*	•	•		52
Beige/Green*	•	•		53
Blue*		•		59
Red*		•		60
Tan*		•		61
Green*		•		62
Green/Green#	•			75
Black/Gray#	•			76
Tan/Tan#	•			77
Green#	•			83

COLOR	CLOTH	VINYL	LEATHER	CODE
Gray#	•			84
Tan#	•			85
Geen#	•			87
Blue#	•			88
Maroon#	•			89

* Convertible only

Newport only

IMPERIAL TRIM

COLOR	CLOTH	VINYL	LEATHER	CODE
Brown/Tan	•			36
Tan	•			37
Blue Gray	•			38
Gray Beige	•			39
Gray	•			40

CROWN IMPERIAL TRIM

COLOR	CLOTH	VINYL	LEATHER	CODE
Brown/Tan	•			20
Tan	•			21
Blue Gray	•			22
Gray Beige	•			23

ENGINE SPECIFICATIONS

ENGINE NUMBER - Located on the left front of the cylinder block.

MODEL	STARTING NUMBER
C48	C48-1001
C49	C49-1001
C50	C50-1001

ROYAL

ENGINE CODE	NO. CYL.	CID	HORSE-POWER	COMP. RATIO	CARB
C48S	6	250	116	7.0:1	1 BC

WINDSOR

ENGINE CODE	NO. CYL.	CID	HORSE-POWER	COMP. RATIO	CARB
C48W	6	250	116	7.0:1	1 BC

SARATOGA

ENGINE CODE	NO. CYL.	CID	HORSE-POWER	COMP. RATIO	CARB
C49K	8	324	135	7.25:1	1 BC

NEW YORKER

ENGINE CODE	NO. CYL.	CID	HORSE-POWER	COMP. RATIO	CARB
C49N	8	324	135	7.25:1	1 BC

CROWN IMPERIAL

ENGINE CODE	NO. CYL.	CID	HORSE-POWER	COMP. RATIO	CARB
C50	8	324	135	7.25:1	1 BC

NOTES

1951 CHRYSLER WINDSOR DELUXE

1951 CHRYSLER

1951 CHRYSLER NEW YORKER

1951 CHRYSLER WINDSOR

1951 CHRYSLER SARATOGA

VEHICLE IDENTIFICATION NUMBER

> **• SERIAL NUMBER •**
> **70,081,001**

The serial number is located on the left front door hinge post. It indicates the series/model and the assembly plant based on numerical sequence.

MODEL NAME	MODEL CODE	ASSEMBLY PLANT	STARTING NUMBERS
Windsor, 6-cyl.	C51W	Detroit	70,081,001
		Los Angeles	65,007,001
Windsor Deluxe 6-cyl.	C51W	Detroit	70,891,001
		Los Angeles	67,026,001
New Yorker, 8-cyl.	C52	Detroit	7,165,001
Crown Imperial, 8-cyl.	C53	Detroit	7,814,501
Imperial, 8-cyl.	C54	Detroit	7,736,501
Saratoga, 8-cyl.	C55	Detroit	76,500,001
		Los Angeles	66,500,001

THE BODY NUMBER PLATE is located on the cowl under the hood. Chrysler did not have body style codes, paint codes or trim codes appearing anywhere on the car. When ordering parts, it was necessary to furnish the factory with both the serial number and body plate number. We have attempted to list codes for paint and trim combinations when available.

> # BODY NUMBER
> # XXX XXXX
> **BRIGGS BODY, DETROIT MICHIGAN**

BODY TYPES

BODY TYPE
WINDSOR - C51-1
2-Dr. Club coupe
4-Dr. sedan
4-Dr. station wagon
4-Dr. sedan, 8-pass. L.W.

WINDSOR DELUXE - C51-2
2-Dr. Club coupe
4-Dr. sedan
4-Dr. Traveler
2-Dr. Newport
4-Dr. sedan L.W.
4-Dr. limo, 8-pass. L.W.

SARATOGA - C55
2-Dr. Club coupe
4-Dr. sedan
4-Dr. Town & Country wagon
4-Dr. sedan, L.W.
4-Dr. limo, 8-pass. L.W.

NEW YORKER - C52
2-Dr. Club coupe
4-Dr. sedan
Convertible
2-Dr. Newport
4-Dr. Town & Country Woodie wagon
2-Dr. Town & country Newport

IMPERIAL - C54
4-Dr. sedan
2-Dr. Club coupe
2-Dr. hardtop
Convertible

THE COLOR CODE indicates the paint color used on the vehicle.

COLOR	CODE
Black	1
Haze Blue	5
Ecuador Blue	6
Newport Blue	7
Foam Green	20
Juniper Green Metallic	21
Continental Green Metallic	22
Quebec Gray	35
Stone Gray	36
Gunmetal Metallic	37
Monitor Gray	38
Arizona Beige	45
Buckskin Tan	46
Indian Brown Metallic	47
Crown Maroon	60
Holiday Red	61
Belvedere Ivory	65
Highland Maroon	*84L

* L indicates lower body color

TWO-TONE COLORS

COLOR	CODE
Quebec Gray/Haze Blue	70
Quebec Gray/Stone Gray	71
Quebec Gray/foam Green	72
Quebec Gray/Juniper Green Poly	73
Quebec Gray/Gunmetal Poly	74
Quebec Gray/Crown Maroon	75
Indian Brown Poly/Buckskin Tan	76
Indian Brown Poly/Arizona Beige	77
Buckskin Tan/Arizona Beige	78
Continental Green Poly/Foam Green	79
Crown Maroon/Quebec Gray	80
Black/Quebec Gray	81
Black/Foam Green	82
Black/Juniper Green Poly	83

* The first code identifies the upper color, the second identifies the lower color.

THE TRIM CODE indicates the color and material scheme used on the vehicle.

WINDSOR TRIM

COLOR	CLOTH	VINYL	LEATHER	CODE
Gray	•			11,19
Tan	•			12,20
Green	•			13,21
Blue	•			22
Brown/Tan	•			69
Brown/Tan*	•			67
Maroon/Tan*	•			15
Green/Green*	•			16
Blue/Gray*	•			17
Red/Red*	•		•	18
Blue*		•		55
Red*		•		56
Tan*		•		57
Green*		•		58
Blue/Gray*	•	•		59
Red/Gray*	•	•		60
Tan/Gray*	•	•		61
Green/Gray*	•	•		62
Green/Green*	•	•		63

* Windsor deluxe only

NEW YORKER TRIM

COLOR	CLOTH	VINYL	LEATHER	CODE
Maroon/Tan	•			15
Green/Green	•			16
Blue/Gray	•			17
Green	•			23
Blue	•			24
Gray	•			25
Tan	•			26
Red/Red	•		•	18
Blue			•	55
Red			•	56
Tan			•	57
Green			•	58
Blue/Gray	•		•	59
Red/Gray	•		•	60
Tan/Gray	•		•	61
Green/Gray	•		•	62
Green/Green	•		•	63,64,71
Black/Gray	•		•	65
Tan/Tan	•		•	66
Brown/Tan	•		•	68

IMPERIAL TRIM

COLOR	CLOTH	VINYL	LEATHER	CODE
Brown/Tan	•			27
Tan	•			28
Blue Gray	•			29
Gray Beige	•			30
Gray	•			36
Gray Shadow	•			31
Green	•			37
Green/Green	•		•	71
Black/Gray	•		•	65
Brown/Tan	•		•	68
Blue			•	55
Red			•	56
Tan			•	57
Green			•	58
Brown/Tan*	•			32
Tan*	•			33
Blue Gray*	•			34
Gray Beige*	•			35
Gray*	•			36
Gray Shadow	•			31
Green	•			37

* Imperial limo only

ENGINE SPECIFICATIONS

ENGINE NUMBER - 6-Cylinder is located on the left front of the cylinder block, V8 on the top of the cylinder block just back of the water pump.

MODEL	STARTING NUMBER
Six	C51-1001
V8	C51-8-1001

WINDSOR

ENGINE CODE	NO. CYL.	CID	HORSE-POWER	COMP. RATIO	CARB
C51	6	250	116	7.0:1	1 BC

NEW YORKER

ENGINE CODE	NO. CYL.	CID	HORSE-POWER	COMP. RATIO	CARB
C52	8	331	180	7.5:1	2 BC

CROWN IMPERIAL

ENGINE CODE	NO. CYL.	CID	HORSE-POWER	COMP. RATIO	CARB
C53	8	331	180	7.5:1	2 BC

IMPERIAL

ENGINE CODE	NO. CYL.	CID	HORSE-POWER	COMP. RATIO	CARB
C54	8	331	180	7.5:1	2 BC

SARATOGA

ENGINE CODE	NO. CYL.	CID	HORSE-POWER	COMP. RATIO	CARB
C55	8	331	180	7.5:1	2 BC

1952 CHRYSLER NEW YORKER

1952 CHRYSLER IMPERIAL

1952 CHRYSLER IMPERIAL

VEHICLE IDENTIFICATION NUMBER

SERIAL NUMBER
70,094,301

The serial number is located on the left front door hinge post. It indicates the series/model and the assembly plant based on numerical sequence.

MODEL NAME	MODEL CODE	ASSEMBLY PLANT	STARTING NUMBERS
Windsor, 6-cyl.	C51W	Detroit	70,094,301
		Los Angeles	65,008,901
Windsor Deluxe 6-cyl	C51W	Detroit	70,952,301
		Los Angeles	67,033,301
New Yorker, 8-cyl.	C52	Detroit	7,199,901
Crown Imperial, 8-cyl.	C53	Detroit	7,815,101
Imperial, 8-cyl.	C54	Detroit	7,753,601
Saratoga, 8-cyl.	C55	Detroit	76,512,101
		Los Angeles	66,501,801

THE BODY NUMBER PLATE is located on the cowl under the hood. Chrysler did not have body style codes, paint codes or trim codes appearing anywhere on the car. When ordering parts, it was necessary to furnish the factory with both the serial number and body plate number. We have attempted to list codes for paint and trim combinations when available.

BODY NUMBER
XXX XXXX
BRIGGS BODY, DETROIT MICHIGAN

BODY TYPES

WINDSOR - C51-1

2-Dr. Club coupe
4-Dr. sedan
4-Dr. Town & Country wagon
4-Dr. sedan, 8-pass. L.W.

WINDSOR DELUXE - C51-2

4-Dr. sedan
2-Dr. convertible coupe
2-Dr. Newport

SARATOGA - C55

2-Dr. Club coupe
4-Dr. sedan
4-Dr. Town & Country wagon
4-Dr. sedan, 8-pass. L.W.

NEW YORKER - C52

4-Dr. sedan
2-Dr. convertible
2-Dr. Newport

IMPERIAL - C54

4-Dr. sedan
2-Dr. Club coupe
2-Dr. hardtop Newport

CROWN IMPERIAL - C53

4-Dr. sedan, 8-pass.
4-Dr. limo, 8-pass.

THE COLOR CODE indicates the paint color used on the vehicle.

COLOR	CODE
Black	1
Superior Blue	5
Huron Blue	7
Florida Green	20
Ivy Green Metallic	21
Jungle Green Metallic	22
Gull Gray	35
Monitor Gray	38
Yuma Beige	45
Sonora Tan	46
Banner Red	61
Majestic Maroon	62
Tuskon Ivory	65
Coffee Brown Metallic	*77U

*U indicates upper body color

TWO-TONE COLORS

COLOR	CODE
Gull Gray/Superior Blue	70
Gull Gray/Ivy Green Metallic	73
Coffee Brown Metallic/Yuma Beige	77
Jungle Green Metallic/Florida Green	79
Black/Gull Gray	81
Black/Florida Green	82
Black/Ivy Green Metallic	83
Gull Gray/Monitor Gray	86

NOTE: The first code identifies the upper color and the second identifies the lower color.

THE TRIM CODE indicates the color and material scheme used on the vehicle.

COLOR	CLOTH	VINYL	LEATHER	CODE
Green	•			16,21,37
Green	•			45
Blue/Gray	•			17
Red/Red	•		•	18
Blue	•			22
Brown/Tan	•			27
Tan	•			28
Blue Gray	•			29,34
Gray/Black	•			31
Tan/Brown	•			33,41,44
Gray/Brown	•			36,43
Green/Brown	•			42
Gray/Blue	•			46
Blue			•	55
Red			•	56
Tan			•	57
Green			•	58
Blue/Blue	•		•	59
Green/Green	•		•	63
Black/Silver Gray	•		•	65
Brown/Tan	•		•	68
Brown/Tan			•	69
Green/Green-Yellow	•		•	71
Black/Gray	•		•	72

ENGINE SPECIFICATIONS

ENGINE NUMBER - 6-Cylinder is located on the left front of the cylinder block, V8 on the top of the cylinder block just back of the water pump.

MODEL	STARTING NUMBER
Six	C52-1001
V8	C52-8-1001

WINDSOR

ENGINE CODE	NO. CYL.	CID	HORSE-POWER	COMP. RATIO	CARB
C51	6	265	119	7.0:1	1 BC

NEW YORKER

ENGINE CODE	NO. CYL.	CID	HORSE-POWER	COMP. RATIO	CARB
C52	8	331	180	7.5:1	2 BC

CROWN IMPERIAL

ENGINE CODE	NO. CYL.	CID	HORSE-POWER	COMP. RATIO	CARB
C53	8	331	180	7.5:1	2 BC

IMPERIAL

ENGINE CODE	NO. CYL.	CID	HORSE-POWER	COMP. RATIO	CARB
C54	8	331	180	7.5:1	2 BC

SARATOGA

ENGINE CODE	NO. CYL.	CID	HORSE-POWER	COMP. RATIO	CARB
C55	8	331	180	7.5:1	2 BC

1953 CHRYSLER

1953 CHRYSLER

1953 CHRYSLER IMPERIAL

VEHICLE IDENTIFICATION NUMBER

SERIAL NUMBER
7 0 , 1 1 0 , 0 0 1

The serial number is located on the left front door hinge post. It indicates the series/model and the assembly plant based on numerical sequence.

MODEL NAME	MODEL CODE	ASSEMBLY PLANT	STARTING NUMBERS
Windsor, 6-cyl.	C60-1	Detroit	70,110,001
		Los Angeles	65,011,001
Windsor Deluxe, 6-cyl.	C60-2	Detroit	71,005,001
		Los Angeles	67,040,001
New Yorker, 8-cyl.	C56-1	Detroit	76,540,001
		Los Angeles	66,506,001
New Yorker Deluxe, 8-cyl.	C56-2	Detroit	7,222,001
		Los Angeles	69,001,001
Crown Imperial, 8-cyl.	C59	Detroit	7,816,001
Custom Imperial, 8-cyl.	C58	Detroit	7,765,001

THE BODY NUMBER PLATE is located on the cowl under the hood. When ordering parts, it was necessary to furnish the factory with both the serial number and body plate number. We have attempted to list codes for paint and trim combinations when available.

CHRYSLER DIVISION

| MODEL | PAINT | TRIM | SCHED | ITEM |

| 25 | 8F | F2 | | 0791515 |

8-31　　　　4

|A|B|C|D|E|F|G|H|J|L|M|N| XXXXXX|

BODY NUMBER　　0000

BODY TYPES

WINDSOR - C60-1
2-Dr. Club coupe
4-Dr. sedan
4-Dr. Town & Country wagon
4-Dr. sedan, 8-pass. L.W.

WINDSOR DELUXE - C60-2
4-Dr. sedan
Convertible
2-Dr. Newport

NEW YORKER - C56-1
2-Dr. Club coupe
4-Dr. sedan
2-Dr. Newport
4-Dr. Town & Country wagon
4-Dr. sedan, 8-pass. L.W.

NEW YORKER DELUXE - C56-2
2-Dr. Club coupe
4-Dr. sedan
Convertible coupe
2-Dr. Newport

IMPERIAL - C58
4-Dr. sedan, 8-pass.
4-Dr. limo, 6-pass.
2-Dr. hardtop

CROWN IMPERIAL - C59
4-Dr. sedan, 8-pass.
4-Dr. limo, 8-pass.

THE COLOR CODE indicates the paint color used on the vehicle.

COLOR	CODE
Black	1
Arctic Blue	5
Erie Blue Metallic	6
Niagara Blue Metallic	7
Columbia Blue	8
Potomac Blue	9
Vermont Green	20
Foliage Green Metallic	21
Everglades Green Metallic	22
Pearl Gray	35
Submarine Gray Metallic	37
Caravan Beige	45
Cinnamon Metallic	46
Cocoa Brown Metallic	47
Hollywood Maroon Met.	60
Pimento Red	61
Casino Cream	65

TWO-TONE COLORS

COLOR	CODE
Pearl Gray/Erie Blue	70
Erie Blue/Pearl Gray	71
Pearl Gray/Submarine Gray Metallic	72
Submarine Gray Metallic/Pearl Gray	73
Vermont Green/Foliage Green Metallic	74
Foliage Green Metallic/Vermont Green	75
Caravan Beige/Cocoa Brown Metallic	76
Cocoa Brown Metallic/Caravan Beige	77
Caravan Beige/Cinnamon Metallic	78
Caravan Beige/Foliage Green Metallic	79
Vermont Green/Everglades Green Metallic	84
Arctic Blue/Columbia Blue Metallic	86
Columbia Blue Metallic/Arctic Blue	87
Caravan Beige/Cinnamon Metallic	88
Pearl Gray/Potomac Blue	89
Potomac Blue/Pearl Gray	90

NOTE: The first color identifies the upper color and the second color identifies the lower color.

THE TRIM CODE indicates the color and material scheme used on the vehicle.

WINDSOR TRIM

COLOR	CLOTH	VINYL	LEATHER	CODE
Gray	•			11,43
Brown/Tan	•		•	69
Green	•			16
Blue	•			17
Red/Red	•		•	18
Gray/Blue	•	•		47
Gray/Green	•	•		48
Gray/Blue			•	55
Gray/Red			•	56
Gray/Brown			•	57
Gray/Green			•	58
Gray Beige/Blue	•		•	59
Gray Beige/Red	•		•	60
Gray Beige/Brown	•		•	61
Gray Beige/Green	•		•	62

NEW YORKER TRIM

COLOR	CLOTH	VINYL	LEATHER	CODE
Two-tone Green*	•			12
Two-tone Blue/Gray*	•			13
Two-tone Gray*	•			14
Two-tone Brown/Tan*	•			15
Green	•			16
Blue	•			17
Red/Red	•		•	18
Gray/Blue	•	•		47
Gray/Green	•	•		48
Gray Beige/Blue	•		•	59
Gray Beige/Red	•		•	60
Gray Beige/Brown	•		•	61
Gray Beige/Green	•		•	62
Tan/Cinnamon Brown*			•	63,75
Tonga Red/Black*			•	64,77
Brown/Tan	•		•	69
Tan/Green*			•	74,76

* New Yorker Deluxe only

IMPERIAL TRIM

COLOR	CLOTH	VINYL	LEATHER	CODE
Green	•			19,37
Blue	•			20
Gray	•			21
Tan	•			22
Gray Shadow	•			31
Blue Gray	•			34
Gray Beige	•			36

ENGINE SPECIFICATIONS

ENGINE NUMBER - 6-Cylinder is located on the left front of the cylinder block, V8 on the top of the cylinder block just back of the water pump.

MODEL	STARTING NUMBER
Six	C53-1001
V8	C53-8-1001

WINDSOR

ENGINE CODE	NO. CYL.	CID	HORSE-POWER	COMP. RATIO	CARB
C60-1	6	265	119	7.0:1	1 BC

WINDSOR DELUXE

ENGINE CODE	NO. CYL.	CID	HORSE-POWER	COMP. RATIO	CARB
C60-2	6	265	119	7.0:1	1 BC

NEW YORKER

ENGINE CODE	NO. CYL.	CID	HORSE-POWER	COMP. RATIO	CARB
C56-1	8	331	180	7.5:1	2 BC

NEW YORKER DELUXE

ENGINE CODE	NO. CYL.	CID	HORSE-POWER	COMP. RATIO	CARB
C56-2	8	331	180	7.5:1	2 BC

CROWN IMPERIAL

ENGINE CODE	NO. CYL.	CID	HORSE-POWER	COMP. RATIO	CARB
C59	8	331	180	7.5:1	2 BC

CUSTOM IMPERIAL

ENGINE CODE	NO. CYL.	CID	HORSE-POWER	COMP. RATIO	CARB
C58	8	331	180	7.5:1	2 BC

1954 CHRYSLER IMPERIAL

1954 CHRYSLER NEW YORKER

1954 CHRYSLER NEW YORKER

1954 CHRYSLER NEW YORKER DELUXE CLUB

VEHICLE IDENTIFICATION NUMBER

```
• SERIAL NUMBER •
   70,141,001
```

The serial number is located on the left front door hinge post. It indicates the series/model and the assembly plant based on numerical sequence.

MODEL NAME	MODEL CODE	ASSEMBLY PLANT	STARTING NUMBERS
Windsor, 6-cyl.	C62	Detroit	70,141,001
		Los Angeles	65,014,001
New Yorker, 8-cyl.	C63-1	Detroit	76,591,001
		Los Angeles	66,510,001
New Yorker Deluxe, 8-cyl.	C63-2	Detroit	7,249,001
		Los Angeles	69,005,001
Imperial, 8-cyl.	C64	Detroit	7,775,001
Crown Imperial, 8-cyl.	C66	Detroit	7,817,001

THE BODY NUMBER PLATE is located on the cowl under the hood. When ordering parts, it was necessary to furnish the factory with both the serial number and body plate number. We have attempted to list codes for paint and trim combinations when available.

```
        CHRYSLER DIVISION

| MODEL | PAINT | TRIM | SCHED | ITEM |

   25      8F      F2        0791515

  O            8-31           4            O

|A|B|C|D|E|F|G|H|J|L|M|N| XXXXXX|

  BODY NUMBER      0000
```

BODY TYPES

WINDSOR DELUXE - C62
2-Dr. Club coupe
4-Dr. sedan
Convertible
2-Dr. Newport
4-Dr. Town & Country wagon, 6-pass.
4-Dr. sedan, 8-pass. L.W.

NEW YORKER - C63-1
2-Dr. Club coupe
4-Dr. sedan
2-Dr. Newport
4-Dr. Town & Country wagon, 6-pass.
4-Dr. sedan, 8-pass. L.W.

NEW YORKER DELUXE - C63-2
2-Dr. Club coupe
4-Dr. sedan
Convertible
2-Dr. Newport

IMPERIAL - C64
4-Dr. sedan
2-Dr. hardtop
4-Dr. limo, 6-pass.

CROWN IMPERIAL - C66
4-Dr. sedan, 8-pass.
4-Dr. limo, 8-pass.

THE COLOR CODE indicates the paint color used on the vehicle.

COLOR	CODE
Black	1
Alpine Blue	5
Flagship Blue	6
Commodore Blue Metallic	7
Glacier Blue	8
Turquoise Blue	9
Peacock Blue Metallic	11
Seabreeze Blue	11
Mint Green	15
Sea Island Green Metallic	16
Everglades Green Metallic	17
Westpoint Gray	30
Ascot Gray	31
Pebble Beige	40
Topaz Tan Metallic	41
Cordovan Brown Metallic	42
Tahitian Beige	43
Torch Red	50
Canary Yellow	55

TWO-TONE COLORS

COLOR	CODE
Flagship Blue/West Point Gray	60
West Point Gray/Flagship Blue	61
Alpine Blue/West Point Gray	62
West Point Gray/Alpine Blue	63
Flagship Blue/Alpine Blue	64
Alpine Blue/Flagship Blue	65
Commodore Blue/Alpine Blue	66
Alpine Blue/Commodore Blue	67
Ascot Gray/West Point Gray	68
West Point Gray/Ascot Gray	69
Everglades Green/Mint Green	70
Mint Green/Everglades Green	71
Mint Green/Sea Island Green	72
Sea Island Green/Mint Green	73
Topaz Tan/Pebble Beige	74
Pebble Beige/Topaz Tan	75
Glacier Blue/Peacock Blue	76
Peacock Blue/Glacier Blue	77
West Point Gray/Torch Red	78
Torch Red/West Point Gray	79
Sea Island Green/Canary Yellow	80
Canary Yellow/Sea Island Green	81
Tahitian Tan/Cordovan Brown	82
Cordovan Brown/Tahitian Tan	83
Black/Turquoise Blue	84
Black/Torch Red	85
Torch Red/Black	86
Black/Canary Yellow	87
Canary Yellow/Black	88

NOTE: The first code identifies the upper color and the second identifies the lower color.

THE TRIM CODE indicates the color and material scheme used on the vehicle.

WINDSOR TRIM

COLOR	CLOTH	VINYL	LEATHER	CODE
Tan/Brown	•			11
Green/Green	•			12
Blue/Blue	•			13
Gray/Gray	•			28
Red/Red	•		•	18
Two-tone Blue	•		•	46
Two-tone Green	•		•	47
Two-tone Brown/Tan	•		•	48
Two-tone Gray/Red	•		•	49
Blue			•	51
Tan			•	53
Two-tone Brown/Tan*	•		•	38
Two-tone Blue*	•		•	39

* Town & Country wagon only

NEW YORKER TRIM

COLOR	CLOTH	VINYL	LEATHER	CODE
Tan/Brown	•			11
Green/Green	•			12
Blue/Blue	•			13
Gray/Gray	•			28
Red/Red	•		•	18
Two-tone Blue	•		•	46
Two-tone Green	•		•	47
Two-tone Brown/Tan	•		•	48
Two-tone Gray/Red	•		•	49
Blue			•	51
Tan			•	53
Two-tone Brown/Tan*	•		•	38
Two-tone Blue*	•		•	39

* Town & Country wagon only

NEW YORKER DELUXE TRIM

COLOR	CLOTH	VINYL	LEATHER	CODE
Two-tone Tan/Brown	•			14
Two-tone Green	•			15
Two-tone Gray	•			16
Two-tone Blue	•			17
Red/Red	•		•	18
Blue			•	51
Tan			•	53
Green			•	59
Red*			•	60
Turquoise/Black	•		•	23

COLOR	CLOTH	VINYL	LEATHER	CODE
Cordovan Brown/ Beige	•		•	24
Black/Red	•		•	25
Blue/Blue	•		•	26
Green/Green	•		•	27
Black/Yellow	•		•	50
Two-tone Blue			•	40
Two-tone Green			•	41
Cordovan Brown/ Beige			•	42
Turquoise/Black			•	44
Black/Red			•	45
Black/Yellow			•	52

* Convertible only

IMPERIAL TRIM

COLOR	CLOTH	VINYL	LEATHER	CODE
Tan	•			19
Green	•			32
Gray	•			33
Blue	•			34
Cordovan Brown/ Beige	•		•	29
Green/Green	•		•	30
Blue/Blue	•		•	31
Two-tone Blue			•	56
Cordovan Brown/Beige			•	57
Two-tone Green			•	58

ENGINE SPECIFICATIONS

ENGINE NUMBER - 6-Cylinder is located on the left front of the cylinder block, V8 on the top of the cylinder block just back of the water pump.

MODEL	STARTING NUMBER
Six	C54-1001
V8	C54-8-1001

WINDSOR

ENGINE CODE	NO. CYL.	CID	HORSE-POWER	COMP. RATIO	CARB
C62	6	265	119	7.0:1	1 BC

NEW YORKER

ENGINE CODE	NO. CYL.	CID	HORSE-POWER	COMP. RATIO	CARB
C63-1	8	331	195	7.5:1	2 BC

NEW YORKER DELUXE

ENGINE CODE	NO. CYL.	CID	HORSE-POWER	COMP. RATIO	CARB
C63-2	8	331	235	7.5:1	4 BC

CUSTOM IMPERIAL

ENGINE CODE	NO. CYL.	CID	HORSE-POWER	COMP. RATIO	CARB
C64	8	331	235	7.5:1	4 BC

CROWN IMPERIAL

ENGINE CODE	NO. CYL.	CID	HORSE-POWER	COMP. RATIO	CARB
C66	8	331	235	7.5:1	4 BC

1955 CHRYSLER 300

1955 CHRYSLER NEW YORKER

1955 CHRYSLER

1955 CHRYSLER

VEHICLE IDENTIFICATION NUMBER

| • W 5 5 L 1 0 0 1 • |

The serial number is located on the left front door hinge post. It indicates the series/model and the assembly plant based on numerical sequence.

FIRST DIGIT: Identifies the car model

MODEL	CODE
Windsor*	W
New Yorker*	N
Imperial/Crown Imperial#	C
Chrysler - C-300B#	3N

* Cars built in Los Angeles and Detroit

\# Cars built in Detroit only

SECOND AND THIRD DIGITS: Identify the model year (1955)

FOURTH DIGIT: (L) Identifies the vehicle as a Los Angeles built car. Los Angeles built cars only, no code for Detroit built cars.

LAST FOUR DIGITS: Identify the basic production sequence number

THE BODY NUMBER PLATE
is located on the cowl under the hood. When ordering parts, it was necessary to furnish the factory with both the serial number and body plate number. We have attempted to list codes for paint and trim combinations when available.

```
┌─────────────────────────────────────────┐
│        CHRYSLER DIVISION                  │
│                                           │
│  | MODEL | PAINT | TRIM | SCHED | ITEM |  │
│                                           │
│    2 5     8 F     F 2      0 7 9 1 5 1 5  │
│   ○          8 - 3 1          4        ○   │
│                                           │
│  |A|B|C|D|E|F|G|H|J|L|M|N| XXXXXX|         │
│   BODY NUMBER      0 0 0 0                 │
└─────────────────────────────────────────┘
```

BODY TYPES

WINDSOR - C67

4-Dr. sedan

convertible

4-Dr. Town & Country wagon

2-Dr. Nassau

2-Dr. Newport

4-Dr. Town & Country wagon

NEW YORKER - C68

4-Dr. sedan

4-Dr. Town & Country wagon, 6-pass.

2-Dr. Newport

Convertible

2-Dr. St. Regis

300-B SERIES - C68

2-Dr. hardtop coupe

IMPERIAL - C69

4-Dr. sedan

2-Dr. hardtop Newport

CROWN IMPERIAL - C70

4-Dr. sedan, 8-pass.

4-Dr. limo, 8-pass.

MODEL NUMBER

MODEL	CODE
Windsor V-8	C67
New Yorker V8	C68
Custom Imperial V8...	C69
Crown Imperial V8...	C70
Chrysler "300"	C68-300

THE COLOR CODE indicates the paint color used on the vehicle.

COLOR	CODE
Black	1
Wisteria Blue	5
Rhapsody Blue Metallic	6
Crown Imperial Blue	7
Porcelain Green	11
Shantung Green Metallic	12
Jade Green Metallic	13
Crown Imperial Green	14
Skyline Gray	16
Embassy Gray Metallic	17
Canyon Tan	20
Desert Sand	21
Tango Red	25
Crown Imperial Maroon	26
Navajo Orange	27
Platinum	30
Nugget Gold Metallic	31
Sunburst Yellow	32
Falcon Green	301
Heron Blue	303

TWO-TONE COLORS

COLOR	CODE
Black/Embassy Gray	35,80
Wisteria Blue/Rhapsody Blue	36,81
Rhapsody Blue/Wisteria Blue	37,82
Porcelain Green/Shantung Green	38,83
Shantung Green/Porcelain Green	39,84
Skyline Gray/Embassy Gray	40,85
Embassy Gray/Skyline Gray	41,86
Canyon Tan/Desert Sand	42,87
Nugget Gold/Platinum	43
Nugget Gold/Platinum#	88
Jade Green/Platinum	44,89
Rhapsody Blue/Platinum	45,90
Navajo Orange/Desert Sand	46
Navajo Orange/Desert Sand#	91
Black/Platinum	47,92
Platinum/Black	48,552
Desert Sand/Canyon Tan*	93
Desert Sand/Navajo Orange*	94
Platinum/Nugget Gold*	95
Platinum/Jade Green*	96
Platinum/Rhapsody Blue*	97
Platinum/Black*	55
Sunburst Yellow/Jade Green*	503
Platinum/Sunburst Yellow*	533
Sunburst Yellow/Jade Green	501,502
Jade Green/Sunburst Yellow	511,512
Sunburst Yellow/Platinum	521,522
Platinum/Sunburst Yellow	531,532
Tango Red/Black	671,672
Black/Tango Red	681,682
Platinum/Tango Red	691,692
Tango Red/Platinum	701,702
Desert Sand/Canyon Tan	721,722
Platinum/Nugget Gold	741,742
Platinum/Jade Green	761,762
Platinum/Rhapsody Blue	781,782
Desert Sand/Navajo Orange	941,942

* New Yorker St. Regis only

Newport only
NOTE: The first color identifies the upper color and the second color identifies the lower color.

THE TRIM CODE indicates the color and material scheme used on the vehicle.

NEW YORKER TRIM

COLOR	CLOTH	VINYL	LEATHER	CODE
Green/Green	•			36
Gray/Gray	•			37
Blue/Blue	•			38
Green/Green			•	62
Gray/Gray			•	63
Blue/Blue			•	64
Brown/Beige*	•		•	23
Gold/White*	•		•	24
Blue/Blue*	•		•	25

* Town & Country wagon only

WINDSOR TRIM

COLOR	CLOTH	VINYL	LEATHER	CODE
Green/Green	•			11
Black/Red	•			12
Blue/Blue	•			13
Green/Green			•	59
Black/Red			•	60,52
Blue/Blue			•	61
Green/White	•		•	14
Black/Red	•		•	15
Blue/White	•		•	16
Green/White			•	51
Blue/White			•	53
Gray/White	•		•	35
Black/White*			•	65

* Town & Country wagon only

ENGINE SPECIFICATIONS

ENGINE NUMBER - Located on the top of the cylinder block just back of the water pump.

MODEL	STARTING NUMBER
C67	WE55-1001
C68	NE55-1001
C69	CE55-1001
C70	CE55-1001
300	3NE55-1001

WINDSOR

ENGINE CODE	NO. CYL.	CID	HORSE-POWER	COMP. RATIO	CARB
C67	8	301	188	8.0:1	2 BC

NEW YORKER

ENGINE CODE	NO. CYL.	CID	HORSE-POWER	COMP. RATIO	CARB
C68	8	331	250	8.5:1	4 BC

CUSTOM IMPERIAL

ENGINE CODE	NO. CYL.	CID	HORSE-POWER	COMP. RATIO	CARB
C69	8	331	250	8.5:1	4 BC

CROWN IMPERIAL

ENGINE CODE	NO. CYL.	CID	HORSE-POWER	COMP. RATIO	CARB
C70	8	331	250	8.5:1	4 BC

CHRYSLER "300"

ENGINE CODE	NO. CYL.	CID	HORSE-POWER	COMP. RATIO	CARB
C68-300	8	331	300	8.5:1	2X4 BC

1956 CHRYSLER NEW YORKER

1956 CHRYSLER WINDSOR NEWPORT

1956 CHRYSLER 300B

1956 CHRYSLER

1956 CHRYSLER

VEHICLE IDENTIFICATION NUMBER

• W 5 6 L 1 0 0 1 •

The serial number is located on the left front door hinge post. It indicates the series/model and the assembly plant based on numerical sequence.

FIRST DIGIT: Identifies the car model

MODEL	CODE
Windsor*	W
New Yorker*	N
Imperial/Crown Imperial#	C
Chrysler - C-300B#	3N

* Cars built in Los Angeles and Detroit

\# Cars built in Detroit only

SECOND AND THIRD DIGITS: Identify the model year (1956)

FOURTH DIGIT: (L) Identifies the vehicle as a Los Angeles built car. Los Angeles built cars only, no code for Detroit built cars.

LAST FOUR DIGITS: Identify the basic production sequence number

---

THE BODY NUMBER PLATE is located on the cowl under the hood. When ordering parts, it was necessary to furnish the factory with both the serial number and body plate number. We have attempted to list codes for paint and trim combinations when available.

CHRYSLER DIVISION

MODEL	PAINT	TRIM	SCHED	ITEM
25	8F	F2		0791515
○	8-31		4	○

| A | B | C | D | E | F | G | H | J | L | M | N | XXXXXX |

BODY NUMBER 0000

BODY TYPES

WINDSOR - C71

4-Dr. sedan

Convertible

4-Dr. Town & Country wagon, 6-pass.

2-Dr. Nassau

2-Dr. Newport

4-Dr. Newport

NEW YORKER - C72

4-Dr. sedan convertible

4-Dr. Town & Country wagon, 6-pass.

2-Dr. Newport

4-Dr. Newport

2-Dr. St. Regis, 6-pass.

300-B SERIES - C72

2-Dr. sport coupe

IMPERIAL - C73

4-Dr. sedan

4-Dr. hardtop Southampton

2-Dr. hardtop Southampton

CROWN IMPERIAL - C70

4-Dr. sedan, 8-pass.

4-Dr. limo, 8-pass.

MODEL	CODE
Crown Imperial V8	C70
Windsor V-8	C71
New Yorker V8	C72
Chrysler "300"	C72-300
Custom Imperial V8	C73

THE COLOR CODE indicates the paint color used on the vehicle.

COLOR	CODE
Black	1
Stardust Blue	5
Mediterranean Blue Metallic	6
Glacier Blue	7
Turquoise	8
Crown Blue Metallic	9
Mint Green	16
Surf Green Metallic	17
Hunter Green Metallic	18
Crown Green Metallic	19
Satin Gray	25
West Point Gray Metallic	26
Sand Dune Beige	30
Rosewood Tan	31
Desert Rose	35
Geranium Red	36
Regimental Red	37
Crown Maroon Metallic	38
Cloud White	41
Nugget Gold Metallic	42
Crocus Yellow	261
Blue Jade	262
Copper Glow Metallic	263

TWO-TONE COLORS

COLOR	CODE
Mediterranean Blue Metallic/Cloud White/ Stardust Blue*	301
Glacier Blue/Raven Black/Turquoise*	302
Cloud White/Surf Green Metallic/Mint Green*	303
Surf Green Metallic/Cloud White/ Hunter Green Metallic*	304
Satin Gray/West Point Gray Metallic/Raven Black*	305
Rosewood Tan/Sand Dune Beige/Raven Black*	306
Raven Black/Desert Rose/Cloud White*	307
Cloud White/Geranium Red/Raven Black*	308
Regimental Red/Cloud White/Raven Black*	309
Nugget Gold Metallic/Raven Black/Cloud White*	310
Raven Black/Cloud White	401
Cloud White/Raven Black	402
Stardust Blue/Cloud White	403
Cloud White/Stardust Blue	404
Mediterranean Blue Metallic/Stardust Blue	405
Stardust Blue/Mediterranean Blue Metallic	406
Mediterranean Blue Metallic/Satin Gray	407
Satin Gray/Mediterranean Blue Metallic	408

COLOR	CODE
Mediterranean Blue Metallic/Cloud White	409
Cloud White/Mediterranean Blue Metallic	410
Glacier Blue/Raven Black	411
Raven Black/Glacier Blue	412
Glacier Blue/West Point Gray Metallic	413
West Point Gray Metallic/Glacier Blue	414
Glacier Blue/Turquoise	415
Turquoise/Glacier Blue	416
Turquoise/Raven Black	417
Raven Black/Turquoise	418
Turquoise/Cloud White	419
Cloud White/Turquoise	420
Mint Green/Raven Black	421
Raven Black/Mint Green	422
Surf Green Metallic/Mint Green	423
Mint Green/Surf Green Metallic	424
Surf Green Metallic/Cloud White	425
Cloud White/Surf Green Metallic	426
Hunter Green Metallic/Mint Green	428
Hunter Green Metallic/Cloud White	429
Cloud White/Hunter Green Metallic	430
Rosewood Tan/Sand Dune Beige	431
Sand Dune Beige/Rosewood Tan	432
Rosewood Tan/Cloud White	433
Cloud White/Rosewood Tan	434
Desert Rose/Raven Black	435
Raven Black/Desert Rose	436
Desert Rose/Cloud White	437
Cloud White/Desert Rose	438
Geranium Red/West Point Gray Metallic	439
West Point Gray Metallic/Geranium Red	440
Geranium Red/Raven Black	441
Raven Black/Geranium Red	442
Geranium Red/Cloud White	443
Cloud White/Geranium Red	444
Regimental Red/Raven Black	445
Raven Black/Regimental Red	446
Regimental Red/Cloud White	447
Cloud White/Regimental Red	448
Nugget Gold Metallic/Raven Black	449
Raven Black/Nugget Gold Metallic	450
Nugget Gold Metallic/Cloud White	451
Cloud White/Nugget Gold Metallic	452
Satin Gray/West Point Gray Metallic	453
West Point Gray Metallic/Satin Gray	454

* The first code identifies the lower color, the second identifies the upper color and the third identifies the roof color.

NOTE: On all the others the first code is the lower color and the second is the upper color.

THE TRIM CODE indicates the color and material
scheme used on the vehicle. No trim codes were available.

WINDSOR TRIM

COLOR	CLOTH	VINYL	LEATHER	CODE
Green/Green	•			
Blue/Blue	•			
Gray/Gray	•			
Brown/Tan	•			
Red/Black	•			
Green/Green		•		
Blue/Blue		•		
Gray/White		•		
Brown/Beige		•		
Red/White		•		
Gray/White	•	•		
Green/Green	•	•		
Gray/Black	•	•		
Tan/Brown	•	•		

NEW YORKER TRIM

COLOR	CLOTH	VINYL	LEATHER	CODE
Green	•			
Blue	•			
Gray	•			
Tan/Brown	•			
Coral/Black	•			
Turquoise/Black	•			
Green	•		•	
Blue	•		•	
Gray/White	•		•	
Tan/Beige	•		•	
Coral/White	•		•	
Turquoise/White	•		•	

ENGINE SPECIFICATIONS

ENGINE NUMBER - Located on the top of the cylinder block just back of the water pump.

MODEL	STARTING NUMBER
C70	CE56-1001
C71	WE56-1001
C72	NE56-1001
C73	CE56-1001
300B	3NE56-1001

WINDSOR

ENGINE CODE	NO. CYL.	CID	HORSE-POWER	COMP. RATIO	CARB
C71	8	331	225	8.5:1	2 BC
	8	331	250	8.5:1	4 BC

NEW YORKER

ENGINE CODE	NO. CYL.	CID	HORSE-POWER	COMP. RATIO	CARB
C72	8	354	280	9.0:1	4 BC

CHRYSLER "300B"

ENGINE CODE	NO. CYL.	CID	HORSE-POWER	COMP. RATIO	CARB
C72-300	8	354	340	9.0:1	2X4 BC
	8	354	355	10.0:1	2X4 BC

IMPERIAL

ENGINE CODE	NO. CYL.	CID	HORSE-POWER	COMP. RATIO	CARB
C73	8	354	280	9.0:1	4 BC

CROWN IMPERIAL

ENGINE CODE	NO. CYL.	CID	HORSE-POWER	COMP. RATIO	CARB
C70	8	354	280	9.0:1	4 BC

1957 CHRYSLER SARATOGA

1957 CHRYSLER NEW YORKER

1957 CHRYSLER

1957 CHRYSLER 300C

1957 IMPERIAL

1957 IMPERIAL

VEHICLE IDENTIFICATION NUMBER

• W 5 7 L 1 0 0 1 •

The serial number is located on the left front door hinge post. It indicates the series/model and the assembly plant based on numerical sequence.

FIRST DIGIT: Identifies the car model

MODEL	CODE
Windsor*	W
New Yorker*	N
Imperial#	C
Saratoga*	L

* Cars built in Los Angeles and Detroit

\# Cars built in Detroit only

SECOND AND THIRD DIGITS: Identify the model year (1957)

FOURTH DIGIT: (L) Identifies the vehicle as a Los Angeles built car. Los Angeles built cars only, no code for Detroit built cars.

LAST FOUR DIGITS: Identify the basic production sequence number

MODEL NUMBER

MODEL	CODE
Windsor V-8	C75-1
Saratoga V8	C75-2
New Yorker V8	C76
Chrysler "300C"	C76-300
Imperial V8	IM-1,2,4

THE BODY NUMBER PLATE is located on the cowl under the hood. When ordering parts, it was necessary to furnish the factory with both the serial number and body plate number. We have attempted to list codes for paint and trim combinations when available.

CHRYSLER DIVISION

MODEL	PAINT	TRIM	SCHED	ITEM
2 5	8 F	F 2		0 7 9 1 5 1 5
○	8 - 3 1		4	○

| A | B | C | D | E | F | G | H | J | L | M | N | X X X X X X |

BODY NUMBER   0 0 0 0

BODY TYPES

WINDSOR - C75-1
4-Dr. sedan
4-Dr. Town & Country wagon, 6-pass.
2-Dr. hardtop
4-Dr. hardtop

SARATOGA - C75-2
4-Dr. sedan
2-Dr. hardtop
4-Dr. hardtop

NEW YORKER - C76
4-Dr. sedan
4-Dr. Town & Country wagon, 6-pass.
2-Dr. hardtop
4-Dr. hardtop
Convertible, 6-pass.

300-B SERIES - C76-300
2-Dr. hardtop coupe, 6-pass.
Convertible, 6-pass.

IMPERIAL - IM1
4-Dr. sedan
4-Dr. hardtop
2-Dr. hardtop

CROWN IMPERIAL
4-Dr. limo, 8-pass.

IMPERIAL CROWN - IM2
4-Dr. Sedan
4 Dr. hardtop Southampton
2 Dr. hardtop Southampton
Convertible

IMPERIAL LEBARON - IM-4
4 Dr. sedan
4 Dr. hardtop Southampton

THE COLOR CODE indicates the paint color used on the vehicle.

COLOR	CODE
Jet Black	A
Horizon Blue	B
Regatta Blue Metallic	C
Regatta Blue Metallic #2	C
Velvet Blue Metallic	C
Sovereign Blue Metallic	D
Seafoam Aqua	E
Parade Green Metallic	F
Forest Green Metallic	G
Mist Gray	H
Gunmetal Gray Metallic	J
Charcoal Gray Metallic	K
Desert Beige	L
Shell Pink	M
Copper Brown Metallic	N
Gauguin Red	P
Regimental Red	R
Sunset Rose	S
Champagne Gold	T
Deep Ruby Metallic	U
Saturn Blue	V
Indian Turquosie	W
Cloud White	X

NOTE: On two-tone and insert combinations the first letter identifies the upper color, the second letter the lower color, the third letter identifies the insert color.

THE TRIM CODE indicates the color and material scheme used on the vehicle.

WINDSOR TRIM

COLOR	CLOTH	VINYL	LEATHER	CODE
Blue/Blue	•	•		53
Green/Green	•	•		54
Tan/Beige	•	•		55
Red/White	•	•		56
Blue/Blue		•		94
Green/Green		•		95
Tan/Beige		•		96
Blue Pattern		•		70
Green Pattern		•		71
Tan Pattern/Beige		•		72

SARATOGA TRIM

COLOR	CLOTH	VINYL	LEATHER	CODE
Blue/Blue	•			11
Green/Green	•			12
Gray/Gray	•			13

COLOR	CLOTH	VINYL	LEATHER	CODE
Blue/Blue		•		88
Green/Green		•		89
Tan/Beige		•		90
Blue Tweed/Blue	•	•		19
Green Tweed/Green	•	•		20
Tan Tweed/Beige	•	•		21
Turquoise Tweed/ Turquoise	•	•		22
Red Tweed/White	•	•		23
Blue Pattern/Blue		•		70
Green Pattern/Green		•		71
Tan Pattern/Beige		•		72
Red Pattern/White		•		74

NEW YORKER TRIM

COLOR	CLOTH	VINYL	LEATHER	CODE
Blue/Blue	•			14
Green/Green	•			15
Gray/Gray	•			16
Brown/Brown	•			17
Blue/Blue			•	91
Green/Green			•	92
Gray/Gray			•	93
Blue/Blue	•	•		24
Green/Green	•	•		25
Black/Gray	•	•		26
Coral/Beige	•	•		27
Turquoise/Turquoise	•	•		28
Blue/Blue		•		75
Green/Green		•		76
Tan/Beige		•		77
Red/White		•		79
Turquoise/Turquoise		•		80
Blue Tweed/Gray*	•	•		29
Green Heather/ Green*	•	•		30
Tan Tweed/Beige*	•	•		31
Tan Tweed/Red*	•	•		32
Green/Green#		•		97
Blue/Blue#		•		98
Tan/Beige#		•		99

* Convertible only

Town & Country wagon only

CONVERTIBLE TOP COLORS

COLOR	CODE
Black	1
Ivory	2
Blue	3
Green	4

ENGINE SPECIFICATIONS

ENGINE NUMBER - Located on the top of the cylinder block just back of the water pump.

MODEL	STARTING NUMBER
C75-1	WE57-1001
C75-2	LE57-1001
C76	NE57-1001
C76-300	3NE57-1001
IM	CE57-1001

WINDSOR

ENGINE CODE	NO. CYL.	CID	HORSE-POWER	COMP. RATIO	CARB
C75-1	8	354	285	9.25:1	2 BC
C75-2	8	354	295	9.25:1	4 BC

SARATOGA

ENGINE CODE	NO. CYL.	CID	HORSE-POWER	COMP. RATIO	CARB
C75-2	8	354	295	9.25:1	4 BC

NEW YORKER

ENGINE CODE	NO. CYL.	CID	HORSE-POWER	COMP. RATIO	CARB
C76	8	392	325	9.25:1	4 BC

CHRYSLER "300B"

ENGINE CODE	NO. CYL.	CID	HORSE-POWER	COMP. RATIO	CARB
C76-300	8	392	375	9.25:1	2X4 BC
C76-300*	8	392	390	10.0:1	2X4 BC

* Optional

IMPERIAL

ENGINE CODE	NO. CYL.	CID	HORSE-POWER	COMP. RATIO	CARB
IM-1	8	392	325	9.25:1	4 BC

CROWN IMPERIAL

ENGINE CODE	NO. CYL.	CID	HORSE-POWER	COMP. RATIO	CARB
IM-2	8	392	325	9.25:1	4 BC

IMPERIAL LEBARON

ENGINE CODE	NO. CYL.	CID	HORSE-POWER	COMP. RATIO	CARB
IM-4	8	392	325	9.25:1	4 BC

1958 IMPERIAL

1958 CHRYSLER WINDSOR

1958 IMPERIAL LEBARON

1958 CHRYSLER SARATOGA

1958 CHRYSLER NEW YORKER

VEHICLE IDENTIFICATION NUMBER

• L C 1 L   1 0 0 1 •

The serial number is located on the left front door hinge post. It indicates the series/model and the assembly plant based on numerical sequence.

FIRST DIGIT: Identifies the model year (L=1958)

SECOND DIGIT: Identifies the car make

MAKE	CODE
Chrysler	C
Imperial	Y

THIRD DIGIT: Identifies the model series

MODEL	CODE
Windsor/Imperial*	1
Saratoga*	2
New Yorker*	3
300D#	4

* Cars built in Los Angeles and Detroit

\# Cars built in Detroit only

FOURTH DIGIT: (L) Identifies the vehicle as a Los Angeles built car. Los Angeles built cars only, no code for Detroit built cars.

LAST FOUR DIGITS: Identify the basic production sequence number

THE BODY NUMBER PLATE is located on the cowl under the hood. When ordering parts, it was necessary to furnish the factory with both the serial number and body plate number. We have attempted to list codes for paint and trim combinations when available.

```
TL   CS   MR   HB   AC   A   SPL

HT PS AG AR PB PF EW S6 RS CU SC

SCH BO NO O BO  PT  TR  CT  TR   O
```

BODY TYPES

WINDSOR - LC1-L
4-Dr. sedan
4-Dr. Town & Country wagon, 6-pass.
4-Dr. Town & country wagon, 9-pass.
2-Dr. hardtop
4-Dr. hardtop

SARATOGA - LC2-M
4-Dr. sedan
2-Dr. hardtop
4-Dr. hardtop

NEW YORKER - LC3-H
4-Dr. sedan
4-Dr. Town & Country wagon, 6-pass.
4-Dr. Town & Country wagon, 9-pass.
2-Dr. hardtop
4-Dr. hardtop
Convertible, 6-pass.

300-B SERIES - C76-300
2-Dr. hardtop coupe
Convertible, 6-pass.

IMPERIAL - LY1-L
4-Dr. sedan
4-Dr. hardtop Southampton
2-Dr. hardtop Southampton

CROWN IMPERIAL - LY1-MC70
4-Dr. sedan, 8-pass.
4-Dr. hardtop Southampton
2-Dr. hardtop Southampton
2-Dr. convertible, 6-pass.

LE BARON - LY1-H
4-Dr. sedan
4-Dr. hardtop

MODEL NUMBER

LC1-L

EXAMPLE:

L ....Model year 1958
C...Car make (Chrysler)
1-L..............................Windsor, low price class

MODEL	CODE
Windsor V-8	LC1-L
Saratoga V8	LC2-M
New Yorker V8	LC3-H
Chrysler "300D"	LC3-S
Imperial V8	LY1-L,M,H

THE COLOR CODE indicates the paint color used on the vehicle.

COLOR	CODE
Raven Black	AAA
Stardust Blue	BBB
Air Force Blue Metallic	CCC
Midnight Blue	DDD
Spring Green	EEE
Cypress Green Metallic	FFF
Mandarin Jade Metallic	GGG
Aztec Turquoise	HHH
Spruce Metallic	JJJ
Satin Gray	KKK
Winchester Gray Metallic	LLL
Mesa Tan	MMM
Sandalwood Metallic	NNN
Tahitian Coral	OOO
Matador Red	PPP
Shell Pink	RRR
Fireglow Metallic	SSS
Garnet Maroon Metallic	TTT
Bamboo Yellow	UUU
Bimini Blue	VVV
Ballet Blue	WWW
Ermine White	XXX
Frosty Tan Metallic	YYY
Champagne Gold	ZZZ

NOTE: On two-tone and insert combinations the first letter identifies the upper color, the second letter the lower color, the third letter identifies the insert color.

THE TRIM CODE indicates the color and material scheme used on the vehicle. We were unable to determine the trim codes for the 1958 Chrysler and Imperial.

ENGINE SPECIFICATIONS

ENGINE NUMBER - Located on the top of the cylinder block just back of the water pump.

MODEL	STARTING NUMBER
LC-1L	58W-1001
LC-2L	58S-1001
LC-3L	58N-1001
LC-3S	58N3-1001
LY1-L,M,H	58C-1001

WINDSOR

ENGINE CODE	NO. CYL.	CID	HORSE-POWER	COMP. RATIO	CARB
LC1-L	8	354	290	10.0:1	2 BC

SARATOGA

ENGINE CODE	NO. CYL.	CID	HORSE-POWER	COMP. RATIO	CARB
LC2-M	8	354	310	10.0:1	4 BC

NEW YORKER

ENGINE CODE	NO. CYL.	CID	HORSE-POWER	COMP. RATIO	CARB
LC3-H	8	392	345	10.0:1	4 BC

CHRYSLER "300D"

ENGINE CODE	NO. CYL.	CID	HORSE-POWER	COMP. RATIO	CARB
LC3-S	8	392	380	10.0:1	2X4 BC
LC3-S	8	392	390	10.0:1	F.I.

IMPERIAL

ENGINE CODE	NO. CYL.	CID	HORSE-POWER	COMP. RATIO	CARB
LY1-L	8	392	345	10.0:1	4 BC

CROWN IMPERIAL

ENGINE CODE	NO. CYL.	CID	HORSE-POWER	COMP. RATIO	CARB
LY1-M	8	392	345	10.0:1	4 BC

IMPERIAL LEBARON

ENGINE CODE	NO. CYL.	CID	HORSE-POWER	COMP. RATIO	CARB
LY1-H	8	392	345	10.0:1	4 BC

1959 CHRYSLER

1959 CHRYSLER 300E

1959 IMPERIAL CROWN SOUTH HAMPTON

1959 CHRYSLER

1959 IMPERIAL LEBARON

VEHICLE IDENTIFICATION NUMBER

`• M 5 5 1   1 0 0 1 •`

The serial number is located on the left cowl under the hood for cars built in Detroit; on the left front door "A" post for cars built in Los Angeles.

FIRST DIGIT: Identifies the model year (M=1959)

SECOND DIGIT: Identifies the car make

MAKE	CODE
Chrysler	5
Imperial	6

THIRD DIGIT: Identifies the model series

MODEL	CODE
Windsor/Imperial Custom	1
Saratoga/Imperial Crown	3
New Yorker/Imperial LeBaron	5
Station Wagons (Windsor or New Yorker	7
300E	9

FOURTH DIGIT: Identifies the vehicle assembly plant

ASSEMBLY PLANT	CODE
Detroit, MI (Jefferson Ave. plant)	1
Los Angeles, CA	4
Detroit, MI (Imperial plant)	7

LAST FOUR DIGITS: Identify the basic production sequence number

THE BODY NUMBER PLATE is located on the cowl under the hood. When ordering parts, it was necessary to furnish the factory with both the serial number and body plate number. We have attempted to list codes for paint and trim combinations when available.

```
TL   CS   MR   HB   AC   A    SPL

HT  PS  AG  AR  PB  PF  EW  S6  RS  CU  SC

SCH  BO  NO  ◯  BO  PT  TR  CT  TR   ◯
```

BODY TYPES

WINDSOR - MC1-L
4-Dr. sedan
4-Dr. Town & Country wagon, 6-pass.
4-Dr. Town & Country wagon, 9-pass.
2-Dr. hardtop
4-Dr. hardtop
Convertible, 6-pass.

SARATOGA - MC2-M
4-Dr. sedan
2-Dr. hardtop
4-Dr. hardtop

NEW YORKER - MC3-H
4-Dr. sedan
4-Dr. Town & Country wagon, 6-pass.
4-Dr. Town & Country wagon, 9-pass.
2-Dr. hardtop
4-Dr. hardtop
Convertible, 6-pass.

300-B SERIES - MC3-H-300
2-Dr. hardtop coupe
Convertible, 6-pass.

IMPERIAL - MY1-L
4-Dr. sedan
4-Dr. hardtop Southampton
2-Dr. hardtop Southampton

CROWN IMPERIAL - MY1-MC70

4-Dr. sedan, 8-pass.

4-Dr. hardtop, 6-pass. Southampton

2-Dr. hardtop Southampton

2-Dr. convertible

LE BARON MY1-H

4-Dr. sedan

4-Dr. hardtop Southampton

MODEL NUMBER

MC1-L

EXAMPLE:

M ....Model year 1959
C ....Car make (Chrysler)
1-L ....Windsor, low price class

MODEL	CODE
Windsor V-8	MC1-L
Saratoga V8	MC2-M
New Yorker V8	MC3-H
Chrysler "300E"	MC3-S
Imperial V8	MY1-L,M,H

THE COLOR CODE indicates the paint color used on the vehicle.

COLOR	CODE
Formal Black	AAA
Normandy Blue	BBB
Nocturne Blue Metallic	CCC
Empress Blue Metallic	DDD
Ballard Green	EEE
Highland Green Metallic	FFF
Sherwood Green Metallic	*GGG
Silverpine Metallic	HHH
Aqua Mist	JJJ
Turquoise Gray Metallic	KKK
Spanish Silver Metallic #1	LLL
Spanish Silver Metallic #2	LLL
Oxford Gray Metallic	*MMM
Storm Gray Metallic	#MMM
Persian Pink	NNN
Carousel Red	PPP
Radiant Red	RRR
Gray Rose Metallic	SSS
Deep Ruby Metallic	TTT
Sandstone	UUU
Cameo Tan Metallic	WWW
Ivory White	XXX
Spun Yellow Metallic	#YYY
Yellow Mist	*YYY
Copper Spice Metallic	ZZZ
Tropic Turquoise	1

* Imperial only

Chrysler only

NOTE: On two-tone and insert combinations the first letter identifies the upper color, the second letter the lower color, the third letter identifies the insert color.

THE TRIM CODE indicates the color and material scheme used on the vehicle. We were unable to determine the trim codes for 1959 Chrysler and Imperial.

ENGINE SPECIFICATIONS

ENGINE NUMBER - Located on the top of the cylinder block just back of the water pump.

MODEL   **STARTING NUMBER**
Windsor/Saratoga MR383-1001
All others MR413-1001

WINDSOR

ENGINE CODE	NO. CYL.	CID	HORSE-POWER	COMP. RATIO	CARB
MC1-L	8	383	305	10.0:1	2 BC

SARATOGA

ENGINE CODE	NO. CYL.	CID	HORSE-POWER	COMP. RATIO	CARB
MC2-M	8	383	325	10.0:1	4 BC

NEW YORKER

ENGINE CODE	NO. CYL.	CID	HORSE-POWER	COMP. RATIO	CARB
MC3-H	8	413	350	10.0:1	4 BC

CHRYSLER "300E"

ENGINE CODE	NO. CYL.	CID	HORSE-POWER	COMP. RATIO	CARB
MC3-S	8	413	380	10.0:1	2X4 BC

IMPERIAL CUSTOM

ENGINE CODE	NO. CYL.	CID	HORSE-POWER	COMP. RATIO	CARB
MY1-L	8	413	350	10.0:1	4 BC

CROWN IMPERIAL

ENGINE CODE	NO. CYL.	CID	HORSE-POWER	COMP. RATIO	CARB
MY1-M	8	413	350	10.0:1	4 BC

IMPERIAL LEBARON

ENGINE CODE	NO. CYL.	CID	HORSE-POWER	COMP. RATIO	CARB
MY1-H	8	413	350	10.0:1	4 BC

1950 DESOTO

1950 DESOTO

1950 DESOTO

VEHICLE IDENTIFICATION NUMBER

• VEHICLE NUMBER •
6,233,501

The serial number is located on the left front door hinge post. It indicates the series and assembly plant where the vehicle was built, based on numerical sequence.

MODEL NAME	MODEL CODE	ASSEMBLY PLANT	STARTING NUMBERS
Deluxe, 6-cyl.	S14-S	Detroit	6,233,501
		Los Angeles	60,005,001
Custom, 6-cyl.	S14-C	Detroit	50,062,001
		Los Angeles	62,011,501

THE BODY NUMBER PLATE

THE BODY NUMBER PLATE is located on the cowl under the hood. The body number was essential in ordering the body parts. DeSoto did not have body style codes, paint codes or trim codes appearing anywhere on the car. When ordering parts, it was necessary to furnish the factory with both the serial number and body plate number. We have attempted to list codes for paint and trim combinations when available.

BODY NUMBER
XXX XXXX
BRIGGS BODY, DETROIT MICHIGAN

No body type codes were used. The bodies were as follows:

DELUXE

4-Dr. sedan
Club coupe
4-Dr. carry-all

DELUXE (LONG WHEELBASE)

4-Dr. sedan, 8-pass.
4-Dr. sedan, 8-pass.

CUSTOM

2-Dr. Club coupe
2-Dr. convertible coupe
4-Dr. sedan
Sportsman hardtop coupe
4-Dr. station wagon, wood
4-Dr. station wagon, steel

CUSTOM (LONG WHEELBASE)

4-Dr. sedan, 8-pass.
4-Dr. Suburban, 9-pass.

THE COLOR CODE indicates the paint color used on the vehicle.

COLOR	CODE
Black	301
Pacific Blue	305
Regal Blue Metallic	306
Midnight Blue	307
Glen Green	320
Andante Green Metallic	321
Cadet Gray	335
Silver Gray	336
Desert Tan	345
Samoa Beige Metallic	346
Royal Maroon	360
Princess Yellow	365
Glade Green Dark Metallic	374U
Nubian Bronze Metallic	375U

U - Indicates color was used on upper body

THE TRIM CODE indicates the color and material scheme used on the vehicle.

CUSTOM

COLOR	CLOTH	VINYL	LEATHER	CODE
Blue			•	401
Red			•	402
Tan			•	403
Green			•	404
Tan		•		446,456,459
Tan		•		480,486
Ivory		•		455,485
Tan/Ivory		•		457,458,487

Leather and bedford cord were available with the following codes (no colors were listed): 421, 422, 423, 424, 481, 482, 483, 484. Broadcloth was available with the following codes (no colors were listed): 934, 935, 936, 953, 954.

DELUXE

COLOR	CLOTH	VINYL	LEATHER	CODE
Tan		•		447
Tan	•	•		449

Broadcloth was available with the following codes (no colors were listed): 932, 933, 947, 948.

ENGINE SPECIFICATIONS

ENGINE NUMBER - Located on the left front of the cylinder block.

MODEL	STARTING NUMBER
S14	S14-1001

DELUXE

ENGINE CODE	NO. CYL.	CID	HORSE-POWER	COMP. RATIO	CARB
S14S	6	237	112	7.0:1	1 BC

CUSTOM

ENGINE CODE	NO. CYL.	CID	HORSE-POWER	COMP. RATIO	CARB
S14C	6	237	112	7.0:1	1 BC

4-4

1951 DESOTO

1951 DESOTO

VEHICLE IDENTIFICATION NUMBER

• VEHICLE NUMBER •
6,269,001

The serial number is located on the left front door hinge post. It indicates the series and assembly plant where the vehicle was built, based on numerical sequence.

MODEL NAME	MODEL CODE	ASSEMBLY PLANT	STARTING NUMBERS
Deluxe, 6-cyl.	S15-S	Detroit	6,269,001
		Los Angeles	60,011,001
Custom, 6-cyl.	S15-C	Detroit	50,155,001
		Los Angeles	62,024,001

THE BODY NUMBER PLATE

THE BODY NUMBER PLATE is located on the cowl under the hood. The body number was essential in ordering the body parts. DeSoto did not have body style codes, paint codes or trim codes appearing anywhere on the car. When ordering parts, it was necessary to furnish the factory with both the serial number and body plate number. We have attempted to list codes for paint and trim combinations when available.

BODY NUMBER
XXX XXXX
BRIGGS BODY, DETROIT MICHIGAN

There were no codes for the body type. They body types are as follows:

DELUXE

club coupe
4-Dr. sedan
4-Dr. sedan, 8-pass.

CUSTOM

Club coupe
Sportsman hardtop
Convertible coupe
4-Dr. sedan
Station wagon, 4-dr., 8-pass.
4-Dr. sedan, 8-pass.
Suburban 4-dr., 9-pass.

THE COLOR CODE indicates the paint color used on the vehicle.

COLOR	CODE
Black	301
Capri Blue	305
Imperial Blue Metallic	306
Midnight Blue	307
Glen Green	320
Andante Green Metallic	321
Dusk Gray	335
Platinum Gray	336
Arizona Beige	345
Morocco Brown Metallic	346
Royal Maroon	360
Ceramic Yellow	365
Samoa Beige Metallic	370U
Glade Green Dark Metallic	374U

U - Indicates color was used on upper body

THE TRIM CODE indicates the color and material scheme used on the vehicle.

CUSTOM TRIM

COLOR	CLOTH	VINYL	LEATHER	CODE
Brown	•			222
Gray	•			223
Blue	•			225
Blue			•	531
Red			•	532
Tan			•	533
Green			•	534
Tan		•		538,547
Tan/Ivory		•		537,539,548
Ivory		•		546
Blue	•		•	541
Red	•		•	542
Tan	•		•	543
Green	•		•	544
Black	•		•	545

DELUXE TRIM

COLOR	CLOTH	VINYL	LEATHER	CODE
Tan		•		535
Tan	•	•		536

ENGINE SPECIFICATIONS

ENGINE NUMBER - Located on the left front of the cylinder block.

MODEL   **STARTING NUMBER**
S15...S15-1001

DELUXE

ENGINE CODE	NO. CYL.	CID	HORSE-POWER	COMP. RATIO	CARB
S15S	6	250	116	7.0:1	1 BC

CUSTOM

ENGINE CODE	NO. CYL.	CID	HORSE-POWER	COMP. RATIO	CARB
S15C	6	250	116	7.0:1	1 BC

1952 DESOTO

1952 DESOTO

1952 DESOTO

VEHICLE IDENTIFICATION NUMBER

```
• VEHICLE NUMBER •
   6,283,601
```

The serial number is located on the left front door hinge post. It indicates the series and assembly plant where the vehicle was built, based on numerical sequence.

MODEL NAME	MODEL CODE	ASSEMBLY PLANT	STARTING NUMBERS
Deluxe, 6-cyl.	S15-S	Detroit	6,283,601
		Los Angeles	60,013,001
Custom, 6-cyl.	S15-C	Detroit	50,230,101
		Los Angeles	62,032,601
V8	S17	Detroit	55,000,001
		Los Angeles	64,001,001

THE BODY NUMBER PLATE is located on the cowl under the hood. The body number was essential in ordering body parts. DeSoto did not have body style codes, paint codes or trim codes appearing anywhere on the car. When ordering parts, it was necessary to furnish the factory with both the serial number and body plate number. We have attempted to list codes for paint and trim combinations when available.

```
BODY  NUMBER
XXX  XXXX
BRIGGS BODY, DETROIT MICHIGAN
```

No body type codes were used. The bodies were as follows:

DELUXE - S15S
Club coupe
4-Dr. sedan
Sedan Carryall, 8-pass.
4-Dr. sedan, 8-pass.

CUSTOM - S15C
Club coupe
Sportsman hardtop coupe
Convertible coupe
4-Dr. sedan
4-Dr. station wagon
4-Dr. sedan, 8-pass.
4-Dr. Suburban, 9-pass.

FIREDOME - S17
Club coupe
Sportsman hardtop
Convertible coupe
4-Dr. sedan
4-Dr. station wagon
4-Dr. sedan, 8-pass.

THE COLOR CODE indicates the paint color used on the vehicle.

COLOR	CODE
Black	301
Capri Blue	305
Imperial Blue Metallic	306
Midnight Blue	307
French Blue	308
Gulf Blue Metallic	309
Midnight Blue Metallic	310
Glen Green	320
Fern Green	322
Marine Green Metallic	323
Dublin Green Metallic	324
Dusk Gray Metallic	335
Platinum Gray	336
Arizona Beige	345
Morocco Brown Metallic	346
Royal Maroon	360
Sovereign Maroon Metallic	361
Ceramic Yellow	365
Samoa Beige Metallic	370U
Glade Green Dark Metallic	374U
Dusk Gray/Platinum Gray	*372
Black/Ceramic Yellow	*376
Gulf Blue/French Blue	*377
Fern Green/Marine Green	*378
Platinum Gray/Sovereign Maroon	*379
Arizona Beige/Morocco Brown	*380

U - Indicates color was used on upper body

* Two-tone colors - First color indicates the upper color; second color indicates the lower color.

THE TRIM CODE indicates the color and material scheme used on the vehicle.

DELUXE

COLOR	CLOTH	VINYL	LEATHER	CODE
Tweed	•			221
Tan	•			535,536

CUSTOM

COLOR	CLOTH	VINYL	LEATHER	CODE
Brown	•			263
Gray	•			265
Blue	•			264
Checkered	•			226

CUSTOM SUBURBAN

COLOR	CLOTH	VINYL	LEATHER	CODE
Tan/Ivory	•			537
Tan	•			538

CUSTOM STATION WAGON

COLOR	CLOTH	VINYL	LEATHER	CODE
Tan/Ivory	•			593

CUSTOM CONVERTIBLE/SPORTSMAN

COLOR	CLOTH	VINYL	LEATHER	CODE
Blue	•		•	541
Red	•		•	542
Tan	•		•	543
Green	•		•	544
Black	•		•	545
Ivory	•			546
Tan	•			547
Tan/Ivory	•			548

ENGINE SPECIFICATIONS

ENGINE NUMBER - 6-cylinders are located on the left front of the cylinder block, the V8's are located on the top of the cylinder block just back of the water pump.

MODEL   **STARTING NUMBER**

S15* S15-1001

S17..S17-1001

* S15 numbers continued from previous year

DELUXE

ENGINE CODE	NO. CYL.	CID	HORSE-POWER	COMP. RATIO	CARB
S15S	6	250	116	7.0:1	1 BC

CUSTOM

ENGINE CODE	NO. CYL.	CID	HORSE-POWER	COMP. RATIO	CARB
S15C	6	250	116	7.0:1	1 BC

FIREDOME

ENGINE CODE	NO. CYL.	CID	HORSE-POWER	COMP. RATIO	CARB
S17	8	276	160	7.1:1	2 BC

1953 DESOTO

1953 DESOTO

VEHICLE IDENTIFICATION NUMBER

```
• VEHICLE NUMBER •
   5 5 , 0 5 0 , 0 0 1
```

The serial number is located on the left front door hinge post. It indicates the series and assembly plant where the vehicle was built, based on numerical sequence.

MODEL NAME	MODEL CODE	ASSEMBLY PLANT	STARTING NUMBERS
Firedome, 8-cyl.	S16	Detroit	55,050,001
		Los Angeles	64,008,001
Powermaster, 6-cyl.	S18	Detroit	50,266,001
		Los Angeles	62,039,001

THE BODY NUMBER PLATE is located on the cowl under the hood. The body number was essential in ordering the body parts. DeSoto did not have body style codes, paint codes or trim codes appearing anywhere on the car. When ordering parts, it was necessary to furnish the factory with both the serial number and body plate number. We have attempted to list codes for paint and trim combinations when available.

```
BODY   NUMBER
XXX  XXXX
BRIGGS BODY, DETROIT MICHIGAN
```

BODY TYPES

POWERMASTER - S18

Club coupe, 6 pass.

4 Dr. sedan

Sportsman hardtop

4 Dr. sedan, 8 pass.

4 Dr. station wagon

FIREDOME - S16

Club coupe

4 Dr. sedan

Sportsman hardtop

Convertible coupe

4 Dr. station wagon

4 Dr. sedan, 8 pass.

THE COLOR CODE indicates the paint color used on the vehicle.

COLOR	CODE
Black	301
French Blue	308
Harbor Blue Metallic	309
Midnight Blue Metallic	310
Spring Green	322
Marine Green Metallic	323
Forest Green Metallic	324
Mist Gray	335
Slate Gray Metallic	336
Arizona Beige	345
Morocco Brown Metallic	346
Sovereign Maroon Metallic	361
Ceramic Yellow	365

THE TRIM CODE indicates the color and material scheme used on the vehicle. We were unable to locate trim codes for 1953 DeSoto.

ENGINE SPECIFICATIONS

ENGINE NUMBER - 6-cylinders are located on the left front of the cylinder block, the V8's are located on the top of the cylinder block just back of the water pump.

MODEL	STARTING NUMBER
S16	S16-1001
S18	S18-1001

POWERMASTER

ENGINE CODE	NO. CYL.	CID	HORSE-POWER	COMP. RATIO	CARB
S18	6	250	116	7.0:1	1 BC

FIREDOME

ENGINE CODE	NO. CYL.	CID	HORSE-POWER	COMP. RATIO	CARB
S16	8	276	160	7.1:1	2 BC

1954 DESOTO

1954 DESOTO

VEHICLE IDENTIFICATION NUMBER

```
•  VEHICLE NUMBER  •
      55,130,001
```

The serial number is located on the left front door hinge post. It indicates the series and assembly plant where the vehicle was built, based on numerical sequence.

MODEL NAME	MODEL CODE	ASSEMBLY PLANT	STARTING NUMBERS
Firedome, 8-cyl.	S19	Detroit	55,130,001
		Los Angeles	64,017,001
Powermaster, 6-cyl.	S20	Detroit	50,306,001
		Los Angeles	62,043,001

THE BODY NUMBER PLATE is located on the cowl under the hood. The body number was essential in ordering body parts. DeSoto did not have body style codes, paint codes or trim codes appearing anywhere on the car. When ordering parts, it was necessary to furnish the factory with both the serial number and body plate number. We have attempted to list codes for paint and trim combinations when available.

```
BODY   NUMBER
XXX   XXXX
BRIGGS BODY, DETROIT MICHIGAN
```

BODY TYPES

POWERMASTER - S-20

Club coupe

Sportsman hardtop coupe

4 Dr. sedan

4 Dr. station wagon

4 Dr. station wagon, 8-pass.

FIREDOME - S-19

Club coupe

Sportsman hardtop coupe

4 Dr. sedan

4 Dr. station wagon

4 Dr. sedan, 8 pass.

THE COLOR CODE indicates the paint color used on the vehicle.

COLOR	CODE
Black	301
Huron Blue	305
Azure Blue Metallic	306
Ensign Blue Metallic	307
Fountain Blue	308
Tropic Blue Metallic	309
Kerry Green	315
Forest Green Metallic	316
Pinehurst Green Metallic	317
June Green	318
Fairway Green Metallic	319
Colonial Gray	330
Slate Gray Metallic	331
Arizona Beige	340
Burma Tan Metallic	341
Cherokee Red	350
Aztec Yellow	355
Cadiz Blue	383L
Sahara Beige	383U

U - Indicates the upper body color

L - Indicates the lower body color

TWO-TONE COLORS

COLOR	CODE
Azure Blue/Huron Blue	360
Huron Blue/Azure Blue	361
Pinehurst Green/Kerry Green	362
Kerry Green/Pinehurst Green	363
Forest Green/Kerry Green	364
Kerry Green/Forest Green	365
Slate Gray/Colonial Gray	366
Colonial Gray/Slate Gray	367
Burma Tan/Arizona Beige	368
Arizona Beige/Burma Tan	369
Black/Cherokee Red	370
Cherokee Red/Black	371
Black/Aztec Yellow	372
Colonial Gray/Azure Blue	374
Azure Blue/Colonial Gray	375
Huron Blue/Colonial Gray	376
Colonial Gray/Huron Blue	377
Black/Colonial Gray	378
Colonial Gray/Black	379
Colonial Gray/Cherokee Red	380
Cherokee Red/Colonial Gray	381
Black/Kerry Green	382

THE TRIM CODE indicates the color and material scheme used on the vehicle.

COLOR	CLOTH	VINYL	LEATHER	CODE
Med. Green/Lt. Green	•			381
Med. Blue/Lt. Blue	•			382
Med. Brown/Dk. Brown	•			383
Med. Green/Dk. Green	•			384
Blue Gray/Blue	•			385
Blue Gray/Black	•			392
Dk. Green/Lt. Green	•	•		386
Black/Red	•	•		387
Black/Black	•	•		388
Brown Plaid/Lt. Brown	•	•		389
Gold Brown/Beige	•	•		390
Red		•		670
Lt. Blue		•		671
Lt. Green		•		672
Black		•		673
Beige		•		674

ENGINE SPECIFICATIONS

ENGINE NUMBER - 6-cylinders are located on the left front of the cylinder block, the V8's are located on the top of the cylinder block just back of the water pump.

MODEL   **STARTING NUMBER**
S19..S19-1001
S20..S20-1001

POWERMASTER

ENGINE CODE	NO. CYL.	CID	HORSE-POWER	COMP. RATIO	CARB
S20	6	250	116	7.0:1	1 BC

FIREDOME

ENGINE CODE	NO. CYL.	CID	HORSE-POWER	COMP. RATIO	CARB
S19	8	276	170	7.5:1	2 BC

1955 DESOTO

1955 DESOTO

1955 DESOTO

1955 DESOTO

1955 DESOTO FIREDOME

VEHICLE IDENTIFICATION NUMBER

• **VEHICLE NUMBER** •
5 0 , 3 3 0 , 0 0 1

The serial number is located on the left front door hinge post. It indicates the series and assembly plant where the vehicle was built, based on numerical sequence.

MODEL NAME	MODEL CODE	ASSEMBLY PLANT	STARTING NUMBERS
Fireflite, 8-cyl.	S21	Detroit	50,330,001
		Los Angeles	62,045,001
Firedome, 8-cyl.	S22	Detroit	55,185,001
		Los Angeles	64,022,001

THE BODY NUMBER PLATE is located on the cowl under the hood. The body number was essential in ordering body parts. Desoto did not have body style codes, paint codes or trim codes appearing anywhere on the car. When ordering parts, it was necessary to furnish the factory with both the serial number and body plate number. We have attempted to list codes for paint and trim combinations when available.

BODY NUMBER

○   **0 0 0   0 0 0 0**   ○

CHRYSLER CORP, DETROIT MICHIGAN

BODY TYPES

FIREDOME - S-22

Special hardtop coupe

Sportsman hardtop coupe

Convertible coupe

4 Dr. sedan

4 Dr. station wagon

FIREFLITE - S 21

Sportsman hardtop coupe

Convertible coupe

4 Dr. sedan

THE COLOR CODE indicates the paint color used on the vehicle.

COLOR	CODE
Black	301
Avon Blue	305
Dolphin Blue	306
Marlin Blue Metallic	307
Cove Green	315
Lexington Green	316
Sherwood Green Metallic	317
Birch Gray	330
Thunder Gray Metallic	331
Jamaica Bronze Metallic	340
Emberglow	350
Carnival Red	351
Surf White	355
Light Taffy/Copper Rose	440

TWO-TONE COLORS

COLOR	CODE
Surf White/Avon Blue	372
Surf White/Dolphin Blue	374
Surf White/Cove Green	382
Surf White/Lexington Green	384
Surf White/Birch Gray	392
Surf White/Jamaica Bronze Metallic	401
Surf White/Emberglow	405
Surf White/Carnival Red	411
Avon Blue/Surf White	419
Dolphin Blue/Surf White	420
Lexington Green/Surf White	421
Cove Green/Surf White	422
Birch Gray/Surf White	423
Carnival Red/Surf White	424
Emberglow/Surf White	425
Jamaica Bronze Metallic/Surf White	426
Coronado Green/Surf White	431
Surf White/Coronado Green	432
Birch Gray/Marlin Blue	376
Carnival Red/Birch Gray	394
Thunder Gray Metallic/Birch Gray	395
Marlin Blue/Avon Blue	371
Avon Blue/Dolphin Blue	373
Avon Blue/Marlin Blue	375
Lexington Green/Cove Green	381
Cove Green/Lexington Green	383
Dolphin Blue/Avon Blue	370
Sherwood Green Metallic/Cove Green	380
Cove Green/Sherwood Green Metallic	386

THE TRIM CODE indicates the color and material scheme used on the vehicle.

COUPE/4-DR. SEDAN

COLOR	CLOTH	VINYL	LEATHER	CODE
Green/Green	•	•		451
Blue/Blue	•	•		453
Gray/Ivory	•	•		457
Coral/Black	•			459
Green/Green	•			460
Gray/Black	•			461
Blue/Blue	•			462

CONVERTIBLE

COLOR	CLOTH	VINYL	LEATHER	CODE
Green/Green	•	•		468
Gray/Black	•	•		469
Blue/Blue	•	•		470
Green		•		759
Ivory/Black		•		761
Blue		•		760
Rose/Ivory	•		•	464
Rose/Ivory			•	752
Red/Ivory	•		•	465
Red/Ivory			•	753
Green/Ivory	•		•	466
Green/Ivory			•	754
Blue/Ivory	•		•	467
Blue/Ivory			•	755

STATION WAGON

COLOR	CLOTH	VINYL	LEATHER	CODE
Ivory/Gray		•		756

ENGINE SPECIFICATIONS

4-24

ENGINE NUMBER - Located on the top of the cylinder block just back of the water pump.

MODEL	STARTING NUMBER
S21	S21-1001
S22	S22-1001

FIREFLITE

ENGINE CODE	NO. CYL.	CID	HORSE-POWER	COMP. RATIO	CARB
S21	8	291	200	7.5:1	4 BC

FIREDOME

ENGINE CODE	NO. CYL.	CID	HORSE-POWER	COMP. RATIO	CARB
S22	8	291	185	7.5:1	2 BC

1956 DESOTO

1956 DESOTO

VEHICLE IDENTIFICATION NUMBER

```
• VEHICLE NUMBER •
  5 5 , 2 5 8 , 0 0 1
```

The serial number is located on the left front door hinge post. It indicates the series and assembly plant where the vehicle was built, based on numerical sequence.

MODEL NAME	MODEL CODE	ASSEMBLY PLANT	STARTING NUMBERS
Firedome, 8-cyl.	S23	Detroit	55,258,001
		Los Angeles	64,028,001
Fireflite, 8-cyl.	S24	Detroit	50,366,001
		Los Angeles	62,048,001
Adventurer, 8-cyl.	S24A	Detroit	50,366,001

THE BODY NUMBER PLATE is located on the cowl under the hood. The body number was essential in ordering body parts. DeSoto did not have body style codes, paint codes or trim codes appearing anywhere on the car. When ordering parts, it was necessary to furnish the factory with both the serial number and body plate number. We have attempted to list codes for paint and trim combinations when available.

```
       B O D Y   N U M B E R

  ◯    0 0 0    0 0 0 0    ◯

  CHRYSLER CORP, DETROIT MICHIGAN
```

No body type codes were used. The bodies were as follows:

FIREDOME S-23

Seville hardtop coupe
4 Dr. Seville hardtop sedan
Sportsman hardtop coupe
4 Dr. Sportsman hardtop sedan
Convertible coupe
4-Dr. sedan
4-Dr. station wagon

FIREFLITE S-24

Sportsman hardtop coupe
4 Dr. Sportsman hardtop sedan
Convertible coupe
Pacesetter convertible coupe
4-Dr. sedan

ADVENTURER S-24A

Hardtop coupe

THE COLOR CODE indicates the paint color used on the vehicle.

COLOR	CODE
Jet Black	301
Dutch Blue	305
Iridescent Blue	306
Light Aqua	315
Sage Green	316
Iridescent Green	317
Pearl Gray	330
Iridescent Gray	331
Shell Pink	350
Iridescent Lavender	351
Iridescent Plum	352
Crimson	353
Sunny Yellow	355
White	356
Adventurer Gold Metallic	438U

U - Indicates the upper body color
L - Indicates the lower body color

TWO-TONE COLORS

COLOR	CODE
Jet Black/Pearl Gray	360
Jet Black/Shell Pink	362
Jet Black/Iridescent Lavender	364
Jet Black/Iridescent Plum	366
Jet Black/Crimson	368
Jet Black/Sunny Yellow	370
Jet Black/White	372
Dutch Blue/Iridescent Blue	380
Dutch Blue/White	382
Iridescent Blue/Pearl Gray	384
Iridescent Blue/White	386
Light Aqua/Sage Green	390
Light Aqua/Iridescent Green	392
Light Aqua/White	394
Sage Green/White	396
Iridescent Green/White	398
Pearl Gray/Iridescent Gray	400
Pearl Gray/Iridescent Plum	402
Pearl Gray/Crimson	404
Pearl Gray/Sunny Yellow	406
Pearl Gray/White	408
Iridescent Gray/Shell Pink	410
Iridescent Gray/Iridescent Lavender	412
Iridescent Gray/Iridescent Plum	414
Iridescent Gray/Crimson	416
Iridescent Gray/Sunny Yellow	418

COLOR	CODE
Iridescent Gray/White	420
Shell Pink/Iridescent Lavender	422
Shell Pink/White	424
Iridescent Lavender/Iridescent Plum	426
Iridescent Lavender/White	428
Iridescent Plum/White	430
Crimson/White	432
Sunny Yellow/White	434
Sunny Yellow/Sage Green	436
White/Gold	438
Gold/Black	440
Pearl Gray/Jet Black	361
Shell Pink/Jet Black	363
Iridescent Lavender/Jet Black	365
Iridescent Plum/Jet Black	367
Crimson/Jet Black	369
Sunny Yellow/Jet Black	371
White/Jet Black	373
Iridescent Blue/Dutch Blue	381
White/Dutch Blue	383
Pearl Gray/Iridescent Blue	385
White/Iridescent Blue	387
Sage Green/Light Aqua	391
Iridesicent Green/Light Aqua	393
White/Light Aqua	395
White/Sage Green	397
White/Iridescent Green	399
Iridescent Gray/Pearl Gray	401
Iridescent Plum/Pearl Gray	403
Crimson/Pearl Gray	405
Sunny Yellow/Pearl Gray	407
White/Pearl Gray	409
Shell Pink/Iridescent Gray	411
Iridescent Lavender/Iridescent Gray	413
Iridescent Plum/Iridescent Gray	415
Crimson/Iridescent Gray	417
Sunny Yellow/Iridescent Gray	419
White/Iridescent Gray	421
Iridescent Lavender/Shell Pink	423
White/Shell Pink	425
Iridescent Plum/Iridescent Lavender	427
White/Iridescent Lavender	429
White/Iridescent Plum	431
White/Crimson	433
White/Sunny Yellow	435
Sage green/Sunny Yellow	437
Gold/White	439
Black/Gold	441

THE TRIM CODE indicates the color and material scheme used on the vehicle.

STATION WAGON

COLOR	CLOTH	VINYL	LEATHER	CODE
Gray		•		858

CONVERTIBLE/SPORTSMAN

COLOR	CLOTH	VINYL	LEATHER	CODE
Green	•	•		566
Blue	•	•		567
Gray	•	•		568
Green		•		863
Blue		•		864
Gray		•		865
Green	•		•	559
Blue	•		•	560
Pink	•		•	561
Gray	•		•	562
Green			•	854
Blue			•	855
Pink			•	856
Gray			•	857

SEVILLE 2-DR./4-DR.

COLOR	CLOTH	VINYL	LEATHER	CODE
Green	•	•		563
Blue	•	•		564
Gray	•	•		565

4-DR. SEDAN

COLOR	CLOTH	VINYL	LEATHER	CODE
Green	•	•		551
Blue	•	•		552
Gray	•	•		553
Green	•			555
Blue	•			556
Pink	•			557
Gray	•			558

ENGINE SPECIFICATIONS

4-28

ENGINE NUMBER - Located on the top of the cylinder block just back of the water pump.

MODEL	STARTING NUMBER
S23	S23-1001
S24	S24-1001
S24A	S24A-1001

FIREDOME

ENGINE CODE	NO. CYL.	CID	HORSE-POWER	COMP. RATIO	CARB
S23	8	330	230	8.5:1	2 BC

FIREFLITE

ENGINE CODE	NO. CYL.	CID	HORSE-POWER	COMP. RATIO	CARB
S24	8	330	255	8.5:1	4 BC

FIREFLITE

ENGINE CODE	NO. CYL.	CID	HORSE-POWER	COMP. RATIO	CARB
S24A	8	341	320	9.25:1	2X4 BC

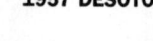

1957 DESOTO

1957 DESOTO FIREFLIGHT

1957 DESOTO

VEHICLE IDENTIFICATION NUMBER

```
• VEHICLE NUMBER •
    55,332,001
```

The serial number is located on the left front door hinge post. It indicates the series and assembly plant where the vehicle was built, based on numerical sequence.

MODEL NAME	MODEL CODE	ASSEMBLY PLANT	STARTING NUMBERS
Firedome, 8-cyl.	S25	Detroit	55,332,001
Fireflite, 8-cyl.	S26	Detroit	50,396,001
Adventurer, 8-cyl.	S26A	Detroit	50,396,001
Firesweep, 8-cyl.	S27	Detroit	58,001,001
		Los Angeles	60,014,001

THE BODY NUMBER PLATE is located on the cowl under the hood. The body number was essential in ordering body parts. DeSoto did not have body style codes, paint codes or trim codes appearing anywhere on the car. When ordering parts, it was necessary to furnish the factory with both the serial number and body plate number. We have attempted to list codes for paint and trim combinations when available.

```
        B O D Y   N U M B E R

O        0 0 0    0 0 0 0        O

    CHRYSLER CORP, DETROIT MICHIGAN
```

BODY TYPES

FIRESWEEP

Sportsman hardtop coupe
Sportsman hardtop sedan
4 Dr. sedan
Shopper wagon 4 Dr., 6 pass.
Explorer wagon 4 Dr., 9 pass.

FIREDOME - S-25

Sportsman hardtop coupe
Sportsman hardtop sedan
Convertible coupe
4 Dr. sedan

FIREFLITE - S-26

Sportsman hardtop coupe
Sportsman hardtop sedan
Convertible coupe
4 Dr. sedan
4 Dr. shopper wagon, 6 pass.
4 Dr. Explorer wagon, 9 pass.

ADVENTURER - S-26A

Hardtop coupe
Convertible coupe

THE COLOR CODE indicates the paint color used on the vehicle.

FIREDOME/FIREFLITE

COLOR	CODE
Black	AAA
Capri Blue	BBB
Azure Blue Metallic	CCC
Seafoam Green	DDD
Tamarack Green Metallic	EEE
Dove Gray	FFF
Charcoal Gray Metallic	GGG
Fiesta Red	HHH
Sunlit Yellow	KKK
White	LLL
Adventurer Gold Metallic	PPP
Mandarin Rust	RRR
Muscatel Maroon	TTT
Sahara Tan	XXX
Spice Brown Metallic	ZZZ

FIRESWEEP

COLOR	CODE
Black	AAA
Lagoon Blue	BBB
Seatone Blue Metallic	CCC
Mist Green	DDD
Leaf Green Metallic	EEE
Dawn Gray	FFF
Slate Gray Metallic	GGG
Fiesta Red	HHH
Sunburst Yellow	KKK
Frosty White	LLL
Light Aqua	MMM
Dusty Orange	NNN
Samoa Green	SSS
Muscatel Maroon	TTT

THE TRIM CODE indicates the color and material scheme used on the vehicle.

FIREDOME 4-DR SEDAN

COLOR	CLOTH	VINYL	LEATHER	CODE
Blue	•	•		501
Green	•	•		502
Black/Silver	•	•		503

FIREDOME CONVERTIBLE/SPORTSMAN

COLOR	CLOTH	VINYL	LEATHER	CODE
Blue	•	•		511
Green	•	•		512
Beige/Gray	•	•		513
Red/Gray	•	•		517
Blue		•		611
Green		•		612
Beige/Gray		•		613
Red/Gray		•		614

FIREFLITE 4-DR. SEDAN

COLOR	CLOTH	VINYL	LEATHER	CODE
Blue	•	•		531
Green	•	•		532
Gray	•	•		533
Gray/Coral	•	•		534

FIREFLITE SPORTSMAN/CONVERTIBLE

COLOR	CLOTH	VINYL	LEATHER	CODE
Blue	•	•		541
Green	•	•		542
Gray/White	•	•		543
Copper	•	•		544
Gray/Red	•	•		545
Blue		•		641
Green		•		642
Gray/White		•		643
Copper		•		644
Gray/Red		•		645
Tan		•		*623

* Station wagon

FIRESWEEP 4-DR. SEDAN

COLOR	CLOTH	VINYL	LEATHER	CODE
Blue	•	•		504
Green	•	•		505
Black/Silver	•	•		506

FIRESWEEP SPORTSMAN

COLOR	CLOTH	VINYL	LEATHER	CODE
Blue	•	•		514
Green	•	•		515
Black/Silver	•	•	•	516
Black/Gold		•		*626

NOTE: On two-tone color combinations the first letter indicates the upper body paint, the second letter indicates the lower body paint, the third letter indicates the color sweep.

ENGINE SPECIFICATIONS

ENGINE NUMBER - Located on the top of the cylinder block just back of the water pump.

MODEL	STARTING NUMBER
S25	S25-1001
S26	S26-1001
S26A	S26A-1001
S27	KDS-1001

FIREDOME

ENGINE CODE	NO. CYL.	CID	HORSE-POWER	COMP. RATIO	CARB
S25	8	341	270	8.25:1	2 BC

FIREFLITE

ENGINE CODE	NO. CYL.	CID	HORSE-POWER	COMP. RATIO	CARB
S26	8	341	295	9.25:1	4 BC

ADVENTURER

ENGINE CODE	NO. CYL.	CID	HORSE-POWER	COMP. RATIO	CARB
S26A	8	345	345	9.25:1	2X4 BC

FIRESWEEP

ENGINE CODE	NO. CYL.	CID	HORSE-POWER	COMP. RATIO	CARB
S27	8	325	245	8.5:1	2 BC
S27*	8	325	260	8.5:1	4 BC

* Power pack

1958 DESOTO FIREDOME

1958 DESOTO SPORTSMAN FIRESWEEP

1958 DESOTO SPORTSMAN FIREFLITE

VEHICLE IDENTIFICATION NUMBER

• L S 3 L 1 0 0 1 •

The serial number is located on the left front door hinge post.

FIRST DIGIT: Identifies the model year (L=1958)

SECOND DIGIT: Identifies the car make (S=Desoto)

THIRD DIGIT: Identifies the model series

MODEL SERIES	CODE
Firesweep	1
Firedome	2
Fireflite/Adventurer	3

FOURTH DIGIT: Identifies the assembly plant if built in Los Angeles, Detroit built cars did not use an assembly plant code

ASSEMBLY PLANT	CODE
Detroit, MI	—
Los Angeles, CA	L

THE LAST FOUR DIGITS: Identify the basic production sequence number

BODY NUMBER PLATE

Located on the cowl under the hood. Body number was essential in ordering body parts.
When ordering parts, it was necessary to furnish the factory with both the seial number and body plate number. We have attempted to list codes for paint and trim combinations when available.

T L	C S	M R	H B	A C	A	S P L
HT	PS	AG	AR	PB	PF	EW	S6	RS	CU	SC
SCH	BO	NO	◯	BO	PT	TR	CT	TR	◯

MODEL NUMBER

LS1-L

EXAMPLE:

L	Model year (1958)
S	Car make (DeSoto)
2	Firesweep chassis
L	Low price class

Fourth digit represents class of car

L	Low price
M	Medium price
H	High price

MODEL NUMBER	CODE
Firesweep V8	LS1-L

Sportsman hardtop coupe
Convertible coupe
4-Dr. sedan
Sportsman hardtop sedan
Shopper wagon, 4-dr.
Explorer wagon, 4-dr.

FIREDOME V8	**LS2-M**

Sportsman hardtop coupe
Convertible coupe
4-Dr. sedan
Sportsman hardtop sedan

FIREFLITE V8	**LS3-H**

Sportsman hardtop coupe
Convertible coupe
4-Dr. sedan
Sportsman hardtop sedan
Shopper wagon, 4-dr.
Explorer wagon, 4-dr.

ADVENTURER V8	**LS3-S**

Hardtop coupe
Convertible coupe

THE COLOR CODE indicates the paint color used on the vehicle.

FIREDOME/FIREFLITE

COLOR	CODE
Black	AAA
Wedgewood Blue	BBB
Haze Blue Metallic	CCC
Midnight Blue	DDD
Willow Green	EEE
Spruce Green Metallic	FFF
Seacoast Aqua	HHH
French Turquoise Metallic	JJJ
Smoke Gray	KKK
Steel Gray Metallic	LLL
Autumn Rust	OOO
Holly Red	PPP

COLOR	CODE
Spring Rose	SSS
Spanish Gold	UUU
Pearl White	XXX

FIRESWEEP

COLOR	CODE
Black	AAA
Wedgewood Blue	BBB
Haze Blue Metallic	CCC
Midnight Blue	DDD
Willow Green	EEE
Spruce Green Metallic	FFF
Arctic Gray Metallic	KKK
Cruiser Gray Metallic	LLL
Rose Beige	MMM
Suede Brown Metallic	NNN
Autumn Rust	OOO
Holly Red	PPP
Sand Dune Yellow	UUU
Pearl White	XXX

NOTE: On two-tone color combinations the first letter indicates the upper body paint, the second letter indicates the lower body paint, the third letter indicates the color sweep.

THE TRIM CODE indicates the color and material scheme used on the vehicle.

FIREDOME SPORTSMAN/CONVERTIBLE

COLOR	CLOTH	VINYL	LEATHER	CODE
Blue		•		731
Green		•		732
Tan		•		733
Turquoise		•		735
Red		•		736
Blue	•	•		631
Green	•	•		632
Tan	•	•		633
Turquoise	•	•		635
Red	•	•		636

FIREDOME 4-DR. SEDAN

COLOR	CLOTH	VINYL	LEATHER	CODE
Blue	•	•		611
Green	•	•		612
Neutral	•	•		613

FIREFLITE 4-DR. SEDAN

COLOR	CLOTH	VINYL	LEATHER	CODE
Blue	•	•		501
Green	•	•		502
Gray	•	•		503

FIREFLITE SPORTSMAN/CONVERTIBLE

COLOR	CLOTH	VINYL	LEATHER	CODE
Blue	•	•		641
Green	•	•		642
Gray	•	•		643
Turquoise	•	•		645
Red	•	•		646
Gray	•	•		*683
Gray		•		*753

* Station wagon

FIRESWEEP 4-DR. SEDAN

COLOR	CLOTH	VINYL	LEATHER	CODE
Blue	•	•		*601
Green	•	•		*602
Beige/Black	•	•		*603
Blue	•	•		#651
Green	•	•		#652
Neutral	•	•		#653

* Standard
# Custom

FIRESWEEP 2-DR./4-DR. SPORTSMAN

COLOR	CLOTH	VINYL	LEATHER	CODE
Blue	•	•		*621
Green	•	•		*622
Beige/Tan	•	•		*623
Blue	•	•		#661
Green	•	•		#662
Black/Tan	•	•		#663
Red	•	•		#666

FIRESWEEP CONVERTIBLE

COLOR	CLOTH	VINYL	LEATHER	CODE
Blue	•	•		*661
Green	•	•		*662
Tan/Black	•	•		*663
Red	•	•		*666
Blue		•		#771
Green		•		#772
Beige/Black		•		#773
Red		•		#776
Beige/Tan	•	•		**673
Beige/Black		•		##763

* Standard
# Custom
** Station wagon

ENGINE SPECIFICATIONS

ENGINE NUMBER - Located on the top of the cylinder block just back of the water pump.

MODEL	STARTING NUMBER
LS-1	L-350-1001
LS-2	L-360-1001
LS-3	L-360-1001

FIRESWEEP

ENGINE CODE	NO. CYL.	CID	HORSE-POWER	COMP. RATIO	CARB
LS1-L	8	350	280	10.0:1	2 BC
LS1-L	8	350	295	10.0:1	4 BC

FIREDOME

ENGINE CODE	NO. CYL.	CID	HORSE-POWER	COMP. RATIO	CARB
LS2-M	8	361	295	10.0:1	2 BC

FIREFLITE

ENGINE CODE	NO. CYL.	CID	HORSE-POWER	COMP. RATIO	CARB
LS3-H	8	361	305	10.0:1	4 BC

ADVENTURER

ENGINE CODE	NO. CYL.	CID	HORSE-POWER	COMP. RATIO	CARB
LS3-S	8	361	345	10.25:1	2-4 BC
LS3-S	8	361	355	10.25:1	F.I.

1959 DESOTO ADVENTURER

1959 DESOTO

VEHICLE IDENTIFICATION NUMBER

● M 4 3 2 1 0 0 1 ●

The serial number is located on the left front door hinge post on all models except the MS-1. On the MS-1, built in Detroit, the serial number is located on the cowl under the hood.

FIRST DIGIT: Identifies the model year (L=1959)

SECOND DIGIT: Identifies the car make (4=Desoto)

THIRD DIGIT: Identifies the model series

MODEL SERIES	CODE
Firewsweep	1
Firedome	3
Fireflite	5
Station wagons	7
Taxi	8
Adventurer	9

FOURTH DIGIT: Identifies the assembly plant code

ASSEMBLY PLANT	CODE
Jefferson Ave., Detroit, MI	1
Dodge Plant, Detroit, MI	2
Los Angeles, CA	4

THE LAST FOUR DIGITS: Identify the basic production sequence number

BODY NUMBER

MS-2 and MS-3 models have the body number stamped on a metal plate attached to the front dust shield between the radiator and grille (right of center). MS-1 models, the body plate is attached to the front top side of cowl panel near right hand hood hinge.

When ordering parts it was necessary to furnish the factory with both the serial number and body plate number. We have attempted to list codes for paint and trim combinations when available.

TL	CS	MR	HB	AC	A	SPL

HT	PS	AG	AR	PB	PF	EW	S6	RS	CU	SC

SCH	BO	NO	◯	BO	PT	TR	CT	TR	◯

MODEL NUMBER

MS1-L

EXAMPLE:

M	Model year (1959)
S	Car make (DeSoto)
1	Firesweep chassis
L	Low price class

FIRST DIGIT: Identifies the year (M=1959)

SECOND DIGIT: Identifies the make(S=DeSoto)

THIRD DIGIT: Identifies the chassis

Firesweep	1
Firedome	2
Fireflite	3

FOURTH DIGIT: Identifies the class

Low price	1
Medium price	2
High price	3

MODEL NUMBER	CODE
FIRESWEEP V8	**MS1-L**

Sportsman hardtop coupe
Convertible coupe
4-Dr. sedan
Sportsman hardtop sedan
Shopper wagon, 4-dr.
Explorer wagon, 4-dr., 9-pass.

FIREDOME V8	**MS2-M**

Sportsman hardtop coupe
Convertible coupe
4-Dr. sedan
Sportsman hardtop sedan

FIREFLITE V8	**MS3-H**

Sportsman hardtop coupe
Convertible coupe
4-Dr. sedan
Sportsman hardtop sedan
Shopper wagon, 4-dr.
Explorer wagon, 4-dr.

ADVENTURER	**MS3-S**

Hardtop coupe
Convertible coupe

THE COLOR CODE indicates the paint color used on the vehicle.

FIREDOME/FIREFLITE

COLOR	CODE
Black	AAA
Bahama Blue	BBB
Caribbean Blue Metallic	CCC
Heather Blue Metallic	DDD
Surf Green	EEE
Forest Green Metallic	FFF
Capri Turquoise Metallic	KKK
Aztec Silver Metallic #1	LLL
Aztec Silver Metallic #2	LLL
French Gray Metallic	MMM
Bimini Coral	PPP
Castillian Red	RRR
Canyon Beige	UUU
Spring Rose	SSS
Golden Tan Metallic	WWW
Pearl White	XXX
Aspen Yellow	YYY

FIRESWEEP

COLOR	CODE
Black	AAA
Catalina Blue	BBB1
Glacier Blue Metallic	CCC1
Heather Blue Metallic	DDD
Spring Green	EEE1
Jade Green Metallic	FFF1
Riviera Turquoise	JJJ1
Aztec Silver Metallic #1	LLL
Aztec Silver Metallic #2	LLL
Dawn Gray Metallic	MMM1
Flamingo Pink	NNN1
Tangier Rose	PPP1
Castillian Red	RRR
Morocco Beige	UUU1
Tropical Tan Metallic	WWW1
Pearl White	XXX
Sunshine Yellow	YYY1

THE TRIM CODE indicates the color and material scheme used on the vehicle. There are no code numbers available.

FIREDOME

COLOR	CLOTH	VINYL	LEATHER	CODE
Blue/Blue	•	•		
Green/Green	•	•		
Tan/Brown	•	•		
Black/Silver/White	•	•		
Red/Gray	•	•		
Blue/Blue		•		
Green/Green		•		
Tan/Brown		•		

FIREFLITE

COLOR	CLOTH	VINYL	LEATHER	CODE
Blue	•	•		
Green	•	•		
Tan/Brown	•	•		
Gray/Silver	•	•		
Red/Gray	•	•		
Blue/Blue		•		
Green/Green		•		
Tan/Beige		•		
Silver/Gray		•		
Gray/Red		•		

FIRESWEEP

COLOR	CLOTH	VINYL	LEATHER	CODE
Blue/Blue	•	•		
Green/Green	•	•		
Tan/Beige	•	•		
Black/Silver	•	•		
Blue/Blue		•		
Green/Green		•		
Brown/Beige		•		
Black/Red		•		

ENGINE SPECIFICATIONS

ENGINE NUMBER - Located on the top of the cylinder block just back of the water pump.

MODEL	STARTING NUMBER
MS-1	ML-361-1001
MS-2	ML-383-1001
MS-3	ML-383-1001

FIRESWEEP

ENGINE CODE	NO. CYL.	CID	HORSE-POWER	COMP. RATIO	CARB
MS-1	8	361	290	10.0:1	2 BC

FIREDOME

ENGINE CODE	NO. CYL.	CID	HORSE-POWER	COMP. RATIO	CARB
MS-2	8	383	305	10.0:1	2 BC

FIREFLITE

ENGINE CODE	NO. CYL.	CID	HORSE-POWER	COMP. RATIO	CARB
MS-3	8	383	325	10.0:1	4 BC

ADVENTURER

ENGINE CODE	NO. CYL.	CID	HORSE-POWER	COMP. RATIO	CARB
MS-3	8	383	350	10.0:1	2X4 BC

1950 DODGE

1950 DODGE

1950 DODGE

1950 DODGE

VEHICLE IDENTIFICATION NUMBER

```
•  VEHICLE NUMBER  •
     37,060,001
```

The serial number is located on the left front door hinge post. It indicates the series/model and assembly plant where the vehicle was built, based on numerical sequence.

MODEL NAME	MODEL CODE	ASSEMBLY PLANT	STARTING NUMBERS
Wayfarer, 6-cyl.	D33	Detroit	37,060,001
		Los Angeles	48,502,001
		San Leandro	48,004,001
S-Meadowbrook Deluxe, C-Coronet Custom/Special Custom, 6-cyl.	D34	Detroit	31,420,001
		Los Angeles	45,505,001
		San Leandro	45,064,001

THE BODY NUMBER PLATE is located on the cowl under the hood. Dodge did not have body style codes, paint codes or trim codes appearing anywhere on the car. When ordering parts, it was necessary to furnish the factory with both the serial number and body plate number. We have attempted to list codes for paint and trim combinations when available.

```
BODY   NUMBER
   XXX   XXXX
BRIGGS BODY, DETROIT MICHIGAN
```

BODY TYPES

WAYFARER - D33
2-Dr. sedan,
2-Dr. coupe
2-Dr. roadster

MEADOWBROOK - D34
4-Dr. sedan

CORONET - D34
4-Dr. sedan
4-Dr. Town sedan
2-Dr. Club coupe
2-Dr. hardtop coupe
2-Dr. convertible coupe
4-Dr. station wagon
4-Dr. metal station wagon
4-Dr. sedan, 8-pass.

THE COLOR CODE indicates the paint color used on the vehicle.

COLOR	CODE
LaPlata Blue	505
Dominion Blue	506
Island Green	520
Hunter Green	521
Gypsy Green Metallic	522
Granite Gray	535
French Gray	536
Nassau Beige	545
Burma Tan Metallic	546
Monarch Maroon	560
Cadet Red	561
Aircruiser Red	562
Victoria Ivory	565
St. Denis Gray	570U
Samoa Beige Metallic	571U
Iceland Gray Metallic	572U
Corva Green	573U
Dawn Gray	574U

U - Indicates color was used on upper body

THE TRIM CODE indicates the color and material scheme used on the vehicle.

COLOR	CLOTH	VINYL	LEATHER	CODE
Blue			•	401
Red			•	402
Tan			•	403
Green			•	404
Blue	•	•		411
Red	•	•		412
Tan	•	•		413
Green	•	•		414
Blue		•		435
Maroon		•		436
Blue	•		•	471
Red	•		•	472
Tan	•		•	473
Green	•		•	474
Maroon	•			930,951
Blue	•			931,952

Broadcloth available with codes: 925, 926, 297, 929, 938, 946

Pile fabric available with codes: 173, 174, 181

ENGINE SPECIFICATIONS

ENGINE NUMBER - Located on the left front of the cylinder block.

MODEL	STARTING NUMBER
D33	D33-1001
D34	D34-1001

WAYFARER

ENGINE CODE	NO. CYL.	CID	HORSE-POWER	COMP. RATIO	CARB
D33	6	230	103	7.0:1	1 BC

CORONET

ENGINE CODE	NO. CYL.	CID	HORSE-POWER	COMP. RATIO	CARB
D34C	6	230	103	7.0:1	1 BC

MEADOWBROOK

ENGINE CODE	NO. CYL.	CID	HORSE-POWER	COMP. RATIO	CARB
D34S	6	230	103	7.0:1	1 BC

1951 DODGE

1951 DODGE WAYFARER

1951 DODGE

VEHICLE IDENTIFICATION NUMBER

• VEHICLE NUMBER •
37,135,001

The serial number is located on the left front door hinge post. It indicates the series/model and assembly plant where the vehicle was built, based on numerical sequence.

MODEL NAME	MODEL CODE	ASSEMBLY PLANT	STARTING NUMBERS
Wayfarer, 6-cyl.	D41	Detroit	37,135,001
		Los Angeles	48,506,001
		San Leandro	48,008,001
S-Meadowbrook Deluxe, C-Coronet Custom, 6-cyl.	D42	Detroit	31,663,001
		Los Angeles	45,518,001
		San Leandro	45,079,001

THE BODY NUMBER PLATE

THE BODY NUMBER PLATE is located on the cowl under the hood. Dodge did not have body style codes, paint codes or trim codes appearing anywhere on the car. When ordering parts, it was necessary to furnish the factory with both the serial number and body plate number. We have attempted to list codes for paint and trim combinations when available.

BODY NUMBER
XXX XXXX
BRIGGS BODY, DETROIT MICHIGAN

BODY TYPES

WAYFARER - D41

2-Dr. sedan

2-Dr. coupe

2-Dr. roadster

MEADOWBROOK - D42

4-Dr. sedan

CORONET - D42

4-Dr. sedan

2-Dr. Club coupe

2-Dr. hardtop coupe

2-Dr. convertible

4-Dr. station wagon

4-Dr. sedan, 8-pass.

THE COLOR CODE

THE COLOR CODE indicates the paint color used on the vehicle.

COLOR	CODE
Pitcairn Blue	505
Dominion Blue	506
Seamist Green	520
Ceram Green	521
Gypsy Green Metallic	522
Kitchener Green Metallic	523
Silhouette Green	524
Manchu Green Metallic	525
Heron Gray	535
Dover Gray	536
Nassau Beige	545
Kachina Bronze Metallic	546
Fawn Beige	547
Oakwood Bronze Metallic	560
Troubador Red	561
Aircruiser Red	562
Dynasty Maroon	563
Victoria Ivory	565
Jungle Lime	566
Iceland Gray Metallic	572U
Corvo Green	573U
Pearl Tan	574U
Eden Green Metallic	575U

U - Indicates color was used on upper body

THE TRIM CODE

THE TRIM CODE indicates the color and material scheme used on the vehicle.

COLOR	CLOTH	VINYL	LEATHER	CODE
Blue	•	•		255,521
Red	•	•		256,522
Tan	•	•		257,523
Green	•	•		258,524
Blue/Blue	•	•		525
Red/Gold	•	•		526
Tan/Gold	•	•		527
Green/Gold	•	•		528
Blue		•		529
Maroon		•		530
Tan		•		540
Blue			•	531,551
Red			•	532,552
Tan			•	533,553
Green			•	534,554

Pile fabric available with codes: 182

Broadcloth available with codes: 211, 213, 214, 215

Textured weave fabric available with codes: 212, 216

Cloth available with codes: 251, 252, 253, 254

1951 DODGE   **CHRYSLER**

ENGINE SPECIFICATIONS

ENGINE NUMBER - Located on the left front of the cylinder block.

MODEL	STARTING NUMBER
D41	D41-1001
D42	D42-1001

WAYFARER

ENGINE CODE	NO. CYL.	CID	HORSE-POWER	COMP. RATIO	CARB
D41	6	230	103	7.0:1	1 BC

CORONET

ENGINE CODE	NO. CYL.	CID	HORSE-POWER	COMP. RATIO	CARB
D42C	6	230	103	7.0:1	1 BC

MEADOWBROOK

ENGINE CODE	NO. CYL.	CID	HORSE-POWER	COMP. RATIO	CARB
D42S	6	230	103	7.0:1	1 BC

1952 DODGE

1952 DODGE

1952 DODGE CORONET SEDAN

VEHICLE IDENTIFICATION NUMBER

> **VEHICLE NUMBER**
> • **37,175,001** •

The serial number is located on the left front door hinge post. It indicates the series/model and assembly plant where the vehicle was built, based on numerical sequence.

MODEL NAME	MODEL CODE	ASSEMBLY PLANT	STARTING NUMBERS
Wayfarer, 6-cyl.	D41	Detroit	37,175,001
		Los Angeles	48,507,601
		San Leandro	48,009,901
S-Meadowbrook Deluxe, C-Coronet Custom, 6-cyl.	D42	Detroit	31,867,801
		Los Angeles	45,527,501
		San Leandro	45,090,601

THE BODY NUMBER PLATE is located on the cowl under the hood. Dodge did not have body style codes, paint codes or trim codes appearing anywhere on the car. When ordering parts, it was necessary to furnish the factory with both the serial number and body plate number. We have attempted to list codes for paint and trim combinations when available.

> **BODY NUMBER**
> **XXX XXXX**
> **BRIGGS BODY, DETROIT MICHIGAN**

BODY TYPES

WAYFARER - D41

2-Dr. sedan

2-Dr. coupe

2-Dr. roadster

MEADOWBROOK - D42

4-Dr. sedan

CORONET - D42

4-Dr. sedan

2-Dr. Club coupe

2-Dr. Diplomat

2-Dr. convertible

4-Dr. station wagon (Sierra)

4-Dr. sedan, 8-pass.

THE COLOR CODE indicates the paint color used on the vehicle.

COLOR	CODE
Pitcairn Blue	505
Dominion Blue	506
Fairfax Blue	507
Seamist Green	520
Gypsy Green Metallic	522
Silhouette Green	524
Manchu Green Metallic	525
Heron Gray	535
Dover Gray	536
Nassau Beige	545
Oakwood Bronze Metallic	548
Aircruiser Red	562
Dynasty Maroon	563
Fiesta Maroon Metallic	564
Victorian Ivory	565
Advance Green Metallic	583L
Riviera Green	583U
Arabian Blue	584L
Pagoda Gray	584U

U - Indicates color was used on upper body

L - Indicates color was used on lower body

THE TRIM CODE indicates the color and material scheme used on the vehicle.

COLOR	CLOTH	VINYL	LEATHER	CODE
Blue	•			251
Red	•			252
Tan	•			253
Green	•			254
Blue	•	•		255
Red	•	•		256
Tan	•	•		257
Green	•	•		258
Blue			•	551
Red			•	552
Tan			•	553
Green			•	554

ENGINE SPECIFICATIONS

ENGINE NUMBER - Located on the left front of the cylinder block.

MODEL	STARTING NUMBER
D41	D41-1001
D42	D42-1001

NOTE: Continued from previous year

WAYFARER

ENGINE CODE	NO. CYL.	CID	HORSE-POWER	COMP. RATIO	CARB
D41	6	230	103	7.0:1	1 BC

CORONET

ENGINE CODE	NO. CYL.	CID	HORSE-POWER	COMP. RATIO	CARB
D42C	6	230	103	7.0:1	1 BC

MEADOWBROOK

ENGINE CODE	NO. CYL.	CID	HORSE-POWER	COMP. RATIO	CARB
D42S	6	230	103	7.0:1	1 BC

1953 DODGE

1953 DODGE CORONET

VEHICLE IDENTIFICATION NUMBER

```
• VEHICLE NUMBER •
   3 4 , 5 0 0 , 0 0 1
```

The serial number is located on the left front door hinge post. It indicates the series/model and assembly plant where the vehicle was built, based on numerical sequence.

MODEL NAME	MODEL CODE	ASSEMBLY PLANT	STARTING NUMBERS
Coronet, 8-cyl.	D44	Detroit	34,500,001
		Los Angeles	41,500,001
		San Leandro	42,500,001
Meadowbrook/Coronet, 6-cyl.	D46	Detroit	32,042,001
		Los Angeles	45,536,001
		San Leandro	45,102,001
Meadowbrook, 6-cyl.	D47	Detroit	37,212,001
		Los Angeles	48,511,001
		San Leandro	48,013,001
Coronet, 8-cyl.	D48	Detroit	38,500,001
		Los Angeles	46,500,001
		San Leandro	47,001,001

THE BODY NUMBER PLATE is located on the cowl under the hood. Dodge did not have body style codes, paint codes or trim codes appearing anywhere on the car. When ordering parts, it was necessary to furnish the factory with both the serial number and body plate number. We have attempted to list codes for paint and trim combinations when available.

```
BODY   NUMBER
XXX   XXXX
BRIGGS BODY, DETROIT MICHIGAN
```

BODY TYPES

MEADOWBROOK - D46

4-Dr. Special sedan

2-Dr. Special sedan

4-Dr. sedan

2-Dr. sedan

MEADOWBROOK - D47

2-Dr. station wagon

CORONET - D44

4-Dr. sedan

2-Dr. sedan

CORONET - D48

2-Dr. Diplomat

2-Dr. convertible

2-Dr. Sierra station wagon

THE COLOR CODE indicates the paint color used on the vehicle.

COLOR	CODE
Bimini Blue	505
Fairfax Blue Metallic	507
Seamist Green	520
Gypsy Green Metallic	522
Silhouette Green	524
Heron Gray	535
Dover Gray	536
Nassau Beige	545
Oakwood Bronze Metallic	548
Esquire Red	562
Fiesta Maroon Metallic	564
Shoreham Ivory	565
Mecca Blue	580L
Shoal Green Metallic	581L
Seashore Green	581U

U - Indicates color was used on upper body

L - Indicates color was used on lower body

THE TRIM CODE indicates the color and material scheme used on the vehicle. Trim codes were not available.

ENGINE SPECIFICATIONS

ENGINE NUMBER - 6-Cylinder is located on the left front of the cylinder block, V8 located on a pad on the left side of the block between 2 and 3 cylinders.

MODEL	STARTING NUMBER
D44	D44-1001
D46	D46-1001
D47	D46-1001
D48	D44-1001

MEADOWBROOK

ENGINE CODE	NO. CYL.	CID	HORSE-POWER	COMP. RATIO	CARB
D46	6	230	103	7.0:1	1 BC
D47	6	230	103	7.0:1	1 BC

CORONET

ENGINE CODE	NO. CYL.	CID	HORSE-POWER	COMP. RATIO	CARB
D44	8	241	140	7.1:1	2 BC
D48	8	241	140	7.1:1	2 BC

1954 DODGE PACE CAR

1954 DODGE PACE CAR

1954 DODGE

VEHICLE IDENTIFICATION NUMBER

```
• VEHICLE NUMBER •
  3 4 , 6 3 5 , 8 0 1
```

The serial number is located on the left front door hinge post. It indicates the series/model and assembly plant where the vehicle was built, based on numerical sequence.

MODEL NAME	MODEL CODE	ASSEMBLY PLANT	STARTING NUMBERS
Meadowbrook, 8-cyl.	D50-1	Detroit	34,635,801
		San Leandro	42,508,001
Meadowbrook, 8-cyl.	D50-1A	Detroit	34,635,801
		San Leandro	42,508,001
Meadowbrook, 6-cyl.	D51-1	Detroit	32,152,901
		San Leandro	45,105,801
Meadowbrook, 6-cyl.	D51-1A	Detroit	32,152,901
		San Leandro	45,105,801
Coronet, 8-cyl.	D50-2	Detroit	34,642,001
		San Leandro	42,510,001
Coronet, 8-cyl.	D50-3	Detroit	39,642,001
		San Leandro	42,510,001
Coronet, 6-cyl.	D51-2	Detroit	32,160,001
		San Leandro	45,110,001
Coronet, 6-cyl.	D52	Detroit	37,227,001
		San Leandro	48,015,001
Sierra, 8-cyl.	D53-2	Detroit	38,525,001
		San Leandro	47,003,001
Royal, 8-cyl.	D53-3	Detroit	38,525,001
		San Leandro	47,003,001

THE BODY NUMBER PLATE is located on the cowl under the hood. Dodge did not have body style codes, paint codes or trim codes appearing anywhere on the car. When ordering parts, it was necessary to furnish the factory with both the serial number and body plate number. We have attempted to list codes for paint and trim combinations when available.

```
BODY   NUMBER
XXX   XXXX
BRIGGS BODY, DETROIT MICHIGAN
```

BODY TYPES

MEADOWBROOK - D51-1A/D51-1
4-Dr. sedan
Club coupe

CORONET - D51-2
4-Dr. sedan
Club coupe

CORONET - D52
2-Dr. station wagon
4-Dr. Sierra station wagon, 6-pass.
4-Dr. Sierra station wagon, 8-pass.

MEADOWBROOK - D50-1/D50-1A
4-Dr. sedan
Club coupe

CORONET - D50-2
4-Dr. sedan
Club coupe

CORONET - D53-2
Hardtop
Convertible
2-Dr. station wagon, 6-pass.
4-Dr. Sierra station wagon, 6-pass.
4-Dr. Sierra station wagon, 8-pass.

ROYAL - D50-3
4-Dr. sedan
Club coupe

ROYAL - D53-3
Hardtop
Convertible

THE COLOR CODE indicates the paint color used on the vehicle.

COLOR	CODE
Bermuda Blue	505
Bedford Blue	506
Lancaster Blue Metallic	507
Willow Green	515
Berkshire Green	516
Cumberland Green Metallic	517
Dawn Gray	530
Wing Gray	531
Sunsand	540
Esquire Red	550
Pace Car Yellow	556
Spanish Coral	580L
Saratoga White	580U
Biscay Green	582

U - Indicates color was used on upper body

L - Indicates color was used on lower body

TWO-TONE COLORS

COLOR	CODE
Dawn Gray/Lancaster Blue Metallic	560
Sunsand/Bedford Blue	561
Bedford Blue/Bermuda Blue	562
Dawn Gray/Winter Gray	563
Bedford Blue/Dawn Gray	564
Bedford Blue/Sunsand	565
Willow Green/Cumberland Green Metallic	566
Willow Green/Berkshire Green	567
Sunsand/Berkshire Green	568
Cumberland Green Metallic/Willow Green	569
Cumberland Green Metallic/Sunsand	570
Sunsand/Esquire Red	571
Esquire Red/Sunsand	572
Esquire Red/Dawn Gray	573
Saratoga White/Spanish Coral	580
Spanish Coral/Saratoga White	581
Saratoga White/Biscay Green	582
Biscay Green/Saratoga White	583

THE TRIM CODE indicates the color and material scheme used on the vehicle. There were no codes available.

MEADOWBROOK TRIM

COLOR	CLOTH	VINYL	LEATHER	CODE
Green	•			
Blue	•			

CORONET TRIM

COLOR	CLOTH	VINYL	LEATHER	CODE
Green	•			
Blue	•			
Red/Gray	•			

ROYAL TRIM

COLOR	CLOTH	VINYL	LEATHER	CODE
Green	•			
Blue	•			
Red/Black	•			

ENGINE SPECIFICATIONS

ENGINE NUMBER - 6-Cylinder is located on the left front of the cylinder block, V8 located on a pad on the left side of the block between 2 and 3 cylinders.

MODEL	STARTING NUMBER
D50	D50-1001
D50-1A	D50A-1001
D50-1	D501-1001
D50-2	D502-1001
D50-3	D503-1001
D51	D51-1001
D51-A	D51-1001
D51-2	D51-1001
D52	D51-1001
D53	D50-1001
D53-2	D502-1001
D53-3	D502-1001

MEADOWBROOK

ENGINE CODE	NO. CYL.	CID	HORSE-POWER	COMP. RATIO	CARB
D51-1	6	230	110	7.25:1	1 BC
D51-1A	6	230	110	7.25:1	1 BC
D50-1	8	241	140	7.1:1	2 BC
D50-1A	8	241	140	7.1:1	2 BC

CORONET

ENGINE CODE	NO. CYL.	CID	HORSE-POWER	COMP. RATIO	CARB
D52	6	230	110	7.25:1	1 BC
D51-2	6	230	110	7.25:1	1 BC
D50-2	8	241	150	7.5:1	2 BC

ROYAL

ENGINE CODE	NO. CYL.	CID	HORSE-POWER	COMP. RATIO	CARB
D50-3	8	241	150	7.5:1	2 BC
D53-3	8	241	150	7.5:1	2 BC

SIERRA

ENGINE CODE	NO. CYL.	CID	HORSE-POWER	COMP. RATIO	CARB
D53-2	8	241	150	7.5:1	2 BC

1955 DODGE

VEHICLE IDENTIFICATION NUMBER

> **VEHICLE NUMBER**
> **34,740,001**

The serial number is located on the left front door hinge post. It indicates the series/model and assembly plant where the vehicle was built, based on numerical sequence.

MODEL NAME	MODEL CODE	ASSEMBLY PLANT	STARTING NUMBERS
Coronet, 8-cyl.	D55-1	Detroit	34,740,001
		Los Angeles	42,518,001
Coronet, 6-cyl.	D56-1	Detroit	32,192,001
		Los Angeles	48,016,001
Royal, 8-cyl.	D55-2	Detroit	34,740,001
		Los Angeles	42,518,001
Custom Royal, 8-cyl.	D55-3	Detroit	34,740,001
		Los Angeles	42,518,001

THE BODY NUMBER PLATE is located on the cowl under the hood. Dodge did not have body style codes, paint codes or trim codes appearing anywhere on the car. When ordering parts, it was necessary to furnish the factory with both the serial number and body plate number. We have attempted to list codes for paint and trim combinations when available.

> **BODY NUMBER**
> ◯ 000 0000 ◯
> **CHRYSLER CORP, DETROIT MICHIGAN**

BODY TYPES

CORONET - D56-1
4-Dr. sedan
2-Dr. sedan
2-Dr. station wagon, 6-pass.
4-Dr. station wagon, 8-pass.

CORONET - D55-1
4-Dr. sedan
2-Dr. sedan
2-Dr. Club sedan
Hardtop coupe
2-Dr. station wagon, 6-pass.
4-Dr. station wagon, 6-pass.
4-Dr. station wagon, 8-pass.

ROYAL - D55-2
4-Dr. sedan
Hardtop coupe
2-Dr. station wagon, 6-pass.
4-Dr. station wagon, 6-pass.
4-Dr. station wagon, 8-pass.

CUSTOM ROYAL - D55-3
4-Dr. sedan
4-Dr. sedan (Lancer)
Hardtop coupe
Convertible

THE COLOR CODE indicates the paint color used on the vehicle.

COLOR	CODE
Halo Blue	505
Parisian Blue	506
Admiral Blue Metallic	507
Chiffon Green	515
Emerald Green	516
Satin Green Metallic	517
Cashmere Gray	530
Heather Rose	550
Cameo Red	551
Regal Burgundy Metallic	552
Sapphire White	555
Fantasy Yellow	556

TWO-TONE COLORS

COLOR	CODE
Halo Blue/Admiral Blue Metallic	560
Admiral Blue Metallic/Halo Blue	561
Sapphire White/Parisian Blue	562
Emerald Green/Satin Green Metallic	563
Satin Green Metallic/Emerald Green	564
Satin Green Metallic/Chiffon Green	565
Emerald Green/Chiffon Green	566
Cameo Red/Cashmere Gray	567
Cameo Red/Sapphire White	570
Heather Rose/Sapphire White	571
Sapphire White/Fantasy Yellow	573
Sapphire White/Regal Burgundy Metallic	575

THE TRIM CODE indicates the color and material scheme used on the vehicle. The trim codes were not available.

ENGINE SPECIFICATIONS

ENGINE NUMBER - 6-Cylinder is located on the left front of the cylinder block, V8 located on a pad on the left side of the block between 2 and 3 cylinders.

MODEL	STARTING NUMBER
D55-1	D551-1001
D55-2	D551-1001
D55-3	D553-1001
D56	D56-1001

CORONET

ENGINE CODE	NO. CYL.	CID	HORSE-POWER	COMP. RATIO	CARB
D56-1	6	230	123	7.4:1	2 BC
D55-1	8	270	175	7.6:1	2 BC

ROYAL

ENGINE CODE	NO. CYL.	CID	HORSE-POWER	COMP. RATIO	CARB
D55-2	8	270	175	7.6:1	2 BC

CUSTOM ROYAL

ENGINE CODE	NO. CYL.	CID	HORSE-POWER	COMP. RATIO	CARB
D55-3	8	270	183	7.6:1	2 BC

ROYAL LANCER

ENGINE CODE	NO. CYL.	CID	HORSE-POWER	COMP. RATIO	CARB
D55-3	8	270	183	7.6:1	2 BC
D55-3	8	270	193	7.6:1	4 BC

1956 DODGE CUSTOM ROYAL V-8 LANCER

1956 DODGE 500

VEHICLE IDENTIFICATION NUMBER

```
• VEHICLE NUMBER •
   3 2 , 2 2 7 , 0 0 1
```

The serial number is located on the left front door hinge post. It indicates the assembly plant where the vehicle was built and whether it was equipped with a 6-cylinder or 8-cylinder engine based on numerical sequence.

MODEL NAME	MODEL CODE	ASSEMBLY PLANT	STARTING NUMBERS
Coronet, 6-cyl.	D62	Detroit	32,227,001
		Los Angeles	48,016,501
Coronet Taxicab	D62	Detroit	32,227,001
Coronet, 8-cyl.	D63-1	Detroit	34,972,001
		Los Angeles	42,608,001
Coronet Taxicab	D63-1	Detroit	34,972,001
Royal, 8-cyl.	D63-2	Detroit	34,972,001
		Los Angeles	42,608,001
Custom Royal, 8-cyl.	D63-3	Detroit	34,972,001
		Los Angeles	42,608,001
	D63-D500	Detroit	34,972,001

THE BODY NUMBER PLATE is located on the cowl under the hood.

Dodge did not have body style codes, paint codes or trim codes appearing anywhere on the car. When ordering parts, it was necessary to furnish the factory with both the serial number and body plate number. We have attempted to list codes for paint and trim combinations when available.

```
┌─────────────────────────────────────┐
│           BODY NUMBER                 │
│  ◯     0 0 0     0 0 0 0     ◯       │
├─────────────────────────────────────┤
│  CHRYSLER CORP, DETROIT MICHIGAN     │
└─────────────────────────────────────┘
```

BODY TYPES

CORONET - D62
4-Dr. sedan
2-Dr. Club sedan
2-Dr. station wagon, 6-pass.

CORONET - D63-1
4-Dr. sedan
4-Dr. hardtop sedan
2-Dr. Club sedan
2-Dr. hardtop coupe
Convertible
2-Dr. station wagon, 6-pass.
4-Dr. station wagon, 6-pass. (Sierra)
4-Dr. station wagon, 8-pass. (Sierra)

ROYAL - D63-2
4-Dr. sedan
4-Dr. hardtop sedan
2-Dr. hardtop coupe
2-Dr. station wagon, 6-pass.
4-Dr. station wagon, 6-pass. (Sierra)
4-Dr. station wagon, 8-pass. (Sierra)

CUSTOM ROYAL - D63-3
4-Dr. sedan
4-Dr. hardtop sedan (Lancer)
Hardtop coupe (Lancer)
Convertible

THE COLOR CODE indicates the paint color used on the vehicle.

COLOR	CODE
Gallant Gold Metallic	PPP
Jewel Black	501
Wedgewood Blue	505
Royal Blue Metallic	506
Aquamarine	515
Neptune Green Metallic	516
Sea Foam Green	517
Jade Green Metallic	518
Cloud Gray	540
Charcoal Metallic	541
Chinese Rose	550
Oriental Coral	551
Garnet Metallic	552
Sapphire White	555
Crown Yellow	556
Misty Orchid	576U
Regal Orchid	576-1L

U - Indicates the upper body color
L - Indicates the lower body color

TWO-TONE COLORS

COLOR	CODE
Sapphire White(U)/Jewel Black(L)	560
Sapphire White(U)/Jewel Black(L)	560-1
Jewel Black(L)/Sapphire White(S)/Oriental Coral (R)	560-4
Royal Blue Metallic(U)/Wedgewood Blue(L)	561
Royal Blue Metallic(U)/Wedgewood Blue(L)	561-1
Wedgewood Blue(L)/Royal Blue Metallic(S)/Sapphire White(R)	561-2
Sapphire White(U)/Royal Blue Metallic(L)	562
Sapphire White(U)/Royal Blue Metallic(L)	562-1
Royal Blue Metallic(L)/Sapphire White(S)/Jewel Black (R)	562-3
Jewel Black(R)/Aquamarine(L)	563
Jewel Black(R)/Aquamarine(L)	563-1
Aquamarine(L)/Jewel Black(S)/Sapphire White(R)	563-2
Sapphire White(U)/Neptune Green Metallic(L)	564
Sapphire White(U)/Neptune Green Metallic(L)	564-1
Neptune Green Metallic(L)/Sapphire White(S)/Jewel Black(R)	564-3
Jade Green Metallic(U)/Sea Foam Green(L)	565
Jade Green Metallic(U)/Sea Foam Green(L)	565-1
Sea Foam Green(L)/Jade Green Metallic(S)/Sapphire White(R)	565-2
Sea Foam Green(U)/Jade Green Metallic(L)	566
Sea Foam Green(U)/Jade Green Metallic(L)	566-1

COLOR	CODE
Jade Green Metallic(L)/Sea Foam Green(S)/Jewel Black(R)	566-3
Iridescent Charcoal Metallic(U)/Cloud Gray(L)	567
Iridescent Charcoal Metallic(U)/Cloud Gray(L)	567-1
Cloud Gray(L)/Iridescent Charcoal Metallic(S)/Sapphire White(R)	567-2
Iridescent Charcoal Metallic(U)/Chinese Rose(L)	568
Iridescent Charcoal Metallic(U)/Chinese Rose(L)	568-1
Chinese Rose(L)/Iridescent Charcoal Metallic(S)/Sapphire White(R)	568-2
Garnet Metallic(U)/Chinese Rose(L)	569
Garnet Metallic(U)/Chinese Rose(L)	569-1
Chinese Rose(L)/Garnet Metallic(S)/Jewel Black(R)	569-3
Sapphire White(U)/Chinese Rose(L)	570
Sapphire White(U)/Chinese Rose(L)	570-1
Chinese Rose(L)/Sapphire White(S)/Jewel Black(R)	570-3
Iridescent Charcoal Metallic(U)/Oriental Coral(L)	571
Iridescent Charcoal Metallic(U)/Oriental Coral(L)	571-1
Oriental Coral(L)/Iridescent Charcoal Metallic(S)/Sapphire White(R)	571-2
Sapphire White(U)/Oriental Coral(L)	572
Sapphire White(U)/Oriental Coral(L)	572-1
Oriental Coral(L)/Sapphire White(S)/Jewel Black(R)	572-3
Jewel Black(U)/Garnet Metallic(L)	573
Jewel Black(U)/Garnet Metallic(L)	573-1
Garnet Metallic(L)/Sapphire White(R)/Jewel Black(S)	573-2
Iridescent Charcoal Metallic(U)/Crown Yellow(L)	574
Iridescent Charcoal Metallic(U)/Crown Yellow(L)	574-1
Crown Yellow(L)/Iridescent Charcoal Metallic(S)/Sapphire White(R)	574-2
Sapphire White(U)/Crown Yellow(L)	575
Sapphire White(U)/Crown Yellow(L)	575-1
Crown Yellow(L)/Sapphire White(S)/Jewel Black(R)	575-3
Misty Orchid(U)/Regal Orchid(L)	576-1

U - Upper body color
L - Lower body color
S - Sweep color
R - Roof color

THE TRIM CODE indicates the color and material scheme used on the vehicle. The trim codes were not available.

ENGINE SPECIFICATIONS

ENGINE NUMBER - 6-Cylinder is located on the left front of the cylinder block, V8 located on a pad on the left side of the block between 2 and 3 cylinders.

MODEL	STARTING NUMBER
D62	D62-1001
D63-1	D63-1-1001
D63-2	D63-3-1001
D63-3	D63-3-1001

CORONET

ENGINE CODE	NO. CYL.	CID	HORSE-POWER	COMP. RATIO	CARB
D62	6	230	131	7.6:1	2 BC
D63-1	8	270	189	8.1:1	2 BC

ROYAL

ENGINE CODE	NO. CYL.	CID	HORSE-POWER	COMP. RATIO	CARB
D63-2	8	315	218	8.1:1	2 BC
D63-2	8	315	230	8.1:1	4 BC

CUSTOM ROYAL

ENGINE CODE	NO. CYL.	CID	HORSE-POWER	COMP. RATIO	CARB
D63-3	8	315	218	8.1:1	2 BC
D63-3	8	315	230	8.1:1	4 BC

DODGE "500"

ENGINE CODE	NO. CYL.	CID	HORSE-POWER	COMP. RATIO	CARB
D500	8	315	260	9.25:1	4 BC
D500	8	315	295	9.25:1	2X4 BC

1957 DODGE CORONET

1957 DODGE LANCER

VEHICLE IDENTIFICATION NUMBER

```
• VEHICLE NUMBER •
    32,255,001
```

The serial number is located on the left front door hinge post. It indicates the assembly plant where the vehicle was built based on numerical sequence.

MODEL NAME	MODEL CODE	ASSEMBLY PLANT	STARTING NUMBERS
Coronet, 6-cyl.	D72-1	Detroit	32,255,001
Coronet Taxicab	D72-1	Detroit	32,255,001
Custom Coronet	D72-2	Detroit	32,255,001
Coronet, 8-cyl.	D66-1	Detroit	35,172,001
		Los Angeles	42,620,001
Coronet Taxicab	D66-1	Detroit	35,172,001
Custom Coronet	D66-2	Detroit	35,172,001
		Los Angeles	42,620,001
Royal, 8-cyl.	D67-1	Detroit	37,240,001
		Los Angeles	45,540,001
Custom Royal, 8-cyl.	D67-2	Detroit	37,240,001
		Los Angeles	45,540,001
Sierra, 8-cyl., Suburban	D70	Detroit	38,001,001
Custom Sierra, Suburban	D71	Detroit	38,535,001
Coronet "501"	D500-1	Detroit	38,172,000
		Los Angeles	42,620,001

THE BODY NUMBER PLATE is located on the cowl under the hood. Dodge did not have body style codes, paint codes or trim codes appearing anywhere on the car. When ordering parts, it was necessary to furnish the factory with both the serial number and body plate number. We have attempted to list codes for paint and trim combinations when available.

```
         BODY NUMBER
  O    000   0000    O
CHRYSLER CORP, DETROIT MICHIGAN
```

BODY TYPES

CORONET - D-72
4-Dr. sedan
2-Dr. Club sedan

CORONET - D-66
4-Dr. sedan
4-Dr. hardtop sedan (Lancer)
2-Dr. Club coupe
2-Dr. hardtop coupe (Lancer)
Convertible

ROYAL - D67-1
4-Dr. sedan
4-Dr. hardtop sedan (Lancer)
2-Dr. hardtop sedan (Lancer)

CUSTOM - D-67-2
4-Dr. sedan
4-Dr. hardtop sedan (Lancer)
2-Dr. hardtop sedan (Lancer)
Convertible

STATION WAGON - D-70
4-Dr. Sierra, 9-pass.
4-Dr. Sierra, 6-pass.
2-Dr. Suburban, 6-pass.

STATION WAGON, CUSTOM - D-71
4-Dr. Sierra, 9-pass.
4-Dr. Sierra, 6-pass.

CORONET - D-501
2-Dr. Club sedan
Convertible

THE COLOR CODE indicates the paint color used on the vehicle. Two-tone combinations were identified by the first letter used as the upper, the second letter as the middle or lower color, the third letter (if it is a three-tone combination) the lower color.

COLOR	CODE
Ice Blue	BBB
Velvet Blue Metallic	CCC
Misty Green	DDD
Forest Green Metallic	EEE
Moonstone Gray	FFF
Metallic Charcoal	GGG
Flame Red	HHH
Sunshine Yellow	KKK
Glacier White	LLL
Turquoise	MMM
Tropical Coral	NNN
Gallant Gold Metallic	PPP
Heather Green	SSS

THE TRIM CODE indicates the color and material scheme used on the vehicle. No code numbers were available.

CORONET TRIM

COLOR	CLOTH	VINYL	LEATHER	CODE
Blue/Blue	•	•		
Green/Green	•	•		
Black/Gold	•	•		
Red*	•			

* Coronet Custom only

ROYAL TRIM

COLOR	CLOTH	VINYL	LEATHER	CODE
Blue/Blue	•	•		
Green/Green	•	•		
Black/Gold	•	•		
Red		•		

CONVERTIBLE TOP COLOR

Black
White
Blue
Green

ENGINE SPECIFICATIONS

ENGINE NUMBER - 6-Cylinder is located on the left front of the cylinder block, V8 located on a pad on the left side of the block between 2 and 3 cylinders.

MODEL	STARTING NUMBER
D72-1 (early)	D72-1001
D72-1 (late)	KDS-1001
D72-2 (early)	D72-1001
D72-2 (late)	KDS-1001
D66-1	KDS-1001
D66-2	KDS-1001
D67-1	KDS-1001
D67-2	KDS-1001
D70	KDS-1001
D71	KDS-1001
D500	KD-501-1001

CORONET

ENGINE CODE	NO. CYL.	CID	HORSE-POWER	COMP. RATIO	CARB
D72-1	6	230	138	8.0:1	1 BC
D66-1	8	325	245	8.5:1	2 BC
D66-2	8	325	260	8.5:1	4 BC
D-500	8	354	285	9.25:1	4 BC
D-500*	8	354	310	9.25:1	2X4 BC
D-500-1	8	354	340	10.0:1	2X4 BC

* Special kit

CUSTOM CORONET

ENGINE CODE	NO. CYL.	CID	HORSE-POWER	COMP. RATIO	CARB
D72-2	6	230	138	8.0:1	2 BC
D66-2	8	325	245	8.5:1	2 BC
D67-2	8	325	260	8.5:1	4 BC
D-500	8	354	285	9.25:1	4 BC
D-500*	8	354	310	9.25:1	2X4 BC
D-500-1	8	354	340	10.0:1	2X4 BC

* Special kit

ROYAL

ENGINE CODE	NO. CYL.	CID	HORSE-POWER	COMP. RATIO	CARB
D67-1	8	325	245	8.5:1	2 BC
D67-2	8	325	260	8.5:1	4 BC
D-500	8	354	285	9.25:1	4 BC
D-500*	8	354	310	9.25:1	2X4 BC

* Special kit

CUSTOM ROYAL

ENGINE CODE	NO. CYL.	CID	HORSE-POWER	COMP. RATIO	CARB
D67-2	8	325	260	8.5:1	4 BC
D-500	8	354	285	9.25:1	4 BC
D-500	8	354	310	9.25:1	2X4 BC

SUBURBAN/SIERRA

ENGINE CODE	NO. CYL.	CID	HORSE-POWER	COMP. RATIO	CARB
D70	8	325	245	8.5:1	2 BC
D67-2	8	325	260	8.5:1	4 BC
D-500	8	354	285	9.25:1	4 BC
D-500*	8	354	310	9.25:1	2X4 BC

* Special kit

CUSTOM SIERRA

ENGINE CODE	NO. CYL.	CID	HORSE-POWER	COMP. RATIO	CARB
D71	8	325	245	8.5:1	2 BC
D67-2	8	325	260	8.5:1	4 BC
D-500	8	354	285	9.25:1	4 BC
D-500*	8	354	310	9.25:1	2X4 BC

* Special kit

1958 DODGE

1958 DODGE STATION WAGON

VEHICLE IDENTIFICATION NUMBER

| • L D 2 L   1 0 0 1 • |

The serial number is located on the left front door hinge post.

FIRST DIGIT: Identifies the model year (L=1958)

SECOND DIGIT: Identifies the car make (D=Dodge)

THIRD DIGIT: Identifies six or eight cylinder chassis

CHASSIS	CODE
6-cyl.	1
8-cyl.	2
8-cyl.	3

FOURTH DIGIT: Identifies the assembly plant

ASSEMBLY PLANT	CODE
Detroit, MI	—
Los Angeles, CA	L
Newark, DE	N

LAST FOUR DIGITS: Identify the basic production sequence number

THE BODY NUMBER PLATE is located on the cowl under the hood. Dodge did not have body style codes, paint codes or trim codes appearing anywhere on the car. When ordering parts, it was necessary to furnish the factory with both the serial number and body plate number. We have attempted to list codes for paint and trim combinations when available.

TL	CS	MR	HB	AC	A	SPL

HT	PS	AG	AR	PB	PF	EW	S6	RS	CU	SC

SCH	BO	NO	◯	BO	PT	TR	CT	TR	◯

BODY TYPES

CORONET - LD1

4-Dr. sedan

2-Dr. Club sedan

2-Dr. hardtop coupe

CORONET - LD2

4-Dr. sedan

4-Dr. hardtop sedan

2-Dr. Club sedan

2-Dr. hardtop coupe

convertible

ROYAL - LD2

4-Dr. sedan

4-Dr. hardtop sedan (Lancer)

2-Dr. hardtop coupe (Laner)

CUSTOM ROYAL - LD3

4-Dr. sedan

4-Dr. hardtop sedan (Lancer)

4-Dr. hardtop coupe (Lancer)

Convertible

Regal hardtop coupe, 2-dr. (Lancer)

STATION WAGON - LD3

4-Dr. Sierra, 9-pass.

4-Dr. Sierra, 6-pass.

2-Dr. Suburban, 6-pass.

Custom 4-dr., 9-pass. (Sierra)

Custom 4-dr., 6-pass. (Sierra)

MODEL NUMBER

LD1-L1

EXAMPLE:

L	Model year (1958)
D	Car make (Dodge)
1	Coronet chassis
L	Low class price
1*	Coronet

* Coronet only - 1 Coronet, 2 Custom Coronet

MODEL	CODE
Coronet 6	LD1-L1
Coronet Custom 6	LD1-L2
Coronet V8	LD2-L1
Coronet Custom V8	LD2-L2
Royal V8	LD2-M
Custom Royal V8	LD3-H
Suburban/Sierra V8	LD3-L
Sierra Custom V8	LD3-H
D500	LD2-S
D500	LD3-S

THE VEHICLE PRICE CODE indicates the price class.

CLASS	CODE
Low	L
Medium	M
High	H
Sport	S

THE COLOR CODE indicates the paint color used on the vehicle. Two-tone combinations are identified by the first letter used as the upper, the second letter as the middle or lower color, the third letter (if it is a three-tone combination) the lower color.

COLOR	CODE
Wedgewood	B
Sapphire Metallic	C
Navy	D
Mint Green	E
Moss Green Metallic	F
Frosted Turquoise Metallic	JJJ
Silver Metallic	K
Charcoal Gray Metallic	L
Beige	M
Sand Metallic	N

COLOR	CODE
Crimson	P
Poppy	RRR
Copper Beige Metallic	T
Paris Rose Metallic	TTT
Sunshine	V
Eggshell	X
Gold Metallic	Z

CONVERTIBLE TOP COLORS

Black
White
Green
Blue

THE TRIM CODE indicates the color and material scheme used on the vehicle. No trim code numbers were available.

COLOR	CLOTH	VINYL	LEATHER	CODE
Blue/Blue	•	•		
Green/Green	•	•		
Tan/Beige	•	•		
Black/Red	•	•		

ENGINE SPECIFICATIONS

ENGINE NUMBER - 6-Cylinder is located on the left front of the cylinder block, V8 located on a pad on the left side of the block between 2 and 3 cylinders, V8-350 located on a boss on the right side of the cylinder block below the distributor.

MODEL	STARTING NUMBER
LD1	L230-1001
LD2	L325-1001
LD3	L350-1001
D500	L350-1001

CORONET

ENGINE CODE	NO. CYL.	CID	HORSE-POWER	COMP. RATIO	CARB
LD1-L1	6	230	138	8.0:1	2 BC
LD2-L1	8	325	252	9.0:1	2 BC
LD2-M	8	325	265	10.0:1	4 BC
D-500	8	361	305	10.0:1	4 BC
D-500	8	361	320	10.0:1	2X4 BC
D-500	8	361	333	10.0:1	F.I.

CUSTOM CORONET

ENGINE CODE	NO. CYL.	CID	HORSE-POWER	COMP. RATIO	CARB
LD1-L2	6	230	138	8.0:1	1 BC
LD2-L2	8	325	252	9.0:1	2 BC
LD2-M	8	325	265	10.0:1	4 BC
D-500	8	361	305	10.0:1	4 BC
D-500	8	361	320	10.0:1	2X4 BC
D-500	8	361	333	10.0:1	F.I.

ROYAL

ENGINE CODE	NO. CYL.	CID	HORSE-POWER	COMP. RATIO	CARB
LD2-L	8	325	252	9.0:1	2 BC
LD2-M	8	325	265	10.0:1	4 BC
D-500	8	361	305	10.0:1	4 BC
D-500	8	361	320	10.0:1	2X4 BC
D-500	8	361	333	10.0:1	F.I.

CUSTOM ROYAL

ENGINE CODE	NO. CYL.	CID	HORSE-POWER	COMP. RATIO	CARB
LD3-H	8	350	295	10.0:1	4 BC
D-500	8	361	305	10.0:1	4 BC
D-500	8	361	320	10.0:1	2X4 BC
D-500	8	361	333	10.0:1	F.I.

SUBURBAN/SIERRA

ENGINE CODE	NO. CYL.	CID	HORSE-POWER	COMP. RATIO	CARB
LD3-L	8	350	295	10.0:1	4 BC
D-500	8	361	305	10.0:1	4 BC
D-500	8	361	320	10.0:1	2X4 BC
D-500	8	361	333	10.0:1	F.I.

CUSTOM SIERRA

ENGINE CODE	NO. CYL.	CID	HORSE-POWER	COMP. RATIO	CARB
LD3-H	8	350	295	10.0:1	4 BC
D-500	8	361	305	10.0:1	4 BC
D-500	8	361	320	10.0:1	2X4 BC
D-500	8	361	333	10.0:1	F.I.

D500

ENGINE CODE	NO. CYL.	CID	HORSE-POWER	COMP. RATIO	CARB
LD2-S	8	361	305	10.0:1	4 BC
D-500	8	361	320	10.0:1	2X4 BC
D-500	8	361	333	10.0:1	F.I.

D500

ENGINE CODE	NO. CYL.	CID	HORSE-POWER	COMP. RATIO	CARB
LD3-S	8	361	305	10.0:1	4 BC
D-500	8	361	320	10.0:1	2X4 BC
D-500	8	361	333	10.0:1	F.I.

1959 DODGE

VEHICLE IDENTIFICATION NUMBER

`• M 3 1 2 1 0 0 0 0 1 •`

The serial number is located on the left front door hinge pillar post on cars built in Los Angeles, it is located on a plate attached to the top front side of the cowl on all other cars.

FIRST DIGIT: Identifies the model year (M=1959)

SECOND DIGIT: Identifies the car make (3=Dodge)

THIRD DIGIT: Identifies the model series

MODEL SERIES	CODE
Coronet, 6-cyl.	0
Coronet	1
Royal	3
Custom Royal	5
Taxi, 6-cyl.	6
Station wagons	7
Taxi, V8	8
Special models	9

FOURTH DIGIT: Identifies the assembly plant

ASSEMBLY PLANT	CODE
Detroit, MI	2
Evansville, IN	3
Los Angeles, CA	4
Newark, DE	5
Valley Park, MO	8

LAST SIX DIGITS: Identify the basic production sequence number

THE BODY NUMBER PLATE is located on the cowl under the hood. Dodge did not have body style codes, paint codes or trim codes appearing anywhere on the car. When ordering parts, it was necessary to furnish the factory with both the serial number and body plate number. We have attempted to list codes for paint and trim combinations when available.

```
TL   CS   MR   HB   AC   A   SPL

HT  PS  AG  AR  PB  PF  EW  S6  RS  CU  SC

SCH  BO  NO  O  BO  PT  TR  CT  TR  O
```

BODY TYPES

CORONET - MD1-L
4-Dr. sedan
4-Dr. Club sedan
4-Dr. hardtop coupe

CORONET - MD2-2
4-Dr. sedan
4-Dr. hardtop (Lancer)
2-Dr. Club sedan
2-Dr. hardtop coupe (Lancer)
Convertible

ROYAL - MD3-M
4-Dr. sedan
4-Dr. hardtop sedan (Lancer)
2-Dr. hardtop coupe (Lancer)

CUSTOM ROYAL - MD3-H
4-Dr. sedan
4-Dr. hardtop sedan (Lancer)
2-Dr. Club sedan
2-Dr. hardtop coupe (Lancer)

SIERRA - MD3-L
4-Dr. station wagon, 9-pass.
4-Dr. station wagon, 6-pass.

SIERRA CUSTOM - MD3-H
4-Dr. station wagon, 9-pass.
4-Dr. station wagon, 6-pass.

MODEL NUMBER

MD1-L

EXAMPLE:

M ....Model year (1959)
D ....Car make (Dodge)
1 ....Coronet chassis
L ....Low class price

MODEL	CODE
Coronet 6	MD1-L
Coronet V8	MD2-L
Royal V8	MD3-M
Custom Royal V8	MD3-H
Sierra V8	MD3-L
Sierra Custom V8	MD3-H

THE VEHICLE PRICE CODE Indicates the price class.

CLASS	CODE
Low	L
Medium	M
High	H

THE COLOR CODE indicates the paint color used on the vehicle. Two-tone color combinations are identified by the arrangement of the paint code letters followed by a paint code number. Example:

CC-1 - Single tone
CB-2 - Fin only. The first letter is the fin color, second letter is the balance of the car.
CB-3 - Fin and lower. The first letter is the fin and lower, the second letter is the balance of the car.
CB-4 - Roof, fins and lower. The first letter is the roof, fins and lower, the second letter is the balance of the car.

COLOR	CODE
Blue Diamond	BB-1
Star Sapphire Metallic	CC-1
Aquamarine	EE-1
Jade Metallic	FF-1
Turquoise	JJ-1
Silver Metallic	LL-1
Silver Metallic #2	LL-1
Pewter Gray Metallic	MM-1
Rose Quartz	NN-1
Coral	PP-1
Ruby	RR-1
Biscuit	UU-1
Mocha Metallic	WW-1
Pearl	XX-1
Canary Diamond	YY-1

THE TRIM CODE indicates the key to the color and material scheme used on the vehicle. No trim code numbers were available.

COLOR	CLOTH	VINYL	LEATHER	CODE
Blue/Blue	•	•		
Green/Green	•	•		
Tan/Beige	•	•		
Black/White	•	•		
Black/Red	•	•		
Black/Turquoise*	•	•		
Black/Yellow*	•	•		

* Custom Royal only

ENGINE SPECIFICATIONS

ENGINE NUMBER - 6-Cylinder is located on the left front of
the cylinder block, V8 located on the top of the cylinder block
behind the water pump.

MODEL	STARTING NUMBER
Six	ML-230-1001
V8-325	ML-325-1001
V8-361	ML-361-1001
V8-383	ML-383-1001

CORONET

ENGINE CODE	NO. CYL.	CID	HORSE-POWER	COMP. RATIO	CARB
MD1-L	6	230	135	8.0:1	1 BC
MD2-L	8	326	255	9.2:1	2 BC
D-500	8	383	320	10.0:1	4 BC
D-500*	8	383	345	10.0:1	2X4 BC

* Super

ROYAL

ENGINE CODE	NO. CYL.	CID	HORSE-POWER	COMP. RATIO	CARB
MD3-M	8	361	295	10.0:1	2 BC
D-500	8	383	320	10.0:1	4 BC
D-500*	8	383	345	10.0:1	2X4 BC

* Super

CUSTOM ROYAL

ENGINE CODE	NO. CYL.	CID	HORSE-POWER	COMP. RATIO	CARB
MD3-H	8	361	305	10.0:1	4 BC
D-500	8	383	320	10.0:1	4 BC
D-500*	8	383	345	10.0:1	2X4 BC

* Super

STATION WAGON

ENGINE CODE	NO. CYL.	CID	HORSE-POWER	COMP. RATIO	CARB
MD3-L	8	361	295	10.0:1	2 BC
D-500	8	383	320	10.0:1	4 BC
D-500*	8	383	345	10.0:1	2X4 BC

* Super

CUSTOM STATION WAGON

ENGINE CODE	NO. CYL.	CID	HORSE-POWER	COMP. RATIO	CARB
MD3-H	8	361	305	10.0:1	4 BC
D-500	8	383	320	10.0:1	4 BC
D-500*	8	383	345	10.0:1	2X4 BC

* Super

1950 PLYMOUTH

1950 PLYMOUTH

1950 PLYMOUTH

1950 PLYMOUTH

VEHICLE IDENTIFICATION NUMBER

Located on the left front door post. The plate indicates only the series, model and assembly plant.

MODEL	SERIES	WHEEL BASE	ASSEMBLY PLANT	NUMBER SEQUENCE
Deluxe	P19	111"	Detroit	18041001
			Los Angeles	28004001
			San Leandro	28503501
			Evansville	24012001
			Windsor	95003001
Deluxe	P20	118 1/2"	Detroit	15359501
			Los Angeles	26030501
			San Leandro	26504001
			Evansville	22097001
			Windsor	95504001
Special Deluxe	20	118 1/2"	Detroit	12384501
			Los Angeles	25097501
			San Leandro	25511001
			Evansville	20367001
			Windsor	96013001

BODY NUMBER

THE BODY NUMBER is located on a tag mounted on the engine side of the firewall, near the left hood hinge. This tag indicates the model/body style, and the sequential body serial number.

BODY NUMBER
XXX XXXX
BRIGGS BODY, DETROIT MICHIGAN

P19 DELUXE

BODY TYPE	CODE
2-Dr. fastback sedan	811
Business coupe, 3-pass.	813
Suburban station wagon (all metal)	817

P20 DELUXE

BODY TYPE	CODE
4-Dr. sedan	800
2-Dr. Club coupe	802

P20 SPECIAL DELUXE

BODY TYPE	CODE
Convertible	804
4-Dr. sedan	805
2-Dr. Club coupe	806

NOTE: Wood body station wagons had a tag with USH-COSW followed by a serial number as these bodies were built by U.S. Body & Forging Co. for Plymouth.

THE TRIM CODE indicates the key to the interior color and material scheme used on the vehicle. This code is not stamped anywhere on Plymouth cars. If this information was needed the owner or dealer was to provide the factory with the car serial number.

COLOR	CLOTH	VINYL	LEATHER	CODE
Green	•			171
Blue	•			172
Blue			•	401
Red			•	402
Tan			•	403
Green			•	404
Blue	•	•		411
Red	•	•		412
Tan	•	•		413
Green	•	•		414
Blue		•		431
Red		•		432,448
Tan		•		433,442,443
Tan		•		444,464,465
Tan		•		469
Green		•		434
Orange		•		441
Maroon Stripe	•			921
Blue Check	•			922
Green Stripe	•			949
Blue Stripe	•			950

THE COLOR CODE indicates the paint color used on the vehicle. This code is not stamped anywhere on Plymouth cars. If this information was needed the owner or dealer was to provide the factory with the car serial number. Paint codes were published by paint suppliers and are included here.

COLOR	CODE
Black	601
Salvador Blue	605
Peru Gray	635
New Brunswick Blue	606
Mexico Red	661
Plymouth Cream	665
Malibu Brown	647
Palm Beige	645
Shore Green	621
Channel Green	620
Gaynor Gray	636
Trinidad Brown	646
Rio Maroon	660

ENGINE SPECIFICATIONS

THE ENGINE NUMBER is located on a flat boss on the left side of the engine block, directly below the cylinder head and directly above the generator. Each engine was stamped with an engineering code matching the model year of the car, followed by a sequential build number. Canadian engines are identified by the code letter C following the engineering code (P20C). Additional information concerning over or undersized bearings installed at the factory is also stamped by the engine number as follows:

A - .020 oversize cylinder bore

B - .010 undersize main and connecting rod bearings

C - .005 oversize rod bearings

AB - .020 oversize cylinders, .010 undersize main
      and connecting rod bearings

ENGINE NUMBER	NO. CYL.	CID	HORSE-POWER	COMP. RATIO	CARB
P20-1001	6	217.8	97	7.0:1	1 BC

1951 PLYMOUTH

1951 PLYMOUTH

VEHICLE IDENTIFICATION NUMBER

VEHICLE 18126001 NUMBER

Located on the left front door post. The plate indicates only the series, model and assembly plant.

MODEL	SERIES	WHEEL BASE	ASSEMBLY PLANT	NUMBER SEQUENCE
Concord	P22	111"	Detroit	18126001
			Los Angeles	28011001
			San Leandro	28513001
			Evansville	24042001
			Windsor	95007001
Cambridge	P23S	118 1/2"	Detroit	15460001
			Los Angeles	26040001
			San Leandro	26512001
			Evansville	22132001
			Windsor	95509001
Cranbrook	P23C	118 1/2"	Detroit	12635001
			Los Angeles	25112001
			San Leandro	25531001
			Evansville	20435001
			Windsor	96030001

BODY NUMBER

THE BODY NUMBER is located on a tag mounted on the engine side of the firewall, near the left hood hinge. This tag indicates the model series, body style, and the sequential body serial number.

BODY NUMBER
XXX XXXX
BRIGGS BODY, DETROIT MICHIGAN

P22 CONCORD

BODY TYPE	CODE
2-Dr. fastback sedan	111
Business coupe, 3-pass.	113
Suburban station wagon	117
Savoy Suburban station wagon	217

P23S CAMBRIDGE

BODY TYPE	CODE
4-Dr. sedan	100
2-Dr. Club coupe	102

P23C CRANBROOK

BODY TYPE	CODE
Belvedere 2-dr. hardtop	103
Convertible	104
4-Dr. sedan	105
2-Dr. Club coupe	106

THE TRIM CODE indicates the key to the interior color and material scheme used on the vehicle. This code is not stamped anywhere on Plymouth cars, except some California and Canadian built cars. If this information was needed the owner or dealer was to provide the factory with the car serial number.

COLOR	CLOTH	VINYL	LEATHER	CODE
Tan	•			201
Blue	•			202
Green	•			203,206,207
Green	•			243
Blue	•			204,244
Red	•			205
Maroon/Red	•	•		205
Black Stripe	•			208
Black/Black	•	•		208
Green/Black	•	•		209
Blue/Red	•	•		210
Black	•	•		245,246,517
Blue	•	•		247,508,521
Maroon	•	•		248
Red/Red	•	•		509,522
Black/Red	•	•		518
Tan/Red	•	•		523
Green/Blue	•	•		524
Blue		•		501,506
Red		•		502,505
Tan		•		503,507
Green		•		504
Blue			•	511
Red			•	512
Tan			•	513
Green			•	514

THE COLOR CODE indicates the paint color used on the vehicle. This code is not stamped anywhere on Plymouth cars, except some California and Canadian built cars. If this information was needed the owner or dealer was to provide the factory with the car serial number. Paint codes were published by paint suppliers and are included here. The letter U indicates an upper body color in two-tone combinations.

COLOR	CODE
Black	601
Nile Green	620
Sherwood Green	621
Sterling Gray	635
Luna Gray	636
Mecca Maroon	660
Champion Blue	676U
Orca Blue	677
Empire Maroon	662
New Brunswick Blue	606
Mexico Red	661
Plymouth Cream	665
Palm Beige	645
Wedgewood Blue	605

ENGINE SPECIFICATIONS

THE ENGINE NUMBER is located on a flat boss on the left side of the engine block, directly below the cylinder head and directly above the generator. Each engine is stamped with an engineering code matching the model year of the car, followed by a sequential build number. Canadian engines are identified by the code letter C following the engineering code (P20C). Additional information concerning over or undersized bearings installed at the factory is also stamped by the engine number as follows:

A - .020 oversize cylinder bore

B - .010 undersize main and connecting rod bearings

C - .005 oversize rod bearings

AB - .020 oversize cylinders, .010 undersize main
     and connecting rod bearings

ENGINE NUMBER	NO. CYL.	CID	HORSE-POWER	COMP. RATIO	CARB
P23-1001/up	6	217.8	97	7.0:1	1 BC

1952 PLYMOUTH BELVEDERE

1952 PLYMOUTH

1952 PLYMOUTH

VEHICLE IDENTIFICATION NUMBER

Located on the left front door post. The plate indicates only the series, model and assembly plant.

MODEL	SERIES	WHEEL BASE	ASSEMBLY PLANT	NUMBER SEQUENCE
Concord	P22	111"	Detroit	18192501
			Los Angeles	28015701
			San Leandro	28519101
			Evansville	24056701
			Windsor	95010001
Cambridge	P23S	118 1/2"	Detroit	15577801
			Los Angeles	26045701
			San Leandro	26518201
			Evansville	22159601
			Windsor	95513701
Cranbrook	P23C	118 1/2"	Detroit	12906701
			Los Angeles	25125301
			San Leandro	25546101
			Evansville	28485001
			Windsor	96044601

BODY NUMBER

THE BODY NUMBER is located on a tag mounted on the engine side of the firewall, near the left hood hinge. This tag indicates the model series, body style, and the sequential body serial number.

BODY NUMBER
XXX XXXX
BRIGGS BODY, DETROIT MICHIGAN

P22 CONCORD

BODY TYPE	CODE
2-Dr. fastback sedan	111
Business coupe, 3-pass.	113
Suburban station wagon	117
Savoy Suburban station wagon	217

P23S CAMBRIDGE

BODY TYPE	CODE
4-Dr. sedan	100
2-Dr. Club coupe	102

P23C CRANBROOK

BODY TYPE	CODE
Belvedere 2-dr. hardtop	103
Convertible	104
4-Dr. sedan	105
2-Dr. Club coupe	106

THE TRIM CODE indicates the key to the interior color and material scheme used on the vehicle. This code is not stamped anywhere on Plymouth cars, except some California and Canadian built cars. If this information was needed the owner or dealer was to provide the factory with the car serial number. No trim codes were available.

THE COLOR CODE indicates the paint color used on the vehicle. This code is not stamped anywhere on Plymouth cars, except some California and Canadian built cars. If this information was needed the owner or dealer was to provide the factory with the car serial number. Paint codes were published by paint suppliers and are included here. The letter U indicates an upper body color and the letter L a lower body color, in two-tone combinations.

COLOR	CODE
Black	601
Wedgewood Blue	605
Belmont Blue	607
Nile Green	620
Lido Geen	622
Sterling Gray	635
Luna Gray	636
Mexico Red	661
Empire Maroon	662
Plymouth Cream	665

TWO-TONE COLORS

COLOR	CODE
Sterling Gray/Belmont Blue Poly (early)	670
Sterling Gray/Coronado Blue Poly (late)	670
Sable Bronze/Suede	671
Dawn Gray/Belmont Blue Poly (early)	674
Dawn Gray/Coronado Blue Poly (late)	674
Dawn Gray/Wedgewood Blue	675
Dawn Gray/Lido Green Sympho	676

ENGINE SPECIFICATIONS

THE ENGINE NUMBER is located on a flat boss on the left side of the engine block, directly below the cylinder head and directly above the generator. Each engine is stamped with an engineering code matching the model year of the car, followed by a sequential build number. Canadian engines are identified by the code letter C following the engineering code (P20C). Additional information concerning over or undersized bearings installed at the factory is also stamped by the engine number as follows:

A   - .020 oversize cylinder bore

B   - .010 undersize main and connecting rod bearings

C   - .005 oversize rod bearings

AB - .020 oversize cylinders, .010 undersize main
     and connecting rod bearings

ENGINE NUMBER	NO. CYL.	CID	HORSE-POWER	COMP. RATIO	CARB
P23-1001/up	6	217.8	97	7.0:1	1 BC

1953 PLYMOUTH SUBURBAN STATION WAGON

1953 PLYMOUTH

1953 PLYMOUTH

VEHICLE IDENTIFICATION NUMBER

Located on the left front door post. Plymouth changed its serial numbers in '53. The serial number no longer indicates the model and series information — only the assembly plant where the vehicle was built.

MODEL	SERIES	ASSEMBLY PLANT	NUMBER SEQUENCE
Cambridge	P24-1	Detroit	13070001
		Los Angeles	25136001
		San Leandro	25560001
		Evansville	20520001
		Windsor	95517201
Cranbrook	P24-2	Detroit	13070001
		Los Angeles	25136001
		San Leandro	25560001
		Evansville	20520001
		Windsor	96057801
Belvedere	P24-3**	Windsor	96900001

** This car line was exclusive to Canadian production

BODY NUMBER

THE BODY NUMBER is located on a tag mounted on the engine side of the firewall, near the left hood hinge. This tag indicates the model series, body style, and the sequential body serial number.

BODY NUMBER
XXX XXXX
BRIGGS BODY, DETROIT MICHIGAN

CRANBROOK

BODY TYPE	CODE
4-Dr. sedan	300
Club coupe	302
Belvedere 2-dr. hardtop	303
Convertible	304
Savoy station wagon	307

CAMBRIDGE

BODY TYPE	CODE
4-Dr. sedan	310
2-Dr. Club sedan	311
Business coupe	313
Suburban station wagon	317

THE TRIM CODE indicates the key to the interior color and material scheme used on the vehicle. This code is not stamped anywhere on Plymouth cars, except some California and Canadian built cars. If this information was needed the owner or dealer was to provide the factory with the car serial number. No trim codes were available.

THE COLOR CODE indicates the paint color used on the vehicle. This code is not stamped anywhere on Plymouth cars, except some California and Canadian built cars. If this information was needed the owner or dealer was to provide the factory with the car serial number. Paint codes were published by paint suppliers and are included here. The letter U indicates an upper body color, the letter L a lower body color, in two-tone combinations.

COLOR	CODE
Black	601
Cactus Green	622
Sonora Bronze	646
Plaza Maroon	662
Coronado Blue	607
Monterey Gray	620
Cortez Gray	635
Pecos Gray	636
Suede	645
Patio Cream	665
Toreador Red	661
Valencia Blue	605

TWO-TONE COLORS

COLOR	CODE
Black/Pecos Gray	670
Valencia Blue/Cortez Gray	671
Coronado Blue Poly/Cortez Gray	672
Monterey Green/Cactus Green Poly	673
Cactus Green Poly/Monterey Green	674
Cortez Gray/Valencia Blue	675
Cortez Gray/Coronado Blue Poly	676
Cortez Gray/Plaza Maroon Poly	677
Pecos Gray/Black	678
Suede/Sonaro Bronze Poly	679
Sonora Bronze Poly/Suede	680
Plaza Maroon Poly/Cortez Gray	681

ENGINE SPECIFICATIONS

THE ENGINE NUMBER is located on a flat boss on the left side of the engine block, directly below the cylinder head and directly above the generator. Each engine is stamped with an engineering code matching the model year of the car, followed by a sequential build number. Canadian engines are identified by the code letter C following the engineering code (P20C). Additional information concerning over or undersized bearings installed at the factory is also stamped by the engine number as follows:

A - .020 oversize cylinder bore

B - .010 undersize main and connecting rod bearings

C - .005 oversize rod bearings

AB - .020 oversize cylinders, .010 undersize main
     and connecting rod bearings

ENGINE NUMBER	NO. CYL.	CID	HORSE-POWER	COMP. RATIO	CARB
P24-1001	6	217.8	100	7.1:1	1 BC

1954 PLYMOUTH

1954 PLYMOUTH

1954 PLYMOUTH

VEHICLE IDENTIFICATION NUMBER

VEHICLE
1 3 5 0 6 0 0 1
NUMBER

Located on the left front door post. The number indicates only the assembly plant where the vehicle was built.

MODEL	SERIES	ASSEMBLY PLANT	NUMBER SEQUENCE
Plaza	P25-1	Detroit	13506001
		Los Angeles	25163001
		San Leandro	25590001
		Evansville	20658001
		Windsor	95524001
Savoy	P25-2	Detroit	13506001
		Los Angeles	25163001
		San Leandro	25590001
		Evansville	20658001
		Windsor	96073001
Belvedere	P25-3	Detroit	13506001
		Los Angeles	25163001
		San Leandro	25590001
		Evansville	20658001
		Windsor	96904001

BODY NUMBER

THE BODY NUMBER is located on a tag mounted on the engine side of the firewall, near the left hood hinge. This tag indicates the model series, body style, and the sequential body serial number.

BODY NUMBER
XXX XXXX
BRIGGS BODY, DETROIT MICHIGAN

PLAZA
BODY TYPE	CODE
4-Dr. sedan	510
Club coupe	513
Business	511
Suburban station wagon	517

SAVOY
BODY TYPE	CODE
4-Dr. sedan	500
Club sedan	502
Club coupe	N/A
Savoy Suburban station wagon	N/A

BELVEDERE
BODY TYPE	CODE
4-Dr. sedan	700
2-Dr. hardtop	703
Convertible	704
Suburban station wagon	707

THE TRIM CODE indicates the interior color and material scheme used on the vehicle. There were no trim codes available.

THE COLOR CODE indicates the paint color used on the vehicle. This code is not stamped anywhere on Plymouth cars, except some California and Canadian built cars. If this information was needed the owner or dealer was to provide the factory with the car serial number. Paint codes were published by paint suppliers and are included here. The letter U indicates an upper body color, the letter L a lower body color, in two-tone combinations.

COLOR	CODE
Black	601
Avalon Blue	606
Shasta Green	616
Mohave Brown	641
San Pedro Blue	607
Modesto Blue	605
San Gabriel Green	618
Berkeley Green	615
Pasadena Gray	630
Cascade Gray	631
Santa Rosa Coral	651
Pomona Beige	640
San Diego Gold	655
Parakeet Green #2	400L
Tinsel Green	403L

TWO-TONE COLORS

COLOR	CODE
Mocha Beige #1/Oriole Orange #2	401
Solitaire Blue #2/Dutch Blue #2	402
Avalon Blue Poly/Pasadena Gray	660
Pasadena Gray/Avalon Blue Poly	661
Pasadena Gray/Modesto Blue	662
Mohave Brown Poly/Pomona Beige	664
Pomona Beige/Mohave Brown Poly	665
Berkeley Green/Shasta Green Poly	666
Shasta Green Poly/Berkeley Green	667
Pasadena Gray/Piedmont Maroon	668
Black/San Diego Gold	670
Black/San Pedro Blue	671
Black/San Gabriel Green	672
Black/Santa Rosa Coral	673
San Leandro Ivory/San Diego Gold	674
San Leandro Ivory/San Pedro Blue	675
San Leandro Ivory/San Gabriel Green	676
San Leandro Ivory/Santa Rosa Coral	677
San Mateo Wheat/San Diego Gold	678
San Mateo Wheat/San Pedro Blue	679
San Mateo Wheat/San Gabriel Green	680
San Mateo Wheat/Santa Rosa Coral	681

ENGINE SPECIFIATIONS

THE ENGINE NUMBER is located on a flat boss on the left side of the engine block, directly below the cylinder head and directly above the generator. Each engine is stamped with an engineering code matching the model year of the car, followed by a sequential build number. Canadian engines are identified by the code letter C following the engineering code (P20C). The larger 230 cid engine has a diamond stamped as a prefix to the engineering code. Additional information concerning over or undersized bearings installed at the factory was also stamped by the engine number as follows:

A - .020 oversize cylinder bore

B - .010 undersize main and connecting rod bearings

C - .005 oversize rod bearings

AB - .020 oversize cylinders, .010 undersize main
     and connecting rod bearings

EARLY 1954

ENGINE NUMBER	NO. CYL.	CID	HORSE-POWER	COMP. RATIO	CARB
P25-1001	6	217.8	100	7.1:1	1 BC

LATE 1954

ENGINE NUMBER	NO. CYL.	CID	HORSE-POWER	COMP. RATIO	CARB
*P25-243001	6	230.2	110	7.25:1	1 BC

1955 PLYMOUTH PLAZA STATION WAGON

1955 PLYMOUTH BELVEDERE

1955 PLYMOUTH PLAZA

1955 PLYMOUTH

1955 PLYMOUTH BELVEDERE

1955 PLYMOUTH BELVEDERE STATION WAGON

VEHICLE IDENTIFICATION NUMBER

Located on the left front door post. The number indicates the assembly plant where the vehicle was built as well as whether it was powered by a six or eight cylinder engine.

PLAZA CYLINDER	SERIES	ASSEMBLY PLANT	NUMBER SEQUENCE
6	P26-1	Detroit	13835001
		Evansville	20745001
		Los Angeles	25180001
		Windsor	95528601
8	P27-1	Detroit	15663001
		Evansville	22182001
		Los Angeles	26524001
		Windsor	96910901

PLAZA CYLINDER	SERIES	ASSEMBLY PLANT	NUMBER SEQUENCE
6	P26-3	Detroit	13835001
		Evansville	20745001
		Los Angeles	25180001
		Windsor	96800001
8	P27-3	Detroit	15663001
		Evansville	22182001
		Los Angeles	26524001
		Windsor	96910901

PLAZA CYLINDER	SERIES	ASSEMBLY PLANT	NUMBER SEQUENCE
6	P26-2	Detroit	13835001
		Evansville	20745001
		Los Angeles	25180001
		Windsor	96088101
8	P27-2	Detroit	15663001
		Evansville	22182001
		Los Angeles	26524001
		Windsor	96910901

BODY NUMBER

THE BODY NUMBER is located on a tag mounted on the engine side of the firewall, near the left hood hinge. This tag indicates the model series, body style, and the sequential body serial number.

BODY NUMBER
○   0 0 0   0 0 0 0   ○
CHRYSLER CORP, DETROIT MICHIGAN

PLAZA
BODY TYPE	CODE
4-Dr. sedan	300
Club coupe	302
Business coupe	N/A
Suburban station wagon, 2-dr.	N/A
Suburban station wagon, 4-dr.	N/A

SAVOY
BODY TYPE	CODE
4-Dr. sedan	110
Club sedan	112

BELVEDERE
BODY TYPE	CODE
4-Dr. sedan	100
Club sedan	102
2-Dr. hardtop	103
Convertible	104
Suburban station wagon, 4-dr.	106

THE TRIM CODE indicates the interior color and material scheme used on the vehicle. There were no trim codes available.

THE COLOR CODE indicates the paint color used on the vehicle. This code is not stamped anywhere on Plymouth cars, except some California and Canadian built cars. If this information was needed the owner or dealer was to provide the factory with the car serial number. Paint codes were published by paint suppliers and are included here. The letter U indicates an upper body color, the letter L a lower body color, in two-tone combinations.

COLOR	CODE
Black	601
Biscayne Blue	606
Gulf Green	661
Largo Green	618
Cypress Brown	641
Bimini Blue-Green	608
Orlando Ivory	655
Sarasota Sand	640
Palm Beach Gray	630
Glades Green	617
Tampa Turquoise	607
Pompano Peach	650
Miami Blue	605
Tamiami Green	615
Seminole Scarlet	651

TWO-TONE COLORS

COLOR	CODE
Biscayne Blue Poly/Miami Blue	661
Orlando Ivory/Miami Blue	662
Miami Blue/Biscayne Blue Poly	663
Saratoga Sand/Biscayne Blue Poly	664
Gulf Green Poly/Tamiami Green	665
Tamiami Green/Gulf Green Poly	666
Saratoga Sand/Gulf Green Poly	667
Cypress Brown Poly/Saratoga Sand	669
Saratoga Sand/Cypress Brown Poly	670
Bimini Blue Green Poly/Tampa Turquoise	677
Saratoga Sand/Tampa Turquoise	678
Black/Tampa Turquoise	679
Largo Green Poly/Glades Green	680
Saratoga Sand/Glades Green	681
Black/Glades Green	682
Cypress Brown Poly/Pompano Peach	683
Saratoga Sand/Pompano Peach	684
Black/Pompano Peach	685
Black/Seminole Scarlet	686
Orlando Ivory/Seminole Scarlet	687
Orlando Ivory/Black	688

ENGINE SPECIFICATIONS

THE ENGINE NUMBER is located on a flat boss on the left side of the engine block, directly below the cylinder head and directly above the generator. Each engine is stamped with an engineering code matching the model year of the car, followed by a sequential build number. Canadian engines are identified by the code letter C following the engineering code (P20C). The larger 230 cid engine has a diamond stamped as a prefix to the engineering code. Additional information concerning over or undersized bearings installed at the factory is also stamped by the engine number as follows:

A - .020 oversize cylinder bore

B - .010 undersize main and connecting rod bearings

C - .005 oversize rod bearings

AB - .020 oversize cylinders, .010 undersize main
     and connecting rod bearings

ENGINE NUMBER	NO. CYL.	CID	HORSE-POWER	COMP. RATIO	CARB
P26-1001	6	230	117	7.4:1	1 BC

ENGINE NUMBER	NO. CYL.	CID	HORSE-POWER	COMP. RATIO	CARB
P27-1001	8	241	157	7.6:1	2 BC
P27-60201	8	259	167	7.6:1	2 BC
*	8	259	177	7.6:1	4 BC

* Plymouth later sold an aftermarket power package for engines after P27-60201 to increase the horsepower from 167 to 177.

1956 PLYMOUTH SAVOY CLUB SEDAN

1956 PLYMOUTH

1956 PLYMOUTH SAVOY

1956 PLYMOUTH PLAZA

1956 PLYMOUTH SUBURBAN STATION WAGON

1956 PLYMOUTH

VEHICLE IDENTIFICATION NUMBER

VEHICLE
14120001
NUMBER

Located on the left front door post. The number indicates the assembly plant where the vehicle was built as well as whether it was powered by a six or eight cylinder engine (Canada production also indicates model and series).

PLAZA CYLINDER	SERIES	ASSEMBLY PLANT	NUMBER SEQUENCE
6	P28-1	Detroit	14120001
		Evansville	20820001
		Los Angeles	25202001
		Windsor	95536401
8	P29-1	Detroit	15873001
		Evansville	22247001
		Los Angeles	26552001
		Windsor	95566501

PLAZA CYLINDER	SERIES	ASSEMBLY PLANT	NUMBER SEQUENCE
6	P28-2	Detroit	14120001
		Evansville	20820001
		Los Angeles	25202001
		Windsor	96107001
8	P29-2	Detroit	15873001
		Evansville	22247001
		Los Angeles	26552001
		Windsor	91677101

PLAZA CYLINDER	SERIES	ASSEMBLY PLANT	NUMBER SEQUENCE
6	P28-3	Detroit	14120001
		Evansville	20820001
		Los Angeles	25202001
		Windsor	95999001
8	P29-3	Detroit	15873001
		Evansville	22247001
		Los Angeles	26552001
		Windsor	96916901

BODY NUMBER

THE BODY NUMBER is located on a tag mounted on the engine side of the firewall, near the left hood hinge. This tag indicates the model series, body style, and the sequential body serial number.

```
┌─────────────────────────────────────────┐
│           B O D Y   N U M B E R           │
├─────────────────────────────────────────┤
│  ◯      0 0 0      0 0 0 0      ◯         │
├─────────────────────────────────────────┤
│   CHRYSLER CORP, DETROIT MICHIGAN         │
└─────────────────────────────────────────┘
```

PLAZA

BODY TYPE	CODE
4-Dr. sedan	101
Club coupe	102
Business coupe	N/A
Suburban station wagon, 2-dr.	106

SAVOY

BODY TYPE	CODE
4-Dr. sedan	201
Club sedan	202
Sport coupe	N/A
Suburban station wagon, 4-dr.	N/A
Suburban station wagon, 2-dr.	N/A

BELVEDERE

BODY TYPE	CODE
4-Dr. sedan	301
Club sedan	N/A
Sport sedan	305
Sport coupe	304
Convertible	309
Suburban station wagon	308

FURY

BODY TYPE	CODE
Sport coupe	404

THE TRIM CODE indicates the interior color and material scheme used on the vehicle. There were no trim codes available.

THE COLOR CODE indicates the paint color used on the vehicle. This code is not stamped anywhere on Plymouth cars, except some California and Canadian built cars. If this information was needed the owner or dealer was to provide the factory with the car serial number. Paint codes were published by paint suppliers and are included here. The letter U indicates an upper body color, the letter L a lower body color, in two-tone combinations.

COLOR	CODE
Jet Black	601
Midnight Blue	609
Pine Green	617
Charcoal Gray	631
Powder Blue	605
Wedgewood Blue	607
Turquoise Blue	608
Seaspray Green	615
Bronze	640
Pearl Gray	630
Briar Rose	651
Cherry Red	650
Canary Yellow	655
Eggshell White	657

TWO-TONE COLORS

COLOR	CODE
Eggshell White/Black	661
Eggshell White/Powder Blue	662
Wedgewood Blue/Powder Blue	663
Eggshell White/Turquoise Blue	664
Eggshell White/Wedgewood Blue	665
Midnight Blue Poly/Turquoise Blue	667
Eggshell White/Midnight Blue Poly	668
Eggshell White/Sea Spray Green	669
Pine Green Poly/Sea Spray Green	670
Eggshell White/Pine Green Poly	671
Eggshell White/Pearl Gray	672
Charcoal Gray Poly/Pearl Gray	673
Eggshell White/Charcoal Gray Poly	674
Eggshell White/Bronze Poly	675
Eggshell White/Cherry Red	677
Black/Cherry Red	678
Eggshell White/Briar Rose	679
Black/Briar Rose	680
Eggshell White/Canary Yellow	681
Black/Canary Yellow	682
Black/Eggshell White	683

ENGINE SPECIFICATIONS

THE ENGINE NUMBER is located on a flat boss on the left side of the engine block, directly below the cylinder head and directly above the generator. Each engine is stamped with an engineering code matching the model year of the car, followed by a sequential build number. Canadian engines are identified by the code letter C following the engineering code (P20C). The larger 230 cid engine has a diamond stamped as a prefix to the engineering code. Additional information concerning over or undersized bearings installed at the factory was also stamped by the engine number as follows:

A - .020 oversize cylinder bore

B - .010 undersize main and connecting rod bearings

C - .005 oversize rod bearings

AB - .020 oversize cylinders, .010 undersize main and connecting rod

bearings

ENGINE NUMBER	NO. CYL.	CID	HORSE-POWER	COMP. RATIO	CARB
P28-1001	6	230	125	7.6:1	1 BC
	6	230	131	7.6:1	2 BC
P29-41001					
P29-250001	8	270	180	8.0:1	2 BC
P29-1001					
P29-80001					
P29-274101	8	277	187	8.0:1	2 BC
P29-1618729	8	277	200	8.0:1	4 BC
P29-1630429*	8	303	240	9.25:1	4 BC

* Fury engine serial number prefixed by the engineering code letters FP.
NOTE: During the model year, a dual 4-barrel carburetor package was released for dealer installation on 277 and 303 Fury engines. When installed on a 277 engine, horsepower was increased to 230 horsepower. Fury horsepower was increased to 270.

1957 PLYMOUTH BELVEDERE

VEHICLE IDENTIFICATION NUMBER

Located on the left front door post. The number indicates the assembly plant where the vehicle was built as well as whether it was powered by a six or eight cylinder engine (Canada production also indicates model and series).

PLAZA CYLINDER	SERIES	ASSEMBLY PLANT	STARTING NUMBER SEQUENCE
6	P30-1	Detroit	14280001
		Evansville	20860001
		Los Angeles	25215001
		Windsor	95545301
8	P31-1	Detroit	16083001
		Evansville	22330001
		Los Angeles	26595001
		Windsor	95569801

PLAZA CYLINDER	SERIES	ASSEMBLY PLANT	NUMBER SEQUENCE
6	P30-2	Detroit	14280001
		Evansville	20860001
		Los Angeles	25215001
		Windsor	96123501
8	P31-2	Detroit	16083001
		Evansville	22330001
		Los Angeles	26595001
		Windsor	96188701

PLAZA CYLINDER	SERIES	ASSEMBLY PLANT	NUMBER SEQUENCE
6	P30-3	Detroit	14280001
		Evansville	20860001
		Los Angeles	25215001
		Windsor	95999101
8	P31-3	Detroit	16083001
		Evansville	22330001
		Los Angeles	26595001
		Windsor	96921601

PLAZA CYLINDER	SERIES	ASSEMBLY PLANT	NUMBER SEQUENCE
8	FP31	Detroit	16083001
		Evansville	22330001
		Los Angeles	26595001
		Windsor	96921601

BODY NUMBER

After the purchase of the Briggs Body in December of 1953, Chrysler began discontinuing the issuance of separate body numbers to denote model or body style.

BODY NUMBER
○   0 0 0   0 0 0 0   ○
CHRYSLER CORP, DETROIT MICHIGAN

THE TRIM CODE indicates the key to the interior color and material scheme used on the vehicle.

FURY TRIM

COLOR	CLOTH	VINYL	LEATHER	CODE
Beige/Brown	•	•		

NOTE: There were no code numbers available.

BELVEDERE TRIM

COLOR	CLOTH	VINYL	LEATHER	CODE
Blue/Blue	•	•		331,341
Green/Green	•	•		332,342
Gold/White	•	•		333,343
Black/White	•	•		334,344
Black/Red	•	•		336,346
Blue/Blue		•		416
Green/Green		•		417
Black/White		•		419
Gold/White		•		420
Black/Red		•		414

SAVOY TRIM

COLOR	CLOTH	VINYL	LEATHER	CODE
Blue/Blue	•	•		311
Green/Green	•	•		312
Tan/Beige	•	•		313
Black/White	•	•		314

PLAZA TRIM

COLOR	CLOTH	VINYL	LEATHER	CODE
Blue/Blue	•	•		301
Green/Green	•	•		302
Tan/White	•	•		303

SUBURBAN TRIM

COLOR	CLOTH	VINYL	LEATHER	CODE
Green/Green	•	•		352
Brown/Beige	•	•		353
Black/White	•	•		354
Tan/White		•		423
Green/Green		•		526
Tan/Beige		•		586
Black/White		•		528
Blue/Blue		•		525

THE COLOR CODE indicates the paint color used on the vehicle. This code is not stamped anywhere on Plymouth cars, except some California and Canadian built cars. If this information was needed the owner or dealer was to provide the factory with the car serial number. Paint codes were published by paint suppliers and are included here. In two-tone or sportone combinations the first letter indicates an upper body color, the second letter a lower body color, the third letter a sportone color.

COLOR	CODE
Sand Dune White	AAA
Jet Black	BBB
Sky Blue	CCC
Marine Blue	DDD
Meadow Green	EEE
Jade Green	FFF
Satin Gray	GGG
Silver Gray	HHH
Carnival Red	JJJ
Ginger	KKK
Canary Yellow	LLL
Burgundy	MMM
Dusty Coral	NNN
Desert Gold	PPP

ENGINE SPECIFICATIONS

THE ENGINE NUMBER is located on a flat boss on the left side of the engine block, directly below the cylinder head and directly above the generator. Each engine is stamped with an engineering code matching the model year of the car, followed by a sequential build number. Canadian engines are identified by the code letter C following the engineering code (P20C). The larger 230 cid engine has a diamond stamped as a prefix to the engineering code. Additional information concerning over or undersized bearings installed at the factory is also stamped by the engine number as follows:

A   - .020 oversize cylinder bore

B   - .010 undersize main and connecting rod bearings

C   - .005 oversize rod bearings

AB - .020 oversize cylinders, .010 undersize main
        and connecting rod bearings

ENGINE NUMBER	NO. CYL.	CID	HORSE-POWER	COMP. RATIO	CARB
P230-1001	6	230	132	8.0:1	1 BC
P31-1001	8	277	197	8.0:1	2 BC
	8	301	215	8.5:1	2 BC
	8	301	235	8.5:1	4 BC
FURY					
FP31	8	318	290	9.25:1	4 BC

1958 PLYMOUTH BELVEDERE

1958 PLYMOUTH SPORT SUBURBAN

VEHICLE IDENTIFICATION NUMBER

> **VEHICLE**
> **LP1-1001**
> **NUMBER**

Located on the left front door post. Plymouth adopted a new system for serial number coding in '58. The letters LP-1 indicates a 6-cylinder engine while LP-2 indicates an 8-cylinder engine. The model codes L, M and H were used to indicate a low priced car, a medium priced car, or a high priced car. The number also indicates the assembly plant where the vehicle was built.

PLAZA CYLINDER	SERIES	ASSEMBLY PLANT	STARTING NUMBER SEQUENCE
6	LP1-L	Detroit	LP1-1001/up
		Evansville	LP1E-1001/up
		Los Angeles	LP1L-1001/up
		Newark	LP1N-1001/up
		Windsor	LP1W-1001/up
8	LP2-L	Detroit	LP2-1001/up
		Evansville	LP2E-1001/up
		Los Angeles	LP2L-1001/up
		Newark	LP2N-1001/up
		Windsor	LP2W-1001/up

PLAZA CYLINDER	SERIES	ASSEMBLY PLANT	NUMBER SEQUENCE
6	LP1-M	Detroit	LP1-1001/up
		Evansville	LP1E-1001/up
		Los Angeles	LP1L-1001/up
		Newark	LP1N-1001/up
		Windsor	LP1W-1001/up
8	LP2-M	Detroit	LP2-1001/up
		Evansville	LP2E-1001/up
		Los Angeles	LP2L-1001/up
		Newark	LP2N-1001/up
		Windsor	LP2W-1001/up

PLAZA CYLINDER	SERIES	ASSEMBLY PLANT	NUMBER SEQUENCE
6	LP1-H	Detroit	LP1-1001/up
		Evansville	LP1E-1001/up
		Los Angeles	LP1L-1001/up
		Newark	LP1N-1001/up
		Windsor	LP1W-1001/up
8	LP2-H	Detroit	LP2-1001/up
		Evansville	LP2E-1001/up
		Los Angeles	LP2L-1001/up
		Newark	LP2N-1001/up
		Windsor	LP2W-1001/up

PLAZA CYLINDER	SERIES	ASSEMBLY PLANT	NUMBER SEQUENCE
8	LP2-S	Detroit	LP2-1001

BODY NUMBER

THE BODY NUMBER is stamped on a metal plate attached to the front top side of the dash panel near the right hand hinge under the hood.

```
TL    CS    MR    HB    AC    A    SPL

HT  PS  AG  AR  PB  PF  EW  S6  RS  CU  SC

SCH  BO  NO  (  )  BO  PT  TR  CT  TR  (  )
```

THE TRIM CODE indicates the interior color and material scheme used on the vehicle. No trim codes were available.

THE COLOR CODE indicates the paint color used on the vehicle. This code is not stamped anywhere on Plymouth cars, except some California and Canadian built cars. If this information was needed the owner or dealer was to provide the factory with the car serial number. Paint codes were published by paint suppliers and are included here. On two-tone combinations, the first letter indicates the upper color, the second letter the lower color, the third letter indicates the lower or insert color.

COLOR	CODE
Jet Black	AAA
Bluebonnet Blue	BBB
Stardust Blue	CCC
Midnight Blue	DDD
Misty Green	EEE
Ivy Green	FFF
Arctic Turquoise	JJJ
Suede	LLL
Buckskin Beige	MMM
Copper Glow	NNN
Toreador Red	OOO
Royal Red	PPP
Sunset Beige	RRR
Coral	SSS
Sunflower Yellow	UUU
Iceberg White	XXX
Canyon Gold	ZZZ

ENGINE SPECIFICATIONS

THE ENGINE NUMBER is located on a flat boss on the left side of the engine block, directly below the cylinder head and directly above the generator. Each engine is stamped with an engineering code matching the model year of the car, followed by a sequential build number. Canadian engines are identified by the code letter C following the engineering code (P20C). The larger 230 cid engine has a diamond stamped as a prefix to the engineering code. Additional information concerning over or undersized bearings installed at the factory is also stamped by the engine number as follows:

A - .020 oversize cylinder bore

B - .010 undersize main and connecting rod bearings

C - .005 oversize rod bearings

AB - .020 oversize cylinders, .010 undersize main
       and connecting rod bearings

ENGINE NUMBER	NO. CYL.	CID	HORSE-POWER	COMP. RATIO	CARB
LP6-1001/up	6	230	132	8.0:1	1 BC
LP230-100001 after 3/58					
LP8-1001/up	8	318	225	9.0:1	2 BC
	8	318	250	9.0:1	4 BC
	8	318	290	9.25:1	4 BC
	8	350	305	10.0:1	2X4 BC
	8	350	315	10.0:1	F.I.

* Some sources indicate the engine codes of LD2 for the small V-8 and LD3 for the 350 large V-8.

1959 PLYMOUTH SPORT FURY

1959 PLYMOUTH STATION WAGON

VEHICLE IDENTIFICATION NUMBER

• M 1 5 6 1 0 0 3 4 5 •

Plymouth adopted an entirely new system of assigning serial numbers in 1959. This system went into effect September 12, 1958. The plate on the left front door post was discontinued and a new plate was mounted on the left side of the top cowl panel under the hood. This serial number indicates the model year, engine, model series designation, assembly plant and production number.

FIRST DIGIT: Identifies the model year (1959)

SECOND DIGIT: Identifies the car line

CAR LINE	CODE
6-cylinder	1
8-cylinder	2

THIRD DIGIT: Identifies the model series

MODEL SERIES	CODE
Savoy	3
Belvedere	5
Fury	6
Station wagons	7
Taxi	8
Sport Fury	9

FOURTH DIGIT: Identifies the assembly plant

ASSEMBLY PLANT	CODE
Evansville, IN	3
Los Angeles, CA	4
Newark, DE	5
Detroit, MI	6
Valley Park, MO	8

LAST SIX DIGITS: Identify the basic production sequence number

BODY NUMBER

THE BODY NUMBER PLATE indicates the model number, body number, paint code, schedule date, model year, number of cylinders, body type, assembly plant and vehicle number.

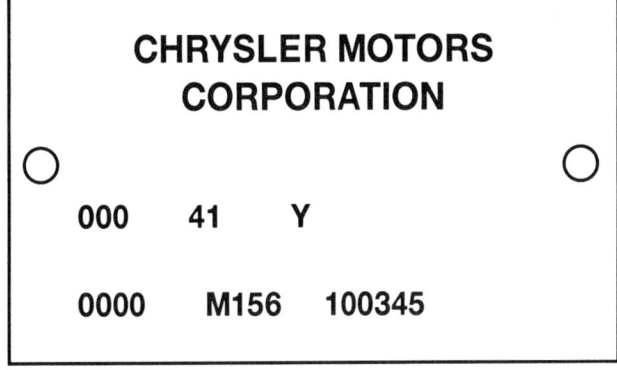

EXAMPLE:

000	Model number
41	4-Dr. sedan
Y	Daffodil Yellow
0000	Schedule date

THE BODY NUMBER is a 2-digit code which indicates the body style.

SAVOY

BODY	CODE
4-Dr. sedan	41
Club sedan	21
Business coupe	22
Station wagon, 4-dr., 6-pass.	45A

BELVEDERE

BODY	CODE
4-Dr. sedan	41
Club sedan	21
Business coupe	22
Station wagon, 2-dr.	25
Station wagon, 4-dr., 6-pass.	45A
Station wagon, 4-dr., 9-pass.	45B
Sport sedan	43
Hardtop, 2-dr.	23
Convertible	27

FURY

BODY	CODE
4-Dr. sedan	41
Station wagon, 4-dr. 6-pass.	45A
Station wagon, 4-dr., 9-pass.	45B
Sport sedan	43
Hardtop, 2-dr.	23

SPORT FURY

BODY	CODE
Hardtop, 2-dr.	23
Convertible	27

THE TRIM CODE indicates the interior color and material scheme used on the vehicle. There were no trim codes available.

THE COLOR CODE indicates the paint color used on the vehicle. On two-tone combinations, the first letter indicates the upper color, the second letter indicates the lower color.

COLOR	CODE
Powder Blue	BB
Starlight Blue	CC
Caribbean Blue	DD
Mint Green	EE
Emerald Green	FF
Apple Green	GG
Turquoise	JJ
Pearl Gray	LL
Silver Gray	MM
Flame	NN
Bronze	TT
Palomino Beige	UU
Bronze	VV
Gold	WW
Sand Dune White	XX
Daffodil Yellow	YY
Bittersweet	ZZ

ENGINE SPECIFICATIONS

THE ENGINE NUMBER is located on a flat boss on the left side of the engine block, directly below the cylinder head and directly above the generator. Each engine is stamped with an engineering code matching the model year of the car, followed by a sequential build number. Canadian engines are identified by the code letter C following the engineering code (P20C). The larger 230 cid engine has a diamond stamped as a prefix to the engineering code. Additional information concerning over or undersized bearings installed at the factory is also stamped by the engine number as follows:

A - .020 oversize cylinder bore

B - .010 undersize main and connecting rod bearings

C - .005 oversize rod bearings

AB - .020 oversize cylinders, .010 undersize main and
     connecting rod bearings

ENGINE NUMBER	NO. CYL.	CID	HORSE-POWER	COMP. RATIO	CARB
	6	230	132	8.0:1	1 BC
	8	318	230	9.0:1	2 BC
	8	318	260	9.0:1	4 BC
	8	361	305	10.0:1	2X4 BC

* Some sources indicate the engine codes of MD2 for the small V-8 and MD3 for the 361 V-8.

1958 EDSEL CITATION

1958 EDSEL CITATION

VEHICLE IDENTIFICATION NUMBER

`• W 8 S H 7 0 0 0 0 1 •`

Located on the left hand front door hinge pillar.

FIRST DIGIT: Identifies the engine

ENGINE	CODE
361, 8-cyl.	W
410, 8-cyl.	X

SECOND DIGIT: Identifies the model year 1958

THIRD DIGIT: Identifies the assembly plant

ASSEMBLY PLANT	CODE
Mahwah, NJ	E
Los Angeles, CA	J
Kansas City, KS	K
San Jose, CA	R
Somerville, MA	S
Louisville, KY	U
Wayne, MI	W

FOURTH DIGIT: Identifies the body style

RANGER/PACER

BODY STYLE	CODE
2-Dr. sedan	C
4-Dr. sedan	F
2-Dr. hardtop	G
4-Dr. hardtop	H
Convertible	R

STATION WAGONS

BODY STYLE	CODE
2-Dr., 6-pass.	S
4-Dr. 6-pass.	T
4-Dr. 9-pass.	V

CORSAIR/CITATION

BODY STYLE	CODE
2-Dr. hardtop	W
4-Dr. hardtop	X
Convertible	Y

LAST SIX DIGITS: Represent the basic production number, 700001/up

PATENT PLATE

Codes are located on the left front body pillar between the front door hinges. The plate consists of the serial number, the body type, exterior paint color, trim scheme and the production code, transmission type and axle type.

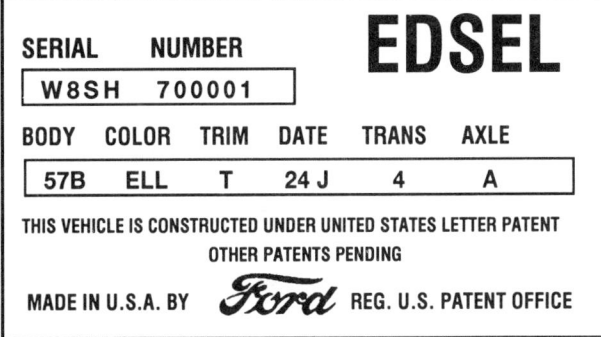

EXAMPLE:

57B	Model (Pacer, 4-dr.)
ELL	Color (Tri-tone, Frost White, Spruce Green, Spruce Green)
T	Trim (Green vinyl/Green cloth)
24	24th Day of Month
J	Month of the Year (September)
4	Automatic Transmission
A	2.91:1 Axle Ratio

THE BODY TYPE CODE indicates the body type.

RANGER

BODY TYPE	CODE
2-Dr. sedan	64A
4-Dr. sedan	58A
2-Dr. hardtop	63A
4-Dr. hardtop	57A
2-Dr. station wagon, Roundup (6-pass.)	59A
4-Dr. station wagon, Villager (6-pass.)	79C
4-Dr. station wagon, Villager (9-pass.)	79A

PACER

BODY TYPE	CODE
4-Dr. hardtop	57B
2-Dr. hardtop	63B
4-Dr. sedan	58B
2-Dr. convertible	76B
4-Dr. station wagon, Bermuda (6-pass.)	79D
4-Dr. station wagon, Bermuda (9-pass.)	79B

CORSAIR

BODY TYPE	CODE
2-Dr. hardtop	63A
4-Dr. hardtop	57A

CITATION

BODY TYPE	CODE
2-Dr. hardtop	63B
4-Dr. hardtop	57B
2-Dr. convertible	76B

THE COLOR CODE indicates the exterior paint colors used on the car.

COLOR	CODE
Jet Black	A
Silver Gray Metallic	B
Ember Red	C
Turquoise	D
Frost White	E
Powder Blue	F
Horizon Blue	G
Royal Blue Metallic	H
Ice Green	J
Spring Green	K
Spruce Green Metallic	L
Charcoal Brown Metallic	M
Driftwood	N
Jonquil Yellow	Q
Sunset Coral	R
Chalk Pink	T
Copper Metallic	U
Gold Metallic	X

THE TRIM CODE indicates the trim color and material for each model series.

RANGER 2-DR/4-DR TRIM

COLOR	CLOTH	VINYL	LEATHER	CODE
Gray/Black	•			C
Green	•			A
Blue	•			B
White/Black	•	•		N
White/Green	•	•		K
White/Blue	•	•		M

RANGER STATION WAGON TRIM

COLOR	CLOTH	VINYL	LEATHER	CODE
Black/Beige	•	•		BC
White/Green		•		BA
White/Blue		•		BB
Red/Beige	•	•		BD

PACER 2-DR/4-DR TRIM

COLOR	CLOTH	VINYL	LEATHER	CODE
Green	•			E
Blue	•			F
Brown	•			D
Green	•	•		T
Blue	•	•		V
White/Red	•	•		AX
White/Brown	•	•		R
White/Turquoise	•	•		AY
White/Coral	•	•		S

PACER CONVERTIBLE TRIM

COLOR	CLOTH	VINYL	LEATHER	CODE
White/Black	•	•		AN
White/Red		•		AZ
White/Turquoise		•		AV
White/Coral		•		AJ

PACER STATION WAGON TRIM

COLOR	CLOTH	VINYL	LEATHER	CODE
Green		•		AS
Blue		•		AT
Driftwood/Brown		•		AU
White/Turquoise		•		AV
White/Coral		•		AJ

CORSAIR 2-DR/4-DR TRIM

COLOR	CLOTH	VINYL	LEATHER	CODE
Green	•	•		D
Blue	•	•		B
Gray/Red	•	•		X
White/Turquoise	•	•		C
White/Gold	•	•		E
White/Copper	•	•		Y

CITATION 2-DR/4-DR TRIM

COLOR	CLOTH	VINYL	LEATHER	CODE
Black/Gray	•	•		AA
Green	•	•		K
Blue	•	•		H
Pink/Brown	•	•		Z
White/Turquoise	•	•		J
White/Gold	•	•		L
White/Copper	•	•		AB

CITATION CONVERTIBLE

COLOR	CLOTH	VINYL	LEATHER	CODE
Red/White		•		AD
Brown/Pink		•		AC
Turquoise/White		•		S
Gold/White		•		T
Copper/White		•		AE

THE PRODUCTION DATE CODE indicates the day of the month the vehicle was built and the letter indicates the month.

MONTH	CODE
January	A
February	B
March	C
April	D
May	E
June	F
July	G
August	H
September	J
October	K
November	L
December	M

THE TRANSMISSION CODE indicates the type of transmission installed in the vehicle.

TYPE	CODE
Standard	1
Overdrive	2
Automatic, lever	3
Automatic, push button	4
Automatic, dual range	5

THE REAR AXLE CODE indicates the ratio of the rear axle installed in the vehicle.

RATIO	CODE
2.91:1	A
3.22:1	B
3.70:1	C
3.89:1	D

ENGINE SPECIFICATIONS

RANGER/PACER, STATION WAGONS

ENGINE CODE	NO. CYL.	CID	HORSE-POWER	COMP. RATIO	CARB
W8	8	361	303	10.5:1	4 BC

CITATION/CORSAIR

ENGINE CODE	NO. CYL.	CID	HORSE-POWER	COMP. RATIO	CARB
X8	8	410	345	10.5:1	4 BC

1959 EDSEL RANGER

1959 EDSEL

1959 EDSEL

VEHICLE IDENTIFICATION NUMBER

• C9UC 700001 •

Located on the left hand front door hinge pillar.

FIRST DIGIT: Identifies the engine

ENGINE	CODE
223, 6-cyl.	A
292, 8-cyl.	C
332, 8-cyl., 2 BC	B
361, 8-cyl.	W

SECOND DIGIT: Identifies the model year 1959

THIRD DIGIT: Identifies the assembly plant

ASSEMBLY PLANT	CODE
Louisville, KY	U

FOURTH DIGIT: Identifies the body style

RANGER

BODY STYLE	CODE
2-Dr. sedan	C
4-Dr. sedan	F
2-Dr. hardtop	G
4-Dr. hardtop	H

CORSAIR

BODY STYLE	CODE
4-Dr. sedan	S
2-Dr. hardtop	W
4-Dr. hardtop	X
Convertible	R

VILLAGER

BODY STYLE	CODE
Station wagon (6-pass.)	T
Station wagon (9-pass.)	V

LAST SIX DIGITS: Represent the basic production number, 700001/up

PATENT PLATE

Codes are located on the left front body pillar between the front door hinges. The plate displays the serial number, the body type, exterior paint color, trim scheme and the production code, transmission type and axle type.

SERIAL NUMBER		MADE IN U.S.A. BY	**MEL**	REG U.S. PAT. OFF
C9UC	700001		FORD MOTOR COMPANY	

BODY	COLOR	TRIM	DATE	TRANS	AXLE
64C	A	50	15 K	3	1

THIS VEHICLE IS CONSTRUCTED UNDER UNITED STATES LETTER PATENT

2 290 927	2 639 936	2 167 571	2 793 532	2 683 578
2 617 681	2 677 572	2 772 114	2 270 122	2 698 012
2 628 833	2 677 974	2 773 396	2 590 719	2 782 722
2 631 694	2 726 894	2 789 621	2 612 829	2 784 863

OTHER PATENTS PENDING

EXAMPLE:

64C	Model (Ranger, 2-dr.)
A	Color (Jet Black)
50	Trim (Gray/Black vinyl/ Black cloth)
15	15th Day of Month
K	Month of the Year (October)
3	Mile-O-Matic Transmission
1	3.10:1 Axle Ratio

THE BODY TYPE CODE indicates the body type.

RANGER

BODY TYPE	CODE
2-Dr. sedan	64C
4-Dr. sedan	58D
2-Dr. hardtop	63F
4-Dr. hardtop	57F

CORSAIR

BODY TYPE	CODE
4-Dr. sedan	58B
2-Dr. hardtop	63B
4-Dr. hardtop	57B
Convertible	76E

VILLAGER

BODY TYPE	CODE
Station wagon, 4-dr. (6-pass.)	71F
Station wagon, 4-dr. (9-pass.)	71E

THE COLOR CODE indicates the exterior paint color used on the car.

COLOR	CODE
Jet Black	A
Moonrise Gray	B
Gold Metallic	C
Redwood	D
Snow White	E
President Red	F
Tailsman Red	G
Desert Tan	H
Velvet Maroon	J
Platinum Gray Metallic	K
Star Blue Metallic	L
Jet Stream Blue	M
Light Aqua	N
Blue Aqua	P
Petal Yellow	Q
Mist Green	R
Jade Glint Green Metallic	S

THE TRIM CODE indicates the trim color and material for each model series.

RANGER TRIM

COLOR	CLOTH	VINYL	LEATHER	CODE
Dk. Green	•	•		23
Dk. Blue	•	•		24
Buff	•	•		25
Black	•	•		50,501

CORSAIR 2-DR/4-DR TRIM

COLOR	CLOTH	VINYL	LEATHER	CODE
Aqua	•	•		38
Redwood	•	•		39
Gold	•	•		40
Black	•	•		51
Dk. Green	•	•		53
Dk. Blue	•	•		54

CORSAIR CONVERTIBLE TRIM

COLOR	CLOTH	VINYL	LEATHER	CODE
Gold/White		•		41
Black/White/Silver		•		42
Aqua/White		•		43
Black/Red		•		44

STATION WAGON TRIM

COLOR	CLOTH	VINYL	LEATHER	CODE
Green	•	•		30
White/Red	•	•		31
Buff/White		•		32
Blue	•	•		52

THE PRODUCTION DATE CODE indicates the day of the month the vehicle was built and the letter indicates the month.

MONTH	CODE
January	A
February	B
March	C
April	D
May	E
June	F
July	G
August	H
September	J
October	K
November	L
December	M

THE TRANSMISSION CODE indicates the type of transmission installed in the vehicle.

TYPE	CODE
Standard	1
Mile-O-Matic (2-speed)	3
Dual power (3-speed)	4

THE REAR AXLE CODE indicates the ratio of the rear axle installed in the vehicle.

RATIO	CODE
3.10:1	1
3.56:1	2
3.70:1	3
3.89:1	4
2.91:1	5
2.69:1	6

ENGINE SPECIFICATIONS

The engine code for the 292 is located on the front of the block at the pushrod cover-to-cylinder block mounting surface. The codes for 223, 332 and 361 are located on the left front of the block below the cylinder head.

RANGER/VILLAGER

ENGINE CODE	NO. CYL.	CID	HORSE-POWER	COMP. RATIO	CARB
A9	6	223	145	8.4:1	1 BC
C9	8	292	200	8.8:1	2 BC
B9	8	332	225	8.9:1	2 BC
W9	8	361	303	9.5:1	4 BC

CORSAIR

ENGINE CODE	NO. CYL.	CID	HORSE-POWER	COMP. RATIO	CARB
B9	8	332	225	8.9:1	2 BC
W9	8	361	303	9.5:1	4 BC

1950 FORD

1950 FORD

1950 FORD

1950 FORD CRESTLINER

1950 FORD

1950 FORD

VEHICLE IDENTIFICATION NUMBER

`• B 0 D A 1 0 0 5 3 2 •`

Located on the plate attached to the front face of the cowl and on top of the right frame side rail just to the rear of the front suspension upper arm.

FIRST DIGIT: Identifies the engine

ENGINE	CODE
226, 6-cyl..	H
239, 8-cyl..	B
255, 8-cyl. (police)	P

SECOND DIGIT: Identifies the model year 1950

THIRD AND FOURTH DIGITS: Identify the assembly plant

ASSEMBLY PLANT	CODE
Atlanta, GA	AT
Buffalo, NY	BF
Chester, PA	CS
Chicago, IL	CH
Dallas, TX..	DL
Highland Park, MI..................................	HM
Dearborn, MI...	DA
Louisville, KY..	LU
Edgewater, NJ.......................................	EG
Kansas City, KS....................................	KC
Long Beach, CA	LB
Memphis, TN	MP
Norfolk, VA	NR
Richmond, VA..	RH
Somerville, MA......................................	SR
Twin City, MN (St. Paul)........................	SP

LAST SIX DIGITS: Represent the basic production number, 100001/up

PATENT PLATE

Codes are located on the front face on the top of the cowl panel. The body type, color and trim codes were revised midway through the 1950 model year.

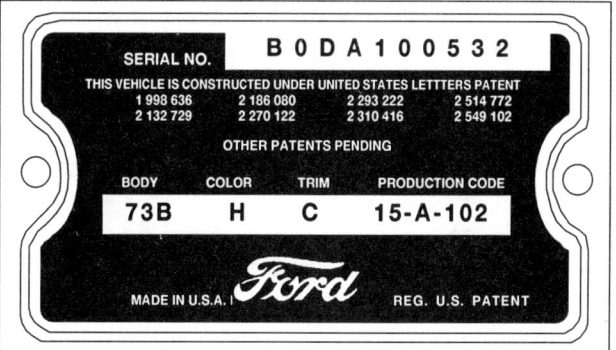

EXAMPLE:

73B	Custom Fordor
H	Palisade Green
A...	Gray Mohair
15	15th day of month
C...	Month of year, (March)
102	Production number

THE BODY TYPE CODE indicates the body type.

BODY TYPE	1ST HALF	2ND HALF
Tudor deluxe..............................	D70	70A
Business coupe, deluxe.............	D72C	72C
Fordor, deluxe	D73	73A
Tudor, custom deluxe	C70	70B
Club coupe, custom deluxe	C72	72B
Fordor, custom deluxe...............	C73	73B
Convertible coupe, custom deluxe	C76	76
Station wagon, custom deluxe Country Squire............................	C79	79
Crestliner	C70C	70C

THE COLOR CODE indicates the paint color used on the car.

BODY TYPE	1ST HALF	2ND HALF
Black	B,3	A
Sheridan Blue	5	B
Bimini Blue	6	C
Dover Grey	11	D
Hawthorne Green	12	E
Sunland Biege	10	F
Cambridge Maroon	7	G
Palisade Green	8	H
Osage Green	9	J
Sportsman's Green*	13	K
Hawaiian Bronze Metallic*		Q
Coronation Red Metallic		R
Silvertone Grey		S
Casino Cream*		T
Matador Red Metallic*		-

* Convertible only

THE TRIM CODE indicates the trim color and material for each model series.

CLOSED MODELS - DELUXE

COLOR	CLOTH	VINYL	LEATHER	1ST HALF	2ND HALF
Gray	•			42	A
Tan	•			43	B

CLOSED MODELS - CUSTOM

COLOR	CLOTH	VINYL	LEATHER	1ST HALF	2ND HALF
Tan		•	•	44	E
Blue/Gray	•			40	C
Blue/Gray	•			41	D

CONVERTIBLE MODELS

COLOR	CLOTH	VINYL	LEATHER	1ST HALF	2ND HALF
Red/Black			•	45	F
Red/Black	•		•	45A	J
Two-Tone Tan		•		—	G
Dk. Brown/ Lt. Brown	•		•	46	—
Lt. Brown/ Dr. Brown	•		•	46A	—
Chartreuse/ Black			•	47	H
Chartreuse/ Black	•			47A	L
Two-Tone Tan	•		•	—	K
Lt. Tan	•			—	M
Lt. Brown	•			48	—

STATION WAGON MODEL

COLOR	CLOTH	VINYL	LEATHER	1ST HALF	2ND HALF
Two-Tone Tan		•		—	T
Lt. Brown		•		49	—

CRESTLINER

COLOR	CLOTH	VINYL	LEATHER	1ST HALF	2ND HALF
Red/Black		•		—	F
Chartreuse/ Black		•		—	H
Two-Tone- Tan		•		—	G

THE PRODUCTION DATE CODE indicates the day, month and the production sequence.

MONTH	CODE
January	A
February	B
March	C
April	D
May	E
June	F
July	G
August	H
September	J
October	K
November	L
December	M

ENGINE SPECIFICATIONS

All engines are stamped with a metal date stamp indicating day, month, and year the engine was built. 8-cylinder engines the code is stamped on the valve chamber cover gasket face on the right side, rear end, and is plainly visible between the edge of the cylinder head and the edge of the valve chamber. On 6-cylinder engines the code appears on the side of the cylinder block in the rear corner and is visible between the cylinder head and intake manifold. The month and year will be coded as follows:

```
M G B L A C K H T R S  E  F
0 1 2 3 4 5 6 7 8 9 10 11 12
```

EXAMPLE: S 15 M

S..October
15 ....Day of month
M...Year (1950)

DELUXE AND CUSTOM MODELS

ENGINE CODE	NO. CYL	CID	HORSE POWER	COMP. RATIO	CARB
H0	6	226	95	6.8:1	1 BC
B0	8	239	100	6.8:1	2 BC
P0	8	255	110	6.8:1	2 BC

1951 FORD

1951 FORD STATION WAGON

1951 FORD

VEHICLE IDENTIFICATION NUMBER

● B 1 D A 1 0 0 5 3 2 ●

Located on the plate attached to the front face of the cowl and on top of the right frame side rail just to the rear of the front suspension control arm.

FIRST DIGIT: Identifies the engine

ENGINE	CODE
226, 6-cyl.	H
239, 8-cyl.	B
255, 8-cyl. (police)	P

SECOND DIGIT: Identifies the model year 1951

THIRD AND FOURTH DIGITS: Identify the assembly plant

ASSEMBLY PLANT	CODE
Atlanta, GA	AT
Buffalo, NY	BF
Chester, PA	CS
Chicago, IL	CH
Dallas, TX	DL
Highland Park, MI	HM
Dearborn, MI	DA
Louisville, KY	LU
Edgewater, NJ	EG
Kansas City, KS	KC
Long Beach, CA	LB
Memphis, TN	MP
Norfolk, VA	NR
Richmond, VA	RH
Somerville, MA	SR
Twin City, MN (St. Paul)	SP

LAST SIX DIGITS: Represent the basic production number, 100001/up

PATENT PLATE

Codes are located on the front face on the top of the cowl panel.

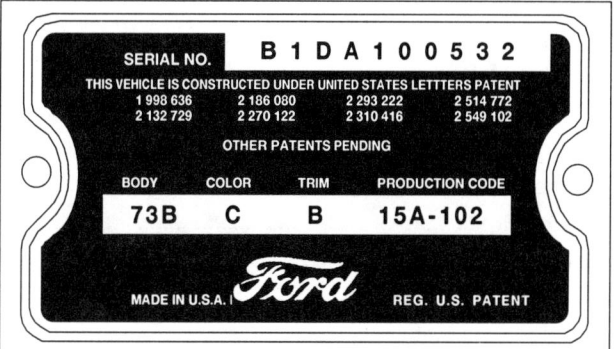

EXAMPLE:

73B	Model (Custom Fordor)
C	Color (Culver Blue Met.)
B	Trim (Black/Blue Mohair)
15	15th day of month
A	Production Month (January)
102	Production number

THE BODY TYPE CODE indicates the body type.

BODY TYPE	CODE
Deluxe tudor	70-A
Deluxe business coupe	72-C
Deluxe fordor	73-A
Custom Victoria	60
Custom tudor	70-B
Custom Crestliner	70-C
Custom 5-pass. coupe	72-B
Custom fordor	73-B
Custom convertible coupe	76
Custom station wagon, Country Squire	79

THE COLOR CODE indicates the paint color used on the car.

COLOR	CODE
Black	A
Sheridan Blue	B
Culver Blue Metallic	C
Alpine Blue	D
Hawthorne Green*	E
Greenbrier Metallic*	F
Sea Island Green	G
Silvertone Gray	H
Mexicalli Maroon Metallic	J
Hawaiian Bronze Metallic*	K
Sportsman Green**	L
Coral Flame Red**	N

* Custom only

** Convertible only

THE TRIM CODE indicates the trim color and material for each model series.

CLOSED MODELS

COLOR	CLOTH	VINYL	LEATHER	CODE
Orange/Gray	•			A
Black/Blue	•			B
Tan/Red	•			C
Gray	•			D
Green	•			E
Two-Tone Brown	•			F

CONVERTIBLE MODELS

COLOR	CLOTH	VINYL	LEATHER	CODE
Red/Black			•	G
Red/Black	•		•	L
Two-Tone Tan			•	H
Chartreuse/Black			•	J
Chartreuse/Black	•		•	N
Blue Green/Black			•	K
Blue Green/Black	•		•	S
Two-Tone Tan	•		•	M

STATION WAGON MODEL

COLOR	CLOTH	VINYL	LEATHER	CODE
Golden Tan/Brown			•	R

THE PRODUCTION DATE CODE indicates the day, month and the production sequence.

MONTH	CODE
January	A
February	B
March	C
April	D
May	E
June	F
July	G
August	H
September	J
October	K
November	L
December	M

ENGINE SPECIFICATIONS

DELUXE AND CUSTOM MODELS

ENGINE CODE	NO. CYL	CID	HORSE POWER	COMP. RATIO	CARB
H1	6	226	95	6.8:1	1 BC
B1	8	239	100	6.8:1	2 BC
P1	8	255	110	6.8:1	2 BC

1952 FORD CRESTLINE VICTORIA

1952 FORD

1952 FORD

1952 FORD RANCH WAGON

1952 FORD

VEHICLE IDENTIFICATION NUMBER

● B 2 D A 1 0 0 5 3 2 ●

The number is located on the plate attached to the right front body pillar below the upper hinge opening, and stamped on the frame in the following places: (1) On top of the right hand reinforcement (side member to No. 1 crossmember). (2) On top of the No. 2 crossmember (part of K member) near the right hand side member (except convertible). (3) Convertible only, on top of the right rear X member near the right hand side member. (4) All passenger models, on top of the rear X member near the right hand end.

FIRST DIGIT: Identifies the engine

ENGINE	CODE
215, 6-cyl.	A
239, 8-cyl.	B
255, 8-cyl. (police)	P

SECOND DIGIT: Identifies the model year 1952

THIRD AND FOURTH DIGITS: Identify the assembly plant

ASSEMBLY PLANT	CODE
Atlanta, GA	AT
Buffalo, NY	BF
Chester, PA	CS
Chicago, IL	CH
Dallas, TX	DL
Dearborn, MI	DA
Louisville, KY	LU
Edgewater, NJ	EG
Kansas City, KS	KC
Long Beach, CA	LB
Memphis, TN	MP
Norfolk, VA	NR
Richmond, VA	RH
Somerville, MA	SR
Twin City, MN (St. Paul)	SP

LAST SIX DIGITS: Represent the basic production number, 100001/up

PATENT PLATE

Codes are located on the right front body pillar below the upper hinge opening. The plate has been redesigned to include the body style, body color and trim scheme, in addition to the serial number. On the late model year on the left front door pillar post.

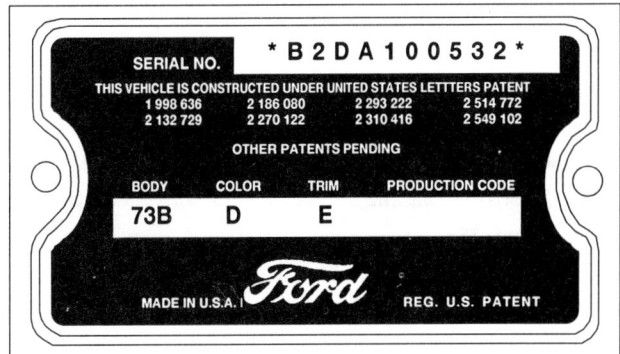

EXAMPLE:

73B	Model (Customline Fordor)
D	Color (Woodsmoke Gray)
E	Trim (Green Stripe Broadcloth)
—	Production Code

THE BODY TYPE CODE indicates the body type.

BODY TYPE	CODE
Mainline ranch wagon	59A
Mainline tudor	70A
Mainline business coupe	72C
Mainline fordor	73A
Crestline Victoria	60B
Crestline Sunliner convertible	76B
Crestline Country Squire	79C
Customline tudor	70B
Customline fordor	73B
Customline club coupe	72B
Customline Country sedan	79B

THE COLOR CODE indicates the paint color used on the car.

COLOR	CODE
Raven Black	A
Sheridan Blue	B
Alpine Blue	C
Woodsmoke Gray	D
Shannon Green Metallic	E
Meadowbrook Green	F
Glenmist Green	G
Carnival Red	H
Hawaiian Bronze	J
Sandpiper Tan	K
Sungate Ivory	L
Coral Flame Red	M
Meadow Green	N
Prime	P
Special Paint	SS

THE TRIM CODE indicates to the trim color and material for each model series.

COLOR	CLOTH	VINYL	LEATHER	CODE
Maroon/Gray	•			A
Tan	•			B
Gray/Red	•			D
Green	•			E
Two-Tone Tan	•			F
Black/Red		•	•	G
Brown/Tan		•	•	H
Green/Ivory		•	•	J
Dk. Blue/Lt. Blue		•	•	K
Green/Gray	•	•		M
Brown/Tan	•	•		N
Blue/Gray	•	•		R
Golden Tan		•		S
Mahogany/Milan	•	•		T
Dk. Blue/Ivory			•	U
Dk. Brown/Ivory			•	V
Dk. Brown/Gray		•		X

THE PRODUCTION DATE CODE indicates the day, month and the production sequence.

MONTH	CODE
January	A
February	B
March	C
April	D
May	E
June	F
July	G
August	H
September	J
October	K
November	L
December	M

ENGINE SPECIFICATIONS

8-12

ENGINE CODE	NO. CYL	CID	HORSE POWER	COMP. RATIO	CARB
A2	6	216	101	7.0:1	1 BC
B2	8	239	110	7.2:1	2 BC
P2	8	255	125	7.2:1	2 BC

1953 FORD

1953 FORD PACE CAR

VEHICLE IDENTIFICATION NUMBER

● B 3 F Y 1 0 0 5 3 2 ●

Located on the plate attached to the left front pillar and stamped on top of the frame right-hand front crossmember to the side member reinforcement.

FIRST DIGIT: Identifies the engine

ENGINE	CODE
215, 6-cyl.	A
239, 8-cyl.	B
255, 8-cyl. (police)	P

SECOND DIGIT: Identifies the model year 1953

THIRD DIGIT: Identifies the assembly plant

ASSEMBLY PLANT	CODE
Atlanta, GA	A
Buffalo, NY	B
Chester, PA	C
Dallas, TX	D
Edgewater, NJ	E
Dearborn, MI	F
Chicago, IL	G
Highland Park, MI	H
Kansas City, KS	K
Long Beach, CA	L
Memphis, TN	M
Norfolk, VA	N
Twin City, MN (St. Paul)	P
Richmond, VA	R
Somerville, MA	S
Louisville, KY	U

FOURTH DIGIT: Identifies the body style

BODY STYLE	CODE
Convertible	C
Ranch Wagon	W
Country sedan	X
Country Squire	Y
Victoria	V
All other (tudor, fordor, coupe)	G

LAST SIX DIGITS: Represent the basic production number, 100001/up

PATENT PLATE

Codes are located on the left front body pillar below the upper hinge opening. The plate displays the serial number, the body type, exterior paint color, trim scheme and the production code.

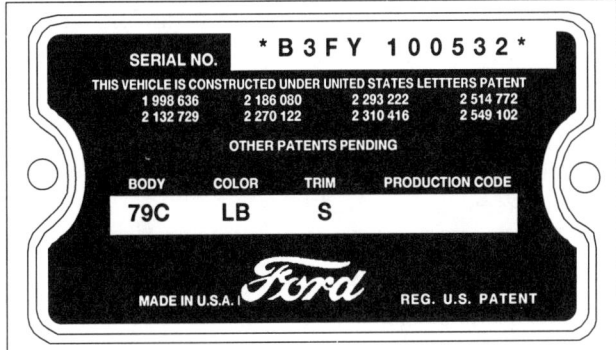

EXAMPLE:

79C	Model (Crestline Country Squire)
L	Sungate Ivory, lower body
B	Sheridan Blue, upper body
S	Trim (Blue/Ivory Vinyl)
—	Production Code

THE BODY TYPE CODE indicates the body type.

BODY TYPE	CODE
Mainline ranch wagon	59A
Mainline tudor	70A
Mainline business coupe	72C
Mainline fordor	73A
Crestline Victoria	60B
Crestline Sunliner convertible	76B
Crestline Country Squire	79C
Customline tudor	70B
Customline fordor	73B
Customline club coupe	72B
Customline Country sedan	79B

THE COLOR CODE indicates the exterior paint color used on the car. A two-tone car has two letters. The first indicates the lower body color, the second the upper body color.

COLOR	CODE
Raven Black	A
Sheridan Blue	B
Glacier Blue	C
Woodsmoke Gray	D
Timberline Green Metallic	E
Fernmist Green	F
Seafoam Green	G
Carnival Red Metallic	H
Polynesian Bronze Metallic	J
Sandpiper Tan	K
Sungate Ivory	L
Coral Flame Red	M
Flamingo Red	S
Prime	P
Special Paint	SS

THE TRIM CODE indicates the trim color and material for each model series.

COLOR	CLOTH	VINYL	LEATHER	CODE
Gray/Yellow	•			B
Two-Tone Gray	•			C
Green	•			D
Two-Tone Tan	•			E
Red/Black			•	F
Brown/Ivory			•	G
Green/Ivory			•	H
Blue/Ivory			•	J
Green		•		K
Tan		•		L
Blue		•		M
Pigskin			•	N
Mahogany/Milan			•	R
Blue/Ivory			•	S
Brown/Ivory			•	T
Dk. Brown			•	U

THE PRODUCTION DATE CODE indicates the day, month and the production sequence.

MONTH	CODE
January	A
February	B
March	C
April	D
May	E
June	F
July	G
August	H
September	J
October	K
November	L
December	M

ENGINE SPECIFICATIONS

ENGINE CODE	NO. CYL	CID	HORSE POWER	COMP. RATIO	CARB
A3	6	215.3	101	7.0:1	1 BC
B3	8	239.4	110	7.2:1	2 BC
P3	8	255	125	7.2:1	2 BC

1954 FORD CRESTLINE

VEHICLE IDENTIFICATION NUMBER

`• U 4 F U 1 0 0 5 3 2 •`

Located on the plate attached to the left front body pillar below the upper hinge opening.

FIRST DIGIT: Identifies the engine

ENGINE	CODE
223, 6-cyl.	A
239, 8-cyl.	U
256, 8-cyl. (police)	P

SECOND DIGIT: Identifies the model year 1954

THIRD DIGIT: Identifies the assembly plant

ASSEMBLY PLANT	CODE
Atlanta, GA	A
Buffalo, NY	B
Chester, PA	C
Dallas, TX	D
Edgewater, NJ	E
Dearborn, MI	F
Chicago, IL	G
Highland Park, MI	H
Kansas City, KS	K
Long Beach, CA	L
Memphis, TN	M
Norfolk, VA	N
Twin City, MN (St. Paul)	P
Richmond, VA	R
Somerville, MA	S
Louisville, KY	U

FOURTH DIGIT: Identifies the body style

BODY STYLE	CODE
Sunliner convertible	C
Skyliner	F
Ranch Wagon*	R
Ranch Wagon+	W
Fordor**	T
Victoria	V
Country Sedan	X
Country Squire	Y
All other (tudor, fordor, coupe)	G

* Customline
** Crestline
+ Mainline

LAST SIX DIGITS: Represent the basic production number, 100001/up

PATENT PLATE

Codes are located on the left front body pillar below the upper hinge opening. The plate consists of the serial number, the body type, exterior paint color, trim scheme and the production code.

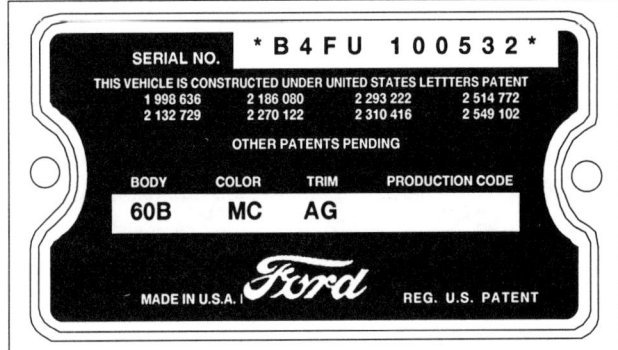

EXAMPLE:

60B	Model (Crestline Victoria)
M	Sandstone White, lower body
C	Cadet Blue, upper body
S	Trim (Lt. Blue/White Vinyl)
—	Production Code

THE BODY TYPE CODE indicates the body type.

BODY TYPE	CODE
Mainline ranch wagon	59A
Mainline tudor	70A
Mainline business coupe	72C
Mainline fordor	73A
Crestline Victoria	60B
Crestline Sunliner convertible	76B
Crestline Skyliner	60F
Crestline Country Squire	79C
Crestline fordor	73C
Customline ranch wagon	59B
Customline tudor	70B
Customline fordor	73B
Customline club coupe	72B
Customline country sedan	79B

THE COLOR CODE indicates the exterior paint color
used on the car. A two-tone car has two letters. The first indicates the lower body color, the second the upper body color.

COLOR	CODE
Raven Black	A
Sheridan Blue	B
Cadet Blue Metallic	C
Glacier Blue	D
Dovetone Gray	E
Highland Green Metallic	F
Killarney Green Metallic	G
Sea Haze Green	H
Lancer Maroon Metallic	J
Sandalwood Tan	L
Sandstone White	M
Torch Red	N
Cameo Coral	R
Primer	P
Special Paint	SS
Golden Rod Yellow	V

THE TRIM CODE indicates the trim color and material for each model series.

COLOR	CLOTH	VINYL	LEATHER	CODE
Gray/Maroon	•			A
Blue	•			B
Green	•			C
Brown	•			D
Brown/Ivory		•		T
White/Brown		•		V
White/Blue		•		X
Brown		•		AA
Black/Lt. Green		•		AB
White/Lt. Blue		•		AC
Black/Coral		•		AD
White/Red		•		AE
Lt. Green/White		•		AF
Lt. Blue/White		•		AG
Coral/White		•		AH
White/Green	•	•		AJ
White/Blue	•	•		AK
White/Coral/Black	•	•		AL
Two-Tone Blue	•			AM
Two-Tone Green	•			AN
Gold/Brown	•			AR
Lt. Blue/Blue/ White		•		AS
Lt. Green/Green/ White		•		AT
White/Red		•		AU
Black/Yellow		•		AX

THE PRODUCTION DATE CODE indicates the
day and the month of the year the car was assembled.

MONTH	CODE
January	A
February	B
March	C
April	D
May	E
June	F
July	G
August	H
September	J
October	K
November	L
December	M

ENGINE SPECIFICATIONS

ENGINE CODE	NO. CYL	CID	HORSE POWER	COMP. RATIO	CARB
A4	6	223	115	7.2:1	1 BC
U4	8	239	130	7.2:1	2 BC
P4	8	256	160	7.5:1	2 BC

1955 FORD CROWN VICTORIA

1955 FORD COUNTRY SQUIRE

1955 FORD THUNDERBIRD

1955 FORD CROWN VICTORIA

VEHICLE IDENTIFICATION NUMBER

• M5FY100532 •

Located on the plate attached to the left front body pillar below the upper hinge opening.

FIRST DIGIT: Identifies the engine

ENGINE	CODE
223, 6-cyl.	A
272, 8-cyl., 4 BC	M
272, 8-cyl., 2 BC	U
292, 8-cyl.	P

SECOND DIGIT: Identifies the model year 1955

THIRD DIGIT: Identifies the assembly plant

ASSEMBLY PLANT	CODE
Atlanta, GA	A
Buffalo, NY	B
Chester, PA	C
Dallas, TX	D
Mahwah, NJ	E
Dearborn, MI	F
Chicago, IL	G
Kansas City, KS	K
Long Beach, CA	L
Memphis, TN	M
Norfolk, VA	N
Twin City, MN (St. Paul)	P
San Jose, CA	R
Somerville, MA	S
Louisville, KY	U

FOURTH DIGIT: Identifies the body style

BODY STYLE	CODE
Convertible, Sunliner	C
Skyliner	F
Ranch Wagon	R
Fairlane (tudor/fordor)	T
Victoria tudor	V
Country Sedan	X
Country Squire	Y
All other (tudor, fordor, Mainline, Customline	G
Special body (solid top)	W

LAST SIX DIGITS: Represent the basic production number, 100001/up

PATENT PLATE

Codes are located on the left front body pillar below the upper hinge opening. The plate consists of the serial number, the body type, exterior paint color, trim scheme and the production code.

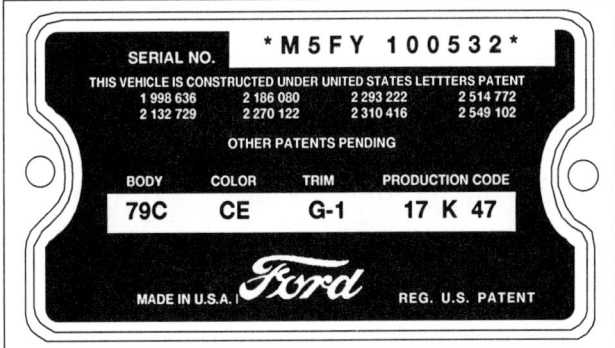

EXAMPLE:

79C	Fairlane Country Squire
C	Aquatone Blue, lower body
E	Shoeshow White, upper body
G	Trim (Dark Blue cloth and Medium Blue cloth)
1	First Trim Deviation
17	17th Day of Month
K	Month of the Year (October)
47	47th Car Produced

THE BODY TYPE CODE indicates the body type.

BODY TYPE	CODE
Mainline ranch wagon	59A
Mainline tudor	70A
Mainline tudor, business	70D
Mainline fordor	73A
Fairlane Victoria	60B
Fairlane Crown Victoria, solid top	64A
Fairlane Crown Victoria, transparent top	64B
Fairlane club sedan	70C
Fairlane town sedan	73C
Fairlane Sunliner convertible	76B
Fairlane Country Squire	79C
Customline ranch wagon	59B
Customline tudor	70B
Customline fordor	73B
Customline country sedan (8-pass.)	79B
Customline country sedan (6-pass.)	79D

THE COLOR CODE indicates the exterior paint color used on the car.

COLOR	CODE
Raven Black	A
Banner Blue	B
Aquatone Blue	C
Waterfall Blue	D
Snowshoe White	E
Pine Tree Green	F
Sea Sprite Green	G
Neptune Green	H
Buckskin Brown	K
Regency Purple	M
Torch Red	R
Sky Haze Green	T
Goldenrod Yellow	V
Tropical Rose	W
Primer	P
Special	S

THE TRIM CODE indicates the key to the trim color and material for each model series.

COLOR	CLOTH	VINYL	LEATHER	CODE
Lt. Gray/Dk. Gray	•	•		A
Dk. Blue/Med. Blue	•	•		C
Med. Turquoise/ Dk. Turquoise	•	•		E
Dk. Blue/Med. Blue	•			G
Med. Copper	•			J
White/Red		•		L
White/Turquoise		•		M
Black/Yellow		•		R
Med. Copper	•	•		Y
White/Red		•		AA
Copper		•		AD
Dk. Copper		•		AE
Lt. Blue/Med. Blue		•		AK
Turquoise		•		AL
Copper		•		AM
Turquoise	•			AR
White/Magenta		•		AS
White/Black	•	•		AT
White/Copper	•	•		AU
White/Red		•		AV
White/Med. Blue		•		AX
Blue		•		AY

THE PRODUCTION DATE CODE indicates the day, month and the production sequence.

MONTH	CODE
January	A
February	B
March	C
April	D
May	E
June	F
July	G
August	H
September	J
October	K
November	L
December	M

ENGINE SPECIFICATIONS

MAINLINE, CUSTOMLINE, FAIRLANE

ENGINE CODE	NO. CYL.	CID	HORSE-POWER	COMP. RATIO	CARB
A5	6	223	120	7.5:1	1 BC
U5	8	272	162	7.6:1	2 BC
M5	8	272	182	8.5:1	4 BC
P5	8	292	198	8.5:1	4 BC
?	8	292	205	?	4 BC

VEHICLE IDENTIFICATION NUMBER

● P5FH100532 ●

Located on the plate attached to the left front body pillar below the upper hinge opening.

FIRST DIGIT: Identifies the engine

ENGINE	CODE
292, 8-cyl.	P

SECOND DIGIT: Identifies the model year 1955

THIRD DIGIT: Identifies the assembly plant

ASSEMBLY PLANT	CODE
Dearborn, MI	F

FOURTH DIGIT: Identifies the body style

BODY STYLE	CODE
Thunderbird	H

LAST SIX DIGITS: Represent the basic production number, 100001/up

PATENT PLATE

The Thunderbird plate is located on the dash panel in the engine compartment. The plate consists of the serial number, the body type, exterior paint color, trim scheme and the production code.

EXAMPLE:

40A	Thunderbird
R	Torch Red
XA	Black/White vinyl
17	17th Day of Month
K	Month of the Year (October)
47	47th car produced

THE BODY TYPE CODE indicates the body type.

BODY TYPE	CODE
Thunderbird	40A

THE COLOR CODE indicates the exterior paint color used on the car.

COLOR	CODE
Raven Black	A
Snowshoe White	E
Torch Red	R
Thunderbird Blue	T
Goldenrod Yellow	V

THE TRIM CODE indicates the key to the trim color and material for each model series.

COLOR	CLOTH	VINYL	LEATHER	CODE
Black/White		•		XA
Red/White		•		XB
Turquoise/White		•		XC
Black/Yellow		•		XD

THE PRODUCTION DATE CODE indicates the
day, month and production sequence.

MONTH	CODE
January	A
February	B
March	C
April	D
May	E
June	F
July	G
August	H
September	J
October	K
November	L
December	M

ENGINE SPECIFICATIONS

ENGINE CODE	NO. CYL.	CID	HORSE-POWER	COMP. RATIO	CARB	TRANS
P5	8	292	193	8.1:1	4 BC	MAN
P5	8	292	198	8.5:1	4 BC	AUTO
P5	8	292	193	8.1:1	4 BC	OD

1956 FORD CUSTOMLINE

1956 FORD PARKLANE STATION WAGON

1956 FORD CROWN VICTORIA

1956 FORD THUNDERBIRD

1956 FORD CROWN VICTORIA

VEHICLE IDENTIFICATION NUMBER

• M 6 F Y 1 0 0 5 3 2 •

Located on the plate attached to the left front body pillar below the upper hinge opening.

FIRST DIGIT: Identifies the engine

ENGINE	CODE
223, 6-cyl.	A
292, 8-cyl.	M
312, 8-cyl.	P
272, 8-cyl.	U

SECOND DIGIT: Identifies the model year 1956

THIRD DIGIT: Identifies the assembly plant

ASSEMBLY PLANT	CODE
Atlanta, GA	A
Buffalo, NY	B
Chester, PA	C
Dallas, TX	D
Mahwah, NJ	E
Dearborn, MI	F
Chicago, IL	G
Kansas City, KS	K
Long Beach, CA	L
Memphis, TN	M
Norfolk, VA	N
Twin City, MN (St. Paul)	P
San Jose, CA	R
Somerville, MA	S
Louisville, KY	U

FOURTH DIGIT: Identifies the body style

BODY STYLE	CODE
Convertible, Sunliner	C
Victoria (Fairlane fordor)	F
Ranch Wagon, Customline	R
Fairlane (tudor/fordor)	T
Victoria tudor	V
Crown Victoria	W
Country sedan	X
Country Squire	Y
All other (tudor, fordor, Mainline, Customline)	G

LAST SIX DIGITS: Represent the basic production number, 100001/up

PATENT PLATE

Codes are located on the left front body pillar below the upper hinge opening. The plate dispalys the serial number, the body type, exterior paint color, trim scheme and the production code.

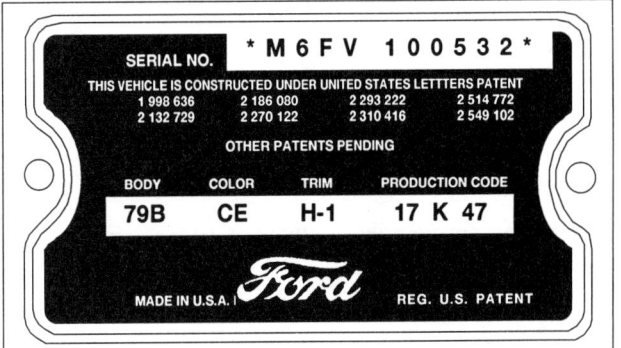

EXAMPLE:

79B	Model Country Squire, Fairlane)
C	Bermuda Blue, lower body
E	Colonial White, upper body
H	Trim (Light Blue/Medium Blue cloth)
1	First Trim Deviation
17	17th Day of Month
K	Month of the Year (October)
47	47th Car Produced

THE BODY TYPE CODE indicates the body type.

BODY TYPE	CODE
Mainline ranch wagon	59A
Mainline tudor	70A
Mainline tudor, business	70D
Mainline fordor	73A
Fairlane Victoria (fordor)	57A
Fairlane Victoria	64C
Fairlane ranch wagon (Parklane)	59C
Fairlane Crown Victoria, solid top	64A
Fairlane Crown Victoria, transparent top	64B
Fairlane club sedan	70C
Fairlane town sedan	73C
Fairlane Sunliner	76B
Fairlane country sedan (8-pass.)	79B
Fairlane Country Squire	79C
Customline ranch wagon	59B
Customline tudor	70B
Customline fordor	73B
Customline country sedan (6-pass.)	79D
Customline Victoria	64D

THE COLOR CODE indicates the exterior paint color used on the car.

COLOR	CODE
Raven Black	A
Nocturne Blue	B
Bermuda Blue	C
Diamond Blue	D
Colonial White	E
Pine Ridge Green	F
Meadowmist Green	G
Platinum Gray	H
Buckskin Tan	J
Fiesta Red	K
Peacock Blue	L
Goldenglow Yellow	M
Mandarin Orange	N
Primer	P
Special Color	S

THE TRIM CODE indicates the key to the trim color and material for each model series.

COLOR	CLOTH	VINYL	LEATHER	CODE
Lt. Blue/Med. Blue	•	•		B
Lt. Green/ Med. Green	•	•		C
Dk. Gray/Lt. Gray	•	•		E
Lt. Blue/Med. Blue	•			H
Green	•			J
Gray	•			L
Green		•		T
Red/White		•		V
White/Black	•	•		AD
Black/Red	•	•		AE
Dk. Brown		•		AJ
White/Peacock	•	•		AN
Green		•		AS
White/Red		•		AT
Blue		•		AV
Brown		•		AX
Brown		•		AZ
Brown		•		BA
Blue		•		BB
Green		•		BC

COLOR	CLOTH	VINYL	LEATHER	CODE
White/Brown		•		BD
Gray	•	•		BE
Gray/Red	•			BF
White/Orange		•		BG
White/Blue		•		BH
Brown	•			BJ
White/Red	•	•		BL
Blue/White		•		BM
Black/White		•		BN
White/Blue		•		BR
White/Blue	•			BS
White/Red		•		BU
White/Blue		•		BV
Blue	•	•		BZ
Green	•	•		CA

THE PRODUCTION DATE CODE indicates the day, month and the production sequence.

MONTH	CODE
January	A
February	B
March	C
April	D
May	E
June	F
July	G
August	H
September	J
October	K
November	L
December	M

ENGINE SPECIFICATIONS

MAINLINE, CUSTOMLINE, FAIRLANE

ENGINE CODE	NO. CYL.	CID	HORSE-POWER	COMP. RATIO	CARB	TRANS
A6	6	223	137	8.0:1	1 BC	MAN/AUTO
U6	8	272	173	8.0:1	2 BC	MAN
U6	8	272	176	8.4:1	2 BC	AUTO
M6	8	292	200	8.0:1	4 BC	MAN
M6	8	292	202	8.4:1	4 BC	AUTO
P6	8	312	215	8.4:1	4 BC	MAN
P6	8	312	225	9.0:1	4 BC	AUTO

VEHICLE IDENTIFICATION NUMBER

• P 6 F H 1 0 0 5 3 2 •

Located on the plate attached to the left front body pillar below the upper hinge opening.

FIRST DIGIT: Identifies the engine

ENGINE	CODE
292, 8-cyl.	M
312, 8-cyl.	P

SECOND DIGIT: Identifies the model year 1956

THIRD DIGIT: Identifies the assembly plant

ASSEMBLY PLANT	CODE
Dearborn, MI	F

FOURTH DIGIT: Identifies the body style

BODY STYLE	CODE
Thunderbird	H

LAST SIX DIGITS: Represent the basic production number, 100001/up

PATENT PLATE

The Thunderbird plate is located on the dash panel in the engine compartment. The plate displays the serial number, the body type, exterior paint color, trim scheme and the production code.

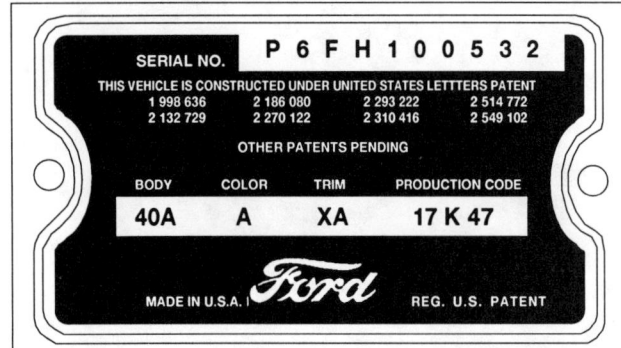

EXAMPLE:

40A	Thunderbird
A	Raven Black
XA	Black/White vinyl
17	17th Day of Month
K	Month of the Year (October)
47	47th car produced

THE BODY TYPE CODE indicates the body type.

BODY TYPE	CODE
Thunderbird	40A

THE COLOR CODE indicates the exterior paint color used on the car.

COLOR	CODE
Raven Black	A
Colonial White	E
Buckskin Tan	J
Fiesta Red	K
Peacock Blue	L
Thunderbird Gray	P
Thunderbird Green	Z
Goldenglow Yellow	M
Sunset Coral	Y

THE TRIM CODE indicates the key to the trim color and material for each model series.

COLOR	CLOTH	VINYL	LEATHER	CODE
Black/White		•		XA
Red/White		•		XB
Peacock/White		•		XC
Tan/White		•		XD
Green/White		•		XF
Brown/White		•		XG

THE PRODUCTION DATE CODE indicates the day, month and production sequence.

MONTH	CODE
January	A
February	B
March	C
April	D
May	E
June	F
July	G
August	H
September	J
October	K
November	L
December	M

ENGINE SPECIFICATIONS

ENGINE CODE	NO. CYL.	CID	HORSE-POWER	COMP. RATIO	CARB	TRANS
M6	8	292	202	8.4:1	4 BC	MAN
P6	8	312	215	8.4:1	4 BC	OD
P6	8	312	225	9.0:1	4 BC	AUTO

1957 FORD CUSTOM

1957 FORD THUNDERBIRD

1957 FORD FAIRLANE

1957 FORD COUNTRY SQUIRE

1957 FORD FAIRLANE 500

1957 FORD THUNDERBIRD

VEHICLE IDENTIFICATION NUMBER

• C7FV100532 •

Located on the plate attached to the left front body pillar below the upper hinge opening.

FIRST DIGIT: Identifies the engine

ENGINE	CODE
223, 6-cyl.	A
272, 8-cyl.	B
292, 8-cyl.	C
312, 8-cyl. (4-BC)	D
312, 8-cyl. (2-4-BC)	E
312, 8-cyl. (supercharged)	F

SECOND DIGIT: Identifies the model year 1957

THIRD DIGIT: Identifies the assembly plant

ASSEMBLY PLANT	CODE
Atlanta, GA	A
Buffalo, NY	B
Chester, PA	C
Dallas, TX	D
Mahwah, NJ	E
Dearborn, MI	F
Chicago, IL	G
Kansas City, KS	K
Long Beach, CA	L
Memphis, TN	M
Norfolk, VA	N
Twin City, MN (St. Paul)	P
San Jose, CA	R
Somerville, MA	S
Louisville, KY	U

FOURTH DIGIT: Identifies the body style

BODY STYLE	CODE
Fairlane 500, convertible	C
Custom/Custom 300, tudor/fordor	G
Custom 300, ranch wagon	R
Fairlane/Fairlane 500, tudor/fordor	T
Fairlane/Falrlane 500, Victoria tudor/fordor	V
Fairlane 500, retactable hardtop	W
Country sedan	X
Country Squire	Y

LAST SIX DIGITS: Represent the basic production number, 100001/up

PATENT PLATE

Codes are located on the left front body pillar below the upper hinge opening. The plate consists of the serial number, the body type, exterior paint color, trim scheme and the production code.

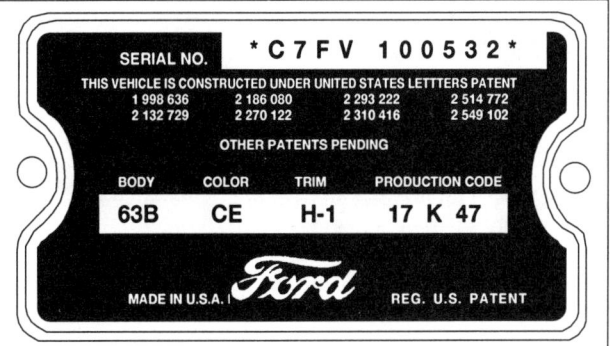

EXAMPLE:

63B	Model (Victoria, Fairlane)
C	Dresden Blue, lower body
E	Colonial White, upper body
H	Trim (Colonial vinyl/Blue cloth)
1	First Trim Deviation
17	17th Day of Month
K	Month of the Year (October)
47	47th Car Produced

THE BODY TYPE CODE indicates the body type.

BODY TYPE	CODE
Fairlane 500, Skyliner (retractable)	51A
Fairlane 500, Victoria, fordor	57A
Fairlane, Victoria, fordor	57B
Fairlane, fordor	58A
Fairlane 500, fordor	58B
Custom, ranch wagon	59A
Custom 300, ranch wagon, Del Rio	59B
Fairlane 500, Victoria, tudor	63A
Fairlane, Victoria, tudor	63B
Fairlane, tudor	64A
Fairlane 500, tudor	64B
Custom, tudor	70A
Custom 300, tudor	70B
Custom, business, tudor	70D
Custom, fordor	73A
Custom 300, fordor	73B
Fairlane 500, convertible	76B
Fairlane 500, country sedan (9-pass.)	79C
Custom 300, country sedan (6-pass.)	79D
Fairlane 500, country squire (8-pass.)	79E

THE COLOR CODE indicates the exterior paint color used on the car.

COLOR	CODE
Raven Black	A
Dresden Blue	C
Colonial White	E
Starmist Blue	F
Cumberland Green	G
Willow Green	J
Silver Mocha	K
Doeskin Tan	L
Gunmetal Gray	N
Woodsmoke Gray	T
Flame Red	V
Dusk Rose	X
Inca Gold	Y
Coral Sand	Z

THE TRIM CODE indicates the key to the trim color and material for each model series.

COLOR	CLOTH	VINYL	LEATHER	CODE
Silver/Gray	•	•		A
Starmist/Blue	•	•		E
Woodsmoke/Gray	•	•		F
Doeskin/Brown	•	•		G
Colonial/Blue	•	•		H
Colonial/Green	•	•		J
Colonial/Gray	•	•		K
Colonial/Brown	•	•		L
Gray	•			R
Brown	•			S
Gold/Black	•			T
Colonial/Black	•			U
Colonial/Blue		•		X
Colonial/Raven		•		AA
Colonial/Blue		•		AB
Colonial/Cumberland		•		AC
Colonial/Red		•		AJ
Willow/Green	•	•		AN
Blue	•			AR
Green	•			AS
Raven/Gold	•	•		AT
Colonial/Flame		•		AU
Doeskin/Tan		•		AX
Colonial/Tan		•		AZ
Blue		•		BC
Green		•		BD
Black		•		BE
Red		•		BF
Brown		•		BG

THE PRODUCTION DATE CODE indicates the day, month and production sequence.

MONTH	CODE
January	A
February	B
March	C
April	D
May	E
June	F
July	G
August	H
September	J
October	K
November	L
December	M

ENGINE SPECIFICATIONS

ENGINE CODE	NO. CYL.	CID	HORSE- POWER	COMP. RATIO	CARB	TRANS
A7	6	223	144	8.6:1	1 BC	MAN/AUTO
B7	8	272	190	8.6:1	2 BC	MAN/AUTO
C7	8	292	206	9.1:1	2 BC	MAN
C7	8	292	212	9.1:1	2 BC	AUTO
D7	8	312	245	9.7:1	4 BC	MAN/AUTO
E7	8	312	270	9.7:1	2-4 BC	MAN
E7	8	312	285	10.0:1	2-4 BC	MAN
F7	8	312	300	8.5:1	SC	MAN
F7	8	312	340	?	SC	MAN

VEHICLE IDENTIFICATION NUMBER

● D 7 F H 1 0 0 5 3 2 ●

Located on the plate attached to the left front body pillar below the upper hinge opening.

FIRST DIGIT: Identifies the engine

ENGINE	CODE
292, 8-cyl.	C
312, 8-cyl., 4 BC	D
312, 8-cyl., 2-4 BC	E
312, 8-cyl., Supercharged	F

SECOND DIGIT: Identifies the model year 1957

THIRD DIGIT: Identifies the assembly plant

ASSEMBLY PLANT	CODE
Dearborn, MI	F

FOURTH DIGIT: Identifies the body style

BODY STYLE	CODE
Thunderbird	H

LAST SIX DIGITS: Represent the basic production number, 100001/up

PATENT PLATE

The Thunderbird plate is located on the dash panel in the engine compartment. The plate consists of the serial number, the body type, exterior paint color, trim scheme and the production code.

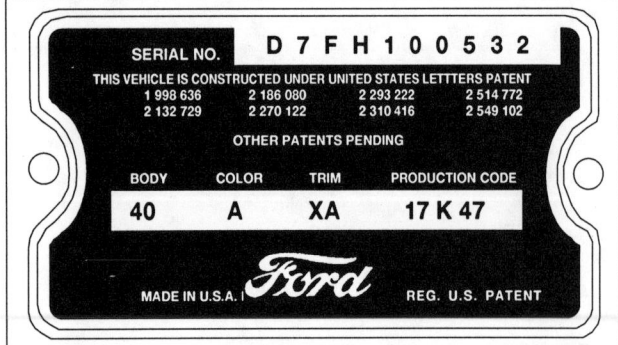

EXAMPLE:

40	Thunderbird
A	Raven Black
XA	Black/White vinyl
17	17th Day of Month
K	Month of the Year (October)
47	47th car produced

THE BODY TYPE CODE indicates the body type.

BODY TYPE	CODE
Thunderbird	40

THE COLOR CODE indicates the exterior paint color used on the car.

COLOR	CODE
Raven Black	A
Starmist Blue	F
Flame Red	V
Inca Gold	Y
Thunderbird Bronze	Q
Gunmetal Gray	N/H
Willow Green	J
Coral Sand	Z
Dusk Rose	X
Colonial White	E
Sun Gold (midyear)	G
Torch Red (midyear)	R
Azure Blue (midyear)	L
Seaspray Green (midyear)	N

THE TRIM CODE indicates the key to the trim color and material for each model series.

COLOR	CLOTH	VINYL	LEATHER	CODE
Black/White		•		XA
Blue/Blue		•		XL
Green/Green		•		XM
Red		•		XH
Copper		•		XJ
White		•		XK

THE PRODUCTION DATE CODE indicates the day, month and production sequence.

MONTH	CODE
January	A
February	B
March	C
April	D
May	E
June	F
July	G
August	H
September	J
October	K
November	L
December	M

ENGINE SPECIFICATIONS

ENGINE CODE	NO. CYL.	CID	HORSE-POWER	COMP. RATIO	CARB	TRANS
C7	8	292	212	9.1:1	2 BC	MAN
D7	8	312	245	9.7:1	4 BC	AUTO/OD
E7	8	312	270	9.7:1	2-4 BC	ALL
F7	8	312	300	8.5:1	SC	ALL

1958 FORD THUNDERBIRD

1958 FORD CUSTOM 300

VEHICLE IDENTIFICATION NUMBER

•B8FT 109299•

Located on the plate attached to the left front body pillar below the upper hinge opening.

FIRST DIGIT: Identifies the engine

ENGINE	CODE
223, 6-cyl.	A
332, 8-cyl.	B
292, 8-cyl.	C
332, 8-cyl.	G
352, 8-cyl.	H
361, 8-cyl. (police)	W

SECOND DIGIT: Identifies the model year 1958

THIRD DIGIT: Identifies the assembly plant

ASSEMBLY PLANT	CODE
Atlanta, GA	A
Buffalo, NY	B
Chester, PA	C
Dallas, TX	D
Mahwah, NJ	E
Dearborn, MI	F
Chicago, IL	G
Kansas City, KS	K
Long Beach, CA	L
Memphis, TN	M
Norfolk, VA	N
Twin City, MN (St. Paul)	P
San Jose, CA	R
Louisville, KY	U

FOURTH DIGIT: Identifies the body style

BODY STYLE	CODE
Fairlane 500, convertible	C
Custom/Custom 300, tudor/ fordor/business	G
Custom/Custom 300, ranch wagon, Del Rio	R
Fairlane/Fairlane 500, tudor/fordor	T
Fairlane/Fairlane 500, Victoria tudor/fordor	V
Country sedan	X
Country Squire	Y
Retractable hardtop	W

LAST SIX DIGITS: Represent the basic production number, 100001/up

PATENT PLATE

Codes are located on the left front door post. The plate consists of the serial number, the body type, exterior paint color, trim scheme and the production code, transmission type and axle type.

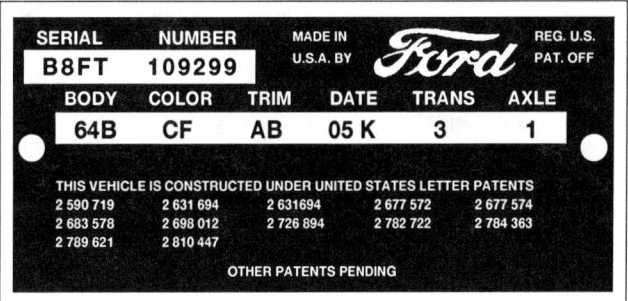

EXAMPLE:

64B	Model (Fairlane 500, tudor)
C	Desert Beige, lower body
F	Silvertone Green, upper body
AB	Beige/Shadow vinyl
05	5th Day of Month
K	Month of the Year (October)
3	Fordomatic Transmission
1	3.10:1 Axle Ratio

THE BODY TYPE CODE indicates the body type.

CUSTOM 300

BODY TYPE	CODE
Ranch wagon, 2-dr.	59A
Tudor	70A
Business, tudor	70D
Fordor	73A
Ranch wagon, 4-dr.	79A

FAIRLANE

BODY TYPE	CODE
Victoria, fordor	57B
Fordor	58A
Victoria, tudor	63B
Tudor	64A

FAIRLANE 500

BODY TYPE	CODE
Retractable hardtop (Skyliner)	51A
Victoria, fordor	57A
Fordor	58B
Victoria, tudor	63A
Tudor	64B
Convertible (Sunliner)	76B
Country sedan (9-pass.)	79C
Country squire (8-pass.)	79E
Country sedan (6-pass.)	79D

THE COLOR CODE indicates the exterior paint color used on the car.

COLOR	CODE
Raven Black	A
Winterset White	B
Desert Beige	C
Palomino Tan	D
Colonial White	E
Silvertone Green	F
Sun Gold	G
Gunmetal Gray	H
Grenadier Red	I
Bali Bronze	J
Everglade Green	K
Azure Blue	L
Gulfstream Blue	M
Seaspray Green	N
Platinum	O
Prime	P
Torch Red	R
Special	S
Silvertone Blue	T
Casino Cream	V
Cameo Rose	W
Cascade Green	X
Monarch Blue	Y
Regatta Blue	Z

THE TRIM CODE indicates the key to the trim color and material for each model series.

COLOR	CLOTH	VINYL	LEATHER	CODE
Silver/Silver	•	•		A
Blue/Blue	•	•		C
Green/Green	•	•		E
Beige/Brown	•	•		F
White/Black	•	•		G
White/Tan	•	•		H
Blue/Blue	•			J
Green/Green	•			K
Brown/Brown	•			L
Black/Gold	•			R
White/Red	•	•		S
Blue/Blue		•		U
Green/Green		•		V
White/Tan		•		X
White/Red		•		Y
White/Black		•		Z
Beige/Shadow		•		AB
Blue/Blue		•		AC
Beige/Brown		•		AH
Gray/Gray	•			AJ
White/Blue	•	•		AK
White/Blue		•		AL
Gold/Black	•	•		AM
Blue/Blue	•	•		*CZ
Green/Green	•	•		*DZ
Gray/Gray	•	•		*EZ

* Used on body types 70B and 73B after 5-9-58

THE PRODUCTION DATE CODE indicates the day and the month of the year the car was produced.

MONTH	CODE
January	A
February	B
March	C
April	D
May	E
June	F
July	G
August	H
September	J
October	K
November	L
December	M

THE TRANSMISSION CODE indicates the type of transmission installed in the vehicle.

TYPE	CODE
Conventional	1
Overdrive	2
Fordomatic	3
Cruise-O-Matic	4

THE REAR AXLE CODE indicates the ratio of the rear axle installed in the vehicle.

RATIO	CODE
2.91:1	0
3.10:1	1
3.56:1	2
3.70:1	3
3.89:1	4

ENGINE SPECIFICATIONS

ENGINE CODE	NO. CYL.	CID	HORSE-POWER	COMP. RATIO	CARB	TRANS
A8	6	223	145	8.6:1	1 BC	MAN/AUTO
C8	8	292	205	9.0:1	2 BC	MAN/AUTO
B8	8	332	240	9.5:1	2 BC	MAN/AUTO
G8	8	332	265	9.6:1	4 BC	MAN/AUTO
H8	8	352	300	10.2:1	4 BC	MAN/AUTO
W8	8	361	303	10.5:1	4 BC	MAN/AUTO

VEHICLE IDENTIFICATION NUMBER

●H8YH 109299●

Located on the plate attached to the left front body pillar below the upper hinge opening.

FIRST DIGIT: Identifies the engine

ENGINE	CODE
352, 8-cyl.	H

SECOND DIGIT: Identifies the model year 1958

THIRD DIGIT: Identifies the assembly plant

ASSEMBLY PLANT	CODE
Wixom, MI	Y

FOURTH DIGIT: Identifies the body style

BODY STYLE	CODE
Hardtop/convertible	H

LAST SIX DIGITS: Represent the basic production number, 100001/up

THE BODY TYPE CODE indicates the body type.

BODY TYPE	CODE
Tudor, hardtop	63A
Convertible	76A

THE COLOR CODE indicates the exterior paint color used on the car.

COLOR	CODE
Raven Black	A
Winterset White	B
Grenadier Red	I
Everglade Green	K
Gulfsteam Blue	M
Platinum	O
Palamino Tan	P
Casino Cream	V
Cameo Rose	W
Cascade green	X
Monarch Blue	Y
Regatta Blue	Z

PATENT PLATE

Codes are located on the left door hinge pillar post. The plate consists of the serial number, the body type, exterior paint color, trim scheme and the production code, transmission type and axle type.

SERIAL	NUMBER		*Thunderbird* ®
H8YH	109299		

BODY	COLOR	TRIM	DATE	TRANS	AXLE
63A	1B	XG	24 M	4	1

THIS VEHICLE IS CONSTRUCTED UNDER UNITED STATES LETTER PATENTS

OTHER PATENTS PENDING

MADE IN U.S.A. BY  REG. U.S. PATENT OFFICE

EXAMPLE:

63A	Model (Tudor, hardtop)
A	Raven Black
XG	Red/White vinyl
24	24th Day of Month
M	Month of the Year (December)
4	Cruise-O-Matic Transmission
1	3.10:1 Axle Ratio

THE TRIM CODE indicates the key to the trim color and material for each model series.

COLOR	CLOTH	VINYL	LEATHER	CODE
Blue/Blue	•	•		XA
Green/Green	•	•		XB
Black/Black	•	•		XC
Blue/White		•		XE
Green/White		•		XF
Red/White		•		XG
Black/White		•		XH
Blue/Blue	•	•		XK
Tan/White		•		XL
Blue/White		•		XM

THE PRODUCTION DATE CODE indicates the day and the month of the year the car was produced.

MONTH	CODE
January	A
February	B
March	C
April	D
May	E
June	F
July	G
August	H
September	J
October	K
November	L
December	M

THE TRANSMISSION CODE indicates the type of transmission installed in the vehicle.

TYPE	CODE
Conventional	1
Overdrive	2
Cruise-O-Matic	4

THE REAR AXLE CODE indicates the ratio of the rear axle installed in the vehicle.

RATIO	CODE
3.10:1	1
3.70:1	3

ENGINE SPECIFICATIONS

ENGINE CODE	NO. CYL.	CID	HORSE-POWER	COMP. RATIO	CARB	TRANS
H8	8	352	300	10.2:1	4 BC	ALL

1959 FORD THUNDERBIRD

1959 FORD COUNTRY SEDAN

1959 FORD THUNDERBIRD

1959 FORD SKYLINER RETRACTABLE

VEHICLE IDENTIFICATION NUMBER

•B9FV 109299•

Located on the plate attached to the left front body pillar below the upper hinge opening.

FIRST DIGIT: Identifies the engine

ENGINE	CODE
223, 6-cyl.	A
332, 8-cyl.	B
292, 8-cyl.	C
352, 8-cyl. (4-BC)	H
430, 8-cyl. (4-BC)	J

SECOND DIGIT: Identifies the model year 1959

THIRD DIGIT: Identifies the assembly plant

ASSEMBLY PLANT	CODE
Atlanta, GA	A
Chester, PA	C
Dallas, TX	D
Mahwah, NJ	E
Dearborn, MI	F
Chicago, IL	G
Loraine, OH	H
Kansas City, KS	K
Long Beach, CA	L
Memphis, TN	M
Norfolk, VA	N
Twin City, MN (St. Paul)	P
San Jose, CA	R
Louisville, KY	U

FOURTH DIGIT: Identifies the body style

BODY STYLE	CODE
Convertible	C
Custom 300, tudor/fordor/ business	G
Ranch wagon, tudor/fordor, country sedans	R
Fairlane 500, Galaxie, tudor/fordor	S
Fairlane, tudor/fordor	T
Fairlane 500, tudor/fordor	V
Retractable hardtop	W
Country Squire	Y

LAST SIX DIGITS: Represent the basic production number, 100001/up

PATENT PLATE

Codes are located on the left front door post. The plate consists of the serial number, the body type, exterior paint color, trim scheme and the production code, transmission type and axle type.

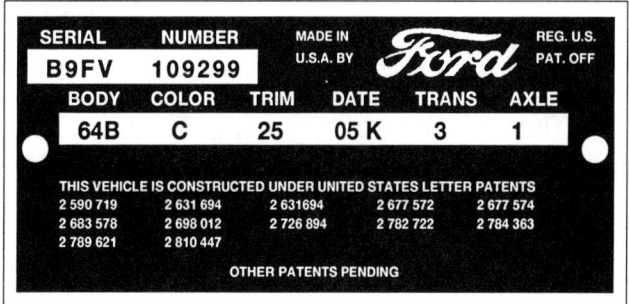

EXAMPLE:

64B	Fairlane 500 Club Sedan
C	Wedgewood Blue
25	Blue vinyl/cloth
05	5th Day of Month
K	Month of the Year (October)
3	Fordomatic Transmission
1	3.10:1 Axle Ratio

THE BODY TYPE CODE indicates the body type.

CUSTOM 300
BODY TYPE	CODE
Tudor sedan (2-dr.)	64F
Fordor sedan (4-dr.)	58E
Business tudor	64G

FAIRLANE
BODY TYPE	CODE
Club sedan (2-dr.)	64A
Town sedan (4-dr.)	58A

FAIRLANE 500
BODY TYPE	CODE
Club sedan (2-dr.)	64B
Town Sedan (4-dr.)	58B
Club Victoria (2-dr.)	63A
Town Victoria (4-dr.)	57A

FAIRLANE 500 GALAXIE

BODY TYPE	CODE
Club sedan (2-dr.)	64H
Town sedan (4-dr.)	54A
Club Victoria (2-dr.)	65A
Town Victoria (4-dr.)	75A
Convertible	76B
Retractable	51A

STATION WAGON

BODY TYPE	CODE
Ranch wagon, 2-dr. (6-pass.)	59C
Ranch wagon, 4-dr. (6-pass.)	71H
Country sedan, 2-dr. Del Rio (6-pass.)	59D
Country sedan, 4-dr. (6-pass.)	71F
Country sedan, 4-dr. (9-pass.)	71E
Country squire, 4-dr. (9-pass.)	71G

THE COLOR CODE indicates the exterior paint color used on the car.

COLOR	CODE
Raven Black	A
Wedgewood Blue	C
Indian Tuquoise	D
Colonial White	E
Fawn Tan	F
April Green	G
Tahitian Bronze	H
Surf Blue	J
Sherwood Green	Q
Torch Red	R
Geranium	T
Inca Gold	Y
Gunsmoke Gray	Z
Prime	P
Special	S
Surf Blue	L
Sherwood Green	M
Tahitian Bronze	K
Gunsmoke Gray	N
Monte Carlo Red	1
Meadowvale Green	4
Belmont Blue	5
Skymist Blue	6
Adriatic Green	W

THE TRIM CODE indicates the key to the trim color and material for each model series.

COLOR	CLOTH	VINYL	LEATHER	CODE
Blue/Blue	•	•		02
Green/Green	•	•		03
Blue/Blue	•			07
Green/Green	•			08
Bronze/Bronze	•			09
Gray/Gray	•			10
Turquoise/Turquoise	•			11
Gray/Gold	•			12
Blue/Blue		•		25
Fawn/Bamboo		•		29
Blue/Blue	•	•		30
Green/Green	•	•		31
Silver/Gunsmoke	•	•		32
Bronze/Bronze	•	•		33
Turquoise/Turquoise	•	•		34
White/Geranium	•	•		37
Gold/Black	•	•		38
Blue/Blue		•		39
Green/Green		•		40
Green/Green	•	•		45
White/Red/Gold		•		46
Bronze/Bronze		•		47
Geranium/Black	•	•		48
Blue/Blue		•		49
Turquoise/Turquoise		•		51
Gold/Black		•		52
Geranium/Black		•		53
Red/Black		•		55
Red/Black		•		56
White/Red		•		57
White/Red		•		58
Blue		•		59
Brown		•		60
Blue/Blue	•	•		032
Turquoise/Turquoise	•			111
Gray/Gold	•			121
Silver/Gunsmoke	•	•		296
Blue/Blue	•	•		301
Blue/Blue	•	•		302
Green/Green	•			311
Green/Green	•	•		312
Gray/Gray	•			323
Bronze/Bronze	•			331
Bronze/Bronze	•	•		332
Turquoise/Turquoise	•	•		341
White/Geranium	•	•		371
Gold/Black	•	•		381
White/Red	•	•		571

THE PRODUCTION DATE CODE indicates the day and the month of the year the car was produced.

MONTH	CODE
January	A
February	B
March	C
April	D
May	E
June	F
July	G
August	H
September	J
October	K
November	L
December	M

THE TRANSMISSION CODE indicates the type of transmission installed in the vehicle.

TYPE	CODE
Conventional	1
Overdrive	2
Fordomatic	3
Cruise-O-Matic	4

THE REAR AXLE CODE indicates the ratio of the rear axle installed in the vehicle.

RATIO	CODE
2.91:1	0
3.10:1	1
3.56:1	2
3.70:1	3
3.89:1	4
2.69:1	6

ENGINE SPECIFICATIONS

ENGINE CODE	NO. CYL.	CID	HORSE-POWER	COMP. RATIO	CARB
A9	6	223	145	8.4:1	1 BC
C9	8	292	200	8.8:1	2 BC
B9	8	332	225	8.9:1	2 BC
H9	8	352	300	9.6:1	4 BC
J9	8	430	350	10.0:1	4 BC

VEHICLE IDENTIFICATION NUMBER

●H9YH 100532●

Located on the plate attached to the left door post.

FIRST DIGIT: Identifies the engine

ENGINE	CODE
352, 8-cyl.	H
430, 8-cyl.	J

SECOND DIGIT: Identifies the model year 1959

THIRD DIGIT: Identifies the assembly plant

ASSEMBLY PLANT	CODE
Wixom, MI	Y

FOURTH DIGIT: Identifies the body style

BODY STYLE	CODE
Tudor, hardtop	H
Convertible	J

LAST SIX DIGITS: Represent the basic production number, 100001/up

PATENT PLATE

Codes are located on the left front door hinge pillar post. The plate consists of the serial number, the body type, exterior paint color, trim scheme and the production code, transmission type and axle type.

SERIAL	NUMBER	*Thunderbird* ®
H9YH	100532	

BODY	COLOR	TRIM	DATE	TRANS	AXLE
63A	A	9X	24 M	4	1

THIS VEHICLE IS CONSTRUCTED UNDER UNITED STATES LETTER PATENTS

OTHER PATENTS PENDING
MADE IN U.S.A. BY  REG. U.S. PATENT OFFICE

EXAMPLE:

63A	Model (Tudor, hardtop)
A	Raven Black
9X	Torch Red/Colonial White vinyl
24	24th Day of Month
M	Month of the Year (December)
4	Cruise-O-Matic Transmission
1	3.10:1 Axle Ratio

THE BODY TYPE CODE indicates the body type.

BODY TYPE	CODE
Tudor, hardtop	63A
Convertible	76A

THE COLOR CODE indicates the exterior paint color used on the car.

COLOR	CODE
Raven Black	A
Baltic Blue	C
Indian Turquoise	D
Colonial White	E
Hickory Tan	F
Glacier Green	G
Tahitian Bronze	H
Steel Blue	J
Sandstone	K
Diamond Blue	I
Doeskin Beige	M
Starlight Blue	N
Sea Reef Green	Q
Brandywine Red	R
Flamingo	T
Cordovan	U
Casino Cream	V
Tamarack Green	W
Platinum	Z

THE TRIM CODE indicates the key to the trim color and material for each model series.

COLOR	CLOTH	VINYL	LEATHER	CODE
Blue/Blue	•	•		1X
Green/Green	•	•		2X
Turquoise/Turquoise	•	•		3X
Black/White	•	•		4X
Blue/Blue		•		5X
Green/White		•		6X
Turquoise/White		•		7X
Black/White		•		8X
Red/White		•		9X
Black			•	1Y
Tan			•	2Y
Turquoise			•	3Y
Red			•	4Y
Tan/White		•		5Y

THE PRODUCTION DATE CODE indicates the day and the month of the year the car was produced.

MONTH	CODE
January	A
February	B
March	C
April	D
May	E
June	F
July	G
August	H
September	J
October	K
November	L
December	M

THE TRANSMISSION CODE indicates the type of transmission installed in the vehicle.

TYPE	CODE
Conventional	1
Overdrive	2
Cruise-O-Matic	4

THE REAR AXLE CODE indicates the ratio of the rear axle installed in the vehicle.

RATIO	CODE
3.10:1	1
3.70:1	3
2.91:1	0

ENGINE SPECIFICATIONS

ENGINE CODE	NO. CYL.	CID	HORSE-POWER	COMP. RATIO	CARB
H9	8	352	300	9.6:1	4 BC
J9	8	430	350	10.0:1	4 BC

1950 LINCOLN

1950 LINCOLN COSMOPOLITAN

VEHICLE IDENTIFICATION NUMBER

● 5 0 L A 1 2 3 4 L ●

Lincoln patent plates are located on the right hand front body hinge pillar, the Lincoln Cosmopolitan patent plates are located on the dash panel to the left of the windshield wiper motor.

FIRST AND SECOND DIGITS: Identify the model year 1950

THIRD AND FOURTH DIGITS: Identify the assembly plant

ASSEMBLY PLANT	CODE
Los Angeles, CA	LA
St. Louis, MO	SL
Lincoln Plant, Detroit, MI	LP

NEXT FOUR DIGITS: Represent the basic production number at each plant

LAST DIGIT: Identifies the car line

CAR LINE	CODE
Lincoln	L
Cosmopolitan	H

BODY PLATE

THE BODY PLATE for the Lincoln is located on the left hand front body hinge pillar on the early 1950 models and on the right-hand front body hinge pillar on the late 1950 models; the Lincoln Cosmopolitan body plate is located directly below the patent plate. The plate indicates the assembly plant, body type, exterior color, trim scheme, day and month the car was assembled, and the production code.

STYLE   LA-72C

BODY NUMBER

03-65-20-L-75

EXAMPLE:

LA	Los Angeles, CA
72C	Custom coupe
03	Banning Blue
65	Gray Stripe Nylon
20	20th day of month
L	Month of year (November)
75	75th Car assembled

THE ASSEMBLY PLANT CODE indicates the plant where the vehicle was assembled.

ASSEMBLY PLANT	CODE
Los Angeles, CA	LA
St. Louis, MO	SL
Lincoln Plant, Detroit, MI	LP

THE BODY TYPE CODE indicates the body type.

LINCOLN

BODY TYPE	CODE
Coupe, 2-dr.	72
Custom coupe, (Lido)	72C
Sport sedan, 4-dr.	74

COSMOPOLITAN

BODY TYPE	CODE
Coupe, 2-dr.	72
Custom coupe (Capri)	72C
Sport sedan, 4-dr.	74
Convertible	76

THE COLOR CODE indicates the paint color used on the car.

COLOR	CODE
Yosemite Green Metallic	—
Admiral Blue Metallic	111
Cosmopolitan Maroon Metallic	112
Nassau Beige Metallic	114
Mallard Green Metallic	115
Arrowhead Gray Metallic	116
Danube Blue Metallic	117
Palomar Green Metallic	118
Chantilly Green	120
Newport Gray	*123
Carlsbad Tan	*127
Glendale Green	*129

* Upper body color

THE TRIM CODE indicates the key to the trim color and material for each model series.
We were unable to locate trim codes for 1950 Lincoln.

THE DAY AND MONTH OF THE YEAR CODE indicates the day and month the car was assembled.

MONTH	CODE
January	A
February	B
March	C
April	D
May	E
June	F
July	G
August	H
September	J
October	K
November	L
December	M

THE ROTATION NUMBER indicates the cars numerical sequence of assembly.

ENGINE SPECIFICATIONS

LINCOLN

ENGINE CODE	NO. CYL	CID	HORSE POWER	COMP. RATIO	CARB
0EL	8	336.7	152	7.0:1	2 BC

COSMOPOLITAN

ENGINE CODE	NO. CYL	CID	HORSE POWER	COMP. RATIO	CARB
0EH	8	336.7	152	7.0:1	2 BC

1951 LINCOLN

1951 LINCOLN

VEHICLE IDENTIFICATION NUMBER

• 5 1 L P 1 2 3 4 5 L •

Lincoln patent plates are located on the right hand front body hinge pillar, the Lincoln Cosmopolitan patent plates are located on the dash panel to the left of the windshield wiper motor.

FIRST AND SECOND DIGITS: Identify the model year 1951

THIRD AND FOURTH DIGITS: Identify the assembly plant

ASSEMBLY PLANT	CODE
Lincoln Plant	LP
Los Angeles, CA	LA

NEXT FIVE DIGITS: Represent the basic production number at each plant

LAST DIGIT: Identifies the car line

CAR LINE	CODE
Lincoln	L
Cosmopolitan	H

BODY PLATE

THE BODY PLATE for the Lincoln is located on the left hand front body hinge pillar on the early models and on the right hand front body hinge pillar on the late models; the Lincoln Cosmopolitan body plate is located just below the patent plate. The plate displays the assembly plant, body type, exterior color, trim scheme, day and month the car was assembled, and the production code.

```
 O                              O

 STYLE      L-74

 BODY NUMBER

 03-65-20-L-75

 O                              O
```

EXAMPLE:

LP	Lincoln Plant
L-74	Sport sedan
03	Banning Blue
65	Gray Stripe Nylon
20	20th day of month
L	Month of year (November)
75	75th Car assembled

THE ASSEMBLY PLANT CODE indicates the plant where the vehicle was assembled.

ASSEMBLY PLANT	CODE
Lincoln Plant	LP
Los Angeles, CA	LA

THE BODY TYPE CODE indicates the body type.

LINCOLN

BODY TYPE	CODE
Coupe, 2-dr.	L72B
Custom coupe (Lido)	L72C
Sport sedan, 4-dr.	L74

COSMOPOLITAN

BODY TYPE	CODE
Coupe, 2-dr.	H72B
Custom coupe (Capri)	H72C
Sport sedan, 4-dr.	H74
Convertible coupe	H76

THE COLOR CODE indicates the paint color used on the car.

COLOR	CODE
Black	01E
Black	01L
Admiral Blue Metallic	02L
Admiral Blue	02AL
Banning Blue Metallic	03E
Cosmopolitan Maroon Metallic	04L
Cosmopolitan Maroon	04AL
Luxor Maroon Metallic	05E
Kent Gray	06E
Kent Gray	06L
Mission Gray	07E
Coppertone Metallic	08L
Coppertone	08AL
Tomah Ivory	09E
Brewster Green Metallic	10L
Brewster Green	10AL
Everglade Green	11E
Saxon Gray Meallic	12E
Saxon Gray	12AL
Sheffield Green	13E
Avon Blue	14E
Avon Blue	14L

COLOR	CODE
Kerry Blue Metallic	15E
Academy Blue	15CE
Radiant Green Metallic	16L
Coventry Green Gray	17E
Bristol Buff	18L
Vassar Yellow	19E
Chantilly Green	20L
Manitou Red Metallic	21
Manitou Red	21AL

* L - Polishing lacquer (Detroit)

* E - Baking Enamel (Los Angeles)

TWO-TONE COLOR

COLORS	CODE
Black*/Tomah Ivory/L#	30E
Tomah Ivory*/Sheffield Green#	31E
Sheffield Green*/Tomah Ivory#	32E
Coventry Green Gray*/Everglade Green#	33E
Everglade Green*/Coventry Green Gray#	34E
Sheffield Green*/Everglade Green#	35E
Everglade Green*/Sheffield Green#	36E
Sheffield Green*/Coventry Green Gray#	37E
Coventry Green Gray*/Sheffield Green#	38E
Mission Gray*/Banning Blue Metallic#	39E
Banning Blue Metallic*/Mission Gray#	40E
Kent Gray*/Avon Blue#	41E/41L
Avon Blue*/Kent Gray#	42E/42L
Kent Gray/Saxon Gray Metallic#	43E/43L
Kent Gray*/Saxon Gray#	43AL
Saxon Gray Metallic*/Kent Gray#	44E/44L
Saxon Gray*/Kent Gray#	44AL
Admiral Blue Metallic*/Kent Gray#	45L
Admiral Blue*/Kent Gray#	45AL
Kent Gray*/Admiral Blue Metallic#	46L
Kent Gray*/Admiral Blue#	46AL
Radiant Green Metallic*/ Brewster Green Metallic#	47L
Radiant Green Metallic*/Brewster Green#	47AL
Brewster Green Metallic*/ Radiant Green Metallic#	48L
Brewster Green*/Radiant Green Metallic#	48AL
Radiant Green Metallic*/Bristol Buff#	49L
Bristol Buff*/Radiant Blue Metallic#	50L
Banning Blue Metallic*/Kent Gray#	51E
Kent Gray*/Banning Blue Metallic#	52E
Bristol Buff*/Copperstone Metallic#	53L
Bristol Buff*/Coppertone#	53AL

* Upper color

Lower color

L Polishing lacquer (Detroit Branch)

E Baking Enamel (Los Angeles Branch)

THE TRIM CODE indicates the key to the trim color and material for each model series.

COLOR	CLOTH	VINYL	LEATHER	CODE
Two-tone Green	•			61,69
Brown		•		63
Brown	•	•		71
Gray		•		65
Gray	•	•		67
Green		•		73
Two-tone Gray	•			75A
Tan/Ivory		•		77
Tan			•	79
Cherry Red			•	81
Med. Green			•	83
Lt. Blue			•	85
Yellow			•	86
Lime Green			•	87
Lt. Blue/Blue	•		•	88
Cherry Red/Tan	•		•	89
Tan	•		•	90
Med. Green/Green	•		•	91
Yellow	•		•	92
Lime Green/Yellow	•		•	93
Cherry Red/Black			•	94
Yellow/Black			•	95
Lt. Blue/Dk. Blue			•	96

THE DAY AND MONTH OF THE YEAR

CODE indicates the day and month the car was assembled.

MONTH	CODE
January	A
February	B
March	C
April	D
May	E
June	F
July	G
August	H
September	J
October	K
November	L
December	M

THE ROTATION NUMBER indicates the cars numerical sequence of assembly.

ENGINE SPECIFICATIONS

LINCOLN

ENGINE CODE	NO. CYL	CID	HORSE POWER	COMP. RATIO	CARB
1EL	8	336.7	154	7.0:1	2 BC

COSMOPOLITAN

ENGINE CODE	NO. CYL	CID	HORSE POWER	COMP. RATIO	CARB
1EH	8	336.7	154	7.0:1	2 BC

1952 LINCOLN

1952 LINCOLN COSMOPOLITAN

VEHICLE IDENTIFICATION NUMBER

● 5 2 L P 5 0 0 1 H ●

The serial number is stamped on the extreme top edge of the Patent Plate.

FIRST AND SECOND DIGITS: Identify the model year 1952

THIRD AND FOURTH DIGITS: Identify the assembly plant

ASSEMBLY PLANT	CODE
Los Angeles, CA	LA
Lincoln Plant	LP
St. Louis, MO	SL

NEXT FOUR DIGITS: Represent the basic production number at each plant

LAST DIGIT: Identifies the car line

CAR LINE	CODE
Lincoln Cosmopolitan	H

PATENT PLATE

THE PATENT PLATE was redesigned to include the body style and body specifications in addition to the car serial number. The plate is located on the right front body pillar just below the upper hinge opening. It displays the serial number, body type, exterior color, trim scheme, day and month the car was assembled, and the production code.

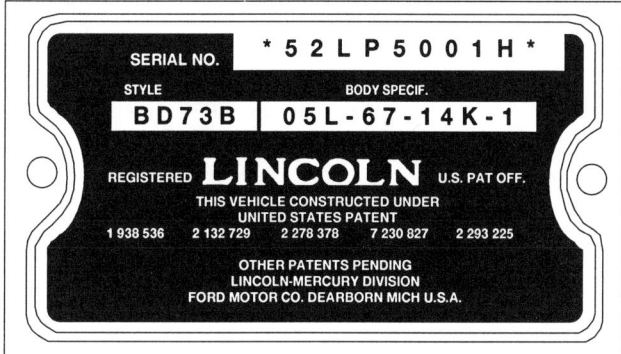

EXAMPLE:

BD73B	Special custom 4-dr. sedan
05L	Newport Gray
67	Green/Silver Stripe nylon
14	14th day of month
K	Month of year (October)
1	First car assembled

THE BODY TYPE CODE indicates the body type.

COSMOPOLITAN

BODY TYPE	CODE
Custom, 4-dr.	73A
Custom, 2-dr.	60C

CAPRI

BODY TYPE	CODE
Special Custom, 4-dr.	73B
Special Custom, 2-dr.	60A
Special Custom, convertible	76A

THE COLOR CODE indicates the paint color used on the car.

COLOR	CODE
Raven Black	01L/01E
Admiral Blue	02L/02E
Fanfare Maroon	04L/04E
Newport Gray	05L/05E
Coppertone	08L
Coppertone Metallic	08E
Pebble Tan	09L/09E
Academy Blue	10L/10E
Hillcrest Green	11L/11E
Lakewood Green	13L/13E
Saxon Gray	15L
Saxon Gray Metallic	15E
Cinabar Red	18L/18E
Vassar Yellow	19L/19E

L - Polishing lacquer (Detroit plant)

E - Baking enamel (all other plants)

TWO-TONE COLOR

COLOR	CODE
Pebble Tan*/Coppertone#	22L
Pebble Tan*/Coppertone Metallic#	22E
Coppertone*/Pebble Tan#	23L
Hillcrest Green*/Newport Gray#	26L/26E
Newport Gray*/Hillcrest Green#	27L/27E
Raven Black*/Newport Gray#	30L/30E
Newport Gray*/Raven Black#	31L/31E
Pebble Tan*/Fanfare Maroon#	32L/32E
Fanfare Maroon*/Pebble Tan#	33L/33E
Raven Black*/Vassar Yellow#	34L/34E
Newport Gray*/Saxon Gray#	36L
Newport Gray*/Saxon Gray Metallic#	36E
Saxon Gray*/Newport Gray#	37L
Saxon Gray Metallic*/Newport Gray#	37E
Newport Gray*/Lakewood Green#	40L/40E
Lakewood Green*/Newport Gray#	41L/41E
Raven Black*/Fanfare Maroon#	42L/42E
Newport Gray*/Academy Blue#	44L/44E
Academy Blue*/Newport Gray#	45L/45E
Raven Black*/Pebble Tan#	46L/46E
Newport Gray*/Admiral Blue#	49L/49E
Admiral Blue*/Newport Gray#	50L/50E
Hillcrest Green*/Vassar Yellow#	52L/52E
Raven Black*/Cinabar Red#	53L/53E
Raven Black*/Lakewood Green#	54L/54E
Raven Black*/Academy Blue#	55L/55E

* Upper color

\# Lower color

L Polishing lacquer (Detroit plant)

E Baking Enamel (all other plants)

THE TRIM CODE indicates the key to the trim color and material for each model series.

COLOR	CLOTH	VINYL	LEATHER	CODE
Green	•			60,63
Brown	•			61
Gray	•			62,65
Tan	•			64
Tan/Ivory	•			66
Green/Silver	•			67
Red/Black	•		•	68
Yellow/Green	•		•	69,69A
Blue	•		•	70
Red/Black			•	71
Yellow/Green			•	72
Dk. Blue/Lt. Blue			•	73
Tan			•	75

THE DAY AND MONTH OF THE YEAR CODE indicates the day and month the car was assembled.

MONTH	CODE
January	A
February	B
March	C
April	D
May	E
June	F
July	G
August	H
September	J
October	K
November	L
December	M

THE ROTATION NUMBER indicates the cars numerical sequence of assembly.

ENGINE SPECIFICATIONS

LINCOLN

ENGINE CODE	NO. CYL	CID	HORSE POWER	COMP. RATIO	CARB
	8	317.5	160	7.5:1	2 BC

1953 LINCOLN CAPRI

VEHICLE IDENTIFICATION NUMBER

● 5 3 W A 5 0 0 1 H ●

The serial number is stamped on the extreme top edge of the Patent Plate.

FIRST AND SECOND DIGITS: Identify the model year 1953

THIRD AND FOURTH DIGITS: Identify the assembly plant

ASSEMBLY PLANT	CODE
Los Angeles, CA	LA
Wayne, MI	WA
St. Louis, MO	SL

NEXT FOUR DIGITS: Represent the basic production number at each plant

LAST DIGIT: Identifies the car line

CAR LINE	CODE
Lincoln	H

PATENT PLATE

THE PATENT PLATE includes the body style and body specifications in addition to the car serial number. The plate is located on the right front body pillar just below the upper hinge opening. It displays the serial number, body type, exterior color, trim scheme, day and month the car was assembled, and the production code.

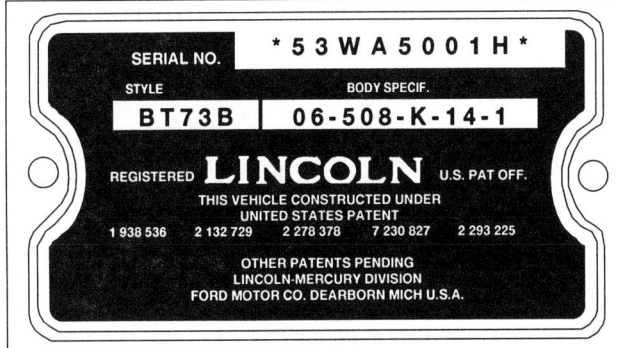

EXAMPLE:

BT73B	Caprl 4-dr. sedan
06	Starlight Gray
508	Dk. Blue/Lt. Blue cloth
K	Month of year (October)
14	14th day of month
1	First car assembled

THE BODY TYPE CODE indicates the body type.

COSMOPOLITAN

BODY TYPE	CODE
4-Dr. sedan	73A
2-Dr. hardtop	60C

CAPRI

BODY TYPE	CODE
4-Dr. sedan	73B
2-Dr. hardtop	60A
2-Dr. convertible	76A

THE COLOR CODE indicates the paint color used on the car.

COLOR	CODE
Regent Black	01
Crown Blue Metallic	02
Majestic Maroon Metallic	04
Kingsbury Gray	05
Embassy Brown Metallic	08
Castle Tan	09
Colonial Blue	10
Esquire Green	12
Empire Green Metallic	14
Oxford Gray Metallic	15
Palace Green Metallic	16
Royal Red	18
Cavalier Yellow	19

TWO-TONE COLORS

COLOR	CODE
Kingsbury Gray*/Crown Blue Metallic#	28
Crown Blue Metallic*/Kingsbury Gray#	29
Regent Black*/Kingsbury Gray#	30
Kingsbury Gray*/Regent Black#	31
Regent Black*/Cavalier Yellow#	34
Castle Tan*/Majestic Maroon Metallic#	38
Majestic Maroon Metallic*/Castle Tan#	39
Empire Green Metallic*/Esquire Green#	48
Esquire Green*/Empire Green Metallic#	49
Palace Green Metallic*/Esquire Green#	50
Esquire Green*/Palace Green Metallic#	51
Oxford Gray Metallic*/Kingsbury Gray#	52
Kingsbury Gray*/Oxford Gray Metallic#	53
Crown Blue Metallic*/Colonial Blue#	54
Colonial Blue*/Crown Blue Metallic#	55
Castle Tan*/Embassy Brown Metallic#	56
Embassy Brown Metallic*/Castle Tan#	57
Regent Black*/Esquire Green#	58
Regent Black*/Castle Tan#	60
Regent Black*/Majestic Maroon Metallic#	61
Regent Black*/Colonial Blue#	62
Regent Black*/Royal Red#	63
Castle Tan*/Royal Red#	64

THE TRIM CODE indicates the key to the trim color and material for each model series.

COLOR	CLOTH	VINYL	LEATHER	CODE
Dk. Gray/Silver	•			301
Dk. Brown/Silver	•			302
Dk. Gray/White	•			303
Dk. Brown/White	•			304
Dk. Green/White	•			305
Dk. Gray/White	•			306
Dk. Blue	•			307
Dk. Brown	•			308
Red/Black	•		•	309
Calf/Black	•		•	310
White/Black	•		•	311
Lt. Blue/Dk. Blue	•		•	312
White/Dk. Blue	•		•	313
Green	•		•	314
White/Dk. Green	•		•	315
Red/Black			•	316
Calf/Black			•	317
White/Black			•	318
Lt. Blue/Dk. Blue			•	319
White/Dk. Blue			•	320
Green			•	321
White/Dk. Green			•	322
White/Calf			•	323
Calf			•	324

THE DAY AND MONTH OF THE YEAR CODE indicates the day and month the car was assembled.

MONTH	CODE
January	A
February	B
March	C
April	D
May	E
June	F
July	G
August	H
September	J
October	K
November	L
December	M

THE ROTATION NUMBER indicates the cars numerical sequence of assembly.

ENGINE SPECIFICATIONS

9-16

LINCOLN

ENGINE CODE	NO. CYL	CID	HORSE POWER	COMP. RATIO	CARB
	8	317.5	205	8.0:1	4 BC

1954 LINCOLN CAPRI

1954 LINCOLN CAPRI

1954 LINCOLN CAPRI

VEHICLE IDENTIFICATION NUMBER

`• 5 4 W A 5 0 0 1 H •`

The serial number is stamped on the extreme top edge of the Patent Plate.

FIRST AND SECOND DIGITS: Identify the model year 1954

THIRD AND FOURTH DIGITS: Identify the assembly plant

ASSEMBLY PLANT	CODE
Los Angeles, CA	LA
Wayne, MI	WA

NEXT FOUR DIGITS: Represent the basic production number at each plant

LAST DIGIT: Identifies the car line

CAR LINE	CODE
Lincoln	H

PATENT PLATE

THE PATENT PLATE includes the body style and body specifications in addition to the car serial number. The plate is located on the right front body pillar just below the upper hinge opening. It displays the serial number, body type, exterior color, trim scheme, day and month the car was assembled, and the production code.

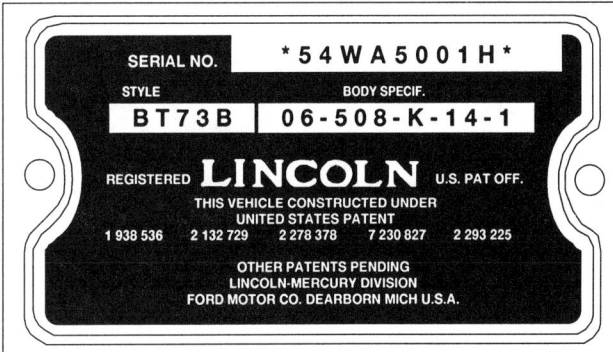

EXAMPLE:

BT73B	Capri 4-dr. sedan
06	Starlight Gray
508	Dk. Blue/Lt. Blue cloth
K	Month of year (October)
14	14th day of month
1	First car assembled

THE BODY TYPE CODE indicates the body type.

COSMOPOLITAN
BODY TYPE	CODE
4-Dr. sedan	73A
2-Dr. hardtop	60C

CAPRI
BODY TYPE	CODE
4-Dr. sedan	73B
2-Dr. hardtop	60A
2-Dr. convertible	76A

THE COLOR CODE indicates the paint color used on the car.

COLOR	CODE
Regent Black	01
Ambassador Blue Metallic	02
Majestic Maroon Metallic	04
Wellington Gray	05
Cadet Gray Metallic	07
Colony Tan	08
Columbia Blue	09
Embassy Brown Metallic	11
Canterbury Green	13
Empire Green Metallic	14
Palace Green Metallic	16
Premier Yellow	19
Royal Red	20
Regal Red	21
Ermine White	23

TWO-TONE COLORS

COLOR	CODE
Regent Black/Premier Yellow	34
Regent Black/Royal Red	38
Colony Tan/Royal Red	39
Empire Green Metallic/Canterbury Green	42
Canterbury Green/Empire Green Metallic	43
Palace Green Metallic/Canterbury Green	45
Canterbury Green/Palace Green Metallic	46
Cadet Gray Metallic/Wellington Gray	47
Wellington Gray/Cadet Gray Metallic	48
Ambassador Blue Metallic/Columbia Blue	49
Columbia Blue/Ambassador Blue Metallic	50
Colony Tan/Embassy Brown Metallic	51
Embassy Brown Metallic/Colony Tan	52
Regent Black/Colony Tan	53
Regent Black/Columbia Blue	54
Regent Black/Canterbury Green	55
Regent Black/Empire Green Metallic	56
Regent Black/Wellington Gray	57
Colony Tan/Palace Green Metallic	58
Colony Tan/Ambassador Blue Metallic	59

TRIM CODE indicates the key to the trim color and material for each model series.

COLOR	CLOTH	VINYL	LEATHER	CODE
Dk. Gray/Silver	•			301
Dk. Brown/Silver	•			302
Dk. Gray/White	•			303
Dk. Brown/White	•			304
Dk. Green/White	•			305
Dk. Gray/White	•			306
Dk. Blue	•			307
Dk. Brown	•			308
Red/Black	•		•	309
Calf/Black	•		•	310
White/Black	•		•	311
Lt. Blue/Dk. Blue	•		•	312
White/Dk. Blue	•		•	313
Green	•		•	314
White/Dk. Green	•		•	315
Red/Black		•		316
Calf/Black		•		317
White/Black		•		318
Lt. Blue/Dk. Blue		•		319
White/Dk. Blue		•		320
Green		•		321
White/Dk. Green		•		322
White/Calf		•		323

COLOR	CLOTH	VINYL	LEATHER	CODE
Calf			•	324
Gray/Silver	•			405
Brown/White	•			406
Green/Silver	•			407
Blue/White	•			408
Calf			•	409
Gray	•			410
Brown	•			411
Green	•			412
Blue	•			413
Red/Black	•		•	414
White/Black	•		•	416
Blue	•			419
White/Dk. Blue	•		•	420
Green	•		•	421
White/Dk. Green	•		•	422
Calf/Beige	•		•	423
Black/Beige	•			424
Black/Red			•	427
Black/White			•	429
Black/Lt. Blue			•	430
Black/Lt. Green			•	431
Dk. Blue/White			•	433
Dk. Green/White			•	435
Calf/White			•	436
Yellow/Black	•			437
Yellow/Black			•	438
Gray		•		501,505
Green		•		503,507
Blue		•		504,508
Brown		•		506
Buff			•	511
White/Lt. Green		•	•	512
White/Lt. Blue		•	•	513
Yellow/Black		•		514
Red/Black		•	•	515
Green		•		517
Blue		•		518
White/Lt. Green			•	519
White/Lt. Blue			•	520
White/Buff			•	523
Yellow/Black			•	524
Red/Black			•	525
White/Black	•		•	527
White/Black			•	528
White/Red			•	529
White/Yellow			•	530
White/Coral			•	531
White/Turquoise			•	532

THE DAY AND MONTH OF THE YEAR
CODE indicates the day and month the car was assembled.

MONTH	CODE
January	A
February	B
March	C
April	D
May	E
June	F
July	G
August	H
September	J
October	K
November	L
December	M

THE ROTATION NUMBER indicates the cars numerical sequence of assembly.

ENGINE SPECIFICATIONS

LINCOLN

ENGINE CODE	NO. CYL	CID	HORSE POWER	COMP. RATIO	CARB
	8	317.5	205	8.0:1	4 BC

1955 LINCOLN CAPRI

1955 LINCOLN CAPRI

1955 LINCOLN CONTINENTAL MARK II

VEHICLE IDENTIFICATION NUMBER

● 5 5 W A 5 0 0 1 H ●

The serial number is stamped on the extreme top edge of the Patent Plate.

FIRST AND SECOND DIGITS: Identify the model year 1955

THIRD AND FOURTH DIGITS: Identify the assembly plant

ASSEMBLY PLANT	CODE
Los Angeles, CA	LA
Wayne, MI	WA

NEXT FOUR DIGITS: Represent the basic production number at each plant

LAST DIGIT: Identifies the car line

CAR LINE	CODE
Lincoln	H

PATENT PLATE

THE PATENT PLATE includes the body style and body specifications in addition to the car serial number. The plate is located on the right front body pillar just below the upper hinge opening. It displays the serial number, body type, exterior color, trim scheme, day and month the car was assembled, and the production code.

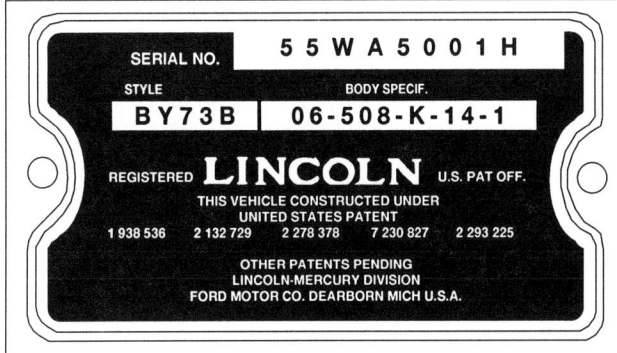

EXAMPLE:

BV73B	Capri 4-dr. sedan
06	Starlight Gray
508	Dk. Blue/Lt. Blue cloth
K	Month of year (October)
14	14th day of month
1	First car assembled

THE BODY TYPE CODE indicates the body type.

CUSTOM

BODY TYPE	CODE
4-Dr. sedan	73A
2-Dr. hardtop	60C

CAPRI

BODY TYPE	CODE
4-Dr. sedan	73B
2-Dr. sedan	60A
2-Dr. convertible	76A

THE COLOR CODE indicates the paint color used on the car.

COLOR	CODE
Executive Black	01
Chalet Blue Metallic	02
Starlight Gray	06
Chancellor Gray Metallic	07
Brunswick Blue	09
Estate Green Metallic	10
Viceroy Brown Metallic	11
Galway Green Metallic	12
Summit Green	13
Sunstone Yellow	19
Huntsman Red	21
Ermine White	23
Palomino Buff	25
Cashmere Coral	27
Taos Turquoise	28
Bahama Blue Metallic	30

TWO-TONE COLORS

COLOR	CODE
Executive Black/Sunstone Yellow	34
Executive Black/Starlight Gray	37
Galway Green Metallic/Summit Green	42
Summit Green/Galway Green Metallic	43
Estate Green Metallic/Summit Green	44
Summit Green/Estate Green Metallic	45
Chancellor Gray Metallic/Starlight Gray	46
Starlight Gray/Chancellor Gray Metallic	47
Chalet Blue Metallic/Brunswick Blue	48
Brunswick Blue/Chalet Blue Metallic	49
Ermine White/Estate Green Metallic	50
Estate Green Metallic/Ermine White	51
Chalet Blue Metallic/Ermine White	52
Ermine White/Chalet Blue Metallic	53
Ermine White/Summit Green	54
Huntsman Red/Ermine White	55
Ermine White/Huntsman Red	56
Ermine White/Brunswick Blue	57
Galway Green Metallic/Ermine White	58
Ermine White/Galway Green Metallic	59
Ermine White/Palomino Buff	60
Palomino Buff/Ermine White	61
Ermine White/Viceroy Brown Metallic	73
Viceroy Brown Metallic/Ermine White	74
Executive Black/Ermine White	75
Ermine White/Executive Black	76
Ermine White/Sunstone yellow	89
Ermine White/Cashmere Coral	90
Cashmere Coral/Ermine White	91
Ermine White/Taos Turquoise	92
Taos Turquoise/Ermine White	93
Executive Black/Huntsman Red	96
Huntsman Red/Executive Black	97
Ermine White/Bahama Blue Metallic	98
Bahama Blue Metallic/Ermine White	99

THE TRIM CODE indicates the key to the trim color and material for each model series.

COLOR	CLOTH	VINYL	LEATHER	CODE
Dk. Gray/Silver	•			301
Dk. Brown/Silver	•			302
Dk. Gray/White	•			303
Dk. Brown/White	•			304
Dk. Green/White	•			305
Dk. Gray/White	•			306
Dk. Blue	•			307
Dk. Brown	•			308
Red/Black	•		•	309
Calf/Black	•		•	310
White/Black	•		•	311
Lt. Blue/Dk. Blue	•		•	312
White/Dk. Blue	•		•	313
Green	•		•	314
White/Dk. Green	•		•	315
Red/Black			•	316
Calf/Black			•	317
White/Black			•	318
Lt. Blue/Dk. Blue			•	319
White/Dk. Blue			•	320
Green			•	321
White/Dk. Green			•	322
White/Calf			•	323
Calf			•	324
Gray/Silver	•			405
Brown/White	•			406
Green/Silver	•			407
Blue/White	•			408
Calf			•	409
Gray	•			410
Brown	•			411
Green	•			412
Blue	•			413
Red/Black	•		•	414
White/Black	•		•	416
Blue	•		•	419
White/Dk. Blue	•		•	420
Green	•		•	421
White/Dk. Green	•		•	422
Calf/Beige	•		•	423
Black/Beige	•		•	424
Black/Red			•	427
Black/White			•	429
Black/Lt. Blue			•	430
Black/Lt. Green			•	431
Dk. Blue/White			•	433

COLOR	CLOTH	VINYL	LEATHER	CODE
Dk. Green/White			•	435
Calf/White			•	436
Yellow/Black	•		•	437
Yellow/Black			•	438
Gray	•			501,505
Green	•			503,507
Blue	•			504,508
Brown	•			506
Buff			•	511
White/Lt. Green	•		•	512
White/Lt. Blue	•		•	513
Yellow/Black	•		•	514
Red/Black	•		•	515
Green	•		•	517
Blue	•		•	518
White/Lt. Green			•	519
White/Lt. Blue			•	520
White/Buff			•	523
Yellow/Black			•	524
Red/Black			•	525
White/Black	•		•	527
White/Black			•	528
White/Red			•	529
White/Yellow			•	530
White/Coral			•	531
White/Turquoise			•	532

THE DAY AND MONTH OF THE YEAR

CODE indicates the day and month the car was assembled.

MONTH	CODE
January	A
February	B
March	C
April	D
May	E
June	F
July	G
August	H
September	J
October	K
November	L
December	M

THE ROTATION NUMBER indicates the cars numerical sequence of assembly.

ENGINE SPECIFICATIONS

LINCOLN

ENGINE CODE	NO. CYL	CID	HORSE POWER	COMP. RATIO	CARB
	8	340.9	225	8.5:1	4 BC

1956 LINCOLN CONTINENTAL MARK II

1956 LINCOLN

1956 LINCOLN CAPRI

1956 LINCOLN CONTINENTAL MARK II

1956 LINCOLN CAPRI

1956 LINCOLN

VEHICLE IDENTIFICATION NUMBER

● 5 6 W A 5 0 0 1 L ●

The serial number is stamped on the extreme top edge of the Patent Plate.

FIRST AND SECOND DIGITS: Identify the model year 1956

THIRD AND FOURTH DIGITS: Identify the assembly plant

ASSEMBLY PLANT	CODE
Los Angeles, CA	LA
Wayne, MI	WA
Wixom, MI	YG

NEXT FOUR DIGITS: Represent the basic production number at each plant

LAST DIGIT: Identifies the car line

CAR LINE	CODE
Lincoln	L

PATENT PLATE

THE PATENT PLATE includes the body style and body specifications in addition to the car serial number. The plate is located on the right front body pillar just below the upper hinge opening. It displays the serial number, body type, exterior color, trim scheme, day and month the car was assembled, and the production code.

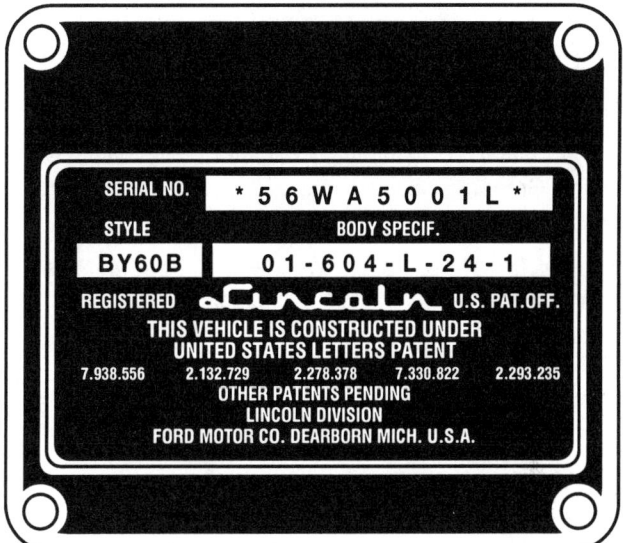

EXAMPLE:

BY60B	Premiere coupe
01	Presidential Black
604	Med. Brown/Dk. Brown cloth
L	Month of year (November)
24	24th day of month
1	First car assembled

THE BODY TYPE CODE indicates the body type.

CAPRI

BODY TYPE	CODE
4-Dr. sedan	73A
2-Dr. hardtop	60E

PREMIERE

BODY TYPE	CODE
4-Dr. sedan	73B
2-Dr. hardtop	60B
2-Dr. convertible	76B

THE COLOR CODE indicates the paint color used on the car.

COLOR	CODE
Presidential Black	01
Admiralty Blue Metallic	02
Centurian Gray	06
Balmoral Gray Metallic	07
Fairmont Blue	09
Shenandoah Green Metallic	10
Briar Brown Metallic	11
Wisteria	12
Summit Green	13
Amethyst	16
Sunburst Yellow	19
Summit Green	18A
Huntsman Red	21
Starmist White	23
Desert Buff	25
Island Coral	27
Taos Turquoise	28
Dubonnet	29
Champlain Blue	30

TWO-TONE COLORS

COLOR	CODE
Black/Dubonnet	33
Presidential Black/Sunburst Yellow	34
Centurian Gray/Dubonnet	35
Dubonnet/Centurian Gray	36
Presidential Black/Amethyst	37
Starmist White/Dubonnet	38
Dubonnet/Starmist White	39
Taos Turquoise/Summit Green	42
Taos Turquoise/Summit Green	42A
Summit Green/Taos Turquoise	43
Summit Green/Taos Turquoise	43A
Shenandoah Green Metallic/Summit Green	44
Shenandoah Green Metallic/Summit Green	44A
Summit Green/Shenandoah Green Metallic	45
Summit Green/Shenandoah Green Metallic	45A
Balmoral Gray Metallic/Centurian Gray	46
Centuran Gray/Balmoral Gray Metallic	47
Admiralty Blue Metallic/Fairmont Blue	48
Fairmont Blue/Admiralty Blue Metallic	49
Starmist White/Shenandoah Green Metallic	50
Shenandoah Green Metallic/Starmist White	51
Admiralty Blue Metallic/Starmist White	52
Starmist White/Admiralty Blue Metallic	53
Starmist White/Summit Green	54
Huntsman Red/Starmist White	55
Huntsman Red/Starmist White	55A
Starmist White/Huntsman Red	56
Starmist White/Huntsman Red	56A
Starmist White/Fairmont Blue	57
Fairmont Blue/Champlain Blue	58
Champlain Blue/Fairmont Blue	59
Starmist White/Desert Buff	60
Starmist White/Centurian Gray	61
Starmist White/Briar Brown	73
Briar Brown/Starmist White	75
Presidential Black/Starmist White	76
Starmist White/Summit Green	79A
Starmist White/Sunburst Yellow	89
Starmist White/Amethyst	90
Starmist White/Island Coral	91
Starmist White/Taos Turquoise	92
Starmist White/Wisteria	93
Presidential Black/Huntsman Red	96
Presidential Black/Huntsman Red	96A
Huntsman Red/Presidential Black	97
Huntsman Red/Presidential Black	97A
Starmist White/Champlain Blue	98
Presidential Black/Island Coral	99

THE TRIM CODE indicates the key to the trim color and material for each model series.

COLOR	CLOTH	VINYL	LEATHER	CODE
Buff			•	600,300,400
Brown	•			604
Brown	•			304
Gray	•			605,305,405
Green	•			606,306,406
Blue	•			607,307,507
White/Red			•	608,308,408
White/Coral			•	609,309,409
White/Black			•	610,310,410
White/Yellow			•	611,311,411
Yellow/Black			•	612,312,412
Green			•	614,314,414
Blue			•	615,315,415
Red/Black			•	617,317,417
Green	•		•	618,318,418
Blue	•		•	619,319,419
White/Black	•		•	620,320,420
Yellow/Black	•		•	621,321,421
Red/Black	•		•	622,322,422
Gray	•			623,323
Gray	•			523,423
Green	•		•	624,324,424
Blue	•			625,325,425
White/Wisteria			•	628,328
White/Amethyst			•	629,329
White/Buff			•	630,330,430
White/Green			•	631,331,431
Amethyst/Black			•	632,332
Coral/Black			•	633,333,433
Wisteria/White	•		•	634,334
Amethyst/White	•		•	635,335
Coral/Black			•	636,336,436
Buff/White	•		•	637,337

THE DAY AND MONTH OF THE YEAR CODE indicates the day and month the car was assembled.

MONTH	CODE
January	A
February	B
March	C
April	D
May	E
June	F
July	G
August	H
September	J
October	K
November	L
December	M

THE ROTATION NUMBER indicates the cars numerical sequence of assembly.

ENGINE SPECIFICATIONS

CAPRI/PREMIERE

ENGINE CODE	NO. CYL	CID	HORSE POWER	COMP. RATIO	CARB
	8	368	285	9.0:1	4 BC

VEHICLE IDENTIFICATION NUMBER

• C 5 6 5 1 0 0 1 •

Located on the Patent Plate.

FIRST DIGIT: Identifies the car line code

CAR LINE	CODE
Continental	C

SECOND AND THIRD DIGITS: Identify the model year 1956

FOURTH DIGIT: Identifies the month the car was assembled (Model year began June, 1955)

NEXT FIVE DIGITS: Represent the basic production number

PATENT PLATE

THE PATENT PLATE includes the body style and body specifications in addition to the car serial number. The plate is located on the right front body pillar just below the upper hinge opening. It indicates the serial number, body type, exterior color, trim scheme, day and month the car was assembled, and the production code.

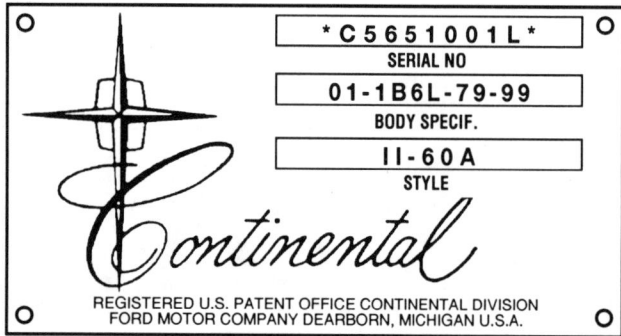

```
*C5651001L*
SERIAL NO
01-1B6L-79-99
BODY SPECIF.
II-60A
STYLE
```
Continental

REGISTERED U.S. PATENT OFFICE CONTINENTAL DIVISION
FORD MOTOR COMPANY DEARBORN, MICHIGAN U.S.A.

EXAMPLE:

01	Black
1B6L	White/Gray leather
7	Month of year (July)
9	9th day of month
99	99th car assembled

THE COLOR CODE indicates the paint color used on the car.

COLOR	CODE
Black	01
Cobalt Blue Metallic	02
Pastorial Blue	04
Forest Green Metallic	05
Naiad Green	07
Briar Brown Metallic	08
Sandalwood	10
Dark Gray Metallic	11
Dark Red	13
Starmist White	14
Medium Blue	15
Medium Green	16
Medium Beige	17
Medium Gray	18

THE TRIM CODE indicates the key to the trim color and material for each model series.

COLOR	CLOTH	VINYL	LEATHER	CODE
Blue			•	1A1A
White/Blue			•	1B6B
White/Green			•	1B6E
White/Beige			•	1B6H
White/Gray			•	1B6K,1B6L
White/Red			•	1B6M
Green			•	1C2D
Beige			•	1D3G
Gray			•	1E4L
Gray/White			•	1E6L
Red/Gray			•	1F4M
Red/White			•	1F6M
Gray/White			•	1G6K
Beige/White			•	1L6H
Green			•	1M6E
Blue/White			•	1N6B
Blue	•		•	2A1A
Green	•		•	2C2D
Beige	•		•	2D3G
Gray/White	•		•	2G6K
Gray	•		•	3E4L
Gray/White	•		•	3E6L
Red/Gray	•		•	3F4M
Red/White	•		•	3F6M

COLOR	CLOTH	VINYL	LEATHER	CODE
Blue	•		•	3H1C
Green	•		•	3J2F
Bronze/Beige	•		•	3K3J
Blue	•			4A1A
Green	•			4C2D
Beige	•			4D3G
Gray	•			5E4L
Red/Gray	•			5F4M
Blue	•			5H1C
Green	•			5J2F
Bronze/Beige	•			5K3J
Gray	•			6E4L
Red/Gray	•			6F4M
Blue	•			6H1C
Green	•			6J2F
Bronze/Beige	•			6K3J

THE DAY AND MONTH OF THE YEAR
CODE indicates the day and month the car was assembled.

MONTH	CODE
January	1
February	2
March	3
April	4
May	5
June	6
July	7
August	8
September	9
October	0
November	A
December	B

THE ROTATION NUMBER indicates the cars numerical sequence of assembly.

THE BODY STYLE indicates the body style of the vehicle.

BODY STYLE	CODE
Coupe	60A

ENGINE SPECIFICATIONS

ENGINE CODE	NO. CYL	CID	HORSE POWER	COMP. RATIO	CARB
	8	368	285	9.0:1	4 BC

1957 LINCOLN

1957 LINCOLN CONTINENTAL MARK II

1957 LINCOLN

1957 LINCOLN CONTINENTAL

VEHICLE IDENTIFICATION NUMBER

● 5 7 W A 5 0 0 1 L ●

The serial number is stamped on the extreme top edge of the Patent Plate.

FIRST AND SECOND DIGITS: Identify the model year 1957

THIRD AND FOURTH DIGITS: Identify the assembly plant

ASSEMBLY PLANT	CODE
Wayne, MI	WA

NEXT FOUR DIGITS: Represent the basic production number at each plant

LAST DIGIT: Identifies the car line

CAR LINE	CODE
Lincoln	L

PATENT PLATE

THE PATENT PLATE includes the body style and body specifications in addition to the car serial number. The plate is located on the right front body pillar just below the upper hinge opening. It displays the serial number, body type, exterior color, trim scheme, day and month the car was assembled, and the production code.

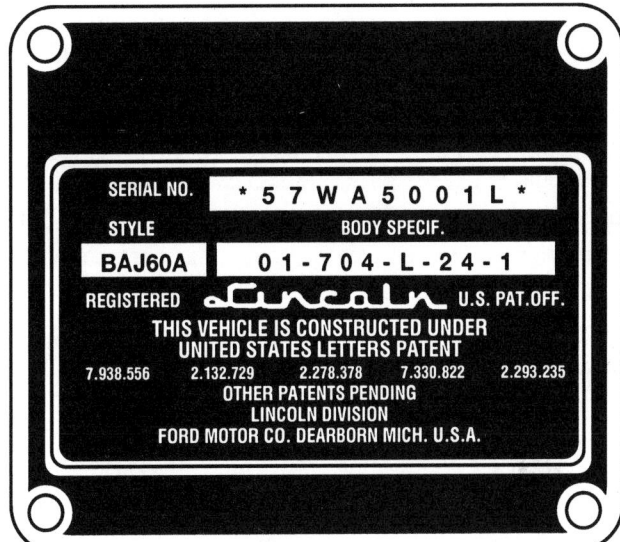

EXAMPLE:

BAJ60A	Capri coupe
01	Presidential Black
704	Dk. Gray/Med. Gray cloth
L	Month of year (November)
24	24th day of month
1	First car assembled

THE BODY TYPE CODE indicates the body type.

CAPRI

BODY TYPE	CODE
4-Dr. sedan	58A
2-Dr. hardtop	60A
4-Dr. hardtop	57A

PREMIERE

BODY TYPE	CODE
4-Dr. sedan	58B
4-Dr. hardtop	57B
2-Dr. hardtop	60B
2-Dr. convertible	76B

THE COLOR CODE indicates the paint color used on the car.

COLOR	CODE
Presidential Black	01
Gainsborough Blue	03
Seascape Blue	04
Horizon Blue	05
Starmist White	06
Ivy Green	07
Willow Green	09
Sand	10
Desert Buff	11
Huntsman Red	12
Saturn Gold	13
Taos Turquoise	14
Dubonnet	15
Cinnamon	16
Bermuda Coral	17
Flamingo	18
Oxford Gray	21
Vermont Green	22

TWO-TONE COLORS

COLOR	CODE
Horizon Blue/Gainsborough Blue	38
Gainsborough Blue/Horizon Blue	39
Seascape Blue/Gainsborough Blue	40
Gainsborough Blue/Seascape Blue	41
Starmist White/Gainsborough Blue	42
Gainsborough Blue/Starmist White	43
Horizon Blue/Seascape Blue	44
Seascape Blue/Horizon Blue	45
Starmist White/Seascape Blue	46
Seascape Blue/Starmist White	47
Starmist White/Horizon Blue	48
Sand/Gainsborough Blue	49
Presidential Black/Horizon Blue	50
Starmist White/Sand	51
Sand/Starmist White	52
Presidential Black/Sand	53
Sand/Presidential Black	54
Sand/Desert Buff	55
Desert Buff/Sand	56
Starmist White/Desert Buff	57
Desert Buff/Starmist White	58
Presidential Black/Dersert Buff	59
Willow Green/Ivy Green	60
Ivy Green/Willow Green	61
Vermont Green/Ivy Green	62
Ivy Green/Vermont Green	63
Starmist White/Ivy Green	64
Ivy Green/Starmist White	65
Willow Green/Vermont Green	66
Vermont Green/Willow Green	67
Starmist White/Willow Green	70
Willow Green/Starmist White	71
Sand/Ivy Green	72
Sand/Vermont Green	73
Presidential Black/Willow Green	74
Presidential Black/Saturn Gold	75
Saturn Gold/Presidential Black	76
Starmist White/Saturn Gold	77
Saturn Gold/Starmist White	78
Starmist White/Presidential Black	79
Presidential Black/Starmist White	80
Presidential Black/Huntsman Red	81
Huntsman Red/Presidential Black	82
Oxford Gray/Huntsman Red	83
Sand/Huntsman Red	84
Starmist White/Huntsman Red	85
Huntsman Red/Starmist White	86
Presidential Black/Taos Turquoise	88
Taos Turquoise/Presidential Black	89
Taos Turquoise/Starmist White	90
Presidential Black/Dubonnet	91
Starmist White/Dubonnet	92
Dubonnet/Starmist White	93
Sand/Dubonnet	94
Presidential Black/Cinnamon	95
Sand/Cinnamon	96
Cinnamon/Sand	97
Starmist White/Cinnamon	98
Cinnamon/Starmist White	99
Presidential Black/Bermuda Coral	100
Bermuda Coral/Presidential Black	101
Starmist White/Bermuda Coral	102
Bermuda Coral/Starmist White	103
Presidential Black/Flamingo	104
Flamingo/Presidential Black	105
Starmist White/Flamingo	106
Flamingo/Starmist White	107
Oxford Gray/Flamingo	108
Flamingo/Oxford Gray	109
Dubonnet/Flamingo	110
Flamingo/Dubonnet	111
Starmist White/Oxford Gray	136
Oxford Gray/Starmist White	137
Starmist White/Vermont Green	146
Vermont Green/Starmist White	147

THE TRIM CODE indicates the key to the trim color and material for each model series.

COLOR	CLOTH	VINYL	LEATHER	CODE
Gray	•			701/701A
Blue	•			702/702A
Green	•			703/703A
Gray	•			704
Blue	•			705
Green	•			706
Gray	•			707/407A
Blue	•			708/708A
Green	•			709/709A
Brown	•			710/710A
Dk. Gray	•			711
Dk. Blue	•			712
Dk. Green	•			713
Blue	•		•	722
Green	•		•	723
White/Champagne			•	724
Turquoise/Black	•		•	725/725A
Beige/Black	•		•	726/726A
Red/Black	•		•	727/727A
Black	•		•	728/728A
Blue			•	729
Green			•	730
White/Red			•	731
White/Turquoise			•	732
White/Yellow			•	733
White/Black			•	734
Beige/Buff			•	735
Black			•	736
Red/White/Black			•	737/737A
Coral/White/Black			•	738/738A
Pink/White/Black			•	739/739A
Turquoise/White/Black			•	740/740A
Yellow/White/Black			•	742/742A
Blue	•		•	744
Green	•		•	745
White/Champagne	•		•	746
Coral/Black	•		•	747/757A
Pink/Black	•		•	748/748A

THE DAY AND MONTH OF THE YEAR CODE indicates the day and month the car was assembled.

MONTH	CODE
January	A
February	B
March	C
April	D
May	E
June	F
July	G
August	H
September	J
October	K
November	L
December	M

THE ROTATION NUMBER indicates the cars numerical sequence of assembly.

ENGINE SPECIFICATIONS

CAPRI/PREMIERE

ENGINE CODE	NO. CYL	CID	HORSE POWER	COMP. RATIO	CARB
	8	368	300	10.0:1	4 BC

VEHICLE IDENTIFICATION NUMBER

• C 5 6 G 1 0 0 1 •

Located on the Patent Plate.

FIRST DIGIT: Identifies the car line code

CAR LINE	CODE
Continental	C

SECOND AND THIRD DIGITS: Identify the model year 1957

FOURTH DIGIT: Identifies the month the car was assembled (May)

NEXT FIVE DIGITS: Represent the basic production number

PATENT PLATE

THE PATENT PLATE includes the body style and body specifications in addition to the car serial number. The plate is located on the right front body pillar just below the upper hinge opening. It displays the serial number, body type, exterior color, trim scheme, day and month the car was assembled, and the production code.

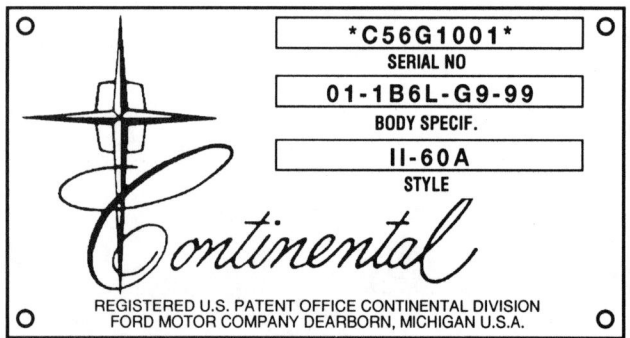

| *C56G1001* |
| SERIAL NO |
| 01-1B6L-G9-99 |
| BODY SPECIF. |
| II-60A |
| STYLE |

REGISTERED U.S. PATENT OFFICE CONTINENTAL DIVISION
FORD MOTOR COMPANY DEARBORN, MICHIGAN U.S.A.

EXAMPLE:

01	Black
1B6L	White/Gray leather
G	Month of year (May)
9	9th day of month
99	99th car assembled

THE COLOR CODE indicates the paint color used on the car.

COLOR	CODE
Black	01
Cobalt Blue Metallic	02
Pastorial Blue	04
Forest Green Metallic	05
Naiad Green	07
Briar Brown Metallic	08
Sandalwood	10
Dark Gray Metallic	11
Dark Red	13
Starmist White	14
Medium Blue	15
Medium Green	16
Medium Beige	17
Medium Gray	18

THE TRIM CODE indicates the key to the trim color and material for each model series.

COLOR	CLOTH	VINYL	LEATHER	CODE
Blue			•	1A1A
White/Blue			•	1B6B
White/Green			•	1B6E
White/Beige			•	1B6H
White/Gray			•	1B6K,1B6L
White/Red			•	1B6M
Green			•	1C2D
Beige			•	1D3G
Gray			•	1E4L
Gray/White			•	1E6L
Red/Gray			•	1F4M
Red/White			•	1F6M
Gray/White			•	1G6K
Beige/White			•	1L6H
Green			•	1M6E
Blue/White			•	1N6B
Blue	•		•	2A1A
Green	•		•	2C2D
Beige	•		•	2D3G
Gray/White	•		•	2G6K
Gray	•		•	3E4L
Gray/White	•		•	3E6L
Red/Gray	•		•	3F4M
Red/White	•		•	3F6M

COLOR	CLOTH	VINYL	LEATHER	CODE
Blue	•		•	3H1C
Green	•		•	3J2F
Bronze/Beige	•		•	3K3J
Blue	•			4A1A
Green	•			4C2D
Beige	•			4D3G
Gray	•			5E4L
Red/Gray	•			5F4M
Blue	•			5H1C
Green	•			5J2F
Bronze/Beige	•			5K3J
Gray	•			6E4L
Red/Gray	•			6F4M
Blue	•			6H1C
Green	•			6J2F
Bronze/Beige	•			6K3J

THE DAY AND MONTH OF THE YEAR CODE indicates the day and month the car was assembled.

MONTH	CODE
January	C
February	D
March	E
April	F
May	G
June	H
July	I
August	J
September	K
October	L
November	M
December	N

THE ROTATION NUMBER indicates the cars numerical sequence of assembly.

THE BODY STYLE indicates the body style of the vehicle.

BODY STYLE	CODE
Coupe	60A

ENGINE SPECIFICATIONS

ENGINE CODE	NO. CYL	CID	HORSE POWER	COMP. RATIO	CARB
	8	368	300	10.0:1	4 BC

1958 LINCOLN CONTINENTAL

1958 LINCOLN

VEHICLE IDENTIFICATION NUMBER

• H 8 Y G 4 0 0 0 0 4 •

Located on the Patent Plate.

FIRST DIGIT: Identifies the engine

ENGINE	CODE
430 cid, 4 BC..H
430 cid, 3-2 BC..J

SECOND DIGIT: Identifies the model year 1958

THIRD DIGIT: Identifies the assembly plant

ASSEMBLY PLANT	CODE
Wixom, MI...Y

FOURTH DIGIT: Identifies the body style

CONTINENTAL MARK III

BODY STYLE	CODE
2-Dr. hardtop ....E
4-Dr. hardtop ....F
4-Dr. sedan...M
2-Dr. convertible..G

CAPRI

BODY STYLE	CODE
2-Dr. hardtop ....A
4-Dr. hardtop ....B
4-Dr. sedan...K

PREMIERE

BODY STYLE	CODE
2-Dr. hardtop C
4-Dr. hardtop ....D
4-Dr. sedan...L

LAST SIX DIGITS: Represent the basic production number

PATENT PLATE

THE PATENT PLATE includes the body style and body specifications in addition to the car serial number. The plate is located on the right front body pillar just below the upper hinge opening. It displays the serial number, body type, exterior color, trim scheme, day and month the car was assembled, and the production code.

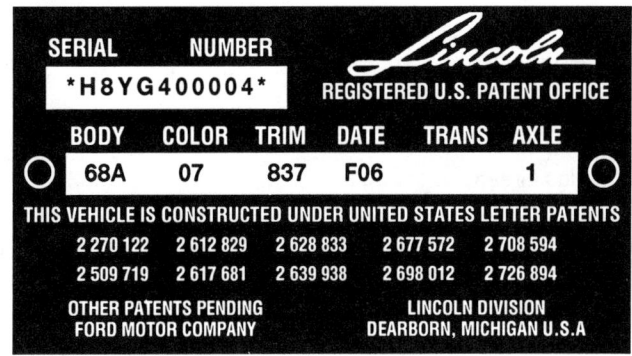

EXAMPLE:

68A...Continental conv.
07 ....Starmist White
837 ....Blue/White leather
F ....Month of year (June)
06 ....6th day of month
....Transmission type
1 ....Axle type

THE BODY TYPE CODE indicates the body type.

CAPRI

BODY TYPE	CODE
4-Dr. sedan..53A
4-Dr. hardtop 57A
2-Dr. hardtop 63A

PREMIERE

BODY TYPE	CODE
4-Dr. sedan..53B
4-Dr. hardtop 57B
2-Dr. hardtop 63B

CONTINENTAL

BODY TYPE	CODE
4-Dr. sedan..54A
4-Dr. hardtop 75A
2-Dr. hardtop 65A
2-Dr. convertible...68A

THE COLOR CODE indicates the paint color used on the car.

COLOR	CODE
Presidential Black	01
Spartan Gray Metallic	02
Athenian Gray	03
Arrowhead Blue Metallic	04
Seneca Blue Metallic	05
Shasta Blue	06
Starmist White	07
Spruce Green Metallic	08
Douglas Green	09
Sequoia Green	10
Jade	11
Suede	12
Deauville Yellow	13
Copper	14
Autumn Rose	15
Sunset	16
Rosemetal	17
Matador Red	18
Claret Metallic	19
Champagne	20
Platinum	23
Silver Metallic	24
Copper Metallic	25
Rosemetal Metallic	26

TWO-TONE COLORS

COLOR	CODE
Athenian Gray (Light)/Presidential Black	40
Athenian Gray (Light)/Spartan Gray Metallic (Dark)	42
Spartan Gray Metallic (Dark)/ Athenian Gray (Light)	43
Starmist White/Spartan Gray Metallic (Dark)	44
Spartan Gray Metallic (Dark)/ Starmist White	45
Starmist White/Athenian Gray (Light)	46
Athenian Gray (Light)/Starmist White	47
Shasta Blue (Light)/Arrowhead Arrowhead Blue Metallic (Dark)/ Shasta Blue (Light)	49
Starmist White/Arrowhead Blue Metallic (Dark)	50
Arrowhead Blue Metallic (Dark)/ Starmist White	51
Shasta Blue (Light)/Seneca Blue Metallic (Medium)	52

Seneca Blue Metallic (Medium)/ Shasta Blue (Light)	53
Starmist White/Seneca Blue Metallic (Medium)	54
Seneca Blue Metallic (Medium)/ Starmist White	55
Starmist White/Shasta Blue (Light)	56
Starmist White/Presidential Black	57
Presidential Black/Starmist White	58
Sequoia Green (Light)/Spruce Green Metallic (Dark)	59
Spruce Green Metallic (Dark)/ Sequoia Green (Light)	60
Starmist White/Spruce Green Metallic (Dark)	61
Sequoia Green (Light)/Douglas Green	62
Jade/Douglas Green	64
Silver Metallic/Jade	65
Starmist White/Silver Metallic	66
Silver Metallic/Starmist White	67
Jade/Sequoia Green (Light)	68
Sequoia Green (Light)/Jade	69
Starmist White/Sequoia Green (Light)	70
Sequoia Green (Light)/Starmist White	71
Presidential Black/Deauville Yellow	72
Deauvile Yellow/Presidential Black	73
Starmist White/Deauville Yellow	74
Deauville Yellow/Rosemetal (Walnut) Metallic	75
Starmist White/Rosemetal (Walnut) Metallic	76
Rosemetal (Walnut) Metallic/ Starmist White	77
Sunset/Rosemetal (Walnut) Metallic	78
Presidential Black/Matador Red	79
Matador Red/Presidential Black	80
Starmist White/Matador Red	81
Matador Red/Starmist White	82
Starmist White/Suede	83
Suede/Starmist White	84
Presidential Black/Jade	85
Starmist White/Jade	87
Jade/Starmist White	88
Starmist White/Sunset	89
Sunset/Starmist White	90
Presidential Black/Autumn Rose	93
Starmist White/Autumn Rose	95
Autumn Rose/Starmist White	96
Starmist White/Copper (Amber) Metallic	97
Copper (Amber) Metallic/Starmist White	98
Starmist White/Claret Metallic	99

COLOR	CODE
Claret Metallic/Starmist White	100
Sunset/Spartan Gray Metallic (Dark)	101
Spartan Gray Metallic (Dark)/Sunset	102
Presidential Black/Champagne	103
Champagne/Presidential Black	104
Starmist White/Champagne	105
Champagne/Starmist White	106
Shasta Blue (Light)/Starmist White	115
Spruce Green Metallic (Dark)/ Starmist White	116
Deauville Yellow/Starmist White	117
Rosemetal (Walnut) Metallic/ Deauville Yellow	118
Rosemetal (Walnut) Metallic/Sunset	119
Champagne/Rosemetal (Walnut) Metallic	120
Rosemetal (Walnut) Metallic/Champagne	121
Champagne/Jade	126
Jade/Champagne	127
Champagne/Douglas Green	128
Athenian Gray (Light)/Matador Red	130
Champagne/Spruce Green Metallic (Dark)	132
Spruce Green Metallic (Dark)/Champagne	133
Sunset/Athenian Gray (Light)	137
Champagne/Matador Red	139
Champagne/Suede	143
Suede/Champagne	144
Deauville Yellow/Suede	145
Suede/Deauville Yellow	146
Champagne/Copper (Amber) Metallic	147
Copper (Amber) Metallic/Champagne	148
Presidential Black/Copper (Amber) Metallic	149
Deauville Yellow/Spartan Gray Metallic (Dark)	159
Spartan Gray Metallic (Dark)/ Deauville Yellow	160
Champagne/Sequoia Green (Light)	163
Sequoia Green (Light)/Champagne	164
Suede/Presidential Black	169
Athenian Gray (Light)/Autumn Rose	173

COLOR	CODE
Presidential Black/Platinum	187
Platinum/Presidential Black	188
Arrowhead Blue Metallic (Dark)/Platinum	189
Platinum/Arrowhead Blue Metallic (Dark)	190
Seneca Blue Metallic (Medium)/Platinum	191
Platinum/Seneca Blue Metallic (Medium)	192
Shasta Blue (Light)/Platinum	193
Platinum/Shasta Blue (Light)	194
Spartan Gray Metallic (Dark)/Platinum	195
Platinum/Spartan Gray Metallic (Dark)	196
Starmist White/Copper Metallic	201
Copper Metallic/Starmist White	202
Silver Metallic/Presidential Black	203
Presidential Black/Silver Metallic	204
Silver Metallic/Starmist White	205
Starmist White/Silver Metallic	206
Silver Metallic/Deauville Yellow	207
Deauville Yellow/Silver Metallic	208
Champagne/Rosemetal Metallic	209
Rosemetal Metallic/Champagne	210
Sunset/Copper Metallic	213
Copper Metallic/Sunset	214
Champagne/Copper Metallic	215
Copper Metallic/Champagne	216
Silver Metallic/Autumn Rose	227
Autumn Rose/Silver Metallic	228
Silver Metallic/Jade	229
Jade/Silver Metallic	230
Silver Metallic/Claret Metallic	233
Claret Metallic/Silver Metallic	234
Silver Metallic/Sunset	237
Sunset/Silver Metallic	238
Silver Metallic/Shasta Blue	243
Shasta Blue/Silver Metallic	244
Rosemetal Metallic/Deauville Yellow	249
Deauville Yellow/Rosemetal Metallic	250
Starmist White/Rosemetal Metallic	251
Rosemetal Metallic/Starmist White	252
Sunset/Rosemetal Metallic	253
Rosemetal Metallic/Sunset	254

THE TRIM CODE indicates the key to the trim color and material for each model series.

COLOR	CLOTH	VINYL	LEATHER	CODE
Gray	•			801
Blue	•			802
Green	•			803
Brown	•			804
Black		•		805
Beige		•		806
Blue/White		•		807
Green/White		•		808
Red/White/Black		•		809
Beige/White/Buff		•		810
Dk. Gray	•			811
Dk. Blue	•			812
Dk. Green	•			813
Brown	•			814
Green	•		•	815
Blue	•		•	816
Green	•		•	817
Beige/Brown	•		•	818
Gray	•		•	819
Blue	•		•	820
Black	•		•	821
White/Black	•		•	822
Red/Black	•		•	823
Green/Gray	•			824
Blue	•			825
Green	•			826
Green	•		•	827
Blue	•		•	828
Green	•		•	829
Brown	•		•	830
Red/Gray	•		•	831
Beige/Brown	•		•	832
Gray	•		•	833
Black	•		•	834
Black			•	835
Beige			•	836
Blue/White			•	837
Green/White			•	838
Red/White/Black			•	839
Beige/White/Buff			•	840
Black/White			•	841
Gray	•			842
Green	•			843
Blue	•			844
Brown	•			845
Black/White			•	846
Special				849

THE DAY AND MONTH OF THE YEAR CODE indicates the day and month the car was assembled.

MONTH	CODE
January	A
February	B
March	C
April	D
May	E
June	F
July	G
August	H
September	J
October	K
November	L
December	M

THE ROTATION NUMBER indicates the cars numerical sequence of assembly.

ENGINE SPECIFICATIONS

9-42

ENGINE CODE	NO. CYL	CID	HORSE POWER	COMP. RATIO	CARB
	8	430	375	10.5:1	4 BC
	8	430	400	10.5;1	3-2 BC

1959 LINCOLN

1959 LINCOLN

VEHICLE IDENTIFICATION NUMBER

`• H9YA400004 •`

Located on the Patent Plate.

FIRST DIGIT: Identifies the engine

ENGINE	CODE
Lincoln	H

SECOND DIGIT: Identifies the model year 1959

THIRD DIGIT: Identifies the assembly plant

ASSEMBLY PLANT	CODE
Wixom, MI	Y

FOURTH DIGIT: Identifies the body series

BODY STYLE	CODE
Lincoln	A
Premiere	B
Continental Mark IV	C

LAST SIX DIGITS: Represent the basic production number

PATENT PLATE

THE PATENT PLATE includes the body style and body specifications in addition to the car serial number. The plate is located on the right front body pillar just below the upper hinge opening. It displays the serial number, body type, exterior color, trim scheme, day and month the car was assembled, and the rear axle ratio.

SERIAL	NUMBER	*Lincoln*
H9YA	400004	REGISTERED U.S. PATENT OFFICE

BODY	COLOR	TRIM	DATE	TRANS	AXLE
63A	01	901	24L		1

THIS VEHICLE IS CONSTRUCTED UNDER UNITED STATES LETTER PATENTS
2 270 122 2 612 829 2 628 833 2 677 572 . 2 708 594
2 509 719 2 617 681 2 639 938 2 698 012 2 726 894

OTHER PATENTS PENDING   LINCOLN DIVISION
FORD MOTOR COMPANY   DEARBORN, MICHIGAN U.S.A

EXAMPLE:

63A	Capri 2-dr. coupe
01	Presidential Black
901	Med. Gray cloth
24	24th day of month
L	Month of year (November)
	Transmission type
1	Axle type

THE BODY TYPE CODE indicates the body type.

LINCOLN
BODY TYPE CODE	
2-Dr. hardtop	63A
4-Dr. hardtop	57A
4-Dr. sedan	53A

PREMIERE
BODY TYPE	CODE
2-Dr. hardtop	63B
4-Dr. hardtop	57B
4-Dr. sedan	53B

CONTINENTAL MARK IV
BODY TYPE	CODE
2-Dr. hardtop	65A
4-Dr. hardtop	75A
4-Dr. sedan	54A
2-Dr. convertible	68A
Executive limo	23A
4-Dr. Formal sedan	23B

THE COLOR CODE indicates the paint color used on the car. On two-tone combinations the first two paint code numbers indicate the upper color, the second two numbers indicate the lower color.

COLOR	CODE
Presidential Black	01
Glacier White	07
Linden Green	15
Palm green	16
Peacock Green Poly	17
Crystal Blue	27
Pearl Blue Poly	28
Midnight Blue Poly	29
Claret Poly	40
Bolero Red	45
Silver Poly	55
Tawn	60
Sunstone	66
Deauville Yellow	75
Platinum	80
Copper Poly	81
Copper Poly	82
Cameo Rose	83
Aquamarine	88
Burnished Gold Poly	92
Sapphire Poly	97

THE TRIM CODE indicates the key to the trim color and material for each model series.

LINCOLN

COLOR	CLOTH	VINYL	LEATHER	CODE
Gray/Gray	•			901
Blue/Blue	•			902
Green/Green	•			903
Gold/Gold	•			904
Gray/Gray	•	•		905
Blue/Blue	•	•		906
Green/Green	•	•		907
Gold/Gold	•	•		908
White/Black	•	•		909

LINCOLN PREMIERE

COLOR	CLOTH	VINYL	LEATHER	CODE
Gray/Gray	•			913
Blue/Blue	•			914
Gold/Gold	•			915
Green/Green	•			916
White/Gold	•		•	917
White/Black	•		•	918
Red/Black	•		•	919
Pink/Black	•		•	920
Beige/Buff	•		•	922
Blue/Blue	•		•	923
Green/Green	•		•	924
White/Black			•	925
Blue/Blue			•	926
Turquoise/Turquoise			•	927
White/Pink			•	928
Beige			•	929

CONTINENTAL MARK IV

COLOR	CLOTH	VINYL	LEATHER	CODE
Gray/Gray	•			934
Blue/Blue	•			935
Gold/Gold	•			936
Blue/Blue	•		•	937
Green/Green	•		•	938
Turquoise/Turquoise	•		•	939
White/Gold	•		•	940
Red/Black	•		•	941
White/Black	•		•	942
Pink/Black	•		•	943
Gray/Gray	•		•	944

COLOR	CLOTH	VINYL	LEATHER	CODE
Gold/Gold	•		•	945
White/Black			•	*946
Blue/Blue			•	*947
Turquoise/Turquoise			•	*948
Gold/Gold			•	*949
White/Pink			•	*950
Beige			•	*951
Red			•	**952
Black			•	**953

* Also used on convertible

** Convertible only

THE DAY AND MONTH OF THE YEAR CODE indicates the day and month the car was assembled.

MONTH	CODE
January	A
February	B
March	C
April	D
May	E
June	F
July	G
August	H
September	J
October	K
November	L
December	M

THE REAR AXLE RATIO CODE indicates the type of rear axle installed in the vehicle.

RATIO	CODE
2:89	1
3:11	2

ENGINE SPECIFICATIONS

The engine production code number indicates the place, day and month of the engine manufacture. It is located on the cylinder block directly in front of the left cylinder head.

ENGINE CODE	NO. CYL	CID	HORSE POWER	COMP. RATIO	CARB
	8	430	350	10.0:1	4 BC

1950 MERCURY MONTEREY

1950 MERCURY

1950 MERCURY

VEHICLE IDENTIFICATION NUMBER

`• 5 0 L A 1 2 3 4 M •`

Located on the right-hand front body hinge pillar.

FIRST AND SECOND DIGITS: Identify the model year 1950

THIRD AND FOURTH DIGITS: Identify the assembly plant

ASSEMBLY PLANT	CODE
Dearborn, MI	DA
Los Angeles, CA	LA
Metuchen, NJ	ME
St. Louis, MO	SL

NEXT FOUR DIGITS: Represent the basic production number at each plant

LAST DIGIT: Identifies the car line code

CAR LINE	CODE
Mercury	M

BODY PLATE

THE BODY PLATE is located on the left hand front body hinge pillar on the early 1950 models and on the right hand front body hinge pillar on the late 1950 models. The plate indicates the assembly plant, body type, exterior color, trim scheme, production code and it's numerical sequence of assembly.

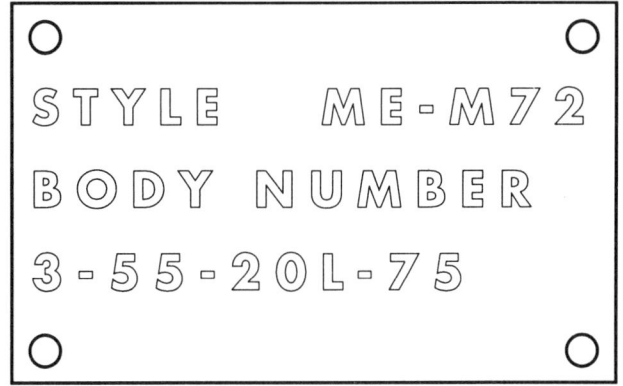

EXAMPLE:

ME	Metuchen, NJ
M72	Mercury 6-pass. coupe
3	Banning Blue
55	Tan Bedford Cord
20	20th day of month
L	Month of year (November)
75	Rotation number

THE ASSEMBLY PLANT CODE indicates the assembly plant.

ASSEMBLY PLANT	CODE
Dearborn, MI	DA
Los Angeles, CA	LA
Metuhen, NJ	ME
St. Louis, MO	SL
Wayne, MI	W

THE BODY TYPE CODE indicates the body type.

BODY TYPE	CODE
Coupe, standard, 6-pass.	M72-A
Coupe, deluxe, 6-pass.	M72-B
Coupe, custom, 6-pass. (Monterey)	M72-C
Sport sedan	M74
Convertible coupe, 6-pass.	M76
Station wagon	M79

THE COLOR CODE indicates the paint color used on the car.

COLOR	CODE
Black	01
Banning Blue	03
Royal Bronze Maroon	05
Trojan Gray	07
Dune Beige	09
Everglade Green	11
Maywood Green	13
Laguna Blue	15
Roanoke Green	17
Mirada Yellow	19

MONTEREY

COLOR	CODE
Black	01
Cortaro Red Metallic	—
Turquoise Blue	203

TWO-TONE COLORS

COLOR	CODE
Maywood Green/Trojan Gray	26
Dune Beige/Penrod Tan	27
Penrod Tan/Dune Beige	31
Trojan Gray/Roanoke Green	33
Roanoke Green/Trojan Gray	35
Trojan Gray/Banning Blue	37
Banning Blue/Trojan Gray	39
Trojan Gray/Laguna Blue	41
Laguna Blue/Trojan Gray	43

* First color is the upper color; second color is the bottom color.

THE TRIM CODE indicates the key to the trim color and material for each model series.

COLOR	CLOTH	VINYL	LEATHER	CODE
Blue	•			52
Tan/Brown	•			55
Blue Gray	•			58
Blue Gray	•			60
Tan Gray	•			62
Tan (two-tone)			•	66
Red/Black			•	68
Blue/Gray			•	70
Tan			•	72
Red			•	74
Green			•	76
Blue/Blue	•		•	81

MONTERY TRIM

COLOR	CLOTH	VINYL	LEATHER
Black/Yellow			•
Red	•		•
Turquoise	•		•

THE DAY AND MONTH OF THE YEAR CODE indicates the day and month the car was assembled.

MONTH	CODE
January	A
February	B
March	C
April	D
May	E
June	F
July	G
August	H
September	J
October	K
November	L
December	M

THE ROTATION NUMBER indicates the cars numerical sequence of assembly.

ENGINE SPECIFICATIONS

ENGINE CODE	NO. CYL	CID	HORSE POWER	COMP. RATIO	CARB
8BA,1BA	8	255	110	6.8:1	2 BC

1951 MERCURY STATION WAGON

1951 MERCURY

1951 MERCURY

1951 MERCURY

1951 MERCURY

VEHICLE IDENTIFICATION NUMBER

`• 5 1 D A 1 2 3 4 5 M •`

Located on the right-hand front body hinge pillar.

FIRST AND SECOND DIGITS: Identify the model year 1951

THIRD AND FOURTH DIGITS: Identify the assembly plant

ASSEMBLY PLANT	CODE
Dearborn, MI	DA
Los Angeles, CA	LA
Metuchen, NJ	ME
St. Louis, MO	SL

NEXT FIVE DIGITS: Represent the basic production number at each plant

LAST DIGIT: Identifies the car line code

CAR LINE	CODE
Mercury	M

BODY PLATE

THE BODY PLATE indicates the assembly plant, body type, exterior color, trim scheme, production code and it's numerical sequence of assembly.

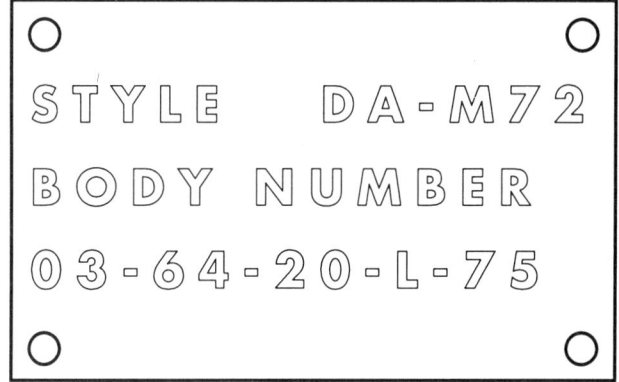

STYLE   DA-M72
BODY NUMBER
03-64-20-L-75

EXAMPLE:

DA	Dearborn, MI
M72	Mercury 6-pass. coupe
03	Banning Blue
64	Gray Block Broadcloth
20	20th day of month
L	Month of year (November)
75	Rotation number

THE ASSEMBLY PLANT CODE indicates the assembly plant.

ASSEMBLY PLANT	CODE
Dearborn, MI	DA
Los Angeles, CA	LA
Metuchen, NJ	ME
St. Louis, MO	SL

THE BODY TYPE CODE indicates the body type.

BODY TYPE	CODE
Coupe, deluxe, 6-pass.	M72-B
Coupe, custom, 6-pass. (Monterey)	M72-C
Sport sedan	M74
Convertible coupe, 6-pass.	M76
Station wagon	M79

THE COLOR CODE indicates the paint color used on the car.

COLOR	CODE
Black	01
Banning Blue Metallic	03
Luxor Maroon Metallic	05
Mission Gray	07
Tomah Ivory	09
Everglade Green	11
Sheffield Green	13
Kerry Blue Metallic	15
Academy Blue	15C
Coventry Green Gray	17
Vassar Yellow	19
Monterey Red	202
Turquoise Blue	203
Brewster Green Metallic	204
Yosemite Green Metallic	204A

TWO-TONE COLORS

COLOR	CODE
Black/Tomah Ivory	30
Tomah Ivory/Sheffield Green	31
Sheffield Green/Tomah Ivory	32
Coventry Green Gray/Everglade Green	33
Everglade Green/Coventry Green Gray	34
Sheffield Green/Coventry Green Gray	37
Coventry Green Gray/Sheffield Green	38
Mission Gray/Banning Blue	39
Banning Blue/Mission Gray	40

* First color is the upper color; second color is the bottom color.

THE TRIM CODE indicates the key to the trim color and material for each model series.

COLOR	CLOTH	VINYL	LEATHER	CODE
Tan	•			60
Tan/Gray	•			62
Gray	•			64
Gray/Rust	•			64A
Blue	•			66
Green	•			68
Red/Black			•	72
Tan/Brown			•	74
Blue/Ivory			•	76
Blue	•		•	78
Red			•	80
Green			•	82
Tan/Rust	•			84
Green	•			97
Brown	•			98
Black/Red			•	202
Brown/Turquoise	•		•	203
White/Green	•		•	204

THE DAY AND MONTH OF THE YEAR CODE indicates the day and month the car was assembled.

MONTH	CODE
January	A
February	B
March	C
April	D
May	E
June	F
July	G
August	H
September	J
October	K
November	L
December	M

THE ROTATION NUMBER indicates the cars numerical sequence of assembly.

ENGINE SPECIFICATIONS

ENGINE CODE	NO. CYL	CID	HORSE POWER	COMP. RATIO	CARB
1CM	8	255.4	112	6.8:1	2 BC

1952 MERCURY MONTEREY

1952 MERCURY

1952 MERCURY

VEHICLE IDENTIFICATION NUMBER

●52SL10005M●

Located on the right-hand front body hinge pillar.

FIRST AND SECOND DIGITS: Identify the model year 1952

THIRD AND FOURTH DIGITS: Identify the assembly plant

ASSEMBLY PLANT	CODE
Lincoln Plant, Detroit, MI	LP
Los Angeles, CA	LA
Metuchen, NJ	ME
St. Louis, MO	SL

NEXT FIVE DIGITS: Represent the basic production number at each plant

LAST DIGIT: Identifies the car line code

CAR LINE	CODE
Mercury	M

PATENT PLATE

THE PATENT PLATE is located on the right front body pillar just below the upper hinge opening. The plate indicates the serial number, assembly plant, body type, exterior color, trim scheme, production code and it's numerical sequence of assembly.

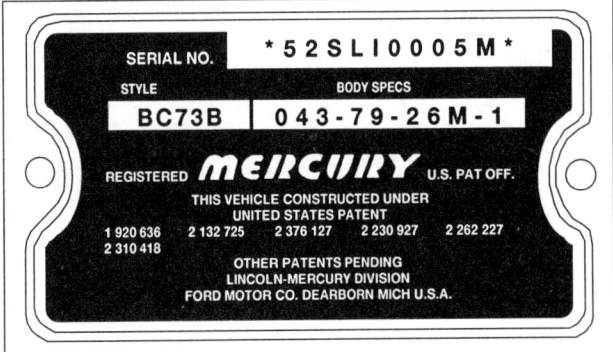

EXAMPLE:

BC73B	4-Dr. sedan
04E	Fanfare Maroon
79	Brown/White Broadcloth
26	26th day of month
M	Month of year (December)
1	Rotation number

THE BODY TYPE CODE indicates the body type.

CUSTOM

BODY TYPE	CODE
2-Dr. coupe	60E
2-Dr. sedan	70B
4-Dr. sedan	73B
4-Dr. station wagon, 6-pass.	79D
4-Dr. station wagon, 8-pass.	79B

MONTEREY

BODY TYPE	CODE
2-Dr. hardtop coupe	60B
4-Dr. sedan	73C
2-Dr. convertible	76B

THE COLOR CODE indicates the paint color used on the car.

COLOR	CODE
Raven Black	01L/01E
Admiral Blue	02L/02E
Fanfare Maroon	04L/04E
Newport Gray	05L/05E
Lucerne Blue	07L/07E
Pebble Tan	09L/09E
Academy Blue	10L/10E
Hillcrest Green	11L/11E
Coventry Green Gray	12L/12E
Lakewood Green	13L/13E
Vassar Yellow	19L/19E

TWO-TONE COLORS

COLOR	CODE
Lucerne Blue/Admiral Blue	20L/20E
Admiral Blue/Lucerne Blue	21L/21E
Hillcrest Green/Coventry Green Gray	24L/24E
Coventry Green Gray/Hillcrest Green	25L
Lakewood Green/Coventry Green Gray	28L/28E
Coventry Green Gray/Lakewood Green	29L/29E
Raven Black/Newport Gray	30L/30E
Newport Gray/Raven Black	31L/31E
Pebble Tan/Fanfare Maroon	32L/32E
Fanfare Maroon/Pebble Tan	33L/33E
Raven Black/Vassar Yellow	34L/34E
Vassar Yellow/Raven Black	35L/35E
Raven Black/Fanfare Maroon	42L/42E
Raven Black/Coventry Green Gray	43L/43E
Newport Gray/Academy Blue	44L/44E
Academy Blue/Newport Gray	45L/45E
Raven Black/Pebble Tan	46L/46E
Raven Black/Lucerne Blue	47L/47E
Raven Black/Lakewood Green	54L/54E

NOTE: First color is upper; second color is lower

L - Polishing Lacquer - Detroit plant

E - Baking Enamel - all other plants

THE TRIM CODE indicates the key to the trim color and material for each model series.

COLOR	CLOTH	VINYL	LEATHER	CODE
Brown/White	•			79
Gray	•			80
Green	•			81
Ivory/Green	•	•		82
Brown	•			83
Blue	•			84
Red	•	•		85
Black/Gray	•			86
Black/Red			•	88
Black/Red		•		88A
Green/Ivory			•	89
Green/Ivory		•		89A
Blue/Ivory			•	90
Blue/Ivory		•		90A
Bittersweet/Ivory			•	91
Bittersweet/Ivory		•		91A
Red/Ivory		•		92
Green/Ivory		•		94
Tan/Brown		•		95

THE DAY AND MONTH OF THE YEAR CODE indicates the day and month the car was assembled.

MONTH	CODE
January	A
February	B
March	C
April	D
May	E
June	F
July	G
August	H
September	J
October	K
November	L
December	M

THE ROTATION NUMBER indicates the cars numerical sequence of assembly.

ENGINE SPECIFICATIONS

ENGINE CODE	NO. CYL	CID	HORSE POWER	COMP. RATIO	CARB
	8	255	125	7.2:1	2 BC
	8	255	125	7.2:1	2 BC

1953 MERCURY MONTEREY

1953 MERCURY

1953 MERCURY

VEHICLE IDENTIFICATION NUMBER

• 5 3 S L 1 0 0 5 M •

Located on the right-hand front body hinge pillar.

FIRST AND SECOND DIGITS: Identify the model year 1953

THIRD AND FOURTH DIGITS: Identify the assembly plant

ASSEMBLY PLANT	CODE
Wayne, MI	WA
Los Angeles, CA	LA
Metuchen, NJ	ME
St. Louis, MO	SL

NEXT FIVE DIGITS: Represent the basic production number at each plant

LAST DIGIT: Identifies the car line code

CAR LINE	CODE
Mercury	M

PATENT PLATE

THE PATENT PLATE is located on the right front body pillar just below the upper hinge opening. The plate indicates the serial number, assembly plant, body type, exterior color, trim scheme, production code and it's numerical sequence of assembly.

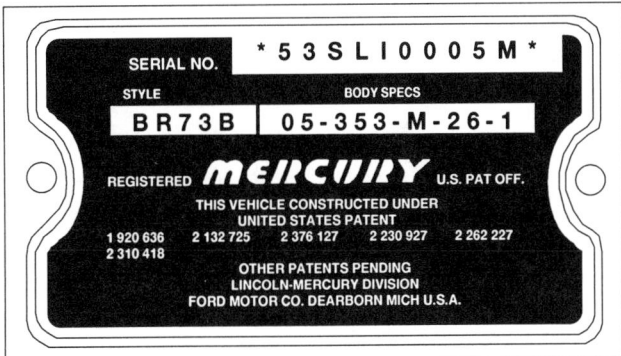

EXAMPLE:

BR73B	4-Dr. sedan
05	Glenwood Gray
353	Dk. Green/White Nylon
M	Month of year (December)
26	26th day of month
1	Rotation number

THE BODY TYPE CODE indicates the body type.

CUSTOM

BODY TYPE	CODE
2-Dr. hardtop	60E
2-Dr. sedan	70B
4-Dr. sedan	73B

MONTEREY

BODY TYPE	CODE
2-Dr. hardtop	60B
4-Dr. sedan	73C
Convertible	76B
4-Dr. station wagon, 8-pass.	79B

THE COLOR CODE indicates the paint color used on the car.

COLOR	CODE
India Black	01
Superior Blue Metallic	02
Mohawk Maroon Metallic	04
Glenwood Gray	05
Beechwood Brown Metallic	06
Brentwood Brown Metallic	06A
Banff Blue	07
Tahiti Tan	09
Sherwood Green Metallic	11
Pinehurst Green	12
Asheville Green	12A
Village Green Metallic	13
Bittersweet	17
Yosemite Yellow	19
Siren Red	20

TWO-TONE COLORS

COLOR	CODE
Banff Blue/Superior Blue Metallic	26
Super Blue Metallic/Banff Blue	27
Glenwood Gray/Superior Blue Metallic	28
Superior Blue Metallic/Glenwood Gray	29
India Black/Glenwood Gray	30
Glenwood Gray/India Black	31
Sherwood Green Metallic/Pinehurst Green	32
Sherwood Green Metallic/Asheville Green	32A
Pinehurst Green/Sherwood Green Metallic	33
Asheville Green/Sherwood Green Metallic	33A
India Black/Yosemite Yellow	34
Yosemite Yellow/India Black	35
Village Green Metallic/Pinehurst Green	36
Village Green Metallic/Asheville Green	36A
Pinehurst Green/Village Green Metallic	37
Asheville Green/Village Green Metallic	37A
Tahiti Tan/Mohawk Maroon Metallic	38
Mohawk Maroon Metallic/Tahiti Tan	39
Tahiti Tan/Beechwood Brown Metallic	40
Tahiti Tan/Brentwood Brown Metallic	40A
Beechwood Brown Metallic/Tahiti Tan	41
Brentwood Brown Metlalic/Tahiti Tan	41A
Tahiti Tan/Bittersweet	42
Bittersweet/Tahiti Tan	43
India Black/Bittersweet	44
Bittersweet/India Black	45
India Black/Banff Blue	46
Banff Blue/India Black	47
India Black/Pinehurst Green	58
India Black/Asheville Green	58A
India Black/Village Green Metallic	59
India Black/Tahiti Tan	60
India Black/Mohawk Maroon Metallic	61
India Black/Siren Red	65
Siren Red/India Black	66
Village Green/Tahiti Tan	67
Tahiti Tan/Village Green	68
Sherwood Green Metallic/Yosemite Yellow	69
Yosemite Yellow/Sherwood Green Metallic	70
Brentwood Brown Metallic/Asheville Green	71
Siren Red/Glenwood Gray	72
Yosemite Yellow/Brentwood Brown Metallic	73

THE TRIM CODE indicates the key to the trim color and material for each model series.

COLOR	CLOTH	VINYL	LEATHER	CODE
Brown/White	•			351
Gray/White	•			352
Green/White	•			353
Gray/White	•			354
Lt. Blue	•			355
Lt. Brown	•			356
Red/Black	•	•		357
Yellow/Black	•	•		358
Turquoise/Black	•	•		359
Blue/Black	•	•		360
Bittersweet/Black	•	•		361
Red/Black	•	•		362
Yellow/Black	•	•		363
Turquoise/Black	•	•		364
Bittersweet/Black	•	•		365
Red/Black		•		366
Yellow/Black		•		367
Turquoise/Ivory		•		368
Blue/Ivory		•		369
Bittersweet/Ivory		•		370
Red/Black			•	371
Yellow/Black			•	372
Turquoise/Ivory			•	373
Blue/Ivory			•	374
Bittersweet/Ivory			•	375
Red/Ivory		•		376
Turquoise/Ivory		•		377
Tan		•		378
Ivory/Dk. Green	•	•		379
Green/White	•			380

THE DAY AND MONTH OF THE YEAR

CODE indicates the day and month the car was assembled.

MONTH	CODE
January	A
February	B
March	C
April	D
May	E
June	F
July	G
August	H
September	J
October	K
November	L
December	M

THE ROTATION NUMBER indicates the cars numerical sequence of assembly.

ENGINE SPECIFICATIONS

ENGINE CODE	NO. CYL	CID	HORSE POWER	COMP. RATIO	CARB
	8	255	125	7.2:1	2 BC

1954 MERCURY

1954 MERCURY

VEHICLE IDENTIFICATION NUMBER

• 5 4 S L 1 0 0 5 M •

Located on the left-hand front body hinge pillar.

FIRST AND SECOND DIGITS: Identify the model year 1954

THIRD AND FOURTH DIGITS: Identify the assembly plant

ASSEMBLY PLANT	CODE
Wayne, MI	WA
Los Angeles, CA	LA
Metuchen, NJ	ME
St. Louis, MO	SL

NEXT FIVE DIGITS: Represent the basic production number at each plant

LAST DIGIT: Identifies the car line code

CAR LINE	CODE
Mercury	M

PATENT PLATE

THE PATENT PLATE is located on the left front body pillar just below the upper hinge opening. The plate indicates the serial number, body type, exterior color, trim scheme, production code and numerical sequence of assembly.

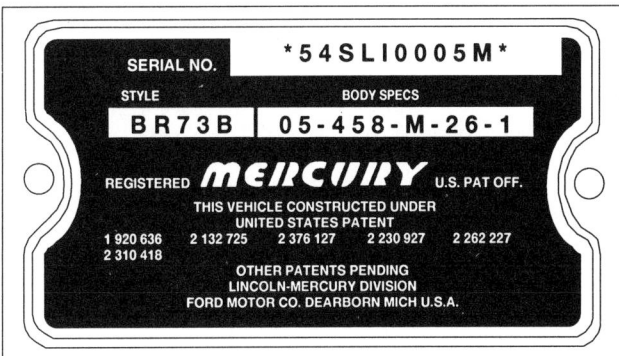

EXAMPLE:

BR73B	4-Dr. sedan
05	Granby Gray
458	Dk. Green/White Nylon
M	Month of year (December)
26	26th day of month
1	Rotation number

THE BODY TYPE CODE indicates the body type.

CUSTOM

BODY TYPE	CODE
2-Dr. hardtop coupe	60E
2-Dr. sedan	70B
4-Dr. sedan	73B

MONTEREY

BODY TYPE	CODE
2-Dr. hardtop coupe	60B
2-Dr. Sun Valley	60F
4-Dr. sedan	73C
2-Dr. convertible	76B
4-Dr. station wagon, 8-pass.	79B

THE COLOR CODE indicates the paint color used on the car.

COLOR	CODE
India Black	01
Atlantic Blue Metallic	02
Lakeland Blue	03
Mohawk Maroon Metallic	04
Granby Gray	05
Country Club Tan	08
Bloomfield Brown Metallic	10
Brentwood Brown Metallic	11
Glenoaks Green Metallic	12
Parklane Green	15
Bittersweet	17
Yosemite Yellow	18
Siren Red	21
Arctic White	22

TWO-TONE COLORS

COLOR	CODE
Bloomfield Green/Parklane Green	28
Arctic White/Parklane Green	29
Arctic White/Glenoaks Green	30
Arctic White/Bloomfield Green Metallic	31
Bloomfield Green/Country Club Tan	36
India Black/Siren Red	37
Arctic White/Atlantic Blue Metallic	40
Atlantic Blue Metallic/Arctic White	41
Arctic White/Lakeland Blue	44
Country Club Tan/Brentwood Brown Metallic	51
Atlantic Blue Metallic/Country Club Tan	60
Atlantic Blue Metallic/Granby Gray	61
Siren Red/Granby Gray	62
Arctic White/India Black	63
Arctic White/Siren Red	64
Arctic white/Bittersweet	65
Bittersweet/Arctic White	66
India Black/Bittersweet	67
India Black/Yosemite Yellow	68
Glenoaks Green Metallic/Yosemite Yellow	69
Bloomfield Green Metallic/Yosemite Yellow	70
Atlantic Blue Metallic/Lakeland Blue	71

NOTE: The first color is the upper color; the second color the lower color.

THE TRIM CODE indicates the key to the trim color and material for each model series.

COLOR	CLOTH	VINYL	LEATHER	CODE
Lt. Gray	•			451
Lt. Green	•			453
Lt. Blue	•			454
Calf		•		455
Dk. Green/White	•			458
Ivory/Dk. Gray	•	•		460
Ivory/Dk. Green	•	•		462
Ivory/Dk. Blue	•	•		463
Chestnut Brown/Calf		•		464
Red/Black	•	•		465
Bittersweet/Black	•	•		466
Turquoise/Ivory	•	•		467
Turquoise/Yellow	•	•		468
Red/Black		•		469

COLOR	CLOTH	VINYL	LEATHER	CODE
Bittersweet/Black		•		470
Turquoise/Yellow		•		471
Red/Ivory		•		473
Bittersweet/Ivory		•		474
Turquoise/Ivory		•		475
Dk. Blue/Ivory		•		476
Red/Black			•	477
Bittersweet/Black			•	478
Turquoise/Yellow			•	479
Red/Ivory			•	481
Bittersweet/Ivory			•	482
Turquoise/Ivory			•	483
Dk. Blue/Ivory			•	484

THE DAY AND MONTH OF THE YEAR

CODE indicates the day and month the car was assembled.

MONTH	CODE
January	A
February	B
March	C
April	D
May	E
June	F
July	G
August	H
September	J
October	K
November	L
December	M

THE ROTATION NUMBER indicates the cars numerical sequence of assembly.

ENGINE SPECIFICATIONS

ENGINE CODE	NO. CYL	CID	HORSE POWER	COMP. RATIO	CARB
EBY	8	256	161	7.5:1	4 BC

1955 MERCURY MONTCLAIR

1955 MERCURY MONTEREY

VEHICLE IDENTIFICATION NUMBER

`●55ME10005M●`

Located on the left-hand front body hinge pillar.

FIRST AND SECOND DIGITS: Identify the model year 1955

THIRD AND FOURTH DIGITS: Identify the assembly plant

ASSEMBLY PLANT	CODE
Wayne, MI	WA
Los Angeles, CA	LA
Metuchen, NJ	ME
St. Louis, MO	SL

NEXT FIVE DIGITS: Represent the basic production number at each plant

LAST DIGIT: Identifies the car line code

CAR LINE	CODE
Mercury	M

PATENT PLATE

THE PATENT PLATE is located on the left front body pillar just below the upper hinge opening. The plate indicates the serial number, body type, exterior color, trim scheme, production code and numerical sequence of assembly.

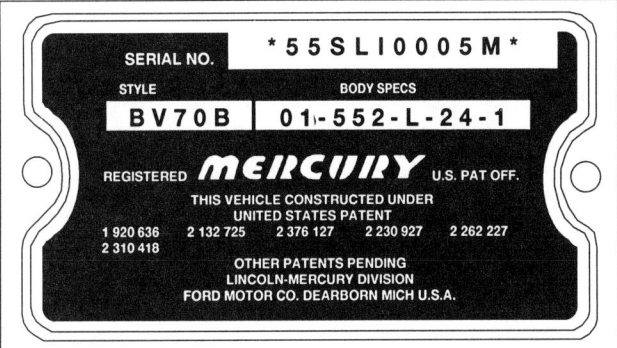

EXAMPLE:

BV70B	2-Dr. sedan
01	Tuxedo Black
552	Green Chevron Nylon
L	Month of year (December)
24	24th day of month
1	Rotation number

THE BODY TYPE CODE indicates the body type.

CUSTOM

BODY TYPE	CODE
2-Dr. hardtop coupe	60E
2-Dr. sedan	70B
4-Dr. sedan	73B
4-Dr. station wagon, 6-pass.	79B

MONTEREY

BODY TYPE	CODE
2-Dr. hardtop coupe	60B
4-Dr. sedan	73C
4-Dr. station wagon, 8-pass.	79C

MONTCLAIR

BODY TYPE	CODE
4-Dr. sedan	58A
2-Dr. hardtop coupe	64A
2-Dr. Sun Valley	64B
2-Dr. convertible	76B

THE COLOR CODE indicates the paint color used on the car.

COLOR	CODE
Tuxedo Black	01
Biltmore Blue	03
Gulfstream Blue Metallic	04
Kingstone Gray	05
Rockdale Gray Metallic	07
Forester Green Metallic	08
Springdale Green	14
Canyon Cordovan Metallic	15
Lime	16
Tropic Blue	17
Yukon Yellow	18
Arbor Green	20
Alaska White	22
Glen Lake Blue Metallic	24
Sea Isle Green Metallic	26
Carmen Red	29
Persimmon	31
Sun Glaze	203

TWO-TONE COLORS

COLOR	CODE
Forester Green Metallic/Springdale Green	32
Springdale Green/Forester Green Metallic	33
Alaska White/Sea Isle Green Metallic	35
Sea Isle Green Metallic/Alaska White	36
Sea Isle Green Metallic/Forester Green Metallic	38
Forester Green Metallic/Alaska White	39
Alaska White/Springdale Green	40
Tuxedo Black/Carmen Red	41
Forester Green Metallic/Yukon Yellow	62
Alaska White/Tuxedo Black	63
Tuxedo Black/Alaska White	64
Alaska White/Carmen Red	65
Carmen Red/Alaska White	66
Gulfstream Blue Metallic/Biltmore Blue	67
Biltmore Blue/Gulfstream Blue Metallic	68
Alaska White/Gulfstream Blue Metallic	69
Gulfstream Blue Metallic/Alaska White	70
Rockdale Gray/Kingstone Gray	71
Alaska White/Lime	72
Tuxedo Black/Yukon Yellow	77
Alaska White/Canyon Cordovan Metallic	78
Canyon Cordovan Metallic/Alaska White	79
Alaska White/Sun Glaze	80
Alaska White/Tropic Blue	81
Tropic Blue/Alaska White	82
Alaska White/Arbor Green	83
Arbor Green/Alaska White	84
Alaska White/Glen Lake Blue Metallic	85
Glen Lake Blue Metallic/Alaska White	86
Alaska White/Biltmore Blue	88
Alaska White/Persimmon	94
Rockdale Gray Metallic/Persimmon	95
Sea Isle Green Metallic/Springdale Green	201
Springdale Green/Sea Isle Green Metallic	202

THE TRIM CODE indicates the key to the trim color and material for each model series.

COLOR	CLOTH	VINYL	LEATHER	CODE
Green	•			552
Blue	•			553
White/Blue	•	•		554
White/Green	•	•		555
White/Red	•	•		556
White/Cordovan	•	•		557

COLOR	CLOTH	VINYL	LEATHER	CODE
Yellow/Black	•	•		558
Blue/White	•	•		559
White/Red		•		560
Yellow/Black		•		561
Green		•		562
Blue		•		563
Blue-Green/White		•		564
Green/White	•	•		565
Red/White	•	•		568
Gray	•			569
Calf		•		570
Black/Yellow	•	•		571
Cordovan/White		•		572
Black/Yellow		•		573
Black/White		•		574
Black/Yellow		•		583
Black/White		•		584
Red/White	•	•		585
Green/White	•	•		586
Blue/White	•	•		587
White/Red	•	•		588
Green	•	•		589
Lt. Blue/Blue	•	•		590
Red/White	•	•		591
Green/White	•	•		592
Blue/White	•	•		593

THE DAY AND MONTH OF THE YEAR

CODE indicates the day and month the car was assembled.

MONTH	CODE
January	A
February	B
March	C
April	D
May	E
June	F
July	G
August	H
September	J
October	K
November	L
December	M

THE ROTATION NUMBER indicates the cars numerical sequence of assembly.

ENGINE SPECIFICATIONS

The engine code is located on the head between the center rocker arm supports and in depression on the lower surface. All early engines had tan rocker arm covers.

ENGINE CODE	NO. CYL	CID	HORSE POWER	COMP. RATIO	CARB	TRANS
ECK	8	292	188	7.6:1	4 BC	ALL
ECL	8	292	198	8.5:1	4 BC	AUTO

1956 MERCURY CUSTOM MEDALIST

1956 MERCURY MEDALIST SERIES

1956 MERCURY MONTCLAIR

1956 MERCURY MONTCLAIR

VEHICLE IDENTIFICATION NUMBER

• 56ME10005M •

Located on the left-hand front body hinge pillar.

FIRST AND SECOND DIGITS: Identify the model year 1956

THIRD AND FOURTH DIGITS: Identify the assembly plant

ASSEMBLY PLANT	CODE
Wayne, MI	WA
Los Angeles, CA	LA
Metuchen, NJ	ME
St. Louis, MO	SL

NEXT FIVE DIGITS: Represent the basic production number at each plant

LAST DIGIT: Identifies the car line code

CAR LINE	CODE
Mercury	M

PATENT PLATE

THE PATENT PLATE is located on the left front body pillar just below the upper hinge opening. The plate indicates the serial number, body type, exterior color, trim scheme, production code and numerical sequence of assembly.

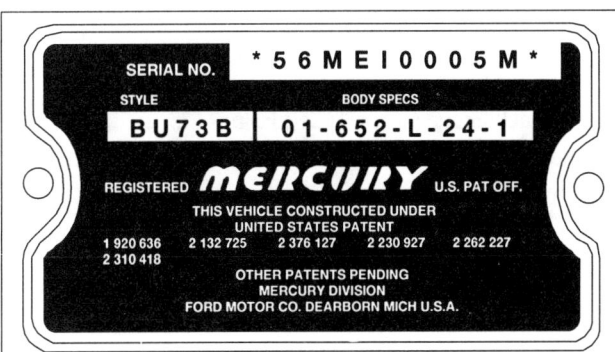

EXAMPLE:

BU73B	2-Dr. sedan
01	Tuxedo Black
652	Med. Blue matelasse/Lt. Blue vinyl
L	Month of year (November)
24	24th day of month
1	Rotation number

THE BODY TYPE CODE indicates the body type.

MEDALIST

BODY TYPE	CODE
4-Dr. hardtop	57D
2-Dr. hardtop	64E
2-Dr. sedan	70C
4-Dr. sedan	73D

CUSTOM

BODY TYPE	CODE
4-Dr. hardtop	57C
2-Dr. hardtop	64D
2-Dr. sedan	70B
4-Dr. sedan	73B
2-Dr. convertible	76A
Station wagon, 8-pass.	79B
Station wagon, 6-pass.	79D

MONTEREY

BODY TYPE	CODE
4-Dr. hardtop	57B
4-Dr. sport sedan	58B
2-Dr. hardtop	64C
4-Dr. sedan	73C
Station wagon, 8-pass.	79C

MONTCLAIR

BODY TYPE	CODE
4-Dr. hardtop	57A
4-Dr. sedan	58A
2-Dr. hardtop	64A
Convertible	76B

THE COLOR CODE indicates the paint color used on the car.

COLOR	CODE
Tuxedo Black	.01
Delta Blue Metallic	.03
Lauderdale Blue	.04
Niagara Blue	.05
London Gray Metallic	.07
Pinewood Green Metallic	.08
Heath Green	.14
Glamour Tan	.15
Grove Green	.17
Verona Green	.18
Saffron Yellow	.19
Cambridge Green	.20
Carousel Red	.21
Classic White	.23
Persimmon	.31

TWO-TONE COLORS

COLOR	CODE
Tuxedo Black/Saffron Yellow	.34
Niagra Blue/Delta Blue Metallic	.40
Delta Blue Metallic/Niagra Blue	.41
Carousel Red/Classic White	.55
Classic White/Carousel Red	.56
Classic White/London Gray Metallic	.62
Niagra Blue/Lauderdale Blue	.63
Lauderdale Blue/Niagra Blue	.64
Classic White/Lauderdale Blue	.65
Lauderdale Blue/Classic White	.66
Classic White/Niagra Blue	.67
Verona Green/Pinewood Green Metallic	.68
Pinewood Green Metallic/Verona Green	.69
Verona Green/Heath Green	.70
Heath Green/Verona Geren	.71
Classic White/Grove Green	.72
Tuxedo Black/Classic White	.75
Classic White/Tuxedo Black	.76
Classic White/Heath Green	.77
Heath Green/Classic White	.78
Classic White/Verona Green	.79
Classic White/Glamour Tan	.80

Glamour Tan/Classic White	.81
Classic White/Persimmon	.82
Persimmon/Classic White	.83
Tuxedo Black/Camridge Green	.86
Tuxedo Black/Grove Green	.87
Classic White/Cambridge Green	.88
Classic White/Saffron Yellow	.89
Persimmon/London Gray Metallic	.94
London Gray Metallic/Persimmon	.95
Tuxedo Black/Carousel Red	.96
Tuxedo Black/Saffron Yellow/Tuxedo Black	234
Saffron Yellow/Tuxedo Black/Saffron Yellow	235
Niagra Blue/Delta Blue Met./Niagra Blue	240
Delta Blue Met./Niagra Blue/Delta Blue	241
Carousel Red/Classic White/Carousel Red	255
London Gray Met./Classic White/London Gray Met.	262
Niagra Blue/Lauderdale Blue/Niagra Blue	263
Lauderdale/Niagra Blue/Lauderdale Blue	264
Lauderdale Blue/Classic White/Lauderdale Blue	266
Niagra Blue/Classic White/Niagra Blue	267
Verona Green/Pinewood Green Met./Verona Green	268
Pinewood Green Met./Verona Green/ Pinewood Green Met.	269
Verona Green/Heath Green/Verona Green	270
Heath Green/Verona Green/Heather Green	271
Grove Green/Classic White/Grove Green	272
Tuxedo Black/Classic White/Tuxedo Black	275
Heath Green/Classic White/Heather Green	278
Verona Green/Classic White/Verona Green	279
Classic White/Glamour Tan/Classic White	280
Glamour Tan/Classic White/Glamour Tan	281
Persimmon/Classic White/Persimmon	283
Tuxedo Black/Cambridge Green/Tuxedo Black	286
Tuxedo Black/Grove Green/Tuxedo Black	287
Cambridge Green/Classic White/Cambridge Green	288
Persimmon/London Gray Met./Persimmon	294
London Gray Met./Persimmon/London Gray Met.	295
Tuxedo Black/Carousel Red/Tuxedo Black	296
Carousel Red/Tuxedo Black/Carousel Red	297

THE TRIM CODE indicates the key to the trim color and material for each model series.

COLOR	CLOTH	VINYL	LEATHER	CODE
Lt. Gray/Black	•	•		650
Gray	•	•		651
Blue	•	•		652
Green	•	•		653
Gray/Black	•	•		654
Blue	•	•		655
Green	•	•		656
White/Black	•	•		657
Yellow/Black	•	•		658
Black/White	•	•		659
Black/Yellow	•	•		660
Blue	•	•		661
Green	•	•		662
Persimmon	•	•		663
Black/Yellow		•		664
Black/White		•		665
Persimmon/White		•		666
Blue		•		667
Green		•		668
Red/Silver	•	•		669
Black/Silver	•	•		670
Gold/Silver	•	•		672
Blue/Silver	•	•		673
Green/Silver	•	•		674
White/Red		•		675
White/Black		•		676
Yellow/Black		•		677
Gold		•		678

COLOR	CLOTH	VINYL	LEATHER	CODE
Persimmon		•		679
White/Black	•	•		680
Blue	•	•		681
Green	•	•		682
White/Black	•	•		683
Blue	•	•		684
Green	•	•		685
White/Black	•	•		686
Blue	•	•		687
Green	•	•		688

THE DAY AND MONTH OF THE YEAR CODE indicates the day and month the car was assembled.

MONTH	CODE
January	A
February	B
March	C
April	D
May	E
June	F
July	G
August	H
September	J
October	K
November	L
December	M

THE ROTATION NUMBER indicates the cars numerical sequence of assembly.

ENGINE SPECIFICATIONS

ENGINE CODE	NO. CYL	CID	HORSE POWER	COMP. RATIO	CARB	TRANS
ECZ-A	8	312	210	8.0:1	4 BC	STD
ECZ-B	8	312	215	8.4:1	4 BC	AUTO
ECZ-C	8	312	225	9.0:1	4 BC	ALL
ECZ-C	8	312	235	9.0:1	4 BC	AUTO
*	8	312	260	9.75:1	2X4 BC	

* The M-260 engine is optional equipment.

1957 MERCURY MONTCLAIR

1957 MERCURY PACE CAR

VEHICLE IDENTIFICATION NUMBER

> • 57ME10005M •

Located on the left-hand front body hinge pillar.

FIRST AND SECOND DIGITS: Identify the model year 1957

THIRD AND FOURTH DIGITS: Identify the assembly plant

ASSEMBLY PLANT	CODE
Wayne, MI	WA
Los Angeles, CA	LA
Metuchen, NJ	ME
St. Louis, MO	SL

NEXT FIVE DIGITS: Represent the basic production number at each plant

LAST DIGIT: Identifies the car line code

CAR LINE	CODE
Mercury	M

PATENT PLATE

THE PATENT PLATE is located on the right front body pillar just below the upper hinge opening. The plate indicates the serial number, body type, exterior color, trim scheme, production code and numerical sequence of assembly.

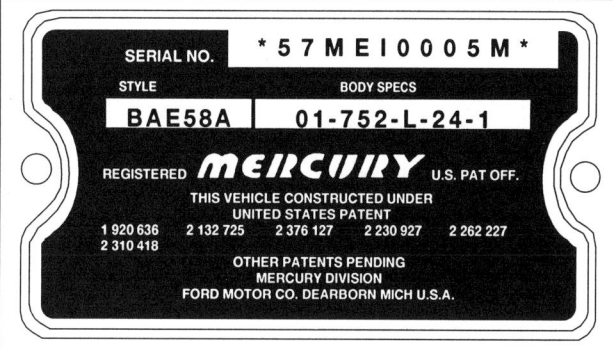

EXAMPLE:

BAE58A	4-Dr. sedan
01	Tuxedo Black
752	Med. Blue vinyl/Dk. Blue Mikato cloth
L	Month of year (November)
24	24th day of month
1	Rotation number

THE BODY TYPE CODE indicates the body type.

MONTEREY

BODY TYPE	CODE
4-Dr. hardtop	57A
4-Dr. sedan	58A
2-Dr. hardtop	63A
2-Dr. sedan	64A
2-Dr. convertible	76A

MONTCLAIR

BODY TYPE	CODE
4-Dr. hardtop	57B
4-Dr. sedan	58B
2-Dr. hardtop	63B
2-Dr. convertible	76B

TURNPIKE CRUISER

BODY TYPE	CODE
2-Dr. hardtop	65A
4-Dr. hardtop	75A
2-Dr. convertible	76S

STATION WAGON

BODY TYPE	CODE
Commuter, 2-dr.	56A
Commuter, 4-dr.	77A
Colony Park, 9-pass.	77B
Commuter, 4-dr., 9-pass.	77C
Voyager, 4-dr., 9-pass.	77D
Voyager, 2-dr.	56B

THE COLOR CODE indicates the paint color used on the car.

COLOR	CODE
Tuxedo Black	.01
Classic White	.06
Tahitian Green	.09
Moonmist Yellow	.13
Regency Gray	.21
Sherwood Green	.22
Pacific Blue	.23
Nantucket Blue	.24
Fiesta Red	.25
Brazilian Bronze	.26
Pastel Peach	.27
Desert Tan	.28
Persimmon	.29
Rosewood	.30
Lexington Green	.31
Sunset Orchid	.32
Sun Glitter	.2000

TWO-TONE COLORS

COLOR	CODE
Classic White/Tahitian Green	.70
Tahitian Green/Classic White	.71
Tuxedo Black/Tahitian Green	.74
Tuxedo Black/Moonmist Yellow	.75
Moonmist Yellow/Tuxedo Black	.76
Classic White/Moonmist Yellow	.77
Moonmist Yellow/Classic White	.78
Classic White/Tuxedo Black	.79
Tuxedo Black/Classic White	.80
Classic White/Regency Gray	.136
Regency Gray/Classic White	.137
Classiç White/Pacific Blue	.138
Pacific Blue/Classic White	.139
Nantucket Blue/Pacific Blue	.140
Pacific Blue/Nantucket Blue	.141
Classic White/Nantucket Blue	.142
Nantucket Blue/Classic White	.143
Nantucket Blue/Tuxedo Black	.144
Tuxedo Black/Nantucket Blue	.145
Classic White/Sherwood Green	.147
Tahitian Green/Sherwood Green	.148
Sherwood Green/Tahitian Green	.149
Pastel Peach/Rosewood	.150
Rosewood/Pastel Peach	.151
Pastel Peach/Tuxedo Black	.152
Tuxedo Black/Pastel Peach	.153
Pastel Peach/Desert Tan	.154
Desert Tan/Pastel Peach	.515
Pastel Peach/Brazilian Bronze	.156
Brazilian Bronze/Pastel Peach	.157
Classic White/Brazilian Bronze	.158
Brazilian Bronze/Classic White	.159
Desert Tan/Tuxedo Black	.160
Tuxedo Black/Desert Tan	.161
Desert Tan/Regency Gray	.162
Regency Gray/Desert Tan	.163
Classic White/Desert Tan	.164
Desert Tan/Classic White	.165
Moonmist Yellow/Regency Gray	.166
Regency Gray/Moonmist Yellow	.167
Classic White/Fiesta Red	.168
Fiesta Red/Classic White	.169
Tahitian Green/Tuxedo Black	.173
Tuxedo Black/Fiesta Red	.181
Fiesta Red/Tuxedo Black	.182
Rosewood/Tuxedo Black	.183
Tuxedo Black/Rosewood	.184
Classic White/Rosewood	.185
Rosewood/Classic White	.186
Classic White/Lexington Green	.187
Lexington Green/Classic White	.188
Classic White/Sunset Orchid	.189
Sunset Orchid/Classic White	.190
Pastel Peach/Persimmon	.191
Persimmon/Pastel Peach	.192
Classic White/Persimmon	.193
Persimmon/Classic White	.194
Sunset Orchid/Tuxedo Black	.195
Tuxedo Black/Sunset Orchid	.196

FLO-TONE COLORS

COLOR	CODE
Classic White/Regency Gray/Classic White	.236
Regency Gray/Classic White/Regency Gray	.237
Classic White/Pacific Blue/Classic White	.238
Pacific Blue/Classic White/Pacific Blue	.239
Nantucket Blue/Pacific Blue/Nantucket Blue	.240
Pacific Blue/Nantucket Blue/Pacific Blue	.241
Classic White/Nantucket Blue/Classic White	.242
Nantucket Blue/Classic White/Nantucket Blue	.243
Nantucket Blue/Tuxedo Black/Nantucket Blue	.244
Tuxedo Black/Nantucket Blue/Tuxedo Black	.245
Classic White/Sherwood Green/Classic White	.246
Sherwood Green/Classic White/Sherwood Green	.247
Tahitian Green/Sherwood Green/Tahitian Green	.248

THE TRIM CODE indicates the key to the trim color and material for each model series.

COLOR	CLOTH	VINYL	LEATHER	CODE
Lt. Gray/Dk. Gray	•	•		750
Gray/Black	•	•		751
Gray/Black/Silver	•	•		751B
Lt. Blue/Dk. Blue	•	•		752
Lt. Green/Dk. Green	•	•		753
Lt. Gold/Gold	•	•		754
White/Black	•	•		755
White/Black/Silver	•	•		755A
Med. Gray/Black/ Silver	•	•		755D
White/Blue	•	•		756
White/Green	•	•		757
Red/Black	•	•		758
Red/Black/Silver	•	•		758A
White/Black	•	•		759
Med. Gray/Black	•	•		759C
White/Dk. Blue	•	•		760
White/Dk. Green	•	•		761
Red/Black	•	•		762
White/Black	•	•		763
Med. Gray/Black	•	•		763A
Blue	•	•		764
Green	•	•		765
Gold	•	•		766
White/Black		•		767
White/Lt. Gold		•		769
Lt. Gold/Gold		•		769B
White/Red		•		770
Black/White		•		771
Med. Blue/White		•		772
Med. Green/White		•		773
Red/White		•		774
White/Black		•		776
White/Dk. Blue		•		777
White/Dk. Green		•		778
White/Red		•		779
White/Black		•		781
White/Dk. Blue		•		782
White/Dk. Green		•		783
White/Red		•		784
White/Black		•		786
White/Red		•		787
White/Med. Blue		•		788
White/Lt. Gold		•		789

COLOR	CLOTH	VINYL	LEATHER	CODE
Lt. Gold/Gold		•		789B
White/Med. Green		•		790
White/Black	•	•		792
White/Dk. Blue	•	•		793
White/Dk. Green	•	•		794
Red/Black	•	•		795
Lt. Gold/White		•		796
Lt. Blue/Dk. Blue	•	•		799
Lt. Green/Dk. Green	•	•		800
Black/Yellow		•		2005

THE DAY AND MONTH OF THE YEAR

CODE indicates the day and month the car was assembled.

MONTH	CODE
January	A
February	B
March	C
April	D
May	E
June	F
July	G
August	H
September	J
October	K
November	L
December	M

THE ROTATION NUMBER indicates the cars

numerical sequence of assembly.

ENGINE SPECIFICATIONS

MONTEREY/MONTCLAIR/STATION WAGONS

ENGINE CODE	NO. CYL.	CID	HORSE-POWER	COMP. RATIO	CARB	TRANS
ECZ	8	312	255	9.75:1	4 BC	ALL
ECU	8	368	290	9.75:1	4 BC	ALL
*	8	368	335	10.0:1	2X4 BC	MAN

* Monterey only

TURNPIKE CRUISER

ENGINE CODE	NO. CYL.	CID	HORSE-POWER	COMP. RATIO	CARB	TRANS
ECU	8	368	290	9.75:1	4 BC	AUTO

1958 MERCURY MONTCLAIR TURNPIKE CRUISER

1958 MERCURY MONTEREY

1958 MERCURY PARK LANE

VEHICLE IDENTIFICATION NUMBER

● M 8 W B 5 0 0 0 0 5 ●

Located on the right-hand front body hinge pillar.

FIRST DIGIT: Identifies the engine

ENGINE	CODE
312	L
383	M
430 (4 BC)	K
430 (3-2 BC)	J

SECOND DIGIT: Identifies the model year 1958

THIRD DIGIT: Identifies the assembly plant

ASSEMBLY PLANT	CODE
Wayne, MI	W
Los Angeles, CA #2	J
Metuchen, NJ	T
St. Louis, MO	Z
Somerville, MA	S

FOURTH DIGIT: Identifies the body type

BODY TYPE	CODE
2-Dr./4-Dr. sedan	A
Hardtop coupes/sedan	B
Convertible	C
Turnpike cruiser	D
2-Dr. station wagon	E
4-Dr. station wagon	F
Park Lane 2-dr./4-dr. hardtop	G
Park Lane convertible	J

FIFTH DIGIT: Identifies the number unique to Mercury line "5"

LAST DIGITS: Represent the basic production number at each plant

PATENT PLATE

THE PATENT PLATE is located on the right front body pillar just below the upper hinge opening. The plate indicates the serial number, body type, exterior color, trim scheme, production code, axle ratio, and transmission type.

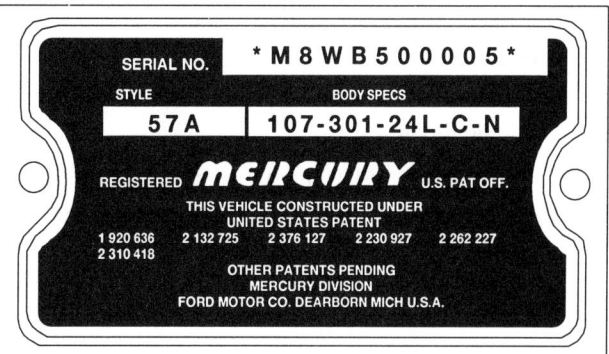

EXAMPLE:

57A	Monterey Phaeton sedan
107	Color (Marble White)
301	Med. Gray/Black vinyl
24	24th day of month
L	Month of year (November)
C	Automatic Transmission
N	2.91:1 Axle ratio

THE BODY TYPE CODE indicates the body type.

STANDARD (MEDALIST)

BODY TYPE	CODE
4-Dr. sedan	58C
2-Dr. sedan	64B

MONTEREY

BODY TYPE	CODE
4-Dr. hardtop	57A
4-Dr. sedan	58A
2-Dr. hardtop	63A
2-Dr. sedan	64A
2-Dr. convertible	76A

MONTCLAIR

BODY TYPE	CODE
4-Dr. hardtop	57B
4-Dr. sedan	58B
2-Dr. hardtop	63B
Turnpike cruiser, 2-dr.	65A
Turnpike cruiser, 4-dr.	75A
2-Dr. convertible	76B

PARKLANE

BODY TYPE	CODE
4-Dr. hardtop	57C
2-Dr. hardtop	63C
2-Dr. convertible	76C

STATION WAGON

BODY TYPE	CODE
2-Dr. commuter	56A
4-Dr. commuter, 6-pass.	77A
4-Dr. commuter, 9-pass.	77C
2-Dr. Voyager, 6-pass.	56B
4-Dr. Colony Park, 9-pass.	77B
4-Dr. Voyager, 9-pass.	77D

THE COLOR CODE indicates the paint color used on the car.

COLOR	CODE
Tuxedo Black	01
Marble White	07
Parisian Green	15
Emerald Metallic	16
Holley Green Metallic	17
Vineyard Blue	30
Jamaican Blue Metallic	31
Flamingo Red	45
Silver Sheen Metallic	55
Oxford Gray metallic	56
Autumn Beige	66
Mayfair Yellow	75
Shadow Rose	87
Golden Dust Metallic	92
Twilight Turquoise	97
Burgundy Metallic	99

NOTE: Exterior paints are prefixed with a single digit number denoting the paint scheme. The numbers following in two digit combinations denote actual area paint colors. On the solid tones the prefix (1) body side moulding area matches surrounding body color. Two-tone and flo-tone colors: The first two numbers indicate the upper body color; the second two numbers indicate the lower body color. On the two-tone color combinations the prefix (2) body side moulding area matches surrounding body color. On the flo-tone color combinations the prefix (4) body side moulding area same as surrounding body color.

THE TRIM CODE indicates the key to the trim color and material for each model series.

COLOR	CLOTH	VINYL	LEATHER	CODE
White/Black			•	102
Lt. Green/Dk. Green			•	120
Lt. Blue/Dk. Blue			•	135
Red			•	140
Gray/Black	•	•		201
White/Black	•	•		202
Green	•	•		215
Green/Dk. Green	•	•		220,221
Green/Dk. Green	•	•		222,223
Green/Dk. Green		•		224
Blue/Med. Blue	•	•		230
Blue/Dk. Blue	•	•		235,236
Blue/Dk. Blue	•	•		237,238
Blue/Dk. Blue		•		239
Med. Gray	•	•		253
Red/Med. Gray		•		254
Gray/Dk. Gray	•	•		256
Med. Gray/Charcoal	•	•		256A
Black/Dk. Gray		•		257
Gray/Black	•	•		257A
Gray/Dk. Gray	•	•		258
Med. Gray/Black	•	•		258A
Gold/Med. Gold	•	•		291,292
Gold/Med. Gold	•	•		293,294
Med. Gray/Black		•		301
Red/Black		•		302
Red/Black	•	•		303
Med. Gray/Black		•		304
Green/Dk. Green	•	•		320
Green/Dk. Green		•		321
Blue/Dk. Blue	•	•		335
Blue/Dk. Blue		•		336
Black/Red		•		340
Lt. Gold		•		390

THE DAY AND MONTH OF THE YEAR CODE indicates the day and month the car was assembled.

MONTH	CODE
January	A
February	B
March	C
April	D
May	E
June	F
July	G
August	H
September	J
October	K
November	L
December	M

THE TRANSMISSION CODE indicates the type of transmission installed in the vehicle.

TYPE	CODE
Conventional	A
Convention w/Overdrive	B
Automatic, single range (LM)	C
Automatic, dual range, multi-drive (LM)	D
Automatic, single range (HX)	E
Atuomatic, dual range, multi-drive (HX)	F

THE REAR AXLE CODE indicates the ratio of the rear axle installed in the vehicle.

RATIO	CODE
2.91:1	N
3.22:1	P
3.70:1	R
3.89:1	T

ENGINE SPECIFICATIONS

The engine codes are located at the lower right front cover bolt. 383 engines with circle "E" on the date code pad have .020" lower head gasket surface and require two head gaskets. The engine date code is stamped on the block in the front of the left cylinder head.

STANDARD (MEDALIST)

ENGINE CODE	NO. CYL.	CID	HORSE-POWER	COMP. RATIO	CARB
ECZ	8	312	255	9.7:1	4 BC

MONTEREY/MONTCLAIR/STATION WAGONS

ENGINE CODE	NO. CYL.	CID	HORSE-POWER	COMP. RATIO	CARB
EDG	8	383	312	10.5:1	4 BC
EDG	8	383	330	10.5:1	4 BC
EDJ	8	430	360	10.5:1	4 BC
EDJ	8	430	400	10.5:1	3X2 BC

PARKLANE

ENGINE CODE	NO. CYL.	CID	HORSE-POWER	COMP. RATIO	CARB
EDJ	8	430	360	10.5:1	4 BC
EDJ	8	430	400	10.5:1	3-2 BC

1959 MERCURY MONTEREY

1959 MERCURY PARK LANE

1959 MERCURY

VEHICLE IDENTIFICATION NUMBER

• N9WA500005 •

Located on the right-hand front body hinge pillar.

FIRST DIGIT: Identifies the engine

ENGINE	CODE
430 (3-2 BC)	K
430, 8-cyl.	L
383, 8-cyl. (4-BC)	M
383, 8-cyl. (2-BC)	N
312, 8-cyl.	P

SECOND DIGIT: Identifies the model year 1959

THIRD DIGIT: Identifies the assembly plant

ASSEMBLY PLANT	CODE
Los Angeles, CA #2	J
Metuchen, NJ	T
Wayne, MI	W
St. Louis, MO	Z

FOURTH DIGIT: Identifies the body type

BODY TYPE	CODE
Monterey	A
Montclair	B
Park Lane	C
Station wagon	D

FIFTH DIGIT: Identifies the number unique to Mercury line "5"

LAST DIGITS: Represent the basic production number at each plant

PATENT PLATE

THE PATENT PLATE is located on the right front body pillar just below the upper hinge opening. The plate indicates the serial number, body type, exterior color, trim scheme, production code, axle ratio, and transmission type.

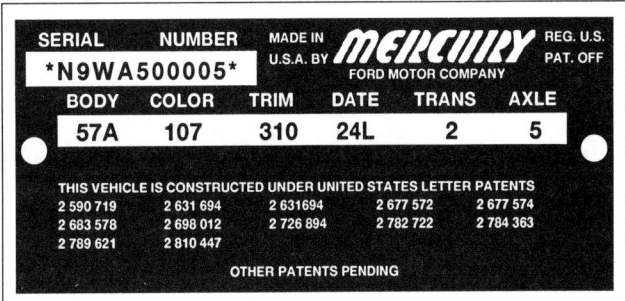

SERIAL	NUMBER	MADE IN U.S.A. BY	MERCURY FORD MOTOR COMPANY		REG. U.S. PAT. OFF
N9WA500005					
BODY	COLOR	TRIM	DATE	TRANS	AXLE
57A	107	310	24L	2	5

THIS VEHICLE IS CONSTRUCTED UNDER UNITED STATES LETTER PATENTS
2 590 719   2 631 694   2 631694   2 677 572   2 677 574
2 683 578   2 698 012   2 726 894   2 782 722   2 784 363
2 789 621   2 810 447

OTHER PATENTS PENDING

EXAMPLE:

57A	Monterey Phaeton sedan
107	Color (Marble White)
310	Lt. Green vinyl/Med. Green cloth
24	24th day of month
L	Month of year (November)
2	Automatic Transmission
5	2.91:1 Axle ratio

THE BODY TYPE CODE indicates the body type.

MONTEREY
BODY TYPE	CODE
4-Dr. hardtop	57A
4-Dr. sedan	58A
2-Dr. hardtop	63A
2-Dr. sedan	64A
2-Dr. convertible coupe	76A

MONTCLAIR
BODY TYPE	CODE
4-Dr. hardtop	57B
4-Dr. sedan	58B
2-Dr. hardtop	63B

PARK LANE
BODY TYPE	CODE
4-Dr. hardtop	57C
2-Dr. hardtop	63C
2-Dr. convertible	76C

STATION WAGONS

BODY TYPE	CODE
Commuter, 6-pass.	56A
Commuter, 6-pass.	77A
Colony Park, 6-pass.	77B
Voyager, 6-pass.	77D

THE COLOR CODE indicates the paint color used on the car.

COLOR	CODE
Tuxedo Black	01
Marble White	07
Sagebrush Green Metallic	16
Sherwood Green Metallic	17
Satellite Blue	27
Blue Ice Metallic	28
Canton Red	45
Silver Green Metallic	55
Charcoal Metallic	56
Autumn Smoke	66
Mederia Yellow	75
Bermuda Sand	83
Silver Beige Metallic	84
Twilight Turquoise	88
Golden Beige Metallic	92
Neptune Turquoise Metallic	97

NOTE: On two-tone color combinations the first two numbers indicate the upper body color; the second two numbers indicate the lower body color. The prefix single number denotes that the projectile area is in contrast to the surrounding body color.

THE TRIM CODE indicates the key to the trim color and material for each model series.

COLOR	CLOTH	VINYL	LEATHER	CODE
White/Black		•		201
Black		•		202
Lt. Blue/Med. Blue		•		225,226
White/Red		•		240
Red		•		242
White/Gold		•		280,281
White/Turquoise		•		282
Turquoise		•		283
White/Black	•	•		301
Green	•	•		310
Med. Green	•	•		311
Green	•	•		313
Blue	•	•		325,326
Med. Blue	•	•		328,329
Red/White	•	•		340
Taupe	•	•		350
Med. Taupe	•	•		351
Rose Beige	•	•		353
Red/Taupe	•	•		354
Med. Gold	•	•		380,381
Med. Gold/White	•	•		382
White/Med. Gold	•	•		383
Turquoise	•	•		384,385
Med. Taupe/White/ Med. Gold	•	•		386

THE DAY AND MONTH OF THE YEAR CODE indicates the day and month the car was assembled.

MONTH	CODE
January	A
February	B
March	C
April	D
May	E
June	F
July	G
August	H
September	J
October	K
November	L
December	M

THE TRANSMISSION CODE indicates the type of transmission installed in the vehicle.

TYPE	CODE
Standard	1
Automatic, single range, PBL-S-7000-B	2
Automatic, dual range, PBL-T-7000-T	3
Automatic, single range, PBM-G-7000-A	4
Automatic, single range, PBL-K-7000-B	5
Automatic, dual range, PBL-L-7000-C	6
Automatic, dual range, PBB-F-7000-F	7

THE REAR AXLE CODE indicates the ratio of the rear axle installed in the vehicle.

RATIO	CODE
2.91:1	1,5
2.71:1	2,3,4
3.10:1	6
3.56:1	7
3.22:1	8
3.89:1	9

ENGINE SPECIFICATIONS

The engine code number indicates the place, day and month of the engine manufacture. The 312 code is located on the front of the cylinder block at the pushrod cover-to-cylinder block mounting surface. The 383 and 430 code is located on the cylinder block directly in front of the left cylinder head.

ENGINE CODE	NO. CYL	CID	HORSE POWER	COMP. RATIO	CARB
P	8	312	210	9.6:1	2 BC
N	8	383	280	9.6:1	2 BC
M	8	383	322	9.2:1	4 BC
L	8	430	345	9.2:1	4 BC

1950 BUICK

1950 BUICK ROADMASTER

1950 BUICK

1950 BUICK SUPER DYNAFLOW

1950 BUICK DYNAFLOW

VEHICLE IDENTIFICATION NUMBER

● 5 3 6 0 0 0 1 ●

Located on a plate on the left front door pillar. The plate indicates the assembly plant and the production sequence number.

FIRST DIGIT: Identifies the assembly plant

ASSEMBLY PLANT	CODE
Flint, MI	1
South Gate, CA	2
Linden, NJ	3
Kansas City, KS	4
Wilmington, DE	5
Atlant, GA	6
Framingham, MA	7

LAST SIX DIGITS: Represent the beginning serial numbers for each assembly plant

SERIAL NUMBERS	PLANT CODE
5360001	1
5370001	2
5374001	3
5380001	4
5388001	5
5393001	6
5397001	7

BODY NUMBER PLATE

Located on the right side of the cowl, under the hood.

```
          BUICK DIVISION
  GENERAL MOTORS CORPORATION
          FLINT, MICH.
   1950     MOD. 56-S
   STYLE Nº. 50 4507
   BODY Nº. 1234
   TRIM Nº. 50
   PAINT Nº.  06
  TOP 00          ACC 00
      BODY BY FISHER
```

EXAMPLE:

50	Model year (1950)
56-S	Super Jetback sedanet
4	Buick Division
5	Super
07	Jetback sedanet
1234	Production sequence
50	Gray pattern cloth
06	Allendale Green

THE MODEL AND STYLE NUMBER indicates the model and body style.

SPECIAL

BODY TYPE	STYLE	MODEL
Tourback sedan	4469	41
Delux Tourback sedan	4469D	41D
Jetback sedan	4408	43
Delux Jetback sedan	4408D	43D
Jetback coupe	4407B	46
Jetback sedanet	4407	46S
Delux Jetback sedanet	4407D	46D

SUPER

BODY TYPE	STYLE	MODEL
Tourback sedan	4569	51
Tourback sedan	4519	52
Tourback sedan	*4519X	52
Jetback sedanet	4507	56S
Convertible	4567	56C
Riviera	4537	56R
Estate wagon	—	59

ROADMASTER

BODY TYPE	STYLE	MODEL
Tourback sedan	4769	71
Tourback sedan	4719	72
Tourback sedan	*4719X	72
Riviera	4737	75R
Jetback sedanet	4707	76S
Convertible	4767	76C
Delux Riviera	4737X	76R
Estate wagon	—	79

* With Hydraulic window lifts

THE BODY NUMBER is the production serial number of the body. The prefix denotes the plant in which the body was assembled.

THE ASSEMBLY PLANT CODE indicates the plant where the vehicle was assembled. No assembly plant codes were available.

THE TRIM CODE indicates the key to the trim color and material for each model series.

COLOR	CLOTH	VINYL	LEATHER	CODE
Gray	•			40,43,50
Gray	•			70,71,78
Gray	•			79,80
Black/Gray			•	44,45,51
Black/Gray			•	72,76
Red			•	53
Blue			•	54,74
Green			•	55,75
Black			•	56
Tan			•	57,77
Red/Gray			•	72,73
Gray/Black	•		•	60
Gray/Red	•		•	61,82
Gray/Tan	•		•	62
Gray/Blue	•		•	63
Gray/Green	•		•	64

THE COLOR CODE indicates the paint color used on the car.

COLOR	CODE
Carlsbad Black	01
Cumberland Gray	02,15
Verde Green	03
Imperial Blue	04
Sunmist Gray	05
Allendale Green	06
Royal Maroon	07
Cirrus Green	08
Old Ivory	09
Olympic Blue	10
Geneva Green	14
Niagara Green	17
Calvin Gray	18
Barton Gray	19
Meredith Green	20
Cloudmist Gray	24
Kashmir Green	25

TWO-TONE COLORS

COLOR	CODE
Verde Green/Cirrus Green	11
Imperial Blue/Olympic Blue	12
Sunmist Gray/Cumberland Gray	13,16
Verde Green/Niagara Green	21
Carlsbad Black/Calvin Gray	22
Imperial Blue/Barton Gray	23

NOTE: The first color identifies the upper body color and the second color identifies the lower body color.

ENGINE SPECIFICATIONS

THE ENGINE NUMBER is located on the boss on the right side of the cylinder block below the pushrod cover. The starting serial numbers are as follows:

SERIES	NUMBERS
40	5568000-4
50	5624734-5
70	5635021-7

NOTE: The last digit identifies the series.

SPECIAL - SERIES 40

ENGINE CODE	NO. CYL.	CID	HORSE-POWER	COMP. RATIO	CARB	TRANS
	8	248	115	6.6:1	2 BC	STD
	8	248	122	7.2:1	2 BC	AUTO

SUPER - SERIES 50

ENGINE CODE	NO. CYL.	CID	HORSE-POWER	COMP. RATIO	CARB	TRANS
	8	263	124	6.9:1	2 BC	STD
	8	263	128	7.2:1	2 BC	AUTO

ROADMASTER - SERIES 70

ENGINE CODE	NO. CYL.	CID	HORSE-POWER	COMP. RATIO	CARB	TRANS
	8	320	152	7.2:1	2 BC	AUTO

1951 BUICK

1951 BUICK

1951 BUICK DYNAFLOW

VEHICLE IDENTIFICATION NUMBER

• 6 0 3 1 3 0 1 •

Located on a plate on the left front door pillar. The plate indicates the assembly plant and the production sequence number.

FIRST DIGIT: Identifies the assembly plant

ASSEMBLY PLANT	CODE
Flint, MI	1
South Gate, CA	2
Linden, NJ	3
Kansas City, KS	4
Wilmington, DE	5
Atlanta, GA	6
Framingham, MA	7

LAST SIX DIGITS: Represent the beginning serial numbers for each assembly plant

SERIAL NUMBERS	PLANT CODE
6031301	1
6050001	2
6055001	3
6061001	4
6070001	5
6075001	6
6080001	7

BODY NUMBER PLATE

Located on the right side of the cowl, under the hood.

BUICK DIVISION
GENERAL MOTORS CORPORATION
FLINT, MICH.
1951   MOD. 56-S
STYLE Nº. 51 4507
BODY Nº. 1234
TRIM Nº. 50
PAINT Nº. 06
TOP 00   **ACC** 00
BODY BY FISHER

EXAMPLE:

51	Model year (1951)
56-S	Super Jetback sedanet
4	Buick Division
5	Super
07	Jetback sedanet
1234	Production sequence
50	Gray cord/cloth
01	Carlsbad Black

THE MODEL AND STYLE NUMBER indicates the model and body style.

SPECIAL

BODY TYPE	STYLE	MODEL
Tourback sedan	4369	41
Delux Tourback sedan	4369D	41D
Riviera	4337	45R
Convertible	4367X	46C
Tourback coupe	4327	46S
Delux Tourback 2-dr. sedan	4311D	48D

SUPER

BODY TYPE	STYLE	MODEL
Tourback sedan	4569	51
Riviera sedan	4519	52
Riviera sedan	*4519X	52
Convertible	4567X	56C
Riviera	4537	56R
Riviera Delux	4537D	56R
Jetback sedanet	4507D	56S
Estate wagon	—	59

ROADMASTER

BODY TYPE	STYLE	MODEL
Riviera sedan	4719	72R
Riviera sedan	*4719X	72R
Convertible	4767X	76C
Riviera	*4737X	76R
Riviera	4737	76MR
Estate wagon	—	79R

* With hydraulic window lifts

THE BODY NUMBER is the production serial number of the body. The prefix denotes the plant in which the body was assembled.

THE ASSEMBLY PLANT CODE indicates the plant where the vehicle was assembled. No assembly plant codes were available.

THE TRIM CODE indicates the key to the trim color and material for each model series.

COLOR	CLOTH	VINYL	LEATHER	CODE
Gray	•			40,64,70
Gray/Gray	•			41,42,50
Green/Green	•			71
Blue/Blue	•			72
Green/Green	•		•	51,78
Blue/Blue	•		•	52,79
Red			•	43,53,59
Blue			•	44,54,58
Green			•	45,55
Black			•	46,56
Tan			•	47,57,77
Gray			•	65,66,67
Gray			•	68,69
Red/Gray			•	60,73
Blue/Blue			•	61,74
Green/Green			•	62,75
Gray/Gray			•	63
Black/Gray			•	76

THE COLOR CODE indicates the paint color used on the car.

COLOR	CODE
Carlsbad Black	01
Verde Green	02
Imperial Blue	03
Geneva Green	04
Barton Gray	05
Olympic Blue	06
Victoria Maroon	07
Sharon Green	08
Cloudmist Gray	09
Old Ivory	10
Sky Gray	17
Calumet Green	19
Venetian Blue	21
Gelena Blue	23
Glenn Green	26

TWO-TONE COLORS

COLOR	CODE
Sky Gray/Verde Green	11
Sky Gray/Olympic Blue	12
Sky Gray/Victoria Maroon	13
Sky Gray/Sharon Green	14
Sky Gray/Cloudmist Gray	15
Imperial Blue/Barton Gray	16
Cloudmist Gray/Sky Gray	18
Sky Gray/Calumet Green	20
Sky Gray/Venetian Blue	22
Sky Gray/Gelena Blue	24
Imperial Blue/Gelena Blue	25
Calumet Green/Glenn Green	28

ENGINE SPECIFICATIONS

THE ENGINE NUMBER is located on the boss on the right side of the cylinder block below the pushrod cover. The starting serial numbers are as follows:

SERIES	STARTING NUMBERS
40	6240100-4
50	6240100-5
70	6240100-7

NOTE: The last digit of the engine number identifies the series.

SPECIAL - SERIES 40

ENGINE CODE	NO. CYL.	CID	HORSE-POWER	COMP. RATIO	CARB	TRANS
	8	263	120	6.6:1	2 BC	STD
	8	263	128	7.2:1	2 BC	AUTO

SUPER - SERIES 50

ENGINE CODE	NO. CYL.	CID	HORSE-POWER	COMP. RATIO	CARB	TRANS
	8	263	124	6.9:1	2 BC	STD
	8	263	128	7.2:1	2 BC	AUTO

ROADMASTER - SERIES 70

ENGINE CODE	NO. CYL.	CID	HORSE-POWER	COMP. RATIO	CARB	TRANS
	8	320	152	7.2:1	2 BC	AUTO

1952 BUICK ROADMASTER

1952 BUICK SPECIAL

1952 BUICK

1952 BUICK ROADMASTER RIVIERA

1952 BUICK

1952 BUICK

VEHICLE IDENTIFICATION NUMBER

• 6 4 3 6 0 0 1 •

Located on a plate on the left front door pillar. The plate indicates the assembly plant and the production sequence number.

FIRST DIGIT: Identifies the assembly plant

ASSEMBLY PLANT	CODE
Flint, MI	1
South Gate, CA	2
Linden, NJ	3
Kansas City, KS	4
Wilmington, DE	5
Atlanta, GA	6
Framingham, MA	7

LAST SIX DIGITS: Represent the beginning serial numbers for each assembly plant

SERIAL NUMBERS	PLANT CODE
6436001	1
6456001	2
6464001	3
6471001	4
6483001	5
6490001	6
6496001	7

BODY NUMBER PLATE

Located on the right side of the cowl, under the hood.

BUICK DIVISION
GENERAL MOTORS CORPORATION
FLINT, MICH.
1952   MOD. 41
STYLE N°. 52 4369
BODY N°. 1234
TRIM N°. 40
PAINT N°. 01
TOP 00   ACC 00
BODY BY FISHER

EXAMPLE:

52	Model year (1952)
41	Special Tourback sedan
4	Buick Division
3	Special
69	Tourback sedan
1234	Production sequence
40	Lt. Gray cloth
01	Carlsbad Black

THE MODEL AND STYLE NUMBER indicates the model and body style.

SPECIAL

BODY TYPE	STYLE	MODEL
Tourback sedan	4369	41
Delux Tourback sedan	4369D	41D
Riviera	4337	45R
Convertible	4367X	46C
Tourback coupe	4327	46S
Delux Tourback 2-dr. sedan	4311D	48D

SUPER

BODY TYPE	STYLE	MODEL
Riviera sedan	4519	52
Riviera sedan	*4519X	52
Convertible	4567X	56C
Riviera	4537	56R
Estate wagon	—	59

ROADMASTER

BODY TYPE	STYLE	MODEL
Riviera sedan	4719	72R
Riviera sedan	*4719X	72R
Convertible	4767X	76C
Riviera	4737X	76R
Estate wagon	—	79R

* With hydraulic window lifts

THE BODY NUMBER is the production serial number

of the body. The prefix denotes the plant in which the body was assembled.

THE ASSEMBLY PLANT CODE indicates the

plant where the vehicle was assembled. No assembly plant codes were available.

THE TRIM CODE indicates the key to the trim color

and material for each model series.

COLOR	CLOTH	VINYL	LEATHER	CODE
Gray	•			40,70,80
Dk. Gray	•			41
Gray/Gray	•			51
Green	•			71,78
Blue	•			72
Red			•	43,53,73,86,97
Blue			•	44,54,74,87,95
Green			•	45,47,55,75,88,96
Black			•	46,56,76,98
Tan			•	57,77,99
Beige/Red	•		•	83
Black/Gray	•			61
Gray/Red	•		•	63
Green/Green	•		•	65,85
Blue/Blue	•		•	84

THE COLOR CODE indicates the paint color used on
the car.

COLOR	CODE
Carlsbad Black	01
Verde Green	02
Imperial Blue	03
Barton Gray	04
Victoria Maroon	05
Seamist Gray	06
Sky Gray	07
Terrace Green	08
Venetian Blue	09
Surf Blue	10
Glenn Green	11
Sequoia Cream	12
Apache Red	13
Nassau Blue	28
Golden Sand	29,40
Coronet Copper	30
Glacier Green	31
Peacock Green	32
Aztec Gold	33
Teal Blue	42
Beach White	43

TWO-TONE COLORS

COLOR	CODE
Sky Gray/Verde Green	14
Sky Gray/Victoria Maroon	15
Sky Gray/Seamist Gray	16
Imperial Blue/Barton Gray	17
Seamist Gray/Sky Gray	18
Sky Gray/Terrace Green	19
Sky Gray/Venetian Blue	20
Sky Gray/Surf Blue	21
Imperial Blue/Surf Blue	22
Terrace Green/Glenn Green	23
Carlsbad Black/Sequoia Cream	24
Carlsbad Black/Apache Red	25
Beach White/Nassau Blue	34
Beach White/Golden Sand	35
Beach White/Coronet Copper	36
Beach White/Glacier Green	37
Beach White/Peacock Green	38
Verde Green/Aztec Gold	39
Beach White/Golden Sand	41
Beach White/Teel Blue	44
Seamist Gray/Beach White	45

NOTE: The first color identifies the upper body color and the second color identifies the lower body color.

ENGINE SPECIFICATIONS

THE ENGINE NUMBER is located on the boss on the right side of the cylinder block below the pushrod cover. The starting serial numbers are as follows:

SERIES	STARTING NUMBERS
40, std.	6646232-4
40, auto	6646230-4
50, std.	6647024-5
50, auto	6646230-5
70, std.	6652000-7
70, power steering	6652220-7

NOTE: The last digit of the engine number identifies the series.

SPECIAL - SERIES 40

ENGINE CODE	NO. CYL.	CID	HORSE-POWER	COMP. RATIO	CARB	TRANS
	8	263	120	6.6:1	2 BC	STD
	8	263	128	7.2:1	2 BC	AUTO

SUPER - SERIES 50

ENGINE CODE	NO. CYL.	CID	HORSE-POWER	COMP. RATIO	CARB	TRANS
	8	263	124	6.9:1	2 BC	STD
	8	263	128	7.2:1	2 BC	AUTO

ROADMASTER - SERIES 70

ENGINE CODE	NO. CYL.	CID	HORSE-POWER	COMP. RATIO	CARB	TRANS
	8	320	170	7.5:1	4 BC	AUTO

1953 BUICK SPECIAL

1953 BUICK SPECIAL

1953 BUICK SUPER

1953 BUICK

1953 BUICK

1953 BUICK SPECIAL

1953 BUICK

1953 BUICK STATION WAGON

VEHICLE IDENTIFICATION NUMBER

```
┌─────────────────────────┐
│  •   6 7 4 0 0 0 1   •  │
└─────────────────────────┘
```

Located on a plate on the left front door pillar. The plate indicates the assembly plant and the production sequence number.

FIRST DIGIT: Identifies the assembly plant

ASSEMBLY PLANT	CODE
Flint, MI	1
South Gate, CA	2
Linden, NJ	3
Kansas City, KS	4
Wilmington, DE	5
Atlanta, GA	6
Framingham, MA	7

LAST SIX DIGITS: Represent the beginning serial numbers for each assembly plant

SERIAL NUMBERS	PLANT CODE
6740001	1
6765001	2
6774001	3
6783001	4
6799001	5
6808001	6
6815001	7

BODY NUMBER PLATE

Located on the right side of the cowl, under the hood.

```
┌───────────────────────────────────────┐
│         BUICK DIVISION                 │
│  GENERAL MOTORS CORPORATION            │
│         FLINT, MICH.                    │
│  1953      MOD. 45-R                    │
│  STYLE Nº. 53 4337                      │
│  BODY Nº. 1234                          │
│  TRIM Nº. 30                            │
│  PAINT Nº.  51                          │
│  TOP  00          ACC  00               │
│         BODY BY FISHER                  │
└───────────────────────────────────────┘
```

EXAMPLE:

53	Model year (1953)
45-R	Special Riviera
4	Buick Division
3	Special
37	Riviera
1234	Production sequence
30	White/Red leather
51	Carlsbad Black

THE MODEL AND STYLE NUMBER indicates the model and body style.

SPECIAL

BODY TYPE	STYLE	MODEL
Delux Tourback sedan	4369D	41D
Riviera	4337	45R
Convertible	4367TX	46C
Delux Tourback sedan	4311D	48D

SUPER

BODY TYPE	STYLE	MODEL
Riviera sedan	4519	52
Riviera sedan	*4519X	52X
Convertible	4567X	56C
Riviera	4537	56R
Estate wagon	—	59

ROADMASTER

BODY TYPE	STYLE	MODEL
Riviera sedan	4719	72R
Riviera sedan	*4719X	72RX
Convertible	4767X	76C
Riviera	4737X	76R
Anniversary convertible	4767SX	76X
Estate wagon	—	79R

* With hydraulic window lifts

THE BODY NUMBER is the production serial number of the body. The prefix denotes the plant in which the body was assembled.

THE ASSEMBLY PLANT CODE indicates the plant where the vehicle was assembled. No assembly plant codes were available.

THE TRIM CODE indicates the key to the trim color and material for each model series.

COLOR	CLOTH	VINYL	LEATHER	CODE
White/Red			•	30,66
Blue/Blue			•	31,74,87
Green/Green			•	32,75,88
Ivory/Tan			•	33
Black/White			•	67
Blue/White			•	68
Green/White			•	69
Red			•	53,73,86
Blue			•	54
Green			•	55
Black			•	56,76
Tan			•	57,77
Gray			•	90,91
Gray			•	92,93
Gray	•			70
Gray/Gray	•			41
Green/Green	•			42,50,52
Green/Green	•			71,78
Blue/Gray	•			43,51
Blue/Blue	•			63,72,79
Green/Green	•		•	60,80
Blue/Blue	•		•	61,81
Black/Red	•		•	62,82
Blue		•		95
Green		•		96
Red		•		97
Black		•		98
Saddle Tan		•		99

THE COLOR CODE indicates the paint color used on the car.

COLOR	CODE
Carlsbad Black	51
Verde Green	52
Imperial Blue	53
Jordan Gray	54
Victoria Maroon	55
Seamist Gray	56
Shell Gray	57
Terrace Green	58
Tyler Blue	59
Ridge Green	60
Osage Cream	61
Matador Red	62
Majestic White	74
Reef Blue	77
Mandarin Red	78
Balsam Green	79
Pinehurst Green	83
Glacier Blue	86

TWO-TONE COLORS

COLOR	CODE
Shell Gray/Verde Green	63
Shell Gray/Victoria Maroon	64
Shell Gray/Seamist Gray	65
Imperial Blue/Jordan Gray	66
Seamist Gray/Shell Gray	67
Ridge Green/Terrace Green	68
Shell Gray/Tyler Blue	69
Terrace Green/Ridge Green	70
Verde Green/Osage Cream	71
Carlsbad Black/Matador Red	72
Seamist Gray/Majestic White	76
Majestic White/Balsam Green	80
Majestic White/Mandarin Red	81
Majestic White/Reef Blue	82
Majestic White/Pinehurst Green	84
Majestic White/Matador Red	85
Imperial Blue/Glacier Blue	87
Jordan Gray/Glacier Blue	88

NOTE: The first color identifies the upper body color and the second color identifies the lower body color.

ENGINE SPECIFICATIONS

THE ENGINE NUMBER is located on the boss on the right side of the cylinder block below the pushrod cover on Series 40. On the other Series it is located on the left side of the cylinder block at the top. The starting serial numbers are as follows:

SERIES	CODE
40, std.	6952425-4
40, auto	6952400-4
50	V-2415-5
70	V-2001-7

NOTE: The last digit of the engine number identifies the series.

SPECIAL - SERIES 40

ENGINE CODE	NO. CYL.	CID	HORSE-POWER	COMP. RATIO	CARB	TRANS
	8	263	125	7.0:1	2 BC	STD
	8	263	130	7.6:1	2 BC	AUTO

SUPER - SERIES 50

ENGINE CODE	NO. CYL.	CID	HORSE-POWER	COMP. RATIO	CARB	TRANS
	8	322	164	8.0:1	2 BC	STD
	8	322	170	8.5:1	2 BC	AUTO

ROADMASTER - SERIES 70

ENGINE CODE	NO. CYL.	CID	HORSE-POWER	COMP. RATIO	CARB	TRANS
	8	322	188	8.5:1	4 BC	AUTO

1954 BUICK CENTURY

1954 BUICK

1954 BUICK

1954 BUICK CENTURY

VEHICLE IDENTIFICATION NUMBER

`• 4 A 3 0 0 1 0 0 1 •`

Located on a plate on the left front door pillar.

FIRST DIGIT: Identifies the series

SERIES	CODE
Special (40)	4
Super (50)	5
Century (60)	6
Roadmaster (70)	7

SECOND DIGIT: Identifies the model year (A=1954)

THIRD DIGIT: Identifies the assembly plant

ASSEMBLY PLANT	CODE
Flint, MI	1
South Gate, CA	2
Linden, NJ	3
Kansas City, KS	4
Wilmington, DE	5
Atlanta, GA	6
Framingham, MA	7
Arlington, TX	8

LAST SIX DIGITS: Represent the basic production sequence

BODY NUMBER PLATE

Located on the right side of the cowl, under the hood.

```
BUICK DIVISION
GENERAL MOTORS CORPORATION
FLINT, MICH.
1954     MOD. 46-R
STYLE Nº. 54 4437
BODY Nº. 1234
TRIM Nº. 40
PAINT Nº. 01
TOP 00          ACC 00
BODY BY FISHER
```

EXAMPLE:

54	Model year (1954)
46-R	Special
4	Buick Division
4	Special
37	Riviera
1234	Production sequence
40	Gray pattern nylon
01	Carlsbad Black

THE MODEL AND STYLE NUMBER indicates the model and body style.

SPECIAL

BODY TYPE	STYLE	MODEL
Delux Tourback sedan	4469D	41D
Riviera	4437	46R
Convertible	4467TX	46C
Delux Tourback 2-dr. sedan	4411D	48D
Estate wagon	4481	49

CENTURY

BODY TYPE	STYLE	MODEL
Tourback sedan	4669	61
Convertible	4667X	66C
Riviera	4637	66R
Estate wagon	4481	69

SUPER

BODY TYPE	STYLE	MODEL
Riviera sedan	4519	52
Convertible	4567X	56C
Riviera	4537	56R

ROADMASTER

BODY TYPE	STYLE	MODEL
Riviera sedan	4719	72R
Riviera	4737X	76RX
Convertible	4767X	76CX
M/100 Skylark convertible	4667SX	100

THE BODY NUMBER is the production serial number of the body. The prefix denotes the plant in which the body was assembled.

THE ASSEMBLY PLANT CODE indicates the plant where the vehicle was assembled. No assembly plant codes were available.

THE TRIM CODE indicates the key to the trim color and material for each model series.

COLOR	CLOTH	VINYL	LEATHER	CODE
Black/Red	•	•		21,22,52
Green/Green	•	•		23,26,28,43,53,63,73,83
Blue/Blue	•	•		24,27,29,44,54,64,74,84
Gray	•			40
Grey/Black	•	•		41
Gray/Red	•	•		42
Black/Red	•	•		62,82
Red		•		45,55
Green		•		46,56
Blue		•		47,57
Green/Green		•		96
Blue/Blue		•		97
Tan/Ivory		•		48,58,98
Red/Ivory		•		95
Black/Cream		•		49,59,99
Blue		•		50,60
Green		•		51,61
Green/Green		•		71
Black/Gray		•		70
Blue/Blue		•		72
Red			•	65,75,85
Green			•	66,76,86
Blue			•	67,77,87
Black/Yellow			•	69
Ivory/Tan			•	78,88
Black/Cream			•	79,89

THE COLOR CODE indicates the paint color used on the car. Solid color cars used only a letter, two-tone paint schemes used a number and a letter.

COLOR	LETTER CODE	NUMBER CODE
Carlsbad Black	A	01
Arctic White	B	02
Casino Beige	C	03
Gull Gray	D	05
Jordan Gray	E	06
Tunis Blue	N	07
Cavalier Blue	F	08
Ranier Blue	G	09
Marlin Blue	H	10
Malibu Blue	P	11
Baffin Green	K	12
Willow Green	L	13
Oceanmist Green	M	14
Aztec Green	—	15
Lido Green	R	16
Titian Red	—	17
Matador Red	—	18
Gulf Turquoise	S	19
Condor Yellow	—	20

ENGINE SPECIFICATIONS

THE ENGINE NUMBER is located on the left side of the cylinder block at the top. The starting serial numbers were as follows:

SERIES	STARTING NUMBERS
40 - Special	4
50 - Super	5
60 - Century	6
70 - Roadmaster	7
100 - Skylark	7

NOTE: The last digit identifies the series.

SPECIAL - SERIES 40

ENGINE CODE	NO. CYL.	CID	HORSE-POWER	COMP. RATIO	CARB	TRANS
	8	264	143	7.1:1	2 BC	STD
	8	264	150	8.1:1	2 BC	AUTO

SUPER - SERIES 50

ENGINE CODE	NO. CYL.	CID	HORSE-POWER	COMP. RATIO	CARB	TRANS
	8	322	177	8.0:1	2 BC	STD
	8	322	182	8.5:1	2 BC	AUTO

CENTURY - SERIES 60

ENGINE CODE	NO. CYL.	CID	HORSE-POWER	COMP. RATIO	CARB	TRANS
	8	322	195	8.0:1	4 BC	STD
	8	322	200	8.5:1	4 BC	AUTO

ROADMASTER - SERIES 70

ENGINE CODE	NO. CYL.	CID	HORSE-POWER	COMP. RATIO	CARB	TRANS
	8	322	200	8.5:1	4 BC	AUTO

SKYLARK - SERIES 100

ENGINE CODE	NO. CYL.	CID	HORSE-POWER	COMP. RATIO	CARB	TRANS
	8	322	200	8.5:1	4 BC	AUTO

1955 BUICK

1955 BUICK RIVIERA

1955 BUICK CENTURY

1955 BUICK CENTURY

1955 BUICK SPECIAL

VEHICLE IDENTIFICATION NUMBER

• 4 B 3 0 0 1 0 0 1 •

Located on a plate on the left front door pillar.

FIRST DIGIT: Identifies the series

SERIES	CODE
Special (40)	4
Super (50)	5
Century (60)	6
Roadmaster (70)	7

SECOND DIGIT: Identifies the model year (B=1955)

THIRD DIGIT: Identifies the assembly plant

ASSEMBLY PLANT	CODE
Flint, MI	1
South Gate, CA	2
Linden, NJ	3
Kansas City, KS	4
Wilmington, DE	5
Atlanta, GA	6
Framingham, MA	7
Arlington, TX	8

LAST SIX DIGITS: Represent the basic production sequence

BODY NUMBER PLATE

Located on the right side of the cowl, under the hood.

```
        BUICK DIVISION
 GENERAL MOTORS CORPORATION
        FLINT, MICH.
  1955      MOD. 43
  STYLE Nº. 55 4439
  BODY Nº. 1234
  TRIM Nº. 440
  PAINT Nº.  A
TOP 00           ACC 00
     BODY BY FISHER
```

EXAMPLE:

55	Model year (1955)
43	Special
4	Buick Division
4	Special
39	Riviera sedan
1234	Production sequence
440	Gray/Gray nylon/vinyl
A	Carlsbad Black

THE MODEL AND STYLE NUMBER indicates the model and body style.

SPECIAL

BODY TYPE	STYLE	MODEL
Tourback sedan	4469	41
Riviera sedan	4439	43
Convertible	4467TX	46C
Riviera	4437	46R
Tourback 2-dr. sedan	4411	48
Estate wagon	4481	49

CENTURY

BODY TYPE	STYLE	MODEL
Tourback sedan	4669	61
Riviera sedan	4639	63
Convertible	4667X	66C
Riviera	4637	66R
Estate wagon	4481	69

SUPER

BODY TYPE	STYLE	MODEL
Sedan	4519	52
Convertible	4567X	56C
Riviera	4537	56R

ROADMASTER

BODY TYPE	STYLE	MODEL
Sedan	4719	72
Convertible	4767X	76C
Riviera	4737X	76R

THE BODY NUMBER is the production serial number of the body. The prefix denotes the plant in which the body was assembled.

THE ASSEMBLY PLANT CODE indicates the plant where the vehicle was assembled. No assembly plant codes were available.

THE TRIM CODE indicates the key to the trim color and material for each model series.

COLOR	CLOTH	VINYL	LEATHER	CODE
Black/Ivory		•		402
Green		•		403,406
Blue		•		404,407
Red		•		405
Maroon/Beige		•		408
Black/Yellow		•		409
Black/Ivory			•	412,432
Red			•	415,435
Green			•	416,433,436
Blue			•	417,434,437
Maroon/Beige			•	418,438
Black/Yellow			•	419,439
Black/Ivory		•		422
Green		•		423,426
Blue		•		424,427
Red		•		425
Maroon/Beige		•		428
Black/Yellow		•		429
Red/Beige		•		495
Green/Beige		•		496
Blue/Ivory		•		497
Tan/Beige		•		498
Maroon/Beige		•		499
Black/Ivory	•	•		446
Black/Beige	•	•		478
Black/Red	•	•		447,452,472

COLOR	CLOTH	VINYL	LEATHER	CODE
Green/Ivory	•	•		448,468,476
Green/Beige	•	•		479
Blue/Ivory	•	•		449,469,477
Black/Ivory	•	•		450,466,475
Blue/Beige	•	•		480
Black/Gray	•	•		455,470
Gray/Gray	•	•		440
Charcoal/Gray	•	•		441,445,460
Charcoal/Gray	•	•		465
Charcoal/Red	•	•		441R,442,462
Blue/Blue	•	•		441B,444,444A
Blue/Blue	•	•		454,464,474
Green/Green	•	•		441G,443,443A
Green/Green	•	•		451,451A,453
Green/Green	•	•		453A,461,463
Green/Green	•	•		473
Black/Red/Ivory	•	•		467
Black/Silver/Ivory	•	•		492
Green/Silver/Ivory	•	•		493
Blue/Silver/Ivory	•	•		494

NOTE: Flint built cars have two digit trim combination numbers stamped on the body name plate.

THE COLOR CODE indicates the paint color used on the car. The paint code consists of 3 letters, the first identifies the upper color, the 2nd identifies the center color, the 3rd identifies the lower color.

COLOR	CODE
Carlsbad Black	A
Dover White	B
Cameo Beige	C
Windsor Gray	D
Temple Gray	E
Colonial Blue	F
Victoria Blue	G
Cascade Blue	H
Stafford Blue	K
Belfast Green	L
Willow Green	M
Galway Green	N
Cadet Blue	P
Titian Red	R
Cherokee Red	S
Gulf Turquoise	T
Condor Yellow	U
Spruce Green	W
Nile Green	X
Mist Green	Y

ENGINE SPECIFICATIONS

THE ENGINE NUMBER is located on the left side of the cylinder block at the top. The starting serial numbers on all series is V-720080 followed by a suffix indicating the series.

SERIES	NUMBER
40 - Special	4
50 - Super	5
60 - Century	6
70 - Roadmaster	7

NOTE: The prefix V is not used after engine #1,000,000.

SPECIAL - SERIES 40

ENGINE CODE	NO. CYL.	CID	HORSE-POWER	COMP. RATIO	CARB	TRANS
	8	264	188	7.8:1	2 BC	STD
	8	264	188	8.4:1	2 BC	AUTO

SUPER - SERIES 50

ENGINE CODE	NO. CYL.	CID	HORSE-POWER	COMP. RATIO	CARB	TRANS
	8	322	188	8.4:1	4 BC	STD
	8	322	236	9.0:1	4 BC	AUTO

CENTURY - SERIES 60

ENGINE CODE	NO. CYL.	CID	HORSE-POWER	COMP. RATIO	CARB	TRANS
	8	322	188	8.4:1	4 BC	STD
	8	322	236	9.0:1	4 BC	AUTO

ROADMASTER - SERIES 70

ENGINE CODE	NO. CYL.	CID	HORSE-POWER	COMP. RATIO	CARB	TRANS
	8	322	236	9.0:1	4 BC	AUTO

1956 BUICK SPECIAL STATION WAGON

1956 BUICK ROADMASTER

1956 BUICK SUPER SERIES

1956 BUICK SPECIAL

1956 BUICK RIVIERA SPECIAL

1956 BUICK CENTURY

VEHICLE IDENTIFICATION NUMBER

`• 4 C 3 0 0 1 0 0 1 •`

Located on a plate on the left front door pillar.

FIRST DIGIT: Identifies the series

SERIES	CODE
Special (40)	4
Super (50)	5
Century (60)	6
Roadmaster (70)	7

SECOND DIGIT: Identifies the model year (C=1956)

THIRD DIGIT: Identifies the assembly plant

ASSEMBLY PLANT	CODE
Flint, MI	1
South Gate, CA	2
Linden, NJ	3
Kansas City, KS	4
Wilmington, DE	5
Atlanta, GA	6
Framingham, MA	7
Arlington, TX	8

LAST SIX DIGITS: Represent the basic production sequence

BODY NUMBER PLATE

Located on the right side of the cowl, under the hood.

BUICK DIVISION
GENERAL MOTORS CORPORATION
FLINT, MICH.
1956   MOD. 43
STYLE Nº. 56 4439
BODY Nº. 1234
TRIM Nº. 400
PAINT Nº. C
BODY BY FISHER

EXAMPLE:

56	Model year (1956)
43	Special
4	Buick Division
4	Special
39	Riviera sedan
1234	Production sequence
400	Red cordaveen
C	Dover White

THE MODEL AND STYLE NUMBER indicates the model and body style.

SPECIAL

BODY TYPE	STYLE	MODEL
Tourback sedan	4469	41
Riviera sedan	4439	43
Convertible	4467TX	46C
Riviera	4437	46R
Tourback 2-dr. sedan	4411	48
Estate wagon	4481	49

CENTURY

BODY TYPE	STYLE	MODEL
Riviera sedan	4639	63
Riviera sedan	4639D	63D
Convertible	4667X	66C
Riviera	4637	66R
Estate wagon	4481	69

SUPER

BODY TYPE	STYLE	MODEL
Sedan	4519	52
Riviera sedan	4539	53
Convertible	4567X	56C
Riviera	4537	56R

ROADMASTER

BODY TYPE	STYLE	MODEL
Sedan	4719	72
Riviera sedan	4739X	73
Convertible	4767X	76C
Riviera	4737X	76R

THE BODY NUMBER is the production serial number of the body. The prefix denotes the plant in which the body was assembled.

THE ASSEMBLY PLANT CODE indicates the plant where the vehicle was assembled. No assembly plant codes were available.

THE TRIM CODE indicates the key to the trim color and material for each model series.

COLOR	CLOTH	VINYL	LEATHER	CODE
Red		•		400,500
Red/Ivory		•		405,605
Black/Ivory		•		530
Blue/Blue		•		520,621,625
Green/Green		•		410,411,510
Green/Green		•		611,615
Green/Green	•	•		412,413,415
Green/Green	•	•		416,417,512
Green/Green	•	•		513,613
Blue/Blue	•	•		420,421,422
Blue/Blue	•	•		423,425,426
Blue/Blue	•	•		427,522,523
Blue/Blue	•	•		623,722,723
Black/Red	•	•		431,433,436
Black/Red	•	•		437,467,531
Black/Red	•	•		533,633,733
Black/Red	•	•		734
Black/Ivory	•	•		432,438,468
Black/Ivory	•	•		532,632
Black/Ivory	•	•		430,434,435
Black/Ivory		•		634,635

COLOR	CLOTH	VINYL	LEATHER	CODE
Tan/Beige		•		445,645
Red/Red		•	•	600
Green/Green		•	•	610,712,713
Blue/Blue		•	•	620
Black/Ivory		•	•	630,731
Red			•	700
Green/Green			•	710
Blue			•	720
Black/Ivory			•	730

THE COLOR CODE indicates the paint color used on the car. The paint code consists of 3 letters. The 1st identifies the upper color, the 2nd identifies the center color, the 3rd identifies the lower color.

COLOR	CODE
Carlsbad Black	A
Castle Gray	B
Dover White	C
Electric Blue	D
Bedford Blue	E
Cadet Blue	F
Cambridge Blue	G
Laurel Green	H
Foam Green	J
Glacier Green	K
Claret Red	L
Seminole Red	M
Tahiti Coral	N
Cameo Beige	P
Harvest Yellow	R
Bitter Sweet	T
Apricot	U

ENGINE SPECIFICATIONS

THE ENGINE NUMBER is located on the left side of the cylidner block at the top. The starting serial number on all series is 1,460,023, followed by a suffix indicating the series.

SPECIAL - SERIES 40

ENGINE CODE	NO. CYL.	CID	HORSE-POWER	COMP. RATIO	CARB	TRANS
	8	322	N/A	7.6:1	2 BC	STD
	8	322	220	8.9:1	2 BC	AUTO

SUPER - SERIES 50

ENGINE CODE	NO. CYL.	CID	HORSE-POWER	COMP. RATIO	CARB	TRANS
	8	322	255	9.5:1	4 BC	AUTO

CENTURY - SERIES 60

ENGINE CODE	NO. CYL.	CID	HORSE-POWER	COMP. RATIO	CARB	TRANS
	8	322	255	9.5:1	4 BC	AUTO

ROADMASTER - SERIES 70

ENGINE CODE	NO. CYL.	CID	HORSE-POWER	COMP. RATIO	CARB	TRANS
	8	322	255	9.5:1	4 BC	AUTO

1957 BUICK CENTURY CABALLERO

1957 BUICK CENTURY

1957 BUICK

1957 BUICK

1957 BUICK RIVIERA

1957 BUICK RIVIERA

1957 BUICK SPECIAL

1957 BUICK

VEHICLE IDENTIFICATION NUMBER

`• 4 D 3 0 0 1 0 0 1 •`

Located on a plate on the left front door pillar.

FIRST DIGIT: Identifies the series

SERIES	CODE
Special (40)..4
Super (50)..5
Century (60)...6
Roadmaster (70)...7

SECOND DIGIT: Identifies the model year (D=1957)

THIRD DIGIT: Identifies the assembly plant

ASSEMBLY PLANT	CODE
Flint, MI 1
South Gate, CA..2
Linden, NJ 3
Kansas City, KS 4
Wilmington, DE 5
Atlanta, GA 6
Framingham, MA 7
Arlington, TX 8

LAST SIX DIGITS: Represent the basic production sequence

BODY NUMBER PLATE

Located on the right side of the cowl, under the hood.

```
        BUICK DIVISION
GENERAL MOTORS CORPORATION
        FLINT, MICH.
  1957      MOD. 43
  STYLE Nº. 57 4439
  BODY Nº. 1234
  TRIM Nº. 400
  PAINT Nº.  C
TOP  00          ACC  00
     BODY BY FISHER
```

EXAMPLE:

57...Model year (1957)
43...Special
4 ....Buick Division
4 ....Special
39..Riviera sedan
1234...Production sequence
400...Red cordaveen
C ....Dover White

THE MODEL AND STYLE NUMBER indicates the model and body style.

SPECIAL

BODY TYPE	STYLE	MODEL
Sedan	4469	41
Riviera sedan	4439	43
Riviera coupe	4437	46R
Convertible	4467TX	46C
2-Dr. sedan	4411	48
Estate wagon	4481	49
Riviera Estate wagon	4482	49D

CENTURY

BODY TYPE	STYLE	MODEL
Sedan	4669	61
Riviera sedan	4639	63
Convertible	4667X	66C
Riviera coupe	4637	66R
Riviera Estate wagon	4682	69

SUPER

BODY TYPE	STYLE	MODEL
Riviera sedan	4539	53
Convertible	4567X	56C
Riviera coupe	4537	56R

ROADMASTER

BODY TYPE	STYLE	MODEL
Riviera sedan	4739DX	73
Riviera sedan	4739X	73A
Riviera sedan	4739SX	75
Riviera coupe	4737SX	75R
Riviera coupe	4737DX	76R
Riviera coupe	4737X	76A
Convertible	4767X	76C

THE BODY NUMBER is the production serial number of the body. The prefix denotes the plant in which the body was assembled.

THE ASSEMBLY PLANT CODE indicates the plant where the vehicle was assembled. No assembly plant codes were available.

THE TRIM CODE indicates the key to the trim color and material for each model series.

COLOR	CLOTH	VINYL	LEATHER	CODE
Red		•		400,500
Red/Ivory		•		405,605,606
Green/Green	•	•		
410,411,412,414				
Green/Green	•	•		416,511,513
Green/Green	•	•		611,613,711
Blue/Blue	•	•		421,422,426
Blue/Blue	•	•		521,523,621
Blue/Blue	•	•		623,721
Black/Ivory	•	•		432,531,533
Black/Ivory	•	•		631,633,731
Black/Red	•	•		442,641
Gray/Ivory	•	•		471,475
Gray/Gray	•	•		473
Rust/Ivory	•	•		482,581,583
Rust/Ivory	•	•		681,683,781
Rust/Beige	•	•		485,685,686
Green/Green	•	•		415,510,615
Green/Green	•			616

COLOR	CLOTH	VINYL	LEATHER	CODE
Blue/Blue		•		420,425,520
Blue/Blue		•		625,626
Black/Ivory		•		430,435,530
Black/Ivory		•		635,636
Tan/Beige		•		465,665,666
Ivory		•		550
Red/Red		•	•	600
Green/Green		•	•	610
Blue/Blue		•	•	620
Black/Ivory		•	•	630,731
Green/Green	•		•	713
Blue/Blue	•		•	723,724
Black/Ivory	•		•	733
Gray/Gray	•		•	773,774,777
Rust/Ivory	•		•	783
Beige/Beige	•		•	791
Red			•	700
Green/Green			•	710
Blue/Blue			•	720
Black/Ivory			•	730
Ivory			•	750
Gray/Gray	•			771

THE COLOR CODE indicates the paint color used on the car. Two-tone combination codes contain two letters, the first letter identifies the upper color and the second letter identifies the lower color.

COLOR	CODE
Carlsbad Black	A
Castle Gray	B
Dover White	C
Starlight Blue	D
Biscay Blue	E
Mariner Blue	F
Dresden Blue	G
Kearney Green	H
Belmont Green	J
Mint Green	K
Jade Green	L
Seminole Red	M
Garent Red	N
Shell Beige	P
Antique Ivory	R
Arctic Blue	S
Dawn Gray	T
Gulf Green	U
Hunter Green	W
Sylvan Gray	X
Dusk Rose	Y

ENGINE SPECIFICATIONS

THE ENGINE NUMBER is located on the cylinder block on the top left side. The engine number is the same as the serial number.

SPECIAL - SERIES 40

ENGINE CODE	NO. CYL.	CID	HORSE-POWER	COMP. RATIO	CARB	TRANS
	8	364	N/A	8.0:1	2 BC	STD
	8	364	250	9.5:1	2 BC	AUTO

SUPER - SERIES 50

ENGINE CODE	NO. CYL.	CID	HORSE-POWER	COMP. RATIO	CARB	TRANS
	8	364	300	10.0:1	4 BC	AUTO
	8	364	N/A	9.5:1	4 BC	AUTO

CENTURY - SERIES 60

ENGINE CODE	NO. CYL.	CID	HORSE-POWER	COMP. RATIO	CARB	TRANS
	8	364	300	10.0:1	4 BC	AUTO
	8	364	N/A	9.5:1	4 BC	AUTO

ROADMASTER - SERIES 70

ENGINE CODE	NO. CYL.	CID	HORSE-POWER	COMP. RATIO	CARB	TRANS
	8	364	300	10.0:1	4 BC	AUTO
	8	364	N/A	9.5:1	4 BC	AUTO

1958 BUICK

1958 BUICK CENTURY

1958 BUICK ROADMASTER

1958 BUICK

1958 BUICK SPECIAL

1958 BUICK

1958 BUICK

VEHICLE IDENTIFICATION NUMBER

• 4 E 3 0 0 1 0 0 1 •

Located on a plate on the left front door pillar.

FIRST DIGIT: Identifies the series

SERIES	CODE
Special (40)	4
Super (50)	5
Century (60)	6
Roadmaster (70)	7
Limited (700)	8

SECOND DIGIT: Identifies the model year (E=1958)

THIRD DIGIT: Identifies the assembly plant

ASSEMBLY PLANT	CODE
Flint, MI	1
South Gate, CA	2
Linden, NJ	3
Kansas City, KS	4
Wilmington, DE	5
Atlanta, GA	6
Framingham, MA	7
Arlington, TX	8

LAST SIX DIGITS: Represent the basic production sequence

BODY NUMBER PLATE

Located on the right side of the cowl, under the hood.

```
BUICK DIVISION
GENERAL MOTORS CORPORATION
FLINT, MICH.
1958      MOD. 43
STYLE Nº.  58 4439
BODY Nº.  1234
TRIM Nº.  431
PAINT Nº.   A
TOP  00          ACC  00
BODY BY FISHER
```

EXAMPLE:

58	Model year (1958)
43	Special
4	Buick Division
4	Special
39	Riviera sedan
1234	Production sequence
431	Gray/White cloth/vinyl
A	Carlsbad Black

THE MODEL AND STYLE NUMBER indicates the model and body style.

SPECIAL

BODY TYPE	STYLE	MODEL
Sedan	4469	41
Riviera sedan	4439	43
Riviera coupe	4437	46R
Convertible	4467TX	46C
2-Dr. sedan	4411	48
Estate wagon	4481	49
Riviera Estate wagon	4482	49D

CENTURY

BODY TYPE	STYLE	MODEL
Sedan	4669	61
Riviera sedan	4639	63
Convertible	4667X	66C
Riviera coupe	4637	66R
Riviera Estate wagon	4682	69

SUPER

BODY TYPE	STYLE	MODEL
Riviera sedan	4539	53
Riviera coupe	4537	56R

ROADMASTER

BODY TYPE	STYLE	MODEL
Riviera sedan	4739X	75
Riviera coupe	4737X	75R
Convertible	4767X	75C

LIMITED

BODY TYPE	STYLE	MODEL
Riviera sedan	4839X	750
Riviera coupe	4837X	755
Convertible	4867X	756

THE BODY NUMBER is the production serial number of the body. The prefix denotes the plant in which the body was assembled.

THE ASSEMBLY PLANT CODE indicates the plant where the vehicle was assembled. No assembly plant codes were available.

THE TRIM CODE indicates the key to the trim color and material for each model series.

COLOR	CLOTH	VINYL	LEATHER	CODE
Green		•		400,405
Green/Green	•	•		401,402,501
Green/Green	•	•		601
Blue/Blue	•	•		511,611
Black/White	•	•		422,521
Black/White	•	•		621
Black/Red	•	•		426,626
Gray/White	•	•		431
Rust/White	•	•		442,541,641
Rust/Beige	•	•		445,645
Gold/White	•	•		446,546,646
Turquoise	•	•		492,591,691
Red		•		450,650
Red/White		•		455,655
Blue		•		415,610,615
Blue/Blue		•		410,411,412
Green		•		600,605
Black/White		•		420,425

COLOR	CLOTH	VINYL	LEATHER	CODE
Black/White		•		620,625
Tan/Beige		•		465,665
Yellow/White		•		680
Green			•	700,702
Blue			•	710,712
Red			•	750
Silver			•	770
Yellow/White			•	780
Green/Green	•		•	701
Blue/Blue	•		•	711,713
Black/Silver	•		•	721
Gray/Silver	•		•	731,733
Beige/Beige	•		•	763
Turquoise	•		•	791

THE COLOR CODE indicates the paint color used on the car. Two-tone combination codes contain two letters, the first letter identifies the upper color and the second letter identifies the lower color.

COLOR	CODE
Carlsbad Black	A
Sylvan Gray	B
Glacier White	C
Spray Green	E
Warwick Blue	G
Dark Turquoise	H
Lt. Turquoise	J
Seminole Red	M
Garnet Red	N
Reef Coral	P
Cobalt Blue	S
Desert Sage	T
Mohave Yellow	U
Canyon Cedar	W
Green Mist	1
Blue Mist	2
Laurel Mist	3
Silver Mist	4
Polar Mist	5
Gold Mist	6

ENGINE SPECIFICATIONS

THE ENGINE NUMBER is located on the front of the cylinder block on the top left side.

SPECIAL - SERIES 40

ENGINE CODE	NO. CYL.	CID	HORSE-POWER	COMP. RATIO	CARB	TRANS
	8	364	N/A	8.0:1	2 BC	STD
	8	364	250	9.5:1	2 BC	AUTO

SUPER - SERIES 50

ENGINE CODE	NO. CYL.	CID	HORSE-POWER	COMP. RATIO	CARB	TRANS
	8	364	300	10.0:1	4 BC	AUTO
	8	364	N/A	9.5:1	4 BC	AUTO

CENTURY - SERIES 60

ENGINE CODE	NO. CYL.	CID	HORSE-POWER	COMP. RATIO	CARB	TRANS
	8	364	300	10.0:1	4 BC	AUTO
	8	364	N/A	9.5:1	4 BC	AUTO

ROADMASTER - SERIES 70

ENGINE CODE	NO. CYL.	CID	HORSE-POWER	COMP. RATIO	CARB	TRANS
	8	364	300	10.0:1	4 BC	AUTO
	8	364	N/A	9.5:1	4 BC	AUTO

LIMITED - SERIES 700

ENGINE CODE	NO. CYL.	CID	HORSE-POWER	COMP. RATIO	CARB	TRANS
	8	364	300	10.0:1	4 BC	AUTO
	8	364	N/A	9.5:1	4 BC	AUTO

1959 BUICK

1959 BUICK LE SABRE

1959 BUICK ELECTRA

VEHICLE IDENTIFICATION NUMBER

● 4 F 3 0 0 1 0 0 1 ●

Located on a plate on the left front door pillar.

FIRST DIGIT: Identifies the series

SERIES	CODE
Le Sabre (4400) 4
Invicta (4600) 6
Electra (4700) 7
Electra "225" (4800) 8

SECOND DIGIT: Identifies the model year (F=1959)

THIRD DIGIT: Identifies the assembly plant

ASSEMBLY PLANT	CODE
Flint, MI 1
South Gate, CA...2
Linden, NJ 3
Kansas City, KS 4
Wilmington, DE 5
Atlanta, GA 6
Framingham, MA 7
Arlington, TX 8

LAST SIX DIGITS: Represent the basic production sequence

BODY NUMBER PLATE

Located on the right side of the cowl, under the hood.

```
STYLE   59 4439
BODY    FB 1234
        BUICK DIVISION
    GENERAL MOTORS CORPORATION
            FLINT, MICH.
TRIM Nº. 432
PAINT Nº.  A
ACC   BFGIU
      BODY BY FISHER
```

EXAMPLE:

59	Model year (1959)
4	Buick Division
4	Le Sabre
39	4-Dr. hardtop
FB	Assembly plant (Flint, MI)
1234	Production sequence
432	Gray cloth/vinyl
A	Sable Black

THE MODEL AND STYLE NUMBER indicates the vehicles body type. The style number is a combination of codes identifying the GM division, series and body type.

LE SABRE

BODY TYPE	STYLE NUMBER
Sedan, 4-dr.	4419
Hardtop, 4-dr.	4439
Hardtop, 2-dr.	4437
Convertible, 2-dr.	4467
Sedan, 2-dr.	4411
Estate wagon, 4-dr.	4435

INVICTA

BODY TYPE	STYLE NUMBER
Sedan, 4-dr.	4619
Hardtop, 4-dr.	4639
Hardtop, 2-dr.	4637
Convertible, 2-dr.	4667
Estate wagon, 4-dr.	4635

ELECTRA

BODY TYPE	STYLE NUMBER
Sedan, 4-dr. 4719	
Hardtop, 4-dr. 4739	
Hardtop, 2-dr. 4737	

"225" ELECTRA

BODY TYPE	STYLE NUMBER
Riviera sedan, 4-dr. 4829	
Hardtop, 4-dr. 4839	
Convertible, 2-dr. 4867	

THE BODY NUMBER is the production serial number of the body. The prefix denotes the plant in which the body was assembled.

THE ASSEMBLY PLANT CODE indicates the plant where the vehicle was assembled. No assembly plant codes were available.

THE TRIM CODE indicates the key to the trim color and material for each model series.

COLOR	CLOTH	VINYL	LEATHER	CODE
Green		•		400,405,409
Green		•		600,609
Blue		•		410,415,419
Blue		•		610,619
Gray		•		430,435,439
Gray		•		630,639
Copper		•		455
Red		•		470,475,479
Red		•		670,679
Green/Green	•	•		401,402,601
Green/Green	•	•		605,701
Blue/Blue	•	•		411,412,611
Blue/Blue	•	•		615,711,713
Gray/Gray	•	•		431,432,631
Gray/Gray	•	•		635,731,733
Gray/Gray	•	•		734
Copper/Copper	•	•		452,651,655
Red/Red	•	•		675
Black/Gray	•	•		721,724
Beige/Beige	•	•		761
Turquoise	•	•		781
Green			•	700,702,809
Blue			•	810,819

COLOR	CLOTH	VINYL	LEATHER	CODE
Gray			•	830,839
Red			•	870,879
Green	•			801
Blue	•			811
Black	•			821
Gray	•			831
Beige	•			861

THE COLOR CODE indicates the paint color used on the car. Two-tone combination codes contain two letters, the first letter identifies the upper color and the second letter identifies the lower color.

COLOR	CODE
Sable Black ....A	
Silver Birch ....B	
Arctic White C	
Sierra Spruce ....D	
Glacier Green ....E	
Shalimar Blue ....H	
Wedgewood Blue ....J	
Turquoise ....K	
Tampico Red L	
Tawny Rose..M	
Lido Lavender ....N	
Pearl Fawn ....P	
Copper Glow ....R	

ENGINE SPECIFICATIONS

THE ENGINE NUMBER is located on the front of the cylinder block on the top left side. The engine number is the same as the serial number.

LA SABRE - SERIES 4400

ENGINE CODE	NO. CYL.	CID	HORSE-POWER	COMP. RATIO	CARB	TRANS
	8	364	210	8.5:1	2 BC	STD
	8	364	250	10.5:1	2 BC	AUTO
	8	364	300	10.5:1	4 BC	AUTO

INVICTA - SERIES 4600

ENGINE CODE	NO. CYL.	CID	HORSE-POWER	COMP. RATIO	CARB	TRANS
	8	401	325	10.5:1	4 BC	AUTO

ELECTRA - SERIES 4700

ENGINE CODE	NO. CYL.	CID	HORSE-POWER	COMP. RATIO	CARB	TRANS
	8	401	325	10.5:1	4 BC	AUTO

ELECTRA "225" - SERIES 4800

ENGINE CODE	NO. CYL.	CID	HORSE-POWER	COMP. RATIO	CARB	TRANS
	8	401	325	10.5:1	4 BC	AUTO

1950 CADILLAC

1950 CADILLAC

1950 CADILLAC COUPE DE VILLE

1950 CADILLAC COUPE DE VILLE

1950 CADILLAC SERIES 61

VEHICLE IDENTIFICATION NUMBER

• 506200123 •

Located on a plate on the flat machined surface of a boss, cast on the right front face of the block, and on the right-hand frame bar just behind the engine support bracket.

FIRST AND SECOND DIGITS: Identify the model year (1950)

THIRD AND FOURTH DIGITS: Identify the series

SERIES	WHEEL BASE	CODE
60S	130"	60
61	122"	61
62	126"	62
75	147"	75
86 Commercial chassis	157"	86

LAST SIX DIGITS: Represent the basic production sequence

BODY NUMBER PLATE

Located on the right side of the cowl just above the battery.

CADILLAC MOTOR DIVISION
GENERAL MOTORS CORPORATION
DETROIT, MICHIGAN

STYLE Nº. 50 6219
BODY Nº. 1234
TRIM Nº. 40
PAINT Nº. 1
TOP 00   ACC 00
BODY BY FLEETWOOD

EXAMPLE:

50	Model year (1950)
62	Series 62
19	4-Dr. sedan
1234	Production sequence
40	Gray bedford cord
1	Black

THE STYLE NUMBER indicates the series and model type.

SERIES 60S
BODY TYPE	STYLE
Fleetwood sedan, 4-dr.	*6019X

SERIES 61
BODY TY8PE	STYLE
Coupe, 2-dr.	6137
Sedan, 4-dr.	6169

SERIES 62
BODY TYPE	STYLE
Sedan, 4-dr.	6219
Sedan, 4-dr.	*6219X
Coupe, 2-dr.	6237
Coupe, 2-dr.	*6237X
Deluxe Coupe DeVille, 2-dr.	*6237DX
Convertible coupe, 2-dr.	*6267X

SERIES 75
BODY TYPE	STYLE
Fleetwood sedan, 4-dr.	*7523X
Fleetwood Imperial sedan, 4-dr.	*7533X

SERIES 86
BODY TYPE	STYLE
Commercial chassis	8680S

* w/ auto window lifts

THE BODY NUMBER is the production serial number of the body. The prefix denotes the plant in which the body was assembled.

THE ASSEMBLY PLANT CODE indicates the plant where the vehicle was assembled. No assembly plant codes available.

THE TRIM CODE indicates the key to the trim color and material for each model series.

SERIES 61

COLOR	CLOTH	VINYL	LEATHER	CODE
Gray	•			30,31
Gray			•	39

SERIES 62

COLOR	CLOTH	VINYL	LEATHER	CODE
Gray	•			40,41
Gray	•			42,43
Blue/Gray	•		•	48
Tan/Tan	•		•	49
Gray			•	47
Tan			•	50
Green/Green			•	51
Blue/Blue			•	52
Red			•	53
Black			•	54

SERIES 60S

COLOR	CLOTH	VINYL	LEATHER	CODE
Gray/Gray	•			60,61
Blue/Blue	•			62,63
Tan/Tan	•			64,65
Green/Green	•			66,67
Gray			•	69

SERIES 75

COLOR	CLOTH	VINYL	LEATHER	CODE
Gray	•			70,71
Tan	•			72,73

THE COLOR CODE indicates the paint color used on the car.

COLOR	CODE
Black	1
Hampden Blue	2
Lynton Green	3
Tyrolian Gray	4
Berkshire Blue	5
El Paso Beige	6
Corinth Blue	7
Savoy Gray	8
Madeira Maroon	9
French Gray	10
Glacier Green	12
Fiesta Ivory	22

TWO-TONE COLORS

COLOR	CODE
Vista Gray/French Gray	15
Marlow Green/Lynton Green	16
French Gray/Berkshire Blue	17
Kingswood Gray/Tyrolian Gray	19
Hampden Blue/Corinth Blue	20
Black/Fiesta Ivory	23

NOTE: The first color identifies the upper color and the second color identifies the lower color.

ENGINE SPECIFICATIONS

THE ENGINE NUMBER is located on the upper right front corner of the block. The engine number is the same as the serial number.

SERIES	ENGINE UNIT NUMBER
61, std.	8-M-1/up
60S,61,62,75, hyd.	9-M-1/up
75,86, std.	2-M-1/up
86, hyd.	7-M-1/up

SERIES 60S

ENGINE CODE	NO. CYL.	CID	HORSE-POWER	COMP. RATIO	CARB
	8	331	160	7.5:1	2 BC

SERIES 61

ENGINE CODE	NO. CYL.	CID	HORSE-POWER	COMP. RATIO	CARB
	8	31	160	7.5:1	2 BC

SERIES 62

ENGINE CODE	NO. CYL.	CID	HORSE-POWER	COMP. RATIO	CARB
	8	331	160	7.5:1	2 BC

SERIES 75

ENGINE CODE	NO. CYL.	CID	HORSE-POWER	COMP. RATIO	CARB
	8	331	160	7.5:1	2 BC

1951 CADILLAC COUPE DE VILLE

1951 CADILLAC

VEHICLE IDENTIFICATION NUMBER

• 5 1 6 2 0 0 1 2 3 •

Located on a plate on the flat machined surface of a boss, cast on the right front face of the block, also on the right-hand frame bar just behind the engine support bracket, and on a plate attached to the left front body pillar.

FIRST AND SECOND DIGITS: Identify the model year (1951)

THIRD AND FOURTH DIGITS: Identify the series

SERIES	WHEEL BASE	CODE
60S	130"	60
61	122"	61
62	126"	62
75	147"	75
86 Commercial chassis	157"	86

LAST SIX DIGITS: Represent the basic production sequence

BODY NUMBER PLATE

Located on the right side of the cowl just above the battery.

CADILLAC MOTOR DIVISION
GENERAL MOTORS CORPORATION
DETROIT, MICHIGAN
STYLE NO. 51 6219
BODY NO. 1234
TRIM NO. 40
PAINT NO. 1
TOP 00   **ACC** 00
BODY BY FLEETWOOD

EXAMPLE:

51	Model year (1951)
62	Series 62
19	4-Dr. sedan
1234	Production sequence
40	Lt. Gray/Dk. Gray cord/cloth
1	Black

THE STYLE NUMBER indicates the series and model type.

SERIES 60S

BODY TYPE	STYLE
Fleetwood sedan, 4-dr.	*6019X

SERIES 61

BODY TYPE	STYLE
Coupe, 2-dr.	6137
Sedan, 4-dr.	6169

SERIES 62

BODY TYPE	STYLE
Sedan, 4-dr.	6219
Sedan, 4-dr.	*6219X
Coupe, 2-dr.	6237
Coupe, 2-dr.	*6237X
Deluxe Coupe DeVille, 2-dr.	*6237DX
Convertible coupe, 2-dr.	*6267X

SERIES 75

BODY TYPE	STYLE
Business sedan, 9-pass.	7523L
Fleetwood sedan, 4-dr.	*7523X
Fleetwood Imperial sedan, 4-dr.	*7533X

SERIES 86

BODY TYPE	STYLE
Commercial chassis	8680S

* With hydraulic window lifts

THE BODY NUMBER is the production serial number of the body. The prefix denotes the plant in which the body was assembled.

THE ASSEMBLY PLANT CODE indicates the plant where the vehicle was assembled. No assembly plant codes were available.

THE TRIM CODE indicates the key to the trim color and material for each model series.

SERIES 61

COLOR	CLOTH	VINYL	LEATHER	CODE
Gray/Gray	•			30,31,34
Tan/Tan	•			32,33,35
Gray			•	38
Tan			•	39

SERIES 62

COLOR	CLOTH	VINYL	LEATHER	CODE
Gray/Gray	•			40,41,42
Tan/Tan	•			43,44,45
Gray			•	48
Tan			•	49,50
Green			•	51
Blue			•	52
Red			•	53
Black			•	54
Green/Green	•		•	57
Blue/Gray	•		•	58
Brown/Beige	•		•	59

SERIES 60S

COLOR	CLOTH	VINYL	LEATHER	CODE
Gray/Gray	•			60,61
Blue/Blue	•			62,63
Tan/Tan	•			64,65
Green/Green	•			66,67
Gray			•	68
Tan			•	69

SERIES 75

COLOR	CLOTH	VINYL	LEATHER	CODE
Gray	•			70,71
Tan	•			72,73

THE COLOR CODE indicates the paint color used on the car.

COLOR	CODE
Black	1
Empress Blue	2
Exeter Green	3
Capri Green	4
Cadet Blue	5
Tucson Beige	6
Corinth Blue	7
Savoy Gray	8
Bolero Maroon	9
Mist Gray	10
Chester Green	12
Fiesta Ivory	22

TWO-TONE COLORS

COLOR	CODE
Chester Green/Exeter Green	16
Argent/Cadet Blue	17
Exeter Green/Chester Green	18
Empress Blue/Corinth Blue	20

NOTE: The first color identifies the upper color and the second color identifies the lower color.

ENGINE SPECIFICATIONS

THE ENGINE NUMBER is located on the upper right front corner of the block. The engine number is the same as the serial number.

SERIES	ENGINE UNIT NUMBER
50-60s,61,62,75, Hyd.	9-N-1/up
51-86, Std.	2-N-1/up
51-86, Hyd.	7-N-1/up

SERIES 60S

ENGINE CODE	NO. CYL.	CID	HORSE-POWER	COMP. RATIO	CARB
	8	331	160	7.5:1	2 BC

SERIES 61

ENGINE CODE	NO. CYL.	CID	HORSE-POWER	COMP. RATIO	CARB
	8	31	160	7.5:1	2 BC

SERIES 62

ENGINE CODE	NO. CYL.	CID	HORSE-POWER	COMP. RATIO	CARB
	8	331	160	7.5:1	2 BC

SERIES 75

ENGINE CODE	NO. CYL.	CID	HORSE-POWER	COMP. RATIO	CARB
	8	331	160	7.5:1	2 BC

1952 CADILLAC SERIES 62

1952 CADILLAC COUPE DE VILLE

1952 CADILLAC COUPE DE VILLE

1952 CADILLAC

1952 CADILLAC 75 IMPERIAL

VEHICLE IDENTIFICATION NUMBER

`• 526200123 •`

Located on a plate on the flat machined surface of a boss, cast on the right front face of the block, also on the right-hand frame bar just behind the engine support bracket, and on a plate attached to the left front body pillar.

FIRST AND SECOND DIGITS: Identify the model year (1952)

THIRD AND FOURTH DIGITS: Identify the series

SERIES	WHEEL BASE	CODE
60S	130"	60
62	126"	62
75	147"	75
86 Commercial chassis	157"	86

LAST SIX DIGITS: Represent the basic production sequence

BODY NUMBER PLATE

Located on the right side of the cowl just above the battery.

CADILLAC MOTOR DIVISION
GENERAL MOTORS CORPORATION
DETROIT, MICHIGAN

STYLE Nº. 52 6219
BODY Nº. 1234
TRIM Nº. 40
PAINT Nº. 1
TOP 00   **ACC** 00
BODY BY FLEETWOOD

EXAMPLE:

52	Model year (1952)
62	Series 62
19	4-Dr. sedan
1234	Production sequence
40	Lt. Gray/Dk. Gray cord/cloth
1	Black

THE STYLE NUMBER indicates the series and model type.

SERIES 60S

BODY TYPE	STYLE
Fleetwood sedan, 4-dr.	*6019X

SERIES 62

BODY TYPE	STYLE
Sedan, 4-dr.	6219
Sedan, 4-dr.	*6219X
Coupe, 2-dr.	6237
Coupe, 2-dr.	*6237X
Deluxe Coupe DeVille, 2-dr.	*6237DX
Convertible coupe, 2-dr.	*6267X

SERIES 75

BODY TYPE	STYLE
Fleetwood sedan, 4-dr.	*7523X
Fleetwood Imperial sedan, 4-dr.	*7533X

SERIES 86

BODY TYPE	STYLE
Commercial chassis	8680S

* With hydraulic window lifts

THE BODY NUMBER is the production serial number of the body. The prefix denotes the plant in which the body was assembled.

THE ASSEMBLY PLANT CODE indicates the plant where the vehicle was assembled. No assembly plant codes were available.

THE TRIM CODE indicates the key to the trim color and material for each model series.

SERIES 62

COLOR	CLOTH	VINYL	LEATHER	CODE
Gray/Gray	•			40,41
Blue/Blue	•			42,43
Tan/Tan	•			44,45
Green/Green	•			46,47
Gray			•	48
Tan/Brown			•	49,50
Green/Green			•	51
Blue/Blue			•	52
Red			•	53
Black			•	54
Gray/Gray	•		•	70
Blue/Blue	•		•	72
Brown/Tan	•		•	74
Green/Green	•		•	76

SERIES 60S

COLOR	CLOTH	VINYL	LEATHER	CODE
Gray/Gray	•			60,61
Blue/Blue	•			62,63
Tan/Tan	•			64,65
Green/Green	•			66,67
Gray			•	68
Tan/Brown			•	69

SERIES 75

COLOR	CLOTH	VINYL	LEATHER	CODE
Gray	•			80,81
Tan	•			84,85

THE COLOR CODE indicates the paint color used on the car.

COLOR	CODE
Black	1
Empress Blue	2
Iverness Green	3
Aleutian Green	4
Nassau Blue	5
Phoenix Beige	6
Olympic Blue	7
Savoy Gray	8
Burgundy Maroon	9
Mist Gray	10
Hillcrest Green	12
Polar Green	13
Opal Gray	14
Sarasota Green	22

TWO-TONE COLORS

COLOR	CODE
Savoy Green/Mist Gray	15
Hillcrest Green/Iverness Green	16
Aleutian Green/Polar Green	17
Iverness Green/Hillcrest Green	18
Savoy Gray/Opal Gray	19
Nassau Blue/Olympic Blue	20
Iverness Green/Sarasota Green	23

NOTE: The first color identifies the upper color and the second color identifies the lower color.

ENGINE SPECIFICATIONS

THE ENGINE NUMBER is located on the upper right front corner of the block. The number is the same as the serial number.

SERIES	ENGINE UNIT NUMBER
52-60s,62,75, Hyd.	9-R-1/up
52-60S,62,75, Power steering/Hyd.	4-R-1/up
52-75,86, Std.	2-R-1/up
52-86, Hyd.	7-R-1/up
52-86, Power steering/Hyd.	5-R-1/up

SERIES 60S

ENGINE CODE	NO. CYL.	CID	HORSE-POWER	COMP. RATIO	CARB
	8	331	190	7.5:1	4 BC

SERIES 62

ENGINE CODE	NO. CYL.	CID	HORSE-POWER	COMP. RATIO	CARB
	8	331	190	7.5:1	4 BC

SERIES 75

ENGINE CODE	NO. CYL.	CID	HORSE-POWER	COMP. RATIO	CARB
	8	331	190	7.5:1	4 BC

1953 CADILLAC

1953 CADILLAC

1953 CADILLAC 62 COUPE DE VILLE

1953 CADILLAC 62 SEDAN

VEHICLE IDENTIFICATION NUMBER

• 5 3 6 2 0 0 1 2 3 •

Located on a plate on the flat machined surface of a boss, cast on the right front face of the block, also on the right-hand frame bar just behind the engine support bracket, and on a plate attached to the left front body pillar.

FIRST AND SECOND DIGITS: Identify the model year (1953)

THIRD AND FOURTH DIGITS: Identify the series

SERIES	WHEEL BASE	CODE
60S	130"	60
62	126"	62
75	147"	75
86 Commercial chassis	157"	86

LAST SIX DIGITS: Represent the basic production sequence

BODY NUMBER PLATE

Located on the right side of the cowl, under the hood, just above the battery.

```
CADILLAC MOTOR DIVISION
GENERAL MOTORS CORPORATION
DETROIT, MICHIGAN

STYLE Nᵒ. 53 6219
BODY Nᵒ. 1234
TRIM Nᵒ. 40
PAINT Nᵒ. 1
   TOP 00          ACC 00
BODY BY FLEETWOOD
```

EXAMPLE:

53	Model year (1953)
62	Series 62
19	4-Dr. sedan
1234	Production sequence
50	Lt. Gray/Dk. Gray cord/cloth
1	Black

THE STYLE NUMBER indicates the series and model type.

SERIES 60S
BODY TYPE	STYLE
Fleetwood sedan, 4-dr.	*6019X

SERIES 62
BODY TYPE	STYLE
Sedan, 4-dr.	6219
Sedan, 4-dr.	*6219X
Coupe, 2-dr.	6237
Coupe, 2-dr.	*6237X
Deluxe Coupe DeVille, 2-dr.	*6237DX
Convertible coupe, 2-dr.	*6267X
El Dorado Special Sport convertible, 2-dr.	*6267SX

SERIES 75
BODY TYPE	STYLE
Fleetwood sedan, 4-dr.	*7523X
Fleetwood Imperial sedan, 4-dr.	*7533X

SERIES 86
BODY TYPE	STYLE
Commercial chassis	8680S

* With hydraulic window lifts

THE BODY NUMBER is the production serial number of the body. The prefix denotes the plant in which the body was assembled.

THE ASSEMBLY PLANT CODE indicates the plant where the vehicle was assembled. No assembly plant codes were available.

THE TRIM CODE indicates the key to the trim color and material for each model series.

SERIES 62

COLOR	CLOTH	VINYL	LEATHER	CODE
Blue/White		•		32,42
Blue		•		33,43
Black/White		•		34
Black		•		35
Red/White		•		38,49
Red		•		39,48
Tan/Brown		•		45
Green/White		•		46
Green		•		47
Gray		•		58
Tan		•		59
Gray/Gray	•			50,51
Gray/Gray	•			60,61
Blue/Blue	•			52,53
Blue/Blue	•			62,63
Tan/Tan	•			54,55
Green/Green	•			56,57
Brown/Tan	•		•	64,65
Green/Green	•		•	66,67

SERIES 60S

COLOR	CLOTH	VINYL	LEATHER	CODE
Gray/Gray	•			70,71,86
Blue/Blue	•			72,73,87
Tan/Tan	•			74,75,88
Green/Green	•			76,77,89
Gray			•	78
Tan/Brown			•	79

SERIES 75

COLOR	CLOTH	VINYL	LEATHER	CODE
Gray	•			80,81
Gray	•			90,91
Blue	•			82,83
Blue	•			92,93
Tan	•			84,85
Tan	•			94,95

THE COLOR CODE indicates the paint color used on the car.

COLOR	CODE
Black	1
Cobalt Blue	2
Forest Green	3
Emerald Green	4
Tunis Blue	5
Phoenix Beige	6
Pastoral Blue	7
Norman Gray	8
Burgundy Maroon	9
Court Gray	10
Crystal Green	12
Gloss Green	13
Artesian Ochre	22
Alpine White	27
Azure Blue	28
Aztec Red	29

TWO-TONE COLORS

COLOR	CODE
Norman Gray/Court Gray	15
Gloss Green/Emerald Green	16
Forest Green/Gloss Green	17
Court Gray/Tunis Blue	18
Cobalt Blue/Pastoral Blue	20
Black/Artisan Ochre	23

NOTE: The first color identifies the upper color and the second color identifies the lower color.

ENGINE SPECIFICATIONS

THE ENGINE NUMBER is located on the upper right front corner of the block. The number is the same as the serial number.

SERIES	ENGINE UNIT NUMBER
53-60S,62,75, Hyd.	9-S-1/up
53-60S,62,75, Hyd./PS	4-S-1/up
53-60S,62,75, Hyd./PS/AC	4-SK-1/up
53-60S,62,75, Hyd./AC	9-SK-1/up
53-75,86, Std.	2-S-1/up
53-75,86, Std./AC	2-SK-1/up
53-86, Hyd.	7-S-1/up
53-86, Hyd./PS	5-S-1/up
53-86/Hyd./AC	7-SK-1/up
53-86, Hyd./PS/AC	5-SK-1/up

PS - Power Steering

AC - Air Conditioning

NOTE: Low compression engines will have suffic "LC" on engine unit number.

SERIES 60S

ENGINE CODE	NO. CYL.	CID	HORSE-POWER	COMP. RATIO	CARB
	8	331	210	8.25:1	4 BC

SERIES 62

ENGINE CODE	NO. CYL.	CID	HORSE-POWER	COMP. RATIO	CARB
	8	331	210	8.25:1	4 BC

SERIES 75

ENGINE CODE	NO. CYL.	CID	HORSE-POWER	COMP. RATIO	CARB
	8	331	210	8.25:1	4 BC

1954 CADILLAC SERIES 60 SPECIAL FLEETWOOD

1954 CADILLAC

1954 CADILLAC ELDORADO SPECIAL

1954 CADILLAC SERIES 62 COUPE DE VILLE

1954 CADILLAC SERIES 62

1954 CADILLAC FLEETWOOD SERIES 75 IMPERIAL

VEHICLE IDENTIFICATION NUMBER

`• 5 4 6 2 0 0 1 2 3 •`

Located on a plate on the flat machined surface of a boss, cast on the right front face of the block, also on the right-hand frame bar just behind the engine support bracket, and on a lubrication plate attached to the left front body pillar. On coupe styles the lubrication plate is located on the left door lock pillar.

FIRST AND SECOND DIGITS: Identify the model year (1954)

THIRD AND FOURTH DIGITS: Identify the series

SERIES	WHEEL BASE	CODE
60S	133"	60
62	129"	62
75	150"	75
86 Commercial chassis	158"	86

LAST SIX DIGITS: Represent the basic production sequence

BODY NUMBER PLATE

Located on the right side of the cowl, under the hood, just above the battery.

CADILLAC MOTOR DIVISION
GENERAL MOTORS CORPORATION
DETROIT, MICHIGAN

STYLE № 54 6219
BODY № 1234
TRIM № 40
PAINT № 1
TOP 00   ACC 00
BODY BY FLEETWOOD

EXAMPLE:

54	Model year (1954)
62	Series 62
19	4-Dr. sedan
1234	Production sequence
50	Lt. Gray/Dk. Gray cloth
1	Black

THE STYLE NUMBER indicates the series and model type.

SERIES 60S

BODY TYPE	STYLE
Fleetwood sedan, 4-dr.	*6019X

SERIES 62

BODY TYPE	STYLE
Sedan, 4-dr.	6219
Sedan, 4-dr.	*6219X
Coupe, 2-dr.	6237
Coupe, 2-dr.	*6237X
Deluxe Coupe DeVille, 2-dr.	*6237DX
Convertible coupe, 2-dr.	*6267X
El Dorado Special Sport convertible, 2-dr.	*6267SX

SERIES 75

BODY TYPE	STYLE
Fleetwood sedan, 4-dr.	*7523X
Fleetwood Imperial sedan, 4-dr.	*7533X

SERIES 86

BODY TYPE	STYLE
Commercial chassis	8680S

* With hydraulic window lifts

THE BODY NUMBER is the production serial number of the body. The prefix denotes the plant in which the body was assembled.

THE ASSEMBLY PLANT CODE indicates the plant where the vehicle was assembled. No assembly plant codes were available.

THE TRIM CODE indicates the key to the trim color and material for each model series.

SERIES 62

COLOR	CLOTH	VINYL	LEATHER	CODE
Black/White		•		30
Black		•		31,41
Blue/White		•		32,42
Blue		•		33,43,58
Black/Yellow		•		34
Yellow		•		35
Red/White		•		38
Red		•		39,49
Beige		•		45
Green/White		•		46
Green		•		47,59
Gray/Gray	•			50,51,503
Gray/Gray	•			513
Blue/Blue	•			52,53,523
Blue/Blue	•			533
Tan/Tan	•			54,543,553
Green/Green	•			56,57,563,573
Black/White	•		•	60
Gray/Gray	•		•	61,603,613
Blue/Blue	•		•	63,623
Tan/Brown	•		•	65,643,653
Green/Green	•		•	67,663

SERIES 60S

COLOR	CLOTH	VINYL	LEATHER	CODE
Blue/Blue			•	78
Green/Green			•	79
Gray/Gray	•			70,71,81
Blue/Blue	•			72,73,83
Blue/Blue	•			723
Tan/Tan	•			74,75,85
Green/Green	•			76,77,87
Green/Green	•			773,893

SERIES 75

COLOR	CLOTH	VINYL	LEATHER	CODE
Gray	•			90,91
Blue	•			92,93
Tan	•			94,95

THE COLOR CODE indicates the paint color used on the car.

COLOR	CODE
Black	1
Newport Blue	2
Viking Blue	3
Iris	4
Cobalt Blue	6
Shoal Green	7
Biscay Green	8
Arlington Green	9
Cabot Gray	10
Gander Gray	12
Russet	13
Driftwood	14
Apollo Gold	16
Aztec Red	17
Alpine White	18
Azure Blue	19

TWO-TONE COLORS

COLOR	CODE
Viking Blue/Newport Blue	2C
Alpine White/Viking Blue	3S
Alpine White/Iris	4S
Arlington Green/Shoal Green	7J
Cabot Gray/Biscay Green	8K
Norman Gray/Cabot Gray	10Y
Copper/Driftwood	14Z
Black/Appollo Gold	16A

ENGINE SPECIFICATIONS

THE ENGINE NUMBER is located on the upper right front corner of the block. The number is the same as the serial number. The engine unit number is located above the cast rib on the rear portion of the crankcase, behind the left hand block.

SERIES	ENGINE UNIT NUMBER
54-60S,62,75, w/o AC	4T1/up
54-60S,62,75, AC	4TK1/up
54-86, PS, w/o AC	5T1/up
54-86, PS/AC	5TK1/up
54-86, w/o PS/AC	7T1/up
54-86, AC, w/o PS	7TK1/up
54-60S,62,75, Syncro-Mesh	9T1/up
54-60S,62,75, Hyd.	9TK1/up

SERIES 60S

ENGINE CODE	NO. CYL.	CID	HORSE-POWER	COMP. RATIO	CARB
	8	331	230	8.25:1	4 BC

SERIES 62

ENGINE CODE	NO. CYL.	CID	HORSE-POWER	COMP. RATIO	CARB
	8	331	230	8.25:1	4 BC

SERIES 75

ENGINE CODE	NO. CYL.	CID	HORSE-POWER	COMP. RATIO	CARB
	8	331	230	8.25:1	4 BC

1955 CADILLAC

1955 CADILLAC SPECIAL FLEETWOOD

1955 CADILLAC SERIES 62

1955 CADILLAC COUPE DE VILLE

1955 CADILLAC SERIES 62 COUPE DE VILLE

1955 CADILLAC SERIES 75 FLEETWOOD

1955 CADILLAC

VEHICLE IDENTIFICATION NUMBER

• 5 5 6 2 0 0 1 2 3 •

Located on a plate on the flat machined surface of a boss, cast on the right front face of the block, also on the right-hand frame bar just behind the engine support bracket, and on a lubrication plate attached to the left front body pillar. On coupe styles the lubrication plate is located on the left door lock pillar.

FIRST AND SECOND DIGITS: Identify the model year (1955)

THIRD AND FOURTH DIGITS: Identify the series

SERIES	WHEEL BASE	CODE
60S	133"	60
62	129"	62
75	150"	75
86 Commercial chassis	158"	86

LAST SIX DIGITS: Represent the basic production sequence

BODY NUMBER PLATE

Located on the right side of the cowl, under the hood, just above the battery.

```
    CADILLAC MOTOR DIVISION
   GENERAL MOTORS CORPORATION
         DETROIT, MICHIGAN

  STYLE Nº. 55 6219X
  BODY Nº. 1234
  TRIM Nº. 40
  PAINT Nº.  30
    TOP 00         ACC 00
      BODY BY FLEETWOOD
```

EXAMPLE:

55	Model year (1955)
62	Series 62
19X	4-Dr. sedan
1234	Production sequence
40	Lt. Gray/Dk. Gray cloth
30	Mist Green

THE STYLE NUMBER indicates the series and model type.

SERIES 60S

BODY TYPE	STYLE
Fleetwood sedan, 4-dr.	*6019X

SERIES 62
BODY TYPE STYLE

BODY TYPE	STYLE
Sedan, 4-dr.	6219
Sedan, 4-dr.	*6219X
Coupe, 2-dr.	6237
Coupe, 2-dr.	*6237X
Deluxe Coupe DeVille, 2-dr.	*6237DX
Convertible coupe, 2-dr.	*6267
El Dorado Special Sport convertible, 2-dr.	*6267

SERIES 75
BODY TYPE STYLE

BODY TYPE	STYLE
Fleetwood sedan, 4-dr.	*7523X
Fleetwood Imperial sedan, 4-dr.	*7533X

SERIES 86
BODY TYPE STYLE

BODY TYPE	STYLE
Commercial chassis	8680S

* With hydraulic window lifts

THE BODY NUMBER is the production serial number of the body. The prefix denotes the plant in which the body was assembled.

THE ASSEMBLY PLANT CODE indicates the plant where the vehicle was assembled. No assembly plant codes were available.

THE TRIM CODE indicates the key to the trim color and material for each model series.

SERIES 62

COLOR	CLOTH	VINYL	LEATHER	CODE
Black			•	31,90,91
Blue/White			•	32
Blue			•	33,92,93
Gray			•	97
Copper/Gray			•	35
Gray/White			•	96
Green/White			•	36
Green			•	37
Red/White			•	38,98
Red			•	39,99
Beige			•	95
Gray/Gray	•			40,41,48
Blue/Blue	•			42,43
Tan/Tan	•			44,49
Green/Green	•			46,47
Gray/Gray	•	•	•	50,51
Blue/Blue	•	•	•	52,53
Tan/Tan	•	•	•	54,55
Green/Green	•	•	•	56,57,63
Black/Copper	•	•	•	61
Gold/White	•	•	•	65

SERIES 60S

COLOR	CLOTH	VINYL	LEATHER	CODE
Gray/Gray	•			70,71,81
Blue/Blue	•			72,73,83
Tan/Tan	•			74,75,85
Green/Green	•			76,77,87
Gray/Gray			•	78
Tan/Tan			•	79
Beige/Copper	•		•	88

SERIES 75

COLOR	CLOTH	VINYL	LEATHER	CODE
Gray/Gray	•			20,21
Blue/Blue	•			22,23
Tan/Tan	•			24,25

THE COLOR CODE indicates the paint color used on the car. Two-Tone colors: The first two digits identify the lower color, the last two digits identify the upper color.

COLOR	CODE
Black	10
Alabaster Gray	12
Ascot Gray	14
Atlantic Gray	16
Ruskin Blue	20
Azure Blue	22
Dresden Blue	24
Cobalt Blue	26
Mist Green	30
Celadon Green	32
Arlington Green	34
Cape Ivory	40
Pecos Beige	42
Cocoabar Brown	46
Pacific Coral	50
Mandan Red	52
Deep Cherry	54
Lt. Wedgewood Green	80
Goddess Gold	84
Alpine White	90
Silver	92
Bahama Blue	94
Copper	96

CONVERTIBLE TOP COLORS

COLOR	CODE
White	1
Black	2
Blue	3
White	4
Beige	5
Green	7
Black	9

ACCESSORY CODES

ACCESSORY	CODE
E Z eye glass	E
Heater	H
Air conditioner (w/shelf outlet)	K
Air conditioner (w/roof ducts)	K2
Electric 4-way control seat	V
Electric vertical lift control	Y

ENGINE SPECIFICATIONS

THE ENGINE NUMBER is located on the upper right front corner of the block. The number is the same as the serial number. The engine unit number is located above the cast rib on the rear portion of the crankcase, behind the left hand block.

SERIES	ENGINE UNIT NUMBER
55-60S,62,75, w/o AC/Dual carbs	4V
55-60S,62,75, w/AC, Dual carbs	4VK
55-86, w/o AC/Dual carbs	5V
55-86, w/AC, w/o/Dual carbs	5VK
55-60S,62, w/Dual carbs, w/o/AC	7V
55-60S,62, w/Dual carbs/AC	7VK

SERIES 60S

ENGINE CODE	NO. CYL.	CID	HORSE-POWER	COMP. RATIO	CARB
	8	331	250	9.1:1	4 BC

SERIES 62

ENGINE CODE	NO. CYL.	CID	HORSE-POWER	COMP. RATIO	CARB
	8	331	250	9.1:1	4 BC

SERIES 62 ELDORADO

ENGINE CODE	NO. CYL.	CID	HORSE-POWER	COMP. RATIO	CARB
	8	331	270	9.1:1	2-4 BC

SERIES 75

ENGINE CODE	NO. CYL.	CID	HORSE-POWER	COMP. RATIO	CARB
	8	331	250	9.1:1	4 BC

1956 CADILLAC SEDAN DE VILLE

1956 CADILLAC

1956 CADILLAC 62 SEDAN

VEHICLE IDENTIFICATION NUMBER

• 5 6 6 2 0 0 1 2 3 •

Located on a plate on the flat machined surface of a boss, cast on the right front face of the block, also on the right-hand frame bar just behind the engine support bracket, and on a lubrication plate attached to the left front body pillar. On coupe styles the lubrication plate is located on the left door lock pillar.

FIRST AND SECOND DIGITS: Identify the model year (1956)

THIRD AND FOURTH DIGITS: Identify the series

SERIES	WHEEL BASE	CODE
60S	133"	60
62	129"	62
75	150"	75
86 Commercial chassis	158"	86

LAST SIX DIGITS: Represent the basic production sequence

BODY NUMBER PLATE

Located on the right side of the cowl, under the hood, just above the battery.

CADILLAC MOTOR DIVISION
GENERAL MOTORS CORPORATION
DETROIT, MICHIGAN

STYLE Nº. 56 6019X
BODY Nº. 1234
TRIM Nº. 60
PAINT Nº. 30
TOP 00   **ACC** 00
BODY BY FLEETWOOD

EXAMPLE:

56	Model year (1956)
60	Series 60S
19X	Fleetwood sedan
1234	Production sequence
60	Lt. Gray cloth
30	Duchess Green

THE STYLE NUMBER indicates the series and model type.

SERIES 60S

BODY TYPE	STYLE
Fleetwood sedan, 4-dr.	*6019X

SERIES 62

BODY TYPE	STYLE
Sedan, 4-dr.	6219
Coupe, 2-dr.	6237
Deluxe Coupe DeVille, 2-dr.	*6237DX
Eldorado Seville coupe, 2-dr.	*6237SDX
Deluxe Sedan DeVille, 4-dr.	*6239DX
Convertible coupe, 2-dr.	*6267X
Eldorado Biarritz Special Sport convertible, 2-dr.	*6267SX

SERIES 75

BODY TYPE	STYLE
Fleetwood sedan, 4-dr.	*7523X
Fleetwood Imperial sedan, 4-dr.	*7533X

SERIES 86

BODY TYPE	STYLE
Commercial chassis	8680S

* With hydraulic window lifts

THE BODY NUMBER is the production serial number of the body. The prefix denotes the plant in which the body was assembled.

THE ASSEMBLY PLANT CODE indicates the plant where the vehicle was assembled. No assembly plant codes were available.

THE TRIM CODE indicates the key to the trim color and material for each model series.

SERIES 62

COLOR	CLOTH	VINYL	LEATHER	CODE
Black			•	11
Black/White			•	10
Blue/White			•	12
Blue			•	13,73
Green/White			•	16
Green			•	17
Red/White			•	18
Red			•	19
Gray/Gray			•	71
Brown/Beige			•	75
Black/White	•		•	20,41,50
Black	•		•	21
Black/Blue	•		•	43
Black/Yellow	•		•	45
Black/Green	•		•	47
Black/Pink	•		•	49
Blue/White	•		•	22
Blue	•		•	42,42A,42B
Blue	•		•	53,73
Turquoise/Black	•		•	23
Beige	•		•	25,54
Green/White	•		•	26,57
Green	•		•	46,77
Red/White	•		•	28,48,58
Red	•		•	29
Gray/White	•		•	40
Gold/White	•		•	44
Gray/Gray	•		•	51
Gray/Gray	•			30
Gray/White	•			31
Blue/Blue	•			32
Blue/White	•			33
Beige/Beige	•			34
Green/Green	•			36
Green/White	•			37

SERIES 60S

COLOR	CLOTH	VINYL	LEATHER	CODE
Gray/Gray	•			60,61
Blue/Blue	•			62,63
Beige/Beige	•			64,65,95
Green/Green	•			66,67
Gray/White	•		•	70
Blue/Blue	•		•	72
Gold/White	•		•	74
Green/Green	•		•	76
Gray			•	78
Brown/Beige			•	79

SERIES 75

COLOR	CLOTH	VINYL	LEATHER	CODE
Gray/Gray	•			80,80A,81A
Gray/Gray	•			81,90
Gray/Gray	•			90A,91
Blue/Blue	•			82,83
Beige/Beige	•			84A,85A
Brown/Beige	•			94A

THE COLOR CODE indicates the paint color used on the car. Two-Tone colors: The first two digits identify the lower color, the second two digits identify the upper color.

COLOR	CODE
Black	10
Canyon Gray	12
Cascade Gray	14
Dawn Gray	16
Camelot Gray	18
Sonic Blue	20
Tahoe Blue	24
Cobalt Blue	26
Duchess Green	30
Princess Green	32
Aquamarine	34
Arlington Green	36
Cape Ivory	40
Goddess Gold	42
Pecos Beige	44
Mountain Laurel	46
Taupe	48
Mandan Red	50
Chantilly Maroon	52
Alpine White	90
Starlight Silver	92
O.A. Starlight Silver	*93
Bahama Blue	94
O.A. Bahama Blue	*95
Emerald Green	96
O.A. Emerald Green	*97

* Acrylic paint

CONVERTIBLE TOP COLORS

COLOR	CODE
Ivory	1
Black	2
Blue	3
Tan	4
Green	5

ACCESSORY CODES

ACCESSORY	CODE
E Z eye glass	E
Heater	H
Air conditioner (w/shelf outlet)	K
Air conditioner (w/roof ducts)	K2
Power lid	S
Electric 6-way control seat	V,Y
Electric window lifts	X

ENGINE SPECIFICATIONS

THE ENGINE NUMBER is located on the upper right front corner of the block. The number is the same as the serial number. The engine unit number is located above the cast rib on the rear portion of the crankcase, behind the left hand block.

SERIES	ENGINE UNIT NUMBER
56-60S,62,75, w/o AC/Dual carbs	4X
56-60S,62,75, w/AC, w/o Dual carbs	4XK
56-86, w/o AC/Dual carbs	5X
56-86, w/AC, w/o Dual carbs	5XK
56-60S,62, w/Dual carbs, w/o AC	7X
56-60S,62, w/Dual carbs/AC	7XK

SERIES 60S

ENGINE CODE	NO. CYL.	CID	HORSE-POWER	COMP. RATIO	CARB
	8	365	285	9.75:1	4 BC

SERIES 62

ENGINE CODE	NO. CYL.	CID	HORSE-POWER	COMP. RATIO	CARB
	8	365	285	9.75:1	4 BC

SERIES 62 ELDORADO

ENGINE CODE	NO. CYL.	CID	HORSE-POWER	COMP. RATIO	CARB
	8	365	305	9.75:1	2x4 BC

SERIES 75

ENGINE CODE	NO. CYL.	CID	HORSE-POWER	COMP. RATIO	CARB
	8	365	285	9.75:1	4 BC

1957 CADILLAC

1957 CADILLAC 62 SEDAN

1957 CADILLAC ELDORADO BIARRITZ

1957 CADILLAC BIARRITZ

1957 CADILLAC ELDORADO BROUGHAM

1957 CADILLAC MODEL 62

1957 CADILLAC ELDORADO SEVILLE

VEHICLE IDENTIFICATION NUMBER

> • 5 7 6 2 0 0 1 2 3 •

Located on a plate on the flat machined surface of a boss, cast on the right front face of the block, also on the right-hand frame bar just behind the engine support bracket, and on a lubrication plate attached to the left front face of the left door lock pillar.

FIRST AND SECOND DIGITS: Identify the model year (1957)

THIRD AND FOURTH DIGITS: Identify the series

SERIES	WHEEL BASE	CODE
60S	133"	60
62	129"	62
70	126"	70
75	150"	75
86 Commercial chassis	156"	86

LAST SIX DIGITS: Represent the basic production sequence

BODY NUMBER PLATE

Located on the right side of the cowl, under the hood, just above the battery.

> **CADILLAC MOTOR DIVISION**
> **GENERAL MOTORS CORPORATION**
> **DETROIT, MICHIGAN**
> **STYLE Nº. 57 6039X**
> **BODY Nº. 1234**
> **TRIM Nº. 60**
> **PAINT Nº. 10**
> **TOP** 00   **ACC** 00
> **BODY BY FLEETWOOD**

EXAMPLE:

57	Model year (1957)
60	Series 60S
39X	Fleetwood 4-dr. sedan
1234	Production sequence
60	Lt. Gray cloth
10	Black

THE STYLE NUMBER indicates the series and model type.

SERIES 60S

BODY TYPE	STYLE
Fleetwood sedan, 4-dr.	*6039X

SERIES 62

BODY TYPE	STYLE
Coupe, 2-dr.	6237
Deluxe Coupe DeVille, 2-dr.	*6237DX
Eldorado Special Sport coupe, 2-dr.	*6237SDX
Sedan, 4-dr.	6239
Deluxe Sedan DeVille, 4-dr.	*6239DX
Convertible coupe, 2-dr.	*6267X
Eldorado Biarritz Special Sport convertible, 2-dr.	*6267SX

SERIES 70

BODY TYPE	STYLE
Eldorado Brougham, 4-dr.	7059X

SERIES 75

BODY TYPE	STYLE
Fleetwood sedan, 4-dr.	*7523X
Fleetwood Imperial sedan, 4-dr.	*7533X

SERIES 86

BODY TYPE	STYLE
Commercial chassis	8680S

* With hydraulic window lifts

THE BODY NUMBER is the production serial number of the body. The prefix denotes the plant in which the body was assembled.

THE ASSEMBLY PLANT CODE indicates the plant where the vehicle was assembled. No assembly plant codes were available.

THE TRIM CODE indicates the key to the trim color and material for each model series.

SERIES 60S

COLOR	CLOTH	VINYL	LEATHER	CODE
Gray/Gray	•			60,61,61A
Blue/Blue	•			62,63
Beige/Beige	•			65,65A
Green/Green	•			66,67
Black/Silver/White	•		•	70,70A
Black/Blue			•	72
Beige/Beige			•	74
Black/Green			•	76
Gray	•		•	96
Beige	•		•	98
Green	•		•	99

SERIES 62

COLOR	CLOTH	VINYL	LEATHER	CODE
Black			•	11
Black/White			•	10
Blue			•	13
Copper			•	15
Green			•	17
Red/White			•	18
Red			•	19
Black/White	•		•	20,20A
Black/Pink	•		•	49
Black/Silver/Pink	•		•	49A
Black/Blue	•		•	53
Black/Copper	•		•	55,58
Black/Green	•		•	56,57
Black	•		•	21
Blue	•		•	22,42,43
Blue	•		•	87
Turquoise/White	•		•	23,23A
Rose	•		•	25
Beige	•		•	25A,44
Green	•		•	26,46,47
Green	•		•	89
Red/White	•		•	28,28A
Red	•		•	29
Gray/White	•		•	40,40A
Gray/White	•		•	86,86A
Silver/White/Gray	•		•	41,41A
Black/Silver/White	•		•	48,50
Gray/Gray	•			30
Gray/White	•			31,31A
Blue/Blue	•			32,33
Beige/Beige	•			34
Green/Green	•			36,37

SERIES 75

COLOR	CLOTH	VINYL	LEATHER	CODE
Gray/Gray	•			80,81,90
Beige/Beige	•			84,85
Brown/Beige	•			94

THE COLOR CODE indicates the paint color used on the car. Two-Tone colors: The first two digits identify the lower color, the second two digits identify the upper color.

COLOR	CODE
Black	10
Alpine White	12
Polo Gray	14
Eton Gray	16
Camelot Gray	18
Orion Blue	20
Tahoe Blue	24
Cobalt Blue	26
Glade Green	30
Thebes Green	32
Turquoise	34
Arlington Green	36
Leghorn Cream	40
Buckskin Beige	44
Mountain Laurel	46
Dusty Rose	48
Amethyst	49
Dakota Red	50
Castile Maroon	52
Olympic White	90
Starlight Silver	92
Bahama Blue	94
Elysian Green	96
Copper	98

CONVERTIBLE TOP COLORS

COLOR	CODE
Ivory	1
Black	2
Med. Blue	3
Beige	4
Green	5
Lt. Blue	7
Copper	8
Lt. Green	9

ACCESSORY CODES

ACCESSORY	CODE
E Z eye glass	E
Heater	H
Air conditioner	K
Power lid	S
Electric 6-way control seat	V,Y
Electric window lifts	X

ENGINE SPECIFICATIONS

THE ENGINE NUMBER is located on the upper right front corner of the block. The engine number is the same as the serial number. The engine unit number is located above the cast rib on the rear portion of the crankcase, behind the left hand block.

SERIES	ENGINE UNIT NUMBER
57-60S,62, w/o AC/Dual carbs	76X
57-60S,62, w/AC, w/o Dual carbs	76K
57-75,86, w/o AC/Dual carbs	77X
57-75,86, w/AC, w/o Dual carbs	77K
57-62, w/Dual carbs, w/o AC	7QX
57-62, w/Dual carbs/AC	7QK

AC - Air conditioning

SERIES 60S

ENGINE CODE	NO. CYL.	CID	HORSE-POWER	COMP. RATIO	CARB
	8	365	300	10.0:1	4 BC

SERIES 62

ENGINE CODE	NO. CYL.	CID	HORSE-POWER	COMP. RATIO	CARB
	8	365	300	10.0:1	4 BC

SERIES 62 ELDORADO

ENGINE CODE	NO. CYL.	CID	HORSE-POWER	COMP. RATIO	CARB
	8	365	325	10.0:1	2x4 BC

SERIES 75

ENGINE CODE	NO. CYL.	CID	HORSE-POWER	COMP. RATIO	CARB
	8	365	300	10.0:1	4 BC

1958 CADILLAC ELDORADO BROUGHAM

1958 CADILLAC COUPE DE VILLE

1958 CADILLAC FLEETWOOD SIXTY SPECIAL

1958 CADILLAC ELDORADO SEVILLE

VEHICLE IDENTIFICATION NUMBER

`• 5 8 F 0 0 1 2 3 4 •`

Located on a plate on the flat machined boss, cast on the upper right hand corner on the front face of the right hand cylinder block, also on the top flange of the frame right hand side member foreward from and adjacent to the number one body bracket, and on a lubrication plate attached to the front face of the left door lock pillar.

FIRST AND SECOND DIGITS: Identify the model year (1958)

THIRD DIGIT: Identifies the body style

SERIES 60

BODY STYLE	CODE
Fleetwood sedan	M

SERIES 62

BODY STYLE	CODE
Coupe	G
Coupe DeVille	J
Eldorado Seville	H
4-Dr. sedan	K
4-Dr. sedan, extended deck	N
Sedan DeVille	L
Convertible	F
Eldorado Biarritz convertible	E

SERIES 70

BODY STYLE	CODE
Brougham	P

SERIES 75

BODY STYLE	CODE
4-Dr. sedan	R
4-Dr. Imperial sedan	S

SERIES 86

BODY STYLE	CODE
Commercial chassis	Z

LAST SIX DIGITS: Represent the basic production sequence

BODY NUMBER PLATE

Located on the top surface of the left air duct cover under the hood, near the cowl.

CADILLAC MOTOR DIVISION
GENERAL MOTORS CORPORATION
DETROIT, MICHIGAN
STYLE Nº. 58 6039X
BODY Nº. 1234
TRIM Nº. 60
PAINT Nº. 30
TOP 00   **ACC** 00
BODY BY FLEETWOOD

EXAMPLE:

58	Model year (1958)
60	Series 60S
39X	Fleetwood 4-dr. sedan
1234	Production sequence
60	Gray/Black/White cloth/leather
30	Acadian Green

THE STYLE NUMBER indicates the series and model type.

SERIES 60S

BODY TYPE	STYLE
Fleetwood sedan, 4-dr.	*6039X

SERIES 62

BODY TYPE	STYLE
Coupe, 2-dr.	6237
Deluxe Coupe DeVille, 2-dr.	*6237DX
Eldorado Seville Special Sport coupe, 2-dr.	*6237SDX
Sedan, 4-dr. (std. deck)	6239
Sedan, 4-dr. (extended deck)	6239E
Deluxe Sedan DeVille, 4-dr. (extended deck)	*6239EDX
Convertible coupe, 2-dr.	*6267X
Eldorado Biarritz Special Sport convertible, 2-dr.	*6267SX

SERIES 70

BODY TYPE	STYLE
Brougham, 4-dr.	7059X

SERIES 75

BODY TYPE	STYLE
Fleetwood sedan, 4-dr.	*7523X
Fleetwood Imperial sedan, 4-dr.	*7533X

SERIES 86

BODY TYPE	STYLE
Commercial chassis	8680S

* With hydraulic window lifts

THE BODY NUMBER is the production serial number of the body. The prefix denotes the plant in which the body was assembled.

THE ASSEMBLY PLANT CODE indicates the plant where the vehicle was assembled. No assembly plant codes were available.

THE TRIM CODE indicates the key to the trim color and material for each model series.

SERIES 60S

COLOR	CLOTH	VINYL	LEATHER	CODE
Gray/Black/White	•		•	60
Gray/Black	•		•	61
Blue/Blue	•		•	63
Beige/Beige	•		•	65
Turquoise/Black	•		•	66
Yellow/Green	•		•	67
Gray	•		•	68
Gray	•			70,71
Blue	•			72,73
Beige	•			74,75
Black/Gray	•		•	96

SERIES 62

COLOR	CLOTH	VINYL	LEATHER	CODE
Black/White	•		•	10,11,20
Black/White	•		•	91
Black	•		•	21
Gray	•		•	12,41,42
Blue	•		•	13,43,52
Copper	•		•	15,54
Green	•		•	17,56
Red/White	•		•	18,28,58
Red	•		•	19,29
Blue/White	•		•	22,93
Coral	•		•	24
Saddle Beige	•		•	25
Yellow-Green/White	•		•	97
Green/White	•		•	26
Black/White/Gray	•		•	86,40
Black/Coral	•		•	44
Black/Pink	•		•	48
Black/Gray	•		•	50,51
Beige	•		•	45
Turquoise	•		•	46
Yellow-Green	•		•	47
Black/White/Gray	•			30
Gray	•			31
Blue	•			33
Black/Coral	•			34
Beige	•			35
Black/Turquoise	•			36
Yellow-Green	•			37

SERIES 75

COLOR	CLOTH	VINYL	LEATHER	CODE
Gray/Gray	•		•	80,81,90
Beige/Beige	•		•	84,85
Brown/Beige	•		•	94

THE COLOR CODE indicates the paint color used on the car. Two-Tone colors: The first two digits identify the lower color, the second two digits identify the upper color.

COLOR	CODE
Black	10
Alpine White	12
Cheviot Gray	14
Prestwick Gray	16
Camelot Gray	18
Daphne Blue	20
Somerset Blue	24
Cobalt Blue	26
Turquoise	28
Peacock	29
Acadian Green	30
Versailles Green	32
Regent Green	36
Calcutta Cream	40
Alamo Beige	42
Buckskin	44
Tahitian Coral	48
Meridian Taupe	49
Dakota Red	50
Olympic White	*90
Rajah Silver	*92
Argyle Blue	*94
Gleneagles Green	*96
Desert Bronze	*98

* Acrylic paint

CONVERTIBLE TOP COLORS

COLOR	CODE
Ivory	1
Black	2
Lt. Blue	3
Beige	4
Lt. Yellow-Green	5
Lt. Green	6
Pale Blue	7
Lt. Copper	8

ACCESSORY CODES

ACCESSORY	CODE
Back rest lock for coupes	C
E Z eye glass	E
Heater	H
Air conditioner	K
Electric door locks	M
Power vent window regulators	N
Remote control trunk lock	S
Electric 6-way control seat	V,Y
Electric window lifts	X

ENGINE SPECIFICATIONS

THE ENGINE NUMBER is located on the upper right front corner of the block. The number is the same as the serial number. The engine unit number is located above the cast rib on the rear portion of the crankcase, behind the left hand block.

SERIES	ENGINE UNIT NUMBER
58-60S,62, w/o AC/three carbs	86X
58-60S,62, w/AC, w/o three carbs	86K
58-75,86, w/o AC/three carbs	87X
58-75,86, w/AC, w/o three carbs	87K
58-60S,62,75, w/three carbs, w/o AC	8QX
58-62, w/three carbs/AC	8QK

AC - Air conditioning

SERIES 60S

ENGINE CODE	NO. CYL.	CID	HORSE-POWER	COMP. RATIO	CARB
	8	365	310	10.25:1	4 BC

SERIES 62

ENGINE CODE	NO. CYL.	CID	HORSE-POWER	COMP. RATIO	CARB
	8	365	310	10.25:1	4 BC

SERIES 62/70 ELDORADO

ENGINE CODE	NO. CYL.	CID	HORSE-POWER	COMP. RATIO	CARB
	8	365	335	10.25:1	3x2 BC

SERIES 75

ENGINE CODE	NO. CYL.	CID	HORSE-POWER	COMP. RATIO	CARB
	8	365	310	10.25:1	4 BC

1959 CADILLAC SIX WINDOW SEDAN

1959 CADILLAC FLEETWOOD SIXTY SPECIAL

1959 CADILLAC SERIES 62

1959 CADILLAC SEDAN DEVILLE

1959 CADILLAC SERIES 64 ELDORADO BIARRITZ

VEHICLE IDENTIFICATION NUMBER

● 5 9 F 0 0 1 2 3 4 ●

Located on a plate on the flat machined boss, cast on the lower left hand side of the cylinder block, also on the top flange of the frame left hand side member forward from and adjacent to the radiator support, and on a lubrication plate attached to the front face of the left door lock pillar.

FIRST AND SECOND DIGITS: Identify the model year (1959)

THIRD DIGIT: Identifies the body style

SERIES 60

BODY STYLE	CODE
Special sedan	M

SERIES 62

BODY STYLE	CODE
4-Dr. sedan	A
Convertible coupe	F
Coupe	G
Standard sedan	K

SERIES 63

BODY STYLE	CODE
Sedan DeVille	B
Coupe DeVille	J
Sedan DeVille	L

SERIES 64

BODY STYLE	CODE
Eldorado Biarritz convertible	E
Eldorado Seville coupe	H

SERIES 67

BODY STYLE	CODE
Limousine, 9-pass.	R
Imperial sedan, 9-pass.	S

SERIES 68

BODY STYLE	CODE
Commercial chassis	Z

SERIES 69

BODY STYLE	CODE
Eldorado Brougham	P

LAST SIX DIGITS: Represent the basic production sequence

BODY NUMBER PLATE

Located on the top surface of the left air duct cover under the hood, near the cowl.

```
CADILLAC DIV.GENERAL MOTORS CORP.
            DETROIT, MICH.
STYLE Nº. 59 6229    BODY Nº. 1234
TRIM Nº. 30          PAINT Nº. 12
     TOP 00          ACC 00
        BODY BY FLEETWOOD
```

EXAMPLE:

59	Model year (1959)
62	Series 62
29	4-Dr. sedan
1234	Production sequence
30	Black/White/Gray cloth
12	Dover White

THE STYLE NUMBER indicates the series and model type.

SERIES 60

BODY TYPE	STYLE
Fleetwood sedan, 4-dr.	*6029

SERIES 62

BODY TYPE	STYLE
Sedan, 4-dr.	6229
Coupe, 2-dr.	6237
Sedan, 4-dr.	6239
Convertible coupe, 2-dr.	*6267
Deluxe Sedan DeVille, 4-dr.	*6339
Deluxe Coupe DeVille, 2-dr.	*6337
Deluxe Sedan DeVille, 4-dr.	*6339
Eldorado Seville Special Sport coupe, 2-dr.	*6437
Eldorado Biarritz Special Sport convertible, 2-dr.	*6467

SERIES 70

BODY TYPE	STYLE
Brougham, 4-dr.	7059X

SERIES 75

BODY TYPE	STYLE
Fleetwood sedan, 4-dr.	*6723
Fleetwood Imperial sedan, 4-dr.	*6733

SERIES 86

BODY TYPE	STYLE
Commercial chassis	6890

* With hydraulic window lifts

THE BODY NUMBER is the production serial number of the body. The prefix denotes the plant in which the body was assembled.

THE ASSEMBLY PLANT CODE indicates the plant where the vehicle was assembled. No assembly plant codes were available.

THE TRIM CODE indicates the key to the trim color and material for each model series.

SERIES 60

COLOR	CLOTH	VINYL	LEATHER	CODE
Black/White	•		•	60,91,96
Gray/White	•		•	92
Blue/White	•		•	93
Gray	•			61
Blue/Blue	•		•	62
Blue	•			63,72
Fawn	•			65,74
Green	•			67
Gray	•			70,71

SERIES 62

COLOR	CLOTH	VINYL	LEATHER	CODE
White			•	10,10B
Black			•	11,11B
Gray			•	12,12B
Blue			•	13,13B,53
Gray-Green			•	17,17B
Plum			•	18,18B
Red			•	19,19B,29
Red/White			•	59
Black/White/Gray	•			30
Gray	•			31
Blue/Black	•			32
Black/Pink	•			34
Fawn	•			35
Black/Turquoise	•			36
Green/Black	•			37
White/Black	•		•	20,86
Black	•		•	21

COLOR	CLOTH	VINYL	LEATHER	CODE
Blue	•		•	23
Saddle	•		•	25
Turquoise	•		•	26
Green	•		•	27
White/Red	•		•	28
Silver/Black/White	•		•	40
Gray/Gray	•		•	41
Blue/Blue	•		•	43,52
Fawn	•		•	45
Med. Green	•		•	46
Turquoise/Black	•		•	47
Pink	•		•	48
White	•		•	50
Gray	•		•	51
Blue	•		•	22,93
Gray-Green	•		•	56
Plum	•		•	58

SERIES 75

COLOR	CLOTH	VINYL	LEATHER	CODE
Gray/Gray	•		•	80,81,90
Fawn/Fawn	•		•	84,85

THE COLOR CODE indicates the paint color used on the car. Two-Tone colors: The first two numbers identify the upper color, the second two numbers identify the lower color.

COLOR	CODE
Ebony Black	10
Dover White	12
Silver Metallic	14
London Gray	16
Breton Blue	20
Georgian Blue	24
Dunstan Blue	26
Vegas Turquoise Metallic	29
Pinehurst Green	30
Inverness Green Metallic	32
Kensington Green Metallic	36
Gotham Gold	40
Beaumont Beige	44
Wood Rose Metallic	49
Seminole Red	50
Olympic White	90
Argent Silver Metallic	92
Argyle Blue Metallic	94
Hampton Green Metallic	96
Persian Sand Metallic	98

CONVERTIBLE TOP COLORS

COLOR	CODE
Ivory	1
Black	2
Plum	3
Med. Green	4
Lt. Buckskin	6
Gray-Green	7
Pale Blue	8

ACCESSORY CODES

ACCESSORY	CODE
Cruise control	C
E Z eye glass	E
Heater	H
Air conditioner	K
Electric door locks	M
Power vent window regulators	N
Remote control trunk lock	S
Electric window lifts	X
Electric 6-way control seat	Y

ENGINE SPECIFICATIONS

THE ENGINE NUMBER is located on the lower left side of the cylinder block. The number is the same as the serial number. The engine unit number is located above the cast rib on the rear portion of the crankcase, behind the left hand block.

SERIES	ENGINE UNIT NUMBER
1959, w/o AC/three carbs	96X
1959, w/AC, w/o three carbs	96K
1959, exc. CC, w/three carbs, w/o AC	96QX
59-60,62, w/three carbs/AC	96QK

AC - Air conditioning

CADILLAC

ENGINE CODE	NO. CYL.	CID	HORSE-POWER	COMP. RATIO	CARB
	8	390	325	10.5:1	4 BC

ELDORADO

ENGINE CODE	NO. CYL.	CID	HORSE-POWER	COMP. RATIO	CARB
	8	390	345	10.5:1	3x2 BC

1950 CHEVROLET DELUXE

1950 CHEVROLET

1950 CHEVROLET

1950 CHEVROLET SYTLELINE DELUXE

VEHICLE IDENTIFICATION NUMBER

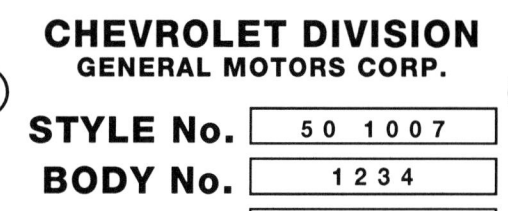

Located on the plate on the left front door hinge pillar.

FIRST DIGIT: Identifies the assembly plant

ASSEMBLY PLANT	CODE
Flint, MI	1
Tarrytown, NY	2
St. Louis, MO	3
Kansas City, MO	5
Oakland, CA	6
Atlanta, GA	8
Norwood, OH	9
Baltimore, MD	14
Los Angeles, CA	20
Janesville, WI	21

SECOND AND THIRD DIGITS: Identify the year, model and series (H=1950)

MODEL	SERIES	CODE
Styleline/Fleetline special	1500	HJ
Styleline/Fleetline deluxe	2100	HK
Sedan delivery	1508	HJ

FOURTH DIGITS: Identifies the month of manufacture

MONTH	CODE
January	A
February	B
March	C
April	D
May	E
June	F
July	G
August	H
September	I
October	J
November	K
December	L

LAST FOUR DIGITS: Represent the basic production number

BODY NUMBER PLATE

Located on the right hand side of the cowl.

CHEVROLET DIVISION
GENERAL MOTORS CORP.

STYLE No.	50 1007
BODY No.	1234
TRIM No.	171
PAINT No.	423

BODY BY FISHER

EXAMPLE:

50	Model year (1950)
10	Fleetline deluxe
07	2-Dr. sedan
1234	Production sequence
171	Gray striped cloth
423	Mayland Black

THE STYLE NUMBER indicates the model and body style.

FLEETLINE DELUXE

BODY STYLE	CODE
2-Dr. sedan	1007
4-Dr. sedan	1008

FLEETLINE SPECIAL

BODY STYLE	CODE
2-Dr. sedan	1207
4-Dr. sedan	1208

STYLELINE DELUXE

BODY STYLE	CODE
2-Dr. sedan	1011
4-Dr. sedan	1069
Station wagon	1062
Convertible	1067
Bel Air	1037
Coupe, 6-pass.	1027

STYLELINE SPECIAL

BODY STYLE	CODE
2-Dr. sedan	1211
4-Dr. sedan	1269
Coupe, 6-pass.	1227
Coupe, 3-pass.	1227B
Sedan delivery	1271

THE BODY NUMBER is the production serial number of the body.

THE COLOR CODE indicates the paint color used on the car.

COLOR	CODE
Mayland Black	423
Oxford Maroon	424
Grecian Gray	425
Crystal Green	426
Falcon Gray	427
Windsor Blue	428
Mist Green	429
Rodeo Beige	430
Moonlite Cream	431
Grecian Gray	437

TWO-TONE COLORS

COLOR	CODE
Falcon Gray/Grecian Gray	432
Crystal Green/Mist Green	433
Mayland Black/Mist Green	434
Grecian Gray/Windsor Blue	435
Falcon Gray/Moonlight Cream	436

NOTE: The first color identifies the upper body color, the second color identifies the lower body color.

THE TRIM CODE indicates the trim color and material for each model series.

COLOR	CLOTH	VINYL	LEATHER	CODE
Gray	•			170,171
Red/Gray	•		•	175
Green/Gray	•		•	176
Blue/Gray	•		•	177
Black/Gray	•		•	179
Red/Gray	•		•	185
Green/Gray	•		•	186
Blue/Gray	•		•	187
Black/Gray	•		•	189
Red/Tan	•		•	195
Green/Tan	•		•	196
Blue/Tan	•		•	197
Black/Tan	•		•	199
Brown		•		163,166

ENGINE SPECIFICATIONS

THE ENGINE NUMBER is located on the right side of the crankcase to the rear of the distributor. The starting engine number is HAA-1001/up - Flint; HAM-1001/up - Tonawanda.

SPECIAL

ENGINE CODE	NO. CYL.	CID	HORSE-POWER	COMP. RATIO	CARB	TRANS
HJ	6	216.5	92	6.6:1	1 BC	STD

DELUXE

ENGINE CODE	NO. CYL.	CID	HORSE-POWER	COMP. RATIO	CARB	TRANS
HK	6	216.5	92	6.6:1	1 BC	STD
HK	6	235.5	105	6.75:1	1 BC	PG

1951 CHEVROLET

1951 CHEVROLET DELUXE

1951 CHEVROLET STYLELINE DELUXE

1951 CHEVROLET

VEHICLE IDENTIFICATION NUMBER

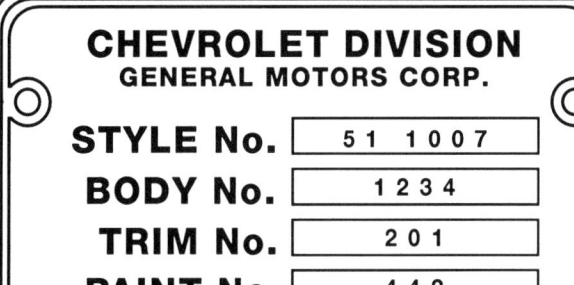

• CHEVROLET •
2 J K B 1 0 0 1

Located on the plate on the left front door hinge pillar.

FIRST DIGIT: Identifies the assembly plant

ASSEMBLY PLANT	CODE
Flint, MI	1
Tarrytown, NY	2
St. Louis, MO	3
Kansas City, MO	5
Oakland, CA	6
Atlanta, GA	8
Norwood, OH	9
Baltimore, MD	14
Los Angeles, CA	20
Janesville, WI	21

SECOND AND THIRD DIGITS: Identify the year, model and series (J=1951)

MODEL	SERIES	CODE
Styleline/Fleetline special	1500	JJ
Styleline/Fleetline deluxe	2100	JK
Sedan delivery	1508	JJ

FOURTH DIGITS: Identifies the month of manufacture

MONTH	CODE
January	A
February	B
March	C
April	D
May	E
June	F
July	G
August	H
September	I
October	J
November	K
December	L

LAST FOUR DIGITS: Represent the basic production number

BODY NUMBER PLATE

Located on the right hand side of the cowl.

CHEVROLET DIVISION
GENERAL MOTORS CORP.

STYLE No. | 51 1007
BODY No. | 1234
TRIM No. | 201
PAINT No. | 442

BODY BY FISHER

EXAMPLE:

51	Model year (1951)
10	Fleetline deluxe
07	2-Dr. sedan
1234	Production sequence
201	Gray striped cloth
442	Mayland Black

THE STYLE NUMBER indicates the model and body style.

FLEETLINE DELUXE

BODY STYLE	CODE
2-Dr. sedan	1007
4-Dr. sedan	1008

FLEETLINE SPECIAL

BODY STYLE	CODE
2-Dr. sedan	1207
4-Dr. sedan	1208

STYLELINE DELUXE

BODY STYLE	CODE
2-Dr. sedan	1011
4-Dr. sedan	1069
Station wagon	1062
Convertible	1067
Bel Air	1037
Coupe, 6-pass.	1027

STYLELINE SPECIAL

BODY STYLE	CODE
2-Dr. sedan	1211
4-Dr. sedan	1269
Coupe, 6-pass.	1227
Coupe, 3-pass.	1227B
Sedan delivery	1271

THE BODY NUMBER is the production serial number of the body.

THE COLOR CODE indicates the paint color used on the car.

COLOR	CODE
Mayland Black	442
Burgundy Red	443
Thistle Gray	444
Fathom Green	445
Shadow Gray	446
Trophy Blue	447
Aspen Green	448
Aztec Tan	449
Moonlite Cream	450

TWO-TONE COLORS

COLOR	CODE
Shadow Gray/Thistle Gray	451
Fathom Green/Aspen Green	452
Mayland Black/Moonlite Cream	453
Thistle Gray/Trophy Blue	454
Thistle Gray/Shadow Gray	455
Aspen Green/Fathom Green	456
Shadow Gray Poly/Thistle Gray	460
Thistle Gray/Shadow Gray Poly	461
Fathom Green/Aspen Green	464
Aspen Green/Fathom Green	465

NOTE: The first color identifies the upper body color, the second color identifies the lower body color.

THE TRIM CODE indicates the trim color and material for each model series.

COLOR	CLOTH	VINYL	LEATHER	CODE
Gray	•			200,201
Red			•	205
Green			•	206
Blue			•	207
Black			•	209
Red/Gray	•		•	185
Green/Gray	•		•	186
Blue/Gray	•		•	187
Black/Gray	•		•	189
Brown		•		163
Tan		•		202
Gray		•		172

ENGINE SPECIFICATIONS

THE ENGINE NUMBER is located on the right side of the crankcase to the rear of the distributor. The starting number on engines is JAA-1001/up - Flint, JAM-1001/up - Tonawanda.

SPECIAL

ENGINE CODE	NO. CYL.	CID	HORSE-POWER	COMP. RATIO	CARB	TRANS
JJ	6	216.5	92	6.6:1	1 BC	STD

DELUXE

ENGINE CODE	NO. CYL.	CID	HORSE-POWER	COMP. RATIO	CARB	TRANS
JK	6	216.5	92	6.6:1	1 BC	STD
JK	6	235.5	105	6.7:1	1 BC	PG

1952 CHEVROLET

1952 CHEVROLET DELUXE

1952 CHEVROLET

VEHICLE IDENTIFICATION NUMBER

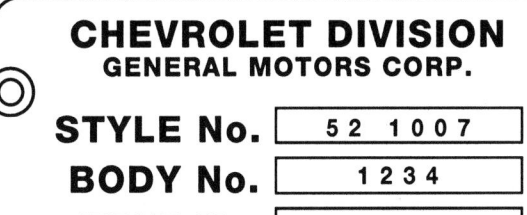

• CHEVROLET •
2 K K B 1 0 0 1

Located on the plate on the left front door hinge pillar.

FIRST DIGIT: Identifies the assembly plant

ASSEMBLY PLANT	CODE
Flint, MI	1
Tarrytown, NY	2
St. Louis, MO	3
Kansas City, MO	5
Oakland, CA	6
Atlanta, GA	8
Norwood, OH	9
Baltimore, MD	14
Los Angeles, CA	20
Janesville, WI	21

SECOND AND THIRD DIGITS: Identify the year, model and series (K=1952)

MODEL	SERIES	CODE
Styleline/Fleetline special	1500	KJ
Styleline/Fleetline deluxe	2100	KK
Sedan delivery	1508	KJ

FOURTH DIGITS: Identifies the month of manufacture

MONTH	CODE
January	A
February	B
March	C
April	D
May	E
June	F
July	G
August	H
September	I
October	J
November	K
December	L

LAST FOUR DIGITS: Represent the basic production number

BODY NUMBER PLATE

Located on the right hand side of the cowl.

CHEVROLET DIVISION
GENERAL MOTORS CORP.
STYLE No. | 52 1007
BODY No. | 1234
TRIM No. | 210
PAINT No. | 465
BODY BY FISHER

EXAMPLE:

52	Model year (1952)
10	Fleetline deluxe
07	2-Dr. sedan
1234	Production sequence
210	Lt. Gray pattern cloth
465	Onyx Black

THE STYLE NUMBER indicates the model and body style.

FLEETLINE DELUXE

BODY STYLE	CODE
2-Dr. sedan	1007

STYLELINE DELUXE

BODY STYLE	CODE
2-Dr. sedan	1011
4-Dr. sedan	1069
Station wagon	1062
Convertible	1067
Bel Air	1037
Coupe, 6-pass.	1027

STYLELINE SPECIAL

BODY STYLE	CODE
2-Dr. sedan	1211
4-Dr. sedan	1269
Coupe, 6-pass.	1227
Coupe, 3-pass.	1227B
Sedan delivery	1271

THE BODY NUMBER is the production serial number of the body.

THE COLOR CODE indicates the paint color used on the car.

COLOR	CODE
Onyx Black	465
Birch Gray	466
Dusk Gray	467
Spring Green	469
Emerald Green	470
Admiral Blue	472
Twilight Blue	477
Sahara Beige	478
Regal Maroon	479
Cherry	481
Honeydew	482
Saddle Brown	483

TWO-TONE COLORS

COLOR	CODE
Dusk Gray Metallic/Birch Gray	468
Emerald Green Metallic/Spring Green	471
Admiral Blue Metallic/Twilight Blue	473
Spring Green/Emerald Green Metallic	474
Birch Gray/Twilight Blue	484
Birch Gray/Spring Green	485
Sahara Beige/Saddle Brown Metallic	486
Sahara Beige/Regal Maroon Metallic	487
Saddle Brown Metallic/Sahara Beige	488
Black/Birch Gray	489
Black/Regal Maroon Metallic	491
Black/Honeydew	493
Birch Gray/Admiral Blue Poly	494

NOTE: The first color identifies the upper body color, the second color identifies the lower body color.

THE TRIM CODE indicates the trim color and material for each model series.

COLOR	CLOTH	VINYL	LEATHER	CODE
Gray	•			210,211
Blue	•			212
Lt. Green	•			213
Tan/Brown			•	224
Red			•	225
Green			•	226
Blue			•	227
Black			•	229
Tan/Brown	•		•	234
Red/Gray	•		•	235
Green	•		•	236
Blue	•		•	237
Black/Gray	•		•	239
White/Coral	•		•	240
Dk. Gray		•		216
Tan		•		218
Gray		•		214

ENGINE SPECIFICATIONS

THE ENGINE NUMBER is located on the right side of the crankcase to the rear of the distributor. The starting serial numbers are as follows:

ENGINE PLANT	STARTING NUMBERS
216" - Flint	KAA-1001/up
216" - Tonawanda	KAM-1001/up

SPECIAL

ENGINE CODE	NO. CYL.	CID	HORSE-POWER	COMP. RATIO	CARB	TRANS
KJ	6	216.5	92	6.6:1	1 BC	STD

DELUXE

ENGINE CODE	NO. CYL.	CID	HORSE-POWER	COMP. RATIO	CARB	TRANS
KK	6	216.5	92	6.6:1	1 BC	STD
KK	6	235.5	105	6.7:1	1 BC	PG

1953 CHEVROLET BEL AIR

1953 CHEVROLET

1953 CHEVROLET CORVETTE

1953 CHEVROLET BEL AIR

1953 CHEVROLET BEL AIR

VEHICLE IDENTIFICATION NUMBER

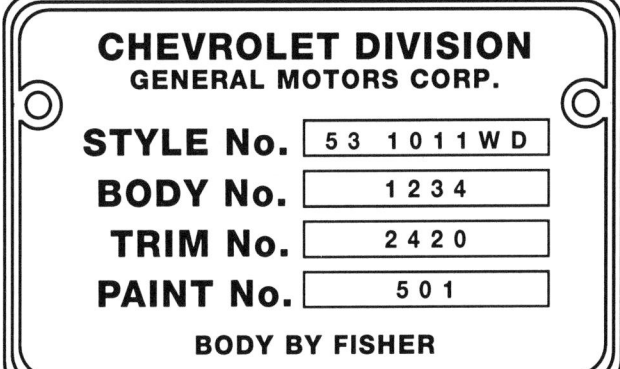

Located on the plate on the left front door hinge pillar.

FIRST DIGIT: Identifies the series and model

MODEL	SERIES	CODE
One-Fifty	1500	A
Two-Ten	2100	B
Bel Air	2400	C
Sedan delivery	1508	D
Corvette	2934	E

SECOND AND THIRD DIGITS: Identify the model year (1953)

FOURTH DIGIT: Identifies the assembly plant

ASSEMBLY PLANT	CODE
Atlanta, GA	A
Baltimore, MD	B
Flint, MI	F
Janesville, WI	J
Kansas City, MO	K
Los Angeles, CA	L
Oakland, CA	O
St. Louis, MO	S
Tarrytown, NY	T
Norwood, OH	N

LAST SIX DIGITS: Represent the basic production number

BODY NUMBER PLATE

Located on the right hand side of the cowl.

CHEVROLET DIVISION
GENERAL MOTORS CORP.

STYLE No.	53 1011WD
BODY No.	1234
TRIM No.	2420
PAINT No.	501

BODY BY FISHER

EXAMPLE:

53	Model year (1953)
10	Bel Air
11D	2-Dr. sedan
1234	Production sequence
242	Blue pattern cloth
501	Regatta Blue

THE STYLE NUMBER indicates the model and body style.

BEL AIR

BODY STYLE	CODE
2-Dr. sedan	1011WD
4-Dr. sedan	1069WD
Sport coupe	1037D
Convertible	1067D

TWO-TEN

BODY STYLE	CODE
2-Dr. sedan	1011W
4-Dr. sedan	1069W
Club coupe	1027
Sport coupe	1037
Station wagon, 8-pass.	1062
Station wagon, 6-pass.	1062F

ONE-FIFTY

BODY STYLE	CODE
2-Dr. sedan	1211
4-Dr. sedan	1269
Club coupe	1227
Business coupe	1227B
Station wagon, 6-pass.	1262F
Sedan delivery	1271

CORVETTE

	CODE
2 Dr.	2934

THE BODY NUMBER is the production serial number of the body.

THE COLOR CODE indicates the paint color used on the car.

COLOR	CODE
Onyx Black	480
Driftwood Gray	490
Dusk Gray	496
Surf Green	498
Woodland Green	499
Regatta Blue	501
Horizon Blue	503
Sahara Beige	504
Madeira Maroon	505
Target Red	506
Campus Cream	507
Sungold	508
Saddle Brown	509

TWO-TONE COLORS

COLOR	CODE
Dusk Gray/Driftwood Gray	497
Woodland Green/Surf Green	500
Regatta Blue/Horizon Blue	502
India Ivory/Horizon Blue	510
India Ivory/Regatta Blue	511
Campus Cream/Woodland Green	512
Woodland Green/Campus Cream	513
Saddle Brown/Sahara Beige	514
Sahara Beige/Saddle Brown	515
India Ivory/Sungold	516
Target Red/India Ivory	517

NOTE: The first color identifies the upper body color, the second color identifies the lower body color.

THE TRIM CODE indicates the key to the trim color and material for each model series.

COLOR	CLOTH	VINYL	LEATHER	CODE
Gray	•			241
Blue	•			242
Green	•			243
Tan/Brown	•			244
Gray	•			245,249
Blue	•			246
Green	•			247
Tan	•			248
Tan	•	•		254
Green	•	•		256
Blue	•	•		257
Yellow/White	•	•		258
Black/White	•	•		259
Brown/Tan		•		284,264
Red		•		285
Green		•		286,266,277
Blue		•		287
Red/White		•		265
Blue		•		267
Yellow/White		•		268
Black/White		•		269
Beige/Brown		•		278
Beige/Green		•		280
Beige		•		276

ENGINE SPECIFICATIONS

THE ENGINE NUMBER is located on the right side of the block to the rear of the distributor. The engine numbers start at 1001 with one of the following prefixes:

ENGINE	FLINT	TONAWANDA
216"	LAG	LAT
216" w/10 3/4" clutch	LAJ	LAV
235"	LAA	LAM
235" w/10 3/4" clutch	LAC	LAP
235" w/PS	LAE	LAR
235" w/aluminum timing gears	LAF	—
235" Powerglide	—	LAQ
235" Powerglide w/PS	—	LAS

PS - Power steering

ONE-FIFTY

NO. CYL.	CID	HORSE-POWER	COMP. RATIO	CARB	TRANS
6	235	108	7.1:1	1 BC	STD
6	235	115	7.5:1	1 BC	PG

TWO-TEN

NO. CYL.	CID	HORSE-POWER	COMP. RATIO	CARB	TRANS
6	235	108	7.1:1	1 BC	STD
6	235	115	7.5:1	1 BC	PG

BEL AIR

NO. CYL.	CID	HORSE-POWER	COMP. RATIO	CARB	TRANS
6	235	108	7.1:1	1 BC	STD
6	235	115	7.5:1	1 BC	PG

CORVETTE

NO. CYL.	CID	HORSE-POWER	COMP. RATIO	CARB	TRANS
6	235	150	8.0:1	3-1 BC	AUTO

1954 CHEVROLET BEL AIR

1954 CHEVROLET BEL AIR

1954 CHEVROLET 210 STATION WAGON

1954 CHEVROLET 210

1954 CHEVROLET BEL AIR

VEHICLE IDENTIFICATION NUMBER

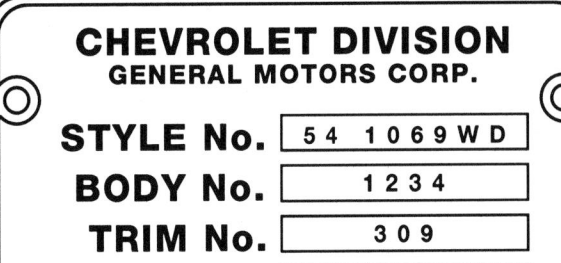

Located on the plate on the left front door hinge pillar.

FIRST DIGIT: Identifies the series and model

MODEL	SERIES	CODE
One-Fifty	1500	A
Two-Ten	2100	B
Bel Air	2400	C
Sedan delivery	1508	D
Corvette	2934	E

SECOND AND THIRD DIGITS: Identify the model year (1954)

FOURTH DIGIT: Identifies the assembly plant

ASSEMBLY PLANT	CODE
Atlanta, GA	A
Baltimore, MD	B
Flint, MI	F
Janesville, WI	J
Kansas City, MO	K
Los Angeles, CA	L
Oakland, CA	O
St. Louis, MO	S
Tarrytown, NY	T
Norwood, OH	N

LAST SIX DIGITS: Represent the basic production number

BODY NUMBER PLATE

Located on the right hand side of the cowl.

CHEVROLET DIVISION
GENERAL MOTORS CORP.
STYLE No. 54 1069WD
BODY No. 1234
TRIM No. 309
PAINT No. 540
BODY BY FISHER

EXAMPLE:

54	Model year (1954)
10	Bel Air
69WD	4-Dr. sedan
1234	Production sequence
309	Gray cloth/vinyl
540	Onyx Black

THE STYLE NUMBER indicates the model and body style.

BEL AIR
BODY STYLE	CODE
2-Dr. sedan	1011WD
4-Dr. sedan	1069WD
Sport coupe	1037D
Station wagon, 8-pass.	1062D
Convertible	1067D

TWO-TEN
BODY STYLE	CODE
2-Dr. sedan	1011W
4-Dr. sedan	1069W
Club coupe	1011WA
Station wagon, 6-pass.	1062F

ONE-FIFTY
BODY STYLE	CODE
2-Dr. sedan	1211W
Utility sedan	1211WB
4-Dr. sedan	1269W
Station wagon, 6-pass.	1262F
Sedan delivery	1271

CORVETTE
2 Dr.	2934

THE BODY NUMBER is the production serial number of the body.

THE COLOR CODE indicates the paint color used on the car.

COLOR	CODE
Onyx Black	540
Surf Green	541
Bermuda Green	542
Horizon Blue	543
Biscayne Blue	544
Shoreline Beige	545
Saddle Brown	546
India Ivory	547
Shadow Gray	548
Morocco Red	549
Romany Red	550
Fiesta Cream	551
Turquoise	552
Pueblo Tan	553
Polo White	*567
Pennant Blue	*570

* Corvette

TWO-TONE COLORS

COLOR	CODE
Shoreline Beige/Bermuda Green	556
India Ivory/Surf Green	555
India Ivory/Horizon Blue	556
India Ivory/Biscayne Blue	557
Bermuda Green/Shoreline Beige	558
Shoreline Beige/Saddle Brown	559
India Ivory/Onyx Black	560
India Ivory/Romany Red	561
Bermuda Green/Fiesta Cream	562
India Ivory/Turquoise	563
Shoreline Beige/Pueblo Tan	564
Morocco Red/Shoreline Beige	563
Shoreline Beige/Morocco Red	566

NOTE: The first color identifies the upper body color, the second color identifies the lower body color.

THE TRIM CODE indicates the trim color and material for each model series.

COLOR	CLOTH	VINYL	LEATHER	CODE
Gray	•			300,304
Blue/White		•		332
Green/White		•		333
Black/White		•		334
Blue	•			305
Green	•			306
Tan/Brown	•			307
Gray	•	•		309
Blue	•	•		310
Green	•	•		311
Beige/Tan	•	•		330
Turquoise/White	•	•		331
Red/White		•		325
Green		•		326
Blue		•		327
Beige/Tan		•		328
Black/White		•		329
Turquoise/White		•		337
Blue	•	•		314
Green	•	•		315
Red/White	•	•		316
Turquoise/White	•	•		317
Beige/Tan	•	•		318
Black/White	•	•		319
Green/Straw		•		323
Beige		•		324
Maroon/Beige		•		322
Gray		•		303
Green		•		371

ENGINE SPECIFICATIONS

THE ENGINE NUMBER is located on the right side of the block to the rear of the distributor. The serial numbers start at 1001. The suffix letter after the engine code identifies the engine plant - "F" - Flint, "T" - Tonawanda. ZC identifies heavy duty clutch, ZH identifies an aluminum cam gear, ZE identifies power steering

ONE-FIFTY

ENGINE CODE	NO. CYL.	CID	HORSE-POWER	COMP. RATIO	CARB	TRANS
Z	6	235	115	7.5:1	1 BC	STD
Y	6	235	125	7.5:1	1 BC	PG

TWO-TEN

ENGINE CODE	NO. CYL.	CID	HORSE-POWER	COMP. RATIO	CARB	TRANS
Z	6	235	115	7.5:1	1 BC	STD
Y	6	235	125	7.5:1	1 BC	PG

BEL AIR

ENGINE CODE	NO. CYL.	CID	HORSE-POWER	COMP. RATIO	CARB	TRANS
Z	6	235	115	7.5:1	1 BC	STD
Y	6	235	125	7.5:1	1 BC	PG

CORVETTE

ENGINE CODE	NO. CYL.	CID	HORSE-POWER	COMP. RATIO	CARB	TRANS
YG	6	235	150	8.0:1	3-1 BC	PG

1955 CHEVROLET

1955 CHEVROLET BEL AIR

1955 CHEVROLET BEL AIR BEAUVILLE STATION WAGON

1955 CHEVROLET BEL AIR

1955 CHEVROLET BEL AIR

1955 CHEVROLET BEL AIR

VEHICLE IDENTIFICATION NUMBER

• CHEVROLET •
C 5 5 F 0 0 1 0 2 3

Located on the plate on the left front door hinge pillar post. The 8-cylinder vehicles have a "V" preceding the first digit.

FIRST DIGIT: Identifies the series and model

MODEL	SERIES	CODE
One-Fifty, 6-cyl.	1500	A
One-Fifty, 8-cyl.	1500	VB
Two-Ten, 6-cyl.	2100	B
Two-Ten, 8-cyl.	2100	VB
Bel Air, 6-cyl.	2400	C
Bel Air, 8-cyl.	2400	VC
Sedan delivery, 6-cyl.	1508	D
Corvette, 6-cyl.	2934	E
Corvette, 8-cyl.	2934	VE

SECOND AND THIRD DIGITS: Identify the model year (1955)

FOURTH DIGIT: Identifies the assembly plant

ASSEMBLY PLANT	CODE
Atlanta, GA	A
Baltimore, MD	B
Flint, MI	F
Janesville, WI	J
Kansas City, MO	K
Los Angeles, CA	L
Oakland, CA	O
St. Louis, MO	S
Tarrytown, NY	T
Norwood, OH	N

LAST SIX DIGITS: Represent the basic production number

BODY NUMBER PLATE

Located on the right hand side of the cowl.

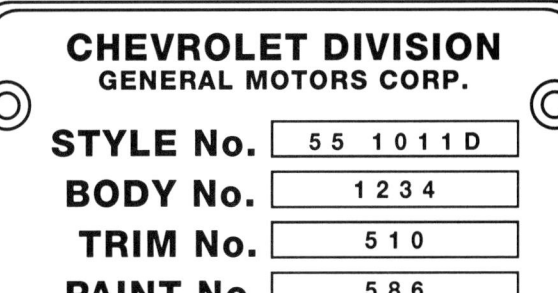

CHEVROLET DIVISION
GENERAL MOTORS CORP.
STYLE No. [55 1011D]
BODY No. [1234]
TRIM No. [510]
PAINT No. [586]
BODY BY FISHER

EXAMPLE:

55	Model year (1955)
10	Bel Air
11D	2-Dr. sedan
1234	Production sequence
510	Green cloth/vinyl
586	Sea Mist Green

THE STYLE NUMBER indicates the model and body style.

BEL AIR

BODY STYLE	CODE
2-Dr. sedan	1011D
4-Dr. sedan	1019D
Sport coupe	1037D
Station wagon (Beauville)	1062DF
Station wagon (Nomad)	1064DF
Convertible	1067D

TWO-TEN

BODY STYLE	CODE
2-Dr. sedan	1011
4-Dr. sedan	1019
Club coupe	1011A
Sport coupe	1037
Station wagon (Townsman)	1062F
Station wagon (Handyman)	1063F

ONE-FIFTY

BODY STYLE	CODE
2-Dr. sedan	1211
Utility sedan	1211B
4-Dr. sedan	1219
Station wagon (Handyman)	1263F
Sedan delivery	1271

CORVETTE

BODY STYLE	CODE
2-Dr.	2934

THE BODY NUMBER is the production serial number of the body.

THE COLOR CODE indicates the paint color used on the car.

COLOR	CODE
Onyx Black	585
Sea Mist Green	586
Neptune Green	587
Skyline Blue	588
Glacier Blue	589
Copper Maroon	590
Shoreline Beige	591
Autumn Bronze	592
India Ivory	593
Shadow Gray	594
Gypsy Red	596
Regal Turquoise	598
Coral	626
Harvest Gold	630
Cashmere Blue	683
Polo White	*
Harvest Gold	*
Gypsy Red	*
Corvette Copper	*

* Corvette

TWO-TONE COLORS

COLOR	CODE
Sea Mist Green/Neptune Green	599
Skyline Blue/Glacier Blue	600
Neptune Green/Shoreline Beige	601
India Ivory/Skyline Blue	602
Autumn Bronze/Shoreline Beige	603
Neptune Green/Sea Mist Green	604
India Ivory/Sea Mist Green	605
Shoreline Beige/Autumn Bronze	606
Glacier Blue/Shoreline Beige	607
India Ivory/Onyx Black	608
Glacier Blue/Skyline Blue	610
India Ivory/Regal Turquoise	612
Shoreline Beige/Neptune Green	613
Shoreline Beige/Glacier Blue	614
Shoreline Beige/Gypsy Red	615
India Ivory/Gypsy Red	617
India Ivory/Shadow Gray	624
Shadow Gray/Coral	627
Onyx Black/India Ivory	628
India Ivory/Coral	629
India Ivory/Harvest Gold	631
India Ivory/Cashmere Blue	682
India Ivory/Navajo Tan	684
India Ivory/Dusk Rose	685

THE TRIM CODE indicates the key to the trim color and material for each model series.

COLOR	CLOTH	VINYL	LEATHER	CODE
Gray	•			500
Gray/Black		•		547
Blue/Beige		•		506
Green/Beige		•		507
Black/Ivory		•		508
Blue	•			503
Green	•			504
Tan/Brown	•			505
Blue	•	•		509
Green	•	•		510
Brown/Beige	•	•		511
Turquoise/Ivory	•	•		513
Gray/Coral	•	•		531
Gray/Ivory	•	•		549
Red/Beige		•		525
Green		•		526
Blue		•		527
Brown/Beige		•		528
Gray/Coral		•		533
Truquoise/Ivory		•		537
Gray/Ivory		•		551
Beige/Blue	•	•		519
Beige/Green	•	•		520
Beige/Red	•	•		521
Beige/Turquoise	•	•		522
Gray/Coral	•	•		532
Gray/Ivory	•			550
Blue/Beige		•		514
Green		•		515
Brown/Beige		•		516
Beige	•	•		517
Beige/Blue	•	•		518
Straw/Brown		•		502,501
Green		•		524

ENGINE SPECIFICATIONS

THE ENGINE NUMBER is located on the right side of the block to the rear of the distributor on the 6-cylinder, on the pad at the front right hand side of the block behind the waterpump on the 8-cylinder. All engine numbers start with 1001. The prefix identifies where the engine was built, model year and model type. (F - Flint, T - Tonawanda)

EXAMPLE: F55GJ 1001

TYPE	CODE	TYPE	CODE
235"	Z	265" V8 3-speed/AC/overdrive	GG
235" w/HD clutch	ZC	265" V8 w/HD clutch	GJ
235" w/aluminum cam gear	ZH	265" V8 w/HD clutch/AC	GK
235" w/HD clutch/cam gear	ZJ	265" V8 w/HD clutch/4-barrel	GL
235" w/Powerglide	Y	265" V8 w/HD clutch/4-barrel/AC	GM
235" Corvette	YG	265" V8 w/Powerglide	F
265" V8 3-speed	G	265" V8 w/Powerglide/4-barrel	FB
265" V8 3-speed/overdrive	GC	265" V8 w/Powerglide/AC	FC
265" V8 3-speed/4-barrel	GD	265" V8 w/Powerglide/AC/4-barrel	FD
265" V8 3-speed/4-barrel/overdrive	GE	265" V8 Corvette	FG
265" V8 3-speed/AC	GF	265" V8 w/standard trans.	GR

ONE-FIFTY

ENGINE CODE	NO. CYL.	CID	HORSE-POWER	COMP. RATIO	CARB
Z	6	235	123	7.5:1	1 BC
Y	6	235	136	7.5:1	1 BC
	8	265	162	8.0:1	2 BC
	8	265	180	8.0:1	4 BC

TWO-TEN

ENGINE CODE	NO. CYL.	CID	HORSE-POWER	COMP. RATIO	CARB
Z	6	235	123	7.5:1	1 BC
Y	6	235	136	7.5:1	1 BC
	8	265	162	8.0:1	2 BC
	8	265	180	8.0:1	4 BC

BEL AIR

ENGINE CODE	NO. CYL.	CID	HORSE-POWER	COMP. RATIO	CARB
Z	6	235	123	7.5:1	1 BC
Y	6	235	136	7.5:1	1 BC
	8	265	162	8.0:1	2 BC
	8	265	180	8.0:1	4 BC

CORVETTE

ENGINE CODE	NO. CYL.	CID	HORSE-POWER	COMP. RATIO	CARB
YG	6	235	150	8.0:1	3-1 BC
FG	8	265	195	8.0:1	4 BC

1956 CHEVROLET NOMAD

1956 CHEVROLET

1956 CHEVROLET BEL AIR NOMAD STATION WAGON

1956 CHEVROLET BEL AIR

1956 CHEVROLET BEAUVILLE

1956 CHEVROLET BEL AIR

VEHICLE IDENTIFICATION NUMBER

● CHEVROLET ●
C56F001023

Located on the plate on the left front door hinge pillar post. The 8-cylinder vehicles have a "V" preceding the first digit.

FIRST DIGIT: Identifies the series and model

MODEL	SERIES	CODE
One-Fifty, 6-cyl.	1500	A
One-Fifty, 8-cyl.	1500	VA
Two-Ten, 6-cyl.	2100	B
Two-Ten, 8-cyl.	2100	VB
Bel Air, 6-cyl.	2400	C
Bel Air, 8-cyl.	2400	VC
Sedan delivery, 6-cyl.	1508	D
Sedan delivery, 8-cyl.	1508	VD
Corvette, 8-cyl.	2934	VE

SECOND AND THIRD DIGITS: Identify the model year (1956)

FOURTH DIGIT: Identifies the assembly plant

ASSEMBLY PLANT	CODE
Atlanta, GA	A
Baltimore, MD	B
Flint, MI	F
Janesville, WI	J
Kansas City, MO	K
Los Angeles, CA	L
Oakland, CA	O
St. Louis, MO	S
Tarrytown, NY	T
Norwood, OH	N

LAST SIX DIGITS: Represent the basic production number

BODY NUMBER PLATE

Located on the right hand side of the cowl.

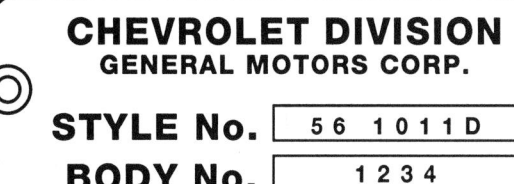

CHEVROLET DIVISION
GENERAL MOTORS CORP.
STYLE No. 56 1011D
BODY No. 1234
TRIM No. 573
PAINT No. 687
BODY BY FISHER

EXAMPLE:

56	Model year (1956)
10	Bel Air
11D	2-Dr. sedan
1234	Production sequence
573	Charcoal/Ivory cloth/vinyl
687	Onyx Black

THE STYLE NUMBER indicates the model and body style.

BEL AIR

BODY STYLE	CODE
2-Dr. sedan	1011D
4-Dr. sedan	1019D
Sport coupe	1037D
Sport sedan	1039D
Station wagon (Beauville)	1062DF
Station wagon (Nomad)	1064DF
Convertible	1067D

TWO-TEN

BODY STYLE	CODE
2-Dr. sedan	1011
4-Dr. sedan	1019
Club coupe	1011A
Sport coupe	1037
Sport sedan	1039
Station wagon (Townsman)	1062F
Station wagon (Beauville)	1062FC
Station wagon (Handyman)	1063F

ONE-FIFTY

BODY STYLE	CODE
2-Dr. sedan	1211
Utility sedan	1211B
4-Dr. sedan	1219
Station wagon (Handyman)	1263F
Sedan delivery	1271

CORVETTE

BODY STYLE	CODE
2-Dr.	2934

THE BODY NUMBER is the production serial number of the body.

THE COLOR CODE indicates the paint color used on the car.

COLOR	CODE
Onyx Black	687
Pinecrest Green	688
Sherwood Green	690
Nassau Blue	691
Harbor Blue	692
Dusk Plum	693
India Ivory	694
Crocus Yellow	695
Matador Red	697
Twilight Turquoise	698
Tropical Turquoise	749
Calypso Cream	750
Inca Silver	752
Onyx Black/Silver panel	*
Aztec Copper/Beige panel	*
Cascade Green/Beige panel	*
Arctic Blue/Silver panel	*
Venetian Red/Beige panel	*
Polo White/Silver panel	*
Inca Silver/Imperial Ivory panel	*

* Corvette

TWO-TONE COLORS

COLOR	CODE
Crocus Yellow/Onyx Black	696
Sierra Gold/Adobe Beige	700
India Ivory/Onyx Black	701
Sherwood Green/Pinecrest Green	702
Harbor Blue/Nassau Blue	703
India Ivory/Pinecrest Green	705
India Ivory/Sherwood Green	706
India Ivory/Nassau Blue	707
India Ivory/Dusk Plum	708
India Ivory/Twilight Turquoise	710
India Ivory/Matador Red	711
Matador Red/Dune Beige	715
Crocus Yellow/Laurel Green	717
India Ivory/Dawn Gray	721
India Ivory/Tropical Turquoise	754
Calypso Cream/Onyx Black	755
Grecian Gold/Calypso Cream	756
Inca Silver/Imperial Ivory	757
Matador Red/Adobe Beige	763

NOTE: The first color identifies the upper body color, the second color identifies the lower body color.

THE TRIM CODE indicates the key to the trim color and material for each model series.

COLOR	CLOTH	VINYL	LEATHER	CODE
Gold	•	•		560
Black/Ivory		•		567
Green/Ivory		•		568
Turquoise/Ivory		•		569
Charcoal	•			564
Green	•			565
Blue	•			566
Charcoal/Ivory	•	•		573
Green	•	•		574
Blue	•	•		575
Turquoise	•	•		577
Charcoal/Yellow	•	•		578
Copper/Tan	•	•		617
Charcoal/Cream	•	•		626
Charcoal/Ivory		•		602
Turquoise/Ivory		•		603
Charcoal/Yellow		•		604
Red/Ivory		•		605
Green		•		606
Blue		•		607
Copper/Tan		•		621
Charcoal/Cream		•		631
Charcoal/Ivory	•	•		579,610
Red Taupe/Red	•	•		629,633,628
Charcoal Yellow/ Cream	•	•		630,632,627
Charcoal/Ivory	•	•		611
Green	•	•		580,590
Blue	•	•		581,591
Red	•	•		593
Turquoise	•	•		584,587,594
Charcoal/Yellow	•	•		585,588,595
Tan/Copper	•	•		618,619,620
Green		•		570
Turquoise		•		572
Charcoal		•		609
Green/Gold		•		562
Gray/Gold		•		616,615

ENGINE SPECIFICATIONS

THE ENGINE NUMBER is located on the right side of the block to the rear of the distributor on the 6-cylinder, on the pad at the right front side of the block behind the water pump on the 8-cylinder. The starting engine numbers are 001001. The prefix identifies the engine plant, model year and model type. (F - Flint, T - Tonawanda)

EXAMPLE: F56GJ 1001

TYPE	CODE
235" 6-cyl., 140 HP	Z
235" 6-cyl. w/HD clutch,140 HP	ZC
235" 6-cyl. w/Powerglide,140 HP	Y
265" 8-cyl. w/3-speed,162 HP	G
265" 8-cyl. w/overdrive,162 HP	GC
265" 8-cyl. w/overdrive/AC,162 HP	GQ
265" 8-cyl. w/overdrive/Powerpack,205 HP	GE
265" 8-cyl. w/AC/3-speed, 162 HP	GF
265" 8-cyl. w/HD clutch, 162 HP	GJ
265" 8-cyl. w/HD clutch/AC, 162 HP	GK
265" 8-cyl. w/Powerglide, 170 HP	GL
265" 8-cyl. w/AC/Powerpack, 205 HP	GM
265" 8-cyl. w/AC/Powerpack/overdrive, 205 HP	GN
265" 8-cyl. w/Powerglide,170 HP	F
265" 8-cyl. w/Powerglide/Powerpack, 205 HP	FB
265" 8-cyl. w/Powerglide/AC, 170 HP	FC
265" 8-cyl. w/Powerglide/Powerpack/AC, 170 HP	FD
265" 8-cyl. Corvette 3-speed, 225 HP	GR
265" 8-cyl. Corvette Powerglide, 225 HP	FG
265" 8-cyl. Corvette 3- Speed, 210 HP	FK
265" 8-cyl. Corvette Powerglide, 210 HP	GV
265" 8-cyl. Corvette 3- Speed, 240 HP	GU

ONE-FIFTY

NO. CYL.	CID	HORSE-POWER	COMP. RATIO	CARB
6	235	140	8.0:1	1 BC
8	265	162	8.0:1	2 BC
8	265	170	8.0:1	2 BC
8	265	205	9.25:1	4 BC
8	265	225	9.25:1	2x4 BC

TWO-TEN

NO. CYL.	CID	HORSE-POWER	COMP. RATIO	CARB
6	235	140	8.0:1	1 BC
8	265	162	8.0:1	2 BC
8	265	170	8.0:1	2 BC
8	265	205	9.25:1	4 BC
8	265	225	9.25:1	2x4 BC

BEL AIR

NO. CYL.	CID	HORSE-POWER	COMP. RATIO	CARB
6	235	140	8.0:1	1 BC
8	265	162	8.0:1	2 BC
8	265	170	8.0:1	2 BC
8	265	205	9.25:1	4 BC
8	265	225	9.25:1	2x4 BC

CORVETTE

NO. CYL.	CID	HORSE-POWER	COMP. RATIO	CARB
8	265	210	9.25:1	4
8	265	225	9.25:1	2x4
8	265	240	9.25:1	2X4

1957 CHEVROLET BEL AIR WAGON

1957 CHEVROLET SPORT COUPE

1957 CHEVROLET CORVETTE

1957 CHEVROLET NOMAD

1957 CHEVROLET BEL AIR

1957 CHEVROLET BEL AIR STATION WAGON

VEHICLE IDENTIFICATION NUMBER

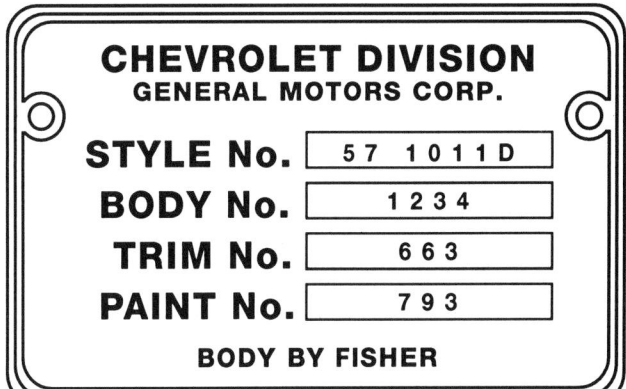

Located on the plate on the left front door hinge pillar post. The 8-cylinder vehicles have a "V" preceding the first digit.

FIRST DIGIT: Identifies the series and model

MODEL	SERIES	CODE
One-Fifty, 6-cyl.	1500	A
One-Fifty, 8-cyl.	1500	VA
Two-Ten, 6-cyl.	2100	B
Two-Ten, 8-cyl.	2100	VB
Bel Air, 6-cyl.	2400	C
Bel Air, 8-cyl.	2400	VC
Sedan delivery, 6-cyl.	1508	D
Sedan delivery, 8-cyl.	1508	VD
Corvette, 8-cyl.	2934	E

SECOND AND THIRD DIGITS: Identify the model year (1957)

FOURTH DIGIT: Identifies the assembly plant

ASSEMBLY PLANT	CODE
Atlanta, GA	A
Baltimore, MD	B
Flint, MI	F
Janesville, WI	J
Kansas City, MO	K
Los Angeles, CA	L
Oakland, CA	O
St. Louis, MO	S
Tarrytown, NY	T
Norwood, OH	N
Willow Run, MI	W

LAST SIX DIGITS: Represent the basic production number

BODY NUMBER PLATE

The first type plate is located on the lower center of the cowl, the second type on the right hand side of the cowl under the heater valve.

CHEVROLET DIVISION
GENERAL MOTORS CORP.

STYLE No.	57 1011D
BODY No.	1234
TRIM No.	663
PAINT No.	793

BODY BY FISHER

EXAMPLE:

57	Model year (1957)
10	Bel Air
11D	2-Dr. sedan
1234	Production sequence
663	Black/Silver cloth/vinyl
793	Onyx Black

THE STYLE NUMBER indicates the model and body style.

BEL AIR

BODY STYLE	CODE
2-Dr. sedan	1011D
4-Dr. sedan	1019D
Sport coupe	1037D
4-Dr. sport sedan	1039D
Station wagon (Townsman)	1062DF
Station wagon (Nomad)	1064DF
Convertible	1067D

TWO-TEN

BODY STYLE	CODE
2-Dr. sedan	1011
4-Dr. sedan	1019
Club coupe	1011A
Sport coupe	1037
4-Dr. sport sedan	1039
Station wagon (Townsman)	1062F
Station wagon (Beauville)	1062FC
Station wagon (Handyman)	1063F

ONE-FIFTY

BODY STYLE	CODE
2-Dr. sedan	1211
Utility sedan	1211B
4-Dr. sedan	1219
Station wagon (Handyman)	1263F
Sedan delivery	1271

CORVETTE

BODY STYLE	CODE
2-Dr.	2934

THE BODY NUMBER is the production serial number of the body.

THE COLOR CODE indicates the paint color used on the car.

COLOR	CODE
Onyx Black	793
Imperial Ivory	794
Larkspur Blue	795
Harbor Blue	796
Surf Green	797
Highland Green	798
Tropical Turquoise	799
Colonial Cream	800
Canyon Coral	801
Matador Red	802
Coronado Yellow	803
Inca Silver	804
Sierra Gold	805
Adobe Beige	806
Dusk Pearl	821
Laurel Green	823

CORVETTE

COLOR	CODE
Onyx Black	704
Aztec Copper	709
Cascade Green	712
Arctic Blue	713
Venetian Red	714
Polo White	718

TWO-TONE COLORS

COLOR	CODE
India Ivory/Onyx Black	807
Imperial Ivory/Inca Silver	808
Harbor Blue/Larkspur Blue	809
India Ivory/Larkspur Blue	810
India Ivory/Tropical Turquoise	811
Surf Green/Highland Green	812
India Ivory/Surf Green	813
India Ivory/Coronado Yellow	814
Colonial Cream/Onyx Black	815
Colonial Cream/India Ivory	816
India Ivory/Canyon Coral	817
Adobe Beige/Sierra Gold	818
India Ivory/Matador Red	819
Colonial Cream/Laurel Green	820
Dusk Pearl/Imperial Ivory	822

NOTE: The first color identifies the upper body color, the second color identifies the lower body color.

THE TRIM CODE indicates the trim color and material for each model series.

COLOR	CLOTH	VINYL	LEATHER	CODE
Black/Gray	•	•		650
Black/Gray		•		651,652
Green/Gray		•		653
Charcoal/Ivory		•		654
Green	•	•		655
Blue	•	•		656
Charcoal/Ivory		•		657
Green		•		658
Beige/Copper		•		659
Charcoal/Ivory		•		660
Green		•		661
Copper/Beige		•		662
Black/Silver	•	•		663
Black/Green	•	•		664
Black/Blue	•	•		665
Black/Turquoise	•	•		666
Black/Copper/Beige	•	•		667
Black/Yellow	•	•		668
Black/Red	•	•		669
Black/Silver	•	•		670
Black/Green	•	•		671
Black/Blue	•	•		672

COLOR	CLOTH	VINYL	LEATHER	CODE
Black/Turquoise	•	•		673
Black/Copper/Beige	•	•		674
Black/Yellow	•	•		675
Black/Red	•	•		676
Silver/Ivory		•		677
Green		•		678
Blue		•		679
Turquoise/Ivory		•		680
Copper/Beige		•		681
Silver/Yellow		•		682
Silver/Red		•		683
Black/Silver		•	•	684
Green		•	•	685
Black/Blue		•	•	686
Black/Turquoise		•	•	687
Black/Copper/Beige	•	•	•	688
Black/Yellow		•	•	689
Black/Red		•	•	690
Black/Silver		•	•	691
Black/Green		•	•	692
Black/Blue		•	•	693
Black/Turquoise		•	•	694
Black/Copper/Beige	•	•	•	695
Black/Yellow		•	•	696
Black/Red		•	•	697

ENGINE SPECIFICATIONS

THE ENGINE NUMBER is located on the right side of the block rear of the distributor on the 6-cylinder, on the pad at the front right side of the block behind the water pump on the 8-cylinder. The engine number includes the engine plant, the month and day it was built and the engine type. (F - Flint, T - Tonawanda)

EXAMPLE: T105C 1001

TYPE	CODE
235" 6-cyl. w/3-speed	A
235" 6-cyl. w/HD clutch	AD
235" 6-cyl. w/Powerglide	B
265" V8 w/3-speed	C
265" V8 w/overdrive	CD
265" V8 w/HD clutch	CE
283" V8 w/4-barrel	E
283" V8 w/fuel injection	EJ
283" V8 w/fuel injection/hi lift cam	EK
283" V8 w/overdrive/4-barrel	EC
283" V8 w/2-4 barrel	EA
283" V8 w/2-4 barrel/hi lift cam	EB
283" V8 w/2-4 barrel/Powerglide	FD
283" V8 w/2-4 barrel/Turboglide	GD
283" V8 w/Powerglide	F
283" V8 w/Powerglide/AC	FA
283" V8 w/Powerglide/4-barrel	FC
283" V8 w/Powerglide/fuel injection	FJ
283" V8 w/Powerglide/AC/4-barrel	FE
283" V8 w/Turboglide	G
283" V8 w/Turboglide/4-barrel	GC
283" V8 w/Turboglide/fuel injection	GF
283" V8 w/Powerglide/2-4 barrel	FD

CORVETTE

	CODE
283" V8 w/3-speed/4-barrel	EF
283" V8 w/3-speed/fuel injection/hi lift cam	EL
283" V8 w/3-speed/fuel injection	EM
283" V8 w/3-speed/cold air injection/fuel injection	EN
283" V8 w/2-4 barrel/hi lift cam	EG
283" V8 w/2-4 barrel	EH
283" V8 w/2-4 barrel/Powerglide	FG
283" V8 w/Powerglide	FH
283" V8 w/Powerglide/fuel injection	FK

ONE-FIFTY/TWO-TEN/BEL AIR

NO. CYL.	CID	HORSE-POWER	COMP. RATIO	CARB
6	235	140	8.0:1	1 BC
8	265	162	8.0:1	2 BC
8	283	185	8.5:1	2 BC
8	283	220	9.5:1	4 BC
8	283	245	9.5:1	4 BC
8	283	250	9.5:1	FI
8	283	270	9.5:1	2x4 BC
8	283	283	10.5:1	FI

CORVETTE

NO. CYL.	CID	HORSE-POWER	COMP. RATIO	CARB
8	283	220	9.5:1	4 BC
8	283	245	9.5:1	4 BC
8	283	250	9.5:1	FI
8	283	270	9.5:1	2x4 BC
8	283	283	10.5:1	FI

1958 CHEVROLET

1958 CHEVROLET IMPALA

1958 CHEVROLET NOMAD STATION WAGON

1958 CHEVROLET BISCAYNE

1958 CHEVROLET IMPALA

VEHICLE IDENTIFICATION NUMBER

• CHEVROLET •
C58F001023

Located on the plate on the left front door hinge pillar post.

FIRST DIGIT: Identifies the series and model

MODEL	SERIES	CODE
Delray/Yeoman wagon (6-cyl.)	1100	A
Delray/Yeoman wagon (8-cyl.)	1200	B
Biscayne/Brookwood wagon (6-cyl.)	1500	C
Biscayne/Brookwood wagon (8-cyl.)	1600	D
Bel Air/Nomad wagon (6-cyl.)	1700	E
Bel Air/Nomad wagon (8-cyl.)	1800	F
Sedan delivery (6-cyl.)	1171	G
Sedan delivery (8-cyl.)	1271	H
Corvette	800	J

SECOND AND THIRD DIGITS: Identify the model year (1958)

FOURTH DIGIT: Identifies the assembly plant

ASSEMBLY PLANT	CODE
Atlanta, GA	A
Baltimore, MD	B
Flint, MI	F
Janesville, WI	J
Kansas City, MO	K
Los Angeles, CA	L
Oakland, CA	O
St. Louis, MO	S
Tarrytown, NY	T
Norwood, OH	N
Willow Run, MI	W

LAST SIX DIGITS: Represent the basic production number

BODY NUMBER PLATE

Located left of center of the cowl down 2" from the top.

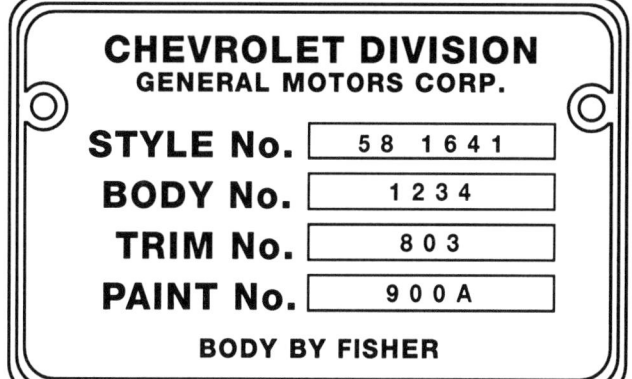

EXAMPLE:

58	Model year (1958)
16	Biscayne
41	2-Dr. sedan
1234	Production sequence
803	Gunmetal/Silver cloth/vinyl
900A	Onyx Black

THE STYLE NUMBER indicates the model and body style.

DELRAY

BODY STYLE	CODE
2-Dr. sedan	1241
4-Dr. sedan	1249
Utility sedan	1221
Sedan delivery	1271

YEOMAN

BODY STYLE	CODE
Station wagon, 2-dr.	1291
Station wagon, 4-dr.	1293

BISCAYNE

BODY STYLE	CODE
2-Dr. sedan	1641
4-Dr. sedan	1649

BROOKWOOD

BODY STYLE	CODE
Station wagon, 4-dr.	1693
Station wagon, 4-dr. (9-pass.)	1694

BEL AIR

BODY STYLE	CODE
Sport coupe	1831
Sport sedan	1839
2-Dr. sedan	1841
4-Dr. sedan	1849

IMPALA

BODY STYLE	CODE
Special sport coupe	1847
Convertible	1867

NOMAD

BODY STYLE	CODE
Station wagon, 4-dr.	1893

CORVETTE

BODY STYLE	CODE
Convertible	867

THE BODY NUMBER is the production serial number of the body.

THE COLOR CODE indicates the paint color used on the car. The suffix letter following the paint code identifies the following:

TYPE	CODE
Single tone	A
Delray/Yeoman two-tone	B
Biscayne/Brookwood two-tone	C
Bel Air/Nomad two-tone	D
Impala two-tone	E

COLOR	CODE
Onyx Black	900A
Glen Green	903A
Forest Green	905A
Cashmere Blue	910A
Fathom Blue	912A
Tropic Turquoise	914A
Aegean Turquoise	916A
Colonial Cream	925A
Silver Blue	930A
Honey Beige	938A
Rio Red	923A
Anniversary Gold	918A
Sierra Gold	920A
Cay Coral	932A
Snowcrest White	936A

CORVETTE

COLOR	CODE
Charcoal	500A
Snowcrest White	510A
Silver Blue	502A
Regal Turquoise	504A
Panama Yellow	508A
Signet Red	506A

TWO-TONE COLORS

COLOR	CODE
Onyx Black/Arctic White	950
Arctic White/Glen Green	953
Forest Green/Glen Green	955
Arctic White/Cashmere Blue	960
Fathom Blue/Cashmere Blue	962
Arctic White/Tropic Turquoise	963
Aegean Turquoise/Arctic White	964
Aegean Turquoise/Tropic Turquoise	966
Arctic White/Sierra Gold	970
Rio Red/Arctic White	973
Colonial Cream/Arctic White	975
Cay Coral/Arctic White	980
Silver Blue/Snowcrest White	982
Anniversary Gold/Honey Beige	986

THE TRIM CODE indicates the trim color and material for each model series.

COLOR	CLOTH	VINYL	LEATHER	CODE
Gunmetal/Silver	•	•		800,803,804
Gunmetal/Silver		•		801,802
Silver/Gunmetal	•	•		805
Gray/Black/				
Turquoise	•	•		806,807,808
Green	•	•		810,812
Green	•	•		813,814
Gray/Green	•	•		815,817
Green	•	•		819
Blue	•	•		820,821,828
Blue	•	•		829,830,832
Gray/Blue	•	•		822,823
Blue	•	•		824,825
Gray/Blue	•	•		826,827
Turquoise	•	•		833,834,835
Gray/Black/				
Turquoise	•	•		836,837,838
Gold/Beige		•		843,844,845
Gold	•	•		846
Beige/Copper/Gold	•	•		847,848
Gold	•	•		849
Gray/Black/Red	•	•		854,855
Coral	•	•		860,861
Coral	•	•		862,863
Gunmetal/Silver	•	•		870,871

ENGINE SPECIFICATIONS

THE ENGINE NUMBER is located on the right side of the block to the rear of the distributor on the 6-cylinder. It is located on the pad on the front right hand side of the block on the 8-cylinder. The number identifies the engine plant, the month and day the engine was built and the engine type. (F - Flint, T - Tonawanda, C - Canada)

EXAMPLE: F203DB 1001

TYPE	CODE
235" 6-cyl. w/3-speed	A
235" 6-cyl. w/HD clutch	AE
235" 6-cyl. w/Powerglide	B
283" V8 w-3-speed	C
283" V8 w/HD clutch	CB
283" V8 w/overdrive	CD
283" V8 w/3-speed/4-barrel	CF
283" V8 w/3-speed/4-barrel/overdrive	CG
283" V8 w/3-speed/fuel injection	CH
283" V8 w/Powerglide	D
283" V8 w/Powerglide/4-barrel	DB
283" V8 w/Powerglide/air suspension	DE
283" V8 w/Powerglide/air suspension/ 4-barrel	DF
283" V8 w/Turboglide	E
283" V8 w/Turboglide/4-barrel	EB
283" V8 w/Turboglide/fuel injection	EC
283" V8 w/Turboglide/air suspension	ED
283" V8 w/Turboglide/air suspension/ 4-barrel	EF
348" V8 w/3-speed	F
348" V8 w/3-speed/3-2 barrel	FA
348" V8 w/3-speed/3-2 barrel/special cam	FB
348" V8 w/Powerglide	G
348" V8 w/Turboglide	H
348" V8 w/Turboglide/3-2 barrel	HA

CORVETTE

283" V8 w/3-speed	CQ
283" V8 w/3-speed/fuel injection	CR
283" V8 w/3-speed/special cam	CS
283" V8 w/3-speed/2-4 barrel	CT
283" V8 w/3-speed/2-4 barrel/special cam	CU
283" V8 w/Powerglide	DG
283" V8 w/Powerglide/fuel injection	DH
283" V8 w/Powerglide/2-4 barrel	DJ

PASSENGER

NO. CYL.	CID	HORSE-POWER	COMP. RATIO	CARB
6	235	145	8.25:1	1 BC
8	283	185	8.5:1	2 BC
8	283	230	9.5:1	4 BC
8	283	250	9.5:1	FI
8	283	290	10.5:1	FI
8	348	250	9.5:1	4 BC
8	348	280	9.5:1	3x2 BC

CORVETTE

NO. CYL.	CID	HORSE-POWER	COMP. RATIO	CARB
8	283	230	9.5:1	4 BC
8	283	250	9.5:1	FI
8	283	290	10.5:1	FI
8	283	245	9.5:1	2x4 BC
8	283	270	9.5:1	2x4 BC

1959 CHEVROLET

1959 CHEVROLET CORVETTE

1959 CHEVROLET BEL AIR

1959 CHEVROLET

1959 CHEVROLET NOMAD STATION WAGON

1959 CHEVROLET BISCAYNE

VEHICLE IDENTIFICATION NUMBER

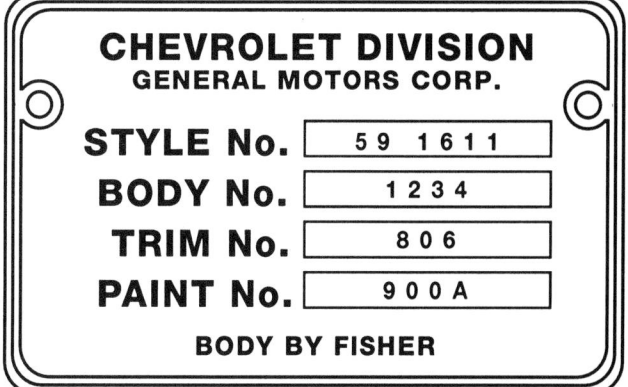

CHEVROLET
D59F001023

Located on the plate on the left front door hinge pillar post.

FIRST DIGIT: Identifies the series and model

MODEL	SERIES	CODE
Biscayne/Brookwood wagon (6-cyl.)	1100	A
Biscayne/Brookwood wagon (8-cyl.)	1200	B
Bel Air/Packwood/Kingswood wagon (6-cyl.)	1500	C
Bel Air/Packwood/Kingswood wagon (8-cyl.)	1600	D
Impala/Nomad wagon (6-cyl.)	1700	E
Impala/Nomad wagon (8-cyl.)	1800	F
Corvette	800	J

SECOND AND THIRD DIGITS: Identify the model year (1959)

FOURTH DIGIT: Identifies the assembly plant

ASSEMBLY PLANT	CODE
Atlanta, GA	A
Baltimore, MD	B
Flint, MI	F
Pontiac, MI	G
Janesville, WI	J
Kansas City, MO	K
Los Angeles, CA	L
Oakland, CA	O
St. Louis, MO	S
Tarrytown, NY	T
Norwood, OH	N
Willow Run, MI	W

LAST SIX DIGITS: Represent the basic production number

BODY NUMBER PLATE

Located left hand top of the cowl.

CHEVROLET DIVISION
GENERAL MOTORS CORP.

STYLE No.	59 1611
BODY No.	1234
TRIM No.	806
PAINT No.	900A

BODY BY FISHER

EXAMPLE:

59	Model year (1959)
16	Bel Air
11	2-Dr. sedan
1234	Production sequence
806	Gunmetal/Silver cloth/vinyl
900A	Onyx Black

THE STYLE NUMBER indicates the model and body style.

BISCAYNE
BODY STYLE	CODE
2-Dr. sedan	1211
Utility sedan	1221
4-Dr. sedan	1219
Sedan delivery	1270

BROOKWOOD
BODY STYLE	CODE
Station wagon, 2-dr.	1215
Station wagon, 4-dr.	1235

EL CAMINO
BODY STYLE	CODE
Pickup delivery	1280

BEL AIR
BODY STYLE	CODE
2-Dr. sedan	1611
4-Dr. sedan	1619
4-Dr. sport sedan	1639

PARKWOOD

BODY STYLE	CODE
Station wagon, 4-dr.	1635

KINGSWOOD

BODY STYLE	CODE
Station wagon, 4-dr. (9-pass.)	1645

IMPALA

BODY STYLE	CODE
4-Dr. sedan	1819
2-Dr. sport coupe	1837
4-Dr. sport sedan	1839
Convertible	1867

NOMAD

BODY STYLE	CODE
Station wagon, 4-dr.	1835

CORVETTE

BODY STYLE	CODE
Convertible	867

THE BODY NUMBER is the production serial number of the body.

THE COLOR CODE indicates the paint color used on the car.

COLOR	CODE
Tuxedo Black	900A
Aspen Green	903A
Highland Green	905A
Frost Blue	910A
Harbor Blue	912A
Gothic Gold	920A
Roman Red	923A
Snowcrest White	936A
Crown Sapphire	914A
Classic Cream	825A
Satin Beige	938A
Grecian Gray	940A
Cameo Coral	942A

CORVETTE

COLOR	CODE
Snowcrest White	510A
Tuxedo Black	503A
Inca Silver	509A
Roman Red	506A
Classic Cream	508A
Frost Blue	502A
Crown Sapphire	504A

TWO-TONE COLORS

COLOR	CODE
Tuxedo Black/Snowcrest White	950
Highland Green/Snowcrest White	953
Harbor Blue/Frost Blue	962
Crown Sapphire/Snowcrest White	963
Gothic Gold/Satin Beige	970
Roman Red/Snowcrest White	973
Frost Blue/Hrabor Blue	987
Grecian Gray/Snowcrest White	988
Cameo Coral/Satin Beige	989
Classic Cream/Aspen Green	990

NOTE: The first color identifies the upper body color, the second color identifies the lower body color.

THE TRIM CODE indicates the trim color and material for each model series.

COLOR	CLOTH	VINYL	LEATHER	CODE
Gray	•	•		800,801,802
Gray	•	•		803,806,807
Gray	•	•		809,810,811
Green/Yellow	•	•		817,818,819
Green	•	•		822,823,825
Green	•	•		826,827
Blue	•	•		833,834,835
Blue	•	•		838
Gray/Blue	•	•		839
Blue	•	•		841,843
Silver/Blue	•	•		842
Turquoise	•	•		849,850,852
Turquoise	•	•		853,854
Copper	•	•		862,863
Copper/Brown	•	•		865,866,867
Red	•	•		873

ENGINE SPECIFICATIONS

THE ENGINE NUMBER is located on the pad on the right side of the block to the rear of the distributor on the 6-cylinder. It is lcoated on the pad at the front right hand side of the block on the 8-cylinder. The engine number identifies the engine plant, the month and day the engine was built and the engine type. (F - Flint, T - Tonawanda, C - Canada)

EXAMPLE: T101C 1001

TYPE	CODE
235" 6-cyl. w/3-speed	A
235" 6-cyl. w/HD clutch	AE
235" 6-cyl. w/Powerglide	B
283" V8 w/3-speed	C
283" V8 w/overdrive	CD
283" V8 w/3-speed/4-barrel	CF
283" V8 w/overdrive/4-barrel	CG
283" V8 w/3-speed/fuel injection	CH
283" V8 w/3-speed/fuel injection/ hi lift cam	CJ
283" V8 w/Powerglide	D
283" V8 w/Powerglide/4-barrel	DB
283" V8 w/Powerglide/air suspension	DE
283" V8 w/Powerglide/air suspension/4-barrel	DF
283" V8 w/Powerglide/AC	DK
283" V8 w/Powerglide/AC/air suspension	DL
283" V8 w/Powerglide/AC/4-barrel	DM
283" V8 w/Powerglide/AC/4-barrel/air suspension	DN
283" V8 w/Powerglide/fuel injection	DP
283" V8 w/Turboglide	E
283" V8 w/Turboglide/4-barrel	EB
283" V8 w/Turboglide/fuel injection	EC
283" V8 w/Turboglide/air suspension	ED
283" V8 w/Turboglide/air suspension/ 4-barrel	EF
283" V8 w/Turboglide/AC	EG
283" V8 w/Turboglide/AC/air suspension	EH
283" V8 w/Turboglide/AC/4-barrel	EJ
283" V8 w/Turboglide/AC/4-barrel/ air suspension	EK
348" V8 w/3-speed	F
348" V8 w/3-speed/3-2 barrel	FA
348" V8 w/3-speed/3-2 barrel/hi lift cam	FB
348" V8 w/hi lift cam	FD
348" V8 w/3-2 barrel/high performance	FE
348" V8 w/high performance	FG
348" V8 w/Powerglide	G
348" V8 w/Powerglide/3-2 barrel	GB
348" V8 w/Powerglide/hi lift cam	GD
348" V8 w/Turboglide	H
348" V8 w/Turboglide/3-2 barrel	HA

CORVETTE

TYPE	CODE
283" V8 w/3-speed	CQ
283" V8 w/3-speed/fuel injection	CR
283" V8 w/3-speed/fuel injection/ hi-lift cam	CS
283" V8 w/3-speed/2-4 barrel	CT
283" V8 w/3-speed/2-4 barrel/hi lift cam	CU
283" V8 w/Powerglide	DG
283" V8 w/Powerglide/fuel injection	DH
283" V8 w/Powerglide/2-4 barrel	DJ

PASSENGER

NO. CYL.	CID	HORSE-POWER	COMP. RATIO	CARB
6	283	135	8.25:1	1 BC
8	283	185	8.5:1	2 BC
8	283	230	9.5:1	4 BC
8	283	250	9.5:1	FI
8	283	290	10.5:1	FI
8	348	250	9.5:1	4 BC
8	348	300	11.0:1	4 BC
8	348	320	11.25:1	4 BC
8	348	280	9.5:1	3x2 BC
8	348	315	11.0:1	3x2 BC
8	348	335	11.25:1	3x2 BC

CORVETTE

NO. CYL.	CID	HORSE-POWER	COMP. RATIO	CARB
8	283	230	9.5:1	4 BC
8	283	245	9.5:1	2x4 BC
8	283	250	9.5:1	FI
8	283	270	9.5:1	2x4 BC
8	283	290	10.5:1	FI

13-46

1950 OLDSMOBILE SERIES 88 FUTURAMIC

1950 OLDSMOBILE SERIES 88 FUTURAMIC

1950 OLDSMOBILE SUPER 88

VEHICLE IDENTIFICATION NUMBER

```
• OLDSMOBILE •
  5 0 6 M 1 0 0 1
```

Located on a plate on the left hand body pillar post.

FIRST AND SECOND DIGITS: Identify the model year (1950)

THIRD DIGIT: Identifies the series

SERIES	CODE
76	6
88	8
98	9

FOURTH DIGIT: Identifies the assembly plant

ASSEMBLY PLANT	CODE
Atlanta, GA	A
Framingham, MA	B
South Gate, CA	C
Kansas City, KS	K
Linden, NJ	L
Lansing, MI	M
Wilmington, DE	W

LAST FOUR DIGITS: Represent the basic production number

BODY NUMBER PLATE

Located on the front of the cowl adjacent to the left hand hinge.

```
OLDSMOBILE DIVISION
GENERAL MOTORS CORPORATION
LANSING, MICH.
STYLE Nº. 50 3769
BODY Nº. L 1234
TRIM Nº. 1
PAINT Nº. 10
TOP 00        ACC 00
BODY BY FISHER
```

EXAMPLE:

50	Model year (1950)
37	"88"
69	4-Dr. sedan
L	Lansing, MI
1234	Production sequence
1	Gray striped cloth
10	Black

THE STYLE NUMBER indicates the model and body style.

"76"

BODY STYLE	CODE
Club sedan	3507
Deluxe club sedan	3507D
2-Dr. sedan	3511
Deluxe 2-dr. sedan	3511D
Club coupe	3527
Deluxe club coupe	3527D
Holiday coupe	3537
Deluxe Holiday coupe	3537D
Station wagon	3562
Deluxe station wagon	3562D
Convertible coupe	3567X
4-Dr. sedan	3569
Deluxe 4-dr. sedan	3569D

"88"

BODY STYLE	CODE
Club sedan	3507
Deluxe club sedan	3707D
2-Dr. sedan	3711
2-Dr. sedan deluxe	3711D
Club coupe	3727
Deluxe club coupe	3727D
Holiday coupe	3737
Deluxe Holiday coupe	3737D
Station wagon	3762
Deluxe station wagon	3762D
Convertible coupe	3767X
4-Dr. sedan	3769
4-Dr. sedan deluxe	3769D

"98"

BODY STYLE	CODE
Club sedan	3807
Deluxe club sedan	3807D
Town sedan	3808
Deluxe town sedan	3808D
Holiday coupe	3837
Deluxe Holiday coupe	3837DX
Deluxe convertible coupe	3867X
4-Dr. sedan	3869
4-Dr. sedan deluxe	3869D

THE BODY NUMBER is the production serial number of the body. The prefix denotes the plant in which the body was assembled.

THE ASSEMBLY PLANT CODE indicates the plant where the vehicle was assembled.

ASSEMBLY PLANT	CODE
Lansing, MI	L
Flint, MI	G
Atlanta, GA	BA
South Gate, CA	BC
Framingham, MA	BF
Kansas City, KS	BK
Linden, NJ	BL
Wilmington, DE	BW
Cleveland, OH	CL

THE TRIM CODE indicates the key to the trim color and material for each model series.

"76" TRIM

COLOR	CLOTH	VINYL	LEATHER	CODE
Gray	•			1
Dk. Gray	•			2
Gray/Red	•		•	5
Gray/Green	•		•	6
Gray/Blue	•		•	7
Gray/Black	•		•	9
Tan			•	14
Red			•	15
Green			•	16
Blue			•	17
Black			•	19

"88" TRIM

COLOR	CLOTH	VINYL	LEATHER	CODE
Gray	•			1,3
Gray/Red	•		•	5,5A
Gray/Green	•		•	6,6A
Gray/Blue	•		•	7,7A
Gray/Black	•		•	9,9A
Tan			•	14
Red			•	15
Green			•	16
Blue			•	17
Black			•	19

"98" TRIM

COLOR	CLOTH	VINYL	LEATHER	CODE
Gray	•			1,3
Gray/Red	•		•	25,25A
Gray/Green	•		•	26,26A
Gray/Blue	•		•	27,27A
Gray/Black	•		•	29,29A
Red			•	35
Green			•	36,36C
Blue			•	37,37C
Black			•	39
Tan		•		44
Red		•		45

THE COLOR CODE indicates the paint color used on the car.

COLOR	CODE
Black	10
Alder Green	11
Garnet Maroon	12
Chariot Red	12C
Dune Biege	13
Canto Cream	13C
Crest Blue	14
Serge Blue	15
Marol Gray	17
Flint Gray	18
Ivy Green	19
Palm Green	20

TWO-TONE COLORS

COLOR	CODE
Alder Green/Ivy Green	11A
Crest Blue/Serge Blue	14A
Marol Gray/Flint Gray	17A
Alder Green/Black	*11H
Canto Cream/Black	*13H
Crest Blue/Black	*14H
Marol Gray/Black	*17H
Palm Green/Sand Beige	*29H

* Holiday coupes

ENGINE SPECIFICATIONS

THE ENGINE NUMBER is located on the left front top corner of the block on the 6-cylinder, on the pad on the left side of the block between #5 & #7 cylinders on the 8-cylinder.

CYLINDERS	STARTING NUMBERS
6-Cyl.	6A97001/up
8-Cyl. (7.25:1 comp. ratio)	8A
Remaining 8-cyl.	194001

NOTE: Suffix H identifies Hydra-Matic

"76" SERIES

ENGINE CODE	NO. CYL.	CID	HORSE-POWER	COMP. RATIO	CARB
	6	257.1	105	6.5:1	1 BC

"88" SERIES

ENGINE CODE	NO. CYL.	CID	HORSE-POWER	COMP. RATIO	CARB
	8	303.7	135	7.25:1	2 BC

"98" SERIES

ENGINE CODE	NO. CYL.	CID	HORSE-POWER	COMP. RATIO	CARB
	8	303.7	135	7.25:1	2 BC

1951 OLDSMOBILE SERIES 98 HOLIDAY

1951 OLDSMOBILE SERIES 88

1951 OLDSMOBILE 88

VEHICLE IDENTIFICATION NUMBER

```
• OLDSMOBILE •
  5 1 6 M 1 0 0 1
```

Located on a plate on the left hand body pillar post.

FIRST AND SECOND DIGITS: Identify the model year (1951)

THIRD DIGIT: Identifies the series

SERIES	CODE
88	7
Super 88	8
98	9

FOURTH DIGIT: Identifies the assembly plant

ASSEMBLY PLANT	CODE
Atlanta, GA	A
Framingham, MA	B
South Gate, CA	C
Kansas City, KS	K
Linden, NJ	L
Lansing, MI	M
Wilmington, DE	W

LAST FOUR DIGITS: Represent the basic production number

BODY NUMBER PLATE

Located on the front of the cowl adjacent to the left hand hinge.

```
OLDSMOBILE DIVISION
GENERAL MOTORS CORPORATION
LANSING, MICH.
STYLE NO. 51 3669D
BODY NO. L 1234
TRIM NO. 3
PAINT NO. 50
TOP 00          ACC 00
BODY BY FISHER
```

EXAMPLE:

51	Model year (1951)
36	Super "88"
69D	Deluxe 4-dr. sedan
L	Lansing, MI
1234	Production sequence
3	Gray striped cloth
50	Black

THE STYLE NUMBER indicates the model and body style.

"88"

BODY STYLE	CODE
2-Dr. sedan	3711
4-Dr. sedan	3769

SUPER "88"

BODY STYLE	CODE
Deluxe 2-dr. sedan	3611D
Deluxe club coupe	3627D
Deluxe Holiday coupe	3637D
Deluxe Holiday coupe*	3637DX
Deluxe convertible coupe*	3667DX
Deluxe convertible coupe**	3667DTX
Deluxe 4-dr. sedan	3669D

"98"

BODY STYLE	CODE
Holiday coupe	3837
Deluxe Holiday coupe*	3837DX
Deluxe convertible coupe*	3867X
Deluxe Holiday sedan#	3869D

* Equipped with all hydraulic controls

** Equipped with hydraulic top control only
# With rear seat center arm rest

THE BODY NUMBER is the production serial number of the body. The prefix denotes the plant in which the body was assembled.

THE ASSEMBLY PLANT CODE indicates the plant where the vehicle was assembled.

ASSEMBLY PLANT	CODE
Lansing, MI	L
Flint, MI	G
Atlanta, GA	BA
South Gate, CA	BC
Framingham, MA	BF
Kansas City, KS	BK
Linden, NJ	BL
Wilmington, DE	BW
Cleveland, OH	CL

THE TRIM CODE indicates the key to the trim color and material for each model series.

"88" TRIM

COLOR	CLOTH	VINYL	LEATHER	CODE
Lt. Gray	•			1,1A,3,3A
Gray/Red	•		•	5
Gray/Green	•		•	6
Gray/Blue	•		•	7
Gray/Black	•		•	9
Red			•	15
Green			•	16
Blue			•	17
Black			•	19

SUPER "88" TRIM

COLOR	CLOTH	VINYL	LEATHER	CODE
Gray	•			3,3A

"98" TRIM

COLOR	CLOTH	VINYL	LEATHER	CODE
Gray	•			1,3
Gray/Red	•		•	25
Gray/Green	•		•	26
Gray/Blue	•		•	27
Gray/Black	•		•	29
Red			•	35
Green			•	36,36C
Blue			•	37,37C
Black			•	39

THE COLOR CODE indicates the paint color used on the car.

COLOR	CODE
Black	50
Cascade Green	51
Empire Maroon	52
Chariot Red	52C
Sand Biege	53
Canto Cream	53C
Otsego Blue	54
Serge Blue	55
Algiers Blue	55C*
Dove Gray	57
Flint Gray	58
Palm Green	59
Shoal Green	59C

* Available only on deluxe convertible coupes

TWO-TONE COLORS

COLOR	CODE
Cascade Green/Palm Green	51A
Cascade Green/Black	51H
Chariot Red/Black	52H
Canto Cream/Black	53H
Otsego Blue/Serge Blue	54A
Otsego Blue/Black	54H
Algiers Blue/Black	55H
Dove Gray/Flint Gray	57A
Dove Gray/Black	57H
Palm Green/Sand Beige	59H

NOTE: Two-tone colors are not available on convertible models.

ENGINE SPECIFICATIONS

THE ENGINE NUMBER is located on the pad on the left side of the block between #5 & #7 exhaust port. The starting engine number is 8C1001/up. The suffix letter "B" identifies a syncro-mesh transmission.

"88" SERIES

ENGINE CODE	NO. CYL.	CID	HORSE-POWER	COMP. RATIO	CARB
	8	303.7	135	7.5:1	2 BC

SUPER "88" SERIES

ENGINE CODE	NO. CYL.	CID	HORSE-POWER	COMP. RATIO	CARB
	8	303.7	135	7.5:1	2 BC

"98" DELUXE SERIES

ENGINE CODE	NO. CYL.	CID	HORSE-POWER	COMP. RATIO	CARB
	8	303.7	135	7.5:1	2 BC

1952 OLDSMOBILE DELUXE 88

1952 OLDSMOBILE SUPER 88 HOLIDAY

VEHICLE IDENTIFICATION NUMBER

```
• OLDSMOBILE •
  5 2 8 M 1 0 0 1
```

Located on a plate on the left hand body pillar post.

FIRST AND SECOND DIGITS: Identify the model year (1952)

THIRD DIGIT: Identifies the series

SERIES	CODE
88	8
98	9

FOURTH DIGIT: Identifies the assembly plant

ASSEMBLY PLANT	CODE
Atlanta, GA	A
Framingham, MA	B
South Gate, CA	C
Kansas City, KS	K
Linden, NJ	L
Lansing, MI	M
Wilmington, DE	W

LAST FOUR DIGITS: Represent the basic production number

BODY NUMBER PLATE

Located on the front of the cowl adjacent to the left hand hinge.

```
        OLDSMOBILE DIVISION
   GENERAL MOTORS CORPORATION
           LANSING, MICH.
   STYLE Nº. 52 3669D
   BODY Nº. L 1234
      TRIM Nº. 6
   PAINT Nº.  40
  TOP 00          ACC 00
       BODY BY FISHER
```

EXAMPLE:

52	Model year (1952)
36	"88"
69D	Deluxe 4-dr. sedan
L	Lansing, MI
1234	Production sequence
6	Gray corded cloth
40	Arctic Blue

THE STYLE NUMBER indicates the model and body style.

"88"

BODY STYLE	CODE
2-Dr. sedan	3611
4-Dr. sedan	3669

SUPER "88"

BODY STYLE	CODE
Deluxe 2-dr. sedan	3611D
Deluxe club coupe	3627D
Deluxe Holiday coupe	3637D
Deluxe convertible coupe**	3667DTX
Deluxe 4-dr. sedan	3669D

"98"

BODY STYLE	CODE
Deluxe Holiday coupe*	3037DX
Deluxe convertible coupe*	3067DX
Deluxe 4-dr. sedan#	3069D

* Equipped with all hydraulic controls

** Equipped with hydraulic top control only

With rear seat center arm rest

THE BODY NUMBER is the production serial number of the body. The prefix denotes the plant in which the body was assembled.

THE ASSEMBLY PLANT CODE indicates the plant where the vehicle was assembled.

ASSEMBLY PLANT	CODE
Lansing, MI	L
Flint, MI	G
Atlanta, GA	BA
South Gate, CA	BC
Framingham, MA	BF
Kansas City, KS	BK
Linden, NJ	BL
Wilmington, DE	BW
Cleveland, OH	CL

THE TRIM CODE indicates the key to the trim color and material for each model series.

"88" TRIM

COLOR	CLOTH	VINYL	LEATHER	CODE
Gray	•			6

SUPER "88" TRIM

COLOR	CLOTH	VINYL	LEATHER	CODE
Lt. Gray	•		•	4
Green	•		•	5
Gray/Red	•		•	15
Green	•		•	16
Gray/Blue	•		•	17
Gray/Black	•		•	19
Red			•	25
Green			•	26C
Blue			•	27C
Black			•	29

"98" TRIM

COLOR	CLOTH	VINYL	LEATHER	CODE
Gray	•			1
Green	•			2
Red			•	45
Green			•	46,46C
Blue			•	47,47C
Black			•	49
Gray/Red	•		•	35
Green	•		•	36
Gray/Blue	•		•	37
Gray/Black	•		•	39

THE COLOR CODE indicates the paint color used on the car.

COLOR	CODE
Black	10
Chariot Red	20
Regent Maroon	21
Cascade Green	30
Shoal Green	31
Palm Green	32
Glade Green	33
Arctic Blue	40
Serge Blue	41
Dove Gray	50
Pearl Gray	51
Canto Cream	60
Sand Biege	61
Aquamarine	70
Royal Turquoise	71

TWO-TONE COLORS

COLOR	CODE
Chariot Red/Black	20B
Cascade Green/Black	30B
Cascade Green/Palm Green	30T
Shoal Green/Swan White	31W
Palm Green/Sand Beige	32T
Glade Green/Sand Beige	33T
Arctic Blue/Black	40B
Arctic Blue/Serge Blue	40T
Arctic Blue/Swan White	40W
Dove Gray/Black	50B
Dove Gray/Pearl Gray	50T
Pearl Gray/Swan White	51W
Canto Cream/Black	60B
Royal Turquoise/Black	71B
Royal Turquoise/Aquamarine	71T
Royal Turquoise/Swan White	71W

NOTE: The first two numbers identify the lower color, the second two numbers identify the upper color. Two-tone colors are not available on convertible models.

ENGINE SPECIFICATIONS

THE ENGINE NUMBER is located on the pad on top of the left hand side of the cylinder block between the center and rear exhaust ports. The starting engine number is R1001/up.

DELUXE "88" SERIES

ENGINE CODE	NO. CYL.	CID	HORSE-POWER	COMP. RATIO	CARB
	8	303.7	145	7.5:1	2 BC

SUPER "88" SERIES

ENGINE CODE	NO. CYL.	CID	HORSE-POWER	COMP. RATIO	CARB
	8	303.7	160	7.5:1	4 BC

"98" DELUXE SERIES

ENGINE CODE	NO. CYL.	CID	HORSE-POWER	COMP. RATIO	CARB
	8	303.7	160	7.5:1	4 BC

1953 OLDSMOBILE CLASSIC 98 HOLIDAY

1953 OLDSMOBILE SUPER 88 HOLIDAY

1953 OLDSMOBILE

VEHICLE IDENTIFICATION NUMBER

```
• OLDSMOBILE •
  5 3 8 M 1 0 0 1
```

Located on a plate on the left hand body pillar post.

FIRST AND SECOND DIGITS: Identify the model year (1953)

THIRD DIGIT: Identifies the series

SERIES	CODE
Deluxe 88	7
Super 88	8
98	9

FOURTH DIGIT: Identifies the assembly plant

ASSEMBLY PLANT	CODE
Atlanta, GA	A
Framingham, MA	B
South Gate, CA	C
Kansas City, KS	K
Linden, NJ	L
Lansing, MI	M
Wilmington, DE	W

LAST FOUR DIGITS: Represent the basic production number

BODY NUMBER PLATE

Located on the front of the cowl adjacent to the left hand hinge.

**OLDSMOBILE DIVISION
GENERAL MOTORS CORPORATION
LANSING, MICH.**

**STYLE Nº. 53 3669D
BODY Nº. L 1234
TRIM Nº. 81
PAINT Nº. 40
TOP** 00   **ACC** 00
BODY BY FISHER

EXAMPLE:

53	Model year (1953)
36	Super "88"
69D	Deluxe 4-dr. sedan
L	Lansing, MI
1234	Production sequence
81	Gray pattern cloth
40	Acacia Blue

THE STYLE NUMBER indicates the model and body style.

DELUXE "88"

BODY STYLE	CODE
2-Dr. sedan	3611
4-Dr. sedan	3669

SUPER "88"

BODY STYLE	CODE
Deluxe 2-dr. sedan	3611D
Deluxe Holiday coupe	3637D
Deluxe Holiday coupe*	3637DX
Deluxe convertible coupe*	3667DX
Deluxe convertible coupe**	3667DTX
Deluxe 4-dr. sedan	3669D

"98"

BODY STYLE	CODE
Deluxe Holiday coupe*	3037DX
Deluxe convertible coupe*	3067DX
Deluxe 4-dr. sedan#	3069D
Deluxe sports convertible*	3067SDX

* Equipped with all hydraulic controls

** Equipped with hydraulic top control only

With rear seat center arm rest

THE BODY NUMBER is the production serial number of the body. The prefix denotes the plant in which the body was assembled.

THE ASSEMBLY PLANT CODE indicates the plant where the vehicle was assembled.

ASSEMBLY PLANT	CODE
Lansing, MI	L
Flint, MI	G
Atlanta, GA	BA
South Gate, CA	BC
Framingham, MA	BF
Kansas City, KS	BK
Linden, NJ	BL
Arlington, TX	BT
Wilmington, DE	BW
Cleveland, OH	CL

THE TRIM CODE indicates the key to the trim color and material for each model series.

DELUXE "88" TRIM

COLOR	CLOTH	VINYL	LEATHER	CODE
Lt. Gray	•		•	61

SUPER "88" TRIM

COLOR	CLOTH	VINYL	LEATHER	CODE
Gray	•			81
Green	•			82
Blue	•			83
Red/Gray	•		•	15
Green	•		•	16
Blue	•		•	17
Black/Gray	•		•	19
Green/Ivory	•		•	63
Blue/Ivory	•	•		73
Green/Black			•	69
Red			•	25
Green			•	26
Blue			•	27
Black			•	29
Red/Ivory			•	35
Green/Ivory			•	36
Blue/Ivory			•	37
Black/Ivory			•	39
Blue/Black			•	79

"98" TRIM

COLOR	CLOTH	VINYL	LEATHER	CODE
Gray	•			91
Green	•			92,94
Blue	•			93
Ivory/Black			•	99
Red			•	45
Green			•	46
Blue			•	47
Black			•	49
Ivory/Red			•	55
Ivory/Green			•	56
Ivory/Blue			•	57
Ivory/Black			•	59
Red/White			•	65
Ivory/Green			•	66
Turquoise/White			•	67
Ivory/Blue			•	77
Gray/Red	•		•	85
Green	•		•	86
Blue	•		•	87
Gray/Black	•		•	89
Green/Ivory	•		•	96
Blue/Ivory	•		•	97

THE COLOR CODE indicates the paint color used on the car. Two-Tone colors: The first two numbers identify the lower body color, the second two numbers identify the upper body color.

COLOR	CODE
Black	10
Agate Red	20
Etna Maroon	21
Fern Green	30
Cove Green	31
Glade Green	32
Acacia Blue	40
Cadet Blue	41
Baltic Blue	42
Mist Gray	50
Pearl Gray	51
Polar White	60
Lotus Cream	61
Monica Tan	62
Burma Brown	*63
Royal Marine	70
Regal Turquoise	71

* Available as top color only

ENGINE SPECIFICATIONS

THE ENGINE NUMBER is located on the left hand side of the cylinder block. The starting number is R-215001/up.

DELUXE "88" SERIES

ENGINE CODE	NO. CYL.	CID	HORSE-POWER	COMP. RATIO	CARB
	8	303.7	150	8.0:1	2 BC

SUPER "88" SERIES

ENGINE CODE	NO. CYL.	CID	HORSE-POWER	COMP. RATIO	CARB
	8	303.7	165	8.0:1	4 BC

"98" DELUXE SERIES

ENGINE CODE	NO. CYL.	CID	HORSE-POWER	COMP. RATIO	CARB
	8	303.7	165	8.0:1	4 BC

1954 OLDSMOBILE

1954 OLDSMOBILE SUPER 88

1954 OLDSMOBILE 98 DELUXE HOLIDAY

VEHICLE IDENTIFICATION NUMBER

```
• OLDSMOBILE •
  5 4 8 M 1 0 0 1
```

Located on a plate on the left hand body pillar post.

FIRST AND SECOND DIGITS: Identify the model year (1954)

THIRD DIGIT: Identifies the series

SERIES	CODE
Deluxe 88	7
Super 88	8
98	9

FOURTH DIGIT: Identifies the assembly plant

ASSEMBLY PLANT	CODE
Atlanta, GA	A
Framingham, MA	B
South Gate, CA	C
Kansas City, KS	K
Linden, NJ	L
Lansing, MI	M
Arlington, TX	T
Wilmington, DE	W

LAST FOUR DIGITS: Represent the basic production number

BODY NUMBER PLATE

Located on the front of the cowl adjacent to the left hand hinge.

```
OLDSMOBILE DIVISION
GENERAL MOTORS CORPORATION
LANSING, MICH.
STYLE Nº. 54 3669D
BODY Nº. L 1234
TRIM Nº. 81
PAINT Nº. 10
TOP 00          ACC 00
BODY BY FISHER
```

EXAMPLE:

54	Model year (1954)
36	Super "88"
69D	Deluxe 4-dr. sedan
L	Lansing, MI
1234	Production sequence
81	Gray pattern cloth
10	Black

THE STYLE NUMBER indicates the model and body style.

DELUXE "88"

BODY STYLE	CODE
2-Dr. sedan	3611
Holiday coupe	3637
4-Dr. sedan	3669

SUPER "88"

BODY STYLE	CODE
Deluxe 2-dr. sedan	3611D
Deluxe Holiday coupe	3637D
Deluxe convertible coupe**	3667DTX
Deluxe 4-dr. sedan	3669D

"98"

BODY STYLE	CODE
Holiday coupe*	3037
Deluxe Holiday coupe*	3037DX
Deluxe convertible coupe*	3067DX
Deluxe 4-dr. sedan#	3069D
Deluxe 4-dr. sedan#*	3069DX

* Equipped with all hydraulic controls

** Equipped with hydraulic top control only

With rear seat center arm rest

THE BODY NUMBER is the production serial number
of the body. The prefix denotes the plant in which the body was assembled.

THE ASSEMBLY PLANT CODE indicates the
plant where the vehicle was assembled.

ASSEMBLY PLANT	CODE
Lansing, MI	L
Flint, MI	G
Atlanta, GA	BA
South Gate, CA	BC
Framingham, MA	BF
Kansas City, KS	BK
Linden, NJ	BL
Arlington, TX	BT
Wilmington, DE	BW
Cleveland, OH	CL

THE TRIM CODE indicates the key to the trim color
and material for each model series.

DELUXE "88" TRIM

COLOR	CLOTH	VINYL	LEATHER	CODE
Gray	•			61,161,261
Gray	•			361
Green	•			62,162,262
Blue	•			63,163,263

SUPER "88" TRIM

COLOR	CLOTH	VINYL	LEATHER	CODE
Gray	•			81
Green	•			82
Blue	•			83
Red/Gray	•		•	15
Green	•		•	16,116
Blue	•		•	17,117
Gray/Ivory	•		•	21
Green/Ivory	•		•	66,166
Blue/Ivory	•		•	73,173
Gray/Red	•		•	115
Red			•	25
Green			•	26
Blue			•	27
Ivory/Turquoise			•	33
Ivory/Red			•	35
Ivory/Blue			•	37,137
Ivory/Green			•	136

"98" TRIM

COLOR	CLOTH	VINYL	LEATHER	CODE
Gray	•			91,191,291
Green	•			92,192,292
Blue	•			93,193,293
Ivory/Gray	•		•	31
Ivory/Turquoise	•		•	53
Red/Gray	•		•	85
Green	•		•	86
Blue	•		•	87
Ivory/Green	•		•	96
Ivory/Blue	•		•	97
Ivory/Turquoise			•	43
Red			•	45
Green			•	46
Blue			•	47
Ivory/Red			•	55
Blue/Ivory			•	57
White/Red			•	165

THE COLOR CODE indicates the paint color used on
the car. Two-Tone colors: The first two numbers identify the lower body color, the second two numbers identify the upper body color.

COLOR	CODE
Black	10
Etna Maroon	21
Flare Red	22
Glacier Green	30
Willow Green	31
Glade Green	32
Sarasota White	33
Capri Blue	40
Cadet Blue	41
Baltic Blue	42
Mist Gray	50
Juneau Gray	51
Polar White	60
Maize Cream	61
Desert Tan	62
Copper Metallic	63
Royal Marine	70
Turquoise	72

ENGINE SPECIFICATIONS

THE ENGINE NUMBER is located on the pad on top of the left side of the cylinder block. The starting engine number is V-1001/up.

DELUXE "88" SERIES

ENGINE CODE	NO. CYL.	CID	HORSE-POWER	COMP. RATIO	CARB
	8	324.3	170	8.25:1	2 BC

SUPER "88" SERIES

ENGINE CODE	NO. CYL.	CID	HORSE-POWER	COMP. RATIO	CARB
	8	324.3	185	8.25:1	4 BC

"98" DELUXE SERIES

ENGINE CODE	NO. CYL.	CID	HORSE-POWER	COMP. RATIO	CARB
	8	324.3	185	8.25:1	4 BC

1955 OLDSMOBILE 98 DELUXE HOLIDAY

1955 OLDSMOBILE 98 STARFIRE

1955 OLDSMOBILE SUPER 88 HOLIDAY

VEHICLE IDENTIFICATION NUMBER

```
• OLDSMOBILE •
  5 5 8 M 1 0 0 1
```

Located on a plate on the left hand body pillar post.

FIRST AND SECOND DIGITS: Identify the model year (1955)

THIRD DIGIT: Identifies the series

SERIES	CODE
Deluxe 88	7
Super 88	8
98	9

FOURTH DIGIT: Identifies the assembly plant

ASSEMBLY PLANT	CODE
Atlanta, GA	A
Framingham, MA	B
South Gate, CA	C
Kansas City, KS	K
Linden, NJ	L
Lansing, MI	M
Arlington, TX	T
Wilmington, DE	W

LAST FOUR DIGITS: Represent the basic production number

BODY NUMBER PLATE

Located on the front of the cowl adjacent to the left hand hinge.

```
OLDSMOBILE DIVISION
GENERAL MOTORS CORPORATION
LANSING, MICH.
STYLE NO. 55 3669D
BODY NO. L 1234
TRIM NO. 382
PAINT NO. 41
TOP 00        ACC 00
BODY BY FISHER
```

EXAMPLE:

55	Model year (1955)
36	Super "88"
69D	Deluxe 4-dr. sedan
L	Lansing, MI
1234	Production sequence
382	Blue pattern cloth
41	Panama Blue

THE STYLE NUMBER indicates the model and body style.

DELUXE "88"

BODY STYLE	CODE
2-Dr. sedan	3611
Holiday coupe	3637
4-Dr. sedan	3669
Holiday sedan	3639

SUPER "88"

BODY STYLE	CODE
Deluxe 2-dr. sedan	3611D
Deluxe Holiday coupe	3637D
Deluxe convertible coupe	3667DTX
Deluxe Holiday sedan	3669SD

"98"

BODY STYLE	CODE
Deluxe Holiday coupe*	3037DX
Deluxe convertible coupe*	3067DX
Deluxe 4-dr. sedan	3069D
Deluxe Holiday sedan*	3039SDX

* Equipped with electric windows/2-way seat

THE BODY NUMBER is the production serial number of the body. The prefix denotes the plant in which the body was assembled.

THE ASSEMBLY PLANT CODE indicates the plant where the vehicle was assembled.

ASSEMBLY PLANT	CODE
Lansing, MI	L
Flint, MI	G
Atlanta, GA	BA
South Gate, CA	BC
Framingham, MA	BF
Kansas City, KS	BK
Linden, NJ	BL
Arlington, TX	BT
Wilmington, DE	BW
Cleveland, OH	CL

THE TRIM CODE indicates the key to the trim color and material for each model series.

DELUXE "88" TRIM

COLOR	CLOTH	VINYL	LEATHER	CODE
Gray	•			361
Green	•			362,342
Blue	•			363
Red/Gray	•			341,385
Coral/Gray	•			344
Ivory/Green	•			347,367
Ivory/Blue	•			348,368
Turquoise/Gray	•			349
Ivory/Gray	•			321

SUPER "88" TRIM

COLOR	CLOTH	VINYL	LEATHER	CODE
Gray	•			381
Green	•			382
Blue	•			383
Gray/Red	•		•	311,315
Green	•		•	312
Gray/Coral	•		•	314
Green/Ivory	•		•	317,377
Blue/Ivory	•		•	318,378
Turquoise/Ivory	•		•	319
Black/Ivory	•		•	371
Ivory/Red			•	320
Green			•	322
Red			•	325
Ivory/Coral			•	326
Ivory/Blue			•	328
Ivory/Turquoise			•	329
Ivory/Red			•	365

"98" TRIM

COLOR	CLOTH	VINYL	LEATHER	CODE
Gray	•			391
Green	•			392
Blue	•			393
Gray/Red	•		•	331,335
Green	•		•	332
Blue	•		•	333
Gray/Coral	•		•	334
Green/Ivory	•		•	337
Blue/Ivory	•		•	338
Turquoise/Ivory	•		•	339
Black/Ivory	•		•	351
Green/Ivory	•		•	387
Blue/Ivory	•		•	388
Red/Ivory	•		•	345,350
Red			•	355
Ivory/Coral			•	356
Ivory/Green			•	357
Ivory/Blue			•	358
Ivory/Turquoise			•	359
Green/Ivory			•	397
Blue/Ivory			•	398
Black/Ivory			•	399

THE COLOR CODE indicates the paint color used on the car. Two-Tone colors: The first two numbers identify the lower body color, the last two numbers identify the upper body color.

COLOR	CODE
Black	10
Burlingame Red	20
Regal Maroon	21
Mint Green	30
Glen Green	31
Grove Green	32
Twilight Blue	40
Panama Blue	41
Bimini Blue	42
Frost Blue	43
Mist Gray	50
Juneau Gray	51
Polar White	60
Caspian Cream	61
Coral	62
Bronze Metallic	63
Chartreuse	64
Shell Beige	65
Turquoise	70

ENGINE SPECIFICATIONS

THE ENGINE NUMBER is located on the pad on the top left hand side of the cylinder block. The starting serial number is V400001.

DELUXE "88" SERIES

ENGINE CODE	NO. CYL.	CID	HORSE-POWER	COMP. RATIO	CARB
	8	324.3	185	8.5:1	2 BC

SUPER "88" SERIES

ENGINE CODE	NO. CYL.	CID	HORSE-POWER	COMP. RATIO	CARB
	8	324.3	202	8.5:1	4 BC

"98" DELUXE SERIES

ENGINE CODE	NO. CYL.	CID	HORSE-POWER	COMP. RATIO	CARB
	8	324.3	202	8.5:1	4 BC

1956 OLDSMOBILE SUPER 88 HOLIDAY

1956 OLDSMOBILE 98

1956 OLDSMOBILE

VEHICLE IDENTIFICATION NUMBER

· OLDSMOBILE ·
5 6 8 M 1 0 0 1

Located on a plate on the left hand body pillar post.

FIRST AND SECOND DIGITS: Identify the model year (1956)

THIRD DIGIT: Identifies the series

SERIES	CODE
Deluxe 88	7
Super 88	8
98	9

FOURTH DIGIT: Identifies the assembly plant

ASSEMBLY PLANT	CODE
Atlanta, GA	A
Framingham, MA	B
South Gate, CA	C
Kansas City, KS	K
Linden, NJ	L
Lansing, MI	M
Arlington, TX	T
Wilmington, DE	W

LAST FOUR DIGITS: Represent the basic production number

BODY NUMBER PLATE

Located on the front of the cowl adjacent to the left hand hinge.

OLDSMOBILE DIVISION
GENERAL MOTORS CORPORATION
LANSING, MICH.

STYLE N⁰. 56 3669
BODY N⁰. L 1234
TRIM N⁰. 361
PAINT N⁰. 10

TOP 00   **ACC** 00

BODY BY FISHER

EXAMPLE:

56	Model year (1956)
36	Deluxe "88"
69	Deluxe 4-dr. sedan
L	Lansing, MI
1234	Production sequence
361	Black/White/Ivory cloth
10	Black

THE STYLE NUMBER indicates the model and body style.

DELUXE "88"

BODY STYLE	CODE
2-Dr. sedan	3611
Holiday coupe	3637
Holiday sedan	3639
4-Dr. sedan	3669

SUPER "88"

BODY STYLE	CODE
Deluxe 2-dr. sedan	3611D
Deluxe 4-dr. sedan	3669D
Deluxe Holiday coupe	3637SD
Deluxe Holiday sedan	3639SD
Deluxe convertible coupe	3667DTX

"98"

BODY STYLE	CODE
Deluxe Holiday coupe*	3037SDX
Deluxe Holiday sedan*	3039SDX
Deluxe convertible coupe*	3067DX
Deluxe 4-dr. sedan	3069D

* Equipped with electric windows/2-way seat

THE BODY NUMBER is the production serial number of the body. The prefix denotes the plant in which the body was assembled.

THE ASSEMBLY PLANT CODE indicates the plant where the vehicle was assembled.

ASSEMBLY PLANT	CODE
Lansing, MI	L
Flint, MI	G
Atlanta, GA	BA
South Gate, CA	BC
Framingham, MA	BF
Kansas City, KS	BK
Linden, NJ	BL
Arlington, TX	BT
Wilmington, DE	BW
Cleveland, OH	CL

THE TRIM CODE indicates the key to the trim color and material for each model series.

DELUXE "88" TRIM

COLOR	CLOTH	VINYL	LEATHER	CODE
Black/White/Ivory	•			361,341
Green/White	•			362
Blue/White	•			363
Beige/White	•			364,344
Black/White/Red	•			345
Green/White/Ivory	•			347
Blue/White/Ivory	•			348
Turquoise/White/ Ivory	•			349
Beige	•			360
Red/Black	•			365
Ivory/Black	•			366
Ivory/Green	•			367
Ivory/Blue	•			368
Ivory/Turquoise	•			369

SUPER "88" TRIM

COLOR	CLOTH	VINYL	LEATHER	CODE
Gray	•			381
Green	•			382
Blue	•			383
Beige	•			384
Ivory/Black	•		•	311,371
Beige	•		•	314,374
Red/Black	•		•	315,375
Green/Ivory	•		•	317,377
Blue/Ivory	•		•	318,378
Turquoise/Ivory	•		•	319,379
Ivory/Red			•	320
Ivory/Black			•	321
Beige			•	324
Red			•	325
Ivory/Green			•	327
Ivory/Blue			•	328
Ivory/Turquoise			•	329

"98" TRIM

COLOR	CLOTH	VINYL	LEATHER	CODE
Gray	•			391
Green	•			392
Blue	•			393
Beige	•			394
Black/Ivory	•		•	331,386
Beige	•		•	334,396
Black/Red	•		•	335,395
Green/Ivory	•		•	337,397
Blue/Ivory	•		•	338,398
Turquoise/Ivory	•		•	339,399
Red/Ivory			•	350
Black/Ivory			•	351
Beige			•	354
Red			•	355
Green/Ivory			•	357
Blue/Ivory			•	358
Turquoise/Ivory			•	359

THE COLOR CODE indicates the paint color used on the car. Two-Tone colors: The first two numbers identify the lower body color, the second two numbers identify the upper body color.

COLOR	CODE
Black	10
Festival Red	20
Ice Green	30
Canyon Green	31
Tropical Green	32
Cirrus Blue	40
Artesian Blue	41
Nordic Blue	42
Sterling Gray	50
Juneau Gray	51
Charcoal	52
Alcan White	60
Citron Cream	61
Terra Cotta	62
Shantung Beige	63
Citation Bronze	64
Lime	65
Island Coral	66
Turquoise	70

ENGINE SPECIFICATIONS

THE ENGINE NUMBER is located on the pad on the top left side of the cylinder block. The starting engine number is V1000001.

"88" SERIES

ENGINE CODE	NO. CYL.	CID	HORSE-POWER	COMP. RATIO	CARB
	8	324.3	230	9.25:1	2 BC

SUPER "88" SERIES

ENGINE CODE	NO. CYL.	CID	HORSE-POWER	COMP. RATIO	CARB
	8	324.3	240	9.25:1	4 BC

"98" DELUXE SERIES

ENGINE CODE	NO. CYL.	CID	HORSE-POWER	COMP. RATIO	CARB
	8	324.3	240	9.25:1	4 BC

1957 OLDSMOBILE SUPER 88 FIESTA

1957 OLDSMOBILE GOLDEN ROCKET 88 HOLIDAY

VEHICLE IDENTIFICATION NUMBER

```
• OLDSMOBILE •
  5 7 8 M 1 0 0 1
```

Located on a plate on the left hand body pillar post.

FIRST AND SECOND DIGITS: Identify the model year (1957)

THIRD DIGIT: Identifies the series

SERIES	CODE
Deluxe 88	7
Super 88	8
98	9

FOURTH DIGIT: Identifies the assembly plant

ASSEMBLY PLANT	CODE
Atlanta, GA	A
Framingham, MA	B
South Gate, CA	C
Kansas City, KS	K
Linden, NJ	L
Lansing, MI	M
Arlington, TX	T
Wilmington, DE	W

LAST FIVE DIGITS: Represent the basic production number

BODY NUMBER PLATE

Located on the front of the cowl adjacent to the left hand hinge.

```
OLDSMOBILE DIVISION
GENERAL MOTORS CORPORATION
LANSING, MICH.
STYLE Nº. 57 3669D
BODY Nº. L 1234
TRIM Nº. 381
PAINT Nº. 10
TOP 00          ACC 00
BODY BY FISHER
```

EXAMPLE:

57	Model year (1957)
36	Super Golden Rocket "88"
69D	Deluxe 4-dr. sedan
L	Lansing, MI
1234	Production sequence
381	Gray cloth
10	Onyx Black

THE STYLE NUMBER indicates the model and body style.

GOLDEN ROCKET "88"

BODY STYLE	CODE
2-Dr. sedan	3611
Holiday coupe	3637
Holiday sedan	3639
Sedan wagon	3662F
Holiday wagon	3665F
Convertible coupe	3667TX
4-Dr. sedan	3669

SUPER GOLDEN ROCKET "88"

BODY STYLE	CODE
Deluxe 2-dr. sedan	3611D
Deluxe 4-dr. sedan	3669D
Deluxe Holiday coupe	3637SD
Deluxe Holiday sedan	3639SD
Deluxe Holiday wagon	3665SDF
Deluxe convertible coupe	3667DTX

STARFIRE "98"

BODY STYLE	CODE
Deluxe Holiday coupe*	3037SDX
Deluxe Holiday sedan*	3039SDX
Deluxe convertible coupe*	3067DX
Deluxe 4-dr. sedan	3069D

* Equipped with electric windows/2-way seat

THE BODY NUMBER is the production serial number
of the body. The prefix denotes the plant in which the body was assembled.

THE ASSEMBLY PLANT CODE indicates the
plant where the vehicle was assembled.

ASSEMBLY PLANT	CODE
Lansing, MI	L
Flint, MI	G
Atlanta, GA	BA
South Gate, CA	BC
Framingham, MA	BF
Kansas City, KS	BK
Linden, NJ	BL
Arlington, TX	BT
Wilmington, DE	BW
Cleveland, OH	CL

THE TRIM CODE indicates the key to the trim color
and material for each model series.

DELUXE "88" TRIM

COLOR	CLOTH	VINYL	LEATHER	CODE
Beige	•			316,366,326
Ivory/Black	•			360,361
Green	•			367
Ivory/Blue	•			368,348,363
Red/Black	•			369,365
Ivory/Charcoal	•			340
Ivory/Green	•			347,362
Ivory/Red	•			349

SUPER "88" TRIM

COLOR	CLOTH	VINYL	LEATHER	CODE
Gray	•			381
Green	•			382
Blue	•			383
Black/Ivory	•		•	380,371,370
Beige	•		•	386,346,376
Green/Ivory	•		•	387,372,377
Blue/Ivory	•		•	388,373,378
Black/Red	•		•	389,375,379
Charcoal/Ivory			•	320
Ivory/Green			•	327
Ivory/Blue			•	328
Red			•	329

"98" TRIM

COLOR	CLOTH	VINYL	LEATHER	CODE
Ivory/Charcoal			•	350
Beige			•	356
Ivory/Green			•	357
Ivory/Blue			•	358
Red			•	359
Black/Ivory	•		•	331,330
Green/Ivory	•		•	332,337
Blue/Ivory	•		•	333,338
Beige	•		•	336,396
Black/Red	•		•	339
Gray	•			391
Green	•			392
Blue	•			393

THE COLOR CODE indicates the paint color used on the car. Two-Tone colors: The first two numbers identify the lower body color, the second two numbers identify the upper body, the third two numbers identify the accent color.

COLOR	CODE
Onyx Black	10
Festival Red	20
Ice Green	30
Allegheny Green	31
Banff Blue	40
Artesian Blue	41
Grenada Gray	50
Juneau Gray	51
Charcoal	52
Alcan White	60
Coronado Yellow	61
Sunset Glow	62
Shantung Beige	63
Cutlass Bronze	64
Desert Glow	65
Royal Glow	66
Victorian White	90
Gold Mist	91
Rose Mist	92
Sapphire Mist	93
Jade Mist	94
Platinum Mist	95

ENGINE SPECIFICATIONS

THE ENGINE NUMBER is located on the pad on the top left hand side of the cylinder block. The starting engine number is A-001001. Export engines are identified by an "E" after the number.

GOLDEN ROCKET "88" SERIES

ENGINE CODE	NO. CYL.	CID	HORSE-POWER	COMP. RATIO	CARB
T-400	8	371	277	9.5:1	4 BC
J-2	8	371	300	10.0:1	3x2 BC

SUPER GOLDEN ROCKET "88" SERIES

ENGINE CODE	NO. CYL.	CID	HORSE-POWER	COMP. RATIO	CARB
T-400	8	371	277	9.5:1	4 BC
J-2	8	371	300	10.0:1	3x2 BC

STARFIRE "98" DELUXE SERIES

ENGINE CODE	NO. CYL.	CID	HORSE-POWER	COMP. RATIO	CARB
T-400	8	371	277	9.5:1	4 BC
J-2	8	371	300	10.0:1	3x2 BC

1958 OLDSMOBILE SUPER 88 HOLIDAY

1958 OLDSMOBILE 98

1958 OLDSMOBILE

VEHICLE IDENTIFICATION NUMBER

```
• OLDSMOBILE •
  5 8 8 M 1 0 0 1
```

Located on a plate on the left hand body pillar post.

FIRST AND SECOND DIGITS: Identify the model year (1958)

THIRD DIGIT: Identifies the series

SERIES	CODE
Dynamic 88	7
Super 88	8
98	9

FOURTH DIGIT: Identifies the assembly plant

ASSEMBLY PLANT	CODE
Atlanta, GA	A
Framingham, MA	B
South Gate, CA	C
Kansas City, KS	K
Linden, NJ	L
Lansing, MI	M
Arlington, TX	T
Wilmington, DE	W

LAST FIVE DIGITS: Represent the basic production number

BODY NUMBER PLATE

Located on the front of the cowl adjacent to the left hand hinge.

```
        OLDSMOBILE DIVISION
    GENERAL MOTORS CORPORATION
            LANSING, MICH.
   STYLE Nº. 58 3669D
    BODY Nº. L 1234
     TRIM Nº. 382
   PAINT Nº.  31
  TOP 00          ACC 00
      BODY BY FISHER
```

EXAMPLE:

58	Model year (1958)
36	Super "88"
69D	Deluxe 4-dr. sedan
L	Lansing, MI
1234	Production sequence
382	Green cloth
31	Onyx Black

THE STYLE NUMBER indicates the model and body style.

DYNAMIC "88"

BODY STYLE	CODE
2-Dr. sedan	3611
Holiday coupe	3637
Holiday sedan	3639
Sedan wagon	3693
Holiday wagon	3695
Convertible coupe	3667TX
4-Dr. sedan	3669

SUPER "88"

BODY STYLE	CODE
Deluxe 4-dr. sedan	3669D
Deluxe Holiday coupe	3637SD
Deluxe Holiday sedan	3639SD
Deluxe Holiday wagon	3695SD
Deluxe convertible coupe	3667DTX

"98"

BODY STYLE	CODE
Deluxe Holiday coupe*	3037SDX
Deluxe Holiday sedan*	3039SDX
Deluxe convertible coupe*	3067DX
Deluxe 4-dr. sedan	3069D

* Equipped with electric windows/2-way seat

THE BODY NUMBER is the production serial number of the body. The prefix denotes the plant in which the body was assembled.

THE ASSEMBLY PLANT CODE indicates the plant where the vehicle was assembled.

ASSEMBLY PLANT	CODE
Lansing, MI	L
Flint, MI	G
Atlanta, GA	BA
South Gate, CA	BC
Framingham, MA	BF
Kansas City, KS	BK
Linden, NJ	BL
Arlington, TX	BT
Wilmington, DE	BW
Cleveland, OH	CL

THE TRIM CODE indicates the key to the trim color and material for each model series.

DYNAMIC "88" TRIM

COLOR	CLOTH	VINYL	LEATHER	CODE
Silver/Charcoal	•			360
Ivory/Black	•			361
Green	•			362,342,367
Ivory/Blue	•			363,343
Beige	•			364,366,316
Red/Black	•			365
Ivory/Charcoal	•			341
Ivory/Red	•			345
Blue	•			368
Red/Charcoal	•			369

SUPER "88" TRIM

COLOR	CLOTH	VINYL	LEATHER	CODE
Gray	•			381
Green	•			382
Blue	•			383
Silver/Charcoal	•		•	371
Green	•		•	372,377,387
Blue/Beige	•		•	373
Beige	•		•	374,376
Beige	•		•	386,314
Red/Charcoal	•		•	375
Charcoal/Ivory/ Silver	•		•	370,380
Ivory/Blue	•		•	378,388
Ivory/Charcoal/Red	•		•	379,389
Silver/Charcoal/ Ivory			•	321
Green			•	322
Blue			•	323
Red			•	325

"98" TRIM

COLOR	CLOTH	VINYL	LEATHER	CODE
Gray	•			391
Green	•			392
Blue	•			393
Charcoal/Ivory/ Silver	•		•	331,330,339
Green	•		•	332,337
Blue/Ivory	•		•	333,338
Beige	•		•	334,336
Charcoal/Ivory/ Silver			•	351
Green			•	352
Blue			•	353
Beige			•	354
Red			•	355

THE COLOR CODE indicates the paint color used on the car. Two-Tone colors: The first two numbers identify the lower body color, the second two numbers identify the upper body color.

COLOR	CODE
Onyx Black	10
Festival Red	20
Surf Green	30
Allegheny Green	31
Banff Blue	40
Marlin Blue	41
Pearl Gray	50
Sterling Gray	51
Charcoal	52
Alaskan White	60
Sandstone	63
Autumn Haze	64
Desert Glow	65
Canyon Glow	66
Heather	67
Mountain Haze	68
Victorian White	90
Champagne Mist	91
Rose Mist	92
Turquoise Mist	93
Jade Mist	94
Tropical Mist	95

ENGINE SPECIFICATIONS

THE ENGINE NUMBER is located on the pad on top of the center exhaust port on the left side of the block. The starting engine number is B001001/up. The letter "E" following the engine number identifies an export engine.

DYNAMIC "88" SERIES

ENGINE CODE	NO. CYL.	CID	HORSE-POWER	COMP. RATIO	CARB
	8	371	265	10.0:1	2 BC
	8	371	312	10.0:1	3x2 BC

SUPER "88" SERIES

ENGINE CODE	NO. CYL.	CID	HORSE-POWER	COMP. RATIO	CARB
	8	371	305	10.0:1	4 BC
	8	371	312	10.0:1	3x2 BC

"98" SERIES

ENGINE CODE	NO. CYL.	CID	HORSE-POWER	COMP. RATIO	CARB
	8	371	305	10.0:1	4 BC
	8	371	312	10.0:1	3x2 BC

1959 OLSMOBILE SUPER 88 FIESTA

1959 OLDSMOBILE SUPER 88 HOLIDAY

1959 OLDSMOBILE SUPER 88 HOLIDAY

VEHICLE IDENTIFICATION NUMBER

• OLDSMOBILE •
598M1001

Located on a plate on the left hand body pillar post.

FIRST AND SECOND DIGITS: Identify the model year (1959)

THIRD DIGIT: Identifies the series

SERIES	CODE
Dynamic 88	7
Super 88	8
98	9

FOURTH DIGIT: Identifies the assembly plant

ASSEMBLY PLANT	CODE
Atlanta, GA	A
Framingham, MA	B
South Gate, CA	C
Kansas City, KS	K
Linden, NJ	L
Lansing, MI	M
Arlington, TX	T
Wilmington, DE	W

LAST FIVE DIGITS: Represent the basic production number

BODY NUMBER PLATE

Located under the hood below the left windshield wiper transmission.

OLDSMOBILE DIV. GENERAL MOTORS CORP.
LANSING, MICH.

STYLE Nº. 59 3519   BODY Nº. LA 1234

TRIM Nº. 331   PAINT Nº. A

ACC 00

THIS CAR FINISHED WITH
Miralite **ACRYLIC LACQUER**
BODY BY FISHER

EXAMPLE:

59	Model year (1959)
35	Super "88"
19	4-Dr. sedan
LA	Lansing, MI
1234	Production sequence
331	Gray cloth
A	Ebony Black

THE STYLE NUMBER indicates the model and body style.

DYNAMIC "88"

BODY STYLE	CODE
2-Dr. sedan	3211
4-Dr. sedan	3219
Fiesta station wagon	3235
Holiday coupe	3237
Holiday sedan	3239
Convertible coupe	3267

SUPER "88"

BODY STYLE	CODE
4-Dr. sedan	3519
Fiesta station wagon	3535
Holiday coupe	3537
Holiday sedan	3539
Convertible coupe	3567

"98"

BODY STYLE	CODE
4-Dr. sedan*	3819
Holiday coupe*	3837
Holiday sedan*	3839
Convertible coupe	3867

* Equipped with electric windows/2-way seat

THE BODY NUMBER is the production serial number of the body. The prefix denotes the plant in which the body was assembled.

THE ASSEMBLY PLANT CODE indicates the plant where the vehicle was assembled.

ASSEMBLY PLANT	CODE
Lansing, MI	LA
Doraville, GA (Atlanta)	BA
South Gate, CA	BC
Framingham, MA	BF
Kansas City, KS	BK
Linden, NJ	BL
Wilmington, DE	BW
Arlington, TX	BT

THE TRIM CODE indicates the key to the trim color and material for each model series.

DYNAMIC "88" TRIM

COLOR	CLOTH	VINYL	LEATHER	CODE
Gray/Ivory	•			311,316,321
Green/Ivory	•			312,317,322
Blue/Ivory	•			313,318,323
Fawn/Beige	•			314
Red/Gray/Ivory	•			315,320
Red/Ivory	•			310,325
Russet/Ivory	•			319
Copper/Ivory	•			324

SUPER "88" TRIM

COLOR	CLOTH	VINYL	LEATHER	CODE
Gray/Ivory	•			331,336,351
Green/Ivory	•			332,337,352
Blue/Ivory	•			333,338,353
Fawn/Beige	•			334,339
Red/Gray/Ivory	•			330
Red/Ivory	•			350
Copper/Ivory	•			359
Red/Ivory			•	360
Russet/Ivory			•	304
Gray/Ivory			•	366
Green/Ivory			•	367
Blue/Ivory			•	368
Fawn/Beige			•	369

"98" TRIM

COLOR	CLOTH	VINYL	LEATHER	CODE
Gray	•			371
Green	•			372
Blue	•			373
Fawn	•			374
Red/Ivory/Gray	•		•	380
Gray/Ivory	•		•	386
Green/Ivory	•		•	387
Blue/Ivory	•		•	388
Fawn/Beige	•		•	389
Red/Ivory/Gray			•	390
Mahogany/Russet/Ivory			•	394
Gray/Ivory			•	396
Green/Ivory			•	397
Blue/Ivory			•	398
Fawn/Beige			•	399

THE COLOR CODE indicates the paint color used on the car. Two-Tone colors: The first letter identifies the lower body color, the second letter identifies the center or accent color, the thrid letter identifies the upper body color, the fourth letter identifies the wheel color.

COLOR	CODE
Ebony Black	A
Silver Mist	B
Polaris White	C
Willow Mist	D
Emerald Mist	E
Crystal Green	F
Sapphire Mist	H
Frost Blue	J
Aqua Mist	K
Cardinal Red	L
Russet	M
Burgundy Mist	N
Golden Mist	P
Bronze Mist	R
Indigo	S

ENGINE SPECIFICATIONS

THE ENGINE NUMBER is located on the pad on top of the center exhaust port on the left side of the cylinder block. The starting engine number is 001001. The prefix letter "C" identifies a 371 engine, the letter "D" a 394 engine. The suffix letter "E" identifies an export engine.

DYNAMIC "88" SERIES

ENGINE CODE	NO. CYL.	CID	HORSE-POWER	COMP. RATIO	CARB
C	8	371	270	9.75:1	2 BC
C	8	371	300	9.75:1	4 BC

SUPER "88" SERIES

ENGINE CODE	NO. CYL.	CID	HORSE-POWER	COMP. RATIO	CARB
D	8	394.3	315	9.75:1	4 BC

"98" SERIES

ENGINE CODE	NO. CYL.	CID	HORSE-POWER	COMP. RATIO	CARB
D	8	394.3	315	9.75:1	4 BC

1950 PONTIAC

VEHICLE IDENTIFICATION NUMBER

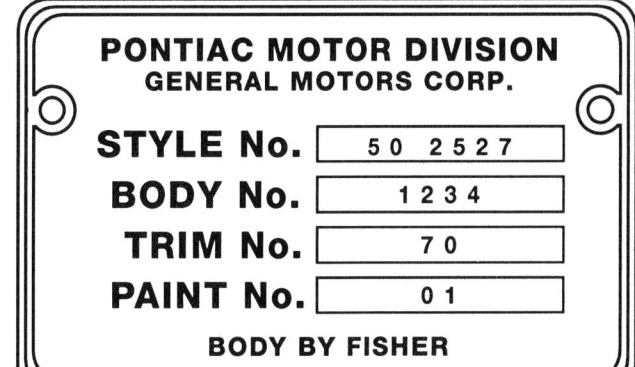

Located on a plate on the lower section of the left front pillar post for convertibles and Catalina's; on the upper section of the left front pillar post for all other models. The serial number is also on the machined pad in the upper left front corner on the cylinder block.

FIRST DIGIT: Identifies the assembly plant

ASSEMBLY PLANT	CODE
Atlanta, GA	A
South Gate, CA	C
Framingham, MA	F
Kansas City, KS	K
Linden, NJ	L
Pontiac, MI	P
Wilmington, DE	W

SECOND DIGIT: Identifies the engine

ENGINE	CODE
6-Cylinder	6
8-Cylinder	8

THIRD DIGIT: Identifies the model year (T=1950)

FOURTH DIGIT: Identifies the transmission type

TYPE	CODE
Hydra-matic	H
Syncro-mesh	S

LAST FOUR DIGITS: Represent the basic production number

BODY NUMBER PLATE

Located under the hood on the right front of the cowl.

PONTIAC MOTOR DIVISION
GENERAL MOTORS CORP.

STYLE No. 50 2527
BODY No. 1234
TRIM No. 70
PAINT No. 01

BODY BY FISHER

EXAMPLE:

50	Model year (1950)
2527	Chieftain sedan coupe
1234	Production sequence
70	Gray striped cloth
01	Starlight Blue

THE STYLE NUMBER indicates the model and body style.

CHIEFTAIN 6-CYL. - 25

BODY STYLE	CODE
Business coupe	2527B
Sedan coupe	2527
Sedan coupe deluxe	2527D
Convertible coupe deluxe	2567DTX
Catalina coupe deluxe	2537D
Catalina coupe Super deluxe	2537SD
2-Dr. sedan	2511
2-Dr. sedan deluxe	2511D
4-Dr. sedan	2569
4-Dr. sedan deluxe	2569D

CHIEFTAIN 8-CYL. - 27

BODY STYLE	CODE
Business coupe	2527B
Sedan coupe	2527
Sedan coupe deluxe	2527D
Convertible coupe deluxe	2567DTX
Catalina coupe deluxe	2537D
Catalina coupe sup. deluxe	2537SD
2-Dr. sedan	2511
2-Dr. sedan deluxe	2511D
4-Dr. sedan	2569
4-Dr. sedan deluxe	2569D

STREAMLINER 6-CYL. - 25

BODY STYLE	CODE
Sedan coupe	2507
Sedan coupe deluxe	2507D
4-Dr. sedan	2508
4-Dr. sedan deluxe	2508D
Station wagon	2562
Station wagon deluxe	2562D
Sedan delivery	2571

STREAMLINER 8-CYL. - 27

BODY STYLE	CODE
Sedan coupe	2507
Sedan coupe deluxe	2507D
4-Dr. sedan	2508
4-Dr. sedan deluxe	2508D
Station wagon	2562
Station wagon deluxe	2562D
Sedan delivery	2571

THE BODY NUMBER is the production serial number of the body.

THE COLOR CODE indicates the paint color used on the car.

COLOR	CODE
Black	00
Starlight Blue	01
Parma Wine	03
Warwick Gray	04
San Pedro Ivory	05
Rio Red	06
Tarragon Green	07
Skylark Blue	08
Cavalier Gray	09
Berkshire Green	10
Solar Gold	11

TWO-TONE COLORS

COLOR	CODE
Cavalier Gray/Warwick Gray	14
San Pedro Ivory/Sierra Rust	15
Tarragon Green/Berkshire Green	17
Skylark Blue/Cavalier Gray	18
Cavalier Gray/Skylark Blue	19

NOTE: The first color identifies the lower body color, the second color identifies the upper body color.

THE TRIM CODE indicates the trim color and material for each model series.

COLOR	CLOTH	VINYL	LEATHER	CODE
Gray	•			70
Dk. Gray	•			71
Brown		•		83
Tan		•		80
Gray/Black	•		•	59,79
Gray/Tan	•		•	64,74
Gray/Red	•		•	65,75,81
Gray/Green	•		•	66,76
Gray/Blue	•		•	67,77
Tan			•	84
Red			•	85
Green			•	86
Blue			•	87
Black			•	89
Rust/Ivory			•	72

ENGINE SPECIFICATIONS

THE ENGINE NUMBER is located on the left upper front corner of the engine block. The number is the same as the VIN number.

NO. CYL.	CID	HORSE-POWER	COMP. RATIO	CARB
6	239.2	90	6.5:1	1 BC
8	268.2	108	6.5:1	2 BC

1951 PONTIAC

VEHICLE IDENTIFICATION NUMBER

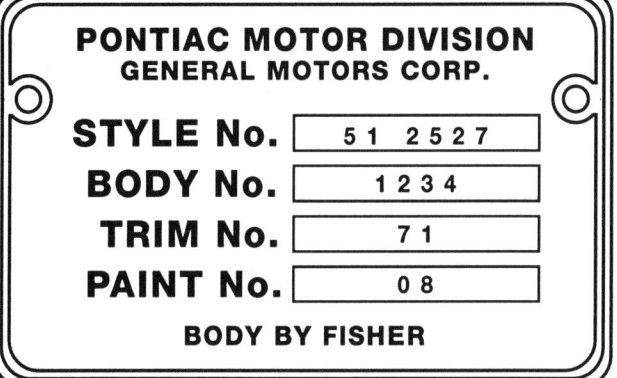

Located on a plate on the lower section of the left front pillar post for convertibles and Catalina's; on the upper section of the left front pillar post for all other models. The serial number is also on the machined pad in the upper left front corner on the cylinder block.

FIRST DIGIT: Identifies the assembly plant

ASSEMBLY PLANT	CODE
Atlanta, GA	A
South Gate, CA	C
Framingham, MA	F
Kansas City, KS	K
Linden, NJ	L
Pontiac, MI	P
Wilmington, DE	W

SECOND DIGIT: Identifies the engine

ENGINE	CODE
6-Cylinder	6
8-Cylinder	8

THIRD DIGIT: Identifies the model year (U=1951)

FOURTH DIGIT: Identifies the transmission type

TYPE	CODE
Hydra-matic	H
Syncro-mesh	S

LAST FOUR DIGITS: Represent the basic production number

BODY NUMBER PLATE

Located under the hood on the right front of the cowl.

PONTIAC MOTOR DIVISION
GENERAL MOTORS CORP.

STYLE No.	51 2527
BODY No.	1234
TRIM No.	71
PAINT No.	08

BODY BY FISHER

EXAMPLE:

51	Model year (1951)
25	Chieftain, 6-cyl.
27	Sedan coupe
1234	Production sequence
71	Gray striped cloth
08	Starmist Blue

THE STYLE NUMBER indicates the model and body style.

SERIES 25, 6-CYL./SERIES 27, 8-CYL. CHIEFTAIN

BODY STYLE	CODE
Business coupe	2527B
Sedan coupe	2527
Sedan coupe deluxe	2527D
Convertible coupe deluxe	2567DTX
Catalina coupe deluxe	2537D
Catalina coupe Super deluxe	2537SD
2-Dr. sedan	2511
2-Dr. sedan deluxe	2511D
4-Dr. sedan	2569
4-Dr. sedan deluxe	2569D

SERIES 25, 6-CYL./SERIES 27/8-CYL. STREAMLINER

BODY STYLE	CODE
Sedan coupe	2507
Sedan coupe deluxe	2507D
Station wagon	2562
Station wagon deluxe	2562D
Sedan delivery	2571

THE BODY NUMBER is the production serial number of the body.

THE COLOR CODE indicates the paint color used on the car.

COLOR	CODE
Black	00
St. Clair Blue	01
Victoria Maroon	03
Yorkshire Gray	04
Malibu Ivory	05
Tripoli Red	06
Palmetto Green	07
Starmist Blue	08
Surf Gray	09
Berkshire Green	10
Saturn Gold	11
Sapphire	12

TWO-TONE COLORS

COLOR	CODE
Surf Gray/Yorkshire Gray	14
Malibu Ivory/Sapphire	15
Palmetto Green/Berkshire Green	17,23
Surf Gray/Starmist Blue	19
Sapphire/Malibu Ivory	22
Lido Beige/Saturn Gold	24
Sand Gray/Imperial Maroon	25
Berkshire Green/Palmetto Green	26
Starmist Blue/St. Clair Blue	28

NOTE: The first color identifies the lower body color, the second color identifies the upper body color.

THE TRIM CODE indicates the trim color and material for each model series.

COLOR	CLOTH	VINYL	LEATHER	CODE
Gray	•			70,71
Tan		•		80
Brown		•		83
Gray/Black	•		•	59,79
Gray/Tan	•		•	64,74
Gray/Red	•		•	65,75,81
Gray/Green	•		•	66,76
Gray/Blue	•		•	67,77
Blue/Ivory	•		•	73
Blue/Ivory			•	72
Tan			•	84
Red			•	85
Green			•	86
Blue			•	87
Black			•	89

ENGINE SPECIFICATIONS

THE ENGINE NUMBER is located on the boss on the left upper front corner of the cylinder block. The number is the same as the VIN number.

NO. CYL.	CID	HORSE-POWER	COMP. RATIO	CARB
6	239.2	96	6.5:1	1 BC
8	268.2	116	6.5:1	2 BC

1952 PONTIAC

VEHICLE IDENTIFICATION NUMBER

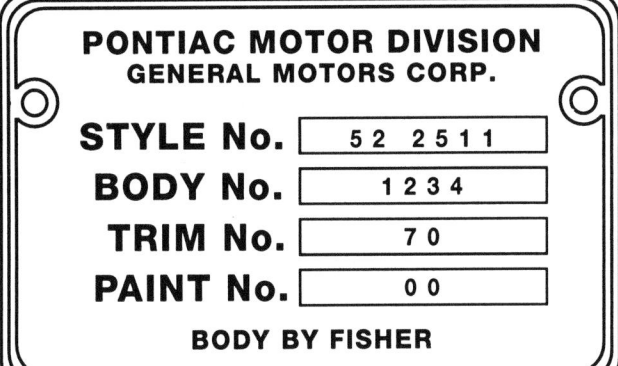

Located on a plate on the lower section of the left front pillar post for convertibles and Catalina's; on the upper section of the left front pillar post for all other models. The serial number is also on the machined pad in the upper left front corner on the cylinder block.

FIRST DIGIT: Identifies the assembly plant

ASSEMBLY PLANT	CODE
Atlanta, GA	A
South Gate, CA	C
Framingham, MA	F
Kansas City, KS	K
Linden, NJ	L
Pontiac, MI	P
Wilmington, DE	W

SECOND DIGIT: Identifies the engine

ENGINE	CODE
6-Cylinder	6
8-Cylinder	8

THIRD DIGIT: Identifies the model year (W=1952)

FOURTH DIGIT: Identifies the transmission type

TYPE	CODE
Hydra-matic	H
Syncro-mesh	S

LAST FOUR DIGITS: Represent the basic production number

BODY NUMBER PLATE

Located under the hood on the right front of the cowl.

PONTIAC MOTOR DIVISION
GENERAL MOTORS CORP.

STYLE No.	52 2511
BODY No.	1234
TRIM No.	70
PAINT No.	00

BODY BY FISHER

EXAMPLE:

52	Model year (1952)
2511	Chieftain, 2-dr. sedan
1234	Production sequence
70	Dk. Gray cloth
00	Black

THE STYLE NUMBER indicates the model and body style.

SERIES 25, 6-CYL./SERIES 27, 8 CYL. CHIEFTAIN

BODY STYLE	CODE
Convertible coupe deluxe	2567DTX
Catalina coupe deluxe	2537D
Catalina coupe Super deluxe	2537SD
2-Dr. sedan	2511
2-Dr. sedan deluxe	2511D
4-Dr. sedan	2569
4-Dr. sedan deluxe	2569D
Station wagon	2562
Station wagon deluxe	2562D
Sedan delivery	2571

THE BODY NUMBER is the production serial number of the body.

THE COLOR CODE indicates the paint color used on the car.

COLOR	CODE
Black	00
Potomac Blue	01
Victoria Maroon	03
Smoke Gray	04
Sea Mist Green	05
Cherokee Red	06
Placid Green	07
Mayflower Blue	08
Shell Gray	09
Forest Green	10
Saturn Gold	11
Belfast Green	12

TWO-TONE COLORS

COLOR	CODE
Shell Gray/Smoke Gray	14
Sea Mist Green/Belfast Green	15
Placid Green/Forest Green	17
Shell Gray/Mayflower Blue	19
Belfast Green/Sea Mist Green	22
Placid Green/Forest Green	23
Lido Beige/Saturn Gold	24
Sand Beige/Imperial Maroon	25
Forest Green/Placid Green	26
Mayflower Blue/Potomac Blue	28

NOTE: The first color identifies the lower body color, the second identifies the upper body color.

THE TRIM CODE indicates the trim color and material for each model series.

COLOR	CLOTH	VINYL	LEATHER	CODE
Blue	•			58,60
Brown	•			61
Gray	•			70,71
Brown		•		83
Tan		•		80
Gray/Black	•		•	59,79
Gray/Red	•		•	65,75
Gray/Green	•		•	66,76
Gray/Blue	•		•	67,77
Blue/Ivory			•	72
Green	•		•	73
Gray/Maroon/Red	•		•	81
Gray/Maroon/Tan	•		•	82
Gray/Maroon/Green	•		•	90
Gray/Maroon/Blue	•		•	91
Gray/Maroon/Black	•		•	92
Dk. Green/Pale Green			•	72
Tan			•	84
Red			•	85
Green			•	86
Blue			•	87
Black			•	89

ENGINE SPECIFICATIONS

THE ENGINE NUMBER is located on the boss on the upper left front corner of the cylinder block. The number is the same as the VIN number.

NO. CYL.	CID	HORSE-POWER	COMP. RATIO	CARB	TRANS
6	239.2	100	6.8:1	1 BC	STD
6	239.2	102	7.7:1	1 BC	HYDRA
8	268.2	118	6.8:1	2 BC	STD
8	268.2	122	7.7:1	2 BC	HYDRA

1953 PONTIAC

1953 PONTIAC CHIEFTAIN

1953 PONTIAC CHIEFTAIN

VEHICLE IDENTIFICATION NUMBER

```
• PONTIAC •
  P8XH1001
```

Located on a plate on the lower section of the left front pillar post for convertibles and Catalina's, on the upper section of the left front pillar post for all other models. The serial number is also on the machined pad in the upper left front corner on the cylinder block.

FIRST DIGIT: Identifies the assembly plant

ASSEMBLY PLANT	CODE
Atlanta, GA	A
South Gate, CA	C
Framingham, MA	F
Kansas City, KS	K
Linden, NJ	L
Pontiac, MI	P
Wilmington, DE	W

SECOND DIGIT: Identifies the engine

ENGINE	CODE
6-Cylinder	6
8-Cylinder	8

THIRD DIGIT: Identifies the model year (X=1953)

FOURTH DIGIT: Identifies the transmission type

TYPE	CODE
Hydra-matic	H
Syncro-mesh	S

LAST FOUR DIGITS: Represent the basic production number

BODY NUMBER PLATE

Located under the hood on the right front of the cowl.

```
PONTIAC MOTOR DIVISION
GENERAL MOTORS CORP.
STYLE No.   53 2511W
BODY No.    1234
TRIM No.    70
PAINT No.   00
BODY BY FISHER
```

EXAMPLE:

53	Model year (1953)
2511W	Chieftain 2-dr. sedan
1234	Production sequence
70	Dk. Gray cloth
00	Raven Black

THE STYLE NUMBER indicates the model and body style.

CHIEFTAIN

BODY STYLE	CODE
Convertible coupe deluxe	2567DTX
Catalina coupe deluxe	2537D
Catalina coupe Super deluxe	2537SD
2-Dr. sedan	2511W
2-Dr. sedan deluxe	2511WD
4-Dr. sedan	2569W
4-Dr. sedan deluxe	2569WD
Station wagon, 2-seat	2562F
Station wagon, 3-seat	2562
Station wagon deluxe	2562DF
Sedan delivery	2571

THE BODY NUMBER is the production serial number of the body.

THE COLOR CODE indicates the paint color used on the car.

COLOR	CODE
Raven Black	00
Caravan Blue	01
Continental Maroon	03
Marathon Gray	04
Milano Ivory	05
Santa Fe Red	06
Linden Green	07
Stardust Blue	08
Cirro Gray	09
Spruce Green	10
Winona Green	11
Laurel Green	12

TWO-TONE COLORS

COLOR	CODE
Cirro Gray/Marathon Gray	14
Milano Ivory/Laurel Green	15
Linden Green/Spruce Green	17
Stardust Blue/Caravan Blue	18
Cirro Gray/Stardust Blue	19
Laurel Green/Milano Ivory	22

NOTE: The first color identifies the lower body color, the second color identifies the upper body color.

THE TRIM CODE indicates the trim color and material for each model series.

COLOR	CLOTH	VINYL	LEATHER	CODE
Blue	•			60
Green	•			61
Gray	•			70,71
Rust		•		80,90
Beige/Black		•		83
Gray/Black	•		•	59,79
Gray/Red	•		•	65,75
Gray/Red	•		•	81,93
Green	•		•	66,76
Green	•		•	82,92
Blue	•		•	67,77
Blue	•		•	91,94
Green/Ivory	•		•	72
Tan			•	84
Red			•	85
Green			•	86
Blue			•	87
Black			•	89

ENGINE SPECIFICATIONS

THE ENGINE NUMBER is located on a pad on the upper left front corner of the cylinder block. The number is the same as the VIN number.

NO. CYL.	CID	HORSE-POWER	COMP. RATIO	CARB	TRANS
6	239.2	115	7.0:1	2 BC	STD
6	239.2	118	7.7:1	2 BC	HYD
8	268.4	118	6.8:1	2 BC	STD
8	268.4	122	7.7:1	2 BC	HYD

1954 PONTIAC STAR CHIEF CUSTOM CATALINA

VEHICLE IDENTIFICATION NUMBER

PONTIAC
P8ZH1001

Located on a plate on the lower section of the left front pillar post for convertibles and Catalina's, on the upper section of the left front pillar post for all other models. The serial number is also on the machined pad in the upper left front corner on the cylinder block.

FIRST DIGIT: Identifies the assembly plant

ASSEMBLY PLANT	CODE
Atlanta, GA	A
South Gate, CA	C
Framingham, MA	F
Kansas City, KS	K
Linden, NJ	L
Pontiac, MI	P
Wilmington, DE	W

SECOND DIGIT: Identifies the engine

ENGINE	CODE
6-Cylinder	6
8-Cylinder	8

THIRD DIGIT: Identifies the model year (Z=1954)

FOURTH DIGIT: Identifies the transmission type

STAR CHIEF

TYPE	CODE
Hydra-matic	A
Syncro-mesh	C

CHIEFTAIN

TYPE	CODE
Hydra-matic	H
Syncro-mesh	S

LAST FOUR DIGITS: Represent the basic production number

BODY NUMBER PLATE

Located under the hood on the right front of the cowl.

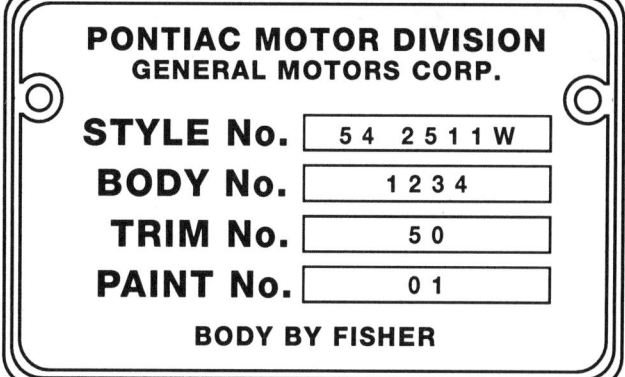

PONTIAC MOTOR DIVISION
GENERAL MOTORS CORP.

STYLE No. 54 2511W
BODY No. 1234
TRIM No. 50
PAINT No. 01

BODY BY FISHER

EXAMPLE:

54	Model year (1954)
2511W	Chieftain 2-dr. sedan
1234	Production sequence
50	Blue cloth
01	San Marino Blue

THE STYLE NUMBER indicates the model and body style.

SERIES 25, 6-CYL./SERIES 27, 8-CYL. CHIEFTAIN

BODY STYLE	CODE
Catalina coupe deluxe	2537D
Catalina coupe sup. deluxe	2537SD
2-Dr. sedan	2511W
2-Dr. sedan deluxe	2511WD
4-Dr. sedan	2569W
4-Dr. sedan deluxe	2569WD
Station wagon, 2-seat	2562F
Station wagon, 3-seat	2562
Station wagon deluxe	2562DF

SERIES 28, 8-CYL. STAR CHIEF

BODY STYLE	CODE
Convertible coupe	2867DTX
Catalina coupe suctom	2837SD
4-Dr. sedan deluxe	2869WD
4-Dr. sedan custom	2869WSD

THE BODY NUMBER is the production serial number of the body.

THE COLOR CODE indicates the paint color used on the car.

COLOR	CODE
Raven Black	00
San Marino Blue	01
Senaca Brown	02
Arlington Maroon	03
Cruiser Gray	04
Maize Yellow	05
Picador Red	06
Shannon Green	07
Mayfair Blue	08
Cirro Gray	09
Brookmere Green	10
Coral Red	11
Biloxi Beige	12
Laurel Green	23
Milano Ivory	24

TWO-TONE COLORS

COLOR	CODE
Shannon Green/Raven Black	13
Cirro Gray/Cruiser Gray	14
Maize Yellow/Winter White	15
Picador Red/Raven Black	16
Shannon Green/Brookmere Green	17
Mayfair Blue/San Marino Blue	18
Cirro Gray/Mayfair Blue	19
Cirro Gray/Raven Black	20
Coral Red/Winter White	21
Biloxi Beige/Winter White	22

NOTE: The first color identifies the upper body color, the second color identifies the lower body color.

THE TRIM CODE indicates the trim color and material for each model series.

COLOR	CLOTH	VINYL	LEATHER	CODE
Blue	•			50,60,62
Green	•			51,61,63
Gray	•			52,64
Gray	•			70,71
Green/Beige		•		80,90
Red/Ivory		•		81,85
Green/Ivory		•		82,86
Blue/Ivory		•		87
Black/Ivory		•		89
Gray/Black	•	•		59
Gray/Red	•	•		65
Green	•	•		66
Blue	•	•		67
Dk. Yellow/Ivory	•		•	55,56
Brown/Ivory	•		•	57,58
Beige/Ivory	•		•	73,74
Yellow/Ivory	•		•	88,92
Coral/Ivory	•		•	91,93
Green			•	30,46
Red			•	38,45
Green/Ivory			•	44
Beige/Ivory			•	72,94
Yellow/Ivory			•	84,96
Coral/Ivory			•	90,97
Blue			•	47
Tan			•	48
Black			•	49

ENGINE SPECIFICATIONS

THE ENGINE NUMBER is located on a pad on the upper left front corner of the cylinder block. The number is the same as the VIN number.

CHIEFTAIN

NO. CYL.	CID	HORSE-POWER	COMP. RATIO	CARB	TRANS
6	239.2	115	7.0:1	2 BC	STD
6	239.2	118	7.7:1	2 BC	HYD
8	268.4	122	6.8:1	2 BC	STD
8	268.4	127	7.7:1	2 BC	HYD

STAR CHIEF

NO. CYL.	CID	HORSE-POWER	COMP. RATIO	CARB	TRANS
8	268.4	122	6.8:1	2 BC	STD
8	268.4	127	7.7:1	2 BC	HYD

1955 PONTIAC STAR CHIEF

1955 PONTIAC STAR CHIEF CUSTOM CATALINA

1955 PONTIAC CHIEFTAIN

1955 PONTIAC

VEHICLE IDENTIFICATION NUMBER

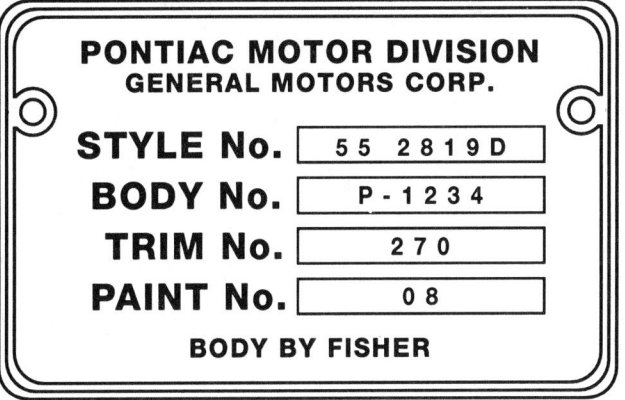

PONTIAC
P 7 5 5 H 1 0 0 1

Located on a plate on the left front hinge pillar post. The serial number is also on the machined pad on the front of the right hand bank of the engine block.

FIRST DIGIT: Identifies the assembly plant

ASSEMBLY PLANT	CODE
Atlanta, GA	A
South Gate, CA	C
Framingham, MA	F
Kansas City, KS	K
Linden, NJ	L
Pontiac, MI	P
Arlington, TX	T
Wilmington, DE	W

SECOND DIGIT: Identifies the series

SERIES	CODE
27 - Chieftain	7
28 - Star Chief	8

THIRD AND FOURTH DIGITS: Identify the model year (1955)

FIFTH DIGIT: Identifies the transmission type

TYPE	CODE
Hydra-matic	H
Syncro-mesh	S

LAST FOUR DIGITS: Represent the basic production number

BODY NUMBER PLATE

Located on the right side of the cowl just under the rear edge of the hood.

PONTIAC MOTOR DIVISION
GENERAL MOTORS CORP.

STYLE No.	55 2819 D
BODY No.	P - 1 2 3 4
TRIM No.	2 7 0
PAINT No.	0 8

BODY BY FISHER

EXAMPLE:

55	Model year (1955)
28	Star Chief
19D	4-Dr. sedan
12345	Production sequence
270	Black/Gray cloth
08	Marietta Blue

THE STYLE NUMBER indicates the model and body style.

SERIES 27 CHIEFTAIN

BODY STYLE	CODE
Catalina coupe deluxe	2537D
2-Dr. sedan	2511
2-Dr. sedan deluxe	2511D
4-Dr. sedan	2519
4-Dr. sedan deluxe	2519D
Station wagon, 4-dr.	2562
Station wagon, 4-dr. deluxe	2562DF
Station wagon, 2-dr.	2563F
Star Chief Custom station wagon	2564DF

SERIES 28 STAR CHIEF

BODY STYLE	CODE
Convertible coupe	2867DTX
Catalina coupe custom	2837SD
4-Dr. sedan deluxe	2819D
4-Dr. sedan custom	2819SD

THE BODY NUMBER is the production serial number of the body.

THE COLOR CODE indicates the paint color used on the car.

COLOR	CODE
Raven Black	00
Beaumont Blue	01
Corsair Tan	02
Persian Maroon	03
Falcon Gray	04
Avalon Yellow	05
Bolero Red	06
Valley Green	07
Marietta Blue	08
Castle Gray	09
Sequoia Green	10
Firegold	11
Turquoise Blue	12
Nautilus Blue	31
Driftwood Beige	41
Polo White	82

TWO-TONE COLORS

COLOR	CODE
Raven Black/Valley Green	13
Falcon Gray Poly/Castle Gray	14
Raven Black/Avalon Yellow	15
Raven Black/Bolero Red	16
Sequoia Green Poly/Valley Green	17
Beaumont Blue Poly/Marietta Blue	18
Marietta Blue/Castle Gray	19
Raven Black/Castle Gray	20
White Mist/Firegold Poly	21
White Mist/Turquoise Blue Poly	22
Castle Gray/Corsair Tan	23
Castle Gray/Nautilus Blue	24
Sequoia Green Poly/Avalon Yellow	25
Nautilus Blue/Castle Gray	26
Avalon Yellow/Raven Black	27
Raven Black/Nautilus Blue	28
Avalon Yellow/Sequoia Green Poly	29
Nautilus Blue/Raven Black	30
Raven Black/Valley green	32
Castle Gray/Falcon Gray Poly	33
Bolero Red/Raven Black	34
Valley Green/Sequoia Green Poly	35

COLOR	CODE
Marietta Blue/Beaumont Blue Poly	36
Castle Gray/Marietta Blue	37
Castle Gray/Raven Black	38
Corsair Tan/Castle Gray	39
Polo White/Driftwood Beige	82

NOTE: The first color identifies the upper body color, the second color identifies the lower body color.

THE TRIM CODE indicates the trim color and material for each model series.

COLOR	CLOTH	VINYL	LEATHER	CODE
Blue	•			248,249,252
Blue	•			256,260
Blue	•			262,279
Green	•			251,257,261
Green	•			263,296,298
Gray	•			255,258,264
Black/Gray	•			270
Gray	•			271
Beige/Copper	•			274
Red/Ivory		•		253,281,285
Green/Ivory		•		254,282,286
Tan/Brown		•		280
Blue/Ivory		•		287
Black/Ivory		•		289
Blue	•	•		250
Gray/Black	•	•		259
Gray/Red	•	•		265
Green	•	•		266,297
Blue	•	•		267
Beige/Copper	•		•	273,274,275
Blue	•		•	277,283,288
Ivory/Copper	•		•	292
Ivory/Blue	•		•	293
Ivory/Copper			•	272,276
Ivory/Blue			•	278,284

ENGINE SPECIFICATIONS

THE ENGINE NUMBER is located on the right front of the cylinder block. The number is the same as the VIN number.

CHIEFTAIN

NO. CYL.	CID	HORSE-POWER	COMP. RATIO	CARB
8	287.3	180	8.0:1	2 BC
8	287.3	180	8.0:1	4 BC
8	287.3	173	7.5:1	2BC

STAR CHIEF

NO. CYL.	CID	HORSE-POWER	COMP. RATIO	CARB
8	287.3	180	8.0:1	2 BC
8	287.3	200	8.0:1	4 BC
8*	287.3	173	7.5:1	2BC

*L- Stamped on engine number pad indicates low compression.

1956 PONTIAC STAR CHIEF CUSTOM CATALINA

1956 PONTIAC 870 STATION WAGON

1956 PONTIAC

1956 PONTIAC 870

VEHICLE IDENTIFICATION NUMBER

• PONTIAC
P756H1001 •

Located on a plate on the left front hinge pillar post. The serial number is also on the machined pad on the front of the right hand bank of the engine block.

FIRST DIGIT: Identifies the assembly plant

ASSEMBLY PLANT	CODE
Atlanta, GA	A
South Gate, CA	C
Framingham, MA	F
Kansas City, KS	K
Linden, NJ	L
Pontiac, MI	P
Arlington, TX	T
Wilmington, DE	W

SECOND DIGIT: Identifies the series

SERIES	CODE
27 - Star Chief Safari, Eight Seventy, Eight Sixty	7
28 - Star Chief	8

THIRD AND FOURTH DIGITS: Identify the model year (1956)

FIFTH DIGIT: Identifies the transmission type

TYPE	CODE
Hydra-matic	H
Syncro-mesh	S

LAST FOUR DIGITS: Represent the basic production number

BODY NUMBER PLATE

Located on the right side of the cowl just under the rear edge of the hood.

**PONTIAC MOTOR DIVISION
GENERAL MOTORS CORPORATION
PONTIAC, MICHIGAN**

STYLE No.	56 2819D
BODY No.	P-12345
TRIM No.	260
PAINT No.	C
TOP	ACC

BODY BY FISHER

EXAMPLE:

56	Model year (1956)
28	Star Chief
19D	4-Dr. sedan
P	Pontiac, MI
12345	Production sequence
260	Blue cloth
C	Olympic Blue

THE STYLE NUMBER indicates the model and body style.

CHIEFTAIN - SERIES 27

BODY STYLE	CODE
Catalina coupe	2737
Catalina coupe deluxe	2737D
Catalina sedan	2739
Catalina sedan deluxe	2739D
2-Dr. sedan	2711
4-Dr. sedan	2719
4-Dr. sedan deluxe	2719D
Station wagon, 4-dr.	2762FC
Station wagon, 4-dr. deluxe	2762DF
Station wagon, 2-dr.	2763F
Star Chief Safari Custom station wagon	2764DF

STAR CHIEF - SERIES 28

BODY STYLE	CODE
Convertible coupe	2867DTX
Catalina coupe custom	2837SD
Catalina sedan custom	2839SD
4-Dr. sedan deluxe	2819D

THE BODY NUMBER is the production serial number of the body. The prefix denotes the assembly plant.

THE COLOR CODE indicates the paint color used on the car. The first digit identifies the lower body color, the second digit identifies the upper body color on the two-tone colors.

COLOR	CODE
Raven Black	A
Chesapeake Blue	B
Olympic Blue	C
Amethyst	D
Phantom Gray	E
Grenada Gold	F
Bolero Red	G
Hialeah Green	H
Malabar Yellow	I
Vista Blue	J
Nimbus Gray	K
Glendale Green	L
Tarragon Green	M
Sandalwood Tan	N,S
Kerry Green	O
Sun Beige	P
Catalina Blue	Q
Camelia Pink	R
Marina Blue	U
Avalon Blue	V
Sun Beige	W
Rodeo Beige	X,Y
Lilac	Z

THE TRIM CODE indicates the trim color and material for each model series.

COLOR	CLOTH	VINYL	LEATHER	CODE
Blue	•			260
Green	•			261
Gray	•			271
Black/Ivory		•		279
Gray		•		280
Red/Ivory		•		281,285
Green/Ivory		•		282,286
Red/Gray		•		292
Blue/Ivory		•		287
Black/Ivory		•		289
Green/Gray		•		293
Black/Gray	•	•		242,264
Black/Ivory	•	•		243,244,253
Blue/Ivory	•	•		245
Green/Ivory	•	•		246
Gray/Ivory	•	•		247,250,265
Blue	•	•		248,251,267
Green	•	•		249,252,266
Black/Red	•	•		258
Gray/Black	•	•		259
Blue/Gray	•	•		262
Green/Gray	•	•		263
Rust/Beige	•		•	255
Blue	•		•	256
Rust/Beige	•		•	273,275
Blue	•		•	277,283
Rust/Beige			•	254,272,276
Blue			•	257,278,284

ENGINE SPECIFICATIONS

THE ENGINE NUMBER is located on a pad on the right front of the cylinder block. The engine number and serial number are the same.

CHIEFTAIN

NO. CYL.	CID	HORSE-POWER	COMP. RATIO	CARB	TRANS
8	316.6	192	7.9:1	2 BC	STD
8	316.6	192	8.9:1	2 BC	STD
8	316.6	216	8.9:1	4 BC	STD
8	316.6	227	8.9:1	4 BC	HYD
8	316.6	205	8.9:1	2 BC	HYD
**8	316.6	285	10.0:1	2x4 BC	

* Special engine for use with regular gas is identified by "L" stamped on the engine number pad.

STAR CHIEF

NO. CYL.	CID	HORSE-POWER	COMP. RATIO	CARB	TRANS
8	316.6	192	7.9:1	2 BC	STD
8	316.6	192	8.9:1	2 BC	STD
8	316.6	216	8.9:1	4 BC	STD
8	316.6	227	8.9:1	4 BC	HYD
8	316.6	205	8.9:1	2 BC	HYD
**8	316.6	285	10.0:1	2x4 BC	

** Optional engine available with all models except ones with air conditioning.

1957 PONTIAC STAR CHIEF

1957 PONTIAC CUSTOM SAFARI

1957 PONTIAC

VEHICLE IDENTIFICATION NUMBER

Located on a plate on the left front hinge pillar post. The serial number is also on the machined pad on the front of the right hand bank of the engine block.

FIRST DIGIT: Identifies the assembly plant

ASSEMBLY PLANT	CODE
Atlanta, GA	A
South Gate, CA	C
Framingham, MA	F
Kansas City, KS	K
Linden, NJ	L
Pontiac, MI	P
Arlington, TX	T
Wilmington, DE	W

SECOND DIGIT: Identifies the series

SERIES	CODE
27	7
28	8

THIRD AND FOURTH DIGITS: Identify the model year (1957)

FIFTH DIGIT: Identifies the transmission type

TYPE	CODE
Hydra-matic	H
Syncro-mesh	S

LAST FOUR DIGITS: Represent the basic production number

BODY NUMBER PLATE

Located on the right side of the cowl just under the rear edge of the hood.

```
PONTIAC MOTOR DIVISION
GENERAL MOTORS CORPORATION
PONTIAC, MICHIGAN
STYLE No.    57 2839SD
BODY No.     P-431
TRIM No.     238
PAINT No.    Q
ACC          BA3X2GJX
BODY BY FISHER
```

EXAMPLE:

57	Model year (1957)
28	Star Chief
39SD	Catalina custom sedan
P	Pontiac, MI
431	Production sequence
238	Silver Beige/Ivory leather
Q	Silver Beige

THE STYLE NUMBER indicates the model and body style.

CHIEFTAIN - SERIES 27

BODY STYLE	CODE
Catalina coupe	2737
Catalina sedan	2739
2-Dr. sedan	2711
4-Dr. sedan	2719
Station wagon, 4-dr.	2762FC
Station wagon, 2-dr.	2763F

SUPER CHIEF - SERIES 27

BODY STYLE	CODE
Caalina coupe	2737D
Catalina sedan	2739D
4-Dr. sedan	2719D
4-Dr. Safari	2762DF
4-Dr. Star Chief Safari Custom	2762SDF
2-Dr. Star Chief Safari Custom	2764DF

STAR CHIEF - SERIES 28

BODY STYLE	CODE
Convertible coupe	2867DTX
Bonneville Custom coupe convertible	2867SDX
Catalina Custom coupe	2837SD
Catalina Custom sedan	2839SD
4-Dr. sedan	2819D
4-Dr. sedan deluxe	2819SD

THE BODY NUMBER is the production serial number of the body. The prefix denotes the assembly plant.

THE COLOR CODE indicates the paint color used on the car. Two-tone color combination consists of three letters. The first letter identifies the lower body color, the second letter identifies the upper body color and the third letter identifies the insert color.

COLOR	CODE
Raven Black	A
Chevron Blue	B
Nassau Green	C
Sapphire Blue	D
Chateau Gray	E
Fontaine Blue	F
Tartan Red	G
Charcoal Gray	H
Lucerne Blue	J
Sheffield Gray	K
Braeburn Green	L
Starlight Yellow	M
Cordova Red	N
Kenya Ivory	P
Silver Beige	Q
Carib Coral	R
Limefire Green	S
Seacrest Green	T
Sage Blue	U
Cascade Blue	V
Mayfair Yellow	W
Iris	X
Bonneville Red	Z

THE TRIM CODE indicates the trim color and material for each model series.

COLOR	CLOTH	VINYL	LEATHER	CODE
Gray		•		209,221,225
Red/Gray		•		210,224,228
Green		•		211,223,227
Blue		•		222,226
Gray/Coral		•		229
Gray	•	•		200,203,215
Blue	•	•		204,216
Green	•	•		205,217
Gray/Coral	•	•		219
Silver Beige/Ivory	•		•	235
Maroon/Ivory	•		•	236
Green	•		•	237
Blue/Ivory	•		•	247,249
Silver Beige/Ivory			•	238,244
Maroon/Ivory			•	239,245
Green			•	240,246
Blue/Ivory			•	248,250,265
Red/Ivory			•	266
Charcoal/Ivory			•	267

ENGINE SPECIFICATIONS

THE ENGINE NUMBER is located on the front right hand side of the cylinder block. The number is the same as the VIN number.

CHIEFTAIN

NO. CYL.	CID	HORSE-POWER	COMP. RATIO	CARB	TRANS
*8	347	227	8.5:1	2 BC	STD
8	347	252	10.0:1	2 BC	HYD
8	347	290	10.0:1	3x2 BC	HYD

SUPER CHIEF

NO. CYL.	CID	HORSE-POWER	COMP. RATIO	CARB	TRANS
*8	347	244	8.5:1	2 BC	STD
8	347	270	10.0:1	4 BC	HYD
8	347	290	10.0:1	3x2 BC	HYD

STAR CHIEF

NO. CYL.	CID	HORSE-POWER	COMP. RATIO	CARB	TRANS
*8	347	244	8.5:1	2 BC	STD
8	347	290	10.0:1	3x2 BC	HYD
8	347	270	10.0:1	4 BC	HYD
**8	347	317	10.0:1	F.I.	HYD

* 8.5:1 Compression engines identified with "L" on engine number.

** Custom Bonneville convertible only.

1958 PONTIAC STATION WAGON

1958 PONTIAC CHIEFTAIN

1958 PONTIAC SUPER CHIEF CATALINA

1958 PONTIAC

VEHICLE IDENTIFICATION NUMBER

```
• PONTIAC •
  P858H1001
```

Located on a plate on the left front hinge pillar post. The serial number is also on the machined pad on the front of the right hand bank of the engine block.

FIRST DIGIT: Identifies the assembly plant

ASSEMBLY PLANT	CODE
Atlanta, GA	A
South Gate, CA	C
Framingham, MA	F
Kansas City, KS	K
Linden, NJ	L
Pontiac, MI	P
Arlington, TX	T
Wilmington, DE	W

SECOND DIGIT: Identifies the series

SERIES	CODE
25 - Bonneville/Chieftain conv.	5
27 - Chieftain/Star Chief station wagon	7
28 - Star Chief/Super Chief	8

THIRD AND FOURTH DIGITS: Identify the model year (1958)

FIFTH DIGIT: Identifies the transmission type

TYPE	CODE
Hydra-matic	H
Syncro-mesh	S

LAST FOUR DIGITS: Represent the basic production number

BODY NUMBER PLATE

Located on the right side of the cowl just under the rear edge of the hood.

```
PONTIAC MOTOR DIVISION
GENERAL MOTORS CORPORATION
PONTIAC, MICHIGAN
STYLE No.    58 2849SD
BODY No.     P-431
TRIM No.     252
PAINT No.    QQQ
ACC          BA3X2GJX
BODY BY FISHER
```

EXAMPLE:

58	Model year (1958)
28	Star Chief
49SD	4-Dr. sedan
P	Pontiac, MI
431	Production sequence
252	Blue cloth/vinyl
QQQ	Deauville Blue

THE STYLE NUMBER indicates the model and body style.

SERIES 25
BONNEVILLE

BODY STYLE	CODE
Sport coupe	2547SD
Convertible coupe	2567SD
Chieftain convertible coupe	2567

SERIES 27
CHIEFTAIN

BODY STYLE	CODE
Catalina coupe	2731
Catalina sedan	2739
2-Dr. sedan	2741
4-Dr. sedan	2749
4-Dr. Safari	2793
4-Dr. Safari	2794
4-Dr. Star Chief Safari deluxe	2793D
4-Dr. Star Chief Safari	2793SD

SERIES 28
SUPER CHIEF

BODY STYLE	CODE
Catalina coupe	2831D
Catalina sedan	2839D
4-Dr. sedan	2849D

STAR CHIEF

BODY STYLE	CODE
Catalina coupe	2831SD
Catalina sedan	2839SD
4-Dr. sedan	2849SD

THE BODY NUMBER is the production serial number of the body. The prefix denotes the assembly plant.

THE COLOR CODE indicates the paint color used on the car. The two-tone color consists of 3 letters. The first letter identifies the lower body color, the second letter identifies the upper body color, the third letter identifies the insert color.

COLOR	CODE
Persian Black	AAA
Ascot Gray	BBB
Palomar Yellow	CCC
Squadron Blue	DDD
Viking Blue	EEE
Darby Green	FFF
Seaforth Green	GGG
Rangoon Red	HHH
Frontier Beige	III
Sunmist Yellow	JJJ
Reefshell Pink	KKK
Tropicana Turquoise	LLL
Lilac Mist	MMM
Mallard Turquoise	NNN
Sunrise Coral	OOO
Marlin Turquoise	PPP
Deauville Blue	QQQ
Kashmir Blue	RRR
Burma Green	SSS
Calypso Green	TTT
Redwood Copper	UUU
Patina Ivory	VVV
Starmist Silver	WWW
Orchid	XXX
Greystone White	YYY

THE TRIM CODE indicates the trim color and material for each model series.

COLOR	CLOTH	VINYL	LEATHER	CODE
Gray	•			225
Blue	•			226
Green	•			227
Gray/Ivory	•	•		201
Blue	•	•		202,209,229
Blue	•	•		237,242,257
Blue	•	•		247,252
Green	•	•		203,210,230
Green	•	•		238,248,253
Green	•	•		258,268
Gray/Red	•	•		206,249
Gray/Ivory	•	•		208,228
Gray/Ivory	•	•		236,246
Red/Ivory	•	•		211,239,240
Gray/Silver	•	•		241,251,256
Gray/Silver	•	•		261,266
Turquoise	•	•		243,254,259
Turquoise	•	•		264,269
Copper/Ivory	•	•		244,255,260
Copper/Ivory	•	•		265,270
Gold/Ivory	•	•		298
Gray/Ivory		•		216,232
Blue		•		217,233
Green		•		218,234
Gray/Pink		•		219
Red/Ivory		•		220,235
Gray/Silver			•	271,277
Gray/Silver			•	285,290
Blue			•	272,278,286
Green			•	273,291
Turquoise			•	274,280
Turquoise			•	287,292
Copper/Ivory			•	275,281
Copper/Ivory			•	288,293
Red/Ivory			•	282,289

ENGINE SPECIFICATIONS

THE ENGINE NUMBER is located on a pad on the front right side of the cylinder block. The number is the same as the VIN number.

BONNEVILLE

NO. CYL.	CID	HORSE- POWER	COMP. RATIO	CARB	TRANS
8	370	255	8.6:1	2 BC	STD
8	370	270	10.0:1	2 BC	STD/HYD
8	370	285	10.0:1	4 BC	STD/HYD
8	370	300	10.5:1	3x2 BC	STD/HYD
8	370	310	10.5:1	F.I.	HYD

CHIEFTAIN

NO. CYL.	CID	HORSE- POWER	COMP. RATIO	CARB	TRANS
8	370	240	8.6:1	2 BC	STD
8	370	285	10.0:1	4 BC	STD
8	370	270	10.0:1	2 BC	STD/HYD
8	370	300	10.5:1	3x2 BC	STD/HYD
8	370	310	10.5:1	F.I.	HYD

STAR CHIEF

NO. CYL.	CID	HORSE- POWER	COMP. RATIO	CARB	TRANS
8	370	255	8.6:1	2 BC	STD
8	370	270	10.0:1	2 BC	STD/HYD
8	370	285	10.0:1	4 BC	STD/HYD
8	370	300	10.5:1	3x2 BC	STD/HYD
8	370	310	10.5:1	F.I.	HYD

SUPER CHIEF

NO. CYL.	CID	HORSE- POWER	COMP. RATIO	CARB	TRANS
8	370	240	8.6:1	2 BC	STD
8	370	285	10.0:1	4 BC	STD/HYD
8	370	270	10.0:1	2 BC	STD/HYD
8	370	300	10.5:1	3x2 BC	STD/HYD
8	370	310	10.5:1	F.I.	HYD

1959 PONTIAC CATALINA

1959 PONTIAC STAR CHIEF

VEHICLE IDENTIFICATION NUMBER

```
┌─────────────────────┐
│ ●  PONTIAC       ●  │
│    1 5 9 P 1 0 0 1   │
└─────────────────────┘
```

Located on a plate on the left front hinge pillar post. The serial number is also on the machined pad on the front of the right hand bank of the engine block.

FIRST DIGIT: Identifies the series

SERIES	CODE
21 - Catalina	1
24 - Star Chief	4
27 - Bonneville Safari	7
28 - Bonneville	8

SECOND AND THIRD DIGITS: Identify the model year (1959)

FOURTH DIGIT: Identifies the assembly plant

ASSEMBLY PLANT	CODE
Atlanta, GA	A
South Gate, CA	C
Framingham, MA	F
Kansas City, KS	K
Linden, NJ	L
Pontiac, MI	P
Arlington, TX	T
Wilmington, DE	W

LAST FOUR DIGITS: Represent the basic production number

BODY NUMBER PLATE

Located on the right side of the cowl just under the rear edge of the hood.

```
┌───────────────────────────────────────────┐
│   PONTIAC DIV. GENERAL MOTORS CORP.        │
│           PONTIAC, MICHIGAN                │
│  STYLE No. 59-2837    BODY No. PO 27       │
│  TRIM No.   270       PAINT No. SC         │
│  ACC 8-1-KX-JX                             │
│         THIS CAR FINISHED WITH            │
│  Magic Mirror ACRYLIC LACQUER              │
│         BODY BY FISHER                     │
└───────────────────────────────────────────┘
```

EXAMPLE:

59	Model year (1959)
28	Bonneville
37	2-Dr. sport coupe
P	Pontiac, MI
27	Production sequence
270	Blue cloth/vinyl
SC	Concord Blue/Cameo Ivory

THE STYLE NUMBER indicates the model and body style.

SERIES 21
CATALINA

BODY STYLE	CODE
2-Dr. sport sedan	2111
4-Dr. sedan	2119
4-Dr. Safari	2135
2-Dr. sport coupe	2137
4-Dr. Vista	2139
4-Dr. Safari	2145
Convertible coupe	2167

SERIES 24
STAR CHIEF

BODY STYLE	CODE
2-Dr. sport sedan	2411
4-Dr. sedan	2419
4-Dr. Vista	2439

SERIES 27
BONNEVILLE

BODY STYLE	CODE
4-Dr. Safari station wagon	2735

SERIES 28
BONNEVILLE

BODY STYLE	CODE
2-Dr. sport coupe	2837
4-Dr. Vista	2839
Convertible coupe	2867

THE BODY NUMBER is the production serial number of the body. The prefix denotes the assembly plant.

THE COLOR CODE indicates the paint color used on the car. The two-tone color combination consists of 2 letters. The first letter identifies the lower body color, the second letter identifies the upper body color.

COLOR	CODE
Regent Black	A
Silvermist Gray	B
Cameo Ivory	C
Dundee Green	D
Jademist Green	E
Seaspray Green	F
Vanguard Blue	H
Castle Blue	J
Gulfstream Blue	K
Mandalay Red	L
Sunset Glow	M
Royal Amethyst	N
Shoreline Gold	P
Canyon Copper	R
Concord Blue	S

THE TRIM CODE indicates the trim color and material for each model series.

COLOR	CLOTH	VINYL	LEATHER	CODE
Gray/Ivory	•	•		201,269
Turquoise	•	•		202,207
Yellow Green	•	•		203,208
Copper/Beige	•	•		204,209,223
Copper/Beige	•	•		232,273
Gray/Ivory	•	•		206
Red/Ivory	•	•		210
Gray/Ivory/Silver	•	•		224,229
Blue	•	•		225,230,270
Green	•	•		226,271
Maroon/Ivory	•	•		228,233,272
Ivory/Gray		•		212
Turquoise		•		213,219
Beige/Copper		•		215,221,249
Beige/copper		•		267,279
Red/Ivory		•		216,222
Yellow Green		•		220
Blue		•		247,264,276
Green		•		248,277
Ivory/Maroon		•		250,266,278
Gray/Silver		•		299
Ivory/Silver/Red			•	288,294
Blue			•	289,295
Ivory/Maroon			•	291,297

ENGINE SPECIFICATIONS

THE ENGINE NUMBER is located on a pad at the front of the right cylinder bank on the block. The number is the same as the serial number. NOTE: Engine identification codes were found on a decal on the left rocker arm cover. On late production models the engine code was stamped in the front of the engine production code located with the engine number. The engine codes and engine production numbers were different than the engine numbers.

EARLY DECAL CODE	LATE ENG. CODE	SERIES	NO. CYL.	HORSE-POWER	CID	COMP. RATIO	CARB	TRANS
—	D	21,24	8	389	245	8.6:1	2 BC	STD
532971	F	27,28	8	389	260	8.6:1	4 BC	STD
531936	ET	21	8	389	215	8.6:1	2 BC	STD
532979	G	ALL	8	389	315	10.5:1	3x2 BC	STD
532972	FP	ALL	8	389	280	10.0:1	4 BC	STD
532977	AL	ALL	8	389	330	10.5:1	4 BC	STD
532981	AN	ALL	8	389	345	10.5:1	3x2 BC	STD
—	ES	ALL	8	389	215	8.6:1	2 BC	STD
531912	DT	21,24	8	389	245	8.6:1	2 BC	STD
531913	H	27,28	8	389	245	8.6:1	2 BC	STD
—	A	21,24	8	389	280	10.0:1	2 BC	HYD
—	B	27,28	8	389	300	10.0:1	4 BC	HYD
—	B	21,24	8	389	300	10.0:1	4 BC	HYD
—	ER	ALL	8	389	215	8.6:1	2 BC	HYD
—	C	ALL	8	389	345	10.5:1	3x2 BC	HYD
532976	BP	ALL	8	389	300	10.0;1	4 BC	HYD
532978	AK	ALL	8	389	330	10.5:1	4 BC	HYD
532982	AM	ALL	8	389	345	10.5:1	3x2	HYD

1950 HUDSON PACEMAKER

VEHICLE IDENTIFICATION NUMBER

SERIAL NUMBER

503101

Located on a plate attached to the right front door hinge pillar, the engine number is stamped on the boss on the top and left side of the cylinder block. The serial number and the engine number are the same.

FIRST AND SECOND DIGITS: Identify the model year (1950)

THIRD DIGIT: Identifes the model

MODEL	CODE
Pacemaker, 6-cyl.	0
Pacemaker Deluxe, 6-cyl.	A
Super, 6-cyl.	1
Commodore, 6-cyl.	2
Super, 8-cyl.	3
Commodore, 8-cyl.	4

THE LAST THREE DIGITS: Represent the basic production sequence number

BODY NUMBER INFORMATION - Hudson did not provide numbers for the individual body styles in each series.

PACEMAKER

BODY TYPE	CODE
Brougham, 2-dr.	500
Sedan, 4-dr.	
Coupe, 3-pass.	
Club coupe, 6-pass.	
Brougham convertible	

PACEMAKER DELUXE

BODY TYPE	CODE
Brougham, 2-dr.	50A
Sedan, 4-dr.	
Club coupe	
Brougham convertible	

SUPER - 6

BODY TYPE	CODE
Brougham, 2-dr.	501
Sedan, 4-dr.	
Club coupe	
Brougham convertible	

COMMODORE - 6

BODY TYPE	CODE
Club coupe	502
Sedan, 4-dr.	
Brougham convertible	

SUPER - 8

BODY TYPE	CODE
Brougham, 2-dr.	503
Sedan, 4-dr.	
Club coupe	

COMMODORE - 8

BODY TYPE	CODE
Sedan, 4-dr.	504
Club coupe	
Brougham convertible	

THE COLOR CODE indicates the paint color used on the car. The code letter or number is stamped on the upper right front door hinge.

COLOR	CODE
Ebony Black	K5
Lagon Blue	B35
Rivard Blue	B38
Riviera Blue	B46
Legion Blue	J38
Bali Blue	J45
Lt. Golden Gray	RR29
Gray Mist	Q24
Field Gray	Q48
Oriental Green	P25
Dark Green Gray	CC30
Peacock Green	S26
Hawaii Green	S49
Texas Tan	H27
Cornish Cream	N37
Revue Red	M28
Twilight Gray	G23
Maroon	HN58

TWO-TONE COMBINATIONS

COLOR	CODE
Riviera Blue/Bali Blue	JB
Twilight Gray/Field Gray	QG
Oriental Green/Hawaii Green	SP
Dark Golden Gray/Light Golden Gray	RC

NOTE: The first color identifies the upper body color, the second color identifies the lower body color.

TRIM CODE - The following is the trim color and material for each model series:

500/50A MODELS

COLOR	CLOTH	VINYL	LEATHER	CODE
Striped Bedford	•	•		

501/503 MODELS

COLOR	CLOTH	VINYL	LEATHER	CODE
Striped Broad cloth	•	•		

502/504 MODELS

COLOR	CLOTH	VINYL	LEATHER	CODE
Blue/Gray	•			
Tan/Brown	•			

CONVERTIBLE MODEL

COLOR	CLOTH	VINYL	LEATHER	CODE
Red*		•		
Maroon#		•		
Blue/Spruce*		•		
Blue#		•		

* 500 and 50A models only

501, 502, 504 models only

ENGINE SPECIFICATIONS

MODEL CODE	NO. CYL.	CID	HORSE-POWER	COMP. RATIO	CARB
500	6	232	112	6.7:1	1 BC
50A	6	232	112	6.7:1	1 BC
501	6	262	123	6.5:1	2 BC
502	6	262	123	6.5:1	2 BC
503	8	254	128	6.5:1	2 BC
504	8	254	128	6.5:1	2 BC

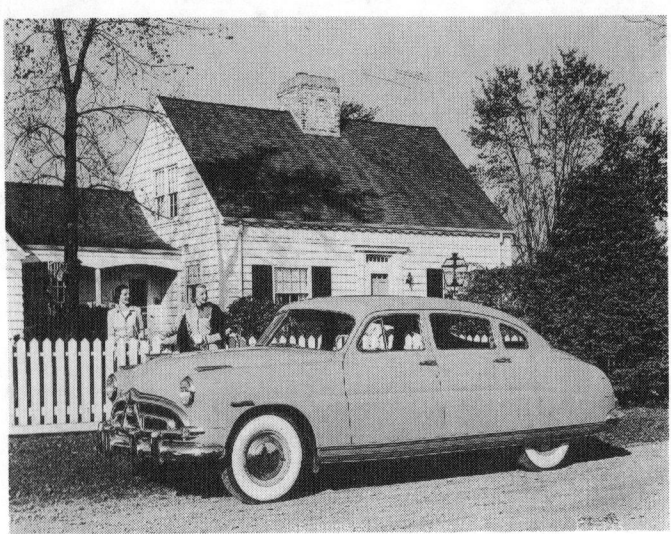

1951 HUDSON

VEHICLE IDENTIFICATION NUMBER

SERIAL NUMBER

4A1001

Located on a plate attached to the right front door hinge pillar. The engine number is stamped on the boss on the top and left side of the cylinder block. Engine and serial number are the same.

FIRST AND SECOND DIGITS: Identify the model

MODEL	CODE
Pacemaker Custom	4A
Super Custom, 6-cyl.	5A
Commodore Custom, 6-cyl.	6A
Hornet	7A
Commodore Custom, 8-cyl.	8A

THE LAST FOUR DIGITS: Represent the basic production sequence number

BODY NUMBER PLATE - Hudson did not provide numbers for the individual body styles in each series.

PACEMAKER CUSTOM SIX

BODY TYPE	CODE
Brougham, 2-dr.	4A
Sedan, 4-dr.	
Coupe, 3-pass.	
Club coupe, 6-pass.	
Brougham convertible	

SUPER SIX CUSTOM

BODY TYPE	CODE
Brougham, 2-dr.	5A
Sedan, 4-dr.	
Club coupe	
Brougham convertible	
Hollywood, 2-dr. hardtop	

COMMODORE SIX CUSTOM

BODY TYPE	CODE
Sedan, 4-dr.	6A
Club coupe	
Brougham convertible	
Hollywood, 2-dr. hardtop	

HORNET SIX

BODY TYPE	CODE
Sedan, 4-dr.	7A
Club coupe	
Brougham convertible, 2-dr.	
Hollywood, 2-dr. hardtop	

COMMODORE CUSTOM - 8

BODY TYPE	CODE
Sedan, 4-dr.	8A
Club coupe	
Hollywood, 2-dr. hardtop	
Brougham convertible	

THE COLOR CODE indicates the paint color used on the car. The code letter or number is stamped on the upper hinge of the right front door.

COLOR	CODE
Ebony Black	K5
Pacific Blue	B59
Admiral Blue	B87
Bali Blue	J45
French Gray	RR72
Newport Gray	Q61
Naples Green	P63
Dark Platinum	CC66
Neptune Blue Green	CC82
Jefferson Green	S62
Texas Tan	H27
Cornish Cream	N37
Toro Red	M64
Northern Gray	G60
Dark Maroon	HN58
Burgundy Maroon	HN83

TWO-TONE COMBINATIONS

COLOR	CODE
Pacific Blue/Bali Blue	JB
Northern Gray/Newport Gray	QG
Pacific Blue/French Gray	RB
Northern Gray/French Gray	RC
Dark Maroon/French Gray	RD
Naples Green/Jefferson Green	SP

NOTE: The first color identifies the upper body color, the second color identifies the lower body color.

TRIM CODE - The following is the trim color and material for each model series:

4A MODELS

COLOR	CLOTH	VINYL	LEATHER	CODE
Gray/Red/Brown	•	•		

5A MODELS

COLOR	CLOTH	VINYL	LEATHER	CODE
Tan/Brown	•	•		

6A,7A,8A MODELS

COLOR	CLOTH	VINYL	LEATHER	CODE
Blue/Gray		•		
Tan/Brown		•		

CONVERTIBLE MODEL

COLOR	CLOTH	VINYL	LEATHER	CODE
Dk. Red			•	
Blue*			•	

* Not available on Model 4A

ENGINE SPECIFICATIONS

16-8

MODEL CODE	NO. CYL.	CID	HORSE-POWER	COMP. RATIO	CARB
4A	6	232	112	6.7:1	1 BC
5A	6	262	123	6.7:1	2 BC
6A	6	262	123	6.7:1	2 BC
7A	6	308	145	6.2:1	2 BC
8A	8	254	128	6.7:1	2 BC

1952 HUDSON

1952 HUDSON COMMODORE 8

1952 HUDSON

1952 HUDSON

1952 HUDSON

VEHICLE IDENTIFICATION NUMBER

SERIAL NUMBER

5 B 1 3 2 9 1 6

Located on a plate attached to the right front door hinge pillar. The engine number is stamped on the boss on the top and left side of the cylinder block. The serial number and engine number are the same.

FIRST AND SECOND DIGITS: Identify the model

MODEL	CODE
Pacemaker	4B
Wasp	5B
Commodore, 6-cyl.	6B
Hornet	7B
Commodore, 8-cyl.	8B

THE LAST SIX DIGITS: Represent the basic production sequence number. The starting number is 132916.

BODY NUMBER INFORMATION - Hudson did not provide numbers for the individual body styles in each series.

PACEMAKER - 6

BODY TYPE	CODE
Brougham, 2-dr.	4B
Sedan, 4-dr.	
Club coupe, 6-pass.	
Business coupe, 3-pass.	

WASP - 6

BODY TYPE	CODE
Brougham, 2-dr.	5B
Sedan, 4-dr.	
Club coupe, 6-pass.	
Hollywood hardtop	
Brougham convertible	

COMMODORE - 6

BODY TYPE	CODE
Sedan, 4-dr.	6B
Club coupe	
Hollywood hardtop	
Brougham convertible	

HORNET - 6

BODY TYPE	CODE
Sedan, 4-dr.	7B
Club coupe	
Hollywood hardtop	
Brougham convertible, 2-dr.	

COMMODORE - 8

BODY TYPE	CODE
Sedan, 4-dr.	8B
Club coupe	
Hollywood hardtop	
Brougham convertible	

THE COLOR CODE indicates the paint color used on the car. The letter or number is stamped on the upper right front door hinge.

COLOR	CODE
Ebony Black	K5
Broadway Blue	B96
Southern Blue	J97
French Gray	RR72
Gulf Green	Q115
Symphony Blue-Green Dark	P124
Symphony Blue-Green Light	CC93
Jefferson Green	S62
Texas Tan	H27
Boston Ivory	N92
Toro Red	M64
Jupiter Gray	G95

TWO-TONE COMBINATIONS

COLOR	CODE
Black/Boston Ivory	RA
Southern Blue/Boston Ivory	RC
Jefferson Green/Boston Ivory	RD
Texas Tan/Boston Ivory	RF
Toro Red/French Gray	RH
French Gray/Black	RI
French Gray/Toro Red	RJ
French Gray/Southern Blue	RK
Symphony Blue-Green/Boston Ivory	RM
Boston Ivory/Symphony Blue-Green	RN
Boston Ivory/Texas Tan	RO
Boston Ivory/Jefferson Green	RP
Symphony Blue-Green Dark/ Symphony Blue-Green Light	RQ
Jefferson Green/Gulf Green	RS

COLOR	CODE
Symphony Blue-Green Light/ Symphony Blue-Green Dark	RT
Gulf Green/Jefferson Green	RU
Boston Ivory/Black	RV
Symphony Blue-Green Light/Black	RW
Southern Blue/Broadway Blue	RX

NOTE: The first letter identifies the lower body color, the second letter identifies the upper body color.

TRIM CODE - The following is the trim color and material for each model series.

PACEMAKER 4B MODELS

COLOR	CLOTH	VINYL	LEATHER	CODE
Gray/Red/Brown	•	•		

WASP 5B MODELS

COLOR	CLOTH	VINYL	LEATHER	CODE
Red/Brown	•	•		

COMMODORE 6B MODELS

COLOR	CLOTH	VINYL	LEATHER	CODE
Tan/Brown	•	•		

HORNET/COMMODORE 8 MODELS

COLOR	CLOTH	VINYL	LEATHER	CODE
Tan/Brown/Gold	•	•		
Blue/Gray	•	•		

CONVERTIBLE MODELS

COLOR	CLOTH	VINYL	LEATHER	CODE
Dk. Red			•	
Blue/Gray			•	
Maroon/Gray			•	

ENGINE SPECIFICATIONS

MODEL CODE	NO. CYL.	CID	HORSE-POWER	COMP. RATIO	CARB
4B	6	232	112	6.7:1*	1 BC
5B	6	262	127	6.7:1*	2 BC
6B	6	262	127	6.7:1*	2 BC
7B	6	308	145	7.2:1#	2 BC
8B	8	254	128	6.7:1*	2 BC

* 7.2:1 optional
# 6.7:1 optional

1953 HUDSON HORNET

VEHICLE IDENTIFICATION NUMBER

Located on a plate attached to the right front door hinge pillar (Jet and Super Jet are found on top of the right frame side rail near the dash). The engine number is stamped on the boss on the top and left side of the cylinder block. The engine number and serial number are the same.

FIRST AND SECOND DIGITS: Identify the model

MODEL	CODE
Jet	1C
Super Jet	2C
Wasp	4C
Super Wasp	5C
Hornet	7C

THE LAST SIX DIGITS: Represent the basic production sequence number

BODY NUMBER INFORMATION - Hudson did not provide numbers for the individual body styles in each series.

JET
BODY TYPE	CODE
Sedan, 4-dr.	1C

SUPER JET
BODY TYPE	CODE
Sedan, 2-Dr.	2C
Sedan, 4-dr.	

WASP
BODY TYPE	CODE
Sedan, 2-dr.	4C
Sedan, 4-dr.	
Club coupe	

SUPER WASP
BODY TYPE	CODE
Sedan, 2-dr.	5C
Sedan, 4-dr.	
Club coupe	
Hollywood hardtop	
Brougham convertible, 2-dr.	

HORNET
BODY TYPE	CODE
Sedan, 4-dr.	7C
Club coupe	
Hollywood hardtop	
Brougham convertible	

THE COLOR CODE indicates the paint color used on the car. The code letter or number is stamped on the upper right door hinge.

COLOR	CODE
Ebony Black	K5
Broadway Blue	B96
Southern Blue	J97
Seal Gray	RR137
Surf Green	Q133
Blue-Grass Green	P136
Robin's Egg Green	CC134
Meadow Green	S132
Texas Tan	H27
Honey Cream	N135
Toro Red	M64
Pearl Gray	G128

TWO-TONE COMBINATIONS
COLOR	CODE
Black/Honey Cream	RA
Southern Blue/Honey Cream	RC
Meadow Green/Honey Cream	RD
Texas Tan/Honey Cream	RF
Toro Red/Black	RH
Seal Gray/Black	RI
Seal Gray/Toro Red	RJ
Seal Gray/Southern Blue	RK
Robin's-Egg Green/Honey Cream	RM
Broadway Blue/Honey Cream	RN
Honey Cream/Texas Tan	RO
Pearl Gray/Black	RP
Robin's-Egg Green/Blue-Grass Green	RQ
Meadow Green/Surf Green	RS
Honey Cream/Meadow Geen	RT
Surf Green/Meadow Green	RU
Surf Green/Honey Cream	RV
Robin's-Egg Green/Black	RW
Southern Blue/Broadway Blue	RX

NOTE: The first letter identifies the lower body color, the second letter identifies the upper body color.

TRIM CODE - The following is the trim color and material for each model series:

JET

COLOR	CLOTH	VINYL	LEATHER	CODE
Red/Brown	•	•		

SUPER JET

COLOR	CLOTH	VINYL	LEATHER	CODE
Green	•	•		
Blue	•	•		

WASP

COLOR	CLOTH	VINYL	LEATHER	CODE
Red/Brown	•	•		

SUPER WASP

COLOR	CLOTH	VINYL	LEATHER	CODE
Green	•	•		
Blue	•	•		

HORNET

COLOR	CLOTH	VINYL	LEATHER	CODE
Green	•	•		
Blue	•	•		

NOTE: Leather is optional on all models in the following colors: Blue/Gray, Maroon/Gray, Green/Gray, Blue, Mraoon, Green.

ENGINE SPECIFICATIONS

MODEL CODE	NO. CYL.	CID	HORSE-POWER	COMP. RATIO	CARB
1C	6	202	104	7.5:1	1 BC
1C	6	202	106	8.0:1	1 BC
1C	6	202	114	8.0:1	2-1 BC
2C	6	202	104	7.5:1	1 BC
2C	6	202	106	8.0:1	1 BC
2C	6	202	114	8.0:1	2-1 BC
4C	6	232	112	6.7:1*	1 BC
5C	6	262	127	6.7:1*	2 BC
7C	8	308	145	7.2:1#	2 BC

* 7.2:1 optional

6.7:1 optional

1954 HUDSON JET

VEHICLE IDENTIFICATION NUMBER

SERIAL NUMBER

1D1269060

Located on a plate attached to the right front door hinge pillar, it is also found on top of the right frame side rail near dash. The engine number is stamped on the boss at the top right corner of the front of the cylinder block. The serial number and engine number are the same.

FIRST AND SECOND DIGITS: Identify the model

MODEL	CODE
Jet, 6-cyl.	1D
Super Jet, 6-cyl.	2D
Jet Liner	3D
Wasp, 6-cyl.	4D
Super Wasp, 6-cyl.	5D
Hornet Special, 6-cyl.	6D
Hornet, 6-cyl.	7D

THE LAST SIX DIGITS: Represent the basic production sequence number

BODY NUMBER INFORMATION - Hudson did not provide numbers for the individual body styles in each series.

JET
BODY TYPE	CODE
Sedan, 4-dr.	1D
Sedan, 2-dr.	
Club sedan	

SUPER JET
BODY TYPE	CODE
Sedan 4-dr.	2D
Club sedan	

JET-LINER
BODY TYPE	CODE
Sedan 4-dr.	3D
Club sedan	

WASP
BODY TYPE	CODE
Sedan 4-dr.	4D
Club sedan	
Club coupe	

SUPER WASP
BODY TYPE	CODE
Sedan 4-dr.	5D
Club sedan	
Club coupe	
Hollywood hardtop	
Brougham convertible	

HORNET SPECIAL
BODY TYPE	CODE
Sedan 4-dr.	6D
Club sedan	
Club coupe	

HORNET
BODY TYPE	CODE
Sedan 4-dr.	7D
Club coupe	
Hollywood hardtop	
Brougham convertible	

THE COLOR CODE indicates the paint color used on the car. The code letter or number is stamped on the upper right door hinge.

COLOR	CODE
Ebony Black	K5
Beret Blue	B158
Silver Blue	J159
St. Clair Gray	RR160
Spring Green	Q161
Pacific Green	P162
Green Gold	P181
Palm Beach Green	CC163
Pasture Green	S164
Roman Bronze	H165
Coronation Cream	N166
Royal Red	M167
Lipstick	M182
Algerian Blue	G168

TWO-TONE COMBINATIONS

COLOR	CODE
Beret Blue/Silver Blue	RX
Coronation Cream/Silver Blue	RC
Beret Blue/Algerian Blue	RP
Coronation Cream/Palm Beach Green	RM
Ebony Black/Palm Beach Green	RW
Pacific Blue Green/Palm Beach Green	RQ
Ebony Black/Royal Red	RH
Royal Red/St. Clair Gray	RJ
Pasture Green/Coronation Cream	RT
Pasture Green/Spring Green	RU
Coronation Cream/Roman Bronze	RF
Ebony Black/Roman Bronze	RO
Lipstick/St. Clair Gray	RJ-183
Ebony Black/Lipstick	RH-184
Coronation Cream/Lipstick	RC-185
Green Gold/Coronation Cream	RT-186
Green Gold/Roman Bronze	RX-187
Green Gold/Pasture Green	RQ-188
St. Clair Gray/Green Gold	RM-189
Ebony Black/Green Gold	RQ-190
Lipstick/Coronation Cream	RX-191
Coronation Cream/Beret Blue	RA-192

NOTE: The first code identifies the upper body color, the second code identifies the lower body color.

THE TRIM CODE indicates the key to the trim color and material for each model series. There were no trim codes available.

ENGINE SPECIFICATIONS

JET SERIES

ENGINE CODE	NO. CYL.	CID	HORSE-POWER	COMP. RATIO	CARB
1D,2D,3D	6	202	104	7.5:1	1 BC
1D,2D,3D	6	202	114	8.0:1	2-1 BC

WASP SERIES

ENGINE CODE	NO. CYL.	CID	HORSE-POWER	COMP. RATIO	CARB
4D	6	232	126	7.0:1	1 BC
4D	6	232	129	7.5:1	1 BC
5D	6	262	140	7.0:1	1 BC
5D	6	262	143	7.5:1	1 BC
5D	6	262	149	7.5:1	2-1 BC

HORNET SERIES

ENGINE CODE	NO. CYL.	CID	HORSE-POWER	COMP. RATIO	CARB
7D	6	308	156	7.0:1	1 BC
7D	6	308	160	7.5:1	1 BC
7D	6	308	170	7.5:1	2-1 BC
6D	6	308	160	7.5:1	2 BC

1955 HUDSON WASP

1955 HUDSON HORNET HOLLYWOOD

1955 HUDSON RAMBLER

1955 HUDSON

VEHICLE IDENTIFICATION NUMBER

```
AMERICAN MOTORS CORPORATION
  MADE IN U.S.A  SERIAL
       XC 1001
```

Located on a plate attached to the right side of the cowl under the hood.

FIRST DIGIT: Identifies the model

MODEL	CODE
Wasp, 6-cyl.	W
Hornet, 6-cyl.	X
Hornet, 8-cyl.	Y

NOTE: If the model number is followed by a C, it indicates the car was assembled in El Segundo, CA; all others were assembled in Kenosha, WI. If followed by KD, it was unassembled for export.

LAST FOUR DIGITS: Represent the basic production sequence number. Ramblers start with 205001 made in Kenosha and 15001 made in El Segundo. All others start with 1001.

BODY NUMBER PLATE

Located on a plate attached to the right side of the cowl under the hood.

```
AMERICAN MOTORS CORPORATION

BODY No.    1001
MODEL No.   35545-1
TRIM No.    N/A
PAINT No.   44
```

EXAMPLE:

1001	Production number
35545-1	Wasp Super 4-dr. sedan
N/A	Trim code
44	Carribean Blue

BODY NUMBER
Identifies the consecutive production number, same as the VIN NUMBER.

MODEL NUMBER

WASP SUPER - 6
BODY TYPE	CODE
Sedan, 4-dr.	35545-1

WASP CUSTOM - 6
BODY TYPE	CODE
Sedan, 4-dr.	35545-2
Hardtop coupe	35547-2

HORNET SUPER - 6
BODY TYPE	CODE
Sedan 4-dr.	35565-1

HORNET CUSTOM - 6
BODY TYPE	CODE
Sedan, 4-dr.	35565-2
Hardtop coupe	35567-2

HORENT SUPER - 8
BODY TYPE	CODE
Sedan 4-dr.	35585-1

HORENT CUSTOM - 8
BODY TYPE	CODE
Sedan 4-dr.	35585-2
Hardtop coupe	35587-2

THE TRIM CODE indicates the key to the paint color and material scheme on the vehicle. There were no trim codes available.

THE COLOR CODE indicates the paint color used on the vehicle. Two-tone combinations: The first set of digits identify the upper body color, the second set of digits identify the lower body color.

COLOR	CODE
Black	P1
Caribbean Blue	P44
Midshipman Blue Dark	P61
Island Green Dark	P62
Rio Red	P64
Coral Red	P66
Sunburst Yellow	P66
Bermuda Green Light	P67
Mist Blue Light	P68
Snowberry White	P69
Palomino Brown	P71

ENGINE SPECIFICATIONS

Engine numbers are different than VIN NUMBERS and are as follows:

MODEL	STARTING NUMBER	LOCATION
Wasp-6 (3554)	M1001/up	Top left front of cyl. block
Hornet-6 (3556)	F1001/up	Top left front of cyl. block
Hornet-8 (3558)	P1001/up	Right rear corner of block below exhaust manifold

ENGINE CODE	NO. CYL.	CID	HORSE-POWER	COMP. RATIO	CARB
3554	6	202	115	7.5:1	1 BC
3554	6	202	126	8.0:1	2-1 BC
3556	6	308	160	7.5:1	1 BC
3556	6	308	170	7.5:1	2-1 BC
3558	8	320	208	7.8:1*	2 BC

* Engine numbers P6001/up have a compression ratio of 8.25:1.

1956 HUDSON HORNET

1956 HUDSON

VEHICLE IDENTIFICATION NUMBER

```
AMERICAN MOTORS CORPORATION
   MADE IN U.S.A   SERIAL
         Z-1001
```

Located on a plate attached to the center of cowl under the hood.

FIRST DIGIT: Identifies the model

MODEL	CODE
Wasp, 6-cyl.	W
Hornet, 6-cyl.	X
Hornet Special, 8-cyl.	Z

NOTE: XD following the letter indicates it was an unassembled model for export, the letter T indicates Canada.

THE LAST FOUR DIGITS: Represent the basic production sequence number

MODEL	PRODUCTION NUMBER
Wasp	8101/up - Canada 1401/up
Hornet	7601/up
Hornet Special	1001/up

BODY NUMBER PLATE

Located on a plate attached to the center of cowl under the hood.

```
AMERICAN MOTORS CORPORATION

BODY No.    1001
MODEL No.   35487-2
TRIM No.    687
PAINT No.   78
```

EXAMPLE:

1001	Production number
35687-2	Hornet V8 Custom 2-dr. hardtop
687	Gray/White cloth/leather
78	Grenedier Red

BODY NUMBER

Identifies the consecutive production number, same as the VIN NUMBER.

MODEL NUMBER

WASP SUPER - 6
BODY TYPE	CODE
Sedan, 4-dr.	35645-1

HORNET SUPER - 6
BODY TYPE	CODE
Sedan, 4-dr.	35665-1

HORNET CUSTOM - 6
BODY TYPE	CODE
Sedan, 4-dr.	35665-2
2-Dr. hardtop	35667-2

HORNET SPECIAL SUPER - 8
BODY TYPE	CODE
Sedan, 4-dr.	35655-1
2-Dr. hardtop	35657-1

HORNET CUSTOM - 8
BODY TYPE	CODE
Sedan 4-dr.	35685-2
2-Dr. hardtop	35687-2

THE TRIM CODE indicates the paint color and the material scheme used on the vehicle.

COLOR	CLOTH	VINYL	LEATHER	CODE
Blue/Blue	•	•		T661,T671
Green/Green	•	•		T663,T673
Gray/White	•	•		T666,T676
Gray/Grenadier Red	•	•		T678
Gray/Ballerina Red	•	•		T679
Gray/Green	•	•		T680
Blue/Blue	•		•	T681
Blue/White	•		•	T682
Green/Green	•		•	T683
Green/White	•		•	T684
Gray/White	•		•	T687
Gray/Grenadier Red	•		•	T688
Gray/Ballerina Red	•		•	T689
Gray/Green	•		•	T690

THE COLOR CODE indicates the paint color used on the vehicle. Two-tone combinations: First set of digits identify the lower body color; the second set identifies the upper body color. Three-tones: The first set of digits identify the lower body color; the second set of digits identify the intermediate body color; the third set of digits identify the upper body color.

COLOR	CODE
Black	P1
Sunburst Yellow	P66
Bermuda Green	P67
Frost White	P72
Willow Green	P73
Crocus Yellow	P74
Polo Green	P75
Golden Brown	P76
Mint Green	P77
Grenadier Red	P78
Boulevard Gray	P80
Solitaire Blue	P81
Pacific Blue	P82
Ballerina Red	P83

ENGINE SPECIFICATIONS

6-cylinder engine number is located on the machined surface on the left side of the cylinder block. Hornet V8 is located vertically on the lower right front corner of the cylinder block.

The beginning engine numbers for all models are as follows:

MODEL	STARTING NUMBER
Wasp, 6-cyl. (35640) M-8701/up
Hornet, 6-cyl. (35660)...F-8601/up
Hornet Special, 8-cyl. (35650) G-1001/up
Hornet, 8-cyl. (35680) P-21001/up

ENGINE CODE	NO. CYL.	CID	HORSE-POWER	COMP. RATIO	CARB.
35640	6	202	120	7.5:1	1 BC
35640	6	202	130	7.5:1	2-1 BC
35660	6	308	165	7.5:1	1 BC
35660	6	308	175	7.5:1	2-1 BC
35650	8	250	190	8.0:1	2 BC
35680	8	352	220	9.55:1	2 BC

1957 HUDSON HORNET

1957 HUDSON HORNET HOLLYWOOD

VEHICLE IDENTIFICATION NUMBER

AMERICAN MOTORS CORPORATION
○ MADE IN U.S.A   SERIAL ○
Y-10501

Located on a plate attached to the center of the cowl under the hood.

FIRST DIGIT: Identifies the model

MODEL	CODE
Hornet, 8-cyl.	Y

THE LAST FIVE DIGITS: Represent the basic production sequence number, 10501 and up.

BODY NUMBER PLATE

Located on a plate attached to the center of cowl under the hood.

AMERICAN MOTORS CORPORATION

BODY No.	**10501**
MODEL No.	**35785-1**
TRIM No.	**N/A**
PAINT No.	**P90**

EXAMPLE:

10501	Production sequence
35785-1	Hornet Super 4-dr. sedan
N/A	Trim number
P90	Mardi Gras Red

BODY NUMBER - Identifies the consecutive production number, same as the VIN NUMBER.

MODEL NUMBER

HORNET SUPER

BODY TYPE	CODE
Sedan, 4-dr.	35785-1
2-Dr., hardtop	35787-1

HORNET CUSTOM

BODY TYPE	CODE
Sedan, 4-dr.	35785-2
2-Dr. hardtop	35787-2

THE TRIM CODE indicates the trim color and material scheme used on the vehicle. There were no trim codes available.

THE COLOR CODE indicates the paint color used on the vehicle. Two-tone combinations: The first set of digits identify the lower body color; the second set of digits identify the upper body color. Three-tones: First set of digits identify the lower body color; the second set of digits identify the intermediate body color; the third set of digits identify the upper body color. If the second digit is "D" it identifies wood-grain.

COLOR	CODE
Classic Black	P1
Bermuda Green	P67
Frost White	P72
Pacific Blue	P82
Glacier Blue	P84
Lagoon Blue	P85
Plum Metallic	P86
Berkshire Green	P87
Oregon Green	P88
Avocado Metallic	P89
Mardi Gras Red	P90
Mojave Yellow	P92
Sierra Peach	P93
Cinnamon Bronze Metallic	P94
Gotham Gray Metallic	P95
Rebel Silver Gray Metallic	P96

ENGINE SPECIFICATIONS

The engine number is located on the lower right front corner of the block,
N-1001 and up.

ENGINE CODE	NO. CYL.	CID	HORSE- POWER	COMP. RATIO	CARB.
35780	8	327	255	9.0:1	4 BC

1950 FRAZER

1950 FRAZER

1950 KAISER

1950 KAISER

VEHICLE IDENTIFICATION NUMBER

• K501001001 •

The Vehicle Identification Number (VIN) is located on the left front door hinge post.

FIRST DIGIT: Identifies the division

DIVISION	CODE
Frazer	F
Kaiser	K

SECOND & THIRD DIGITS: Identify the model year 1950

FOURTH DIGIT: Identifies the body style

BODY STYLE	CODE
Kaiser Special	1
Kaiser Deluxe	2
Frazer	5
Frazer Manhattan	6

LAST SIX DIGITS: Represent the basic production numbers 001001 and up. A prefix in the serial number denotes the assembly plant.

ASSEMBLY PLANT	CODE
Detroit, MI	B
Muskegon, MI	C

BODY NUMBER PLATE

The body number plate is located on a plate attached to the right side of the cowl under the hood.

KAISER-FRAZER CORP.

MODEL	BODY	PAINT	TRIM	DR	KL	TR	RO	HR	AG	SL	SB	AR
491	1	150	8007	1		4			1			

CT	WL	TS	M1	M2	M3	M4	SPEC-FO	M5	M6	SCHED	ITEM NO.

BODY NUMBER

THE MODEL NUMBER CODE consists of three digits. The first two digits identify the year 1949 (1950 models were actually 1949 models with renumbered serial numbers. Body number plates were not renumbered). The third digit identifies the model type.

MODEL TYPE	CODE
Kaiser Special	1
Kaiser Deluxe	2
Frazer	5
Frazer Manhattan	6

THE BODY NUMBER CODE indicates the body type.

KAISER SPECIAL

BODY	CODE
Sedan, 4-dr.	1
Traveler, 4-dr.	5
Taxicab	6

KAISER DELUXE

BODY	CODE
Sedan, 4-dr.	1
Convertible, 4-dr.	2
Virginian	3
Vagabond	5

FRAZER

BODY	CODE
Sedan, 4-dr.	1

FRAZER MANHATTAN

BODY	CODE
Sedan, 4-dr.	1
Convertible, 4-dr.	2

THE PAINT CODE consists of 3 digits and indicates the color used on the car.

COLOR	CODE
Sportsman Beige Metallic	105
Buckeye Maroon	110
Cardinal	110
Polar Gray	115
Flax	120
Hickory Brown Metallic	125
Horizon Blue	130
Academy Blue Metallic	135
Onyx	140
Wedgewood Blue Metallic	145
Crystal Green	150
Dubonnet	155
Teal Blue	160
Ranger Gray	165
Executive Green	170
Yale Blue Metallic	175
Bermuda Tan	180
Ranger Gray Metallic	185
Executive Green Metallic	190
Caribbean Coral Metallic	195
Adirondack Gray	200
Parakeet Green Metallic	205
Linden Green Metallic	210
Glass Green	215
Bermuda Tan Metallic	220
Mineral Gray Metallic	225
Blade Green Metallic	230
Saddle Bronze Metallic	235
Horizon Blue Metallic	245
Ocean Spray Green Metallic	250
Green Spray	255
Sportsman Beige	260
Garden Green Metallic	265
Suede Gray Metallic	270
Wedgewood Blue	275
Pearl Mist Gray	280
Green Spray Metallic	285
Doeskin	290
Blue Satin Metallic	295
Indian Ceramic	300
Turf/Linden Green	511
Silver Fox Gray Metallic	610

THE TRIM CODE indicates the interior color and material scheme.

KAISER STANDARD 4-DR TRIM

COLOR	CLOTH	VINYL	LEATHER	CODE
Sahara Tan	•			111,121
Sahara Tan	•			1108,1110
Solar Gray	•			116,126
Solar Gray	•			1109,1122
Linden Green	•			1118
Cardinal	•			3005
Green/Sahara Tan	•			8004
Sandtone Beige/ Maroon	•			8005
Sandtone Beige/ Blue	•			8006
Green	•			8007

KAISER STANDARD VAGABOND TRIM

COLOR	CLOTH	VINYL	LEATHER	CODE
Red	•			203
Executive Green		•		1501
Cardinal		•		1502
Oakwood Brown		•		1503
Light Green		•		1508
Sahara Tan/ Oakwood Brown		•		1509
Maroon/Cardinal		•		1510
Executive Green	•	•		1514
Solar Gray/ Executive Green	•	•		1517
Solar Gray/ Cardinal	•	•		1518
Linden Green/ Oakwood Brown	•	•		1519
Horizon Blue/ Oakwood Brown	•	•		1520
Collegiate/ Executive Green	•	•		1521

KAISER DELUXE 4-DR TRIM

COLOR	CLOTH	VINYL	LEATHER	CODE
Flag/Havanna Blue	•			202
Tuscany/Canyon Rose	•			207
Executive Green	•			211
Horizon Blue	•			216,236,247
Horizon Blue	•			286
Solar Gray	•			221
Executive Green	•			226
Linden Green	•			231
Sunset Beige	•			241
Blue/Beige	•			242
Alamo E	•			246
Turquoise	•			251
Linden Green		•		252
Hickory Brown	•			261
Tuscany Rose/Canyon Rose	•			271
Hickory Brown	•			276
Havana Blue	•			280
Blade/Ocean Spray Green	•			291
Polar Gray	•			296
Sahara Tan	•			2104
Sunset Beige	•			2111
Tuscany Rose/Canyon Rose	•			2113

KAISER DELUXE CONVERTIBLE TRIM

COLOR	CLOTH	VINYL	LEATHER	CODE
Indian Ceramic		•		366,367
Black		•		371,372
Garden Green	•	•		376,377
Black		•	•	2202
Brown		•	•	2214

KAISER DELUXE VIRGINIAN TRIM

COLOR	CLOTH	VINYL	LEATHER	CODE
Horizon Blue	•			401
Tuscany/Canyon Rose	•			402
Executive Green	•			406,411
Linden Green	•			416
Horizon Blue	•			421
Horizon Blue		•		427
Horizon Blue		•	•	2302
Cardinal Red		•		422
Solar Gray	•			426
Tuscany Rose/Canyon Rose	•			431
Linden Green		•		432
Oakwood Brown		•		437
Sunset Beige	•			441
Pigskin/Caribbean Coral	•	•		442
Black		•		447
Turquoise	•			461
Alamo E	•			466
Hickory Brown	•			471,2315
Ocean Spray Green	•			476
Havana Blue	•			481
Blade/Ocean Spray Green	•			486
Hickory Brown/Chamois	•			491
Flag/Havanna Blue	•			496
Linden Green		•	•	2303
Black		•	•	2306
Turquoise		•		2314
Pepper Red		•	•	2319
Teal Blue		•	•	2320

KAISER SPECIAL VAGABOND TRIM

COLOR	CLOTH	VINYL	LEATHER	CODE
Pepper Red		•		2501
Pepper Red		•	•	2509
Oakwood Brown		•		2502
Oakwood Brown		•	•	2510
Executive Green		•		2504
Cardinal Red		•		2508
Cardinal Red		•	•	2513

FRAZER STANDARD 4-DR TRIM

COLOR	CLOTH	VINYL	LEATHER	CODE
Hickory Brown	•			501
Horizon Blue	•			506,521
Green Brown	•			511
Dubonnet	•			516
Blade Green	•			526

FRAZER DELUXE 4-DR TRIM

COLOR	CLOTH	VINYL	LEATHER	CODE
Wedgewood Blue		•		607
Saddle Bronze	•			616
Hickory Brown	•			620,626
Garden Green	•			631
Teal Blue	•			636,691
Dubonnet	•			641,642,661
Blade Green	•			646
Academy Blue	•			651
Zero Gray	•			656
Aztec Copper	•			686
Cardinal Red		•		696
Jasper Green	•			9001,9002
Emblem Blue	•			9003
Cardinal	•			9004

FRAZER DELUXE CONVERTIBLE TRIM

COLOR	CLOTH	VINYL	LEATHER	CODE
Blue Satin	•	•		761,762
Green Spray		•		771,772
Saddle Bronze	•	•		766,767
Pepper Red		•		776,777
Green		•	•	6216
Cardinal		•	•	6221
Brown/Green	•		•	6223
Brown & Rose/				
Saddle Bronze	•		•	6224

THE TRANSMISSION CODE is a single digit under "TR" on the body plate that indicates the transmission used.

TYPE	CODE
3-Speed conventional	1
3-Speed conventional	2
3-Speed overdrive	4

THE ACCESSORY GROUP CODE under "AG" on the body number plate indicates the accessory group.

THE SPECIAL FACTORY ORDER CODE under the "SPEC-FO" on the bottom line indicates that the car was custom ordered. Special order numbers start with the following:

Kaiser	K
Frazer	F

THE ENGINE NUMBER CODE is located on the left side of the engine at the upper front, on plate attached to the left side of the crankcase.

KAISER SPECIAL

ENGINE CODE	NO. CYL.	CID	HORSE-POWER	COMP. RATIO	CARB
K-M10001	6	226	100	7.3:1	1 BC

KAISER DELUXE

ENGINE CODE	NO. CYL.	CID	HORSE-POWER	COMP. RATIO	CARB
K-M10001	6	226	112	7.3:1	1 BC

FRAZER

ENGINE CODE	NO. CYL.	CID	HORSE-POWER	COMP. RATIO	CARB
F-M10001	6	226	112	7.3:1	1 BC

ENGINE SUFFIX LETTERS

Letters suffixes in connection with engine numbers denote the following:

A - Designates .010 undersize main and rod bearings

N - Designates .020 oversize pistons

AN - Designates .010 undersize main and rod bearings and .020 oversize pistons

1951 FRAZER

1951 KAISER

VEHICLE IDENTIFICATION NUMBER

$\boxed{\bullet\,\text{K}\,5\,1\,1\,0\,0\,1\,0\,0\,1\,\bullet}$

The Vehicle Identification Number (VIN) is located on the left front door hinge post.

FIRST DIGIT: Identifies the division symbol

DIVISION	CODE
Frazer	F
Kaiser	K

SECOND & THIRD DIGITS: Identifies the model year 1951

FOURTH DIGIT: Identifies the body style

BODY STYLE	CODE
Kaiser Special	1
Kaiser Deluxe	2
Henry J, 4-cyl.	3
Henry J, 6-cyl.	4
Frazer	5
Frazer Manhattan	6

LAST SIX DIGITS: Represent the basic production numbers - 001001 and up. Prefix letter denotes assembly plant other than Willow Run. A - Long Beach, CA; B - Jackson, MI; C - Portland, OR.

BODY NUMBER PLATE

The body number plate is located on the right side of the cowl under the hood.

KAISER-FRAZER CORP.

MODEL	BODY	PAINT	TRIM	DR	KL	TR	RO	HR	AG	SL	SB	AR
511	1	076	1170	1		4			1			

C T	W L	T S	M 1	M 2	M 3	M 4	SPEC-FO	M 5	M 6	SCHED	ITEM NO.

BODY NUMBER

THE MODEL NUMBER CODE consists of three digits. The first two digits identify the year 1951. The third digit identifies the model type.

MODEL TYPE	CODE
Kaiser Special	1
Kaiser Deluxe	2
Henry J, 4 cyl.	3
Henry J, 6 cyl.	4
Frazer	5
Frazer Manhattan	6

THE BODY NUMBER CODE indicates the body type.

KAISER SPECIAL

BODY TYPE	CODE
Sedan, 4-dr.	1
Business coupe	3
Sedan, 2-dr.	4
Traveler, 4-dr.	5
Taxi	6
Club coupe	7
Traveler, 2-dr.	0

KAISER DELUXE

BODY TYPE	CODE
Sedan, 4-dr.	1*
Sedan, 2-dr.	4
Traveler, 4-dr.	5
Club coupe	7
Traveler, 2-dr.	0

* Dragons interior option

FRAZER

BODY TYPE	CODE
Sedan, 4-dr.	1
Vagabond, 4-dr.	5

FRAZER MANHATTAN

BODY TYPE	CODE
Sedan, 4-dr., hardtop	1
Convertible, 4-dr.	2

HENRY J

BODY TYPE	CODE
Sedan, 2-dr.	4

THE PAINT CODE consists of 3 digits that indicates the color used on the car.

COLOR	CODE
Caribbean Coral Metallic	065
Garden Green Metallic	076
Mariner Gray	077,088
Horizon Blue	078
Blue Satin	079
Oakwood Brown Metallic	080
Ceramic Green	081
Tropical Green Metallic	084,090
Arena Yellow	087,570
Cape Verde Green	089
Sportsman Beige	105
Cardinal	110
Polar Gray	115
Flax	120
Horizon Blue	130
Onyx	140
Crystal Green	150
Teal Blue	171
Caribbean Coral Metallic	195
Glass Green	215
Blade Green Metallic	230
Saddle Bronze Metallic	235
Garden Green Metallic	265
Cape Verde Green Metallic	325
Blue Satin	330
Oakwood Brown Metallic	335
Ceramic Green	355
Mariner Gray	370,375
Aloha Green	390
Pasadena Yellow	391

THE TRIM CODE indicates the interior color and material scheme.

KAISER STANDARD UTILITY 2-DR TRIM

COLOR	CLOTH	VINYL	LEATHER	CODE
Cardinal Red		•		1051
Garden Green		•		1052
Oakwood Brown		•		1053
Horizon Blue		•		1054
Executive Green		•		1055

KAISER STANDARD 4-DR TRIM

COLOR	CLOTH	VINYL	LEATHER	CODE
Explorer Gray		•		1123
Explorer Gray	•			1130
Chocolate Brown	•			1131
Gunmetal	•			1139
Forest Green	•			1170
Gray	•			1174
Caribbean Coral	•			1178
Green	•			1182
Light Brown	•			1186

KAISER STANDARD BUSINESS COUPE TRIM

COLOR	CLOTH	VINYL	LEATHER	CODE
Explorer Gray	•			1330
Chocolate Brown	•			1331
Oakwood Brown	•			1355

KAISER STANDARD 2-DR TRIM

COLOR	CLOTH	VINYL	LEATHER	CODE
Explorer Gray	•			1430
Chocolate Brown	•			1431

KAISER STANDARD UTILITY 4-DR TRIM

COLOR	CLOTH	VINYL	LEATHER	CODE
Cardinal Red		•		1561
Garden Green		•		1562
Oakwood Brown		•		1563
Horizon Blue		•		1564
Executive Green		•		1565

KAISER DELUXE UTILITY 2-DR TRIM

COLOR	CLOTH	VINYL	LEATHER	CODE
Cardinal		•		2051
Garden Green		•		2052
Oakwood Brown		•		2053
Horizon Blue		•		2054
Executive Green		•		2055

KAISER DELUXE 4-DR TRIM

COLOR	CLOTH	VINYL	LEATHER	CODE
Gray	•			2134,2185
Gray	•			2145
Caribbean Coral	•			2135,2802
Caribbean Coral	•			2808
Caribbean Coral		•		2823
Blue	•			2136
Blue Satin	•			2803,2809
Light Green	•			2139
Tropical Green		•		2824,2848
Cardinal	•			2146
Green	•			2150
Green		•		2829
Explorer Gray	•			2801,2807
Cape Verde Green	•			2804,2810
Cape Verde Green		•		2822,2847
Chukkar Tan	•			2805,2811
Garden Green	•			2806,2812
Red		•	•	2818
Black		•	•	2819
Black		•		2820,2826
Black		•		2845
Burma Brown		•		2821
Scarlet		•		2825,2846

KAISER DELUXE 2-DR TRIM

COLOR	CLOTH	VINYL	LEATHER	CODE
Explorer Gray	•			2407,2413
Explorer Gray	•			2436,2446
Caribbean Coral	•			2408,2414
Caribbean Coral	•			2435
Blue Satin	•			2409,2415
Cape Verde Green	•			2410,2416
Chukkar Tan	•			2411,2417
Garden Green	•			2412,2418
Cardinal	•			2445

KAISER DELUXE UTILITY 4-DR TRIM

COLOR	CLOTH	VINYL	LEATHER	CODE
Cardinal		•		2560
Garden Green		•		2561
Oakwood Brown		•		2562
Horizon Blue		•		2563
Executive Green		•		2564
Caribbean Coral		•		2575

KAISER DELUXE CLUB COUPE TRIM

COLOR	CLOTH	VINYL	LEATHER	CODE
Explorer Gray	•			2711,2717
Explorer Gray	•			2734
Caribbean Coral	•			2712,2718
Caribbean Coral	•			2745
Blue Satin	•			2713,2719
Cape Verde Green	•			2714,2720
Chukkar Tan	•			2715,2721
Garden Green	•			2716
Executive Green	•			2737
Cardinal	•			2746

KAISER DELUXE - DRAGONS TRIM

COLOR	CLOTH	VINYL	LEATHER	CODE
Black		•		2820,2845
Black		•		2826
Burma Brown		•		2821
Cape Verde Green		•		2822
Caribbean Coral		•		2823
Tropical Green		•		2824
Scarlet		•		2825,2846
Straw		•		2848

HENRY J 4-CYL. 2-DR TRIM

COLOR	CLOTH	VINYL	LEATHER	CODE
Gray	•			3401
Brown	•			3402
Green/Gray	•	•		3403
Brown/White	•			3405
Black/White	•			3406

HENRY J 6-CYL. 2-DR TRIM

COLOR	CLOTH	VINYL	LEATHER	CODE
Shepherd Plaid/ Burma Brown		•		4403
Hickory Brown/ Burma Brown	•	•		4404
Hickory Brown	•			4423
Green/Cape Verde Green	•	•		4425
Blue Satin	•			4427
Burma Brown		•		4429
Cardinal	•			4431
Blue	•			4433
Garden Green	•			4435
Burma Brown		•		4436

FRAZER STANDARD 4-DR TRIM

COLOR	CLOTH	VINYL	LEATHER	CODE
Mariner Gray	•			5153,5164
Executive Green	•			5160
Garden Green	•			5161
Horizon Blue	•			5167,5181
Oakwood Brown	•			5168
Green	•			5170
Hickory Brown	•			5171
Academy Blue	•			5172
Brown	•			5174
Olive Green	•			5175
Dark Blue	•			5177
Buckeye Maroon	•			5178
Dark Blue	•			5179,5180
Cardinal	•			5182

FRAZER STANDARD UTILITY 4-DR TRIM

COLOR	CLOTH	VINYL	LEATHER	CODE
Horizon Blue		•		5550
Cardinal		•		5551
Hickory Brown		•		5553
Garden Green		•		5554
Blue		•	•	5555
Green		•		5557
Blue		•		5559
Green		•		5560,5561
Black		•	•	5562
Black		•		5567

FRAZER DELUXE CONVERTIBLE

COLOR	CLOTH	VINYL	LEATHER	CODE
Red		•	•	6260
Brown		•	•	6261,6263
Black		•	•	6265
Blue		•	•	6281

THE TRANSMISSION CODE is a single digit under "TR" on the plate that indicates the transmission used.

TYPE	CODE
3-Speed conventional	2
3-Speed overdrive	4
Automatic	6

THE ACCESSORY GROUP CODE under "AG" on the body number plate indicates the accessory group.

THE SPECIAL FACTORY ORDER CODE

under the "SPEC-FO" on the bottom line indicates that the car was custom ordered. Special order numbers start with the following:

Kaiser	K
Frazer	F

THE KAISER-FRAZER ENGINE NUMBER CODE is located on the left side of the engine at the upper front and on the plate attached to the left side of the crankcase. The Henry J is located on the right side of the engine on the block at upper front, also located on the plate attached to the left side of the center of the crankcase.

KAISER

1ST ENGINE NUMBER	NO. CYL.	CID	HORSE-POWER	COMP. RATIO	CARB
1100000	6	226	115	7.3:1	1 BC
2000000	6	226	115	7.3:1	1 BC

FRAZER

1ST ENGINE NUMBER	NO. CYL.	CID	HORSE-POWER	COMP. RATIO	CARB
1000001	6	226	115	7.3:1	1 BC
2300000	6	226	115	7.3:1	1 BC

HENRY J

1ST ENGINE NUMBER	NO. CYL.	CID	HORSE-POWER	COMP. RATIO	CARB
3500000	4	134	68	7.0:1	1 BC
3000001	6	161	80	7.0:1	1 BC

ENGINE SUFFIX LETTERS
Letter suffixes in connection with engine numbers denote the following:

A - Designates .010 undersize main and rod bearings
N - Designates .020 oversize pistons
AN - Designates .010 undersize main and rod bearings and .020 oversize pistons

1952 HENRY J

1952 HENRY J

VEHICLE IDENTIFICATION NUMBER

•K 5 2 4 1 2 0 0 0 0 1•

The Vehicle Identification Number (VIN) is located on the left front door hinge post.

FIRST DIGIT: Identifies the division symbol

Kaiser ....K

SECOND & THIRD DIGITS: Identify the model year 1952

FOURTH DIGIT: Identifies the body style

BODY STYLE	CODE
Virginian Special	1
Virginian Deluxe	2
Kaiser Deluxe	1
Kaiser Manhattan	2
Henry J, 4-cyl.	3
Henry J, 6-cyl.	4

LAST SEVEN DIGITS: Represent the basic production numbers. 1000001 and up - Virginian, Virginian Deluxe & Henry J Vagabond. 1,200,000 and up - Deluxe, Manhattan and Henry J Corsair. Prefix letter denotes assembly plant other than Willow Run. A - Long Beach, CA; B - Jackson, MI; C - Portland, OR.

BODY NUMBER PLATE

THE BODY NUMBER PLATE is located on the right side of the cowl under the hood.

KAISER-FRAZER CORP.

MODEL	BODY	PAINT	TRIM	DR	KL	TR	RO	HR	AG	SL	SB	AR
524	4	087	4451	1		4			1			

C T L	W L	T S	M 1	M 2	M 3	M 4	SPEC-FO	M 5	M 6	SCHED	ITEM NO.

BODY NUMBER

THE MODEL NUMBER CODE consists of three digits. The first two digits identify the year 1952. The third digit identifies the model type.

MODEL TYPE	CODE
Kaiser Virginian Special	1
Kaiser Virginian Deluxe	2
Kaiser Deluxe	1
Kaiser Manhattan	2
Henry J Vagabond, 4 cyl.	3
Henry J Vagabond Deluxe, 6 cyl.	4
Henry J Corsair, 4-cyl.	3
Henry J Corsair Deluxe, 6-cyl.	4

THE BODY NUMBER CODE indicates the body type.

KAISER VIRGINIAN SPECIAL

BODY TYPE	CODE
Sedan, 4-dr.	1
Business coupe	3
Sedan, 2-dr.	4
Traveler, 4-dr.	5
Traveler, 2-dr.	0

KAISER VIRGINIAN DELUXE

BODY TYPE	CODE
Sedan, 4-dr.	1
Sedan, 2-dr.	4
Traveler, 4-dr.	5
Club coupe	7
Traveler, 2-dr.	0

KAISER DELUXE

BODY TYPE	CODE
Sedan, 4-dr.	1
Sedan, 2-dr.	4
Club Coupe	7

KAISER MANHATTAN

BODY TYPE	CODE
Sedan, 4-dr.	1
Sedan, 2-dr.	4
Club coupe	7

HENRY J

BODY TYPE	CODE
Sedan, 2-dr.	4

THE PAINT CODE consists of 3 digits and indicates the color used on the car.

COLOR	CODE
Arena Yellow	087
Cardinal	110
Onyx	140
Crystal Green	150
Caribbean Coral Metallic	195
Blade Green Metallic	230
Saddle Bronze Metallic	235
Garden Green Metallic	265
Claypipe Gray	310
Cape Verde Green Metallic	325
Blue Satin	330
Ceramic Green	355
Mariner Gray	370,375
Pasadena Yellow	391
Turquoise Blue	394
Gunmetal Gray	397
Cerulean Blue	398
Willow Gray	399
Pasadena Yellow	406
Crystal Green	409
Caribbean Coral Metallic	425
Blue Satin Metallic	561
Oakwood Brown Metallic	572
Cape Verde Green Metallic	576
Caribbean Coral Metallic	577
Blue Satin	579
Mineral Gray	580
Crystal Green	582
Onyx	584

THE TRIM CODE indicates the interior color and material scheme.

KAISER DELUXE 2-DR TRIM

COLOR	CLOTH	VINYL	LEATHER	CODE
Gunmetal	•			1412
Explorer Gray	•			1414
Chocolate Brown	•			1415
Forest Green	•			1419
Blue Satin	•			1421
Caribbean Coral	•			1422
Chukkar Tan	•			1423

KAISER DELUXE UTILITY 4-DR TRIM

COLOR	CLOTH	VINYL	LEATHER	CODE
Burma Brown		•		1530
Caribbean Coral		•		1531
Scarlet		•		1532
Cardinal Red		•		1561

KAISER DELUXE 4-DR TRIM

COLOR	CLOTH	VINYL	LEATHER	CODE
Explorer Gray	•			1802
Chocolate Brown	•			1803
Forest Green	•			1807
Blue Satin	•			1809
Caribbean Coral	•			1810
Chukkar Tan	•			1811

KAISER MANHATTAN 2-DR TRIM

COLOR	CLOTH	VINYL	LEATHER	CODE
Gunmetal Gray	•			2421
Saddle Bronze	•			2422
Forest Green	•			2424
Turquoise	•			2425
Blue Satin	•			2426
Chukkar Tan	•			2428
Explorer Gray	•			2429

KAISER MANHATTAN UTILITY 4-DR TRIM

COLOR	CLOTH	VINYL	LEATHER	CODE
Caribbean Coral		•		2515
Scarlet		•		2516

KAISER MANHATTAN 4-DR TRIM

COLOR	CLOTH	VINYL	LEATHER	CODE
Gunmetal	•			2860
Saddle Bronze	•			2861
Forest Green	•			2863
Turquoise	•			2864
Blue Satin	•			2865
Caribbean Coral	•			2866
Chukkar Tan	•			2867
Explorer Gray	•			2868
Garden Green	•			2869

HENRY J 4-CYL. 2-DR TRIM

COLOR	CLOTH	VINYL	LEATHER	CODE
Brown Shepherd	•			3407,3461
Black Shepherd	•			3408,3460
Shepherd	•			3456,3486
Caribbean	•			3457,3487
Shepherd/Burma	•	•		3478,3479
Caribbean/Forest Green	•	•		3480,3481

HENRY J 6-CYL. 2-DR TRIM

COLOR	CLOTH	VINYL	LEATHER	CODE
Shepherd Plaid/ Burma Brown	•	•		4420,4451
Shepherd Plaid/ Burma Brown	•	•		4482,4485
Caribbean/Cape Verde Green	•	•		4421,4453
McDonnell Plaid	•			4464,4481
Swiss Chalet Plaid	•			4465,4480

THE TRANSMISSION CODE is a single digit under "TR" on the plate that indicates the transmission used.

TYPE	CODE
3-Speed conventional	2
3-Speed overdrive	3
3-Speed overdrive	4
3-Speed overdrive	6
Automatic	7

THE ACCESSORY GROUP CODE under "AG" on the body number plate indicates the accessory group.

THE SPECIAL FACTORY ORDER CODE

under the "SPEC-FO" on the bottom line indicates that the car was custom ordered. Special order numbers start with the following:

Kaiser ....K

THE ENGINE NUMBER CODE for Kaiser is located on the left side of the engine at the upper front, and also on the plate attached to the left side of the crankcase. The Henry J engine code is located on the top of the water pump boss on the front of the engine, and on the engine name plate on the right side of the crankcase.

VIRGINIAN

ENGINE NUMBER	NO. CYL.	CID	HORSE-POWER	COMP. RATIO	CARB	TRANS
1100000/up	6	226	115	7.3:1	1 BC	MAN

DELUXE MANHATTAN

ENGINE NUMBER	NO. CYL.	CID	HORSE-POWER	COMP. RATIO	CARB	TRANS
1165001	6	226	115	7.3:1	1 BC	MAN
2114001/	6	226	115	7.3:1	1 BC	AUTO
2218001						

HENRY J

ENGINE NUMBER	NO. CYL.	CID	HORSE-POWER	COMP. RATIO	CARB	TRANS
3,500,001/up	4	134	68	7.0:1	1 BC	MAN
3,000,001/up	6	161	80	7.0:1	1 BC	MAN

ENGINE SUFFIX LETTERS

Lertter suffixes in connection with engine numbers denote the following:

A - Designates .010 undersize main and rod bearings
N - Designates .020 oversize pistons
AN - Designates .010 undersize main and rod bearings and .020
    oversize pistons

1953 HENRY J

1953 KAISER

VEHICLE IDENTIFICATION NUMBER

• K 5 3 1 0 0 1 0 0 1 •

The Vehicle Identification Number (VIN) is located on the left front door hinge post.

FIRST DIGIT: Identifies the division symbol

DIVISION	CODE
Kaiser ....K

SECOND & THIRD DIGITS: Identifies the model year 1953

FOURTH DIGIT: Identifies the body style

BODY STYLE	CODE
Kaiser Dragon 0
Kaiser Deluxe 1
Kaiser Manhattan.....................................2
Henry J Corsair 3
Henry J Corsair Deluxe............................4
Kaiser Carolina 8

LAST SIX DIGITS: Represent the basic production numbers - 001001 and up.

BODY NUMBER PLATE

THE BODY NUMBER PLATE is located on the right side of the cowl under the hood.

KAISER-FRAZER CORP.

MODEL	BODY	PAINT	TRIM	DR	KL	TR	RO	HR	AG	SL	SB	AR
531	1	597	5003	1		4			1			

CT	WL	TS	M1	M2	M3	M4	SPEC-FO	M5	M6	SCHED	ITEM NO.

BODY NUMBER

THE MODEL NUMBER CODE consists of three digits. The first two digits identify the year 1953. The third digit identifies the model type.

MODEL TYPE	CODE
Kaiser Dragon 0
Kaiser Deluxe 1
Kaiser Manhattan.....................................2
Henry J Corsair 3
Henry J Corsair Deluxe............................4
Kaiser Carolina 8

THE BODY NUMBER CODE indicates the body type.

KAISER DRAGON

BODY TYPE	CODE
Sedan, 4-dr. 1

KAISER DELUXE

BODY TYPE	CODE
Sedan, 4-dr. 1
Sedan, 2-dr. 4
Traveler, 4-dr. 5

KAISER MANHATTAN

BODY TYPE	CODE
Sedan, 4-dr. 1
Sedan, 2-dr. 4

KAISER CAROLINA

BODY TYPE	CODE
Sedan, 4-dr. 1
Sedan, 2-dr. 4

HENRY J

BODY TYPE	CODE
Sedan, 2-dr. 4

THE PAINT CODE consists of 3 digits and indicates the color used on the car.

COLOR	CODE
Onyx	096,140
Stardust Ivory	097,106,214
Jade Tint	098
Frosted Holly Green	099,643
Maroon Velvet Metallic	107
Cardinal	110
Jade Green Metallic	202,643
Peacock Blue	203,644
Sabre Jet Blue	204,646
Persian Gray Metallic	207,297,648
Anchor Gray	208
Pine Tint Green	228
Powder Blue	229
Australian Beige	213
Tropical Green Metallic	395
Crystal Green	582
Robinhood Green	582
Cardinal	597
Tropical Green Metallic	603
Cerulean Blue	604,398
Copper Dust Metallic	647,206
Anchor Gray	649
Australian Beige	653
Pine Tint	668

THE TRIM CODE indicates the interior color and material scheme.

KAISER DELUXE 4-DR TRIM

COLOR	CLOTH	VINYL	LEATHER	CODE
Chocolate Brown/ Burma	•	•		5000
Chukkar Tan/ Burma	•	•		5002
Explorer Gray/ Burma	•	•		5003
Blue Satin/ Leather Tan	•	•		5004
Blue Satin/ Leather Tan	•	•		5005
Forest Green/ Leather Tan	•	•		5006
Forest Green/ Leather Tan	•	•		5007
Gunmetal/Burma	•	•		5008
Caribbean Coral/ Burma Brown	•	•		5015
Caribbean Coral/ Burma Brown	•	•		5016
Saddle Bronze/ Leather Tan	•	•		5017
Turquoise/Leather Tan	•	•		5019
Persian Gray/ Black	•	•		5021
Honey Beige/ Burma Brown	•	•		5022

KAISER CAROLINA 4-DR TRIM

COLOR	CLOTH	VINYL	LEATHER	CODE
Sportsman Beige/ Burma Brown	•	•		5020,5023

KAISER DELUXE TRAVELER 4-DR TRIM

COLOR	CLOTH	VINYL	LEATHER	CODE
Burma Brown		•		5125
Caribbean Coral		•		5126
Scarlet Dinosaur		•		5127
Forest Green		•		5128
Tropical Green		•		5129

KAISER DELUXE 2-DR TRIM

COLOR	CLOTH	VINYL	LEATHER	CODE
Chocolate Brown/ Burma Brown	•	•		5200
Chukkar Tan/ Burma Brown	•	•		5202
Explorer Gray/ Burma Brown	•	•		5203
Blue Satin/ Leather Tan	•	•		5204
Blue Satin/ Leather Tan	•	•		5205
Forest Green/ Leather Tan	•	•		5206
Foest Green/ Leather Tan	•	•		5207
Gunmetal/Burma Brown	•	•		5208
Caribbean Coral/ Burma Brown	•	•		5215
Caribbean Coral/ Burma Brown	•	•		5216
Saddle bronze/ Leather Tan	•	•		5217
Turquoise/ Leather Tan	•	•		5219
Persian Gray/Black	•	•		5221
Honey Beige/Burma Brown	•	•		5222

KAISER CAROLINA 2-DR TRIM

COLOR	CLOTH	VINYL	LEATHER	CODE
Sportsman Beige Burma Brown	•	•		5220
Persian Gray/ Black	•	•		5221
Honey Beige/ Burma Brown	•	•		5222
Sportsman Beige/ Burma Brown	•	•		5223

KAISER MANHATTAN 4-DR TRIM

COLOR	CLOTH	VINYL	LEATHER	CODE
Persian Gray/ Bleached Bambu	•	•		5300
Copperdust/ Bleached Bambu	•	•		5301
Peacock Blue/ Bleached Bambu	•	•		5302
Jade Green/ Bleached Bambu	•	•		5303
Tropical Green/ Bleached Bambu	•	•		5304
Australian Beige/ Brown Bambu	•	•		5305
Copperdust/ Bleached Bambu	•	•		5310

KAISER DRAGON 4-DR TRIM

COLOR	CLOTH	VINYL	LEATHER	CODE
Black/Beige/ Bleached Bambu	•	•		5308
Green/Beige/ Green Bambu	•	•		5309
Green/Green Bambu	•	•		5311
White/Green Bambu	•	•		5312
Maroon/Beige/ Maroon Bambu	•	•		5313

KAISER MANHATTAN 2-DR TRIM

COLOR	CLOTH	VINYL	LEATHER	CODE
Persian Gray/ Black Bambu	•	•		5400
Copperdust/ Bleached Bambu	•	•		5401
Peacock Blue/ Bleached Bambu	•	•		5402
Jade Green/ Bleached Bambu	•	•		5403
Tropical Green/ Bleached Bambu	•	•		5404
Australian Beige/ Brown Bambu	•	•		5405
Copperdust/ Bleached Bambu	•	•		5410

HENRY J CORSAIR 2-DR TRIM

COLOR	CLOTH	VINYL	LEATHER	CODE
Copperweave	•			5500*
Copperweave	•			5501#

* Folding seat

\# Stationary seat

HENRY J CORSAIR DELUXE 2-DR TRIM

COLOR	CLOTH	VINYL	LEATHER	CODE
Caribbean Plaid	•			5504,5505
Swiss Chalet/ Burma Brown	•	•		5506,5507
Caribbean Plaid	•			5509
Swiss Chalet/ Burma Brown	•	•		5510
McDonnell Plaid	•			5511
Australian Beige/ Burman Brown	•	•		5602
Persian Gray/ Burma Brown	•	•		5603

THE TRANSMISSION CODE is a single digit under "TR" on the plate that indicates the transmission type.

TYPE	CODE
3-Speed conventional	2
3-Speed overdrive	3
3-Speed overdrive	4
3-Speed overdrive	6
Automatic	7

THE ACCESSORY GROUP CODE under "AG" on the body number plate indicates the accessory group.

THE SPECIAL FACTORY ORDER CODE under the "SPEC-FO" on the bottom line indicates that the car was custom ordered. Special order numbers start with the following:

Kaiser ....K

THE ENGINE NUMBER for the Kaiser is located on the left side of the engine at the upper front and also on the plate attached to the left side of the crankcase. The engine number for the Henry J is located on the top of the water pump boss on the front of the engine and on the engine name plate on the right side of the crankcase.

KAISER

ENGINE NUMBER	NO. CYL.	CID	HORSE-POWER	COMP. RATIO	CARB	TRANS
2059001	6	226	118	7.3:1	1 BC	MAN
2130001	6	226	118	7.3:1	1 BC	AUTO

HENRY J

ENGINE NUMBER	NO. CYL.	CID	HORSE-POWER	COMP. RATIO	CARB	TRANS
3560068/up	4	134	68	7.0:1	1 BC	MAN
3065713/up	6	161	80	7.0:1	1 BC	MAN

KAISER SUFFIX LETTERS

Letter suffixes in connection with engine numbers denote the following:

A - Designates .010 undersize main and rod bearings
N - Designates .020 oversize pistons
AN - Designates .010 undersize main and rod bearings and .020
    oversize pistons

1954 KAISER DARRIN

1954 KAISER DARRIN

VEHICLE IDENTIFICATION NUMBER

The Vehicle Identification Number (VIN) for the Kaiser and Henry J is located on the left front door hinge post. The VIN for the Kaiser-Darrin is located on the plate attached to the cowl under the hood.

KAISER

```
• K 5 4 3 0 0 1 0 0 1 •
```

FIRST DIGIT: Identifies the division symbol

DIVISION	CODE
Kaiser	K

SECOND & THIRD DIGITS: Identify the model year 1954

FOURTH DIGIT: Identifies the body style

BODY STYLE	CODE
Kaiser Manhattan	2
Henry J Corsair	3
Henry J Corsair Deluxe	4
Kaiser Special	5

LAST SIX DIGITS: Represent the basic production numbers - 001001 and up.

KAISER - DARRIN

```
• 1 6 1 - 0 0 1 0 0 1 •
```

FIRST THREE DIGITS: Identify the model number

MODEL	CODE
Darrin Sports Car	161

LAST SIX DIGITS: Represent the basic production numbers - 001001 and up.

THE BODY NUMBER PLATE

The body number plate is located on the right side of the cowl under the hood.

KAISER-FRAZER CORP.

MODEL	BODY	PAINT	TRIM	DR	KL	TR	RO	HR	AG	SL	SB	AR
542	1	597	5003	1		4			1			

C T	W L	T S	M 1	M 2	M 3	M 4	SPEC-FO	M 5	M 6	SCHED	ITEM NO.

BODY NUMBER

* Kaiser-Darrin plate says WILLYS MOTORS.

THE MODEL NUMBER CODE consists of three digits. The first two digits identify the year 1954. The third digit identifies the model type.

MODEL TYPE	CODE
Kaiser Manhattan	2
Henry J Corsair	3
Henry J Corsair Deluxe	4
Kaiser Special	5
Darrin Sports Roadster	7

THE BODY NUMBER CODE indicates the body type.

KAISER

BODY TYPE	CODE
Sedan, 4-dr.	1
Sedan, 2-dr.	4

HENRY J

BODY TYPE	CODE
Sedan, 2-dr.	4

THE PAINT CODE consists of 3 digits that indicates the color used on the car.

KAISER-WILLYS

COLOR	CODE
Beryl Green	035
Bristol Red	036
Cardinal	110
Pine Tint	117
Onyx	140,239
Champagne	153
Pine Tint	154
Red Sail	156
Yellow Satin	157
Gunmetal Metallic	161
Jade Green Metallic	202
Persian Gray Metallic	207
Stardust Ivory	214
Palm Beach Ivory	218
Blue Comet Metallic	224
Signal Gray Metallic	226
Island Green Metallic	227
Powder Blue	229

KAISER-DARRIN

COLOR	CODE
Champagne	153
Pine Tint	154
Red Sail	156
Yellow Satin	157

THE TRIM CODE indicates the interior color and material scheme.

KAISER SPECIAL 4-DR TRIM

COLOR	CLOTH	VINYL	LEATHER	CODE
Australian Beige	•	•		5030
Persian Gray	•	•		5031
Persian Gray/ Bleached Bambu	•	•		5300
Copperdust/ Bleached Bambu	•	•		5301,5310
Peacock Blue/ Bleached Bambu	•	•		5302
Jade Green/ Bleached Bambu	•	•		5303
Tropical Green/ Bleached Bambu	•	•		5304
Australian Beige/ Brown Bambu	•	•		5305

KAISER MANHATTAN 4-DR TRIM

COLOR	CLOTH	VINYL	LEATHER	CODE
Ivory/Copperdust	•	•		5320,5322
Ivory/Green	•	•		5321
Gray/Blue	•	•		5323,5330
Gray/Black	•	•		5324
Red		•	•	5324
Green		•		5325

KAISER SPECIAL 2-DR TRIM

COLOR	CLOTH	VINYL	LEATHER	CODE
Persian Gray/ Black Bambu	•	•		5400
Copperdust/ Bleached Bambu	•	•		5401,5410
Peacock Blue/ Bleached Bambu	•	•		5402
Jade Green/ Bleached Bambu	•	•		5403
Tropical Green/ Bleached Bambu	•	•		5404
Australian Beige/ Bleached Bambu	•	•		5405

KAISER MANHATTAN 2-DR TRIM

COLOR	CLOTH	VINYL	LEATHER	CODE
Ivory/Copperdust	•	•		5420,5422
Ivory/Green	•	•		5421
Gray/Blue	•	•		5423
Gray/Black	•	•		5424
Green		•		5425

HENRY J CORSAIR 2-DR TRIM

COLOR	CLOTH	VINYL	LEATHER	CODE
Copperweave	•			5500,5501
Caribbean Plaid	•			5504,5505
Swiss Chalet/ Burma Brown		•		5506
Swiss Chalet/ Burma Brown		•		5507

HENRY J CORSAIR DELUXE 2-DR TRIM

COLOR	CLOTH	VINYL	LEATHER	CODE
McDonnell Plaid	•			5507,5511
Caribbean Plaid	•			5509
Swiss Chalet/ Burma Brown	•	•		5510

KAISER DARRIN SPORTS ROADSTER TRIM

COLOR	CLOTH	VINYL	LEATHER	CODE
Red			•	7200,7202
Red			•	7208
Pine Tint			•	7203
Yellow Satin			•	7204
Black			•	7205
White			•	7209

THE TRANSMISSION CODE is a single digit under "TR" on the plate that indicates the transmission type.

TYPE	CODE
3-Speed conventional	2
3-Speed overdrive	3
3-Speed overdrive	4
3-Speed overdrive	6
Automatic	7

THE ACCESSORY GROUP CODE under "AG" on the body number plate indicates the accessory group.

THE SPECIAL FACTORY ORDER CODE under the "SPEC-FO" on the bottom line indicates that the car was custom ordered. Special order numbers start with the following:

Kaiser ....K

Darrin ....KD

THE ENGINE NUMBER of the Kaiser is located on the left side of the engine at the upper front and on the plate attached to the left side of the crankcase. The Henry J engine number is located on the top of the water pump boss on the front of the engine and on the engine name plate on the right side of the crankcase. The Darrin engine number is located on the boss on the top right front corner of the block.

HENRY J

ENGINE NUMBER	NO. CYL.	CID	HORSE-POWER	COMP. RATIO	CARB	TRANS
3560068 Up	4	134	68	7.0:1	1 BC	
3065713 Up	6	161	80	7.0:1	1 BC	

KAISER SPECIAL

ENGINE NUMBER	NO. CYL.	CID	HORSE-POWER	COMP. RATIO	CARB	TRANS
2059001/Up	6	226	118	7.3:1	1 BC	Man
2130001/Up	6	226	118	7.3:1	1BC	Auto

KAISER MANHATTAN

ENGINE NUMBER	NO. CYL.	CID	HORSE-POWER	COMP. RATIO	CARB	TRANS
K542-001001	6	226	140	7.3:1	SC	

KAISER-DARRIN

ENGINE NUMBER	NO. CYL.	CID	HORSE-POWER	COMP. RATIO	CARB	TRANS
2063001/Up	6	161	90	7.6:1	1 BC	

ENGINE SUFFIX LETTERS

Letter suffixes in connection wit engine numbers denote the following:

A - Designates .010 undersize main and rod bearings
N - Designates .020 oversize pistons
AN - Designates .010 undersize main and rod bearings and .020
    oversize pistons

1955 KAISER

1955 KAISER

VEHICLE IDENTIFICATION NUMBER

● 5 1 3 6 7 5 0 0 1 ●

The Vehicle Identification Number (VIN) is located on the left front door hinge post.

FIRST FIVE DIGITS: Identify the model number

MODEL NUMBER	CODE
Kaiser Manhattan 4-dr.	51367
Kaiser Manhattan 2-dr.	51467
Kaiser Manhattan, 4-dr. (export)	51363

LAST FOUR DIGITS: Represent the basic production numbers - 5001 and up.

THE BODY NUMBER PLATE is on the right side of the cowl under the hood.

KAISER-FRAZER CORP.											
MODEL	BODY	PAINT	TRIM	DR	KL	TR	RO	HR	AG	SL	SB	AR
542	1	035	5320	1		6			1		

C T	W L	T S	M 1	M 2	M 3	M 4	SPEC-FO	M 5	M 6	SCHED	ITEM NO.

BODY NUMBER

THE MODEL NUMBER CODE consists of three digits. The first two digits identify the year 1955. The third digit identifies the model type.

MODEL TYPE	CODE
Manhattan	2

THE BODY NUMBER CODE indicates the body type.

BODY TYPE	CODE
Sedan, 4-dr.	1
Sedan, 2-dr.	4

THE PAINT CODE consists of 3 digits that indicates the color used on the car.

COLOR	CODE
Raven Black	80
Beryl Green	92
Artic White	94
Island Green Poly	100
Copper Dust Poly	102
Blue Comet Poly	104A
Powder Blue	105
Palm Beach Ivory	106
President Red	108
Steelglow Gray Poly	109
Julep Green Poly	110
Transport Yellow	111
Pine Tint	117
Concert Ivory	118

THE TRIM CODE indicates the interior color and material scheme.

KAISER MANHATTAN 4-DR TRIM

COLOR	CLOTH	VINYL	LEATHER	CODE
Ivory/Copperdust	•	•		5320,5322
Ivory/Green	•	•		5321
Gray/Blue	•	•		5323,5330
Gray/Black	•	•		5324
Red		•	•	5324
Green		•		5325

KAISER MANHATTAN 2-DR TRIM

COLOR	CLOTH	VINYL	LEATHER	CODE
Ivory/Copperdust	•	•		5420,5422
Ivory/Green	•	•		5421
Gray/Blue	•	•		5423
Gray/Black	•	•		5424
Green		•		5425

THE TRANSMISSION CODE is a single digit under "TR" on the plate that indicates the transmission type.

TYPE	CODE
3-Speed conventional	2
3-Speed overdrive	6
Automatic	7

THE ACCESSORY GROUP CODE under "AG" on the body number plate indicates the accessory group that car came equipped with.

THE SPECIAL FACTORY ORDER CODE under the "SPEC-FO" on the bottom line indicates that the car was custom ordered. Special order numbers start with the following:

Kaiser .... K

THE ENGINE NUMBER is located on the left side of the engine at the upper front, and on the plate attached to the left side of the crankcase.

ENGINE NUMBER	NO. CYL.	CID	HORSE-POWER	COMP. RATIO	CARB.
2063001/Up	6	226	140	7.3:1	SC

ENGINE SUFFIX LETTERS
The letters used as suffixes in connection with engine numbers denote the following:

A - Designates .010 undersize main and rod bearings
N - Designates .020 oversize pistons
AN - Designates .010 undersize main and rod berings and .020
    oversize pistons

1950 NASH RAMBLER

1950 NASH RAMBLER

1950 NASH RAMBLER

VEHICLE IDENTIFICATION NUMBER

● R - 5 5 6 0 0 1 ●

Located on the right side of the cowl under the hood.

FIRST DIGIT: Identifies the model

MODEL	CODE
Rambler	D
Statesman	K
Ambassador	R

NOTE: C following the letter identifies a car built in El Segundo; a Canada car carries a T: a D identifies an unassembled export unit. If there was no second code the car was built in Kenosha.

LAST SIX DIGITS: Identify the basic production sequence number

Rambler   - 1001/up

Ambassador - 556001 (El Segundo 3501/up)

Statesman - 34001/up (El Segundo 9501/up)

BODY PLATE NUMBER

Located on the right side of the cowl under the hood.

NASH KELVINATOR CORPORATION
NASH MOTORS DIVISION
BODY PLANT

BODY Nº. 1234
MODEL Nº. 5021
TRIM Nº. T47
PAINT Nº. 13

MODEL NUMBER

RAMBLER SERIES 10

BODY STYLE	CODE
Convertible Landau, 2-dr.	5021
Station wagon, 2-dr.	5024

STATESMAN SERIES 40 - DELUXE

BODY STYLE	CODE
Business coupe, 2-dr.	5032

STATESMAN SERIES 40 - SUPER

BODY STYLE	CODE
Sedan, 4-dr.	5048
Sedan, 2-dr.	5049
Club coupe, 2-dr.	5043

STATESMAN SERIES 40 - CUSTOM

BODY STYLE	CODE
Sedan, 4-dr.	5058
Sedan, 2-dr.	5059
Club coupe, 2-dr.	5053

AMBASSADOR SERIES 60 - SUPER

BODY STYLE	CODE
Sedan, 4-dr.	5068
Sedan, 2-dr.	5069
Club coupe, 2-dr.	5063

AMBASSADOR SERIES 70 - CUSTOM

BODY STYLE	CODE
Sedan, 4-dr.	5078
Sedan, 2-dr.	5079
Club coupe, 2-dr.	5073

THE COLOR CODE indicates the paint color used on the vehicle. Two-tone combinations: The first set of letter and numbers identifies the lower body color, the second letter and numbers identifies the upper body color.

COLOR	CODE
Black	*P1
Sunset Maroon Light	*P3
Fawn Brown Medium	P7
Nile Green Light	P8
Seal Brown Dark	P13
Midnight Blue Dark	P16
Sherwood Green Dark	P17
Surf Green Medium	*P18
Cruiser Gray Dark	P19
Sea Mist Gray Light	*P20
Strata Blue Light	P21
Bermuda Blue Medium Metallic	*P22
Champagne Ivory	*P23
Carioca Rust	P24
Ocean Blue Medium	P25
Pan American Red	*27
Blue Black	1

* Also Rambler colors

THE TRIM CODE indicates the key to the color and material scheme used on the vehicle.

TRIM CODE

COLOR	CLOTH	VINYL	LEATHER	CODE
Blue/Taupe	•			T4
Brown/Taupe	•			T4
Taupe/Brown	•			T4
Blue/Gray/Taupe/ Brown/Black	•			T4
Gray/Gray	•			T7
Blue/Green/Gray	•			T6
Blue/Taupe/Brown	•			T6
Black/Gray	•			T8
Rust/Gray	•			T8
Green/Gray	•			T8
Blue/Gray	•			T8
Tan		•		T5
Blue		•		T5
Red		•		T5

RAMBLER WAGON TRIM

COLOR	CLOTH	VINYL	LEATHER	CODE
Tan		•		
Ivory		•		
Rust		•		
Rust	•			
Green	•			
Blue	•			
Black	•			

ENGINE SPECIFICATIONS

ENGINE NUMBER - Ambassador number is located on the upper right hand corner of the engine block; Statesman and Rambler numbers are located on a machined surface on the right side of the engine block just above the exhaust pipe. NOTE: Near the engine number is a three letter code: first letter refers to the cylinder bore; second letter refers to the crankshaft main bearings; third letter refers to the size of the connecting rod bearings. Letter "A" means standard, letter "B" means .010 undersize, letter "C" means .010 oversize. Engines not marked are standard in all respects.

RAMBLER

ENGINE NO.	NO. CYL.	CID	HORSE-POWER	COMP. RATIO	CARB
F1001/UP	6	172.6	82	7.25:1	1 BC

STATESMAN

ENGINE NO.	NO. CYL.	CID	HORSE-POWER	COMP. RATIO	CARB
S-92001/UP	6	184	85	7.0:1	1 BC
S-92001/UP	6	184	N/A	7.35:1	1 BC

AMBASSADOR

ENGINE NO.	NO. CYL.	CID	HORSE-POWER	COMP. RATIO	CARB
A-46001/UP	6	234.8	115	7.0:1	1 BC
A-46001/UP	6	234.8	N/A	7.5:1	1 BC

1951 NASH

1951 NASH RAMBLER

1951 NASH RAMBLER

1951 NASH

1951 NASH

VEHICLE IDENTIFICATION NUMBER

• A - 6 0 0 5 0 1 •

Located on the right side of the cowl under the hood.

FIRST DIGIT: Identifies the model

MODEL	CODE
Rambler	D
Statesman	K
Ambassador	R

NOTE: C following the letter identifies a car built in El Segundo. If there is no second code, the car was built in Kenosha.

LAST SIX DIGITS: Identify the basic production sequence number

Rambler   - 12501/up

Ambassador - 600501 (El Segundo 8701/up)

Statesman - 438001/up (El Segundo 23501/up)

BODY PLATE NUMBER

Located in the same location as the serial number plate.

NASH KELVINATOR CORPORATION
NASH MOTORS DIVISION
BODY PLANT

BODY Nº. 12501

MODEL Nº. 5114

TRIM Nº. 54

PAINT Nº. 33

MODEL NUMBER

RAMBLER SERIES 10 - SUBURBAN

BODY STYLE	CODE
Station wagon, 2-dr.	5114

RAMBLER SERIES 20 - CUSTOM

BODY STYLE	CODE
Convertible Landau, 2-dr.	5121
Station wagon, 2-dr.	5124
Hardtop coupe (Country Club)	5127

STATESMAN SERIES 40 - DELUXE

BODY STYLE	CODE
Business coupe, 2-dr.	5132

STATESMAN SERIES 40 - SUPER

BODY STYLE	CODE
Sedan, 4-dr.	5148
Sedan, 2-dr.	5149
Club coupe, 2-dr.	5143

STATESMAN SERIES 40 - CUSTOM

BODY STYLE	CODE
Sedan, 4-dr.	5158
Sedan, 2-dr.	5159
Club coupe, 2-dr.	5153

AMBASSADOR SERIES 60 - SUPER

BODY STYLE	CODE
Sedan, 4-dr.	5168
Sedan, 2-dr.	5169
Club coupe, 2-dr.	5163

AMBASSADOR SERIES 60 - CUSTOM

BODY STYLE	CODE
Sedan, 4-dr.	5178
Sedan, 2-dr.	5179
Club coupe, 2-dr.	5173

THE COLOR CODE indicates the paint color used on the vehicle. Two-tone combinations: The first letter and numbers identify the lower body color; the second letter and numbers identify the upper body color.

STATESMAN/AMBASSADOR

COLOR	CODE
Black	P1
Nile Green Light	P8
Cruiser Gray Dark	P19
Sea Mist Gray Light	P20
Champagne Ivory	P23
Light Harvard Maroon	P28
Oxford Dark Blue	P29
Forest Dark Green	P30
Greenwich Medium Green Metallic	P31
Light Cadet Blue	P32
Medium Klondike Brown Metallic	P33
Medium Arctic Blue Metallic	P34

RAMBLER

COLOR	CODE
Black	P1
Sunset Maroon	P3
Surf Green Medium (Tan top)	P18
Sea Mist Gray Light	P20
Bermuda Blue Medium (Tan top)	P22
Champagne Ivory (Black top)	P23
Carioca Rust	P24
Pan American Red (Black top)	P27

THE TRIM CODE indicates the color and material scheme used on the vehicle.

COLOR	CLOTH	VINYL	LEATHER	CODE
Brown/Gray	•			T45
Herringbone/Rust	•	•		T50
Brown/Gray	•			T52
Blue/Brown/Gray	•			T53
Brown/Rust	•	•		T54
Blue/Blue	•	•		T55
Gray/Med. Gray/ Dark Maroon	•			T69
Gray/Dark Gray/ Dark Maroon	•			T70
Gray/Black/Gray	•			T93,T94
Gray/Black/Rust	•			T95
Gray/Black/Green	•			T96
Gray/Black/Blue	•			T97
Tan			•	T56
Blue			•	T57
Red			•	T58
Black/Gray	•			*T111
Rust/Gray	•			*T112
Green/Gray	•			*T113
Tan/Ivory/Rust	•			*T114

* Rambler combinations

ENGINE SPECIFICATIONS

ENGINE NUMBER - Ambassador number is located on the upper right hand corner of the engine block; Statesman and Rambler numbers are located on a machined surface on the right side of the engine block above the exhaust pipe. NOTE: Near the engine number is a three letter code: first letter refers to the cylinder bore; second letter refers to the crankshaft main bearings; third letter refers to the size of the connecting rod bearings. Letter "A" means standard, letter "B" means .010 undersize, letter "C" means .010 oversize. Engines not marked are standard in all respects.

Rambler - F-13001/up

Ambassador - A-97001/up

Statesman - S-207001/up

RAMBLER

ENGINE NO.	NO. CYL.	CID	HORSE-POWER	COMP. RATIO	CARB
F13001/UP	6	172.6	82	7.25:1	1 BC

STATESMAN

ENGINE NO.	NO. CYL.	CID	HORSE-POWER	COMP. RATIO	CARB
S-207001/UP	6	184	85	7.0:1	1 BC
S-207001/UP	6	184	N/A	7.35:1	1 BC

AMBASSADOR

ENGINE NO.	NO. CYL.	CID	HORSE-POWER	COMP. RATIO	CARB
A-97001/UP	6	234.8	115	7.3:1	1 BC
A-97001/UP	6	234.8	N/A	7.5:1	1 BC

1952 NASH RAMBLER HAMILTON 480

1952 NASH AMBASSADOR GOLDEN ANNIVERSARY

1952 NASH STATESMAN

1952 NASH RAMBLER COUNTRY CLUB

VEHICLE IDENTIFICATION NUMBER

• D C - 7 9 5 0 0 1 •

Located on the right hand wheelhouse panel under the hood on the Rambler, located on the plate attached to the cowl under the hood on the Statesman and Ambassador.

FIRST DIGIT: Identifies the model

MODEL	CODE
Rambler	D
Statesman	K
Ambassador	R

SECOND DIGIT: Identifies the assembly plant. If there is no second letter, the car was assembled in Kenosha, WI.

ASSEMBLY PLANT	CODE
El Segundo, CA	C
Toronto, CANADA	T

LAST SIX DIGITS: Identify the basic production sequence number

RAMBLER

Kenosha, WI	79501/up
El Segundo, CA	4101/up
Toronto, CAN	1001/up

STATESMAN

Kenosha, WI	656001/up
El Segundo, CA	14501/up

AMBASSADOR

Kenosha, WI	519001/up
El Segundo, CA	37001/up
Toronto, CAN	6101/up

BODY PLATE NUMBER

Located in the same location as the serial number plate.

NASH KELVINATOR CORPORATION
NASH MOTORS DIVISION
BODY PLANT

BODY Nº. 79501
MODEL Nº. 5227
TRIM Nº. —
PAINT Nº. 28

MODEL NUMBER

RAMBLER - SUPER

BODY STYLE	CODE
Station wagon, 2-dr.	5214

RAMBLER - CUSTOM

BODY STYLE	CODE
Hardtop coupe	5227
Convertible Landau, 2-dr.	5221
Station wagon, 2-dr.	5224

STATESMAN - SUPER

BODY STYLE	CODE
Sedan, 4-dr.	5245
Sedan, 2-dr.	5246

STATESMAN - CUSTOM

BODY STYLE	CODE
Sedan, 4-dr.	5255
Sedan, 2-dr.	5256
Hardtop coupe, 2-dr.	5257

AMBASSADOR - SUPER

BODY STYLE	CODE
Sedan, 4-dr.	5265
Sedan, 2-dr.	5266

AMBASSADOR - CUSTOM

BODY STYLE	CODE
Sedan, 4-dr.	5275
Sedan, 2-dr.	5276
Hardtop coupe, 2-dr.	5277

THE COLOR CODE indicates the paint color used on the vehicle. Two-tone combinations: The first set of numbers identifies the lower body color; the second set of numbers identifies the upper body color.

COLOR	CODE
Cruiser Gray Dark	P19
Sea Mist Gray Dark	P20
Champagne Ivory	P23
Pan American Red	27
Harvard Maroon	P28
Forest Green	P30
Greenwich Green Metallic	P31
Meadow Green	35
Willow Green	P37
Tuxedo Blue Dark	38
Academy Blue Metallic	39
Skyline Blue	P40
Trooper Tan Metallic	41
Autumn Rust Metallic	42
Anniversary Gold Metallic	P43
Caribbean Blue	P44
Blue Black	1

THE TRIM CODE indicates the color and material scheme used on the vehicle. Trim codes were not available.

ENGINE SPECIFICATIONS

ENGINE NUMBER - Ambassador number is located on the upper right hand corner of the engine block; Statesman and Rambler numbers are located on a machined surface on the right side of the engine block above the exhaust pipe. NOTE: Near the engine number is a three letter code: first letter refers to the cylinder bore; second letter refers to the crankshaft main bearings; third letter refers to the size of the connecting rod bearings. Letter "A" means standard, letter "B" means .010 undersize, letter "C" means .010 oversize. Engines not marked are standard in all respects.

Rambler - F-85001/up

Ambassador - A-165001/up

Statesman - S-308001/up

RAMBLER

ENGINE NO.	NO. CYL.	CID	HORSE-POWER	COMP. RATIO	CARB
F-85001/UP	6	172.6	82	7.25:1	1 BC

STATESMAN

ENGINE NO.	NO. CYL.	CID	HORSE-POWER	COMP. RATIO	CARB
S-308001/UP	6	195.6	88	7.1:1	1 BC

AMBASSADOR

ENGINE NO.	NO. CYL.	CID	HORSE-POWER	COMP. RATIO	CARB
A-165001/UP	6	252.6	120	7.3:1	1 BC
	6	252.6	140	8.0:1	2-1 BC

1953 NASH AMBASSADOR

1953 NASH HEALY

1953 NASH RAMBLER

1953 NASH

VEHICLE IDENTIFICATION NUMBER

`• DC-795001 •`

Located on the plate attached to the cowl under the hood.

FIRST DIGIT: Identifies the model

MODEL	CODE
Rambler	D
Statesman	K
Ambassador	R

SECOND DIGIT: Identifies the assembly plant. If there is no second digit, the car was assembled in Kenosha, WI.

ASSEMBLY PLANT	CODE
El Segundo, CA	C
Kenosha, WI	—
Toronto, CAN	T

LAST SIX DIGITS: Identify the basic production sequence number

RAMBLER

Kenosha, WI	127501/up
El Segundo, CA	9001/up
Toronto, CAN	1901/up

STATESMAN

Kenosha, WI	563501/up
El Segundo, CA	43001/up
Toronto, CAN	6901/up

AMBASSADOR

Kenosha, WI	692101/up
El Segundo, CA	19001/up

BODY PLATE NUMBER

Located in the same location as the serial number plate. (On the first 12,000 Ramblers the serial number is located on a plate attached to the right front wheelhouse panel.)

```
NASH KELVINATOR CORPORATION
       NASH MOTORS DIVISION
            BODY PLANT
   BODY Nº.  127501
   MODEL Nº. 5314
   TRIM Nº.  —
   PAINT Nº.  19
```

MODEL NUMBER

RAMBLER - SUPER

BODY STYLE	CODE
Station wagon, 2-dr.	5314

RAMBLER - CUSTOM

BODY STYLE	CODE
Hardtop coupe	5327
Convertible sedan, 2-dr.	5321
Station wagon, 2-dr.	5324

STATESMAN - SUPER

BODY STYLE	CODE
Sedan, 4-dr.	5345
Sedan, 2-dr.	5346

STATESMAN - CUSTOM

BODY STYLE	CODE
Sedan, 4-dr.	5355
Sedan, 2-dr.	5356
Hardtop coupe, 2-dr.	5357

AMBASSADOR - SUPER

BODY STYLE	CODE
Sedan, 4-dr.	5365
Sedan, 2-dr.	5366

AMBASSADOR - CUSTOM

BODY STYLE	CODE
Sedan, 4-dr.	5375
Sedan, 2-dr.	5376
Hardtop coupe, 2-dr.	5377

THE COLOR CODE indicates the paint color used on the vehicle. Two-tone combinations: The first set of numbers identifies the lower body color; the second set of numbers identifies the upper body color.

COLOR	CODE
Cruiser Gray	P19
Sea Mist Gray	P20
Champagne Ivory	P23
Willow Green	P37
Skyline Blue	P40
Autumn Rust Metallic	42
Anniversary Gold Metallic	P43
Caribbean Blue	P44
Hunter Green	P45
Village Green Metallic	P46
Pingree Blue	P47
Horizon Blue Metallic	P48
University Maroon	P49
Dawn Gray Metallic	P50
Spanish Red	P51
Blue Black	1

THE TRIM CODE indicates the color and material scheme used on the vehicle. The trim codes were not available.

ENGINE SPECIFICATIONS

ENGINE NUMBER - Ambassador number is located on the upper right corner of the engine block; Statesman and Rambler numbers are located on a machined surface on the right side of the engine block above the exhaust pipe. NOTE: Near the engine number is a three letter code: first letter refers to the cylinder bore; second letter refers to the crankshaft main bearings; third letter refers to the size of the connecting rod bearings. Letter "A" means standard, letter "B" means .010 undersize, letter "C" means .010 oversize. Engines not marked are standard in all respects.

RAMBLER

ENGINE NO.	NO. CYL.	CID	HORSE-POWER	COMP. RATIO	CARB	TRANS
F-14001/UP	6	184	85	7.25:1	1 BC	MAN
H-1001/UP	6	195.6	90	7.3:1	1 BC	AUTO

STATESMAN

ENGINE NO.	NO. CYL.	CID	HORSE-POWER	COMP. RATIO	CARB	TRANS
S-365001/UP	6	195.6	100	7.45:1	1 BC	ALL

AMBASSADOR

ENGINE NO.	NO. CYL.	CID	HORSE-POWER	COMP. RATIO	CARB	TRANS
A-21001/UP	6	252	120	7.3:1	1 BC	ALL
LMA*	6	252	140	8.0:1	2-1 BC	ALL

* LeMans dual Jetfire

1954 NASH RAMBLER

1954 NASH RAMBLER

1954 NASH RAMBLER

1954 NASH

VEHICLE IDENTIFICATION NUMBER

• D C - 1 7 1 5 0 1 •

Located on the plate attached to the cowl under the hood on the right side.

FIRST DIGIT: Identifies the model

MODEL	CODE
Rambler	D
Statesman	K
Ambassador	R

NOTE: C following the letter indicates the car was assembled in El Segundo.

LAST SIX DIGITS: Identify the basic production sequence number

RAMBLER

Kenosha, WI	171501/up
El Segundo, CA	12301/up

AMBASSADOR

Kenosha, WI	722501/up
El Segundo, CA	22001/up

STATESMAN

Kenosha, WI	615501/up
El Segundo, CA	47201/up

BODY PLATE NUMBER

Located at the same location of the serial number plate.

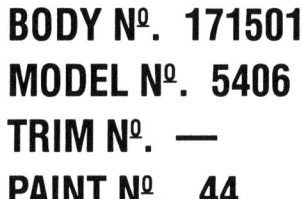

NASH KELVINATOR CORPORATION
NASH MOTORS DIVISION
BODY PLANT

BODY Nº. 171501
MODEL Nº. 5406
TRIM Nº. —
PAINT Nº. 44

MODEL NUMBER

RAMBLER - DELUXE
BODY STYLE	CODE
Club sedan, 2-dr.	5406

RAMBLER - SUPER
BODY STYLE	CODE
Station wagon, 2-dr.	5414
Sedan, 4-dr.	5415
Club sedan, 2-dr.	5416
Hardtop coupe, 2-dr.	5417

RAMBLER - CUSTOM
BODY STYLE	CODE
Hardtop coupe	5427
Convertible sedan, 2-dr.	5421
Station wagon, 2-dr.	5424
Sedan, 4-dr.	5425
Station wagon, 4-dr.	5428

STATESMAN - SUPER
BODY STYLE	CODE
Sedan, 4-dr.	5445
Sedan, 2-dr.	5446

STATESMAN - CUSTOM
BODY STYLE	CODE
Sedan, 4-dr.	5455
Sedan, 2-dr.	5456
Hardtop coupe, 2-dr.	5457

AMBASSADOR - SUPER

BODY STYLE	CODE
Sedan, 4-dr.	5465
Sedan, 2-dr.	5466

AMBASSADOR - CUSTOM

BODY STYLE	CODE
Sedan, 4-dr.	5475
Hardtop coupe, 2-dr.	5477

THE COLOR CODE indicates the paint color used on the vehicle. Two-tone combinations: The first set of digits identify the lower body color; the second set of digits identify the upper body color.

COLOR	CODE
Black	P1
Willow Green	P37
Anniversary Gold Metallic	P43
Caribbean Blue	P44
Spanish Red	P51
Remington Gray Metallic	P52
Pinehurst Green	P53
Sherwood Green Metallic	P54
Brussels Blue Metallic	P55
Parisian Blue	P56
Collegiate Maroon Metallic	P57
Malibu Ivory	P58
Mist Gray Green	P59
Croton Green	P60

THE TRIM CODE indicates the color and material scheme used on the vehicle. There were no trim codes available.

ENGINE SPECIFICATIONS

ENGINE NUMBER - Ambassador number is located on the upper right hand corner of the engine block; Statesman and Rambler numbers are located on a machined surface on the right side of the engine block just above the exhaust pipe. NOTE: Near the engine number is a three letter code: first letter refers to the cylinder bore; second letter refers to the crankshaft main bearings; third letter refers to the size of the connecting rod bearings. Letter "A" means standard, letter "B" means .010 undersize, letter "C" means .010 oversize. Engines not marked are standard in all respects.

RAMBLER

ENGINE NO.	NO. CYL.	CID	HORSE-POWER	COMP. RATIO	CARB
F-17001/UP	6	184	85	7.25:1	1 BC
H-12001/UP	6	196	90	7.3:1	1 BC

STATESMAN

ENGINE NO.	NO. CYL.	CID	HORSE-POWER	COMP. RATIO	CARB
S-43001/UP	6	196	100	7.45:1	1 BC
J-1001/UP	6	196	110	8.5:1	2-1 BC

AMBASSADOR

ENGINE NO.	NO. CYL.	CID	HORSE-POWER	COMP. RATIO	CARB
A-246001/UP	6	252	130	7.6:1	1 BC
LMA-246001/UP	6	252	140	8.0:1	2-1 BC

1955 RAMBLER SUBURBAN

1955 RAMBLER COUNTRY CLUB

1955 NASH AMBASSADOR

1955 NASH STATESMAN

1955 NASH RAMBLER COUNTRY CLUB

1955 NASH AMBASSADOR

VEHICLE IDENTIFICATION NUMBER

• D - 2 0 5 0 0 1 •

Located on the plate attached to the cowl under the hood on the right side.

FIRST DIGIT: Identifies the model

MODEL	CODE
Rambler	D
Statesman	K
Ambassador - 6	R
Ambassador - V8	V

NOTE: C following the letter indicates the car was assembled in El Segundo. If there is no second code, the car was built in Kenosha, WI.

LAST SIX DIGITS: Identify the basic production sequence number

RAMBLER
Kenosha, WI	205001/up
El Segundo, CA	15001/up

STATESMAN
Kenosha, WI	35001/up
El segundo, CA	48101/up

AMBASSADOR - 6
Kenosha, WI	742901/up
El Segundo, CA	23001/up

AMBASSADOR - V8
Kenosha, WI	1001/up
El Segundo, CA	1001/up

BODY PLATE NUMBER

Located at the same location of the serial number plate.

AMERICAN MOTORS CORPORATION

BODY No.	**742901**
MODEL No.	**5565-1**
TRIM No.	**539**
PAINT No.	**67**

EXAMPLE:

742901	Ambassador
5565-1	4-Dr. sedan
T-539	Green cloth/vinyl
67	Bermuda Green

THE BODY NUMBER is the same as the VIN number.

MODEL NUMBER

RAMBLER - DELUXE
BODY STYLE	CODE
Sedan, 4-dr.	5515
Club sedan, 2-dr.	5516
Business sedan, 2-dr.	5512
Station wagon, 2-dr.	5514

RAMBLER - SUPER
BODY STYLE	CODE
Station wagon, 2-dr.	5514-1
Sedan, 4-dr.	5515-1
Club sedan, 2-dr.	5516-1
Station wagon, 4-dr.	5518-1

RAMBLER - CUSTOM
BODY STYLE	CODE
Sedan, 4-dr.	5515-2
Hardtop coupe (Country Club)	5517-2
Station wagon, 4-dr. (Cross Country)	5518-2

STATESMAN - SUPER
BODY STYLE	CODE
Sedan, 4-dr.	5545-1

STATESMAN - CUSTOM

BODY STYLE	CODE
Sedan, 4-dr.	5545-2
Hardtop coupe (Country Club)	5547-2

AMBASSADOR 6 - SUPER

BODY STYLE	CODE
Sedan, 4-dr.	5565-1

AMBASSADOR 6 - CUSTOM

BODY STYLE	CODE
Sedan, 4-dr.	5565-2
Hardtop coupe (Country Club)	5567-2

AMBASSADOR V8 - SUPER

BODY STYLE	CODE
Sedan, 4-dr.	5585-1

AMBASSADOR V8 - CUSTOM

BODY STYLE	CODE
Sedan, 4-dr.	5585-2
Hardtop coupe (Country Club)	5587-2

THE COLOR CODE indicates the paint color used on the vehicle. Two-tone combinations: The first set of digits identify the lower body color; the second set of digits identify the upper body color.

COLOR	CODE
Black	P1
Caribbean Blue	P44
Midshipman Blue	P61
Island Green	P62
Rio Red	P64
Coral Red	P65
Sunburst Yellow	P66
Bermuda Green	P67
Mist Blue	P68
Snowberry White	P69
Palomino Brown	P71

THE TRIM CODE indicates the color and material scheme used on the vehicle.

STATESMAN SUPER

COLOR	CLOTH	VINYL	LEATHER	CODE
Blue/Blue	•	•		T531
Green/Green	•	•		T532

AMBASSADOR SUPER

COLOR	CLOTH	VINYL	LEATHER	CODE
Gray/Green	•	•		T537
Gray/Red/Blue	•	•		T538
Green/Green	•	•		T539
Green/White	•	•		T545
Gray/White	•	•		T546
Blue/White	•	•		T547

STATESMAN/AMBASSADOR CUSTOM

COLOR	CLOTH	VINYL	LEATHER	CODE
Green/White	•	•		T541
Gray/White	•	•		T542
Blue/White	•	•		T544

STATESMAN/AMBASSADOR (OPTIONS)

COLOR	CLOTH	VINYL	LEATHER	CODE
Green/White	•		•	T551
Gray/White	•		•	T552
Blue/White	•		•	T554
Black/Red	•		•	T553

ENGINE SPECIFICATIONS

ENGINE NUMBER - Ambassador number is located on the upper right hand corner of the engine block; Statesman and Rambler numbers are located on a machined surface on the right side of the cylinder block above the exhaust pipe. NOTE: Near the engine number is a three letter code: first letter refers to the cylinder bore; second letter refers to the crankshaft main bearings; third letter refers to the size of the connecting rod bearings. Letter "A" means standard, letter "B" means .010 undersize, letter "C" means .010 oversize. Engines not marked are standard in all respects.

RAMBLER

ENGINE NO.	NO. CYL.	CID	HORSE-POWER	COMP. RATIO	CARB
H-45001/UP	6	196	90	7.3:1	1 BC

STATESMAN

ENGINE NO.	NO. CYL.	CID	HORSE-POWER	COMP. RATIO	CARB
S-44001/UP	6	196	100	8.5:1	1 BC
J-30001/UP	6	196	110	8.0:1	2-1 BC

AMBASSADOR

ENGINE NO.	NO. CYL.	CID	HORSE-POWER	COMP. RATIO	CARB
A-27001/UP	6	252	130	7.6:1	1 BC
LMA-27001/UP	6	252	140	7.6:1	2-1 BC
P-1001/UP	8	320	208	7.8:1*	2 BC

* After engine number P-6001 the compression ratio went to 8.25:1

1956 NASH

1956 NASH RAMBLER

1956 NASH AMBASSADOR

1956 NASH RAMBLER

1956 NASH STATESMAN

VEHICLE IDENTIFICATION NUMBER

• D-276101 •

Located on the plate attached to the cowl under the hood.

FIRST DIGIT: Identifies the model

MODEL	CODE
Rambler	D
Statesman	K
Ambassador - 6 cyl.	R
Ambassador Special V8	U
Ambassador - 8 cyl.	V

LAST SIX DIGITS: Identify the basic production sequence number

Rambler	276101/up
Statesman	649201/up
Ambassador - 6	757901/up
Ambassador - V8	11501/up
Ambassador Special - V8	1001/up

BODY NUMBER PLATE

Located at the same location as the serial number plate.

AMERICAN MOTORS CORPORATION

BODY No.	757901
MODEL No.	5615-2
TRIM No.	633
PAINT No.	77

EXAMPLE:

5615	Sedan, 4-dr.
T-633	Green cloth/vinyl
77	Mint Green

THE BODY NUMBER is the same as the VIN number.

MODEL NUMBER

RAMBLER - DELUXE

BODY STYLE	CODE
Sedan, 4-dr.	5615

RAMBLER - SUPER

BODY STYLE	CODE
Sedan, 4-dr.	5615-1
Station wagon, 4-dr.	5618-1

RAMBLER - CUSTOM

BODY STYLE	CODE
Sedan, 4-dr.	5615-2
Hardtop sedan, 4-dr.	5619-2
Station wagon, 4-dr. (Cross Country)	5618-2
Station wagon, 4-dr., hardtop (Cross Country)	5613-2

STATESMAN 6

BODY STYLE	CODE
Sedan, 4-dr.	5645-1

AMBASSADOR 6 - SUPER

BODY STYLE	CODE
Sedan, 4-dr.	5665-1

AMBASSADOR V8 - SUPER

BODY STYLE	CODE
Sedan, 4-dr.	5685-1

AMBASSADOR V8 - CUSTOM

BODY STYLE	CODE
Sedan, 4-dr.	5685-2
Hardtop coupe (Country Club)	5687-2

AMBASSADOR V8 SPECIAL - SUPER

BODY STYLE	CODE
Sedan, 4-dr.	5655-1
Hardtop coupe (Country Club)	5667-1

AMBASSADOR V8 SPECIAL - CUSTOM

BODY STYLE	CODE
Sedan, 4-dr.	5655-2
Sedan, 2-dr.	5657-2

THE COLOR CODE indicates the paint color used on the vehicle. Two-tone combinations: The first set of digits identifies the lower body color; the second set of digits identifies the upper body color. Special two-tone combinations: The first digits identify the upper body color; the second digits identify the intermediate body color; the third digits identify the lower body color.

COLOR	CODE
Black	P1
Sunburst Yellow	P66
Bermuda Green	P67
Frost White	P72
Willow Green	P73
Crocus Yellow	P74
Polo Green	P75
Golden Brown	P76
Mint Green	P77
Grenadier Red	P78
Boulevard Gray	P80
Solitaire Blue	P81
Pacific Blue	P82
Ballerina Red	P83

THE TRIM CODE indicates the color and material scheme used on the vehicle.

STATESMAN/AMBASSADOR SUPER - 6-CYL.

COLOR	CLOTH	VINYL	LEATHER	CODE
Blue/Blue	•	•		T631
Green/Green	•	•		T633
Gray/White	•	•		T636

AMBASSADOR SUPER - 8-CYL.

COLOR	CLOTH	VINYL	LEATHER	CODE
Blue/Blue	•	•		T641
Green/Green	•	•		T643
Gray/White	•	•		T646
Gray/Grenadier Red	•	•		T648
Gray/Ballerina Red	•	•		T649
Gray/Green	•	•		T650

AMBASSADOR CUSTOM

COLOR	CLOTH	VINYL	LEATHER	CODE
Blue/Blue	•		•	T651
Blue/White	•		•	T652
Green/Green	•		•	T653
Green/White	•		•	T654
Gray/White	•		•	T657
Gray/Grenadier Red	•		•	T658
Gray/Ballerina Red	•		•	T659
Gray/Green	•		•	T660

NOTE: These trims are optional on the Ambassador Super 6-cyl.

ENGINE SPECIFICATIONS

ENGINE NUMBER - Ambassador number is located on the upper right hand corner of the engine block; Statesman and Rambler numbers are located on a machined surface on the right side of the engine block just above the exhaust pipe. NOTE: Near the engine number is a three letter code: first letter refers to the cylinder bore; second letter refers to the crankshaft main bearings; third letter refers to the size of the connecting rod bearings. Letter "A" means standard, letter "B" means .010 undersize, letter "C" means .010 oversize. Engines not marked are standard in all respects.

RAMBLER

ENGINE NO.	NO. CYL.	CID	HORSE-POWER	COMP. RATIO	CARB
B-1001/UP	6	196	120	7.47:1	1 BC

STATESMAN

ENGINE NO.	NO. CYL.	CID	HORSE-POWER	COMP. RATIO	CARB
DB-1001/UP	6	196	130	7.47:1	2 BC

AMBASSADOR

ENGINE NO.	NO. CYL.	CID	HORSE-POWER	COMP. RATIO	CARB
A-279001/UP	6	252	135	7.6:1	1 BC
LMA-277001/UP	6	252	145	7.6:1	2-1 BC
P-21001/UP	8	352	220	9.55:1	2 BC
G-1001/UP	8	250	190	8.0:1	2 BC

1957 RAMBLER

1957 RAMBLER

1957 NASH AMBASSADOR SUPER

1957 NASH REBEL

VEHICLE IDENTIFICATION NUMBER

```
• Y - 1 6 5 1 0 1 •
```

Located on the plate attached to the cowl under the hood on the right side.

FIRST DIGIT: Identifies the model

MODEL	CODE
Rambler - 6	D
Rambler - V8	A
Rebel	F
Ambassador - V8	V

LAST SIX DIGITS: Identify the basic production sequence number

Rambler - 6	341001/up
Rambler - V8	1001/up
Rebel	1001/up
Ambassador - V8	16501/up

BODY NUMBER PLATE

Located at the same location as the serial number plate.

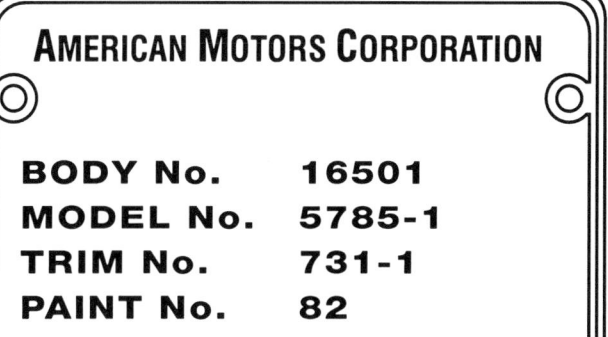

```
AMERICAN MOTORS CORPORATION

BODY No.     16501
MODEL No.    5785-1
TRIM No.     731-1
PAINT No.    82
```

EXAMPLE:

Sedan, 4-dr. Ambassador V-8 Super	5785-1
Blue/White cloth/vinyl	T-731-1
Pacific Blue	P82

THE BODY NUMBER is the same as the VIN number.

MODEL NUMBER

RAMBLER-6 - DELUXE

BODY STYLE	CODE
Sedan, 4-dr.	5715

RAMBLER-6 - SUPER

BODY STYLE	CODE
Sedan, 4-dr.	5715-1
Hardtop sedan, 4-dr.	5719-1
Station wagon, 4-dr. (Cross Country)	5718-1

RAMBLER-6 - CUSTOM

BODY STYLE	CODE
Sedan, 4-dr.	5715-2
Station wagon, 4-dr.	5718-2

RAMBLER-V8 - SUPER

BODY STYLE	CODE
Sedan, 4-dr.	5725-1
Station wagon, 4-dr.	5728-1

RAMBLER-V8 - CUSTOM

BODY STYLE	CODE
Sedan, 4-dr.	5725-2
Hardtop sedan, 4-dr.	5729-2
Station wagon, 4-dr.	5728-2
Hardtop, 4-dr. (Cross Country)	5723-2

REBEL

BODY STYLE	CODE
Hardtop sedan, 4-dr.	5739-3

AMBASSADOR-V8 - SUPER

BODY STYLE	CODE
Sedan, 4-dr.	5785-1
Sedan, 2-dr.	5787-1

AMBASSADOR V8 - CUSTOM

BODY STYLE	CODE
Sedan, 4-dr.	5785-2
Hardtop, 2-dr. (Country Club)	5787-2

THE COLOR CODE indicates the paint color used on the vehicle. Two-tone combinations: The first digits identify the lower body color; the second digits identify the upper body color. Three-tone combinations: The first digits identify the lower body color; the second digits identify the intermediate body color; the third digits identify the upper body color.

COLOR	CODE
Classic Black	P1
Bermuda Green	P67
Frost White	P72
Pacific Blue	P82
Glacier Blue	P84
Lagoon Blue	P85
Plum Metallic	P86
Berkshire Green	P87
Oregon Green	P88
Avocado Metallic	P89
Mardi Gras Red	P90
Mojave Yellow	P92
Sierra Peach	P93
Cinnamon Bronze Metallic	P94
Gotham Gray Metallic	P95
Rebel Silver	P96

THE TRIM CODE indicates the color and material scheme used on the vehicle.

RAMBLER

COLOR	CLOTH	VINYL	LEATHER	CODE
Blue/White	•	•		T702,T737
Gray/White	•	•		T707,T739
Green/White	•	•		T725,T738
Coral Saran/White	•	•		T732
Black/Red	•	•		T712
Black/Peach	•	•		T718
Black/Avocado	•	•		T720
Blue/Blue	•	•		T721
Green/Green	•	•		T723
Gray/Red	•	•		T713
Gray/Avocado	•	•		T730
Brown		•		T714
Blue/Blue	•		•	T708
Green/Green	•		•	T710
Gray/Red	•		•	T740
Gray/Green	•		•	T741
Black/Red	•		•	T743
Black/White	•		•	T744

AMBASSADOR

COLOR	CLOTH	VINYL	LEATHER	CODE
Blue/White	•	•		T731-1
Green/White	•	•		T733-1
Gray/White	•	•		T736-1
Black/Red	•	•		T755
Black/Peach	•	•		T748
Black/Avocado	•	•		T750
Blue/Blue	•	•		T751
Blue/White	•	•		T752
Green/Green	•	•		T753
Green/White	•	•		T754
Gray/Red	•	•		T756
Gray/Peach	•	•		T758
Gray/Avocado	•	•		T760
Blue/Blue	•		•	T767
Green/Green	•		•	T769
Black/Red	•		•	T771
Gray/Red	•		•	T772
Gray/Green	•		•	T774

ENGINE SPECIFICATIONS

ENGINE NUMBER - V8 numbers are located on the machined surface on the lower right front corner of the cylinder block; 6-cylinder numbers are located on the right side front of the cylinder block; 6-cylinders with air conditioning are located on the left side front corner of the cylinder block. NOTE: Near the engine number is a three letter code: first letter refers to the cylinder bore; second letter refers to the crankshaft main bearings; third letter refers to the size of the connecting rod bearings. Letter "A" means standard; letter "B" means .010 undersize; letter "C" means .010 oversize. Engines not marked are standard in all respects.

RAMBLER

ENGINE NO.	NO. CYL.	CID	HORSE-POWER	COMP. RATIO	CARB
B-73001/UP	6	196	120	8.0:1	1 BC
CB-2001/UP	6	196	135	8.0:1	2 BC
G-7501/UP	8	250	190	8.0:1	2 BC
CG-1001/UP	8	250	203	8.0:1	4 BC

REBEL

ENGINE NO.	NO. CYL.	CID	HORSE-POWER	COMP. RATIO	CARB
CN-1001/UP	8	327	255	9.5:1	4 BC

AMBASSADOR

ENGINE NO.	NO. CYL.	CID	HORSE-POWER	COMP. RATIO	CARB
N-1001/UP	8	327	288	9.5:1	F.I.

NASH

ENGINE NO.	NO. CYL.	CID	HORSE-POWER	COMP. RATIO	CARB
V-16501/UP	8	327	255	9.0:1	4 BC

1958 RAMBLER AMERICAN

1958 RAMBLER REBEL

1958 RAMBLER

VEHICLE IDENTIFICATION NUMBER

| ● | M - 1 0 0 1 | ● |

Located on the plate attached to the cowl under the hood.

FIRST DIGIT: Identifies the model

MODEL	CODE
Rambler - 6	D
Rambler American	M
Rebel V8	A
Ambassador V8	V

LAST FOUR DIGITS: Identify the basic production sequence number

Rambler American	1001/up
Rambler - 6	409001/up
Rebel V8	16001/up
Ambassador - V8	27001/up

BODY NUMBER PLATE

Located at the same location as the serial number plate.

AMERICAN MOTORS CORPORATION

BODY No.	1001
MODEL No.	5806
TRIM No.	—
PAINT No.	97

EXAMPLE:

Rambler American Deluxe Sedan, 2-dr.	5806
Trim no.	—
Frost White	72

THE BODY NUMBER is the same as the VIN number.

MODEL NUMBER

RAMBLER AMERICAN - DELUXE
BODY STYLE	CODE
Sedan, 2-dr.	5806
Business coupe, 2-dr.	5802

RAMBLER AMERICAN - SUPER
BODY STYLE	CODE
Sedan, 2-dr.	5806-1

RAMBLER-6 - DELUXE
BODY STYLE	CODE
Sedan, 4-dr.	5815
Station wagon, 4-dr. (Cross Country)	5818

RAMBLER-6 - SUPER
BODY STYLE	CODE
Sedan, 4-dr.	5815-1
Station wagon, 4-dr. (Cross Country)	5818-1
Hardtop sedan, 4-dr. (Country Club)	5819-1

RAMBLER-6 - CUSTOM
BODY STYLE	CODE
Sedan, 4-dr.	5815-2
Station wagon, 4-dr.	5818-2

REBEL-V8 - DELUXE
BODY STYLE	CODE
Sedan, 4-dr.	5825

REBEL-V8 - SUPER
BODY STYLE	CODE
Sedan, 4-dr.	5825-1
Station wagon, 4-dr. (Cross Country)	5828-1

REBEL-V8 - CUSTOM
BODY STYLE	CODE
Sedan, 4-dr.	5825-2
Hardtop sedan, 4-dr. (Country Club)	5829-2
Station wagon, 4-dr. (Cross Country)	5828-2

AMBASSADOR-V8 - SUPER
BODY STYLE	CODE
Sedan, 4-dr.	5885-1
Station wagon, 4-dr. (Cross Country)	5888-1

AMBASSADOR-V8 - CUSTOM

BODY STYLE	CODE
Station wagon, 4-dr.	5883-2
Sedan, 4-dr.	5885-2
Station wagon, 4-dr. (Cross Country)	5888-2
Hardtop sedan, 4-dr. (Country Club)	5889-2

THE COLOR CODE indicates the paint color used on the vehicle. Two-tone combinations: The first set of digits identify the body color; the second set of digits identify the accent color.

COLOR	CODE
Kimberly Blue	P2
Saranac Green	P3
Alamo Beige	P4
Autumn Yellow	P5
Georgian Rose	P6
Mariner Turquoise Metallic	P7
Frost White	P72
Mardi Gras Red	P90
Cinnamon Bronze Metallic	P94
Gotham Gray Metallic	P95
Brentwood Green	P97
Lakeshore Blue	P98
Frontenac Gray	P99

THE TRIM CODE indicates the color and material scheme used on the vehicle. There were no trim codes available.

ENGINE SPECIFICATIONS

ENGINE NUMBER - 6-Cylinder numbers are located on the machined surface on the upper left front corner of the cylinder block; V-8 numbers are located on the lower front of the cylinder block. NOTE: Near the engine number is a three letter code: first letter refers to the cylinder bore; second letter refers to the crankshaft main bearings; third letter refers to the size of the connecting rod bearings. Letter "A" means standard, letter "B" means .010 undersize, letter "C" means .010 oversize. Engines not marked are standard in all respects.

RAMBLER AMERICAN

ENGINE NO.	NO. CYL.	CID	HORSE-POWER	COMP. RATIO	CARB
E-1001/UP	6	196	90	8.0:1	1 BC
B-145001/UP	6	196	127	8.7:1	1 BC
CB-9001/UP	6	196	138	8.7:1	2 BC

REBEL

ENGINE NO.	NO. CYL.	CID	HORSE-POWER	COMP. RATIO	CARB
G-24001/UP	8	250	215	8.7:1	4 BC

AMBASSADOR

ENGINE NO.	NO. CYL.	CID	HORSE-POWER	COMP. RATIO	CARB
N-17001/UP	8	327	270	9.7:1	4 BC

1959 RAMBLER

1959 RAMBLER AMERICAN

1959 RAMBLER AMERICAN

1959 RAMBLER

VEHICLE IDENTIFICATION NUMBER

| • | M - 1 0 0 1 | • |

Located on the plate attached to the cowl under the hood.

FIRST DIGIT: Identifies the model

MODEL	CODE
Rambler - 6	D
Rambler American	M
Rebel V8	A
Ambassador V8	V

LAST FOUR DIGITS: Identify the basic production sequence number

Rambler American	32001/up
Rambler - 6	516001/up
Rebel V8	26101/up
Ambassador - V8	41501/up

BODY NUMBER PLATE

Located at the same location as the serial number plate.

AMERICAN MOTORS CORPORATION

BODY No.	**321001**
MODEL No.	**5906**
TRIM No.	**—**
PAINT No.	**14**

EXAMPLE:

American Deluxe Sedan, 2-dr.	5906
Trim no.	—
Caramel Copper Metallic	14

THE BODY NUMBER is the same as the VIN number.

MODEL NUMBER

RAMBLER AMERICAN - DELUXE
BODY STYLE	CODE
Business sedan, 2-dr.	5902
Station wagon, 2-dr.	5904
Sedan, 2-dr.	5906

RAMBLER AMERICAN - SUPER
BODY STYLE	CODE
Sedan, 2-dr.	5906-1
Station wagon, 2-dr.	5904-1

RAMBLER-6 - DELUXE
BODY STYLE	CODE
Sedan, 4-dr.	5915
Country station wagon, 4-dr.	5918

RAMBLER-6 - SUPER
BODY STYLE	CODE
Sedan, 4-dr.	5915-1
Hardtop sedan, 4-dr.	5919-1
Country station wagon, 4-dr.	5918-1

RAMBLER-6 - CUSTOM
BODY STYLE	CODE
Sedan, 4-dr.	5915-2
Country station wagon, 4-dr.	5918-2

REBEL-V8 - DELUXE
BODY STYLE	CODE
Sedan, 4-dr.	5925

REBEL-V8 - SUPER
BODY STYLE	CODE
Sedan, 4-dr.	5925-1
Country station wagon, 4-dr.	5928-1

REBEL-V8 - CUSTOM
BODY STYLE	CODE
Sedan, 4-dr.	5925-2
Hardtop sedan, 4-dr.	5929-2
Country station wagon, 4-dr.	5928-2

AMBASSADOR-V8 - DELUXE
BODY STYLE	CODE
Sedan, 4-dr.	5985

AMBASSADOR-V8 - SUPER
BODY STYLE	CODE
Sedan, 4-dr.	5985-1
Country station wagon, 4-dr.	5988-1

AMBASSADOR-V8 - CUSTOM

BODY STYLE	CODE
Sedan, 4-dr.	5985-2
Hardtop sedan, 4-dr.	5989-2
Country station wagon, 4-dr.	5988-2
Station wagon, 4-dr.	5983-2

THE COLOR CODE indicates the paint color used on the vehicle. Two-tone combinations: The first set of digits identify the body color; the second set of digits identify the accent color.

COLOR	CODE
Classic Black	P1
Alamo Beige	P4
Autumn Yellow	P5
Chatsworth Green	P8
Pine Ridge Green Metallic	P9
Placid Blue	P10
Nocturne Blue Metallic	P11
Aladdin Gray Metallic	P12
Oriental Red	P13
Caramel Copper Metallic	P14
Aqua Mist Metallic	P15
Cotillion Mauve	P16
Hibiscus Rose	P17
Frost White	P72
Frontenac Gray	P99

THE TRIM CODE indicates the color and material scheme used on the vehicle. There were no trim codes available.

ENGINE SPECIFICATIONS

ENGINE NUMBER - 6-Cylinder numbers are located on the machined surface on the upper left front corner of the cylinder block; V-8 numbers are located on the lower front of the cylinder block. NOTE: Near the engine number is a three letter code: first letter refers to the cylinder bore; second letter refers to the crankshaft main bearings; third letter refers to the size of the connecting rod bearings. Letter "A" means standard, letter "B" means .010 undersize, letter "C" means .010 oversize. Engines not marked are standard in all respects.

5901 - E-33001/up

5910, 1 BC - B-227001/up

5910, 2 BC - CB-36001/up

5920 - G-34501/up

5980 - N-32501/up

RAMBLER AMERICAN

ENGINE NO.	NO. CYL.	CID	HORSE-POWER	COMP. RATIO	CARB
E-33001/UP	6	196	90	8.0:1	1 BC
B-227001/UP	6	196	127	8.7:1	1 BC
CB-36001/UP	6	196	138	8.7:1	2 BC

REBEL

ENGINE NO.	NO. CYL.	CID	HORSE-POWER	COMP. RATIO	CARB
G-34501/UP	8	250	215	8.7:1	4 BC

AMBASSADOR

ENGINE NO.	NO. CYL.	CID	HORSE-POWER	COMP. RATIO	CARB
N-32501/UP	8	327	270	9.7:1	4 BC

1950 PACKARD CUSTOM

1950 PACKARD DELUXE EIGHT

1950 PACKARD

VEHICLE IDENTIFICATION NUMBER

Located on the left side of the cowl under the hood. Identifies series, year, model name and chassis number by using the body style number. The remaining figures constitute the consecutive number of the car.

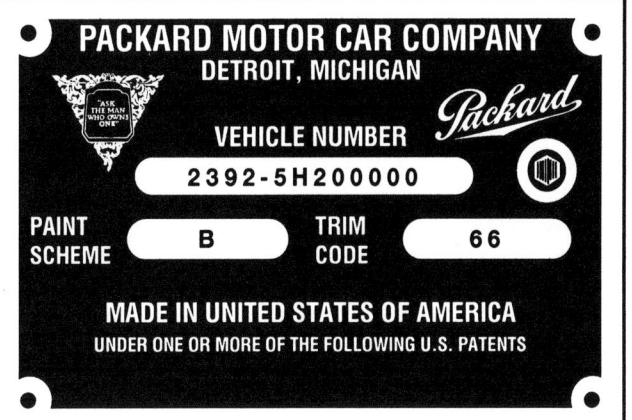

EXAMPLE:

2392-5	Standard 8 4 Dr. Sedan
B	Packard Blue Metallic
66	Gray/Blue Cloth\

THE FIRST FIVE DIGITS: Identify the body style number

STANDARD 8 - SERIES 23

BODY STYLE	CODE
Sedan, 4-dr.	2392-5
Club sedan	2395-5
Station sedan	2393-5
Used with Chassis No.	2301-5

STANDARD 8 DELUXE - SERIES 23

BODY STYLE	CODE
Sedan, 4-dr.	2362-5
Club sedan	2365-5
Used with Chassis No.	2301-5

SUPER STANDARD 8 - SERIES 23

BODY STYLE	CODE
Sedan, 4-dr.	2382-5
Club sedan	2385-5
Used with Chassis No.	2302-5

SUPER STANDARD 8 DELUXE - SERIES 23

BODY STYLE	CODE
Sedan, 4-dr.	2372-5
Club sedan	2375-5
Used with Chassis No.	2302-5
Convertible	2379-5
Used with Chassis No.	2332-5

CUSTOM STANDARD 8 - SERIES 23

BODY STYLE	CODE
Sedan, 4-dr.	2352-5
Used with Chassis No.	2306-5
Convertible	2359-5
Used with Chassis No.	2333-5

LAST SEVEN DIGITS: Identify the basic production sequence number

NOTE: 1950 numbers are a continuation of 1949 numbers.

Standard Eight	H200000/up
Super Eight	H400000/up
Custom Eight	H600001/up

THE COLOR CODE indicates the paint color used on the vehicle.

COLOR	CODE
Lowell Gray Metallic	A
Packard Blue Metallic	B
Egyptian Sand	C
Granada Gray	C
Spruce Green Metallic	D
Corona Cream	F
Argentine Gray Metallic	G
Yosemite Blue Metallic	H
Valiant Green Metallic	K
Sylvan Green Metallic	N
Grenadier Maroon Metallic	P
Ash Green	Q
Coronet Blue Metallic	S
Turquoise Blue Lt.	S
Turquoise Blue	T
Matador Maroon Metallic	U
Arizona Beige	W
Seminole Beige	W
Black	X
Astral Blue Metallic	Y
Maumee Maize	Z

THE TRIM CODE indicates the key to the interior color and material scheme used on the vehicle.

COLOR	CLOTH	VINYL	LEATHER	CODE
Tan	•			46,61,69
Tan	•			79,501
Gray/Blue	•			66
Gray	•			68,78
Green	•			502
Blue	•			503
Maroon	•			504
Tan		•		314
Tan		•		614,624
Tan/Brown		•		724
Tan/Red		•		726
Red		•		316,626
Blue		•		319
Tan			•	524,824
Red			•	526,826
Blue			•	829

ENGINE NUMBER

Located on the upper left side of the cylinder block, same as the serial number.

Standard Eight H200000
Super Eight H400000
Custom Eight...H600001
* - An asterisk appearing after engine code indicates engine is bored .020" oversize.

ENGINE CODES

ENGINE MODEL	NO. CYL.	CID	HORSE-POWER	COMP. RATIO	CARB
2301-5	8	288	135	7.0:1	2 BC
2302-5/ 2332-5	8	327	150	7.0:1	2 BC
2306-5/ 2333-5	8	356	160	7.0:1	2 BC

1951 PACKARD

VEHICLE IDENTIFICATION NUMBER

Located on the left front door hinge post. Identifies series, year, model name and chassis number by using the body style number. The remaining figures constitute the consecutive number of the car.

PACKARD MOTOR CAR COMPANY
DETROIT, MICHIGAN

Packard

VEHICLE NUMBER

2492J200000

PAINT SCHEME   B   TRIM CODE   45

MADE IN UNITED STATES OF AMERICA
UNDER ONE OR MORE OF THE FOLLOWING U.S. PATENTS

EXAMPLE:

2492.."200" Standard 8, 4 Dr. Sedan
B...Packard Blue Metallic
45...Blue Cloth

FIRST FOUR DIGITS: Identify the body style number

"200" STANDARD 8 - SERIES 24

BODY STYLE	CODE
Sedan, 4-dr.	2492
Club sedan	2495
Business coupe	2498
Used with Chassis No.	2401

"200" DELUXE STANDARD 8 - SERIES 24

BODY STYLE	CODE
Sedan, 4-dr.	2462
Club sedan	2465
Used with Chassis No.	2401

"250" STANDARD 8 - SERIES 24

BODY STYLE	CODE
Sports coupe, Mayfair	2467
Convertible	2469
Used with Chassis No.	2401

"300" STANDARD 8 - SERIES 24

BODY STYLE	CODE
Sedan, 4-dr.	2472
Used with Chassis No.	2402

"400" STANDARD 8 DELUXE - SERIES 24

BODY STYLE	CODE
Sedan, 4-dr.	2452
Used with Chassis No.	2406

LAST SEVEN DIGITS: Identify the basic production sequence number

200	J200001
250	J400001
300	J400001
400	J600001

2nd Line of Serial Number Plate

THE COLOR CODE indicates the paint color used on the vehicle.

COLOR	CODE
Lowell Gray Metallic	A
Packard Blue Metallic	B
Granada Gray	C
Corona Cream	F
Argentine Gray Metallic	G
Yosemite Blue Metallic	H
Valiant Green Metallic	K
Sunset Red Metallic	L
Twilight Taupe Metallic	M
Ash Green	Q
Turquoise Blue Lt.	S
Packard Ivory	T
Matador Maroon Metallic	U
Seminole Beige	W
Black	X
Astral Blue Metallic	Y
Maumee Maize	Z

THE TRIM CODE indicates the interior color and material scheme used on the vehicle.

COLOR	CLOTH	VINYL	LEATHER	CODE
Gray	•			43,47,49
Gray	•			71,71A
Blue	•			45,63,503
Blue	•			603
Tan	•			501,601
Green	•			502,602
Green		•		312
Red		•		316
Blue		•		319
Black	•		•	691
Red	•		•	696
Green			•	822
Tan			•	824
Red			•	826
Blue			•	829

ENGINE NUMBER

Stamped on upper left side of cylinder block, same as the serial number.

200 ....J200001
250 400001
300 400001
400 600001

* A "Star" appearing after engine code indicates engine is bored .020" oversize.

ENGINE CODES

2401 SERIES

ENGINE MODEL	NO. CYL.	CID	HORSE-POWER	COMP. RATIO	CARB
200	8	288	135	7.0:1	2 BC
250	8	327	150	7.0:1	2 BC

2402 SERIES

ENGINE MODEL	NO. CYL.	CID	HORSE-POWER	COMP. RATIO	CARB
300	8	327	150	7.0:1	2 BC

2406 SERIES

ENGINE MODEL	NO. CYL.	CID	HORSE-POWER	COMP. RATIO	CARB
400	8	327	155	7.8:1	2 BC

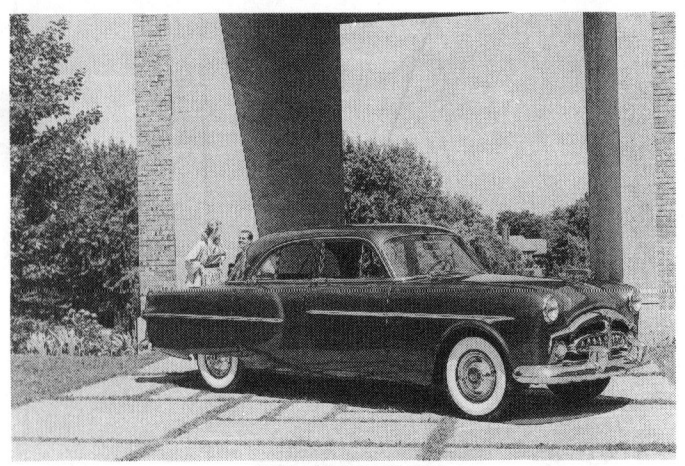

1952 PACKARD 300

1952 PACKARD MAYFAIR

1952 PACKARD CLIPPER

VEHICLE IDENTIFICATION NUMBER

Located on the left front door hinge post. Identifies series, year, model name and chassis number by using the body style number. The remaining figures constitute the consecutive number of the car.

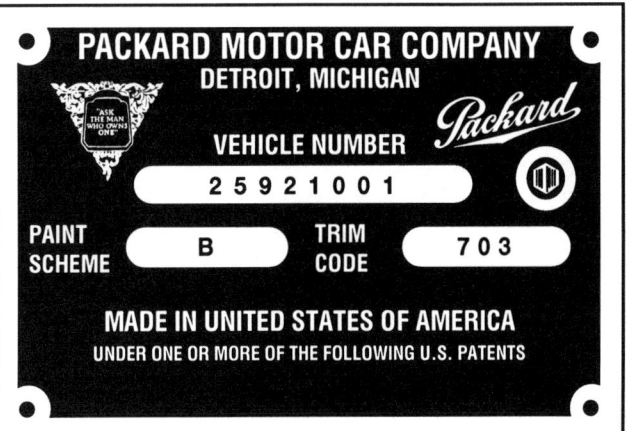

PACKARD MOTOR CAR COMPANY
DETROIT, MICHIGAN
Packard

VEHICLE NUMBER
2 5 9 2 1 0 0 1

PAINT SCHEME   B   TRIM CODE   7 0 3

MADE IN UNITED STATES OF AMERICA
UNDER ONE OR MORE OF THE FOLLOWING U.S. PATENTS

EXAMPLE:

2592	"200" 4 Dr. Sedan
B	Packard Blue Metallic
703	Blue/Gray Cloth

FIRST FOUR DIGITS: Identify the body style number

"200" STANDARD 8 - SERIES 25

BODY STYLE	CODE
Sedan, 4-dr.	2592
Club sedan	2595
Used with Chassis No.	2501

"200" DELUXE STANDARD 8 - SERIES 25

BODY STYLE	CODE
Sedan, 4-dr.	2562
Club sedan	2565
Used with Chassis No.	2501

"250" STANDARD 8 - SERIES 25

BODY STYLE	CODE
Sports coupe, Mayfair	2577
Convertible	2579
Used with chassis	2531

"300" STANDARD 8 - SERIES 25

BODY STYLE	CODE
Sedan, 4-dr.	2572
Used with Chassis No.	2502

"400" DELUXE STANDARD 8 - SERIES 25

BODY STYLE	CODE
Sedan, 4-dr.	2552
Used with Chassis No.	2506

LAST SEVEN DIGITS: Identify the basic production sequence number

200	K200001
250	K400001
300	K400001
400	K600001

THE COLOR CODE indicates the paint color used on the vehicle.

COLOR	CODE
Packard Blue Metallic	B
Labrador Gray	D
Argentine Gray Metallic	G
Yosemite Blue Metallic	H
Gallant Green Metallic	J
Sunset Red Metallic	L
Twilight Taupe Metallic	M
Aspen Green	O
Turquoise Blue Lt.	S
Packard Ivory	T
Matador Maroon Metallic	U
Jet Black	X

THE TRIM CODE indicates the key to the interior color and material scheme used on the vehicle.

COLOR	CLOTH	VINYL	LEATHER	CODE
Black/Gray	•			44,64,66
Black/Gray	•			74,76
Gray	•			71,71A,704
Brown/Tan	•			701
Green/Tan	•			702
Blue/Gray	•			703
Green/Gray	•			705
Green		•		312
Tan		•		314
Red		•		316
Blue		•		319
Black/Gray	•		•	491
Red/Gray	•		•	496
Black/Ivory			•	791
Red/Ivory			•	796
Green			•	822
Tan			•	824
Red			•	826,896
Blue			•	829
Black			•	891

ENGINE NUMBER

Stamped on the upper left side of the cylinder block, same as the serial number.

200	K200001
250	K400001
300	K400001
400	K600001

* A "Star" appearing after the engine code indicates engine is bored .020" oversize.

ENGINE CODES

ENGINE MODEL	NO. CYL.	CID	HORSE-POWER	COMP. RATIO	CARB
2601	8	288	135	7.0:1	2 BC
2631	8	327	150	7.0:1	2 BC
2602	8	327	150	7.0:1	2 BC
2606	8	327	155	7.8:1	2 BC

1953 PACKARD

1953 PACKARD CARIBBEAN

VEHICLE IDENTIFICATION NUMBER

Located on the left front door hinge post. Identifies series, year, model name and chassis number by using the body style number. The remaining figures constitute the consecutive number of the car.

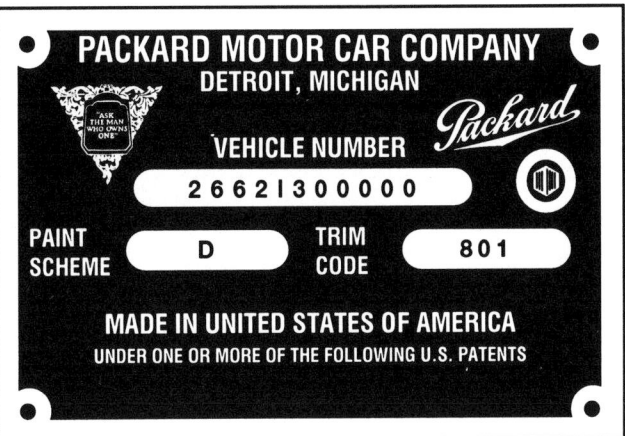

EXAMPLE:

2662 ....Clipper Deluxe 4 Dr. Sedan
D ....Carolina Cream
801 ....Brown/Tan Vinyl

FIRST FOUR DIGITS: Identify the body style number

CLIPPER STANDARD 8 - SERIES 26

BODY STYLE	CODE
Sedan, 4-dr.	2692
Club sedan	2695
Sportster	2697
Used with Chassis No.	2601

CLIPPER DELUXE STANDARD 8 - SERIES 26

BODY STYLE	CODE
Sedan, 4-dr.	2662
Club sedan	2665
Used with Chassis No.	2611

CAVALIER STANDARD 8 - SERIES 26

BODY STYLE	CODE
Sedan, 4-dr.	2672
Used with Chassis No.	2602

STANDARD 8 - SERIES 26

BODY STYLE	CODE
Mayfair	2677
Caribbean	2678
Convertible	2679
Used with Chassis No.	2631

PATRICIAN STANDARD DELUXE 8 - SERIES 26

BODY STYLE	CODE
Sedan, 4-dr.	2652
Formal sedan	2653
Used with Chassis No.	2606

CUSTOM STANDARD 8 - SERIES 26

BODY STYLE	CODE
Sedan, 4-dr.	2651
Limousine	2650
Used with Chassis No.	2626

LAST SEVEN DIGITS: Identify the basic production sequence number

Clipper	L200000
Clipper Deluxe	L300000
Cavalier	L400000
Standard 8	L400000
Patrician	L600000
Custom Standard	L600000

THE COLOR CODE indicates the paint color used on the vehicle. Two-tone combinations: The first letter identifies the upper body color, the second letter identifies the lower body color.

COLOR	CODE
Regimental Gray Metallic	A
Meridian Blue	B
Polaris Blue	C
Carolina Cream	D
Dresden Gray	F
Yosemite Blue Metallic	H
Galahad Green Metallic	K
Sunset Red Metallic	L
Topeka Tan	M
Orchard Green	O
Turquoise Blue Lt.	S
Packard Ivory	T
Matador Maroon Metallic	U
Sahara Sand	W
Black	X

THE TRIM CODE indicates the key to the interior color and material used on the vehicle.

COLOR	CLOTH	VINYL	LEATHER	CODE
Green	•			32,32A,52
Blue	•			33,33A,53
Blue	•			805
Gray	•			34,34A,54
Gray	•			804
Brown	•			807
Green/Green	•			82,802
Blue/Gray	•			83,803
Gray/Gray	•			84
Brown/Tan	•			801
Green		•		12,312A
Blue		•		13
Gray		•		14
Tan		•		314A
Red		•		316A
Green/Green			•	2
Gray/Blue			•	3
Gray/Gray			•	4
Green/White			•	72
Blue/White			•	73
Maroon/White			•	76
Black/White			•	77
Maroon			•	96
Black			•	97
Blue			•	829A
Black/Cream			•	91,98,198
Black/Ivory			•	198A
Maroon/Cream			•	94,194
Maroon/Ivory			•	94A,194A
Maroon/Tan	•		•	95
Maroon/Gray	•		•	46
Black/Gray	•		•	47
Cream/Blue	•		•	93
Ivory/Blue	•		•	93A
Ivory/Maroon	•	•		92A
Maroon/Tan	•	•		95
Ivory/Blue	•	•		93A

ENGINE NUMBER

The engine number is located on the upper left side of the cylinder block, same as the serial number.

Clipper L200000

Clipper Deluxe L300000

Cavalier..L400000

Standard 8 ....L400000

Patrician...L600000

Custom Standard.....................................L600000

* A "Star" appearing after the engine code indicates the engine is bored .020" oversize.

ENGINE CODES

2601 SERIES

ENGINE MODEL	NO. CYL.	CID	HORSE-POWER	COMP. RATIO	CARB
2601	8	288	150	7.7:1	2 BC
2611	8	327	160	8.0:1	2 BC
2602/2606/2626/2631	8	327	180	8.0:1	4 BC

1954 PACKARD CLIPPER PANAMA

VEHICLE IDENTIFICATION NUMBER

Located on the left front door hinge post. Identifies series, year, model name and chassis number by using the body style number. The remaining figures constitute the consecutive number of the car.

EXAMPLE:

5485 ....Clipper Special Club Sedan
C ....Polaris Blue
53 ....Blue Cloth

FIRST FOUR DIGITS: Identify the body style number

CLIPPER SPECIAL - SERIES 54

BODY STYLE	CODE
Sedan, 4-dr.	5482
Club sedan	5485
Used with Chassis No.	5400

CLIPPER DELUXE - SERIES 54

BODY STYLE	CODE
Sedan, 4-dr.	5492
Club sedan	5495
Sportster	5497
Used with Chassis No.	5401

CLIPPER SUPER - SERIES 54

BODY STYLE	CODE
Sedan, 4-dr.	5462
Club sedan	5465
Panama, hardtop	5467
Used with Chassis No.	5411

CAVALIER - SERIES 54

BODY STYLE	CODE
Sedan, 4-dr.	5472
Used with Chassis No.	5402

STANDARD 8 - SERIES 54

BODY STYLE	CODE
Pacific, hardtop	5477
Caribbean convertible	5478
Convertible	5479
Used with Chassis No.	5431

PATRICIAN - SERIES 54

BODY STYLE	CODE
Sedan, 4-dr.	5452
Formal sedan	5453
Used with Chassis No.	5406

CUSTOM - SERIES 54

BODY STYLE	CODE
Sedan, 4-dr.	5451
Limousine, 4-dr.	5450
Used with Chassis no.	5426

LAST SEVEN DIGITS: Identify the basic production sequence number

Clipper Special	M200000
Clipper Deluxe	M300000
Clipper Super	M300000
Cavalier	M400000
Standard 8 - 5431	M600000
Patrician	M600000
Custom Standard	M600000

THE COLOR CODE indicates the paint color used on the vehicle. Two-tone combinations: The first letter identifies the upper body color, the second letter identifies the lower body color.

COLOR	CODE
Varsity Gray Metallic	A
Meridian Blue Metallic	B
Polaris Blue	C
Mackinaw Gray	F
Chariot Red	G
Bikini Blue	H
Gulf Green	J
Galahad Green Metallic	K
Orchard Green	O
Bellevue Green	N
Packard Ivory	T
Matador Maroon Metallic	U
Sahara Sand	W
Black	X

THE TRIM CODE indicates the key to the interior color and material scheme used on the vehicle.

COLOR	CLOTH	VINYL	LEATHER	CODE
Green	•			32A,55
Green	•			975,975A
Green/Green	•			32B,45,52A
Green/Green	•			58,65,75,95
Green/Green	•			82A
Blue	•			33A,53
Blue	•			976,976A
Blue/Blue	•			46,66,76,96
Blue/Blue	•			83A
Gray/Blue	•			33B,53A,54
Gray	•			34A,57,59
Gray/Gray	•			34B,47,54A
Gray/Gray	•			67,77,84A,97
Brown	•			50
Tan	•			51
Brown/Tan	•			52
Gray/Green	•			56
Maroon	•			973,973A
Black	•			978,978A
Green/Green			•	5,205
Blue/Gray			•	6
Gray/Gray			•	7
Green/White			•	82
Blue/White			•	83
Red/White			•	86
Black/White			•	87
Red			•	203
Black			•	208
Black/Ivory			•	209
Red/Ivory			•	206
Red/Black			•	207
Green/Green		•		25
Blue/Gray		•		26
Gray/Gray		•		27
Maroon/Black	•		•	113,123
Green/Green	•	•		115,125,325
Ivory/Blue	•		•	116,126
Ivory/Black	•	•		118,128,329
Black/White	•		•	324
Black/Yellow	•		•	326
Red/Black	•		•	327

ENGINE NUMBER

Located on the upper left side of the cylinder block, same as the serial number.

Clipper Special M200000

Clipper Deluxe M300000

Cavalier...M300000

Standard 8 - 5431 ....M600000

Patrician M600000

Custom Standard..M600000

* A "Star" appearing after the engine code indicates the engine bore .020"
  oversize.

ENGINE CODES

ENGINE MODEL	NO. CYL.	CID	HORSE-POWER	COMP. RATIO	CARB
5400	8	288	150	7.7:1	2 BC
5401/5411	8	327	165	8.0:1	2 BC
5402	8	327	185	8.0:1	4 BC
5406/5426/5431	8	359	212	8.7:1	4 BC

1955 PACKARD 400

1955 PACKARD

1955 PACKARD

1955 PACKARD CLIPPER

VEHICLE IDENTIFICATION NUMBER

● 5 5 2 2 1 0 0 1 ●

Located on the left front door hinge post. Identifies series, year, model name and chassis number by using the body style number. The remaining figures constitute the consecutive number of the car.

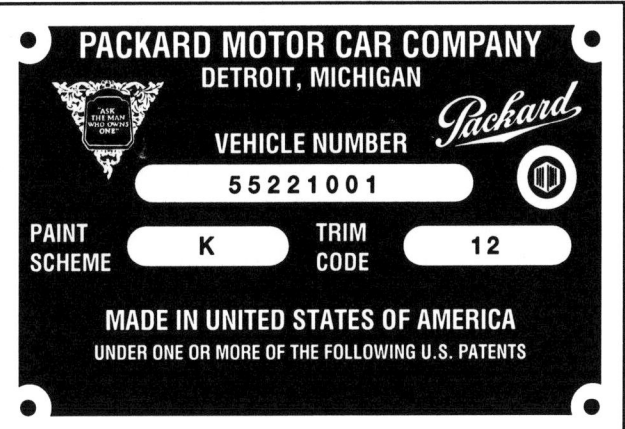

EXAMPLE:

5522	Clipper Deluxe 4 Dr.
K	Topaz Metallic
12	Blue Cloth

FIRST FOUR DIGITS: Identify the body style number

CLIPPER DELUXE - SERIES 55

BODY STYLE	CODE
Sedan, 4-dr.	5522
Used with Chassis No.	5540

CLIPPER SUPER - SERIES 55

BODY STYLE	CODE
Sedan, 4-dr.	5542
Panama, hardtop	5547
Used with Chassis No.	5540

CLIPPER CUSTOM - SERIES 55

BODY STYLE	CODE
Sedan, 4-dr.	5562
Constellation, hardtop	5567
Used with Chassis No.	5560

PACKARD - SERIES 55

BODY STYLE	CODE
Patrician, 4-dr.	5582
Four Hundred hardtop	5587
Caribbean convertible	5588
Used with chassis	5580

LAST FOUR DIGITS: Identify the basic production sequence number

All series start with 1001

THE COLOR CODE indicates the paint color used on the vehicle. Two-tone combinations: The first letter identifies the upper body color, the second letter identifies the lower body color.

COLOR	CODE
Jade	A
Tourmaline	B
Emerald Metallic	C
Zircon	D
Ultramarine Metallic	E
Sapphire Metallic	F
Moonstone	G
Gray Pearl Metallic	H
Fire Opal	I
Topaz Metallic	K
Turquoise	L
White Jade	M
Agate	N
Citrine	P
Sardonyx	R
Rose Quartz	U
Onyx	V

THE TRIM CODE indicates the key to the interior color and material scheme used on the vehicle.

CLIPPER TRIM

COLOR	CLOTH	VINYL	LEATHER	CODE
Gray/Black	•			11,21,41
Blue/Blue	•			12,22,42
Green/Green	•			13,23,43
Green/Green		•		3
Blue/Blue		•		2
Gray/Black		•		5
Green/Green			•	3,6
Blue/Blue			•	2,7
Red/Black			•	4
Charcoal/White	•	•		40,50
Gray/Black	•	•		31
Blue/Blue	•	•		32,52
Green/Green	•	•		33,53
Black/Turquoise	•	•		54
Black/Red	•	•		56
Black/Yellow	•	•		57

PACKARD TRIM

COLOR	CLOTH	VINYL	LEATHER	CODE
Blue/Blue	•		•	62
Green/Green	•		•	63
Gray/Gray	•		•	65
Tan/Brown	•		•	69
Blue/White	•		•	82
Green/White	•		•	83
Tan/White	•		•	81
Black/White	•		•	85
Black/White/ Turquoise	•		•	84
Black/White/Red	•		•	86
Black/White/ Yellow	•		•	87
Tan/White/Brown	•		•	89
Green/Green			•	72,6
Blue/Blue			•	73,60,7
Red/Black			•	9
White/Blue			•	92
White/Green			•	93
White/Red/Black			•	96
White/Fuchsia/Gray			•	97

ENGINE NUMBER

Located on the front end of the block between the cylinder banks, directly behind the water pump, same as the serial number.

Example: 5522-1001

All series start with a four digit model number and a 4-digit consecutive number starting with 1001.

ENGINE CODE

ENGINE MODEL	NO. CYL.	CID	HORSE-POWER	COMP. RATIO	CARB
5540	8	320	225	8.5:1	4 BC
5560	8	352	245	8.5:1	4 BC
5580	8	352	260	8.5:1	4 BC
5588	8	352	275	8.5:1	2-4 BC

1956 PACKARD

1956 PACKARD CLIPPER

1956 PACKARD CARIBBEAN

1956 PACKARD CARIBBEAN

VEHICLE IDENTIFICATION NUMBER

Located on the left front door hinge post. Identifies series, year, model name and chassis number by using the body style number. The remaining figures constitute the consecutive number of the car.

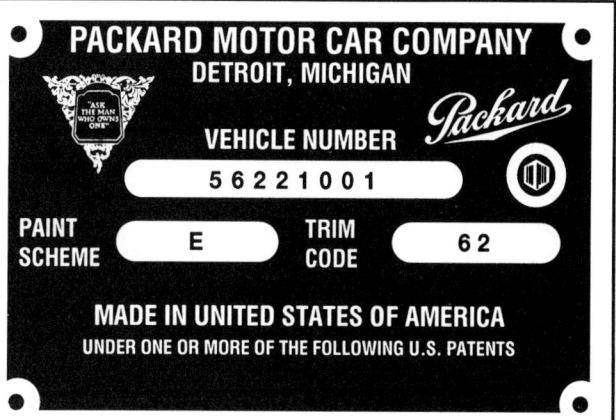

PACKARD MOTOR CAR COMPANY
DETROIT, MICHIGAN

Packard

VEHICLE NUMBER

5 6 2 2 1 0 0 1

PAINT SCHEME — E   TRIM CODE — 62

MADE IN UNITED STATES OF AMERICA
UNDER ONE OR MORE OF THE FOLLOWING U.S. PATENTS

EXAMPLE:

5622	Clipper Deluxe 4 Dr. Sedan
E	Danube Blue
62	Blue Cloth and Leather

FIRST FOUR DIGITS: Identify the body style number

CLIPPER DELUXE - SERIES 56

BODY STYLE	CODE
Sedan, 4-dr.	5622
Used with Chassis No.	5640

CLIPPER SUPER - SERIES 56

BODY STYLE	CODE
Sedan, 4-dr.	5642
Hardtop	5647
Used with Chassis No.	5640

CLIPPER CUSTOM - SERIES 56

BODY STYLE	CODE
Sedan, 4-dr.	5662
Constellation, hardtop	5667
Used with Chassis No.	5660

EXECUTIVE - SERIES 56

BODY STYLE	CODE
Sedan, 4-dr.	5672A
Hardtop	5677A
Used with Chassis No.	5670

PACKARD - SERIES 56

BODY STYLE	CODE
Patrician, 4-dr.	5682
Four Hundred hardtop	5687
Used with Chassis No.	5680

CARIBBEAN - SERIES 56

BODY STYLE	CODE
Hardtop	5697
Convertible	5699
Used with Chassis No.	5688

LAST FOUR DIGITS: Identify the basic production sequence number

All series start with 1001

THE COLOR CODE indicates the paint color used on the vehicle. Two-tone combinations: The first letter identifies the upper body color, the second letter identifies the lower body color.

COLOR	CODE
Shannon Green	A
Tahitian Jade	B
Eire Green	C
Norwegian Forest	D
Danube Blue	E
Holland Blue	F
Aegian Blue	G
Adriatic Blue	H
Tangier Red	J
Scottish Heather	K
Persian Aqua	L
Dover White	M
Maltese Gray	N
Jamaican Yellow	P
Mohave Tan	R
Roman Copper Metallic	S
Naples Orange	T
Corsican Black	V

THE TRIM CODE indicates the key to the interior color and material scheme used on the vehicle.

PATRICIAN TRIM

COLOR	CLOTH	VINYL	LEATHER	CODE
Gray/Gray	•		•	61
Blue/Blue	•		•	62
Green/Green	•		•	63
Copper/Copper	•		•	69
Blue/White	•		•	72,162
Green/White	•		•	73,163
Black/White	•		•	75,165
Copper/White	•		•	79,169

FOUR HUNDRED TRIM

COLOR	CLOTH	VINYL	LEATHER	CODE
Blue/White	•		•	82
Green/White	•		•	83
Black/White/ Turquoise	•		•	84
Black/White	•		•	85
Black/Red/White	•		•	86
Copper/White	•		•	89
Black/Yellow/White	•		•	87
Blue/White			•	182
Green/White			•	183
Black/White			•	185
Red/White/Black			•	186
Copper/White			•	189

CARIBBEAN CONVERTIBLE TRIM

COLOR	CLOTH	VINYL	LEATHER	CODE
White/Black/ Vermillion	•		•	90
White/Copper/ Blue			•	92
Copper/White/Blue	•		•	92
Gray/Vermillion/ White	•		•	290
Vermillion/Black/ White			•	290
Copper/Blue/White			•	292
Blue/Copper/White	•		•	292
Gray/White/Green	•		•	93
White/Black/Green			•	03
Gray/White/Red	•		•	96
White/Gray/Red			•	96
Gray/Green/White	•		•	293
Green/Black/White			•	293
Gray/Red/White	•		•	296
Red/Gray/White			•	296

CLIPPER TRIM

COLOR	CLOTH	VINYL	LEATHER	CODE
Gray/Black	•	•		11,31
Blue/Blue	•	•		12,32,52
Green/Green	•	•		13,33,53
Gray/Black	•			21,41
Blue/Blue	•			22,42
Green/Green	•			23,43
Black/Turquoise	•	•		54
Black/White	•	•		55
Black/Red	•	•		56
Black/Yellow	•	•		57
White/Blue			•	112,122
White/Green			•	113,123
White/Black			•	115,125

ENGINE NUMBER

19-28

Located on the front end of the block between the cylinder banks, directly behind the water pump, same as the serial number. All series start with a four digit model number, and a 4-digit consecutive number starting with 1001.

Example: 5622-1001

ENGINE CODES

ENGINE MODEL	NO. CYL.	CID	HORSE-POWER	COMP. RATIO	CARB
5540	8	352	240	9.5:1	4 BC
5560	8	352	275	9.5:1	4 BC
5570	8	352	275	9.5:1	4 BC
5580	8	374	290	10.0:1	4 BC
5588	8	374	310	10.0:1	2-4 BC

1957 PACKARD CLIPPER

VEHICLE IDENTIFICATION NUMBER

● 5 7 L Y 8 1 0 0 1 ●

Located on the left front door hinge post. Identifies year, model and consecutive number of the car.

FIRST THREE DIGITS: Identify the model

MODEL	CODE
Clipper	57L

FOURTH AND FIFTH DIGITS: Identify the body style

BODY STYLE	CODE
Sedan, 4-dr.	Y8
Station wagon	P8

LAST FOUR DIGITS: Identify the basic production sequence number

All series start with 1001

BODY NUMBER PLATE

Located on the engine cowl. Identifies the car model, body style and body number.

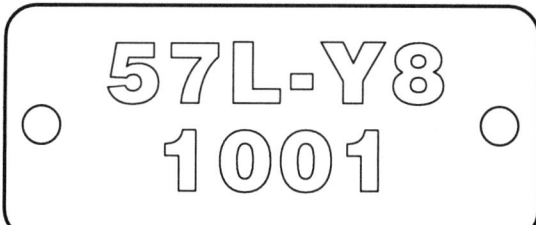

EXAMPLE:

57L	Clipper
Y8	4-Dr. sedan
1001	Production sequence

THE MODEL NUMBER CODE indicates the model type.

MODEL	CODE
1957 Clipper	57L

THE BODY STYLE indicates the body style of the vehicle.

BODY STYLE	CODE
Sedan, 4-dr.	Y8
Station wagon, 4-dr.	P8

THE BODY NUMBER starts with 1001/up.

THE PAINT CODE is located on a sticker attached to the underneath portion of the instrument panel directly under the glove compartment.

THE COLOR CODE indicates the paint color used on the vehicle.

COLOR	CODE
Arctic White	1026-BBA
Glendale Green Metallic	1033-BBH
Wedgewood Blue	1035-BBJ
Turquoise	1036-BBK
Taupe Metallic	1037-BBL
Coppertone Metallic	1030-BBE
Tiara Gold Metallic	1031-BBF
Woodsmoke Gray Metallic	1032-BBG
Azure Blue Metallic	1034-BBI
Cumberland Gray	1044-BBT
Lilac	1042-BBR
Regal Red	1043-BBS

THE TRIM CODE indicates the key to the interior color and material scheme used on the vehicle. The trim codes are not available.

ENGINE NUMBER

Located on the machined pad on top of the cylinder block. All series start with LS-101.

ENGINE CODES

ENGINE MODEL	NO. CYL.	CID	HORSE-POWER	COMP. RATIO	CARB
57LY	8	289	275	7.5:1	2 BC*
57LP	8	289	275	7.5:1	2 BC*

* Supercharged

1958 PACKARD

VEHICLE IDENTIFICATION NUMBER

$\bullet$ V 8 - 5 8 L - 6 1 0 1 $\bullet$

Located on the left front door hinge post. Identifies year, model and consecutive number of the car.

FIRST DIGITS: Identify the year and model

MODEL	CODE
Packard	58L
Hawk	58LS

LAST FOUR DIGITS: Identify the basic production sequence number

All sedan, hardtop and station wagon series start with 6101. Packard Hawk starts with 1001.

BODY NUMBER PLATE

Located on the engine cowl. Identifies the car model, body style and body number.

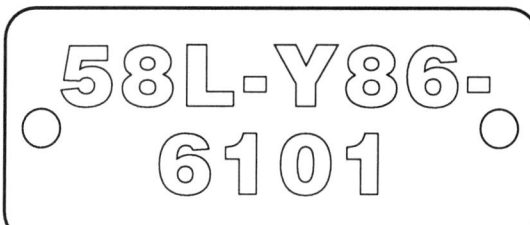

EXAMPLE:

58L	Packard
Y8	4-Dr. sedan
6101	Production sequence

THE MODEL NUMBER CODE indicates the model type.

MODEL	CODE
Packard	58L
Hawk	58LS

THE BODY STYLE indicates the body style of the vehicle.

BODY STYLE	CODE
Sedan, 4-dr.	Y8
Hardtop	J8
Station wagon, 4-dr.	P8
Hawk hardtop	K9

THE BODY NUMBER for Packard starts with 6101/up; Hawk starts with 1001/up.

THE PAINT CODE is located on a sticker attached to the underneath portion of the instrument panel directly under the glove compartment.

THE COLOR CODE indicates the paint color used on the vehicle.

COLOR	CODE
Glasgow Gray	1065-BCO
Parchment White	1066-BCP
White Gold Metallic	1061-BCK
Canyon Copper Metallic	1062-BCL
Parade Red	1068-BCR
Cliff Gray	1054-BCD
Mountain Blue Metallic	1057-BCG
Jewel Beige	1060-BCJ
Glen Green	1063-BCM
Loch Blue	1064-BCN
Bluff Gray Metallic	1055-BCE
Waterfall Blue	1056-BCF
Surf Green	1058-BCH
Park Green Metallic	1059-BCI

THE TRIM CODE indicates the key to the interior color and material scheme used on the vehicle. No trim codes were available.

ENGINE NUMBER

Located on the machined pad on top of the cylinder block. All series start with three digit model number and consecutive number starting with 101. Hawk starts with LS-5201.

ENGINE CODES

ENGINE MODEL	NO. CYL.	CID	HORSE- POWER	COMP. RATIO	CARB
58L	8	289	225	8.3:1	4 BC
58LS	8	289	275	7.8:1	2 BC*

* Supercharged

NOTE: THE PACKARD LINE WAS DISCONTINUED AFTER THE 1958 MODEL YEAR.

1950 STUDEBAKER

1950 STUDEBAKER

1950 STUDEBAKER

VEHICLE IDENTIFICATION NUMBER

● G - 4 6 8 1 0 ●

The VIN number is located on the plate on the left front door pillar post.

The letter and numbers identify the model number, starting production numbers and assembly plant.

MODEL	STARTING NO./ASSY. PLANT South Bend, IN	STARTING NO./ASSY. PLANT Los Angeles, CA
Champion	G-46810/up	G-851801/up
Commander	4398601/up	4839001/up

BODY NUMBER PLATE

Located on the cowl under the hood.

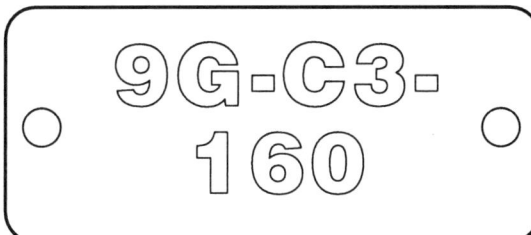

EXAMPLE: 10G-C3-160

9G	1950 Champion
C3	Deluxe coupe, 5-pass.
160	160th car produced

The first series of numbers and letters indicates the model.

MODEL	CODE
Champion	9G
Commander	17A

The second series of digits indicates the body type.

CHAMPION

BODY TYPE	CODE
Deluxe coupe, 5-pass.	C3
Deluxe sedan, 2-dr.	F3
Deluxe coupe, 3-pass.	Q1
Deluxe sedan, 4-dr.	W3
Custom coupe, 5-pass.	C1
Custom sedan, 2-dr.	F1
Custom coupe, 3-pass.	Q4
Custom sedan, 4-dr.	W1
Regal coupe, 5-pass.	C5
Regal sedan, 2-dr.	F5
Regal coupe, 3-pass.	Q2
Regal convertible	S2
Regal sedan, 4-dr.	S5

COMMANDER

BODY TYPE	CODE
Regal coupe, 5-pass.	C3
Regal sedan, 2-dr.	F3
Regal sedan, 4-dr.	W3
State coupe, 5-pass.	C5
State sedan, 2-dr.	F5
State convertible	S2
State sedan, 4-dr.	W5
State Land Cruiser, 4-dr.	Y5

The third series of digits indicates the particular body number of that type manufactured.

THE COLOR CODE indicates the paint color used on the vehicle. The code is located in the glove box.

COLOR	CODE
Velvet Black	W-ND
Aqua Green	W-VT
Surf Gray	W-VR
Midnight Blue	8303W-UP
Bahama Mist Metallic	8263W-UF
Highland Mist Metallic	8266W-UG
Plaza Gray	8283W-UL
Concord Blue	8293W-UN
Bermuda Green	8307W-UR
Copper Mist Metallic	8318W-UT
Black Cherry	8336W-UY
Comanche Red	8337W-UZ
Grove Green	8338W-VA
Falcon Gray	8339W-VB
Aqua Green	W-VC
Steel Mist Metallic	8341W-VD
Fiesta Tan	8364W-VF
Rio Green	8382W-VY
Maui Blue	8388W-VZ
Shenandoah Green	8401W-VO
Old Ivory	8405W-VP
Aero Blue	8417W-VT
Tulip Cream	W-SS

THE TRIM CODE indicates the trim color and material scheme used on the vehicle. There were no trim codes available.

ENGINE SPECIFICATIONS

The engine number is located on a pad on the upper front left corner of the engine block. The starting engine numbers are as follows:

MODEL	ENGINE NUMBER
Champion	521,001/up
Commander	H-370,001/up

ENGINE NUMBER	NO. CYL.	CID	HORSE-POWER	COMP. RATIO	CARB
9G	6	170	85	7.0:1	1 BC
17A	6	246	102	7.0:1	1 BC

1951 STUDEBAKER

1951 STUDEBAKER CHAMPION

1951 STUDEBAKER

1951 STUDEBAKER CHAMPION

VEHICLE IDENTIFICATION NUMBER

• G-1000001 •

The VIN number is located on the plate on the left front door pillar post.
The letter and numbers identify the model number, starting production numbers and assembly plant.

MODEL	STARTING NO./ASSY. PLANT South Bend, IN	STARTING NO.ASSY. PLANT Los Angeles, CA
Champion	G-1000001/up	G-889101/up
Commander	8110001/up	8800001/up

BODY NUMBER PLATE

Located on the cowl under the hood.

10G	1951 Champion
W3	Deluxe sedan, 4-dr.
160	160th car produced

The first series of numbers and letters indicates the model.

MODEL	CODE
Champion	10G
Commander	H

The second series of digits indicates the body type.

CHAMPION

BODY TYPE	CODE
Deluxe coupe, 5-pass.	C3
Deluxe sedan, 2-dr.	F3
Deluxe coupe, 3-pass.	Q1
Deluxe sedan, 4-dr.	W3
Custom coupe, 5-pass.	C1
Custom sedan, 2-dr.	F1
Custom coupe, 3-pass.	Q4
Custom sedan, 4-dr.	W1
Regal coupe, 5-pass.	C5
Regal sedan, 2-dr.	F5

Regal sedan, 4-dr.	W5
Regal coupe, 3-pass.	Q2
Regal convertible (hardtop)	K2
Regal convertible (folding top)	S2

COMMANDER

BODY TYPE	CODE
Regal coupe, 5-pass.	C3
Regal sedan, 2-dr.	F3
Regal sedan, 4-dr.	W3
State coupe, 5-pass.	C5
State sedan, 2-dr.	F5
State convertible (hardtop)	K2
State convertible (folding top)	S2
State sedan, 4-dr.	W5
State Land Cruiser, 4-dr.	Y5

The third series of digits indicates the particular body number of that type manufactured.

THE COLOR CODE indicates the paint color used on the vehicle. The code is located in the glove box.

COLOR	CODE
Velvet Black	W-ND
Aqua Green	W-VC
Surf Gray	W-VR
Plaza Gray	8283W-UL
Concord Blue	8293W-UN
Black Cherry	8336W-UY
Comanche Red	8337W-UZ
Shenandoah Green	8401W-VO
Sahara Sand	8444W-VX
Rio Green	8448W-VY
Maui Blue	8452W-VZ
Tulip Cream	W-SS
Old Ivory	W-VP
Aero Blue	W-VT

THE TRIM CODE indicates the trim color and material scheme used on the vehicle. There were no trim codes available.

ENGINE SPECIFICATIONS

The engine number is located on a boss on the top left front corner of the cylinder block. The starting engine numbers are as follows:

MODEL	ENGINE NUMBER
Champion	778,001/up
Commander	V-101/up

ENGINE NUMBER	NO. CYL.	CID	HORSE-POWER	COMP. RATIO	CARB
10G	6	170	85	7.0:1	1 BC
H	6	233	120	7.0:1	2 BC

1952 STUDEBAKER

1952 STUDEBAKER COMMANDER

VEHICLE IDENTIFICATION NUMBER

• G-115501 •

The VIN number is located on the plate on the left front door pillar post.

The letter and numbers identify the model number, starting production numbers and assembly plant.

MODEL	STARTING NO./ASSY. PLANT South Bend, IN	STARTING NO./ASSY. PLANT Los Angeles, CA
Champion	G-115501/up	G-907301/up
Commander	8217001/up	8816001/up

BODY NUMBER PLATE

Located on the cowl under the hood.

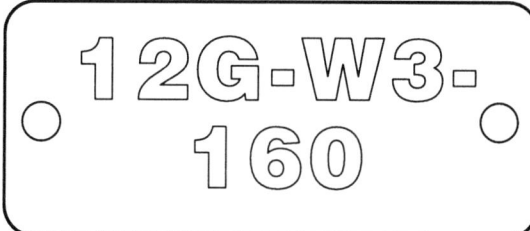

12G	1952 Champion
W3	Deluxe sedan, 4-dr.
160	160th car produced

The first series of numbers and letters indicates the model.

MODEL	CODE
Champion	12G
Commander	3H

The second series of digits indicates the body type.

CHAMPION

BODY TYPE	CODE
Deluxe coupe, 5-pass.	C3
Deluxe sedan, 2-dr.	F3
Deluxe sedan, 4-dr.	W3
Custom coupe, 5-pass.	C1
Custom sedan, 2-dr.	F1
Custom sedan, 4-dr.	W1
Regal coupe, 5-pass.	C5
Regal sedan, 2-dr.	F5
Regal sedan, 4-dr.	W5
Regal convertible (hardtop)	K2
Regal convertible (folding top)	S2

COMMANDER

BODY TYPE	CODE
Regal coupe, 5-pass.	C3
Regal sedan, 2-dr.	F3
Regal sedan, 4-dr.	W3
State coupe, 5-pass.	C5
State sedan, 2-dr.	F5
State convertible (hardtop)	K2
State convertible (folding top)	S2
State sedan, 4-dr.	W5
State Land Cruiser, 4-dr.	Y5

The third series of digits indicates the particular body number of that type manufactured.

THE COLOR CODE indicates the paint color used on the vehicle. The code is located in the glove box.

COLOR	CODE
Velvet Black	W-ND
Aqua Green	W-VC
Concord Blue	8293W-UN
Surf Gray	8409W-VR
Sahara Sand	8444W-VX
Rio Green	8448W-VY
Maui Blue	8452W-VZ
Cuban Red	8488W-WD
Nocturne Blue	8491W-WE
Tahoe Green	8494W-WF
Piedmont Gray	8498W-WG
Venice Red	8508W-WK
Spartan Rust	8511W-WL
Corning Olive	8514W-WM
Shell Ivory	8517W-WN
London Gray	8520W-WO
Shadow Green	8523W-WP
Walnut Brown	8526W-WR

THE TRIM CODE indicates the color scheme used on the vehicle. No trim codes were available.

ENGINE SPECIFICATIONS

The Champion engine number is located on a boss on the top left front corner of the cylinder block, the commander engine number is located on the boss at the top rear end of the cylinder block. The starting engine numbers are as follows:

MODEL	ENGINE NUMBER
Champion	911,501/up
Commander	V-123001/up

ENGINE NUMBER	NO. CYL.	CID	HORSE-POWER	COMP. RATIO	CARB
12G	6	170	85	7.0:1	1 BC
3H	8	233	120	7.0:1	2 BC

1953 STUDEBAKER

1953 STUDEBAKER COMMANDER STARLINER

1953 STUDEBAKER

1953 STUDEBAKER CHAMPION STARLITE

1953 STUDEBAKER

VEHICLE IDENTIFICATION NUMBER

● G - 1 1 9 7 5 0 1 ●

The VIN number is located on the plate on the left front door pillar post.

The letter and numbers identify the model number, starting production numbers and assembly plant.

MODEL	STARTING NO./ASSY. PLANT South Bend, IN	STARTING NO./ASSY. PLANT Los Angeles, CA
Champion	G-1197501/up	G-917701/up
Commander	8290001/up	8826801/up

BODY NUMBER PLATE

Located on the cowl under the hood.

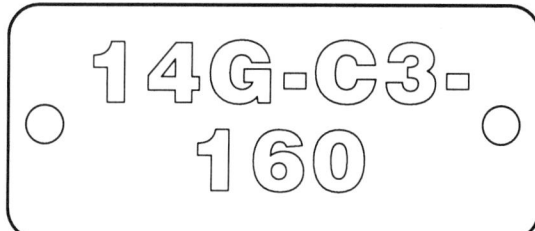

14G	1953 Champion
C3	Deluxe coupe, 5-pass.
160	160th car produced

The first series of numbers and letters indicate the model.

MODEL	CODE
Champion	14G
Commander	4H

The second series of digits indicates the body type.

CHAMPION

BODY TYPE	CODE
Deluxe coupe, 5-pass.	C3
Deluxe sedan, 2-dr.	F3
Deluxe sedan, 2-dr., w/wraparound windshield	F4
Deluxe sedan, 4-dr.	W3
Deluxe sedan, 4-dr., w/wraparound windshield	W4
Custom sedan, 2-dr.	F1
Custom sedan, 2-dr., w/wraparound windshield	F2
Custom sedan, 4-dr.	W1
Custom sedan, 4-dr., w/wraparound windshield	W2
Regal sedan, 2-dr.	F5
Regal sedan, 4-dr.	W5
Regal sedan, 4-dr., w/wraparound windshield	W6
Regal hardtop, 5-pass.	K5

COMMANDER

BODY TYPE	CODE
Custom sedan, 2-dr.	F1
Custom sedan, 2-dr., w/wraparound windshield	F2
Deluxe coupe, 5-pass.	C3
Deluxe sedan, 2-dr.	F3
Deluxe sedan, 2-dr., w/wraparound windshield	F4
Deluxe sedan, 4-dr.	W3
Deluxe sedan, 4-dr., w/wraparound windshield	W4
Deluxe sedan, 4-dr. (long wheelbase)	Y3
Deluxe sedan, 4-dr. (long wheelbase w/wraparound windshield	Y4
Custom sedan, 4-dr.	W1
Custom sedan, 4-dr. w/wraparound windshield	W2
Regal coupe, 5-pass.	C5
Regal sedan, 2-dr.	F5
Regal sedan, 4-dr.	W5
Regal sedan, 4-dr., w/wraparound windshield	W6
Regal hardtop, 5-pass.	K5
Regal Land Cruiser, 4-dr.	Y5
State coupe, 5-pass.	C5

The third series of digits indicates the particular body number of that type manufactured.

THE COLOR CODE indicates the paint color used on the vehicle. The code is located in the glove box.

COLOR	CODE
Velvet Black	W-ND
Ivory Mist	8574W-XI
Coral Red	8577W-XJ
Manchester Maroon	8580W-XK
Monterey Beige	8583W-XL
Olympic Gray	8586W-XM
Chippewa Green	8592W-XO
Lombard Green	8595W-XP
Tacoma Gray	8607W-XS
Bombay Red	8650W-XZ
Salem White	8653W-YA
Nocturne Blue	8491W-WE
Maui Blue	8452W-VZ
Tahoe Green	8494W-WF

THE TRIM CODE indicates the trim color and material scheme used on the vehicle. No trim codes were available.

ENGINE SPECIFICATIONS

The engine number is located on a boss on the top front of the cylinder block. The starting engine numbers are as follows:

MODEL	ENGINE NUMBER
Champion	1,004,001/up
Commander	V-207,001/up

ENGINE NUMBER	NO. CYL.	CID	HORSE-POWER	COMP. RATIO	CARB	TRANS
14G	6	170	85	7.0:1	1 BC	STD
14G	6	170	85	7.5:1	1 BC	AUTO
4H	8	233	120	7.0:1	2 BC	

1954 STUDEBAKER

1954 STUDEBAKER STATION WAGON

1954 STUDEBAKER

VEHICLE IDENTIFICATION NUMBER

`• G-1274001 •`

The VIN number is located on the plate on the left front door pillar post.

The letter and numbers identify the model number, starting production numbers and assembly plant.

MODEL	STARTING NO./ASSY. PLANT South Bend, IN	STARTING NO./ASSY. PLANT Los Angeles, CA
Champion	G-1274001/up	G-927401/up
Commander/ Land Cruiser	8354901/up	8836801/up

BODY NUMBER PLATE

Located on the cowl under the hood.

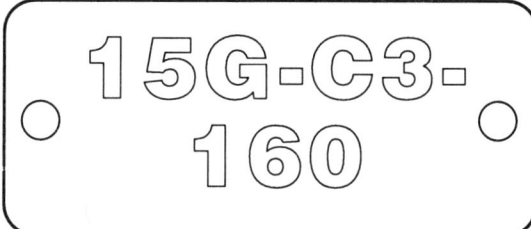

15G	1954 Champion
C3	Deluxe coupe, 5-pass.
160	160th car produced

The first series of numbers and letters indicates the model.

MODEL	CODE
Champion	15G
Commander	5H
Land Cruiser	5HY

The second series of digits indicates the body type.

CHAMPION

BODY TYPE	CODE
Deluxe coupe, 5-pass.	C3
Deluxe station wagon	D3
Deluxe station wagon, w/wraparound windshield	D4
Deluxe sedan, 2-dr.	F3
Deluxe sedan, 2-dr., w/wraparound windshield	F4
Deluxe sedan, 4-dr.	W3
Deluxe sedan, 4-dr., w/wraparound windshield	W4
Custom sedan, 2-dr.	F1
Custom sedan, 2-dr., w/wraparound windshield	F2
Custom sedan, 4-dr.	W1
Custom sedan, 4-dr., w/wraparound windshield	W2
Regal station wagon	D5
Regal station wagon, w/wraparound windshield	D6
Regal sedan, 2-dr.	F5
Regal sedan, 4-dr.	W5
Regal sedan, 4-dr., w/wraparound windshield	W6
Regal hardtop, 5-pass.	K5

COMMANDER

BODY TYPE	CODE
Custom sedan, 2-dr.	F1
Custom sedan, 2-dr., w/wraparound windshield	F2
Custom sedan, 4-dr.	W1
Custom sedan, 4-dr., w/wraparound windshield	W2
Deluxe coupe, 5-pass.	C3
Deluxe station wagon	D5
Deluxe station wagon, w/wraparound windshield	D6
Deluxe sedan, 2-dr.	F3
Deluxe sedan, 2-dr., w/wraparound windshield	F4
Deluxe sedan, 4-dr.	W3
Deluxe sedan, 4-dr., w/wraparound windshield	W4
Deluxe sedan, 4-dr. (long wheelbase)	Y3
Deluxe sedan, 4-dr. (long wheelbase w/wraparound windshield	Y4
Regal coupe, 5-pass.	C5
Regal sedan, 2-dr.	F5
Regal sedan, 4-dr.	W5
Regal sedan, 4-dr., w/wraparound windshield	W6
Regal hardtop, 5-pass.	K5
Regal Land Cruiser, 4-dr.	Y5
State coupe, 5-pass.	C5

The third series of digits indicates the particular body number of that type manufactured.

THE COLOR CODE indicates the paint color used on the vehicle. The code is located in the glove box.

COLOR	CODE
Velvet Black	W-DD
Safford Cream	8669W-YD
Sandusky Beige	8673W-YE
Lance Green	8677W-YF
Chadron Red	8681W-YG
Cadet Gray	8697W-YK
Azore Green	8693W-YJ
Shoshone Red	8685W-YH
Ontario Blue	8732W-YX
Nocturne Blue	8491W-WE
Alberta Blue	8665W-YC
Elko Gray	8689W-YI
Vista Green	8705W-YM
Vienna Blue	8701W-YL
Mesa Tan	8713W-YM

THE TRIM CODE indicates the trim color and material scheme used on the vehicle. No trim codes were available.

ENGINE SPECIFICATIONS

20-20

The engine number is located on a boss on the top front of the cylinder block. The starting engine numbers are as follows:

MODEL	ENGINE NUMBER
Champion	1,090,001/up
Commander	V-282501/up

ENGINE NUMBER	NO. CYL.	CID	HORSE-POWER	COMP. RATIO	CARB
15G	6	170	85	7.5:1	1 BC
5H,5HY	8	233	120	7.5:1	2 BC

1955 STUDEBAKER

1955 STUDEBAKER COMMANDER

VEHICLE IDENTIFICATION NUMBER

● G-1316501 ●

The VIN number is located on the plate on the left front door pillar post.
The letter and numbers identify the model number, starting production numbers and assembly plant.

MODEL	STARTING NO./ASSY. PLANT South Bend, IN	STARTING NO./ASSY. PLANT Los Angeles, CA
Champion	G-1316501/up	G-932501/up
Commander	8380601/up	8841201/up
President	7150001	7805001

BODY NUMBER PLATE

Located on the cowl under the hood.

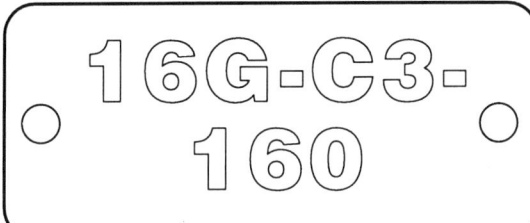

16G6	1955 Champion
C3	Deluxe coupe, 5-pass.
160	160th car produced

The first series of numbers and letters indicates the model.

MODEL	CODE
Champion	16G6
Commander	16G8
President	6H

The second series of digits indicates the body type.

CHAMPION

BODY TYPE	CODE
Deluxe coupe, 5-pass.	C3
Deluxe station wagon	D3
Deluxe station wagon, w/wraparound windshield	D4
Deluxe sedan, 2-dr.	F3
Deluxe sedan, 2-dr., w/wraparound windshield	F4
Deluxe sedan, 4-dr.	W3
Deluxe sedan, 4-dr., w/wraparound windshield	W4
Custom sedan, 2-dr.	F1
Custom sedan, 2-dr., w/wraparound windshield	F2
Custom sedan, 4-dr.	W1
Custom sedan, 4-dr., w/wraparound windshield	W2
Regal coupe, 5-pass.	C5
Regal station wagon	D5
Regal station wagon, w/wraparound windshield	D6
Regal sedan, 2-dr.	F5
Regal sedan, 4-dr.	W5
Regal sedan, 4-dr., w/wraparound windshield	W6
Regal hardtop, 5-pass.	K5

COMMANDER

BODY TYPE	CODE
Custom sedan, 2-dr.	F1
Custom sedan, 2-dr., w/wraparound windshield	F2
Custom sedan, 4-dr.	W1
Custom sedan, 4-dr., w/wraparound windshield	W2
Deluxe coupe, 5-pass.	C3
Deluxe station wagon	D3
Deluxe station wagon, w/wraparound windshield	D4
Deluxe sedan, 2-dr.	F3
Deluxe sedan, 2-dr., w/wraparound windshield	F4
Deluxe sedan, 4-dr.	W3
Deluxe sedan, 4-dr., w/wraparound windshield	W4
Regal coupe, 5-pass.	C5
Regal station wagon	D5
Regal station wagon, w/wraparound windshield	D6
Regal sedan, 2-dr.	F5
Regal sedan, 4-dr.	W5
Regal sedan, 4-dr., w/wraparound windshield	W6
Regal hardtop, 5-pass.	K5

PRESIDENT

BODY TYPE	CODE
State coupe, 5-pass.	C5
State hardtop	K5
State sedan, 4-dr.	Y5
State sedan, 4-dr., w/wraparound windshield	Y6
Deluxe station wagon, 2-dr.	D3
Deluxe station wagon, 2-dr. w/wraparound windshield	D4
Deluxe sedan, 4-dr.	Y3
Deluxe sedan, 4-dr., w/wraparound windshield	Y4
Speedster hardtop	K7

The third series of digits indicates the particular body number of that type manufactured.

THE COLOR CODE indicates the paint color used on the vehicle. The code is located in the glove box.

COLOR	CODE
Velvet Black	W-NA
Hialeah Green Metallic	W-ZV
Sun Valley Yellow	W-ZW
Pimlico Gray Metallic	W-ZX
Congo Ivory	W-ZY
Coraltone	1001B-AB
Alpena Blue	8751W-ZA
Shasta White	8746W-YZ
Cascade Green	8752W-ZB
Pima Red	8753W-ZC
Encino Cream	8754W-ZD
Sheridan Green	8755W-ZE
Tilden Gray	8756W-ZF
Saginaw Green	8757W-ZG
Windsor Blue	8758W-ZH
Sonora Beige	8759W-ZI
Rancho Red	8848W-ZZ

THE TRIM CODE indicates the trim color and material scheme used on the vehicle. No trim codes were available.

ENGINE SPECIFICATIONS

The engine number is located on a boss on the top front of the cylinder block. The starting engine numbers are as follows:

MODEL	STARTING ENGINE NUMBERS South Bend, IN	STARTING ENGINE NUMBERS Los Angeles, CA
Champion	1,138,001/up	L-101/up
Commander (early series)	V-312,701/up	VL-312,701/up
Commander (late series)	V-331101	VL-101/up
President	P-101	PL-101/up

ENGINE NUMBER	NO. CYL.	CID	HORSE-POWER	COMP. RATIO	CARB	TRANS
16G6	6	186	101	7.5:1	1 BC	
16G8*	8	224	140	7.5:1	2 BC	
16G8#	8	259	162	7.5:1	2 BC	
6H*	8	259	175	7.5:1	4 BC	
6H#	8	259	185	7.5:1	4 BC	

* Early series

Late series

1956 STUDEBAKER GOLDEN HAWK

1956 STUDEBAKER HAWK

1956 STUDEBAKER CHAMPION

1956 STUDEBAKER

VEHICLE IDENTIFICATION NUMBER

$\boxed{\bullet\ \text{G - 1 3 5 7 5 0 1}\ \bullet}$

The VIN number is located on the plate on the left front door pillar post.
The letter and numbers identify the model number, starting production numbers and assembly plant.

MODEL	STARTING NO./ASSY. PLANT South Bend, IN	STARTING NO./ASSY. PLANT Los Angeles, CA
Champion	G-1357501/up	G-936701/up
Commander	8429601/up	8849101/up
President	7171001	7808501
Golden Hawk	6030001	6800001

BODY NUMBER PLATE

Located on the cowl under the hood.

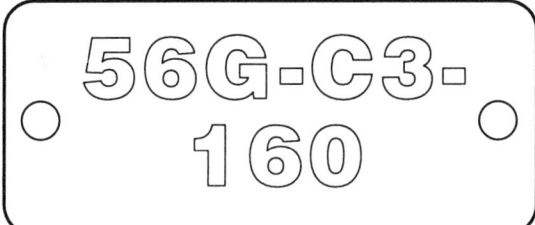

56G	1956 Champion
C3	Deluxe coupe, 5-pass.
160	160th car produced

The first series of numbers and letters indicates the model.

MODEL	CODE
Champion	56G
Commander	56B
President	56H
Golden Hawk	56J

The second series of digits indicates the body type.

CHAMPION

BODY TYPE	CODE
Flight Hawk coupe, 5-pass.	C3
Flight Hawk hardtop, 5-pass.	K7
Silver Hawk coupe, 5-pass.	C3
Pelham station wagon, 2-dr. w/wraparound windshield	D4
Deluxe sedan, 2-dr., w/wraparound windshield	F4
Custom sedan, 4-dr. w/wraparound windshield	W2
Deluxe sedan, 4-dr. w/wraparound windshield	W4
Custom sedan, 2-dr., w/wraparound windshield	F2

COMMANDER

BODY TYPE	CODE
Power Hawk coupe, 5-pass.	C3
Custom sedan, 2-dr.	F1
Custom sedan, 2-dr., w/wraparound windshield	F2
Sedan, 4-dr., w/wraparound windshield	W2
Parkview station wagon, 2-dr., w/wraparound windshield	D4
Deluxe sedan, 2-dr., w/wraparound windshield	F4

PRESIDENT

BODY TYPE	CODE
Pinehurst station wagon, 2-dr. w/wraparound windshield	D6
Sedan, 4-dr., w/wraparound windshield	F6
Sky Hawk hardtop, 5-pass.	K7
Sedan, 4-dr.	W6
Classic sedan, 4-dr., w/long wheelbase	Y6

GOLDEN HAWK

BODY TYPE	CODE
Hardtop, 5-pass.	K7

The third series of digits indicates the particular body number of that type manufactured.

THE COLOR CODE indicates the paint color used on the vehicle. The code is located in the glove box.

COLOR	CODE
Midnight Black	1000-BAA
Rosebud	1001-BAB
Sunglow Gold	1002-BAC
Romany Red	1003-BAD
Seaside Green	1004-BAE
Daybreak Blue	1005-BAF
Snowcap White	1006-BAG
Cambridge Gray Metallic	1007-BAH
Air Force Blue Metallic	1008-BAI
Glenbrook Green Metallic	1009-BAJ
Ceramic Green Metallic	1010-BAK
Doeskin	1011-BAL
Mocha	1012-BAM
Yellowstone	1013-BAN
Tangerine	1015-BAP
Redwood Metallic	1027-BBB

THE TRIM CODE indicates the color scheme used on the vehicle. No trim codes were available.

ENGINE SPECIFICATIONS

The engine number is located on a boss on the top front of the cylinder block. The starting engine numbers are as follows:

MODEL	STARTING ENGINE NUMBERS South Bend, IN	STARTING ENGINE NUMBERS Los Angeles, CA
Champion	1,180,251/up	L-3201/up
Commander	V-363,751/up	VL-6301/up
President	P-22001	PL-2701/up
Golden Hawk (overdrive)	K-1001	K-1001
Golden Hawk (ultramatic)	S-1001	S-1001

ENGINE NUMBER	NO. CYL.	CID	HORSE-POWER	COMP. RATIO	CARB
56G	6	185	101	7.5:1	1 BC
56B	8	259	170	7.8:1	2 BC
56B	8	259	185	7.8:1	4 BC
56H	8	289	210	7.8:1	4 BC
56H	8	289	195	7.8:1	4 BC
56J	8	352	275	9.5:1	4 BC

1957 STUDEBAKER

VEHICLE IDENTIFICATION NUMBER

• G - 1 3 7 9 2 0 1 •

The VIN number is located on the plate on the left front door pillar post.

The letter and numbers identify the model number, starting production numbers and assembly plant.

MODEL	STARTING NUMBER
Champion	G-1379201/up
Commander	8454101/up
President	7188901
Golden Hawk	6100001

BODY NUMBER PLATE

Located on the cowl under the hood.

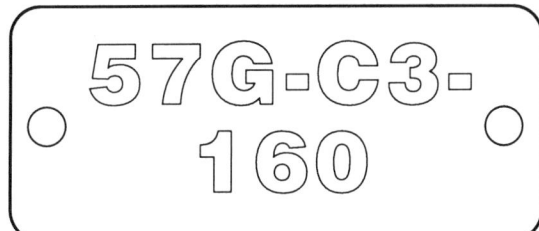

57G	1957 Champion
C3	Coupe, 5-pass.
160	160th car produced

The first series of numbers and letters indicates the model.

MODEL	CODE
Champion	57G
Commander	57B
President	57H
Golden Hawk	57H

The second series of digits indicates the body type.

CHAMPION

BODY TYPE	CODE
Silver Hawk coupe, 5-pass.	C3
Silver Hawk hardtop, 5-pass.	K3
Pelham station wagon, 2-dr. w/wraparound windshield	D4
Scotsman sedan, 2-dr. w/wraparound windshield	F1
Custom sedan, 2-dr., w/wraparound windshield	F2
Deluxe sedan, 2-dr., w/wraparound windshield	F4
Scotsman sedan, 4-dr. w/wraparound windshield	W1
Custom sedan, 4-dr. w/wraparound windshield	W2
Deluxe sedan, 4-dr., w/wraparound windshield	W4
Regal sedan, 4-dr., w/wraparound windshield	W6

COMMANDER

BODY TYPE	CODE
Silver Hawk coupe, 5-pass.	C3
Silver Hawk hardtop, 5-pass.	K3
Parkview station wagon, 2-dr.	D4
Custom sedan, 2-dr., w/wraparound windshield	F2
Deluxe sedan, 2-dr., w/wraparound windshield	F4
Custom sedan, 4-dr., w/wraparound windshield	W2
Provincial station wagon, 4-dr., w/wraparound windshield	P4
Deluxe sedan, 4-dr., w/wraparound windshield	W4

PRESIDENT

BODY TYPE	CODE
Silver Hawk coupe, 5-pass.	C3
Parkview station wagon, 2-dr. w/wraparound windshield	D4
Provincial station wagon, 4-dr., w/wraparound windshield	P4
Broadmoor station wagon, 4-dr., w/wraparound windshield	P6
Custom sedan, 2-dr., w/wraparound windshield	F2
Deluxe sedan, 2-dr., w/wraparound windshield	F4
Regal sedan, 2-dr., w/wraparound windshield	F6
Custom sedan, 4-dr., w/wraparound windshield	W2
Deluxe sedan, 4-dr., w/wraparound windshield	W4
Regal sedan, 4-dr., w/wraparound windshield	W6
Classic sedan, 4-dr., w/long wheelbase	Y6

GOLDEN HAWK

BODY TYPE	CODE
Hardtop, 5-pass.	K7

The third series of digits indicates the particular body number of that type manufactured.

THE COLOR CODE indicates the paint color used on the vehicle. The code is located in the glove box.

COLOR	CODE
Lilac	1042-BBR
Regal Red	1043-BBS
Cumberland Gray	1044-BBT
Arctic White	1026-BBA
Apache Red	1029-BBD
Coppertone Metallic	1030-BBE
Tiara Gold Metallic	1031-BBF
Woodsmoke Gray Metallic	1032-BBG
Glendale Green Metallic	1033-BBH
Turquoise	1036-BBK
Azure Blue Metallic	1034-BBI
Wedgewood Blue	1035-BBJ
Taupe Metallic	1037-BBL
Admiral Blue	1041-BCA
Highland Gray	1050-BBZ
Lombard Green	8595-WXP

THE TRIM CODE indicates the trim color and material scheme used on the vehicle. There were no trim codes available.

ENGINE SPECIFICATIONS

The engine number is located on a boss on the top front of the cylinder block on 6-cylinders, on the top front of the cylinder blocks on the V-8s. The starting engine numbers are as follows:

	STARTING
MODEL	**ENGINE NUMBERS**
Champion	1,202,101/up
Commander	V-390,001/up
President	P-39601
Golden Hawk	PS-1001

ENGINE NUMBER	NO. CYL.	CID	HORSE-POWER	COMP. RATIO	CARB
57G	6	185	101	7.8:1	1 BC
57B	8	259	180	8.0:1	2 BC
57B	8	259	195	8.0:1	4 BC
57H	8	289	210	8.0:1	2 BC
57H	8	289	225	8.0:1	4 BC
57H/K7	8	289	275	7.5:1	2 BC*

* Supercharged

1958 STUDEBAKER GOLDEN HAWK

1958 STUDEBAKER

1958 STUDEBAKER

1958 STUDEBAKER HAWK

1958 STUDEBAKER

VEHICLE IDENTIFICATION NUMBER

• G-1405401 •

The VIN number is located on the plate on the left front door pillar post.
The letter and numbers identify the model number, starting production numbers and assembly plant.

MODEL	STARTING NUMBER
Champion	G-1405401/up
Commander	8471601/up
President	7210001
Golden Hawk	6104501

BODY NUMBER PLATE

Located on the cowl under the hood.

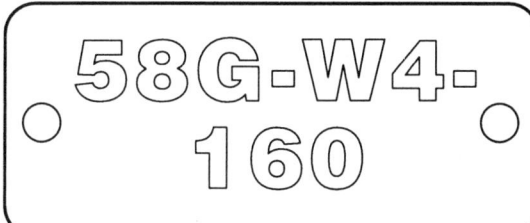

58G	1958 Champion
W4	Sedan, 4-dr.
160	160th car produced

The first series of numbers and letters indicates the model.

MODEL	CODE
Champion	58G
Commander	58B
President	58H
Golden Hawk	58H

The second series of digits indicates the body type.

CHAMPION

BODY TYPE	CODE
Silver Hawk coupe, 5-pass.	C3
Scotsman station wagon, 2-dr.	D1
Scotsman sedan, 2-dr.	F1
Scotsman sedan, 2-dr.	F4
Scotsman sedan, 4-dr.	W1
Sedan, 4-dr.	W4

COMMANDER

BODY TYPE	CODE
Silver Hawk coupe, 5-pass.	C3
Scotsman station wagon, 2-dr.	D1
Scotsman sedan, 2-dr.	F1
Marshal sedan, 4-dr.	W1
Marshal sedan, 4-dr.	W4
Provincial station wagon, 4-dr.	P4

PRESIDENT

BODY TYPE	CODE
Silver Hawk coupe, 5-pass.	C3
Marshal sedan, 2-dr.	F1
Sedan hardtop, 2-dr.	J6
Sedan, 4-dr.	Y6

GOLDEN HAWK

BODY TYPE	CODE
Sport hardtop, 5-pass.	K7

The third series of digits indicates the particular body number of that type manufactured.

THE COLOR CODE indicates the paint color used on the vehicle. The code is located in the glove box.

COLOR	CODE
Apache Red	1029-BBD
Waterfall Blue	1056-BGF
Mountain Blue Metallic	1057-BCG
Sherwood Green Metallic	1039-BBN
Academy Blue	1040-BBO
Surf Green	1058-BCH
Jewel Beige	1060-BCJ
Cliff Gray	1054-BCD
Bluff Gray Metallic	1055-BCF
Canyon Copper Metallic	1062-BCL
White Cold Metallic	1061-BCK
Parchment White	1066-BCP
Parade Red	1068-BCR
Loch Blue	1064-BCN
Glen Green	1063-BCM
Glasgow Gray	1065-BCO

THE TRIM CODE indicates the trim color and material scheme used on the vehicle. There were no trim codes available.

ENGINE SPECIFICATIONS

The engine number is located on a boss on the top front of the cylinder block on 6-cylinders, and on the top front of the cylinder block on the V-8. The starting engine numbers are as follows:

MODEL	STARTING ENGINE NUMBERS
Champion	1,228,401/up
Commander	V-407,501/up
President	P-60701
Golden Hawk	PS-5501

ENGINE NUMBER	NO. CYL.	CID	HORSE-POWER	COMP. RATIO	CARB
58G	6	185	101	7.8:1	1 BC
58B	8	259	180	8.3:1	2 BC
58H	8	289	225	8.3:1	4 BC
58H	8	289	210	8.3:1	2 BC
58H	8	289	275	7.8:1	2 BC*

* Supercharged

1959 STUDEBAKER HAWK

1959 STUDEBAKER HAWK

1959 STUDEBAKER LARK

VEHICLE IDENTIFICATION NUMBER

• 59S-1001 •

The VIN number is located on the plate on the left front door pillar post.
The letter and numbers identify the model number, starting production numbers and assembly plant.

THE FIRST AND SECOND DIGITS: Identify the model year (1959)

THE THIRD DIGIT: Identifies the engine type

TYPE	CODE
6-Cylinder	S
8-Cylinder	V

THE LAST FOUR DIGITS: Identify the production sequence number, 1001/up

BODY NUMBER PLATE

Located on the cowl under the hood.

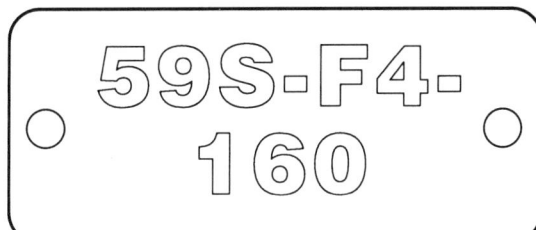

59S	1959 6-cylinder
F4	Sedan, 2-dr.
160	160th car produced

The first series of numbers and letters indicates the year and the engine type.

MODEL YEAR/ENGINE TYPE	CODE
1959 6-cyl.	59S
1959 8-cyl.	59V

The second series of digits indicates the body type.

LARK DELUXE

BODY TYPE	CODE
2-Dr. sedan	F4
4-Dr. sedan	W4
2-Dr. station wagon	D4

LARK REGAL

BODY TYPE	CODE
2-Dr. sedan hardtop	J6
4-Dr. sedan	W6
2-Dr. station wagon	D6

SILVER HAWK

BODY TYPE	CODE
Sport coupe	C6

The third series of digits indicates the particular body number of that type manufactured.

THE COLOR CODE indicates the paint color used on the vehicle. The code is located in the glove box.

COLOR	CODE
Velvet Black	1084-BDH
Bahama Blue	1100-BDX
Bamboo Yellow	1101-BDY
Cameo Beige	1102-BDZ
Seamist Green	1103-BEA
White Sand	1082-BDF
Alaskan Blue	1083-BDG
Hawaiian Green	1087-BDK
Tahiti Coral	1085-BDI
Silvertone Gray	1086-BDJ
Campfire Red	1081-BDE

THE TRIM CODE indicates the trim color and material scheme used on the vehicle. There were no trim codes available.

ENGINE SPECIFICATIONS

The engine number is located on a machined pad at the upper front of the cylinder block. The starting engine numbers are as follows:

MODEL	STARTING ENGINE NUMBERS
59S	S-10001/up
59V	V-418701/up

ENGINE NUMBER	NO. CYL.	CID	HORSE-POWER	COMP. RATIO	CARB
59S	6	170	90	8.3:1	1 BC
59V	8	259	180	8.8:1	2 BC
59V	8	259	195	8.8:1	4 BC

1952 WILLYS

VEHICLE IDENTIFICATION NUMBER

Located on the left front door pillar. The serial number is prefixed by the model number.

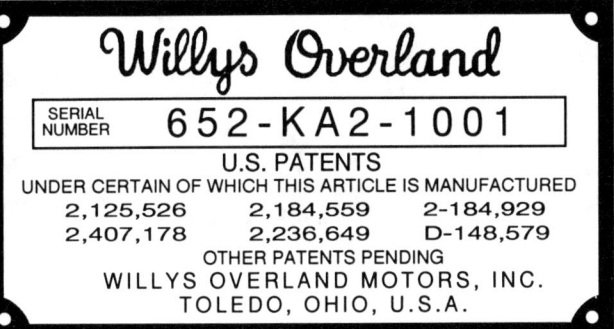

SERIAL NUMBER: 1001/up, preceded by the model code

MODEL TYPE	CODE
Aero Lark 675	652-KA2
Aero Wing Super Deluxe 685	652-LAI
Aero Ace Custom 685	652-MAI
Aero Eagle 685	652-MCI

MODEL TYPE	CODE
Aero Lark Deluxe 2-dr. sedan	675
Aerper deluxe, 2-dr. sedan	685
Aero Ace Custom, 2-dr. sedan	685
Aero Eagle, 2-dr. hardtop sedan	685

THE COLOR CODE indicates the paint color used on the vehicle.

COLOR	CODE
Bermuda Blue	—
Cherokee Red Metallic	—
Duchess Gray	—
Hampshire Green Metallic	—
Hatteras Green	—
Inverness Green Metallic	—
Mediterranean Blue Metallic	—
Riviera Gray	—
Shadow Gray Mtallic	—
Smoked Ruby	—
Oxford Gray Metallic	—

TRIM CODES

Trim codes were unavailable for the 1952 Willys.

ENGINE SPECIFICATIONS

The engine number is located on the water pump boss at the front of the cylinder block. The engine number is the same as the serial number.

ENGINE NUMBER	NO. CYL.	CID	HORSE-POWER	COMP. RATIO	CARB
652-KA2	6	161	75	6.9:1*	1 BC
652-LA1	6	161	90	7.6:1**	1 BC

* L-Head

** F-Head

1953 WILLYS

1953 WILLYS

VEHICLE IDENTIFICATION NUMBER

Located on the left front door pillar. The serial number is prefixed by the model number.

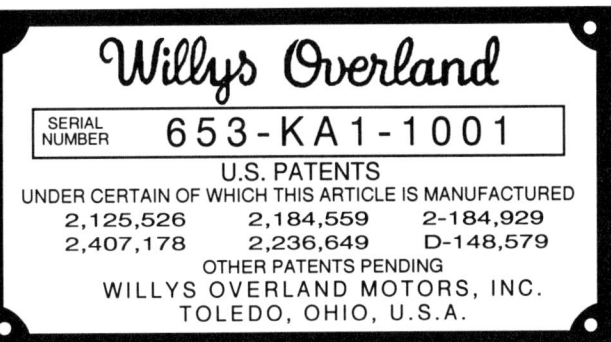

MODEL TYPE	CODE
Aero Lark Deluxe, 2-dr. sedan	453-KA1
Aero Lark Deluxe, 4-dr. sedan (475)	453-KB1
Aero Lark Deluxe, 4-dr. sedan (675)	653-KB1
Aero Lark Deluxe, 2-dr. sedan (675)	653-KA1
Aero Ace Custom, 4-dr. sedan (685)	653-MB1
Aero Ace Custom, 2-dr. sedan (685)	653-MA1
Aero Eagle hardtop sedan (685)	653-MC1
Aero Falcon Super Deluxe, 4-dr. sedan (675)	653-PB1
Aero Falcon Super Deluxe, 2-dr. sedan (675)	653-PA1

MODEL NUMBERS

MODEL TYPE	CODE
Aero Lark Deluxe, 4-cyl.	475A
Aero Lark Deluxe	675A
Aero Wing Super Deluxe	685A
Aero Ace Custom	685A
Aero Eagle	685A

THE COLOR CODE indicates the paint color used on the vehicle.

COLOR	CODE
Cadet Gray	—
Coronado Sand	—
Mediterranean Blue Metallic	—
Pacific Glow	—
Riviera Gray	—
Woodstock Green Metallic	2
Admiral Blue	3
Willow Green Metallic	4
Cadet Gray Metallic	6
Sabre Rouge	7
Jasper Green Metallic	8

THE TRIM CODE indicates the key to the trim color and material used on the vehicle. There were no trim codes available.

ENGINE SPECIFICATIONS

The engine number is located on the water pump boss at the front of the cylinder block. All, except Aero 4-cylinder are consecutive with 1952 production.

4-Cyl. Aero 4P-10001
6-Cyl. Aero ....W/1952 prod.

ENGINE NUMBER	NO. CYL.	CID	HORSE-POWER	COMP. RATIO	CARB
453-KA1,KB1	4	134	72	7.4:1	1 BC
653-KB1,KA1,PB1,PA1	6	161	75	6.9:1*	1 BC
653-MB1,MA1,MC1	6	161	90	7.6:1**	1 BC

* L-Head

** F-Head

1954 WILLYS

VEHICLE IDENTIFICATION NUMBER

Located on the left front door pillar. All numbers start at 5001 with a prefix for each model.

```
Willys Overland
SERIAL
NUMBER    6 5 4 - K A 3 - 5 0 0 1
              U.S. PATENTS
UNDER CERTAIN OF WHICH THIS ARTICLE IS MANUFACTURED
    2,125,526     2,184,559     2-184,929
    2,407,178     2,236,649     D-148,579
          OTHER PATENTS PENDING
      WILLYS OVERLAND MOTORS, INC.
          TOLEDO, OHIO, U.S.A.
```

MODEL TYPE	CODE
Aero Lark, 2-dr. sedan (675)	654-KA3
Aero Lark, 4-dr. sedan (675)	654-KB3
Aero Ace, 4-dr. sedan (685)	654-MB2
Aero Ace, 2-dr. sedan (685)	654-MA2
Aero Eagle, 2-dr. hardtop coupe (685)	654-MC3
Aero Eagle hardtop coupe (226)	654-MC1
Aero Eagle Custom hardtop coupe (226)	654-MC2
Aero Ace, 4-dr. sedan (226)	654-MB1
Aero Ace, 2-dr. sedan (226)	654-MA1

MODEL NUMBERS

MODEL TYPE	CODE
Aero Lark	675B
Aero Ace	685B
Aero Eagle	685B
Aero Ace	6-226
Aero Eagle	6-226

THE COLOR CODE indicates the paint color used on the vehicle.

COLOR	CODE
Arctic White	—
Blue Comet Metallic	—
Copper Dust Metallic	—
Coronado Sand	—
Palm Beach Ivory	—
Raven	21
Granada Green Metallic	31
Gulf Blue Metallic	32
Coral Rust Metallic	33
Gale Gray Metallic	34
Beryl Green	35
Bristol Red	36
Pine Tint	117
Persian Gray Metallic	207
Signal Green Metallic	226
Island Green Metallic	227
Powder Blue	229

THE TRIM CODE indicates the trim color and material used on the vehicle. There were no trim codes available.

ENGINE SPECIFICATIONS

The engine number is located on the top front of the cylinder block.

ENGINE NUMBER	NO. CYL.	CID	HORSE-POWER	COMP. RATIO	CARB
685(F)	6	161	75	6.9:1	1 BC
685(F)	6	161	90	7.6:1	1 BC
226(L)	6	226	115	7.3:1	2 BC

1955 WILLYS

VEHICLE IDENTIFICATION NUMBER

Located on the left front door pillar. All numbers start at 10001 with a prefix for each model.

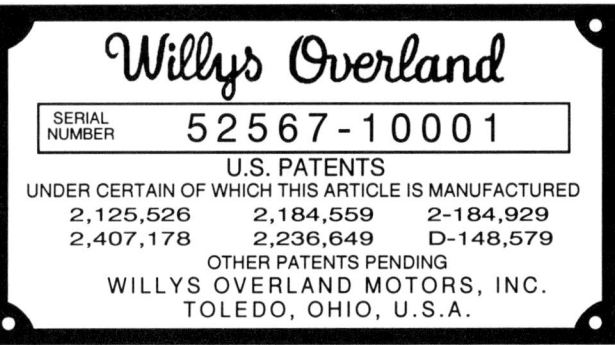

MODEL TYPE	CODE
Bermuda hardtop (6-226)	52567
Custom, 4-dr., 5-pass. (6-226)	52367
Custom, 2-dr., 5-pass. (6-226)	52467

THE COLOR CODE indicates the paint color used on the vehicle.

COLOR	CODE
Arctic White	—
Blue Comet Metallic	—
Copper Dust Metallic	—
Palm Beach Ivory	—
Steel Glow Gray Metallic	—
Beryl Green	92
Bristol Red	93
Island Green Metallic	100
President Red	108
Julep Green Metallic	110
Transport Yellow	111
Pine Tint	117
Concert Ivory	118
Powder Blue	104A

THE TRIM CODE indicates the trim color and material used on the vehicle. There were no trim codes available.

ENGINE SPECIFICATIONS

The engine number is located on the top front of the cylinder block.

ENGINE NUMBER	NO. CYL.	CID	HORSE-POWER	COMP. RATIO	CARB
6-226	6	226	115	7.3:1	2 BC

NOTES

cop. 1

21-11